The Phoenix Moment

Praful Bidwai (1949–2015) was a journalist, political analyst, author and activist. He started his journalistic career as a columnist for the *Economic and Political Weekly*, beginning in 1972. He then worked for magazines and newspapers including *Business India*, *Financial Express* and *The Times of India*. His articles were published regularly in the *Hindustan Times*, *Frontline*, Rediff.com, and other outlets. He had also been published in *The Guardian*, *The New Statesmen* and *Society* (London), *The Nation* (New York), *Le Monde Diplomatique* (Paris), and *Il Manifesto* (Rome).

A veteran peace activist, he helped found the Movement in India for Nuclear Disarmament (MIND), based in New Delhi, was a member of the International Network of Engineers and Scientists against Proliferation, and was one of the leaders of the Coalition for Nuclear Disarmament and Peace, India.

He is the author of *The Politics of Climate Change and the Global Crisis: Mortgaging Our Future* (Orient Blackswan, 2011). He has co-authored *Testing Times: The Global Stake in a Nuclear Test Ban* (Dag Hammerskjöld Foundation: Uppsala, 1996), *New Nukes: India, Pakistan and Global Nuclear Disarmament* (Interlink, 1999), both with Achin Vanaik; *Religion, Religiosity and Communalism*, with Harbans Mukhia and Achin Vanaik (South Asia Books, 1996); and *India Under Siege: Challenges Within and Without*, with Muchkund Dubey, Anuradha Chenoy and Arun Ghosh (South Asia Books, 1995). He was the co-editor (with M.N.V. Nair) of *The History of the Trade Union Movement in India, 1941–47* (Indian Council of Historical Research, 2005).

He passed away on 23 June 2015 while attending a conference in Amsterdam. Bidwai was a fellow at the Transnational Institute in Amsterdam in the Netherlands.

Praise for the book

'This book addresses a subject of significant importance in contemporary Indian politics: the decline of the Left during the era of neo-liberalism and communalism and its future prospects. Scanning through its history, the author highlights its strength and weakness in theoretical formulations and political practices. Although the Left had a fairly large following among the intelligentsia, had ruled West Bengal for thirty-four years, had intermittently come to power in Kerala and is still the dominant political force in Tripura, it is facing what the author calls an 'existential crisis'. Whether the Left 'ideologies, strategies and programmes' are adequate to deal with this challenge is the central theme of the book. The author's analysis and conclusions compel serious engagement, both by academics and political leaders, who believe in the relevance of the Left for the future of Indian democracy and its socialist transformation.'

—**K.N. Panikkar**, former professor, Jawaharlal Nehru University

'A detailed history of the Left in India going back to the 1920s that leads to a sympathetic critique of its role in independent India, the book argues how, even from its current low point, the Left can rebuild itself and have a say in the direction of change in India.'

—**Rammanohar Reddy**, editor, *Economic & Political Weekly*

'*The Phoenix Moment* focuses on the history and role of Left movements in India working within the system of Indian democracy. It provides not just a chronicle of events but also a wide-ranging discussion of the many facets relating to the politics and actions of these movements and parties. It does not hesitate to be critical wherever the author feels that criticism is required. Praful Bidwai's assessments will undoubtedly trigger further discussion. In the present Indian context of neoliberalism and the increasing resort to the politics of religious communities, alternatives to social and political functioning need to be considered. The main question that the book addresses is how the emergence of new Left movements could work towards ensuring a democratic and secular future.'

—**Romila Thapar**, professor emerita, Jawaharlal Nehru University

'If, like me, you know little about the Indian Left, I guarantee that Praful Bidwai will be a reliable, insightful and well-informed guide. If, like so many of his readers in India, you are well informed, I feel confident that he raises the right questions and is scrupulously fair. And, whoever you are, you will find his writing is, as always, a pleasure to read.'

—**Susan George**, president, Transnational Institute, Amsterdam

The Phoenix Moment

Challenges Confronting the Indian Left

Praful Bidwai

HarperCollins *Publishers* India

First published in India in 2015 by
HarperCollins *Publishers* India

Copyright © Praful Bidwai 2015

P-ISBN: 978-93-5177-516-4
E-ISBN: 978-93-5177-517-1

2 4 6 8 10 9 7 5 3 1

HarperCollins *Publishers*
A-75, Sector 57, Noida, Uttar Pradesh 201301, India
1 London Bridge Street, London, SE1 9GF, United Kingdom
Hazelton Lanes, 55 Avenue Road, Suite 2900, Toronto, Ontario M5R 3L2
and 1995 Markham Road, Scarborough, Ontario M1B 5M8, Canada
25 Ryde Road, Pymble, Sydney, NSW 2073, Australia
195 Broadway, New York, NY 10007, USA

Typeset in 10.5/13.5 Adobe Caslon Pro
By Saanvi Graphics Noida

Printed and bound at
Thomson Press (India) Ltd

Contents

Preface

India has long been a social–political oddity: a country with widespread poverty and wretched deprivation, but where the underprivileged find no voice in most political parties; one of the world's fastest-growing economies, where less than a tenth of the population has regular jobs and where a quarter-million farmers have recently committed suicide; a democracy with largely free and fair elections, which has failed to establish the rule of law and where human rights violations are rampant amidst caste- and religion-driven hatred and vicious discrimination against women.

A pertinent question is why left-wing politics has not flourished in India as a vital source of legitimacy for parties to the extent that might be expected in a society with a million injustices and growing inequalities, recently worsened by Hindutva and neo-liberal capitalism. Historically, left politics in India has shrunk in range and variety.

It was once a rainbow comprising breathtakingly different currents, including parliamentary and non-parliamentary communist parties; socialists of different hues ranging from the Congress Socialist Party (CSP) to the Gandhians, to followers of the viscerally anti-Congress Ram Manohar Lohia. It also encompassed anti-caste movements with radical agendas associated with Ambedkar's Republican Party of India (RPI) or later with the Dalit Panthers; and Maoists and Marxist–Leninist parties which believe in an insurrectionary seizure of power. There also used to be independent groups such as the Peasants and Workers Party (PWP) and Lal Nishan Party in Maharashtra or the Revolutionary Communist Party of India in West Bengal and Assam which set regionally limited agendas; there were currents like the Chhattisgarh Mukti Morcha (CMM) of Shankar Guha Niyogi which aimed to create embryos of workers' and peasants' republics; and there were many smaller progressive currents which aimed to rescue revolutionary Marxist politics from its 'distortions', active not just within the intelligentsia, but also in unions and other formations.

The rainbow has contracted in size and lost some of its hues. Many political currents have shrunk in variety and waned, while a few new ones have taken root. The socialists have long ceased to have a coherent organizational expression (barring the largely caste- and community-based, family-driven Samajwadi Party), but groupings like Samajwadi Samagam have grown. The once-strong PWP is now a feeble force. The CMM has split irrevocably. Liberal social democracy, always weak in India, which found expression in the Congress and other centrist parties, no longer exists as a force.

New differentiations have appeared within the Left spectrum, the most important of which is the division between the party Left and non-party political Left, the latter is comprised of 'people's movement' structures and federations of civil society groups like the National Alliance of People's Movements, National Fishworkers' Forum, All India Union of Forest Working People, Mazdoor Kisan Shakti Sangathan, Indian Social Action Forum, New Trade Union Initiative, Shramik Mukti Dal, New Socialist Initiative, Radical Socialist, and Campaign for Survival and Dignity.

The party Left is now reduced primarily to two currents: the mainstream parliamentary communist parties and their affiliates, and non-parliamentary Maoist or Marxist–Leninist groupings. The first is a parliamentary alliance and campaigning bloc which is mainly comprised of the Communist Party of India (Marxist) or CPI(M), the Communist Party of India (CPI), the Revolutionary Socialist Party (RSP), and the All India Forward Bloc (FB), recently joined by the Communist Party of India (Marxist-Leninist)-Liberation and Socialist Unity Centre of India (Communist).

The Maoist groupings—more than thirty at last count—are ideologically variegated and geographically dispersed, but the most important current is the Communist Party of India (Maoist), formed in 2004 after a merger between the People's War Group (PWG) and the Maoist Communist Centre of India (MCCI). It is particularly active in India's well-forested and mineral-rich tribal heartland, which extractive capitalism wants to exploit rapaciously. Some eighty-odd districts there are declared by the Indian state as dangerously affected by 'left-wing extremism' where paramilitary troops and special police forces rule rather than the civilian administration. The Maoists have waxed and waned, and now seem to be in decline, with the recent arrest or effective immobilization of some of their top leaders.[1]

The present book has an admittedly narrow focus: it deals primarily with the parliamentary communist parties. This focus arises from three factors. First, the mainstream bloc has had the longest and richest experience of trying to grapple with India's bourgeois–liberal democratic system, which despite limitations, enjoys a fair degree of popular legitimacy, and offers opportunities for progressive change and potentially transformative politics. Parties working within the system face obvious constraints: of having to operate within the four corners of the Constitution, and to fight elections, which are increasingly becoming a big-money game. They also run the risk of being co-opted by the system and rendered utterly ineffective.

However, the greatest challenge for left politics in India lies precisely in the bourgeois-democratic arena, and the possibilities it contains both within the state and in society, the latter with its own institutions, organizations, and freedoms of association and action. The Maoists, despite their admirable commitment and dedication, have totally retreated from this challenge. And the non-party political Left does not directly engage with it—often for well-considered reasons—through state-level participation, as distinct from popular education and mobilization, or advocacy and lobbying.

Second, the mainstream bloc is the biggest of all Left currents, and has had the longest continuous organized existence, notwithstanding various splits, dissensions and mutual rivalries. It also shares many ideological and strategic premises, which are today in need of revision.

If the Left summons up the will to revisit its strategic perspectives and undertake course correction, its relative cohesion and access to resources can reduce its vulnerability and offer it some protection. The opposite can happen if the bloc remains ideologically rigid. This book attempts to create a basis for understanding which way the mainstream Left might be headed.

Third, astonishing as this might seem, there is very little recent analytical literature on the mainstream Left at the national level—as distinct from state-specific studies and articles.[2] The present book will hopefully help fill this void by combining an analysis of the state- and national-level performance of the Left parties with a critical appraisal of their ideological premises, strategic perspectives, political mobilization approaches, and organizational doctrines and practices.

The real lessons for the future lie in how well the mainstream Left acquits itself in the face of the challenge of working within the bourgeois-democratic system and uses the freedoms available within it to expand the space for radical politics, empower the exploited and oppressed, and work for a transition to a post-capitalist society. On test is the ability of its national leadership to overcome the grave crisis they confront today as the Left faces its Phoenix Moment.

This book was planned well before the downslide of India's mainstream communist parties became apparent in electoral terms. Indeed, it should have been written ten, if not twenty, years ago. It is a coincidence that it is being published just when the Left parties find themselves in the grip of their worst-ever crisis. What is not a coincidence is the persistence of some of the long-term processes that drove my decades-long analytical interest in the Left—its ideological deficiencies, theoretical rigidity, aridity in programme formulation, and undemocratic organizational practices.

A brief personal note is in order here. I have for more than four decades considered myself a socialist who broadly accepts Marx's analysis of capitalism. I was exposed to the working-class movement in my student days in Bombay and worked with trade unions and Dalit youth in the slums of Matunga Labour Camp (a part of Dharavi). I never joined a Left political party because I found none of them sufficiently undogmatic or open to new ideas—in particular receptive to my staunchly anti-Stalinist views—but I have worked closely and happily with members of a variety of Left parties all my life.

In the early 1970s, I was associated with the Magowa Group and the Shramik Sanghatana which were active among the Bhil tribals in northern Maharashtra, where I worked briefly. Later, I was also part of what mutated from the Revolutionary Bolshevik Circle to the Platform Tendency, based in Delhi, Bombay and Bangalore, which took theory extremely seriously and exposed its members to Marxism as an intellectual adventure—with an amazingly rich repertoire of literature, views and ideas on a stunning variety of subjects.

I was fortunate enough to be able to research the history of the Indian communist and trade union movements of the 1940s, and also to combine this with union activism with outstanding labour organizers like D. Thankappan of the Kamani Workers' Union, and later, the Centre for Workers' Management. I spent a fruitful period in Europe in the late 1970s, and observed the communist parties as well as the then vibrant Far Left in France and Italy go through a fateful transition, which was, alas, aborted after the Soviet collapse. My education in science, technology, economics and philosophy, my interests in the social sciences, and my career in analytical journalism, helped me understand issues like ecology and energy and integrate some of the insights I thus gained into my understanding of socialism.

I hope the present book reflects a small part of this. It is divided into four parts. The first part analyses the Left's rise, and its overall achievements, strengths and weaknesses as it struggled to define a strategic framework in which to practise its politics, itself part of an ambitious long-term project of social transformation. It argues that the struggle was at best partially successful thanks to the Left's persistent ideological–theoretical and programmatic weaknesses. The first part also looks at the Left's foray into national politics and then its growing regionalization, especially after the CPI–CPI(M) split of 1964.

The Left's growth as a force in national politics became dependent on its strategy of allying either with the ruling Congress or its major adversaries. Here the two parties took the opposite approach. This benefited both to an extent in different ways, but extracted a high price through ideological confusion and political disarray. The Left acquired the profile of a kingmaker in the 1990s, but committed a 'historic blunder' by refusing to lead a non-BJP, non-Congress government in 1996.

The second part deals with West Bengal and Kerala. In Bengal, the Left Front set an international record by being elected to power consecutively for seven terms. Its ascent to office in 1977, followed by land reforms and Panchayati Raj, opened up the space for progressive change. Unfortunately, it squandered that opportunity by limiting the land reforms, imposing a narrowly partisan agenda on the panchayats, and neglecting social development agendas. This caused an ossification of the Left's structures, entry of opportunists into its ranks, and loss of legitimacy especially after it embraced neo-liberal economic policies—leading to its ignominious exit from power in 2011.

The Kerala drama began with the Left's involvement in social reform movements and workers' and peasants' mobilizations, which brought the Communist Party of India to power in 1957 in a democratic election—for the first time anywhere in the world. The communists initiated what is known the world over as the Kerala Model.

In spite of their considerable achievements, the Left parties were unable to reinvent the model or break the caste and community mould in which Kerala's politics has long been set. Their social base has shrunk perceptibly in recent years (although not as severely as in West Bengal), but despite their decline, they still have a fighting chance to revitalize themselves in Kerala.

The book's third part concentrates on the period 2004–08 when the Left lent the Congress-led United Progressive Alliance (UPA) 'outside' support. This gave the Left a unique opportunity to push the UPA towards progressive agendas. However, the Left gave up the fight midway when it withdrew support to the UPA on the US–India nuclear deal in 2008. Thus began the Left's secular slide leading to the debacle of 2014.

The last part of the book deals with the urgent need for the Left to re-examine its theoretical–ideological premises, and revisit its political strategy, tactics and organizational practices—a precondition for its recovery and rejuvenation. If the Left fails to do this and goes into terminal decline, can independent Marxist groups, civil society organizations, people's movements and the progressive intelligentsia create the conceptual embryo of a new Left?

This is not an easy question to answer. I can only hope that this book will persuade at least some readers to believe, like me, that the Left is indispensable to the health of Indian democracy. If it did not exist, we would have to invent it.

1

The Rise and Decline of the Left

Origins, Achievements, Strengths and Weaknesses

India is by far the world's most important country which still has a significant and relatively powerful communist movement today, despite its decline in recent years and the massive setbacks its communist parties have suffered, especially in and since the 2014 national elections. The movement, originally inspired by anti-feudal, anti-imperialist and anti-capitalist ideals, was born during India's anti-colonial struggle, which it tried to influence with its own programmes and agendas. It has had a virtually uninterrupted, nine decades-long distinctive political presence in the form of mainstream parties, coalitions, associations and a variety of non-party groupings, as well as a smaller, more radical, armed expression in the Maoist insurgency since the late 1960s.

The impact of the movement at the parliamentary level was first felt in 1957, when the then still-undivided Communist Party of India became the world's first communist party to rule a sizeable state (Kerala) following a free and fair election in a democracy. Its government was dismissed in 1959 by the constitutionally authorized, if politically controversial, procedure of president's rule, but not before it had set in motion a number of substantial reforms, including changes in tenancy laws and education, grant of homestead lands to the landless and a series of other pro-poor measures. These reforms, including actual land redistribution from rich to poor, would soon make Kerala India's most advanced state in human development.

Since then, communist parties have been a significant component of the Indian political spectrum, represented in virtually every state of the country in trade unions, peasant associations, women's organizations and student unions, and in state legislatures, municipal bodies and village councils. They have ruled at various times in three states and been among the larger opposition parties in the national parliament, holding seven to eleven per cent of all seats in its Lower House.

Besides practising radical politics, and instituting reforms to bring about progressive change in society and governance, communist parties have made a significant, often vibrant, and in many ways unique, contribution to Indian society. Their contribution to people's capacity for self-organization, to culture, the arts and intellectual life, and to conceptions and agendas of social emancipation over a long span of time is highly disproportionate to their size or strength in legislatures.

The left parties represent one of the few currents in the Indian political mainstream (and arguably the most important one), which base themselves on an analysis of the relations of exploitation and oppression that underlie India's iniquitous social system and recognize the central importance of social bondage and economic servitude in sustaining its unequal political order. They profess a serious commitment to the uplift and empowerment of exploited and oppressed classes such as workers and peasants and other poor and marginalized groups, joined to a project of radical social transformation with the avowed goal of establishing a socialist society.

The CPI(M) and the CPI are both cadre-based parties. Between them, they count more than 1.7 million members,[1] who as a rule are considerably more committed and active than members of most other parties. They have close to 130,000 branches/units, and a strong presence, running into more than fifty million members, in trade unions, kisan sabhas (peasant associations), landless agricultural workers' unions and women's organizations, not to speak of youth and student associations, spread across India.[2] The CPI(M) is the world's second-largest communist party in size of membership, next only to the Chinese party.

The communist Left occupies a unique position within the Indian political–cultural spectrum as a formation overwhelmingly inspired and driven by principle and ideology. It gained social and political relevance early on, indeed a good deal of moral credibility and prestige, because it concentrated its energies on organizing and empowering exploited and underprivileged people on a programmatic basis, informed by a rich theoretical framework and a long-term vision. It addressed this task with unparalleled dedication, idealism and intelligence despite having to work in adverse circumstances, and made that task's achievement its central mission.

Equally important, the thrust of the Left's politics corresponded relatively closely to what might be termed the 'natural' centre of political gravity in a poor, extremely hierarchical and unequal society like India's. Yet the fact that communist parties did not develop such a strong base in other countries that were comparably poor and unequal heightens the mystery of what makes the Indian communist movement exceptional.

The communist movement's success during its heyday must be seen to lie in the enduring presence and growth of two large cadre-based parties, and the wide range of movements and organizations associated with them, which contributed to defending, deepening and enriching Indian democracy, and to extending the working people's rights and freedoms. The formidable influence that the communist parties wielded both nationally and in a large number of states enabled them to shape the ideological debate and policy agenda, and offer an alternative pole of attraction to generations of idealistic intellectuals and activists fighting for radical social change.

The Origins

The Indian Left was born late. Communist and socialist ideas arrived in India early in the twentieth century, and communists like M.N. Roy made a mark in debates within the Communist International (Comintern) in the very early 1920s. But left-wing ideas only found a political–organizational expression some decades after the middle-of-the-road or bourgeois-nationalist Indian National Congress was established (in 1885). The Congress, which led the movement for independence from British rule, had by the 1920s evolved into a party with a substantial national presence and a base among varied social layers thanks to Gandhi's non-cooperation movement.

By contrast, the Communist Party of India was only founded in 1925,[3] and the socialists had to wait until 1934 before emerging organizationally as a party. The CPI—which was periodically banned, with its publications proscribed and its leaders detained on 'conspiracy' charges by the colonial state—could at best establish a relatively weak and unstable presence by the mid-1930s, confined for all intents and purposes to a few big cities and some rural pockets. Its membership was limited to a few hundred in the early 1930s and reached a few thousand only after a major wave of strikes in the late 1930s, involving railway, tram and jute industry workers, in which the communists played an active, sometimes leading, role.[4]

The CPI's leadership had a relatively narrow social base and was dominated by upper-caste Hindus, with a sprinkling of educated middle-class Muslims (especially in Bengal) and Christians (in Kerala). There were hardly any women or Dalits and very few workers, poor peasants or landless labourers among its early leaders. The CPI did not hold its first congress until 1943.

The circumstance of late birth was crucial in setting the main terrain of domestic political contestation for the Left. No less vital was the international context. The Communist Party of India was formed and shaped in the era of high Stalinism, and derived its theoretical and strategic frameworks, and its basic understanding of politics, from the Communist International, which by the late 1920s had been fully subordinated to the Communist Party of the Soviet Union. The Comintern's Sixth Congress (1928)[5] furnished what became the formative influence for the CPI. Central to adherence to the Comintern were the tenets of 'socialism in one country' and defence of the Soviet Union as the paramount objective to be pursued by communist parties the world over.

Contrary to what some analysts argue, the Comintern's views, and its changing 'lines' from one Congress to the next, were not so much imposed on the CPI as accepted by it voluntarily—although they became a hindrance to understanding the complex specificities of Indian reality. Most CPI theoreticians of the early period believed that the 'actually existing socialism' of the Soviet Union, then invested with unparalleled revolutionary prestige, was the only kind of socialism possible. They had no exposure to any other doctrine or approach, nor access to Marxist literature except what came via the Comintern or the Soviet–British route—leave alone Left-wing literature critical of the CPSU or Comintern. They knew little about the Moscow Trials (1936–38), in which Stalin purged the entire Bolshevik old guard, barring himself; or they denied that these were staged.

In particular, Indian communists remained unacquainted with the theoretical tradition of Western Marxism,[6] with its rich discourse on the nature of capitalism, the modern state, and the peculiarities of the exercise of power in bourgeois democracy. Most of them had no opportunity even to read the more serious theoretical work of Marx or Lenin—and had to be content with Stalin's *Dialectical and Historical Materialism*, or even more formulaic and crude booklets and pamphlets by lesser ideologues.

At the same time, most Indian communists' dogmatic theoretical frameworks did not encourage them to explore valuable non-Marxist analyses of Indian society, caste and class relations and politics. This, among other factors, limited the CPI's ability both to comprehend Marxist theory holistically and to apply the Marxist method creatively and independently in order to develop an understanding of India's specific social, cultural and political realities and forge relevant strategic approaches.

The key strategic concepts that India's communist parties have always worked with originated in the Comintern tradition: including the notion of a 'two-stage revolution' in backward-capitalist or 'semi-feudal, semi-colonial' societies which have not undergone a bourgeois (or 'democratic') revolution; and the idea of a multi-class people's or national democratic front (comprising the working class, peasantry, petty bourgeoisie, and at times, the 'national bourgeoisie') under the 'vanguard role' of the party, which would eventually lead to 'the dictatorship of the proletariat' and to socialism.

Many of these tenets still remain central to the Indian communist parties' theoretical apparatus, as does the notion and organizational practice of 'democratic centralism', which allows limited internal debate in party congresses and other major forums, but requires that the majority decisions reached after such debate must bind all members; they cannot express dissenting views between congresses.

Similarly, the socialists were circumscribed by the theoretical framework of the Second International and its intense political rivalry with the Comintern. The two currents diverged from each other in their understanding of capitalism, the goals of the working class movement and threats to the socialist project from fascism and Nazism. Many socialists emphasized the relevance for India of labour-intensive small-scale production, while communists as a rule believed in heavy industry as the key to economic development along the Soviet model. The two currents also had a different understanding of the question of ends and means. The Indian socialists showed less theoretical rigidity than the communists in grappling with caste and some other India-specific issues, but they were reluctant to embrace class-based approaches and work jointly with the communists.

The socialists were the most important, if not the only, left current in India to have set up an organization that would counter the Rashtriya Swayamsevak Sangh (RSS) and the Hindu Mahasabha at the grass roots. This was the Rashtra Seva Dal (RSD), set up in Maharashtra in 1941, which aimed at the 'moral–intellectual development' of young people by inculcating in them the values of 'democratic socialism, secular nationalism ... equality, social justice, fraternity and rule of law'. The Dal set up schools and would hold periodic camps during school and college vacations. Had other Left currents supported the Dal or taken similar initiatives, India would have seen more resistance to Hindu communalism.[7]

Erosion of Left Diversity

A great deal of variety or diversity came to prevail by the 1940s within the Left spectrum in politics, in keeping with Indian society's pluralism and the wide range of its popular movements. Besides the communist and socialist parties, the Left formations included independent Marxist currents which rejected the Third International and Stalinist legacies, 'indigenist' and nationalist groupings (e.g., the Forward Bloc) with their own definitions of socialism, regional parties which emphasized social reform and Dalit liberation, and smaller currents which espoused quasi-Gandhian egalitarianism, some of whom later evolved into radical versions of 'Sarvodaya'.

A whole range of different ideologies and doctrines, with divergent characterizations of the nature of Indian society and state, and with different political goals and strategies, thrived in the country's Left, ranging from parliamentarism, workers' self-organization and grass-roots mobilization focused on the peasantry, to adherence to the perspective of an armed agrarian revolution.

There was some dialogue and contestation between these currents and their ideological approaches—always against the backdrop of the great wave of workers' strikes, peasant struggles and nationalist mobilizations that broke out in the decade or so before Independence. Although the dialogue was sometimes fractious, it was often productive. Later, however, some of the smaller streams got absorbed in the Congress and mainstream Left parties. The socialists underwent four major splits in the short span of seventeen years between 1955 and 1972.[8] Yet other currents disintegrated owing to personality clashes or under the force of state repression. The resultant diminution of diversity within the Left was to exact a toll on all currents, in particular the communists.

The undivided CPI had a complex, largely fraternal but at times contradictory, relationship with the socialists.[9] They shared a common critique of imperialism, feudalism and capitalism, and brought that to the freedom movement. Like the socialists, many individual communist party members also joined the Congress Socialist Party (CSP), a party/bloc within the parent body, in the 1930s. In some provinces, for example Kerala, the two currents worked together fruitfully. In others, their relations were far from cordial. But the CPI had little to do with, and was often hostile towards, B.R. Ambedkar, who led a new, sharply focused movement for the emancipation of the Dalits. This, as we shall see, had major consequences for the communists' approach to the caste question.

The first three decades of India's communist movement were turbulent, marked by major shifts of strategy, swings between armed struggle and parliamentarism, fraught relations with other Left currents, and inner-party factional strife and internal splits, some related to differences within the international communist movement, and others to the stance to be adopted vis-à-vis the independence movement, Partition, and national, regional and ethnic–linguistic questions.

It was not easy for the communist movement, either before or immediately after Independence, to identify which classes or social groups were its potential allies and which the main enemies, or to chart out its strategic line of march and decide on its tactics and methods of struggle. It oscillated between condemnation of the Congress as a conservative party reluctant to fight the British for full independence, and cooperation with the Congress in the CSP and the All-India Trade Union Congress (AITUC) and other mass organizations until the late 1940s. It adopted an ambivalent, often adversarial, and far-from-consistent, attitude towards the Congress, and its two main leaders, Gandhi and Nehru.

Comintern's Toxic Influence

The influence of the Comintern and the Communist Party of Great Britain (CPGB), as well as the Eurocentric thinking of early Indian communist leaders such as M.N. Roy—which ignored the India-specific context and characteristics of the fight for socialism, including caste, religion, gender and regional and linguistic diversity—was decisive in shaping the strategy and tactics of the CPI along doctrinaire or formulaic lines. A particularly toxic influence was exercised by CPGB theoretician Rajani Palme Dutt,[10] who was close to the Comintern leadership and became the CPI's most important adviser. The Comintern-dictated Eurocentric approach was carried over beyond Roy and Dutt by major CPI leaders such as Shripad Amrit Dange and Gangadhar Adhikari.

Following the Comintern's 'ultra-left' Sixth Congress line, the CPI in 1928 termed the Congress a 'bourgeois-nationalist' party opposed to the interests of workers and peasants, and declared Gandhism 'an openly counter-revolutionary force'.[11] That is one reason why the CPI suffered a decline in the strength and influence that had been gained through its painstaking organizing among workers.

Later, under the Seventh Congress (1935) line of the Comintern, the CPI executed another U-turn. It renounced the anti-capitalist struggle and endorsed strategic collaboration with the Congress's dominant leadership—just when the Congress in a rightward shift was giving up its demand for a full-fledged Constituent Assembly within a completely independent India. The CPI largely ignored the challenge posed by Subhas Chandra Bose to Gandhi. It made no sustained effort to build links with progressive elements in the Congress and to contain or isolate its right wing. Despite this, the CPI by the late 1930s had sunk popular roots in different provinces and acquired a base in the workers' and peasants' movements through sheer hard work.

When World War II broke out, the CPI, like communist parties the world over, first termed it 'an imperialist war'. Faced with a wrenching challenge in 1941 after Hitler invaded the Soviet Union, the CPI made a wholesale shift, characterizing the war as 'a people's war'. The party's support for the war effort isolated its leadership from the freedom movement and pitted it against the Congress-led 'Quit India' movement.[12] But unlike, say, M.N. Roy and some other supporters of the 'people's war' thesis, CPI leaders refused to collaborate with the colonial state, or to suspend the workers' and peasants' struggles they led.[13] Nevertheless, this stand was to cause the party a loss of part of its working class support base, especially in the vitally important Bombay cotton mill industry, where a Congress-led conservative union soon entrenched itself and right-wing Congress politicians like S.K. Patil virulently attacked the communists.

However, even this inconsistency, grave as it was, pales into insignificance beside the about-turn the CPI executed on the critical question of a separate state of Pakistan, based on religion, followed by a series of spectacularly contradictory positions on India's partition. In September 1942, an enlarged plenum of the CPI's central committee passed a resolution, 'Pakistan and National Unity', expressing support for the 'just essence of the Pakistan demand', which was later confirmed by the first congress of the party in May 1943.

The CPI's support for Pakistan was based on party theoretician Gangadhar Adhikari's analysis, which literally followed Stalin's definition of the nation and nationality, based on religion, among other attributes.[14] Integral to it was the principle of self-determination for nationalities and minorities, to the point of secession. The CPI had made 'the right to self-determination, including that of complete separation' part of its draft programme in 1930,[15] and reiterated it in 1941. At the historic 'Quit India' session of the Congress Working Committee (CWC) in August 1942, communist committee members opposed the majority demand for an immediate British withdrawal and called instead for a prior agreement with the Muslim League.[16]

In its November 1942 'manifesto' for 'Unity Week', the CPI rooted for a Congress–Muslim League agreement to create a 'provisional national government' based on Hindu–Muslim unity.[17] The party came under sharp attack from the Congress leadership, including Nehru, for advocating this. Communists were expelled from the All-India Congress Committee (AICC) and provincial organs in December 1945. None of this deterred the CPI from presenting a memorandum to the British Cabinet Mission in April 1946, which set forth its support for self-determination in unambiguous terms.[18] The same party would later condemn Partition as an 'imperialist conspiracy'.

The CPI's pro-Pakistan position turned a blind eye to the highly problematic nature of creating a nation state primarily on the basis of religion, and to Partition's likely communal and human consequences. But as Partition approached, the party changed its stance. In June 1947, it described India's imminent 'independence' as short of 'complete' freedom, and yet 'a weapon in the hands of the people' and 'an advance' towards freedom. On 3 August 1947, the CPI dedicated 'itself anew to fight … to win complete independence for our country', and to 'establish fraternal cooperation between India and Pakistan as a first step towards voluntary reunion of our motherland'.[19]

Soon after Partition, the CPI encouraged several of its 'Muslim' members to migrate to Pakistan. Among them was litterateur and Progressive Writers' Association founder Sajjad Zaheer, who was despatched in 1948 to West Pakistan to set up the communist party there.[20] The arrangement did not work. Zaheer was constantly harassed and then gaoled for four years in the trumped-up Rawalpindi conspiracy case.[21] He was deported to India in 1955, but 'under Nehru's protection and on the undertaking that he would never interfere in the internal affairs of Pakistan again'.[22]

In August 1948, the CPI adopted another extreme stand on the Pakistan issue. In a pamphlet entitled *Who Rules Pakistan?*, it condemned the 'fake freedom and fake leadership' prevalent in Pakistan, termed it a predatory bourgeois-landlord stooge of 'imperialism' and 'foreign exploiters'. It accused the 'exploiting landlords and capitalists of Pakistan' of thriving 'on communal passions' and 'secretly striking a deal with foreign capitalists for the joint exploitation of Pakistan'. It said the Pakistani state is based on violations of 'civil liberties and democratic rights', and cannot guarantee 'freedom from religious obscurantism'. Yet, it also said: 'The people of Pakistan like the people of India have yet to liberate themselves and save their country from being sold to foreign exploiters.'[23]

On Jammu and Kashmir too, the CPI took a series of inconsistent positions. It first welcomed the state's accession to India; but in retrospect, the party said it wrongly 'made the Kashmiri people believe' that the Indian Army's march into Kashmir was 'the march of the democratic forces'. In February–March 1948 (i.e., during the Ranadive period,)[24] it repudiated this as a 'mistake', derived from the erroneous presumption that the Indian Union is 'progressive' and Pakistan is 'reactionary'. Besides, 'there can be no question of accession [of Jammu and Kashmir to either India or Pakistan] before the complete victorious people's democratic revolution has been achieved ... before princely aristocracy has been liquidated and power has passed into the hands of the masses.'[25] This represented sharp opposition to the partition formula devised by the colonial state, under which the rulers of the princely states would choose whether to accede to India or to Pakistan.

In August 1948, the CPI condemned the so-called tribal incursion from Pakistan into Kashmir. It said Pakistan's leaders had embarked on this 'adventurous policy' 'at the behest of the British imperialists', and 'entered into a virtual war against the people of Kashmir and the government of the Indian Union',[26] thus by implication supporting the latter. However, in a document titled 'Imperialist Aggression in Kashmir',[27] also belonging to Ranadive period, the party attributed the Kashmir crisis to the 'aggressive designs of the Anglo–American imperialist bloc'.

The bloc, said the CPI, not only wanted to play India and Pakistan off against each other and 'aggravate religious-communal hostilities in order to maintain their domination over the whole sub-continent', but 'control areas of military-strategic importance, particularly the Northern Region of Kashmir where the borders of the Soviet Union and China meet'; the 'essence' of the imperialist design was 'the preparation for a war against the Soviet Union'.

The CPI also vehemently condemned Nehru's Kashmir policy of 1947–50, which it said aimed to 'grab' and exploit Kashmir's 'rich territory' by forcing Sheikh Abdullah into a 'heinous compromise' with the 'tyrannical Maharaja', and making the latter accede to India; Abdullah merely lent a 'democratic garb' to the 'treacherous accession'.[28] Later, the CPI radically revised this position, accepting the maharaja's decision to accede to the Indian Union as legitimate—just as it moved over from a 'hard' insurrectionist line in 1948 to a 'soft' parliamentary stance in 1953, and from support for radical federalism and separatism, to acceptance of 'national unity'.[29]

These zigzag turns, breathtaking in their swings between extremes, betray near-total servility on the part of the CPI to an ideological–theoretical framework borrowed from the Comintern and the CPSU, the party's passive acceptance of Moscow's tactical line on a range of issues, and its own leaders' failure or inability to develop an independent analytical perspective or political strategy. When CPI leaders differed among themselves on strategic or major tactical issues, they would ask the CPSU to mediate or advise them, as happened in 1951 when Stalin himself intervened (discussed in the next chapter).

More generally, all this speaks of a persistent weakness in the Indian communists' theoretical apparatus and analysis, itself rooted in a lack of exposure to and systematic education in Marxism and the absence of a tradition of robust internal debate. The absence is partly attributable to their compulsions of having had to work underground or in otherwise straitened circumstances for long periods, an organizational culture that inhibits respect for intellectual difference and dissent, and a lack of interest in theoretical matters. Put simply, theory—unlike good, vigorous activism or dedicated mass-organizing and party-building work—has never been a forte of Indian communists.

The turns on Pakistan, the national question and Kashmir were some of the worst misadventures in Indian communism's history and exacted a heavy price from the CPI. Remarkably, however, the party was able to overcome the opprobrium resulting from its maverick and controversial positions relatively quickly, and regain legitimacy. The process began as early as 1943, with the CPI tripling its membership.[30]

The process gathered pace thanks to a strengthening of the party's base among trade unions and kisan sabhas in the mid- and late 1940s across different states through mass struggles, which earned the CPI more relevance and respectability. In the early 1950s, the party changed its top leadership, abandoned the 'fake independence' line, made a solemn commitment to abide by parliamentary democracy and the brand-new Indian Constitution, affirmed its support to India's territorial claims over Jammu and Kashmir, and started behaving like a 'responsible' mainstream political party.

The CPI performed remarkably well in independent India's first general election in 1951–52 and emerged as the largest opposition party. Even greater mainstream acceptance followed when the party softened its stand on the Congress partly under Soviet influence, itself traceable to Nehru's pursuit of a policy of bloc neutrality in the cold war, his advocacy of a 'mixed economy' strategy based on indicative planning, and his openness to taking Soviet assistance for the construction of a modern steel mill, which the West refused to offer.

This caused tensions within the CPI, some of whose leaders were opposed to subordinating the party's line to the foreign policy interests of the Soviet state. An even more important source of inner-party dissension was the historic schism between the USSR and China under Mao Zedong following the Twentieth Congress of the CPSU and Nikita Khrushchev's proclamation of a policy of 'peaceful coexistence' between socialism and capitalism.[31]

Inner-party tensions were greatly exacerbated by the Sino-Indian border war of 1962; CPI leaders were sharply divided over supporting the Indian government on the dispute. Several were arrested on suspicion that they opposed the Indian government's line, yet the top leadership backed the government on manifestly 'patriotic' grounds. These differences played a significant role in the CPI split of 1964, leading to the formation of the CPI(M), which advocated a more militant line against the Congress government.

Five years later, in the wake of the Naxalbari armed uprising in West Bengal in 1967, the CPI(M) itself split, resulting in the formation of the All-India Coordination Committee of Communist Revolutionaries, and in 1969, the birth of the CPI (Marxist-Leninist), i.e., CPI (ML), or the Naxalites. The Naxalites underwent a series of splits, mergers and further splits and were greatly weakened until two of their major factions eventually coalesced in 2004 to form the CPI (Maoist).

Meanwhile, in 1957, the still undivided CPI became the world's first communist party to come to power by winning a free and fair election in a sizeable state in a democracy—in Kerala.[32] This was to mark the CPI's long-term transition to 'the parliamentary road to socialism'. The CPI(M) and the CPI have since practised quasi-'normal' parliamentary politics and shared power in three states—under the Left Front banner in West Bengal and Tripura, and in a broader coalition called the Left Democratic Front (LDF) in Kerala.

The Left Front's record in government in West Bengal, which it ruled for an uninterrupted thirty-four years since 1977, is analysed in depth in Chapters 4 and 5; suffice it to say here that its early exuberance and promise soon faded. After its first decade in power, the Front got de-radicalized in ideological, programmatic and organizational terms. It moved more and more towards maintaining the status quo, turned bureaucratic, routinist and conservative in its methods even as it continued to win state assembly and panchayat elections. It gave up transformative agendas like land confiscation and redistribution, and opted for a much more modest programme of registration and protection of tenants through Operation Barga. It turned its face against organizing a union of landless agricultural workers separate from the kisan sabhas representing landowning peasants, including rich and middle peasants who employ labourers.

A question that has long intrigued both scholars and activists in India and abroad is why the communist parties' greatest political strength and influence—reflected in their long tenure or repeated stints in power—

remained confined to West Bengal and Kerala (and tiny Tripura), which also account for more than 70 per cent of their membership. The reasons, discussed in the chapters devoted to those states, obviously have to do with their social and cultural specificities, the peculiarities of their class and caste structures, and these states' special histories of political mobilization.

These 'initial conditions' matter greatly and explain why the communist movement sank its roots relatively early in these states and grew there to the point of making a bid for power. Yet, these conditions are not so overwhelmingly location- or culture-specific as to limit the movement's spread to these states alone. Many other states/ regions also had strong Left movements, accompanied by radical trade unionism, kisan sabha mobilization, feminism and other forms of social activism. Notable among them are Andhra Pradesh/Telangana, Bihar, Maharashtra, Tamil Nadu, Punjab, Jharkhand, Assam, and not least, parts of Uttar Pradesh.

Similarly, the dissimilarities between Kerala and West Bengal in social, political and cultural features, and in the Left's achievements, are as important as their similarities. In Kerala, the Left instituted serious social and political reforms through programmes of popular participation and empowerment, radical decentralization, and schemes for affordable access to food, education and social security. It invested substantive content into formal democracy and radicalized it. In West Bengal, however, it started on a much more conservative base, adopted mild versions of land and governance reforms, and allowed initiatives like panchayati raj to get bureaucratized under party control. Eventually, it embraced a quasi-neo-liberal industrialization policy. The reasons for these differences are discussed in the respective chapters.

At any rate, there is hardly a state in India without a history of Left-wing politics. Networks of blue- and white-collar workers' unions, women's organizations, and associations of teachers, students, lawyers and other professionals, which have a Left connection or outlook, have thrived in every nook and corner of the country. Some of these movements were not sustained, and some atrophied, because the local balance of class forces turned adverse, the organized working class shrank in relative weight, certain kinds of identity politics came to hold sway (e.g., Mandalism in the Hindi belt), the Left parties' social base shifted towards the middle class, or their organizational and cadre-building resources proved inadequate. Some of these reasons are analysed below. But the movements flourished for decades in numerous states and have left their mark; they cannot be written off even today.

The Left parties' presence and strength was regionally always uneven and unbalanced. In some cases, e.g., Kerala and Andhra, they grew rapidly precisely because they expressed regional aspirations for ethno-linguistic autonomy and right of self-determination, especially in the 1940s and early 1950s. Yet, it would be wrong to view these parties primarily through the prism of regional politics. The Left movement has always had a national profile, self-perception and perspective—and an India-wide presence. In recent years, the movement's national role has grown disproportionately in relation to its influence in the states, barring West Bengal and Kerala.

Indeed, with the effective end of one-party rule at the Centre in 1989, the Left parties acquired unprecedented influence in national politics. They played what has been called the kingmaker's role in installing the V.P. Singh–led coalition government in New Delhi (1989–91). Dependent on the two opposite ends of the spectrum, the Left Front and the Bharatiya Janata Party (BJP), the government did not last long. But as India's politics turned increasingly multipolar (at least until 2014), Left parties came to be seen as legitimate contenders for sharing national power or becoming arbiters in its distribution—not least because of their image as 'serious', 'responsible' parties, and the prestige they enjoyed.

Thus, in 1996, long-standing West Bengal chief minister Jyoti Basu, considered the tallest leader in the non-Congress-non-BJP camp, was unanimously offered the prime minister's post by a multiparty coalition. His party, the CPI(M), made him turn down the offer. Basu later called this 'a historic blunder' as such an opportunity is unlikely to return in the near future.

The Left parties' role in national politics and their alliance strategies are discussed in depth in Chapters 2 and 3. Their support from the 'outside' was critical to the formation of the Congress party-led United Progressive Alliance government after the 2004 national election, which ended the six-year spell of the Bharatiya Janata Party–led

National Democratic Alliance (NDA). Although the 'outside' support arrangement broke down in 2008, the Left played no mean role in drafting the UPA's Common Minimum Programme (CMP) and influencing some of its social and economic agendas, and to a lesser extent, foreign and security policies.

However, prolonged experience of limited power at the state level—as opposed to national power, which proved beyond their reach—became the Indian Left's distinguishing mark. This was both similar to and different from the Italian and French communist parties' long-lasting sway over scores of city and provincial governments between the 1960s and the 1980s, where they in some cases implemented radical programmes. Wielding state-level power, itself circumscribed by the supervening authority of the Centre, has confronted the Indian Left with the prospect of 'regionalization'—a strong presence and consolidation in a handful of states, but with relatively feeble and declining strength nationally, and in particular, in the populous Hindi belt.

It was not easy for the Left to make the watershed decision it made in the 1960s to form governments in the states in the knowledge that in India's semi-federal political system, the distribution of power is strongly biased in favour of the Central government and leaves very little policy space for the states. The memory of the dismissal of Kerala's first communist government in 1959 also weighed heavily on the minds of the Left's leaders. They decided that they would nevertheless participate in state governments through which they would have a degree of freedom to implement policies of their choice in order to bring 'limited relief' to the people.

The experience of wielding state-level power has not been consistently happy for the Left. Both the Left Front in West Bengal and Left Democratic Front in Kerala instituted impressive reforms, especially in the early years of their tenure. But they soon made compromises, whose merits have long been debated both within and outside the Left. The question is discussed at greater length in Chapters 4 to 7. It bears mentioning here, however, that in West Bengal in particular, the Left drifted into conservative approaches to social development, economic growth and industrialization. The result was to alienate its social base and eventually lead to a loss of state power.

The socialists, who were highly influential in Indian politics and more numerous than the communists at one time, but marked by greater individualism and weak, if less-than-rigid organization, submerged their identities in the Janata Party in 1977, and got fragmented in its various factional offshoots after the party split two years later. Most socialists now remain scattered among a myriad different parties, including low-caste-based formations and even explicitly right-wing parties like the BJP. The socialist current has ceased to have a distinct organizational, and even ideological, expression in India, although a tiny, nominally national-level Socialist Party (India) still exists[33] and attempts are being made to reunite former socialists who were part of the Janata ensemble.

To all intents and purposes, the Indian Left is now reduced to the mainstream parties listed above—and a younger non-parliamentary Left current composed of Maoist or Naxalite groupings, which believe in the armed overthrow of the state. These groupings are implacably hostile to the mainstream Left parties, which they regard as 'revisionist' and part of the existing system of power. They are active in the forested central and south-eastern adivasi (tribal) belt, and in pockets of Orissa and West Bengal. This belt is home to some of India's most impoverished and marginalized people, whose livelihoods are gravely endangered by predatory mining, power generation and industrial projects. Known for audacious armed attacks on their adversaries, including police and other state personnel, these guerrillas constitute one of the biggest Maoist movements in the world.

The Maoists have suffered several desertions and losses in recent years thanks to state repression and non-judicial executions. Although they now seem to be in decline, they have succeeded in mobilizing large numbers of adivasis on livelihood issues and against the deprivation of their traditional access to natural resources like water, forests and land (jal, jungle, zameen). The Indian state has responded to this mobilization with savage military force and blatant human rights violations, including sponsorship and arming of militias like Salwa Judum in the central Indian state of Chhattisgarh. But the political impasse continues in the tribal belt; state repression has not succeeded in destroying the Maoist movement.

The state's approach towards the Maoist movement highlights

profound weaknesses in India's political system and the shallowness of its liberal-democratic claims. The mainstream parliamentary Left parties, in particular the CPI(M), do not focus enough on these weaknesses or advocate a qualitatively different non-coercive approach, they largely reciprocate the Naxalites' hostility towards them. When in power in West Bengal, they pursued policies similar to the Centre's own militarized approach against the Maoists, especially in the state's Jangalmahal region in the west which has a significant Adivasi population. Unless there is a dialogue with the Maoists, which addresses their legitimate concerns and helps them enter the political mainstream, the parliamentary Left will not be able to help break the impasse.

My focus, however, is primarily on the mainstream Left parties, and I attempt an analysis of their ideological premises, theories, strategic visions and programmatic perspectives. I do not attempt an analysis of non-party radical movements on social, environmental and livelihood issues, new forms of labour unions, women's organizations, progressive civil society groups,[34] and mobilizations of what may be called the 'social Left', including the intelligentsia. India is distinguished by a staggering variety of such movements, with a remarkable range of interests, great vigour and ability to mobilize large numbers. Few other countries match India in this regard.

A study of such movements would be fascinating and hugely rewarding, being long overdue. However, it is beyond the scope of this book, which is limited to noting the broad relationship between the waxing and waning of the organized Left, on the one hand, and on the other, the trajectories of social movements on issues that are not of immediate consequence to the Left's political success or failure, but which nevertheless define the larger ecosystem within which it works. The question is discussed in Chapter 8 and argues that the Left flourishes best when it acts as a bold avant-garde force for social emancipation and radical transformation and becomes a beacon to progressive social movements; the Left fails and falters in situations where it tails such movements or lacks the audacity to question the status quo radically enough.

The Left's struggle to remain relevant to Indian reality and grow into a larger force for emancipatory change has only been partially successful.

It has often been problematic and deeply fraught with inconsistencies and contradictions. Not only has the Left sometimes made compromises with its own principles and stated policy positions; it has also neglected a number of major social agendas, both theoretical and strategic, or at best developed an unbalanced or distorted perspective on them.

For instance, the Left has never adequately theorized caste or religion, despite their signal importance in India. Nor has it given the issue of gender the salience it deserves in India's patriarchal and viciously male-supremacist society. And it has failed to incorporate the question of ecology and destruction of nature centrally into its critique of capitalism. It has thus not developed an argument for socialism as an altogether novel economic system or form of social organization based on a qualitatively transformed relationship between natural resources, human society, and production and consumption—different from anything known in history. Nor does the Left have an understanding of caste that enables it to relate that concept, along with the notion of class, to the nature of social hegemony that is specific to India, and to integrate it into its conception of the structure of political power. This needs a major modification of conventional Marxist theory without losing sight of its foundational anti-capitalist tenets or the goal of socialism.

As we shall see below, it is simply not enough, indeed it is basically wrong, to reduce caste to a relic of feudalism or semi-feudalism. Caste is very much a contemporary phenomenon. Although it has increasingly taken on a political expression, caste remains central to the relations of exploitation and oppression that are at the heart of India's hierarchical society. Similarly, the Left has by and large not theorized identity politics of the Other Backward Classes (OBCs) and kindred varieties, although it first vacillated on and then supported the demand for OBC reservations under the Mandal formula.

Over the years, much of the Left has relatively uncritically accepted the standard mainstream discourse about the freedom movement, Partition and formation of the Indian state, including the accession of Jammu and Kashmir to the Indian Union. As in the standard nationalist narrative, the Left too holds the Muslim League primarily responsible for Partition, and sees in the division of India a conspiracy on the part of the departing British colonialists. In truth, as many scholars have recently argued, the Congress, thanks to its refusal to share power with the League within a federal structure, was in no small measure culpable for the chain of events that resulted in Partition.[35]

Until the 1940s, a multiplicity of views about the nature of the emerging Indian state and the Congress leadership prevailed within the Left. For many years after Independence, both the communist Left and other progressive streams debated a variety of approaches on building an alternative to the degraded, semi-authoritarian liberal-democratic political order that came to prevail in the country. This alternative would not be confined to formal parliamentary or power-oriented politics alone, but encompass civil society and the organization of producers both as workers and as citizens who empower themselves through self-activity.

The Left thus struggled to articulate a new vision of society based on the extension of the idea of freedom through the self-organization of the working people. Collective modes and new cultures of self-expression would be important here in realizing the notion of the Left not just as a party or organization, but as a living, throbbing movement that represents new critical, radical thinking about society, the state, the economy, human relationships, lifestyles, work and play, the family, culture, education, leisure, everything under the sun. Integral to this would be an effort to combine the mundane and the quotidian with the long-term goals and ideals central to what has been called the Grand Narrative or Discourse of history.[36]

During its best phase, the Left formed itself and educated itself through several kinds of activities or practices: first, a lively interaction and dialogue with the trade unions, kisan sabhas and other mass organizations in whose work it participated; second, its own theoretical reflection developed in intellectual debates in party and non-party circles; third, its participation in social and cultural initiatives and its conversation with grass-roots movements active on these issues; and finally, its practice of standard or conventional parliamentary politics, including the exercise of state power.

The first of the three exposed it to new ideas and experiences, for which the last would provide a vehicle of translation or realization into practice. The Left attempted with varying success to establish a strong, structured relationship between these non-parliamentary activities and its parliamentary work. This was a unique combination of features, not replicated, indeed not even attempted, in most other political formations or movements in India.

Contribution to Social Change

The Left parties struggled to create a new culture of politics. They represented their core constituencies of workers, peasants, the poor, the landless, artisans and other disadvantaged sections with great passion, as no other current or party did. They struggled for and achieved rights and benefits on their behalf, which were among the greatest gains that the underprivileged have made. Some of the factors underlying their success are discussed in the following chapters. They include an analysis of social relations and of the state derived from Marxist theory, an international perspective on capitalism, a long-term vision of socialism, a systematic effort to evolve a relatively coherent domestic political strategy, keenness to organize and sink roots among exploited and oppressed strata, a disciplined party organization and an extraordinarily talented, remarkably diligent and fiercely dedicated cadre.

So are some of the weaknesses of these parties. These include a rigid, ossified ideological–theoretical framework, inadequate comprehension of the peculiarities of Indian capitalism (especially since the 1980s), flawed conjunctural analysis and absence of a tradition of open and free debate on issues of strategy. They are magnified by an authoritarian organizational form congealed in the practice of democratic centralism, and not least, failure to build an internally democratic and balanced Left Front not subject to any one party's overwhelming influence or control. These weaknesses proved disabling in the face of new challenges confronting the communist parties from the 1990s on, especially in respect of policies to promote economic growth and industrialization, within a cogently anti-neo-liberal framework. They partially explain their decline—and equally, the failure to comprehend it and take corrective steps.

The Left has over the years tried, with varying degrees of success, to apply Marxist theory to understand Indian reality and to reinterpret, adapt and enrich that theory. It has also tried to deploy the resulting analysis to develop a vision of social emancipation from which to derive its own programmes, policies and practices aimed at bringing about radical change, both through popular mobilization and the use of state power.

This book asks how far and in what manner the Left has accomplished this goal; whether it could have achieved more; what is the Left's likely future prospect given its present shrunken state; and whether its core agenda of progressive or socialist transformation can still be reinvented and restored to relevance either with its own agency or through other forces, formations and initiatives.

A tentative answer to the first question is that the Left's contribution to transformative social change in India has been substantial, indeed salutary, and in many ways irreplaceable. But the value of the contribution lies more in the Left's role in generating forums and platforms of radical ideas, and in organizing and leading popular mobilizations around them, than in its use of instruments of state power to institute various reform measures, significant as these might have been in promoting the interests of workers, peasants and other underprivileged groups.

Second, the Left could have achieved much more had it set its sights higher and adopted a less conformist and more questioning, even irreverent, stance vis-à-vis the institutions of India's bourgeois democracy and attempted to radicalize these through mass-movement pressure. Put more bluntly, the Left parties are partially responsible for failing to achieve their potential or fulfil their own long-term promise.[37] This is not only because they had a limited or narrow conception of what they could achieve within the limits of what they considered to be *feasible*, but more importantly, because they had a limited Horizon of the Possible[38] within their political imagination and strategic thinking. They were not ambitious enough.

Third, the Left today faces a grim crisis of an existential nature and of multiple dimensions. It stands at a fork in history. I suggest that it could rejuvenate itself, but only on condition that it acknowledges the gravity of the crisis and its leaders' responsibility for it, undertakes painfully self-critical introspection into its flaws and weaknesses, and pulls itself up by the bootstraps through radical course correction. The likely alternative, if it does not do so, is terminal decline—through further electoral losses, cadre demoralization and defection, growing erosion of social base, intellectual confusion, and organizational disarray and disintegration. It is not clear if the Left has the will, and the ideological, intellectual, political and organizational resources to pursue the first path.

Finally, even if the political Left as it is currently constituted fails to rejuvenate and reinvent itself, many of its ideas, strategies and social–political agendas will retain their relevance and must be taken up, perhaps in other organizational forms, by what might be termed the broad 'social Left', as well as mass organizations like trade unions and kisan sabhas, civil society groups and people's movements. The book considers some tentative ideas and proposals in this regard in Chapter 10.

Surviving the Soviet Collapse

A remarkable feature of the Indian Left's recent history is that its membership continued to grow for more than two decades after the collapse of the Soviet Union and the demise of international socialism in 1991. Although membership growth slowed down in some states during the second half of the first decade of the twenty-first century, and the number of party members stagnated or decreased in some others, including West Bengal and Uttar Pradesh, the overall national trend was one of growth until recently. For instance, the CPI(M)'s overall membership rose by 6.4 per cent to 1.045 million between 2007 and 2011. And although the CPI's strength saw ups and downs in recent years, and peaked at a little under 666,000 members in 2010, it grew by 7.4 per cent between 2007 and 2011.[39]

This set the CPI(M) and the CPI apart from most conventional communist parties (CPs) the world over which inherited the legacy of the Third (or Communist) International.[40] These include large communist parties in the developed countries, including France, Italy and Spain, which commanded a formidable presence after World War II, but declined to near-irrelevance soon after the collapse of the Berlin Wall in 1989. Barring a few exceptions like Nepal and South Africa, the CPs in most countries could not survive the Soviet Union's disintegration. They soon lost much of their political credibility, suffered electoral defeats and an exodus of their members, splintered into factions—and went into extinction. The Indian communist movement endured, even flourished, for several years after the disintegration not just of the USSR, but of many communist regimes in eastern Europe too.

The Indian Left's post-1991 expansion seemed—at least until the electoral setbacks beginning in 2009 and ending in a debacle five years on—to be an impressive achievement in and of itself. It spoke of the continuing relevance of the Left parties' programmes and policies for Indian society, and their roots among the masses. But their expansion was in many ways shallow and uneven.

Although the Left parties' parliamentary representation grew, reaching in 2004 an all-time peak of sixty-one Lok Sabha seats (of a total of 543), their base became progressively narrower and more regionalized, being confined primarily to West Bengal (not to be underrated: its ninety-one-million population is higher than that of any West European country)[41], Kerala (population thirty-three million), and Tripura (population 3.7 million) in the north-east. Equally important, by the early 1990s, if not earlier, the Left's intellectual–moral appeal began to wane. Stagnation set in at the level of ideas and political strategies, and policy conservatism grew and got consolidated, especially in the states where the Left was in power.

Crucially, India's communist parties failed to draw any lessons from the collapse of the Soviet Union, for long their ideal and their prime model of socialism. In fact, they had no explanation to offer for what was a catastrophe for their own ideology and belief system, certainly not an explanation based on 'internal' conditions, including the structural factors and long-term causal processes which underlay the extreme bureaucratization of the Communist Party of the Soviet Union (CPSU) soon after the Revolution, the rapid degeneration of the state which the party dominated, the consolidation of a parasitic leadership at its apex, and growing unpopularity and loss of legitimacy of the Soviet system, which eventually put a question mark over its viability.[42]

The Indian CPs did not recognize these longer-term processes and phenomena as the necessary, or prior and enabling, conditions for the implosion produced by the combination of a dysfunctional economy, social crisis and internal political dissonance in the mid-1980s, which finally led to the disintegration of the USSR. Rather, they attributed the collapse of the Soviet Union to contingent or tactical factors, including external ones, and subjective 'errors' by Soviet leaders.

Indian communists did not develop a critique of some of the basic ideological tenets of the CPSU in the early period, including its flawed analysis of global capitalism, statist notion of socialism, vanguardism, bureaucratic and hierarchical political practices, and some of its regressive positions under Stalin on nationalism, on 'socialism in one country' and on social issues. These were among the more salient causes for the degeneration of the Soviet system.

The Indian CPs largely ignored or rationalized the terrible cruelties and privations imposed upon the USSR's public by Stalin's policies and methods, and the absence of democracy and civil and political rights that became integral to the Soviet governing system. The Soviet crisis had deep roots going back to the 1920s, if not earlier. It got aggravated over succeeding decades and led to a hollowing out of all progressive content from the Soviet system under a variety of regimes and governments led by Khrushchev and Brezhnev, and after them.

Nor did the Indian CPs attempt an independent critical analysis of the USSR's post-war social and economic policies, its extravagant military postures during the cold war and its international policy failures, which compounded the crisis.[43] By the 1980s, the Soviet economy had faltered, military spending became unsustainable, and alternatives—however flawed—towards greater political freedom became visible to the public, along with the lure of comparatively higher living standards in the West. The public was now willing to abandon socialism and embrace capitalism, albeit of a degraded, criminalized variety.

Instead of analysing the deep structural or systemic causes of the collapse of the USSR and 'actually existing socialisms' in eastern and central Europe, the Indian CPs attributed it to Gorbachev's 'mistakes' in instigating glasnost and perestroika. They also blamed interventions by 'imperialism', the 'subjective' errors of the CPSU leadership in embracing 'revisionism', its negation of socialism's 'glorious' past achievements, its failure to raise the 'ideological consciousness' of the masses, and its eventual abandonment of the class struggle, the 'dictatorship of the proletariat' and 'democratic centralism' in favour of social democracy and legalization of private property for the dismantling of socialism in the USSR and the demise of international socialism which followed.

The Indian CPs' failure to subject the Soviet model of socialism to critical scrutiny and to diagnose the pathology of the CPSU and the Soviet system that eventually resulted in the cataclysm of 1991 was not merely ideological. It was closely related to, or it derived from, the fact that the Indian Left would have had to apply that diagnosis to itself—because its own organization mirrored that of the CPSU to a considerable extent.

Until the Soviet model itself broke down, it remained the Indian communist parties' sole template, which was unaffected by the Hungarian crisis (1956) and the Prague Spring (1968). Bereft of a thorough, radical critique of the Soviet model, the Left could not develop an *independent* alternative conception of socialism based on coherent and secure ideological–political foundations which correspond to contemporary reality and are yet in broad consonance with Marxism or Historical Materialism.

This stands in sharp contrast to, say, the new Latin American Left, which built an altogether different relationship—in relation to the traditional Left—with autonomous grass-roots movements on issues such as workers' rights, participatory budgeting, environmental protection, land, agricultural labour rights and urban affairs.[44] The Indian Left's failure to do anything comparable has affected, and will probably continue to impair, its capacity to acknowledge and learn from its mistakes by using independent criteria of its own and to undertake course correction. The failure is not only ideological, but also strategic and organizational.

Since the early 1990s, the Left has had to confront yet another major challenge—the Indian state's pursuit of neo-liberal economic policies, which have spawned, and in turn have been buttressed by, a rapid spread of reactionary social-Darwinist ideas. These have had a corrosive impact on the tenor of public discourse. Neo-liberal policies have resulted in the growth and consolidation of a sizeable, propertied, consumerist–hedonist and socially conservative middle class, and further shifted the overall balance of class forces in favour of the Right, in particular the Hindu political Right, much to the Left's disadvantage. This led to the drying up of a part of the Left's support base among the urban middle class, which could now as easily be drawn towards the Right as it had earlier been attracted to the Left. This shrank the pool for recruiting Left-wing cadres.

Yet, the Left managed—almost miraculously, some analysts would say—to survive these adversities for two decades, albeit with some losses and after paying a price through policy compromises in the states where it was in power, especially West Bengal. By the mid-1990s, these compromises became manifest in an uncritical embrace of industrialization based on private capital investment, and later, in gravitation towards the very same neo-liberal policies for which the Left pilloried the Central government, and which increasingly alienated it from the plebeian layers of the population.

At the same time, the Left neglected, particularly in West Bengal, vital social development agendas such as health care, nutrition, education, employment, food security and environmental protection, as well as inclusive policies for the substantial Muslim minority, estimated at over one-fourth of the state's population. As we shall see below, especially in Chapters 5 and 7, the Left would pay dearly for this neglect after the early 2000s.

A Part of India's Political Modernity

Between the late 1980s and the middle of first decade of the twenty-first century, the Left substantially expanded its political strength and membership. The mass organizations it led added sizeable numbers to their ranks. The Left's parliamentary strength also grew rapidly. Its relative success was attributable in no small measure to its legacy of committed partisanship of underprivileged, marginalized and poor people. As noted above, the Left spoke and acted, for many decades, for these groups in a far more principled, consistent and organic way than did any other major political current in India. In a society marked by mass poverty, multiple forms of deprivation and extreme economic inequalities, this partisanship created a great deal of legitimacy, goodwill and respect for the Left. Along with its intellectual and political capital, its early work among workers and peasants and its energetic organizational capacity building, these furnished the basis of the Left's gains and achievements over many decades.

A major argument of this book is that the Left must be understood not just as a political entity, or a phenomenon expressed merely through parties and associated organizations, but rather as a *movement*, a living social–cultural organism with deep roots in civil society and people's mobilizations, which aspires to institute a new notion of citizenship through the self-organization of the working people and by struggling to foster critical, radical thinking about society, the state, the economy, human relationships, lifestyles, work and play, the family, culture, education, leisure and so on.

These aspirations did not always fructify, but the periods during which they came close to realization were the Left's most creative and vibrant phases. Crucial to the Left's success was its ability to articulate practical agendas such as land reforms, decentralization of power, expanded rights for the working people and social security programmes. It could often link these to a perspective of freeing the underprivileged from bondage and oppression, as part of the goal of creating an egalitarian and just society with human dignity and social cohesion.

Historically, the social ideals and political agendas that the Left fought for, defended, and disseminated, based on socialism and Marxism, became an integral part of India's political modernity. They significantly shaped some of the forward-looking ideas contained in the Indian nation-building project for nearly a century. The Left brought a refreshingly new critical perspective to this project by anchoring it in the empowerment of the dispossessed and powerless. It advocated a radical notion of democracy, waged intransigent struggles against the rich and powerful (and policies that favour them), defended dissent and the right to dissent, and championed pro-poor alternative policies. Insofar as India has registered moral progress over these long decades, the Left significantly contributed to it. This is no mean achievement.

The communists were probably the first political current in India, barring the revolutionary terrorists of the freedom movement, to demand full sovereign independence for the country, as distinct from limited Home Rule, to which the Congress party confined itself until the late

1920s.[45] Even as a fledgling force, they assertively tried, through their leadership of the workers' movement, to press the Congress to adopt that demand. For instance, in December 1928 in Calcutta, they organized an assembly of 20,000 workers from a variety of trades and invaded the compound where the Congress's annual session was being held. They forced prominent Congress leaders, including Jawaharlal Nehru, to address them and passed a resolution which said: '... we the workers and peasants of the land shall not rest content till complete independence is established and all exploitation from capitalism and imperialism cease[s]. We do call upon the National Congress to keep that goal before them and organize the national forces for that purpose'.[46]

No less significant was the role that communist and socialist thought played in the 1920s and 1930s in influencing the freedom movement to adopt a progressive Left-leaning, anti-imperialist, anti-feudal agenda.[47] Eventually, this agenda was powerfully reflected in the Directive Principles of State Policy of the Indian Constitution, probably its most radical chapter. The roots of the Principles are traceable to the Congress party's '1931 Karachi Resolution, or farther, and to the two streams of socialist and nationalist sentiments in India that had been flowing ever faster since the late 1920s'.[48]

Indian communists and socialists fought for the idea of building an open, modern, free, and democratic society unburdened by hierarchy, ignorance and superstition. They demanded that the state in independent India must bear a major responsibility for the welfare of its citizens. They tried to infuse into the struggle against imperialism agendas of workers' rights, restructuring of agrarian relations through the demand for 'land to the tiller', and other elements of economic equality and social justice—agendas which the Congress proposed, but often did not seriously pursue.

The Left parties played a pioneering role in organizing industrial workers in trade unions, peasants in kisan sabhas and the landless in agricultural workers' unions. Right from the 1920s, they mobilized millions of people around the right to form unions, and for better wages, humane working conditions and the right to employment; right to food and food security; participation in democratic decision making; devolution of power to local governments; and many other agendas of popular empowerment. The rich experience of struggles led by the Left proved invaluable to the working people: it raised their political consciousness, self-confidence, and capacity for self-organization.

The Left parties' origins and early history are inseparable from the history of the Indian workers' movement, of which they have been a leading component. Basing themselves on the experience of the earliest industrial trade unions formed in India, they immersed themselves in unionizing workers across a range of industries while building an organic relationship with working class activists. The Left has led a majority of the important strikes organized in India. It also ventured into spaces and sectors which most political parties shun, by organizing marginal and dispossessed social groups like nomadic communities, seasonal labourers and home-based workers. It built networks of associations and unions of women, white-collar employees, youth, writers, lawyers and other professional groups, and politicized them.

The Left parties also fought spirited battles against casteism, gender inequality, various forms of social hierarchy and oppression, superstition and, above all, communalism and religious identity-based politics. Indeed, these parties were long seen as India's greatest secular bulwark against Hindutva or Hindu-supremacism, which threatens pluralist democracy. This helped the Left build a bond with the progressive intelligentsia which abhors bigotry and respects tolerance.

Deep into Cultural Movements

The Left has had a strong spontaneous awareness of, and affinity towards, culture. Its past interventions in the cultural field, especially through the Progressive Writers' Association (PWA) and Indian People's Theatre Association (IPTA) (both formally established between the mid-1930s and mid-1940s) remain unmatched for their aesthetic quality and imaginativeness as well as their value as instruments of public education and mass mobilization.[49] For decades, the Left was the natural or favoured pole of attraction for progressive poets, novelists, literary critics, musicians, balladeers, theatre persons, dancers, folk artistes and other creative people, who associated it with free thought, enlightened modernity and the values and agendas of social liberation.

Avant-garde painters, sculptors, potters and photographers from some of the most creative and influential schools and movements in the field were naturally drawn to the Left. They included the Bombay Progressives (such as M.F. Hussain, F.N. Souza, S.H. Raza, Tyeb Mehta, S.K. Bakre, Akbar Padamsee, Ram Kumar and V.S. Gaitonde), the Calcutta Group (including Pradosh Dasgupta, Paritosh Sen and Gopal Ghose) and radicals from the Baroda and Santiniketan schools. Many were card-carrying members of the communist and socialist parties. So were scholars and critics like Kamaladevi Chattopadhyay who worked with traditional handicrafts people and folk artistes and documented the enormous aesthetic value and wealth of knowledge they brought to their vocations.

The great photographer Sunil Janah, who poignantly documented the ravages of the Bengal Famine of 1943, was a long-standing member of the CPI. The party organ *People's War* was the first periodical to publish his work, as well as the woodcuts and paintings of outstanding visual artists such as Chittaprasad and Somnath Hore. In this regard, the Left press was far more advanced than the mainstream media of the time.

The Left deeply influenced progressive currents in both popular and auteur cinema from the 1930s to the 1970s. Insofar as there was a radical film culture which engaged with contemporary social questions, people's movements, workers' rights and issues like communalism and secularism, it was inseparable from the Left: the best of directors, actors, composers, lyricists and musicians belonged to it. The Left also created a whole new audience for quality cinema, whose lasting impact was felt especially in Kerala.

The Left, the communists in particular, but to an extent the socialists too, stood against the prevalent social–cultural status quo and advocated a critical and sceptical approach to received wisdom and values promoted in the name of 'tradition', 'convention' and 'custom'. In the decades of the 1930s and 1940s, when the hold of conservative, patriarchal and hierarchical ideas on Indian society was formidable, they challenged these, often at the cost of attracting disapproval or censure.

The communists of this period not only advocated an alternative, radical vision of society and of life, but also tried to practise it in their individual conduct and personal relationships. Many questioned monogamy, traditional 'family values' and child-rearing norms, and the conventional division of labour between the sexes that is usually taken for granted in Indian society.[50] They experimented with collective ways of living, caring and sharing, and working together in participatory, non-hierarchical ways. Many lived in party communes and entered into unconventional relationships with one another, through which deep human bonds were built and the personal and the political fused.[51]

Commune members received equal (and equally frugal) wages from the party. Any additional income earned through writing, speaking, editing or acting was shared, as were domestic tasks, including childcare, cooking and cleaning. Apart from small circles of socialists and Left-inclined radical Gandhians, the communists were the only organized group in India to have built communes and attempted to give a deeply personal expression to their collectivist ideals. Remarkably, communes were set up not just in big cities like Bombay and Calcutta, but also in a number of small or provincial towns across India.[52]

The Left's commitment to promoting a radical and critical outlook was reflected in many other ways. Its members pioneered literacy campaigns, newspaper- and book-reading clubs and 'people's science' movements through initiatives such as the Kerala Sasthra Sahithya Parishad, a remarkable organization which launched many social, environmental and popular education campaigns, sometimes in opposition to the official party line. Activists of the Left later became leading participants in the Bharat Gyan Vigyan Samiti and the All-India People's Science Network. These encouraged people to develop a scientific temper and question what passes for conservative notions of 'common sense' and received wisdom.

The Left's Great Strengths

Besides enthusiastically spreading literacy, promoting the reading habit, popularizing science, introducing ordinary people to high-quality theatre, dance and cinema, combating superstition and questioning tradition-based authority, the people's science movement also made major contributions to raising ecological awareness, especially in Kerala, where it has had the greatest impact. These were all significant accomplishments in a society in which naive piety, blind faith and servility towards or worship of authority are widely prevalent.

By the late 1960s, Left parties became a major influence on the Indian cultural-social-political mainstream and emerged as an alternative pole of attraction for many Left-leaning currents even in middle-of-the-road bourgeois parties, including the Congress. Sympathizers of the Left formed 'ginger groups' like the 'Young Turks' in the Congress, which lobbied for policies like abolition of the 'privy purses' of the former princes and nationalization of major commercial banks. Indira Gandhi adopted these during her famous 'left turn' during the Congress split of 1969 and beyond. Left-of-Centre caucuses and pressure groups sprang up within and across parties, often named after Nehru, which strongly defended economic planning, economic self-reliance and distributive justice.

The CPI had a particularly close relationship with these currents and individuals. Indeed, some party members, most famously Mohan Kumaramangalam, formally joined the Congress and accepted ministerial berths in its government at the Centre. Many leaders of the CPI, especially on its Right, such as former party chairman Sripad Amrit Dange and ideologue Mohit Sen, strongly favoured a working alliance, coordination or understanding with the Congress, which would help push it leftwards. Irrespective of whether they were right or wrong, the pertinent point is that leftists became hugely influential at the national level in the 1970s.

By the late 1960s, the Left parties had become major contenders for power in West Bengal, where they won substantial vote shares in elections and formed two coalition governments under the banner of the United Front. In Kerala, the communists, now split between the CPI and the CPI(M), returned to power in the late 1960s. Equally important, communist parties emerged as a salient force in the growing popular mobilizations of the time on labour and land issues and the radical students' movement nationally, and the 'food movement' in eastern India. They acquired political influence in several other states including major ones like Bihar, Andhra Pradesh, Maharashtra and Tamil Nadu; their own membership and the strength of their mass fronts also grew in other states. The Left could now claim a significant national presence.

The eruption of an insurrectionary movement in Naxalbari in West Bengal in 1967, and the spread of Maoism elsewhere in India, especially in Andhra Pradesh and the tribal belt of central India, greatly inspired students and youth all over the country because it seemed imbued with the spirit of revolutionary idealism and rejection of compromises with the existing order.

Although the Naxalite movement condemned the parliamentary communist parties as 'revisionist', Naxalism had great influence in radicalizing their cadres. It also catalysed broader mass participation in many 'anti-systemic' struggles, including, perhaps most importantly, the so-called 'land grab' movement of the late 1960s in West Bengal and Bihar, and to an extent, Assam, based on peasant seizures of lands belonging to large landowners, which exceeded the legal ceiling, but which they refused to surrender to the state.

The two main communist parties suffered setbacks during the Emergency (1975–77)—the CPI(M) owing to state repression, and the CPI because of its support for and collaboration with the ruling Congress until late 1976—but they recovered when the Emergency was lifted, making way for the rule of the Janata Party. The two CPs soon built a mutually cooperative or fraternal relationship with each other. Following the disintegration of the Janata Party in 1979, and with it the splintering of the socialists, they emerged as the principal alternative pole of attraction to the Congress, at least ideologically, if not politically or electorally.

The Left presented a relatively coherent critique of the status quo, which was itself shaken by a growing crisis of the Nehruvian model and the self-evident failure of official policies to ameliorate grinding poverty, hunger, multiple forms of deprivation, and gross inequality. The Left also presented what seemed to many a persuasive case for progressive social change.

In the more recent past, the Left parties tried to offer an alternative, however imperfect and inadequate, to the dominant discourse on a range of domestic and international issues. They have been more trenchant and consistent than other parties in articulating a critique of capitalism in its neo-liberal avatar, and in particular the policies of globalization, liberalization, deregulation and privatization pursued since the early

1990s by successive Indian governments. These policies have created new structural distortions in the Indian economy and failed to significantly reduce—leave alone eradicate—poverty, deprivation and lack of social opportunity. They have also greatly increased inequalities of wealth and income, and widened regional disparities.

The Left has at the national level advocated economic policies which defend the public sector, oppose the unbridled economic penetration of multinational corporations and liberalization of trade, strengthen indigenous industrial and technological capacities, prevent monopolies and stringent intellectual property regimes, and oppose the rampant privatization of natural resources.

True, much of such advocacy has been at the level of policy statements unaccompanied by actual grass-roots mobilization that effectively combats and stops neo-liberal globalization. Yet, there is some value in providing a counterpoint even at the rhetorical level to an official policy orientation which promotes a brazenly corporate-driven growth model. The Left has also called for social development policies which favour the working people. But as we shall see below, it was less than consistent in its own social development practices in the states where it held power. In recent years, it also compromised with and even internalized neo-liberal approaches.

The Left has tried to debunk the Indian elite's pretensions to be leading the nation's emergence as one of the 'great powers' of the world. It questions the objective of achieving such status within a skewed world order and instead advocates South–South solidarity and close cooperation among the developing countries. It also lays emphasis on India's many unfulfilled social and economic domestic agendas and priorities, including poverty eradication, universal provision of public services, and equal access to affordable health care, safe drinking water, sanitation, education and energy.

Critiquing International Policies

On international issues, the Left has always articulated strong positions. It has been a vocal critic of the current unequal global political and strategic order and the institutions through which it is expressed and sustained. It is far more unrelenting than other parties in opposing Western policies of global domination or 'imperialism', and in particular, the United States' military interventions in numerous countries.[53] The Left stands for an equitable multipolar global order, based on multilateral institutions. It is also a staunch advocate of India's foreign and security policy independence, and non-alignment in the conventional sense.

The Left is distinguished by its unrelenting opposition to the US–India 'strategic partnership' which has been consolidated over the past decade and more, under which India has participated in or collaborated with Washington's global system of alliances and has often taken positions contrary to its own citizens' interests, e.g., on the Iran–Pakistan–India gas pipeline project. The 'partnership' resulted in the inking of the US–India civilian nuclear cooperation deal in 2005, which the Left fiercely opposed. In 2008, when the deal was about to be finalized, it withdrew support to the United Progressive Alliance government, triggering a controversy in its own ranks, in particular within the CPI(M).

The Left parties are the only part of the domestic party-political spectrum to have condemned India's 1998 nuclear tests (albeit with some initial hesitation). They called for a rolling back of the Indian (and Pakistani) nuclear weapons programmes and demanded that India return to the global nuclear disarmament agenda. The left parties' stance against militarism, and their relatively non-chauvinist position as regards Pakistan and India's other neighbours, set them apart from most political formations in a country marked by extreme nationalism, growing jingoism, and increasing gravitation towards militarization of foreign policy, especially in the South Asian region.

The Left has relentlessly criticized the international financial institutions for promoting and enforcing neo-liberal policies, corporate-led globalization and unequal trade and intellectual property regimes which aggravate North–South economic imbalances. It has offered a far more cogent analysis than other Indian parties of the causes of the post-2008 global great recession, and the false solutions promoted to resolve it. Its positions on these issues have earned the Left goodwill and respect both in India and abroad among the progressive intelligentsia.

Domestically, the Left parties have traditionally been respected for espousing enlightened and lofty universal values, rejecting parochial, social, regional, linguistic, male-supremacist and casteist agendas, resisting the growing corrosion and degradation of India's democratic institutions, and trenchantly and consistently opposing corruption in public life. They are widely seen as India's cleanest and most scrupulous parties which have no stake in corruption—increasingly a rarity in a country where an overwhelming majority of parties are mired in bribery, nepotism and favouritism, and where they pillage public resources in collusion with corporations.

The Left pursues, and is widely seen to meet, far higher standards of personal probity, political morality and ethics than most political parties; it remains relatively untainted by venality and dynastic notions of leadership. The Left also stands out for its respect for the integrity of democratic institutions, advocacy of transparency in public life, record of accountable and participatory governance, and willingness to disclose the sources of its funds and donations. By contrast, most other parties show little respect for democratic institutions and procedures of accountability. They rule with a heavy hand, and without consultation with, and participation of, citizens. Many are family-centred parties, rife with nepotism. And they are opaque about their funding sources.

The Left therefore continued, at least until recently, to enjoy high, indeed enviable, legitimacy, moral and political prestige and respect despite the recent ascendancy of right-wing ideas, and a general decline in the appeal of socialism and Marxism both worldwide and in India.

Another important source of prestige and goodwill for the Left parties was their performance, especially until the 1990s, as the leaders of the governments of West Bengal, Kerala and Tripura, where they could claim credit for some of the best land reforms and progressive changes effected in governance anywhere in India. In West Bengal, they instituted a large-scale tenancy reform programme and pioneered panchayati raj which devolves power to elected village councils.

In Kerala, they undertook India's most thoroughgoing land redistribution, and stabilized a social development model whose achievements remain unparalleled even in India's more prosperous states despite the latter's considerably higher GDP growth rates. Under the Left's leadership, Tripura has the distinction of having become India's first fully literate state. Its government has also managed to contain a difficult ethnic insurgency while successfully decentralizing power to local bodies.

The Left parties earned near-universal respect because they generally tried to derive their policy stances systematically, from coherent, well-thought-out frameworks, and to link their practice to theory. This lent relative stability and reliability to their policies. Even when engaging in electoral politics, they tended—at least until very recently—to be choosey about picking their allies, in keeping with their 'political line'. This set them apart from most parties, which typically have loosely defined, vague or incoherent programmes based on caste and/or regional interests, pursue ad hoc policies and form opportunistic alliances largely for short-term power-related goals.

Principle apart, some leading personalities of the Left have distinguished themselves as eminent thinkers, writers, artists, critics and educators. The Left has traditionally attracted men and women of exceptional intelligence, erudition and idealism, who inspired entire generations of people. They made brilliant contributions to artistic, cultural and literary fields and to social science disciplines, including history, sociology, economics, political science and cultural anthropology. It is hard to think of another stream or school of scholars and thinkers which can parallel the contribution made by Marxists to India's intellectual discourse.[54]

This distinctive combination of intellectual integrity, moral prestige, theory–practice relationship and commitment to grass-roots work historically set the Indian Left apart from other political currents. It equipped the Left with a certain resilience, which enabled it to cope with all manner of adversity, including repeated proscription of its organizations, prolonged detention of its top leaders by the state, accusations of being 'anti-national' and 'foreign-inspired', smear campaigns in the media and, not least, physical attacks by repressive governments and political opponents.

Weaknesses and Recent Decline

However, in recent years, the Left has suffered a generalized decline in its political strength, stature, intellectual–moral influence and an erosion of its support base. One consequence has been a series of electoral reverses. Prominent among the reasons for the Left's decline is its embrace of aggressively top-down, indeed predatory, land acquisition policies to promote elitist, environmentally destructive forms of urban development and a pattern of industrialization that is hard to demarcate from neo-liberalism.

The neo-liberal drift became starkly evident in 2006–08 when the Left Front government in West Bengal had an ugly confrontation with segments of its own base among the peasantry and artisans at Singur, 40 km from Kolkata (where the Tatas proposed to set up a car factory), and at Nandigram in East Medinipur (earmarked for a chemicals production 'hub' by Indonesia's tainted Selim group). In March 2007, the police opened fire on protesters at Nandigram, killing fourteen of them. Later that year, CPI(M) cadres brutally 'recaptured' the area by unleashing violence against ordinary peasants.

The Singur and Nandigram crises were symptoms, not causes, of the malaise that afflicted the Left—a culmination of longer-term processes leading it into the abyss of ideological conservatism and economic policy myopia. These crises not only damaged the Left's reputation nationwide and beyond, but proved precursors to the setbacks it received in the panchayat elections of 2008, and its cascading defeats in the Lok Sabha and state assembly elections which followed.

The electoral setbacks have proved especially severe in West Bengal, where an early recovery looks highly unlikely. The Left could regain some lost ground in Kerala. But significant recovery at the national level, leave alone expansion, seems improbable in the short run. The prospect of an even steeper decline now stares the Left in the face. As we shall see later in the book, the Left has already lost the profile of a dynamic or vibrant force that can influence social and political agendas and shape mass mobilizations even when it is not in power. The Left space has shrunk in the academic world, larger public sphere and media—in the last case because of growing corporatization of media institutions and increasing marginalization of independent journalists and progressive commentators.

While the mainstream Left parties are in steep and generalized decline, they still remain relevant because of their role in popular struggles, leadership of mass organizations and the quality of their parliamentary interventions. However, their long-term project of transforming India along socialist lines seems distant—deeply troubled and unsupported by transitional or incremental steps towards the goal. They can no longer even articulate a holistic and realizable agenda of humane social development. They now experience a serious crisis of credibility, indeed an existential crisis.

Some of the conservative policies that the Left recently supported, and the culture of crude pragmatism and opportunism that some of its leaders exhibit, are alienating it further from its core constituency—workers, peasants, artisans and other underprivileged people. The leadership–cadre dissonance is growing as the Left's regional leaders remain in denial of the gravity of the recent setbacks to their parties and refuse to acknowledge their role in causing them. Their party cadres' morale is low and falling. This is preventing them from confronting their opponents, especially in West Bengal, on issues such as major corruption scandals (especially the Saradha Ponzi scheme scam), breakdown of law and order, and violence against women, and thus regain popular support. Indeed, they offer little resistance to the violence and intimidation they face.

Eroding Influence

In recent years, Left's role as a movement has become increasingly peripheral to its identity and self-definition and as a source of attraction for potential cadres. The Left parties have ignored the agendas of mass agitation and mobilization and become increasingly parliamentary in orientation and practice. They have come to be judged by more mundane criteria, close to the kind that are usually applied to ordinary, fairly 'normal', power-oriented political formations. The Left still enjoys a modicum of prestige in some circles because it has now displaced the effete Congress as the foremost champion and representative of the

Nehruvian legacy of democracy, secularism, 'socialism' (understood as distributive justice), and non-alignment; but this is a non-radical, tame, variant of what the Left used to stand for.

Equally important, the Indian Left is widely seen by some mainstream commentators as 'antiquated' ('so twentieth century') because of its defence of collectivism, state intervention and the public sector; they regard it as a declining political force which has 'finally' fallen in line with the global trend of socialism's eclipse and demise, as it was destined to. These commentators are wrong, as we shall see below. Collectivist socialist agendas still remain relevant—the colossal failure of the neo-liberal project has demonstrated this the world over. The Indian Left is not destined to go into oblivion. To regain its relevance, it must undoubtedly modernize itself in numerous ways and relate to contemporary concerns, especially those of the young generation. This book argues that it can do so, indeed it can become a vibrant force in society and politics.

That said, the Left has undeniably suffered major and repeated electoral setbacks beginning with the national elections of 2009, which saw its Lok Sabha tally plummet by over 60 per cent to twenty-four seats, thus significantly reducing its national-level political influence at a critical juncture. It then lost power in the 2011 assembly elections in both Kerala (narrowly) and West Bengal (humiliatingly). The West Bengal assembly rout was followed by major losses in both rural panchayat and municipal polls in the state.

The Left's debacle in 2014[55] saw it winning its lowest-ever number (ten)[56] of the 543 Lok Sabha seats, with the CPI(M) falling below its score even in 1967, the very first national election it contested after it was formed in 1964. The Left parties' combined national vote share shrank from the traditional 7 to 11 per cent to just 5 per cent.[57] In West Bengal, the CPI(M), despite winning 23 per cent of the popular vote, suffered the ignominy of being reduced to the same seat tally (two) as that of the BJP, which won 17 per cent of the vote.

In Kerala, the trend of the Left Democratic Front and the Congress-led United Democratic Front winning alternating Lok Sabha elections was broken when the LDF won only eight of twenty seats in 2014. The BJP won its highest-ever vote share (11 per cent) in that election. The

Kerala Left has witnessed a significant loss in its traditional class- and caste-based support. It is only in Tripura that the Left retained both its seats, winning an impressive 64 per cent of the vote.

More generally and damagingly, the Left parties' links with the trade unions and kisan sabhas have been weakened, their general moral–intellectual capital stands depleted, and their cadres are badly demoralized, especially in West Bengal, where they face violent attacks from the ruling Trinamool Congress. Meanwhile, the Hindu Right has come to power nationally under one of its most rabidly communal leaders. The Right's ascendancy will mount further pressure on the Left, aggravating its crisis.

To borrow a term from thermodynamics, the Indian Left finds itself in a state of entropy—or a gradual process of dissipation of energy, decline into uncertainty, disorder, fragmentation and degeneration, which is inevitable in a closed system. This can only change if the Left opens itself up and receives an infusion of new energies. The present entropy is ultimately rooted in a long-term erosion in the Left's social base and political influence.

It is not clear if the Left's leaders can summon up the ideological, intellectual and political resources needed to explain the erosion as a consequence of the Left's ideological ossification, failure to evolve programmatic perspectives and political mobilization strategies appropriate to Indian conditions, of its outmoded 'vanguardist' notions of leadership, and its less-than-democratic organizational practices. Without such an explanation, they cannot possibly hope to analyse, leave alone resolve, the crisis.

The Indian Left, then, stands at a historic crossroads—a make-or-break moment. Either it engages in critical introspection into its flaws and weaknesses, analyses why it is losing support within its core constituencies, and undertakes radical course correction; or it chooses soft options, persists with the political practices and policy approaches that have alienated its support base, and fails to break with the status quo of its political mobilization strategies.

The second course could see the Left suffer erosion at an accelerating pace, leading to demoralization among its cadres and leaders, especially as the Left gets increasingly marginalized in electoral politics. Under this trajectory, the Left could drift into irrelevance and fade into history, as has happened with many communist parties the world over. As of now, the Left seems disinclined to adopt the first course. Its organizational culture, based on 'democratic centralism' and virtual outlawing of dissent, is not conducive to open debate and introspection.

This spells a dismal prospect for the Left in its present political form and organizational shape. Yet, even assuming that much of the actually existing organized Left collapses, many of the principles, ideas and agendas it has historically championed will remain relevant as an important part of the Indian people's struggles for freedom, self-empowerment and justice. The mantle of salvaging their rational core and building on them will fall on the shoulders of grass-roots people's movements, the social Left, radical civil society groups and progressive intellectuals. It is of course possible that sections of the existing Left may opt for the first course.

How these grass-roots people's movements, working with such sections, might be able to gather the fragments, rescue what is valuable and worthy, and reinvent the Left in a new, more relevant, creative and attractive form is discussed in the last chapter—less as a series of prescriptions, but more in the spirit of making suggestions for launching a cooperative or collective endeavour, based on a shared solidarity, to draw up a people's charter which might fulfil the potential for the emancipatory transformation thay Indian society still cries out for.

2

Search for a Strategic Framework

'Two-Stage' Revolution, Bourgeois Democracy,
the Question of Hegemony

If one were to split the history of India's Left in a brutally schematic manner into the pre- and post-Independence periods, the movement's search for a strategic framework for advancing its long-term goal could be best understood in terms of two sets of questions. First, how to forge a strategy to fight its powerful early opponents simultaneously: the British colonial state, and the domestic bourgeoisie which had already launched a national liberation movement through the 'moderate' Indian National Congress.

One part of the challenge lay in participating in the national movement even while effectively resisting the bourgeoisie's effort at hegemonizing it—itself a formidable task. The other part of the challenge consisted in choosing the right model for bringing about radical change: Would it be an urban working class insurrection (as in Europe) or an armed agrarian revolution (as in China)? Or would it consist of organizing radical struggles of workers and peasants while building a united front with progressive sections of the national movement by using both parliamentary and non-parliamentary means? Would it be some combination of the two, or a model that was sui generis?

In the second period, the principal question before the Left was how to deal with the reality that 'Independence ushered in a form, however backward, of nationally based capitalism, and that the mode of class rule, however weak in comparison with the West, has remained essentially bourgeois-democratic since 1947'.[1] After Independence, the Left—specifically, the communist parties—would have to work within the framework of bourgeois democracy, with all its limitations, imperfections, distortions and tendencies towards authoritarianism, but also with its undeniable merits, and the considerable public legitimacy it enjoyed.

The CPI first declared India's Independence a chimera and opted for an insurrectionary model, which failed disastrously, as we shall see. But by the early 1950s, it came around to working within a broadly liberal parliamentary system, and yet struggled to transcend the system's limitations. This orientation was further strengthened in 1957, when the CPI won the Kerala assembly elections.

However, neither the CPI, nor later the CPI(M), adequately theorized this transition. Nor did they explicitly acknowledge that it signified a paradigm shift: from a strategy of insurrection/armed agrarian revolution which smashes the state, as Lenin put it, to one which seeks to transform it through a protracted *war of position*. This would entail struggling to change the state from within through increasingly radical and anti-capitalist policy thrusts, while amplifying and supplementing that effort through militant mass mobilization from the outside, based on an intransigent commitment to long-term transformatory change.

The central challenge for the Left in the second period, then, would be how to combine its non-parliamentary agenda of mass mobilization with its parliamentary work in a manner which preserves the primacy of the former. And yet such a dual approach must allow the Left to use all the opportunities the bourgeois democratic system offers, while resisting the pressures and temptations to be co-opted into it. This would approximate what Antonio Gramsci termed as the struggle to establish an alternative working class or socialist hegemony—a formidable task of great complexity.

The two paradigms pertaining to the two different periods are expectedly dissimilar and offer strikingly different benchmarks. Yet both raise the question: Did the Left grapple hard enough with the problem of comprehending the character and resilience of the Indian bourgeoisie? Despite inheriting the structures of a backward capitalism with vestiges of landlordism in agriculture and its own lack of industrial entrepreneurship, the bourgeoisie used different state instruments, and took advantage of various international and domestic institutions, to entrench itself in power. How early or late did the Left understand that bourgeois democracy would sink deep roots in India, and thus determine the scope of the strategies, degrees of freedom and room for manoeuvre available to it?

The rest of this chapter attempts to assess whether the Left engaged with these issues sufficiently deeply and how far it succeeded in developing a strategic framework that is theoretically well-founded, politically robust and yet capable of tactical resilience and flexibility.

CPI's 'Oscillating Pattern'

From its birth in 1925 until Independence, the Left had to confront two mighty adversaries: British imperialism, and the Indian bourgeoisie which had by the early 1920s developed enough economic strength, consciousness of its conflict of interest with metropolitan capital, and political confidence, to make a bid for the leadership of the freedom struggle through the Indian National Congress (established in 1885) under Mohandas Karamchand Gandhi's stewardship.

The minuscule communist cadres—who numbered only about fifty in 1926, a year after the Communist Party of India held its first conference at Kanpur in 1925, compared to about 30,000 in China[2]—faced severe repression at the hands of the colonial state. This state regarded them as part of a diabolical global network led by the Soviet Union to instigate a revolution and impose communism upon the world. It adopted a particularly vengeful policy towards them, missing no opportunity to harass, arrest and immobilize them. Especially noteworthy were the successive 'conspiracy' cases filed against the communists, including Peshawar (1922–23), Kanpur (1924) and Meerut (1929–33), which prevented CPI cadres and sympathizers from disseminating their literature, recruiting members and supporters, and playing an active role in the growing workers' movement.

At the same time, the communists were called upon to compete in the freedom struggle with the much larger and far better-ramified Congress. With the advent of Gandhi, the Congress evolved from a small organization composed of tiny sections of the economic elite and urban professionals who favoured gradual reform, into a major national-level party with a sizeable base comprising a coalition between the urban elite and the peasantry, whose mobilization shifted the agrarian balance of class forces against the zamindars, and politically strengthened an otherwise weak bourgeoisie.[3]

The Congress-led non-cooperation and civil disobedience campaigns generated pressure on the colonial state to grant concessions to the freedom struggle, including limited rights of association and political representation. The Congress crafted a strategy of carefully ratcheting up such pressure through mass mobilization—only to reach periodic compromises with the state and strengthen itself.

However, while mobilizing the highly differentiated peasant masses in the anti-colonial struggle, the Congress suppressed and minimized internal caste and class differences within their various strata and subordinated agrarian conflict to class conciliation in the larger 'nationalist' cause. It never mobilized plebeian—and increasingly rebellious—groups such as landless labourers or poor and marginal peasants on the basis of their specific interests or by granting them agency as an independent political force. It kept their mobilizations under careful control by adopting methods that preclude or discourage independent mass initiatives which might spontaneously radicalize the struggles into armed rebellions or develop their potential for social revolution.[4]

The challenge confronting the CPI from the 1920s until Independence, viz., participating in and strengthening the freedom struggle while organizing effective resistance to the bourgeoisie's effort at hegemonizing it, was doubtless daunting. It entailed analysing the structures of Indian society in depth, grasping the dual character of the Congress as both party and social movement with all its strengths and weaknesses, and developing a convincing critique of the changing tactics of the freedom struggle under Gandhi's astute leadership. Only thus could the CPI have forged a political strategy which is both consistently anti-imperialist and anti-capitalist, but which leaves room for great tactical flexibility necessitated by the waxing and waning of the balance of power between the Indian and metropolitan bourgeoisies.[5]

Simply put, the CPI largely failed to rise to this challenge. Instead of combining anti-imperialism with anti-capitalism, it alternated between them, and fell into 'an oscillating pattern': sterile denunciation of the Congress, and uncritical support for it.[6] The CPI made little attempt to grasp the specificities of the Indian state and society that set them apart from, say, China, and which would render the prospect of an armed revolution against colonial rule bleak, if not impossible. India by the early twentieth century had a strong, unified colonial state, which enjoyed a certain amount of authority partly because it had established quasi-modern systems of law, administration and education. By contrast, central power had collapsed in China and warlordism was rampant.

The CPI did not consistently carry forward the mass political work which individual communists had begun especially among urban workers, and which the party itself took up after its formation. In the late 1920s, the CPI set about building workers' and peasants' parties in different provinces as mass fronts based on a general agenda of working people's rights. It also played an active role in the labour movement which saw an eruption of strikes and fervent activism—the landmark Bombay textile strike of April–October 1928, a coalminers' strike in Jharia in Bihar and railway and jute workers' industrial actions in Bengal.[7] The CPI tried to create a broad left-leaning platform within the Congress, which was itself undergoing a process of radicalization which would soon result in the civil disobedience movement of the early 1930s.

However, the 'Third Period' line of the Comintern[8] intervened, just as new opportunities arose for a united-front approach towards the progressive section of the Congress which would promote political differentiation within that party. This line directed communists to reject joint mass work with any section of the Congress and to denounce the more radical Nehru wing as the 'Left face of imperialism', akin to the European communist parties' characterization of social democracy as 'social fascism' or the 'Left face of fascism'.[9]

Labour militancy declined after 1928–29, and the CPI was greatly weakened by the arrests of party leaders in the Meerut conspiracy case of 1929. Just then began the communists' left-sectarian phase, in which they specifically targeted the Congress's left-nationalists, 'expelling Nehru from the League Against Imperialism in April 1930, and quarrelling with Bose to the point of bringing about a second split in the AITUC at its Calcutta session in July 1931 ... They kept aloof from Civil Disobedience, and spent most of their energies quarrelling among themselves'.[10]

This line led to a disastrous fall in the CPI's already tiny membership, to about twenty. It is only during 1934 that its membership rose, to a less embarrassing 150, thanks to its shift to a united front tactical line. But soon, under the Comintern's Seventh Congress (1935) line, the CPI abandoned its anti-capitalist agenda, and plunged headlong into collaboration with the Congress's dominant leadership—just when the Congress was shifting rightwards. These about-turns extracted a heavy political price from the CPI in the very first decade of its formation. They both exposed and reinforced its dependence on the Comintern and the Communist Party of Great Britain for strategy and tactics.

Confused about its main strategic line of march, the CPI experimented with two divergent models of revolution—probably the best known models in the 1940s. The first was based on an urban insurrectional general strike amidst a grave crisis of the state and great advances in the political consciousness of workers and other plebeian layers. In this model, collapse of state authority precipitates a situation of 'dual power', in which the old state apparatus is no longer able to perform critical functions, and new organs of popular power emerge, which suddenly change the relationship of political forces, potentially allowing a new class to take power. This is what happened in Russia and in some European countries in the first quarter of the twentieth century.

The second model is based on agrarian struggle—a long-drawn-out, often territorially based, war against relatively weak or dysfunctional states which lack popular legitimacy, as in China, Vietnam or Yugoslavia. Here, typically, the agrarian question or issues of national liberation predominate and large numbers of peasants are mobilized in armed guerrilla warfare under a radical leadership. 'Dual power' takes a different form and has a dissimilar trajectory from the urban insurrectionary pathway.

Telengana: Heroic *and* Tragic

The CPI experimented with the second model in the Telengana armed struggle (1946–1951), which broke out in Hyderabad state. Telengana was India's longest-sustained agrarian insurgency. The struggle began by mobilizing tenants and landless labourers against rapacious landlords (zamindars and jagirdars) who were part of the Nizam's revenue collection system. One of its early targets was the practice of forced unpaid labour; another was usury, which pitted ruthless moneylenders against the poor. But the struggle soon evolved into an explicitly political anti-Nizam movement under the banner of the Andhra Mahasabha which demanded an ethno-linguistic state.

As the princely state repressed it brutally, the movement retaliated by using armed force and driving landlords out of their fiefdoms. This phase began in September 1947, just after the Nizam refused to accede to the Indian Union and deployed a fierce militia called Razakars against his adversaries. These adversaries happened, like in many others of India's 500-odd princely states, to be primarily communists and socialists—not least because the Congress treated the states' rulers as potential allies and did not organize mass agitations against them. The Telengana peasantry fought heroic battles against the Nizam and occupied the lands it had long cultivated with its labour for landlords. It burned the moneylenders' books and established autonomous village panchayats. The struggle succeeded in abolishing jagirdari and forced labour and 'liberating' 4,000 villages, distributing one million acres of land to tenant-cultivators and reducing the concentration of landownership. As peasants fought the Razakars with exemplary determination, a situation of dual power emerged in large parts of the Telengana region.

Meanwhile, the Central government led by Prime Minister Jawaharlal Nehru and Home Minister Vallabhbhai Patel reached a compromise called 'standstill' agreement with the Nizam, which entirely bypassed the Telengana struggle and its support base. The movement gathered yet more momentum. Amidst this volatile situation, the Indian government in September 1948 launched its 'police action', a euphemism for a brutal large-scale military operation under Gen. J.N. Chaudhury.

The ostensible goal of the action was to force the Nizam to accede to the Indian Union, but as historian Sumit Sarkar says, the operation was 'probably undertaken in large part ... to halt the communist advance, for otherwise New Delhi and particularly Patel had seemed quite willing to strike a deal with the Nizam ...'[11] The army used indiscriminate force against communist cadres and supporters; hundreds of activists were killed and subjected to cruel forms of torture. Worse, huge anti-Muslim pogroms broke out, especially in the state's Marathwada region, aided and abetted by soldiers and policemen. The Centre sent a three-person 'goodwill' delegation to Hyderabad, headed by Pandit Sundarlal, in November–December 1948. Its report made the 'very conservative estimate' that between 27,000 and 40,000 people were killed 'during and after the police action'.[12] This was probably India's worst post-Partition civilian massacre.

The CPI leadership did not anticipate the army action or communal pogroms, it was divided over whether and how to resist the Indian troops. There was no way the cadres of the party, with their primitive weapons, could have fought the Indian Army. Hundreds of communists were killed. Some fled to nearby hills and forests. Finally, the armed struggle was withdrawn in October 1951—after enormous losses and human suffering.[13]

Despite repression, the state could not eliminate communist influence from Telengana. In the 1952 Lok Sabha election from Nalgonda, Ravi Narayan Reddy, a hero of Telengana, won the highest number of votes in India, and a margin bigger than Nehru's. Communists also won every assembly seat from Telengana's Nalgonda and Warangal districts.[14]

During 1948–50, the CPI flirted with the other, urban, model of insurrection in industrial centres like Bombay, Calcutta, Madras and Coimbatore under the adventurist line laid down by its new general secretary B.T. Ranadive. This line condemned India's independence as 'fake' and declared the Nehru government illegitimate; the time was ripe for toppling it. Party cadres were ordered to launch strikes and violent all-out confrontations with the police and the army.

Thousands of communists were jailed. They were forced to undertake prolonged hunger strikes and offer militant resistance to the authorities who opened fire upon them: more than eighty cadres died in the prison firings. Cadres who were not arrested were asked to attack jail gates, and were shot down. More than 3,700 communists perished in the savage state repression—an enormous loss.[15]

The CPI's membership plummeted disastrously, from over 89,000 in 1948 to 20,000 in 1950; it would take another four years for it to reach 75,000.[16] It soon became clear that the communist movement would have to rethink the use of insurrectionary methods unsupported by large numbers of the public; it would need another strategy and model of mobilization.

Underestimating Bourgeois Democracy

Given its theoretical confusion, lack of clarity about Indian society and politics, history of political zigzags—and not least, its condemnation of independence as 'fake'—the CPI was poorly equipped to understand and acknowledge that an essentially bourgeois-democratic system got instituted in India in 1947, itself a big advance over military or authoritarian rule.

The system, based on the right to private property and unequal distribution of wealth and power, obviously had its constraints and imperfections, but it also had its strengths and advantages, including formal citizen equality, and constitutional guarantees of the freedom of expression, conscience and association. It created opportunities, absent under army-dominated dictatorships or out-and-out authoritarian states, to educate, organize and politicize workers and peasants, to represent them in unions and elected legislatures, and to build civil society organizations and political coalitions. Bourgeois democracy therefore commanded a certain degree of public legitimacy.

The CPI underrated these freedoms and opportunities and saw bourgeois democracy largely as a sham, at least until the mid-1950s. It also neglected the agenda of deepening democracy—i.e., demanding fidelity to the rule of law, extending civil and political liberties and fighting for greater social and economic rights. It did not theorize these issues as an integral part of its political strategy.

Nevertheless, the CPI in the early 1950s moved towards political moderation under the leadership of Ajoy Ghosh and especially P.C.

Joshi. This was less a well-theorized decision than the result of these leaders' instinctive pragmatism, 'friendly' advice from Stalin,[17] and a softer Soviet stand towards Nehru. A turning point was the CPI decision to participate in legislative elections, beginning with the general elections of 1952. It emerged from these as India's second largest party. The new pragmatism would soon see the CPI accept the Nehruvian paradigm of 'democracy', 'secularism', 'non-alignment', and 'socialism' or a 'socialistic pattern of society' (meaning a modicum of redistributive justice within a market economy) as the context within which it would operate.

The CPI notched up a dramatic success by winning the 1957 assembly elections in Kerala—on a reform platform that was originally advocated by the Congress, but which that party had absolutely no will to implement.[18] The land reform initiated by the CPI in Kerala enabled it to move to a potentially more radical perspective and politics; it also pointed to the way in which the limitations of working within the parliamentary system could be transcended in practice.

This was a major political advance. Yet, Indian communists did not in the 1950s or 1960s analyse their society—with its class–caste peculiarities, gender iniquities, economic dynamics, power structures and state character—in India-specific frameworks. Rather, they conceptualized that complex reality in simplistic or formulaic categories inherited from a schematic, mechanical, sclerotic Marxism in which Stalin's exegeses on *Dialectical and Historical Materialism* were the final word. While theorizing their strategic perspectives, they would use holdall terms like 'semi-feudal semi-colonial' social formations, which fail to take into account the pattern of combined and uneven development specific to India and all but erase crucial differences between India and other former colonies.

In this respect, the Indian communists were no exception to most member parties of the Third International located in the underdeveloped world and in the early phase of their formation. They all adopted a strategic perspective based on the notion of a 'two-stage' revolution: first, a bourgeois or 'democratic' stage, followed by a socialist one which would establish the 'dictatorship of the proletariat' and eventually create a qualitatively new social order.

This sequence would conform strictly, in textbook fashion, to a succession of 'stages' of history, progressing through different modes of production, from slavery, to feudalism, to capitalism, to socialism, and communism. These would correspond to different levels of 'development of the productive forces', as outlined by Marx in his famous but poorly understood *Preface to the Critique of Political Economy.*

The Indian communists too shared the critical premise that the bourgeoisie of the former colonies was too weak, and too compromised with the imperial powers as well as with domestic landlord-dominated 'semi-feudal' agrarian structures, to be able to lead a democratic revolution, as the bourgeoisie had done in France and England.[19]

That task would fall in the former colonies to the industrial working class, presumably led by the communists, which would build a multi-class alliance against the 'semi-colonial semi-feudal' state and complete the 'democratic' stage of the revolution by abolishing landlordism and creating conditions for indigenous industrial development. This would then pave the way for the revolution's second, 'socialist', stage.

This analysis did demarcate India's social formation from those of the developed capitalist countries, as was self-evidently necessary. But it ignored the fundamentally *capitalist* logic of the Indian economy and its expression in the state. Space does not permit a detailed discussion here of the specificities of India's backward capitalism; suffice it to say that although the Indian state might have, to an extent, protected landlordism and retained remnants of feudal elements, its main function and preoccupation has long been to develop capitalism.[20] Capitalist relations have grown steadily and penetrated society in keeping with this logic.

The 'two-stage' formulation also prevents a clear, unambiguous characterization of the Indian state as quintessentially bourgeois-democratic (albeit of a backward type) and implies that non-participation in its institutions or their outright rejection would somehow be essential to bringing about transformative change—a questionable proposition. And it ignores the inherently radicalizing dynamic of mass mobilizations. For instance, czarist Russia was also a backward-capitalist society, yet the revolutionary process there did not stop at the 'democratic' stage, but followed the momentum all the way to socialism.

Different versions prevailed among Indian communists as regards the classes which would form the multi-class alliance leading the revolution's first stage, and their roles in it, but there was broad agreement that they would include various layers of the peasantry, the urban petty bourgeoisie and the intelligentsia. There were sharp differences, however, on the importance of the role of a 'national bourgeoisie' within the alliance. This stratum was identified as that section of the bourgeoisie, including its 'non-monopoly' interests, which had a stake in indigenous industrialization based on developing the 'home market', and which was contrasted with other sections of the industrial capitalist class that were deeply dependent on and allied with imperial interests—in particular, the 'comprador' bourgeoisie, a concept derived from the Communist Party of China (CPC).

Alliances against Semi-Feudalism

Differences over the 'national bourgeoisie' surfaced repeatedly in the CPI in the 1940s and 1950s and simmered for a long time despite efforts to reconcile them. They finally found their sharpest expression in the split in the Communist Party of India in 1964, which led to the formation of the Communist Party of India (Marxist), in the shadow of the great Sino-Soviet ideological–political schism. The CPI adopted the strategy of a 'National Democratic Revolution', in which the 'national bourgeoisie', sections of which were supposedly represented in the Congress, would play a prominent role, besides the working class. The National Democratic Front (NDF) would include the peasantry and the petty bourgeoisie too.

The CPI(M) also advocated a four-class alliance. But it adopted a 'People's Democratic Revolution' perspective, which emphasized opposition to the Congress as a 'bourgeois-landlord' party dominated by the 'big bourgeoisie' or by 'monopoly capital'. The Maoist CPI(Marxist-Leninist), which split from the CPI(M) during 1967–69, adopted the programme of what it called, following the Chinese model, a 'New Democratic Revolution', but similar to the 'People's Democratic Revolution'.[21]

CPI–CPI(M) differences were rooted in their divergent characterizations of the Indian state, and differences in the leadership of the two Fronts. The CPI regarded the Indian state as 'the organ of the national bourgeoisie as a whole. In the formation and exercise of governmental power, the big bourgeoisie wields considerable influence. The national bourgeoisie compromises with the landlords, admits them in the ministries and governmental composition, especially at the state levels ...' But it held that in the NDF, 'the exclusive leadership of the working class is not yet established, though the exclusive leadership of the bourgeoisie no longer exists ... the [NDF] will draw into its ranks not only the masses following the Congress but also its progressive sections'.[22]

By contrast, the CPI(M) characterized 'the present Indian state' as 'the organ of the class rule of the bourgeoisie and landlords, led by the big bourgeoisie'. It said the peasantry, including the rich peasantry, can 'by and large' be 'brought into' the People's Democratic Front (PDF), as can the middle classes and 'the national bourgeoisie', which however 'exhibits extreme vacillation between the imperialists and their native big bourgeois accomplices on the one hand and the People's Democratic Front on the other'.

Unlike the CPI's NDF, which is led jointly by the working class and the national bourgeoisie, the PDF advocated by the CPI(M) would be a 'united front from below': 'Ours is a democratic revolution in an entirely new epoch of world history, where the proletariat and its political party is destined to assume its leadership and not leave it to the bourgeois class to betray it in the middle ... Hence it is not the old-type bourgeois-led democratic revolution but a new type of People's Democratic Revolution, organized and led under the hegemony of the working class'.[23]

The two parties thus adopted sharply contrasting attitudes towards the Congress. The CPI(M) was totally opposed to it. One of its main goals was to end the Congress's 'one-party monopoly' of Indian politics. The CPI could extend qualified support to 'progressive' elements in the Congress while generally opposing it. For instance, in the 1965 assembly elections in Kerala, the CPI(M) was willing to join hands with any party which opposed the Congress; it even cooperated with the Muslim League. But the CPI refused to ally with 'communal' parties like the League in Kerala (and the Jana Sangh elsewhere). It later formed a ruling coalition with the Congress in Kerala.

In practice, the CPI lent a degree of legitimacy to the Congress as a party with a 'progressive' component in it, and was open to forming alliances with it—a policy which continued until the 1970s. The CPI(M), by contrast, challenged and tried to weaken the Congress's political hegemony, sometimes by helping the forces of the Right, but without correspondingly strengthening the Left movement as a whole.

Despite these differences, the two parties identified 'semi-feudalism' as being at the heart of the agrarian question. It must be fought by building a broad front including all layers of the landowning peasantry, as well as landless labourers. For both, eradication of landlordism, seen as the mainstay of the 'semi-feudal' order—based on the extraction of rent or a share of the crop from tenants—would be a critical, if not the most important, component of the first stage of the revolution.

Stalin's Advice on the Agrarian Revolution

Stalin played a direct personal role in influencing the CPI's strategic thinking by defining the Indian revolution as 'mainly agrarian'. He met CPI leaders C. Rajeswara Rao, S.A. Dange, Ajoy Ghosh and M. Basavapunnaiah on 9 February 1951 in Moscow. During a three-hour-long discussion, he told them: 'We, Russians, look at this revolution as mainly agrarian. It signifies the liquidation of feudal property, the division of the land amongst the peasantry and it becoming their personal property. It means the liquidation of feudal private property in the name of the affirmation of the private property of the peasantry. As we see this, none of this is socialist. We do not consider that India stands before the socialist revolution.'[24]

He said: 'This is that Chinese path which is spoken of everywhere, i.e., the agrarian, anti-feudal revolution without any confiscation or nationalization of the property of the national bourgeoisie. This is the bourgeois-democratic revolution or the first stage of the people's democratic revolution. The people's democratic revolution that began in the eastern countries of

Europe, even before it did in China, has two stages. The first stage [is] agrarian revolution or agrarian reform, as you desire.'

'The countries of people's democracy in Europe', Stalin said, 'went through this stage in the very first year after the war. China stands now at this first stage. India is approaching this stage. The second stage of the people's democratic revolution as shown in Eastern Europe is characterized by the agrarian revolution passing over to the expropriation of the national bourgeoisie. This is already the beginning of the socialist revolution. In all of the people's democratic countries of Europe the plants, factories, banks are nationalized and handed over to the state. China is still far from this second stage. This stage is also far off in India or India is far from this stage.'

Stalin also opposed the demand for nationalization of land in India. 'At the given stage you do not need to advance this demand, never, on the one side, put forward the demand for the division of the landlords' land and simultaneously say that the land must be given to the state … It would be disadvantageous now for you to advance the demand for nationalization.'

Stalin also commented on the Telangana armed peasant movement in progress since 1946 in Hyderabad state as 'the first sprouts of civil war', but added that 'one does not need to rely on partisan war alone. It, of course, renders assistance but itself it is in need of help … It is necessary to have bigger work amongst the people, amongst the workers, in the army, amongst the intelligentsia, the peasantry … In general, out of all the classes of society the peasants have great trust in the working class. It is necessary to unite these two forms of struggle—the struggle of the workers and peasants, the peasant uprising and the march of the workers.'

According to other accounts, Stalin advised the CPI to call off the armed struggle and surrender the arms it had collected, and asked its general secretary Rajeswara Rao to personally supervise and lead the entire operation.[25]

When the CPI leaders thanked Stalin for the discussion and declared that on the basis of his 'instructions', they would 'reconsider all of their activity and would act in correspondence' with them, Stalin said, 'I have given you no instructions, this is advice, it is not obligatory for you, you may or may not adopt it'.[26]

But the message had gone home. Following the discussion, the CPI formulated a perspective on strategy and tactics for the first time, and prepared two new party documents in 1951. The Tactical Line document was illegally circulated in April 1951. Its legal version was adopted at a specially convened party conference in Calcutta in October 1951, which also approved the Party Programme of a 'People's Democratic Revolution' as part of a 'two-stage' perspective.[27] The CPI(M) was later to adopt this very programme and accuse the CPI of reneging on it.

Despite sharp CPI–CPI(M) differences over its content, the obsession with the 'two-stage' revolution proved durable. Meanwhile, a serious, prolonged, often lively if sometimes fractious, debate broke out in the 1960s partly against the backdrop of the recently launched Green Revolution on the issue of the mode of production in Indian agriculture (discussed in Appendix 1).

Arrayed on one side were eminent intellectuals, especially economists, including Utsa Patnaik, Amit Bhaduri, Amiya K. Bagchi, Pradhan H. Prasad, Nirmal Chandra, and in the beginning, Ashok Rudra, who argued that Indian agriculture continued to be dominated by pre-capitalist or 'semi-feudal' relations of production under the system of landlordism and tenancy. Although there was a tendency for capitalist relations of production to grow, definite limits were set on it by the prevalent high levels of 'pre-capitalist ground rent'.

This was contested by equally eminent theorists such as Jairus Banaji, Sulekh Gupta, Kathleen Gough, Jan Breman, Ashwani Saith, Gail Omvedt, and later (especially forcefully) by Ashok Rudra. They argued that a transition to agrarian capitalism was already under way despite the persistence of tenancy, which is not necessarily a feature of 'semi-feudalism' and is perfectly compatible with capitalist relations of production.

By confusing forms of exploitation with relations of production, these scholars argued, the adherents of the semi-feudal thesis failed to recognize that a new class of capitalist farmers disguised as landlords already wielded enormous power, and bourgeois production relations with associated trade and moneylending interests had irreversibly penetrated agriculture.[28] The discussants made no reference to Robert Brenner's famous argument about tenancy and capitalism, published in *New Left Review* in 1977, as the Indian mode of production debate was coming to a close; but in retrospect, the argument would clearly seem to carry major implications for the debate's content.[29]

To return to the early 1980s, when the mode of production debate ended, the majority opinion among participants had crystallized in favour of the view that capitalism had achieved dominance in Indian agriculture as part of a long-term process of transition or a paradigm shift in the character of the Indian economic system. This happened despite the persistence of forms of tenancy and unfree labour historically associated with pre-capitalist societies.[37]

Major shifts had by then become visible in the dynamic of the larger economic system, related to industrial decontrol and new investment flows, altered balances in capital accumulation between agriculture and industry, as well as increased crop production for the market based on the more explicit use of hired labour. The use of Green Revolution inputs like irrigation, hybrid seeds, fertilizer and pesticides raised yields and productivity; consequently, capital intensity increased and penetration of capitalist production relations deepened in agriculture.

Poverty of Theory

The mode of production debate was one of the most exciting and intellectually stimulating exchanges in Marxist theory to have occurred in India, which spanned a number of disciplines and attracted international scholarly participation. Yet, neither the CPI nor the CPI(M) participated in it or related to it as parties in a major way—although it would have consequences for their political strategy and tactics. This testifies to their lack of interest in theoretical matters and the relatively low priority accorded to Marxist theory, as distinct from programmatic and practical matters, in party education. The low priority went hand in hand with Indian communist leaders' dependence in respect of theoretical analysis, and in getting the political line 'right', on British communists like Rajani Palme Dutt,[30] whom they held in great awe.

Although Palme Dutt visited India only once, in 1946, he wrote with great authority on Indian society and politics.[31] His *India Today* (first published in 1940, and revised several times) remained the communist primer on India right until the 1970s. Palme Dutt mentored many Indian communists who studied in Britain. He became the CPI's most important adviser and often 'officially' communicated the Comintern line to the party leadership.[32]

The Indian communist parties attracted the brightest of intellectuals and scholars, but they did not create or foster an internal climate where their theoretical abilities and analytical talent would be encouraged and original work rewarded. Paucity of original Marxist or socialist literature inhibited theoretical education and debate until the 1950s.[33] But even after that ceased being the case, there was very little generation of theoretical work from within the CPs.

Indeed, it is hard to come across even a serious reference to Marx's *Capital*, not to speak of a commentary on it, in the writings of party intellectuals, however voluminous. Most first-generation communist party leaders this writer has known never read *Capital* or other serious theoretical work by Marx such as *Economic and Philosophical Manuscripts* or the *Grundrisse*, nor, to take random examples, Marxists like Rosa Luxemburg or Antonio Gramsci.[34] *Capital* was translated into Indian languages many decades after it was published in English; it was first published in Marathi in 1943, in Hindi in 1965, and in Malayalam in 1968.[35] It was not translated into Bengali until 1984.[36]

There was very little ideological–theoretical debate in the Indian CPs on such diverse issues as the question of Stalin and the Twentieth Congress of the CPSU, the nature of post-war capitalism, the politics of production or the labour process, the content of 'socialism' in the USSR, China, Yugoslavia, Vietnam, North Korea or Cuba (or more recently, Dengism and the embrace of the market and the neo-liberal turn in

China), feminism and the communist movement, the changing nature of North–South relations, ecology and socialism, party–mass-organization–civil society relations, or new forms of global solidarity in the post-Soviet era, to mention only a few. Even when the CPs in practice adopted worthy positions on the issues of the day, which they often did, they did not theorize them or develop them through rigorous analysis, particularly where strategic or programmatic matters were concerned. Sometimes, they merely ratified in their congress or central committee resolutions major policy shifts and decisions that had already been made by their state units. (For instance, the CPI(M)'s fifteenth congress at Chandigarh (1995) ratified the new industrial policy announced by the Left Front government in West Bengal in 1994, including its decision to invite private and foreign capital to industrialize the state.)

The economy-wide capital accumulation process got intensified in later years and culminated in India's embrace of neo-liberalism in the early 1990s. This led to India's deeper integration into the world capitalist market and global financial system. Far-reaching changes occurred in the economy's external linkages and internal structures, and in the balance between agriculture, industry and services. Thanks to relatively rapid GDP growth, India would soon be perceived as one of the world's 'emerging economies' and as a 'regional' or 'sub-imperial' power, at least in the making.

Today, it would be manifestly absurd to characterize India as a remotely pre-capitalist or 'semi-feudal', leave alone a 'semi-colonial', society. Indeed, that has long been true. Yet, the characterization remained a strategic beacon for most currents of the communist Left for half a century and more, and influenced its programmatic perspectives, policy frameworks, self-identity and practical actions—in particular, its priorities in organizing the peasantry. It survives today in its purest form in the CPI (Maoist), which continues to adhere to the 'semi-feudal, semi-colonial' thesis.

This thesis and the associated agrarian programme meant that communists would organize, and invest their rural energies largely in mobilizing the peasantry as a whole, including rich peasants, as well as middle and poor peasants[38], against landlords. At the centre of their land reform agenda lay the abolition of tenancy—seen as the core of 'semi-feudal' relations—and 'land to the tiller' even if that promotes capitalist agriculture. For instance, E.M.S. Namboodiripad argued in 1952 that land reform should lead to the abolition of feudalism and generation of capitalist relations in agriculture through the building of a 'rich peasant economy' along the lines of the Chinese Revolution.[39]

Low Priority for the Landless

The greatest early rural mobilizations under communists followed the all-peasant-unity approach. Besides Telengana, these include the Tebhaga tenants' movement in Bengal in the 1940s for a higher crop share (one of the greatest and longest mobilizations of its kind); movements in Uttar Pradesh, Bihar, Maharashtra, Andhra, Punjab, Tamil Nadu, Assam and many other states, in which the undivided CPI allied with other progressive groupings including the socialists and, it bears mentioning, remnants of Swami Sahajanand Saraswati's[40] movement in Bihar. This approach marks a majority of the hundreds of peasant movements that have occurred in India since the 1930s.[41]

Some of the central demands of the kisan sabhas in recent years too have focused on higher prices for agricultural output, subsidies for fertilizer, irrigation and electricity, and guaranteed state procurement of grain and cash crops like cotton. These tend to favour (admittedly not always) peasants, including rich peasants, who produce primarily for the market and not for self-consumption or subsistence, as poorer peasants often do. The bias towards landowning peasants is strong in regions like Punjab, Haryana, western Uttar Pradesh, coastal Andhra and parts of Tamil Nadu, which are major grain producers, as various kisan sabha reports suggest.

Higher food prices benefit farmers in general and big farmers in particular, but raise the cost of living for agricultural labourers and marginal peasants, who are net consumers rather than net producers of foodgrains. Thus the notion of unity between all strata or layers of the landowning peasantry, and the landless, is problematic, if not chimerical. In recent years, the chasm between the two groups or classes has widened because of the Mahatma Gandhi National Rural Employment Guarantee Act (MGNREGA), which has tended to raise the general level of rural wages by offering jobs for 100 days a year for village households at minimum wages, thus creating a wage floor.

It can thus be argued that communists should have accorded a high priority to organizing landless agricultural labourers, not least because they are the poorest of all rural classes, but also because they are exploited as wage workers by peasant proprietors including, seasonally, small or poor peasants. This ethical–political consideration, based on solidarity with the most disadvantaged, would of course have to be balanced vis-à-vis the pragmatic or electoral requirements of making alliances with forces sufficiently large and powerful to propel the CPs to power. Such forces would have to include the landowning peasantry, but need not exclude the landless altogether.

The alliance building would have to be done with sensitivity to specific contexts and local configurations of class forces. But trying to achieve the right balance is one thing; abandoning the agenda of organizing the landless quite another. In the long run, the second choice would work against even short-term political logic: the number of the landless has steadily grown since Independence in virtually every state. In some regions, it has grown especially rapidly in the past two decades. The landless there, although not a majority, form the single largest bloc of votes, which is critical to winning elections in India's first-past-the-post system.

In practice, Kerala was a significant exception to this all-peasant-unity approach, Namboodiripad's 'rich peasant economy' advocacy notwithstanding. There, the CPI, first through the Congress Socialist Party, and later independently, organized the rural landless, in particular casual farm labourers, coir workers, toddy tappers, etc., at an early stage. This in part explains why the CPI acquired both an enduring influence among such plebeian layers and a relatively radical political orientation even before it was elected to lead India's first communist government in 1957.

Nationally, the early communist perspective on the agrarian question mandated or permitted alliances with all manner of non-plebeian classes, including rich peasants and agents of rural commercial capital like traders and rice millers.[42] Also included were 'mixed' categories like tenants (including some with sizeable plots), smallholders practising intensive cultivation (who greatly depend on hired labour), poor peasants (who use it during planting, harvesting or threshing), and lower intermediate strata. These latter subsist precariously, by cultivating tiny 'home-garden'-size parcels, and by hiring out their labour power for agricultural or non-agricultural work on a casual basis.

Given the fluidity and context-specific nature of these various categories, and their openness to interpretation even within the Marxist tradition, it was never easy to translate them into practical terms by identifying which political parties or factions represent them. Diverse state and local units of the CPs would identify them differently while strategizing 'all-peasant unity'. This often led to unprincipled, opportunistic alliances and compromises with dominant agrarian interests, which typically worked against the landless and the more vulnerable of poor people.

In the cities too, the mandated multi-class coalition—which would include the blue-collar industrial working class and the petty bourgeoisie (presumably comprising small traders, white-collar workers but also supervisory staff, students, undefined layers of the 'youth', etc.)—produced not just confusion over the priorities to be adopted, but also misalliances which subordinated the interests of the working class and the truly underprivileged. There was, of course, the opposite danger, of the CPs' base getting restricted to numerically small groups. Finding the right balance was certainly a challenge; choosing the easiest option could mean running away from the challenge.

This does not argue against alliances, but only for carefully and clearly stating some broad criteria for regarding certain forces or groups as potential allies. Absence of such criteria could produce bizarre results. Thus, the Shiv Sena, a Marathi-chauvinist party of the lumpen proletariat cynically employed by Bombay's industrialists to break strikes and undermine communist-led trade unions, was characterized by a section of the Left as a party representing the unemployed children of workers formerly employed in the textile mills, and therefore a force worthy of support or alliance.[43]

On organizing agricultural workers, the CPI and the CPI(M) differ somewhat. The CPI is perhaps more flexible about organizing landless workers, including seasonal labourers, rather than concentrating on landowning peasants—especially in Punjab, Bihar and Maharashtra. Yet at the theoretical level, the semi-feudal characterization persisted in the mainstream Left until recently.

As we shall see later, the all-peasant-unity orientation was to de-radicalize the communist movement, limit its potential for bringing about structural change, and to an extent alienate it from the poorest strata of the population, especially landless agricultural workers. For instance, in West Bengal—where landlessness runs at almost 50 per cent—the CPI(M)-led kisan sabha for decades opposed the formation of a separate agricultural workers' union, in contrast to its policy at the all-India level. The union is still in its infancy.[44]

Industrialization through Private Capital

Even more important, the 'two-stage revolution' perspective ordained that the communists support and bring about a transition from agrarian reform and development to industrialization, itself considered the key to further developing the 'productive forces' within the first, 'democratic' or bourgeois, stage of the revolution. In West Bengal, this led the Left Front to adopt an aggressive strategy of industrial promotion in the mid-1980s beginning with the Haldia petrochemicals complex. The first major industrial project initiated by the government after it assumed office in 1977, this was set up as a joint venture with a private company, a major change in party policy.[45]

The Haldia decision set the stage for greater reliance on private capital for industrialization, and not only in West Bengal. Soon after the Berlin Wall fell and the Soviet crisis broke out, a CPI(M) central committee resolution (1990) publicly acknowledged 'the role of the market' in building socialism. At its fourteenth congress (1992), the party adopted a resolution on 'the necessity' of the market in a period of socialist transformation, based on the Soviet failure and the experience of China.[46]

Then followed West Bengal's new industrial policy of 1994, announced and passed in the legislative assembly without discussion in the Left Front or the CPI(M) state committee. This opened the floodgates to industrialization-at-any-cost based on unbridled private investment—even if that meant confiscating poor people's lands, offering unconscionable tax rebates and other 'incentives' to Big Business, creating and aggravating ecological imbalances, and increasing the financial burden on the state and thus greatly reducing its capacity to invest in public welfare.

An odious example of such caving in to capital was Tata Motors' Nano car project at Singur. Eminent economist and former West Bengal finance minister Ashok Mitra estimated that the Tatas were offered subsidies equivalent to nearly one-half of the cost of the project.[47] Yet, as a senior CPI(M) functionary put it, if industrialization is an imperative, and if that means inviting the Tatas, the Ambanis and the Birlas to invest on their terms, to maximize their profits, 'so be it'.[48]

All told, the 'two-stage' perspective visited enormous damage on the Left. It entailed that the Left *manage* capitalism rather than transform it or radically reshape its character by imposing a new social discipline on capital and regulating it in the public interest. After the mid-1990s, the Left Front increasingly stopped negotiating with prospective investors conditions such as local content requirements and guarantees of job creation, environmental protection and other safeguards. The investors set the terms, the Left Front passively accepted them. Even the line of demarcation between managing capitalism and promoting it indiscriminately got blurred.

Singur and Nandigram were the logical culmination of this process of de-radicalization—and by no means an aberration or a mere 'tactical' mistake. But despite the great harm they caused to the Left's image worldwide and to its cadres' morale in Bengal, the Front, in particular the CPI(M), refused in later years to take decisions which could have limited or counteracted the original damage by facilitating an alternative approach. The party leadership acted as if its public relations apparatus spoke the truth to its own cadres: no course correction was needed.

Few Takers for Workers' Takeovers

Another effect of adherence to a 'two-stage revolution' perspective was the neglect of agendas to promote cooperative or collective forms of organization, production and distribution in various fields, including agriculture, industry, health care, housing, education, urban affairs, rural governance, and so on. Such measures were often seen as belonging to the 'next' (socialist or post-bourgeois) stage of development, and therefore either too 'advanced' for the present stage of struggle, or otherwise unworthy of immediate pursuit.

The Left has been inconsistent in supporting workers' initiatives for takeover of closed industries even where the initiatives arise out of spontaneous struggles and could result in viable enterprises. Such support should have normally been the Left's natural response. But in West Bengal, Left-led unions were hostile to two such major takeover attempts—Sonali Tea Garden in Jalpaiguri (1974–78),[49] and Kanoria Jute Mill in Calcutta (1993-94).[50] By contrast, in Kerala, the Left supported employee cooperatives such as Kerala Dinesh Beedi Workers Central Cooperative Society at Kannur (which has since diversified into garments, food, and information technology, etc.), and Kanan Devan Hills Plantation Company at Munnar, which involved workers' takeover and management.[51]

In the case of Kamani Tubes Ltd in Bombay, a fairly large industrial factory with 700 workers, the Left failed to support or help a workers' cooperative which took over the company in 1988 and ran it remarkably successfully for seven years.[52] Kamani Tubes was the biggest and one of the longest-sustained instances of a workers' takeover; its continuation beyond 1997 would have had a salutary effect in stimulating similar efforts in other industries and states.

Yet many Left leaders refused to support the Kamani Tubes initiative because it would only create 'a socialist island' in a sea of capitalism— as if a wholly capitalist ocean was preferable—or at best promote 'workers' capitalism', thus diverting attention away from the struggle for socialism.[53] The Left also remained passive in the face of closure of many other enterprises in Maharashtra and other states including Kerala, where the closure of state-owned companies in electronics and other industries could have been prevented with solidarity action.

Similarly, the Left should have logically been in the forefront of mobilizations demanding agricultural cooperatives, especially of subsistence farmers, based on the sharing of inputs including seeds, fertilizers and bullock power, and on joint harvesting efforts, as well as the marketing of agricultural produce. It could have called for special credit lines for small and marginal peasants' cooperatives and consolidation of tiny below-subsistence holdings to make them viable.

However, the Left was generally absent from such movements—even in states like Maharashtra, Gujarat and Karnataka, and later on, Punjab, Tamil Nadu and Andhra Pradesh, which launched initiatives to set up agricultural credit and marketing cooperatives. In the absence of a Left influence, many of these adopted limited, often conservative, agendas focused on farmers with a marketable surplus, rather than subsistence-oriented peasants.

Such cooperatives naturally excluded small or marginal peasants, not to speak of the landless and land-poor. They were typically captured and dominated by the upper and middle strata of farmers and helped shift the balance of rural political power further in favour of the propertied classes. This became particularly evident in western Maharashtra where cane growers' cooperatives, and sugar mills and alcohol distilleries based on them, proliferated from the 1950s to the 1980s. They gave the Congress and other rich farmer-oriented parties a new social base, leading to the marginalization of the forces that sustained the Left. These cooperatives also resulted in growing iniquities in the use of scarce inputs like irrigation water, which further compromised the interests of the underprivileged, besides aggravating ecological imbalances and water scarcity in drought-prone areas.

Equally significant was the communists' and socialists' early failure to engage with issues like education, health and housing. They could have demanded large-scale literacy promotion programmes and a 'socialist-style' state-funded common school system with equal access for all. They could have outlined a radical health care programme with emphasis on preventive and community medicine, sanitation, nutrition and primary health; and affordable public housing and municipal amenities, including supply of safe water on an equitable basis for the vast majority of the population that lacked it. Such programmes could have been launched through workers' and peasants' cooperatives and integrated with schemes to empower local government institutions.

Like the right to work and the right to a living wage, which were taken up by the Left-led trade union movement, these agendas have long been part of the working people's aspirations for a life with human dignity. They should have been integrated into the Left's political work. But they rarely found expression in its educational, propaganda and agitational activities. Indeed, they received scarce attention even in its theorizing of programmes and policies—partly because they were considered 'too advanced' for this 'democratic (bourgeois) stage' of the revolution.[54]

Consistently missing from the Left's programmes and agitational platforms was the pivotal notion of *prefiguration* of what a future, more equitable and just society would look like, and attempts to bring it into being, however imperfectly, through collective action. The rise of workers' industrial cooperatives, and workers' control over factories and collective forms of management, should not have to await the 'second' stage of the revolution. Its immediacy was felt during the industrial reorganization that took place in India during and immediately after World War II.

There were other early examples too. For instance, Mondragon town in the Basque region of northern Spain—established and run by labour cooperatives[55]—was a reality by the 1930s. Mondragon is today a €15-billion enterprise which acts as the parent company to 111 small, medium-sized and large cooperatives and employs 84,000 people. Despite the criticism it has drawn for being an allegedly 'quasi-corporate' enterprise, Mondragon is a monument to the creative power of the working class. Similarly, by the 1960s, Yugoslavia had created many examples of joint workers' management, especially in public enterprises, which were worthy of emulation. But while the Nehruvian model of planned development and public-sector-led investment attracted fulsome praise from many sections of the Left, especially the CPI, these examples never did.

Nor did the Left—despite the substantial presence of the trade unions led by it in India's large public sector factories in steel, fertilizer, heavy industries and machine tools, and in state-owned banks and insurance companies—demand an enhanced role for workers in their management or systematic consultation with the unions in their working. A greater role for employees would have helped them develop expertise and technical skills in the field, raised their bargaining power, improved the working of these enterprises, and strengthened the unions. This has happened to a limited extent in public sector banks where the unions have become vocal in protesting against questionable loans which result in non-performing assets.

Following the Nehruvian Paradigm

At the national level, the communists from the early 1950s onwards largely accepted the Nehruvian paradigm of democracy, 'secularism', 'non-alignment', and 'socialism' (a degree of redistributive justice) as the crucible or context in which they would practise their politics. The paradigm emphasized gradual poverty alleviation through (capitalist) growth, import-substituting industrialization and piecemeal change, rather than through sweeping redistributive measures which might lead to a loss of support to the Indian state from the propertied classes.

The paradigm did not accord a high priority to investment in human capacity building, in particular health care, sanitation, literacy, education, housing and public provision of other basic needs. It failed to redress the by-then-evident growing inequalities of wealth and income. But barring land reform, the CPI and the CPI(M) did not sufficiently distance themselves from the paradigm by agitating for radically different priorities with ambitious redistributive programmes and large-scale investment in human development. Even when the Nehruvian growth model unravelled in the late 1960s, they failed to acknowledge the contradictions, flaws and weaknesses responsible for its breakdown, or to press for a more progressive alternative.

The CPI and the CPI(M) were notably uncritical of two features of the Nehruvian paradigm: its advocacy of a specific kind of 'developmentalism' or 'idea of progress' based on large-scale projects, and its nationalist ambition to make India a major world power. The first was summed up in Nehru's description of large irrigation dams and industrial factories as 'the temples of modern India'. This 'idea of progress' was based on a crudely utilitarian greatest-good-of-the-greatest-number calculus, which ignored the social and ecological costs of 'development', including the displacement of millions of people, many of them vulnerable, and environmental destruction and damage.

As many as sixty million Indians, roughly equivalent to the population of France or Britain, are estimated to have been displaced in the name of development since Independence.[56]

The second feature was captured in Nehru's abiding faith in 'India's Tryst with Destiny',[57] which would 'naturally' give India prominence in world affairs. Nehru not only regarded India as the rightful inheritor of the British Empire and potentially a great power in its own right because of its history and size, he also believed that India is special or exceptional, like no other nation. India's foreign policy, including non-alignment, prioritizing of Afro-Asian solidarity, search for a larger role in the United Nations and multilateral organizations, and later its nuclear ambitions, reflected this.[58] The Left did not distance itself consistently from this hubris-driven nationalism, nor did it criticize India's arrogant conduct vis-à-vis its smaller neighbours, which later resulted in military interventions in Sri Lanka and Maldives and an economic blockade of Nepal.

In practical domestic politics, the CPI firmly embraced parliamentarism and a peaceful transition to socialism, and invested its energies until the late 1970s in attempts to find ways to build a multi-class 'National Democratic Front' by allying with the Congress and trying to push it in a leftward direction—as if the Nehruvian paradigm still prevailed. Indira Gandhi's 'left turn' of the late 1960s and early 1970s, including the abolition of privy purses, nationalization of banks, and her Garibi Hatao slogan, seemingly legitimized this approach and impelled the CPI to support or ally with the Indira Congress and try and isolate factions and parties to its right.

However, the 1970s witnessed a grave crisis of the Indian developmental state,[59] with 'de-institutionalization', widespread public revulsion against corruption and concentration of power, loss of legitimacy and breakdown of what was termed the 'Congress system'— and the imposition of Emergency in June 1975. The CPI supported the Emergency in part because right-wing organizations like the RSS were proscribed under it. It is only after the CPI was itself victimized and demonized by Sanjay Gandhi, presumably with his mother's consent, from late 1976 onwards, that the party revised its stand and apologized publicly for it at the 1978 Bhatinda congress.[60]

As for the CPI(M), it largely pursued a staunchly anti-Congress policy to the point of aligning with right-wing parties like the Jana Sangh in the 1967 elections and later—although it did support some of Indira Gandhi's 'progressive' measures and regarded the right ('Syndicate') faction of the Congress as the greatest threat to democracy. Yet after the eclipse of the Nehruvian model, the CPI(M) did not acknowledge that a change had taken place in the balance of class forces nationally: it probably remained too preoccupied with the dismissal of the two United Front ministries in West Bengal during 1967–70 and the savage repression it was subjected to in the years that followed.[61]

The CPI(M) continued until 1977 to espouse popular mobilizations around revolutionary demands against the state, with the rhetoric of 'subverting the system from within' as the ultimate aim. Its party programme (adopted in 1964) warned: 'The threat to parliamentary system and democracy comes not from working people and the parties which represent their interests … [but] from the exploiting classes. It is they who undermine parliamentary system both from within and without by making it an instrument to advance their narrow interests…. When the people begin to use parliamentary institutions for advancing their cause … these classes do not hesitate to trample underfoot parliamentary democracy as was done in Kerala in 1959. When their interest demands they do not hesitate to replace parliamentary democracy by military dictatorship. It will be a serious error and a dangerous illusion to imagine that our country is free from such threats …'[62]

It also said: '… it needs always to be borne in mind that the ruling classes never relinquish their power voluntarily. They seek to defy the will of the people …[with]… violence. It is therefore, necessary for the revolutionary forces to be vigilant and so orientate their work that they can face up to all contingencies, to any twist and turn in the political life of the country …'[63]

However, the CPI(M) was pragmatic enough to continue with the policy of relying on parliamentary politics and contesting elections. This indeed reflected an inescapable dilemma that radical parties face in liberal democracy. The dilemma is structural or inherent to the system because of its democratic promise and, to an extent, the reality of citizens' political equality—despite social and economic inequalities between them. The crucial issue is how to resolve the dilemma without falling into the trap of what the party called 'Right revisionism', viz., abandoning the perspective of radical change. The CPI(M) would soon confront the issue of the real *purpose* of parliamentary politics, when a practical chance materialized to come to power at the regional/state level by peaceful means.

The closest the CPI(M) came to defining that purpose, and outlining its notion of a non-insurrectionary capture of political power, especially at the level of the states, was a paragraph (number 112) in its party programme, which stated: 'The Party will obviously have to work out various interim slogans in order to meet the requirements of a rapidly changing political situation. Even while keeping before the people the task of dislodging the present ruling classes and establishing a new democratic state and government based on [a] firm alliance of the working class and peasantry, the Party will utilise all the opportunities that present themselves of bringing into existence governments pledged to carry out a modest programme of giving immediate relief to the people.'

'The formation of such governments', the text added, 'will give [a] great fillip to the revolutionary movement of the working people and thus help the process of building the democratic front. It, however, would not solve the economic and political problems of the nation in any fundamental manner. The Party, therefore, will continue to educate the masses of the people of the need for replacing the present bourgeois-landlord state ... even while utilising all opportunities for forming such governments of a transitional character which gives immediate relief to the people and thus strengthen the mass movement'.[64] The criteria of what constitutes such 'relief' were left unstated.

Towards a 'Left and Democratic Front'

This paved the way for the CPI(M)'s alliances with other parties and its participation in the United Front governments in West Bengal in the late 1960s and various coalition regimes in Kerala and Tripura. Such participation was confined to the states, which used to be looked at with suspicion or hostility by the Centre. There was no possibility then of the Left joining an alternative to the Congress nationally, which would probably have attracted the charge of 'revisionism' from within.

But the Indian political climate changed dramatically after the Emergency, with the installation of the Janata Party government at the Centre. The formation of an alternative alliance at the national level in which the Left parties would participate no longer remained just a remote possibility. After all, the CPI(M) had lent full-throated support to the formation of the Janata Party government in 1977.

At its tenth congress in Jalandhar in 1978, the CPI(M) agreed in principle to participate in a 'Left and Democratic Front' (LDF) government at the Centre. What would have been considered 'revisionist' in the 1960s found acceptance and respectability in the changed context of the late 1970s and subsequent years. But the CPI(M) and other Left parties never addressed the question of the central objective behind building and participating in an LDF, and precisely what could be achieved through it: what long-term strategy and tactics would they deploy to accomplish a gradual transition to their avowed goal of a democratic revolution?

Yet, just when the opportunity to join a broadly centre-left government presented itself in 1996—when West Bengal chief minister Jyoti Basu was unanimously offered the prime minister's post in the United Front government—the party's central committee famously turned down the offer, a decision that Basu termed 'a historic blunder'.[65]

Basu later said that paragraph 112 referred to the states: 'Earlier, we thought they [the bourgeois-landlord state] would never allow us to function even in the states, but things changed.' As for coming to power at the Centre, 'We thought it was absolutely a dream now, it would come later. But things have happened since then: in the Centre too, we have to play a part ...'[66] That prospect evidently receded after the electoral setback the Left parties suffered in 2009. After the rout of 2014, it has become remote.

Regardless of the balance of political forces and its own prospects at different times, the Left did not grapple hard enough with the problem of comprehending the resilience of the Indian bourgeoisie and its astute use of various institutions, including political parties and the bureaucracy, to capture and retain power. Even less did the Left understand that bourgeois democracy—albeit of a devalued, degraded, authoritarian variety, which violates the tenets of the Constitution that lies at the very foundation of its legitimacy—would sink deep roots in India. This limited the scope of the strategies, degrees of freedom, and room for manoeuvre available to the Left but at the same time, created new opportunities and campaign platforms.

The Left grasped these opportunities to some extent, but did it grasp them sufficiently to fashion a strategy of working within the political–institutional confines of bourgeois democracy to promote radical change through a resilient but clear programme and policy agenda? Could it have been more effective in doing so? The answer that emerges from the chapters that follow is that the Left could probably have been more effective had it formulated the various conceptual issues and choices involved more sharply than it did—for instance, not merely by asking if it should participate in a national-level LDF, but precisely defining the very minimum that it would seek to achieve through such participation, and where it should draw the line.

As noted earlier, the central challenge for the Left in this protracted war of position would be how to combine its non-parliamentary agenda of mass mobilization with its (limited) election- and power-oriented work, but always by subordinating the second to the first and never losing sight of the primacy of conceptually developing and practically working for radical, comprehensive and holistic alternatives to what centrist and right-wing programmes have to offer. In Gramscian terms, this would mean a struggle to establish a new, alternative working class or socialist hegemony.

The key to building the alternative would lie in evolving an emancipatory vision of future social arrangements and relations and fighting for programmes and practices that reflect that vision. Struggling to do so while strengthening social solidarity is a prerequisite for empowering the dispossessed and marginalized, enabling and catalysing their self-organization, expanding the freedom available to them, and broadening and deepening formal democracy into a system that is substantive and transformative.

Only thus could the Left interrogate, critique, and show up the inconsistencies in the ideological hegemony (in the Gramscian sense) of bourgeois ideas which sustain the present system of power, and eventually delegitimize it by creating the core of a popular or plebeian *counter-hegemony*. The true challenge for the Indian Left has always been how to infuse radical perspectives into real, live, vibrant social movements based on people's needs and aspirations, and how to integrate the lessons learnt from such movements into state policies through mass-mobilization pressure.

As we shall see in the following chapters, the Left allowed its vision to be narrowed—whether through the dogma of a multi-stage revolution in a 'semi-feudal' society, or via a preoccupation with working within the bourgeois-democratic system *without* trying to radically transform it (what Lenin called 'parliamentary cretinism'). It therefore largely failed to rise to the challenge; indeed, it fled from it by setting its sights too low and has progressively marginalized itself.

The Left has so far not just taken a limited, conservative view of what is feasible in the existing circumstances, but also adopted a constricted 'Horizon of the Possible'. It has endeavoured to take state power within the bourgeois-democratic framework and successfully hold on to it for varying periods at the regional (state) level, but without sufficient clarity about the larger ends to which the power would be used. It has participated half-heartedly in popular mobilizations without learning enough from them in a spirit of humility. On the other hand, it has often failed to radicalize them sufficiently when it has had an opportunity to do so.

The Left's search for a strategic framework within which to fight for transformative social change based on popular counter-hegemony remains both inadequately theorized and practically unrealized. If the Left is to rejuvenate itself, it will have to return to this unfulfilled agenda with all seriousness, and with fresh ideas that expand its political horizons. There is no alternative to this.

3

Forward March in National Politics

Rising Influence, Twin Evils or One?, 'Historic Blunder',
Incoherent Third-frontism

When World War II ended, the Communist Party of India almost miraculously emerged as India's third largest party, next only to the Indian National Congress and the Muslim League.[1] This came about although the CPI had been repeatedly banned and repressed, and despite the setbacks that it suffered owing to its own misjudgements and mistakes during the war. These included its characterization of it as a 'People's War' after Hitler's invasion of the Soviet Union, and the 'Adhikari thesis' of August–September 1942 on 'Pakistan and National Unity'.[2]

The CPI's rapid expansion in the 1940s, and especially in the post-war years, is explained largely by the upsurge of popular struggles that took place during that period, of which the party was a major and integral part. It registered impressive, often dramatic, growth in membership and influence despite its vacillations and about-turns on important issues like the question of Pakistan and the integration of Jammu and Kashmir into the Indian Union. The CPI supplemented its work in the trade unions and kisan sabhas with participation in parliamentary politics. In India's first general elections, held in 1951–52, it emerged as the principal opposition party.

This chapter analyses how the communist movement acquired a strong national identity and presence and the extent to which it was able to develop a hegemonic perspective for radical social change during its heyday. It examines the course of the movement's growth through and beyond the split in the CPI and the formation of the Communist Party of India (Marxist) in 1964, and a further schism in the CPI(M) caused by the Naxalite movement.[3] It analyses the strategies and tactics deployed by the CPI and CPI(M) to gain national-level influence and the reasons for their growing 'regionalization' after the Emergency, which limited their ability to influence major developments which reshaped Indian society and politics in the last quarter of the twentieth century and beyond.

This chapter also takes a critical look at the organizational legacy of the communist movement, in particular the doctrine of 'democratic centralism', which prevented serious inner-party deliberation on critically important issues. These include, most vitally, the nature and composition of the ruling class and its relationship to different political parties and currents, the form of the governance system within the broad framework of bourgeois democracy, the 'weak links' in the prevailing chain of power, and opportunities for the working people to advance their interests. Such debate would have furnished the basis necessary to set the Left's priorities and enabled it to develop coherent strategies.

The CPI was by the mid-1940s well implanted in urban working class trade unions—the membership of the All-India Trade Union Congress (AITUC) doubled between 1942 and 1944—and among organizations of agricultural workers and sharecroppers in Telangana, Kerala, coastal Andhra and North Bengal, and 'some pockets in Punjab, Maharashtra and Tamil Nadu'.[4] Its anti-fascist platform during World War II also helped the CPI gain significant influence in sections of the intelligentsia which were not narrowly nationalist, but aware of the global issues that lay at the heart of the war, including the importance of defeating the forces of Nazism and fascism.

Strong Cultural Work

The CPI was legalized by the colonial state in July 1942—after having been hounded and persecuted by it right since the 1920s, and formally proscribed in 1934. Legalization, and the ability to work openly, gave the CPI a huge boost. Its membership rose dramatically from 4,000 in

1942, to 15,000 in May 1943, when the party held its first congress in Bombay. Membership more than tripled to 53,000 in mid-1946, and crossed 100,000 at the time of the second CPI congress in February 1948.[5] As its membership increased impressively, the party's influence in mass organizations and among students also grew rapidly.

Equally important was the CPI's pioneering work in the cultural field through the Indian People's Theatre Association (IPTA) and the Progressive Writers' Association. IPTA was at its creative peak in raising public awareness about the Bengal Famine and collecting funds for relief, in providing which the party's cadres immersed themselves with great dedication. IPTA acquired unparalleled influence in middle-class cultural life through its plays, musical performances and countrywide public education campaigns. It attracted a galaxy of talented people such as Balraj Sahni, Khwaja Ahmad Abbas, Prithviraj Kapoor, Sunil Janah, Kaifi Azmi, Salil Chowdhury, Shombhu Mitra, Amar Shaikh and Annabhau Sathe. In Bengal, Jyotirindra Maitra's *Nabajivaner Gan* and Bijon Bhattacharya's play *Nabanna* 'marked major cultural departures' and IPTA became a magnet for extraordinarily creative artists, writers and poets including Chittaprasad, Somnath Hore, Debabrata Biswas, Suchitra Mitra, Sukanta Bhattacharya, Manik Bandyopadhyay, Bishnu De and Samar Sen.

The CPI was deeply involved in, and in many cases in the forefront of, the great wave of strikes, upsurges and armed revolts that broke out during 1945–47, including the Telengana peasant insurgency in Hyderabad state, the Tebhaga sharecroppers' movement in Bengal, the Punnapra–Vayalar revolt in Travancore, the Warli movement in Maharashtra's Thane district,[6] and not least, the Royal Indian Navy mutiny of 1946 in Bombay, and the nationwide campaign for the release of members of Subhas Chandra Bose's Indian National Army who had been taken prisoner.

There was massive unrest among workers and students in India during July–September 1946, including a rash of strikes by railway workers, miners, textile millworkers, white-collar employees in post offices and banks, military establishment employees, local transport workers, and even the police in different cities, along with large-scale solidarity actions, including general strikes.[7] These urban-industrial and agrarian upheavals—the last to occur before a series of communal riots broke out in several Indian cities, paving the way for Partition—were unprecedented in their sweep, scale and potential. But they 'lacked a pattern, there was no common direction or similarity of purpose and goal, and therefore there was little possibility of unification under a common leadership'.[8]

The CPI was in no position to provide that leadership. It had little capacity or time to reflect on these movements in depth or to set up a dialogue between their dispersed participants and leaders, ranging from rural Telengana and Kerala to cities such as Bombay, Calcutta and Kanpur. It made no attempt to evolve a coordinated strategy—except briefly and awkwardly via the 1948 Ranadive line, which declared Indian independence a chimera and saw in every local protest a 'general leftward swing' and a potential for a revolutionary breakthrough.

A deeper cause for the CPI's leadership deficit in this period lay in its members' rather limited acquaintance with Marxist theory and the history of debates within the international communist movement on broad-horizon programmatic perspectives and issues of strategy and tactics. Most party leaders' exposure to these issues was circumscribed by a lack of access to Marxist literature, especially the original theoretical work of Marx and other major socialist thinkers, including Lenin and Luxemburg, leave alone Bukharin or Trotsky, who was reviled within the Communist International from the 1920s onwards.

For the most part, it is Stalin's crude, formulaic, schematized and dogma-ridden texts like *Dialectical and Historical Materialism* and *A History of the Communist Party of the Soviet Union (Bolshevik)* that formed the staple of the Marxist 'education' of CPI cadres. Such 'education' could not have stimulated rigorous or serious Marxist analysis, not to speak of creative thinking free of dogma. Indeed, it did not even inculcate respect for the battle of ideas or tolerance for unorthodox opinions which questioned the 'party line'.

The CPI leadership did not display much interest in ideological and theoretical matters even when these were of immediate, crucial significance in defining the foundational framework for the party's own political activities, and for giving them coherence. Thus, for some thirty years, the CPI functioned without a party programme or a clearly formulated statement of policy or tactical line. It held its first two party congresses without debating or adopting a programme or a broad policy statement. It only adopted these in 1951—and that too under external (ironically, Stalin's) goading![9]

'Official' Marxists' Rigidity

Within the CPI, there was very little in-depth discussion of theoretical issues in study circles or party schools/classes; nor was analytical work greatly valued; very few communist leaders, including those with a British education, could claim to be generally well read or well versed with contemporary Marxist discourse.[10] There was no dialogue between what D.D. Kosambi called 'official Marxists' (CPI members) and non-party social scientists or scholars even of a Marxist bent of mind or persuasion. The quality of the party leadership's theoretical analysis, its grasp of complex ideological issues, or its intellectual maturity, rarely rose to the level of its dedication to the socialist cause, its fiery idealism, its spirit of self-sacrifice, and its immense practical inventiveness.

Within the CPI's prevalent organizational culture, party members shunned non-party intellectuals and often viewed them with suspicion. It bears recalling that much of the formative ideological influence on India's communists until at least the mid-1930s, if not later, came from the sectarian line of the Sixth Congress of the Comintern (1928), which described the social democrats as 'social fascists' and collaborators of Nazism'.[11] This partly explains the CPI's allergy to accommodating different tendencies and views within its ranks and also its propensity to splits, factional divisions and expulsions. The sectarianism also bred a degree of cynicism towards intellectual pursuits.

The CPI was unable to analyse the significance of the popular upheavals from the mid-1940s to the early 1950s within a coherent yet resilient political framework.[12] The result was that the party had as many as four distinct political 'lines' between April 1946 and October 1951: cooperation with the 'popular ministries' of the Congress and Muslim League, in the 'people's common interest' (1946); 'revolutionary defence' against the 'collaborationist' Congress, which 'had gone over to the camp of imperialism' (December 1947); refusal to recognize that India became independent in August 1947, and insistence that it was a 'satellite state', which calls for a guerrilla war following the 'Chinese way' (the Ranadive line of 1948); and Ranadive's replacement as CPI general secretary by C. Rajeswara Rao in June 1950,[13] and adoption of the draft programme and tactical line (October 1951).[14]

These different lines reflected persistent differences within the undivided CPI on assessing the character of the Indian bourgeoisie, which dominated the inner-party debate all the way to the CPI–CPI(M) split and the formation of the CPI(M-L) in the late 1960s, and beyond. The question of whether the bourgeoisie is anti-imperialist, collaborates with imperialism, or plays a dual role vis-à-vis imperialism would determine the fault lines in the communist movement.

To return to the late 1940s, the CPI faced great hostility from the Congress party as the latter prepared to take the reins of government in independent India on the basis of a fundamental continuity with colonial rule and its instruments. Fearful of popular 'excesses' (read, 'widespread agrarian revolt, labour trouble, army disaffection, and the presence of INA men with some military expertise')[15] Congress leaders clung to the path of negotiation and compromise with the British and the Muslim League and eventually accepted Partition. They dropped the demand for a Constituent Assembly elected on the basis of universal franchise and diluted and reneged on some of their pledges to incorporate expansive social rights in the Constitution, which came into force in 1950.

Not only was the Telengana uprising crushed; the CPI found itself beleaguered even after it abandoned the Ranadive line. It was hard put to contend with both the internal problem of defining its strategic line of march, and coping with the momentous political developments that occurred soon after Independence, including India's adoption of planning, the announcement of the first general elections based on adult franchise in 1951–52, and a softening of the Soviet Union's attitude towards the Nehru government in view of its policy of bloc neutrality in the cold war.

The CPI nevertheless performed remarkably well in the first general elections, emerging as the main opposition party with a 3.3 per cent national vote share and sixteen of a total of 489 Lok Sabha seats. It also did reasonably well in the 1952 and 1953 state assembly elections in Andhra Pradesh, and made its electoral presence felt in a few other states. However, it did not generally develop a well-thought-out strategy to combine its parliamentary leverage with grass-roots work. The exception was Kerala, where the party, with the independent candidates backed by it, won a majority in the landmark assembly elections of 1957.

The Regional Route?

In the 1950s, the CPI fashioned a strategy to join popular struggles for the creation of linguistic states, a demand it had long supported as part of its quasi-federal agenda. The Congress also supported the demand before Independence, but dragged its feet on its implementation later. The CPI's role in such agitations was especially important among the Telugu-speaking people of Andhra Pradesh (comprising the Nizam's Hyderabad state and parts of the Madras province), Malayalam-speaking people of Kerala (reuniting the princely state of Travancore–Cochin with Malabar, which was part of Madras), Marathi-speaking people (mainly of the bilingual Bombay state, but also some parts of Mysore, later Karnataka), and Gujarati-speaking people (who demanded separation from Bombay state).

These movements, respectively called Vishal Andhra, Aikya Keralam, Samyukta Maharashtra and Maha-Gujarat, wholly or largely succeeded in winning their demands. The CPI reaped great benefits from participation in the first two cases, but the results were somewhat mixed in the other two. Communist cadres participating in the Samyukta Maharashtra Samiti and the Maha-Gujarat movements sometimes found themselves fighting on opposing sides. The Samiti movement attracted large-scale popular, in particular working class, support from 1956 to 1960, and was led by the Communist Party of India, the Praja Socialist Party, the Peasants and Workers Party and the Republican Party. These parties and independents associated with the Samiti contested the 1957 general elections and secured 132 of the 397 seats in the Bombay Legislative Assembly. The Samiti also won a large number of local bodies including the Bombay and Poona municipal corporations.

Yet there was very little that held the Samiti together except the desire for a unified Maharashtra and opposition to the Congress.

Eventually, on 1 May 1960, the new state of Maharashtra was created in accordance with most, though not all, of the Samiti's demands. The Samiti soon went into oblivion. The CPI gained significantly through its membership of the Samiti by joining the 'mainstream' cause of linguistic provincialism as one of its leading parties, if not the most important one.[16]

However, there was a price to pay. The Samiti promoted the cult of Shivaji as a Maratha hero, and did not demarcate itself sufficiently from the chauvinist sentiment that was among the driving forces of the agitation. The Shiv Sena, born in the mid-1960s, cynically capitalized on both the sentiment and the cult. Exploiting the situation of growing unemployment, it fanned rank Maharashtrian chauvinism, attributing joblessness among Bombay's working class youth to the domination of the city's industrial economy by non-Maharashtrian interests. It soon forged itself into a strike-breaking force in the service of unscrupulous industrial magnates, and specifically targeted skilled workers from the south, who had emerged as the best organized and most dedicated militant force in the trade unions, especially in the engineering, chemicals and pharmaceuticals industries.

With the patronage of the Congress-led state government and its police, and backed to the hilt by industrialists, the Sena soon became a powerful anti-communist force, which would physically attack CPI cadres, set up company-sponsored unions and terrorize whole working class neighbourhoods. In 1967, Sena chief Bal Thackeray openly declared that his objective was the 'emasculation of the communists'.[17] The CPI offered some resistance to the Sena's roguish conduct and goon tactics by setting up physical self-defence units. Particularly noteworthy was the work of its central Bombay MLA Krishna Desai in training working class youth in self-defence methods.

On 5 June 1970, Krishna Desai was hacked to death by the Shiv Sena's goons, reportedly on Thackeray's orders. Tens of thousands of working class people spontaneously joined the funeral procession to Dadar, only a short distance from Shivaji Park, where the Sena's headquarters is located. They all shouted anti–Shiv Sena slogans and wanted to register their outrage by marching to the Sena's headquarters. Dange and other senior communist leaders prevented them from doing so, counselled against 'direct action', but promised to hold peaceful protests later.[18] This never happened. The workers were bitterly disappointed and demoralized.

Thackeray brazenly defended and even celebrated Desai's assassination and threatened to carry out more such 'actions'. The CPI's supine response further bolstered the Shiv Sena's hubris. The Sena displayed shameless triumphalism when Desai's widow contested and lost the by-election that followed. This was a historic defeat for the communist movement, which had already been weakened by the CPI–CPI(M) split. It probably lost the allegiance of thousands of working class supporters who expected it to punish and avenge Desai's murder *politically*, by integrating active resistance and self-defence into its political strategy.[19]

Since the early 1970s, there has been very little deep reflection within the CPI or the CPI(M) on federalism,[20] and the wisdom of supporting linguistic states or allying with regional forces. The CPI(M) in 1972 formulated a new position on 'the national question in India', which reversed the conventional communist stand, by resolving not to support movements for linguistic states on the ground that they are mostly led by 'bourgeois and petty-bourgeois parties', and because the real issue is "not one oppressor nation dominating, economically and politically, one or several oppressed nations, but ... of the big-bourgeois-landlord classes of different big and small nationalities ... holding political power and pursuing the capitalist path of development ..."[21]

This view is vulnerable to the criticism that it largely ignores the aspirations of sub-nationalities and small ethnic groups within states which share a common language, who however believe that their primary cultural identities are different; their distinctive identities would develop better under separate, more homogeneous, states. Often the 'common' language characterization is a holdall category that suppresses significant differences between the tongues/languages actually used in diverse regions. It can also be argued that it might be easier to administer smaller, but agro-climatically and culturally similar, units than mega-states like Uttar Pradesh (population 200 million).

Since the 1970s, the CPI(M), unlike the CPI, has opposed any further division of linguistic states, including the formation of

Uttarakhand, Jharkhand and Chhattisgarh[22] on the ground that this deviates from the linguistic principle of statehood followed in India since the mid-1950s. It instead demanded 'regional self-government' (like 'autonomous' district councils) within existing states in areas inhabited by 'tribes, or communities with distinct social and cultural traits'—a position reiterated in the party programme of 2000. But the CPI(M) was not consistent in applying the linguistic identity criterion when it opposed the creation of Gorkhaland out of West Bengal: the region's people do not speak Bengali, but a distinctly different language (Gorkhali or Nepali) and have a different culture from the rest of the state.

This recently pitted the CPI and the CPI(M) against each other on the issue of separation of Telangana from Andhra.[23] The CPI(M) also opposes separate statehood for Vidarbha (Maharashtra), Harit Pradesh, Avadh or Purvanchal (Uttar Pradesh), Mithila or Bhojpur (Bihar), and so on. Unless these differences are resolved through a deeper theoretical discussion, they hold the potential for dividing the Left and preventing it from intervening effectively in such movements.

Big Gains in Bihar

The 1960s and '70s saw the growth of radical politics and popular mobilizations in a large number of states and regions. The CPI acquired a sizeable or significant presence in Bihar (including Jharkhand, which was later separated from it), Andhra Pradesh (including Telangana), Maharashtra, Tamil Nadu and Punjab. It could not be ignored in the industrial centres of Uttar Pradesh, Madhya Pradesh (including today's Chhattisgarh) and Karnataka, or in peasant unions in the Hindi belt.

The CPI's growth and influence was attributable to its participation in a wide array of mass activity and cultural work, illustrated through the following examples. In Bihar, the CPI grew rapidly through its anti-zamindari campaign and took over the leadership of the Kisan Sabha, launched by Swami Sahajanand Saraswati, which by 1938 had recruited over 250,000 members; this made it 'by far the largest such provincial body in India'. It established 'impregnable citadels like the Begusarai belt in central Bihar where a village is known till today as the "Stalingrad of Bihar"'.[24] It also built a strong trade union presence in south Bihar's colliery and industrial belts.

The Bihar CPI was founded by Rahul Sankrityayan, B.B. Mishra and Sunil Mukherjee. By the 1970s, it was in the forefront of India's Left movement, and had legendary leaders like Jagannath Sarkar, Yogendra Sharma, Indradeep Sinha, Ali Ashraf, Karyanand Sharma, Bhogendra Jha and Chaturanan Mishra. Between the 1960s and 1980s, the CPI in Bihar grew in what might be called synergistic competition with the socialists, in particular the Samyutka Socialist Party (SSP).

Especially noteworthy was the CPI–SSP 'joint action' agrarian struggle programme of 1964–67, which the CPI(M) too joined as a junior partner. This 'brought great strength to the CPI as well as the SSP'.[25] The CPI already had a strong mass base in Bihar. The SSP had by the early 1970s developed a base among the low and middle castes, officially termed the Other Backward Classes (OBCs). The CPI declined in later years as Bihar's politics got 'Mandalized' or came under the spell of OBC mobilization to the exclusion of class-based movements and organizations—to the point of splitting even the pro-Mandal SSP into caste-based splinters.

In Andhra, the CPI built on its work among the Telangana peasantry. It organized, sponsored and led many units of the Andhra Mahasabha, a broad-based organization created 'to promote the cultural and political interests' of Telugu-speaking people, and the Progressive Writers' Association. Although the Andhra PWA held its first session in 1943, one of its main leaders, the legendary poet Sri Sri (Srirangam Srinivasa Rao), credited with 'epoch-making' work, was inspired by the original PWA manifesto drawn up in London in 1936.

In 1967, the CPI had as many as 118 MLAs in thirteen states, including twenty-four in Bihar, fourteen in Uttar Pradesh, ten each in Andhra and Maharashtra, besides nineteen in Kerala and sixteen in West Bengal. The CPI had a national parliamentary presence though its 4.95 per cent share of the all-India vote and twenty-three Lok Sabha MPs in 1967 (and a lower vote share of 4.73 per cent, with the same number of MPs in 1971). Even more important was its work in the AITUC, the Kisan Sabha, a range of public sector industrial unions, and white-collar bank and insurance employees' associations spread all over the country.

The CPI(M) too built a significant presence in Tamil Nadu, Andhra, Tripura, Maharashtra and Assam, besides its strong bases of Kerala and

West Bengal. By 1971, it overtook the CPI in its national vote share (5.12 per cent) and number of MPs (twenty-five to twenty-three). The lead would persist thereafter. In electoral terms, a key to the CPI(M)'s expansion outside West Bengal and Kerala in the 1970s was its post-Emergency alliance with the Janata Party. The political key to its success was its participation in agitations against state repression and its work on the issue of federalism, which led to the setting up of the Sarkaria Commission on Centre–state relations—a long-term national gain.

Gradually, however, the link between the communist parties' parliamentary work and their mass-level and intellectual–cultural activities got weakened. One reason for this was the CPI–CPI(M) split of 1964, which ruptured the strong connection between their intellectual leaders, on the one hand, and their mass organizations and cadres, on the other. The bulk of the former (with rare exceptions such as E.M.S. Namboodiripad, and at a stretch, B.T. Ranadive and M. Basavapunnaiah) stayed with the CPI, while a majority of the cadres went over to the CPI(M). This also created an imbalance between their West Bengal and Kerala units, dominated by the CPI(M), and the rest, in which the CPI remained important. This spurred the further regionalization of communist politics.

Costly Election Alliances

Both parties became preoccupied with electoral politics beginning in 1967, when the Congress party suffered its first major setbacks in state assembly elections in the north, especially in Uttar Pradesh and Bihar. The CPI, after some hesitation and debate, decided to join the non-Congress Samyukta Vidhayak Dal (SVD) governments formed in UP and Bihar in 1967, which included the Hindu-communal Jana Sangh. The decision was justified on the ground that the Jana Sangh had been included in them 'on the basis of a concrete programme … which is non-communal in character'. The CPI joined an Akali Dal–led government in Punjab too.

The CPI(M) denounced the CPI's participation in the SVD governments and kept out of the Punjab ministry—although it lent it support from the 'outside', with Harkishan Singh Surjeet acting as the convenor of the ruling front's coordination committee. The CPI(M) adopted a totally different position in Kerala, where its own poor performance in the 1965 assembly elections had come as a shock to it. It concluded that survival necessitated building alliances, however opportunistic. This sent it into the arms of the Muslim League in 1967, damaging its secular credentials, and undermining its chances of freeing the Muslim masses of Malabar from the League's toxic influence.

Both parties became more introverted and joined alliances guided by their assessments of the nature of the Congress and their own short-term interest, based primarily on expediency. Wielding power in the states became a high priority for them. In West Bengal, the CPI(M) and the CPI both allied with the Bangla Congress, with which they had little in common, to form two unstable United Front governments in 1967 and 1969. In the late 1960s, however, Indira Gandhi largely succeeded in weaning the CPI away from the CPI(M). This further widened the rift between them—until after the state of Emergency (1975–77) was lifted.

Meanwhile, the Naxalbari upsurge broke out in 1967 in West Bengal and the CPI(M) itself split, leading to the formation of the CPI (Marxist-Leninist) in 1969. The Naxalite movement directly threatened the CPI(M) from the Left, and to an extent radicalized its cadre then active in the 'land grab' agitation. The state government (the CPI(M) was a partner in the coalition government with the Bangla Congress), brutally repressed the Naxalite movement and its sympathizers in the cities, causing gross human rights violations. The movement spread to Andhra Pradesh, Bihar, and in a limited way, to some other states such as Kerala and Maharashtra, and later powerfully, to present-day Chhattisgarh and Jharkhand.

The CPI(M)–Naxalite split had organizational consequences too. The CPI(M)'s hostility towards the Naxalites, coupled with the vicious attacks that it itself faced from the West Bengal's Congress-led government in the early 1970s, strengthened the hardliners in the party who were not averse to using strong-arm methods to deal with the challenge from the Left. This raised the hardliners' weight in the CPI(M)'s organizational apparatus, tightly controlled by Promode Dasgupta.[26]

A disastrous consequence of the growing CPI–CPI(M) rivalry was the split, first, in the All-India Kisan Sabha in 1968,[27] and then, in the

AITUC in 1970. The CPI(M)'s decision to form the Centre of Indian Trade Unions (CITU) sent out the message that the communists, who swear by working class unity, have little respect for it in practice and are prepared to sacrifice it to narrow party-political or parochial ends. This weakened both union federations on the eve of an industrial transition, which would see a massive attack on working class organizations by employers and the beginning of deindustrialization in cities like Bombay and Ahmedabad.

Three other developments were to shape the evolution of the two communist parties from the early 1970s onwards: the rise or increased activity of independent radical groups among workers, peasants and tribals; growing mobilization by non-party Left currents, especially from the Indian equivalent of the '1968 generation', of campaigns focused on environmental and developmental issues; and the rise of feminist consciousness and an independent women's movement.

Lal Nishan, Niyogi, Roy, Magowa, URG

The first trend manifested itself in a variety of currents: the Lal Nishan Party in Maharashtra, which had broken away from the CPI in the 1940s; the Chhattisgarh Mukti Morcha of Shankar Guha Niyogi; the militant unionism of A.K. Roy in south Bihar (later Jharkhand); the Shramik Sanghatana and Magowa group in Maharashtra, with their work on land and wage issues; and a network of independent plant-based union activists spread in different cities, to mention a few. The communist parties were either indifferent, or decidedly unsympathetic or hostile, to these groupings and their activities.

The Lal Nishan Party started with a significant working class base in the textile mills and engineering factories of Bombay and Poona and became particularly active in plant-based unions in suburban factories like Mukand Iron and Steel and Kamani Engineering Corporation. It earned a reputation for its non-sectarian approach to trade unionism and its ability to work with diverse political currents, on account of which it was sometimes called narrowly 'workerist'; unlike the communist parties, it did not campaign for its own brand of politics and did not have a strong parliamentary orientation, although some of its leaders like Datta Deshmukh were elected MLAs.

In the late 1960s, the Lal Nishan Party (LNP) pioneered unionization among informal sector and seasonal rural workers like sugar cane cutters, and also launched a campaign for an employment guarantee scheme (EGS), which would be integrated with a programme to provide relief to people affected by a severe drought in Maharashtra in 1972–73. The LNP developed a remarkable analysis of the use and abuse of water, linked it to the predatory cooperative sugar industry in Maharashtra, and succeeded in getting the EGS implemented—India's first programme of its kind, and a very early precursor to the Mahatma Gandhi National Rural Employment Guarantee Act, which came three decades later.[28] The CPs refused to join such initiatives wholeheartedly or take them on board. The LNP split in 1989, but both its factions remain active in various unions among engineering and municipal workers, as well as anganwadi workers in Mumbai and Pune.

Shankar Guha Niyogi was a strikingly original political and union leader committed to a unique breadth of agendas which go beyond the eight hours that workers daily spend at the workplace: including health, literacy and education; the right to clean drinking water; struggles against casteism, communalism and women's oppression; unorganized and contract workers' rights; issues of adivasi identity and autonomy; and enrichment of economic, social and civil–political democratic rights. His Chhattisgarh Mines Shramik Sangh (CMSS) had as many as eighteen different wings or departments, devoted to subjects such as culture, education, libraries, women's issues, the environment, community kitchens and housing—in addition to hard-core trade union work.[29]

Niyogi started his career in Chhattisgarh as an unskilled worker in an iron ore mine, and later joined the Bhilai Steel Plant, where he earned an engineering degree. By the mid-1960s, he became an organizer of the Blast Furnace Action Committee, which played a major role in a post-riot anti-communal mobilization. He was briefly associated with the All-India Coordination Committee of Communist Revolutionaries, the CPI(M-L)'s precursor, and the party itself. He was detained for thirteen months during the Emergency for his work among quartzite miners. Niyogi established the CMSS in 1977 at Dalli-Rajhara near Bhilai.

CMSS was India's only trade union to set up a public hospital with self-generated funds—a shining example of health care provided 'by the labouring masses for the labouring masses'. The Shaheed (martyrs') Hospital has inspired countless activists, including the physician and outstanding human rights fighter Binayak Sen, who worked there during 2001–09.[30] The CMSS mobilized tens of thousands of workers in the steel plant's ancillary and satellite units, and in limestone, dolomite and iron ore mines. Its key demands were abolition of contract labour and assignment of work to labour cooperatives and major increases in the near-starvation wages paid in this desperately backward adivasi region.

The CMSS evolved an innovative plan for 'semi-mechanization' of factories and mines, which would increase production without retrenching workers. It also gave high representation to women in its decision-making committees and fought against their sexual exploitation. The union, along with the Chhattisgarh Mukti Morcha, became a major site of 'Sangharsh aur Nirman' (struggle for social change and constructive work): to transform people's lives and create prefigurations of a future society. Niyogi was assassinated in September 1991 by goons hired by industrialists in the eleventh month of a strike by over 100,000 workers. Eventually, in a testimony to India's appallingly dysfunctional justice delivery system, the Supreme Court in 2005 acquitted all the industrialists, and convicted one of the hired killers.

A.K. Roy was the key figure in the Jharkhand Colliery Kamgar Union (JCKU) in and around Dhanbad, the theatre of militant unionism for more than two decades. Earlier, he was active in unions in the state-owned fertilizer complex at Sindri, where he lost his job as an engineer because he opposed the management's move to get white-collar staff to man industrial operations during a workers' strike. Roy joined the CPI(M) in the mid-1960s and won two elections to the Bihar state assembly, where he made powerful interventions on the problems of workers and of adivasis who formed a substantial proportion of the area's coal miners. By the late 1960s, he had built a formidable trade union base known for its democratic internal functioning and militant resistance to sustained violence and intimidation from the Dhanbad coal mafia (which pilfered coal on a huge scale), and the nexus of labour contractors and right-wing political leaders which dominated the area.

Although Roy never joined the Naxalite movement, he was sympathetic to it and impressed by its appeal among radical youth. He wrote an essay, 'Vote and Revolution', in *Frontier* in 1971, which led to his expulsion from the CPI(M). In 1972, he formed the Marxist Coordination Committee, which the Jharkhand leader Shibu Soren briefly joined. Roy's support for the demands for autonomy and recognition of the rights of tribals led him to work closely with the movement for a separate Jharkand state. He coined the slogan 'Jharkhand [is] Lalkhand'. When the Jharkhand Mukti Morcha came into being in 1973, Roy was lauded as its source of inspiration and unsung patron.

Roy won the 1977 Lok Sabha election with a huge margin with the support of Jayaprakash Narayan, and went on to win the 1980 election too. Soon, however, the workers' movement in Jharkhand took a huge downturn, from which it has not yet recovered. Over the past decade or so, Roy has become marginal in Jharkhand politics, now swamped by egregious forms of identity-based communal tokenism and opportunism which the BJP has cynically exploited. But Roy is still known and will be remembered as an incorruptible trade union leader and a Gandhian ascetic who fought heroically against heavy odds to defend workers' rights.[31]

The Shramik Sanghatana (SS), set up in northern Maharashtra in 1971, was a coalition between two different currents: adivasis (mainly Bhils) organized by Amber Singh Suratwanti, a local tribal leader earlier associated with the Sarvodaya Mandal, and educated middle class young radicals inspired by Marxism, but fiercely independent of any political party, who decided to settle in the villages.[32] It launched a Bhoo-Mukti Andolan (land liberation campaign) to recover tribal land that had been appropriated by kulak-moneylenders, and politicized large numbers of adivasis. The SS also took up the issue of wages for agricultural workers in this highly fertile and productive belt in the Tapti–Narmada valley, and developed a broad agenda cutting across class, caste, tribe and gender divides.

The SS used a range of methods, including gheraos, roadblocks, picketing of government offices, litigation in the courts, boycotts of landlords and long marches to recapture over 4,000 acres of land during 1972–74 along the lines of the kisan sabha model. Its demands included registration of land in the names of the tribals, cultivating forest land, cancelling tribal debts, distribution of land among cultivators and withdrawal of police cases against them. It also took up the demand for work in the government's Employment Guarantee Scheme. The SS built up a union membership of 15,000 to 20,000. Funds came from the membership base and from an effective urban support network. The network's presence in the media gave the movement an edge.

By 1979, nine of the Sanghatana's fourteen full-time activists were tribals, six of them from agricultural worker or poor peasant backgrounds. The SS initiated large-scale mobilization of women for equal rights. The SS inspired large numbers of urban men and women in Maharashtra, some of whom spent considerable periods of time in the area. It catalysed the formation of the Shramik Mukti Sanghatana, which took up issues of reform of customary tribal law and women's property rights, opposed patriarchal Bhil rituals and superstition and soon embraced explicitly feminist goals. These organizations had a lasting presence and impact in Dhulia and Nandurbar districts and beyond.

Among other initiatives outside the traditional Left parties was the Union Research Group (URG) in Bombay,[33] a site of highly productive interaction between gifted social science researchers and grass-root worker-activists. URG for the first time produced systematic high-quality analysis of the wage bargaining process, especially in plant-based independent unions, which themselves saw an efflorescence of radicalism until the 1980s. This was similar to the 'workers' inquiries' initiative then under way in western Europe. URG collected and analysed several thousand wage agreements.

URG also analysed how managements broke the unions through subcontracting, voluntary retirement schemes, and the arbitrary manipulation of categories (the issue of who is and is not a 'workman' under the Industrial Disputes Act). Managements fought hard to restrict the meaning of 'workman' to the narrowest possible group after the 1980s. URG's work helped unions drive better wage bargains and raise workers' awareness in a number of areas. It led to the creation of the Trade Union Solidarity Committee, which dealt with the issue of industrial closures and sustained the kind of radicalism that drove workers' takeover of industries such as Kamani Tubes Ltd.[34]

Not Learning from Others

The mainstream Left parties could have learned a great deal from this rich repertoire of experience: for instance, CMSS's participatory organizing methods and its success in broadening workers' struggles beyond the point of production to encompass other determinants of the quality of life. They could similarly have related more positively to the Shramik Sanghatana's work among adivasis and women, organized solidarity campaigns in support of A.K. Roy, and used URG's splendid resources. The communist parties were reluctant to do so largely because these were independent, often Far Left, highly democratic and inclusive initiatives not amenable to conventional methods of control.

The Emergency marked a turning point in Indian politics. It weakened the forces of the Left and also led to further deterioration in CPI–CPI(M) relations. Differences between the two parties had become manifest even earlier in their positions on the Nav Nirman movement in Gujarat (1973–74), the railway strike of 1974, and the 'Total Revolution' movement in Bihar led by Jayaprakash Narayan (JP). The CPI opposed the Gujarat and Bihar movements as agitations led and controlled by 'the forces of reaction' represented by landlords and the petty bourgeoisie,[35] but it extended support to the railway strike led by socialist leader George Fernandes.[36] The CPI's opposition to JP's movement was especially strong in Bihar, its 'home state', where it had emerged as a mass party; but the CPI later diluted its opposition somewhat.

By contrast, the CPI(M) by and large supported these agitations in line with its general opposition to the Congress. In particular, it only had a feeble critique to offer of the Total Revolution movement's stated objectives—dissolution of parliament and state assemblies by compelling MPs and MLAs to resign, Indira Gandhi's replacement by a national government; and the ushering in of a new political system based on party-less democracy.[37] With the growth of the JP movement, 'there were hesitant moves towards cooperation' on the part of the CPI(M), 'which never achieved formal status or proved of much significance …'[38]

The CPI(M) analysed the Emergency as an 'authoritarian' form of 'one-party' rule, without adequate explanation of what authoritarianism as a right-wing phenomenon meant in that specific context, and with no comment on how the decision to impose the Emergency was made by a small cabal within the Congress, which carried out what in effect was a coup in order to take over the party by marginalizing leaders suspected to be disloyal to Gandhi.

Dissonance on Alliances

There were differences within the CPI(M) on these issues, especially the party's 'political-tactical line'. Some members felt the party was not doing enough on its own to fight the Emergency. Some dissenters were especially unhappy that the CPI(M) had entered into indirect collaboration with the Jana Sangh by supporting JP-style movements. These dissenting views were voiced by no less than the CPI(M)'s first general secretary, P. Sundarayya.[39] The differences remained unresolved, and led to Sundarayya's withdrawal from active leadership. In 1977 E.M.S. Namboodiripad formally replaced him as general secretary. In West Bengal as well, there was 'considerable introspection among the Leftist cadre ... [and] a general dissatisfaction with the inactivity of the ... leadership in the face of repression, and its failure to launch any mass movement or even organize an underground network capable of avoiding arrest in a period of crisis'.[40]

The Emergency regime treated the two parties very differently. It arrested and detained a large number of 'ground-level' CPI(M) activists in West Bengal, where the party was already in a state of retreat and hibernation since 1972 following the attacks launched by the Congress regime of Siddhartha Shankar Ray.[41] But the state government took care not to arrest any of its top leaders out of fear—and a warning from an intelligence report—that this would radicalize the CPI(M) or drive it underground, as had happened during the food movement of the 1960s.[42]

The West Bengal CPI(M) remained united under the iron hand of state party secretary Promode Dasgupta. But it suffered a decline in party membership of 9 per cent between 1975 and 1976 as a result of 'expulsion of dissidents and dropouts',[43] and a steeper fall of 20 per cent between 1972 and 1976.[44] The announcement of the 1977 elections came as a godsend to the CPI(M), which made a quick transition from inactivity and demoralization to an energetic electoral machine[45].

The Congress treated the CPI—which supported Indira Gandhi's measures against 'Right reactionaries' and her twenty-point programme—as an ally until late 1976, at which point Sanjay Gandhi launched a virulent attack on the party. His mother too became publicly critical of the CPI after its MPs opposed the postponement of the general elections, announced in October 1976, and voted against the draconian forty-fourth constitution amendment bill. The CPI said: '… while the government correctly started by delivering stunning blows against the reactionaries, the emergency powers are now being used more and more against the democratic forces and the common people'.[46]

The CPI paid a heavy price for supporting the Emergency in the 1977 Lok Sabha elections, when it won just seven seats with 2.82 per cent of the national vote, in place of the twenty-three seats it had won in 1971 with 4.73 per cent of the vote.[47] It recanted its line and undertook some candid self-criticism at its eleventh congress at Bhatinda in 1978: '… it would have been prudent on our part to have waited to grasp the full implications of the Emergency instead of rushing to support it … Even if the initial mistake of supporting the Emergency was made, there was no reason to continue it till the very fag end.

'If our support to the Emergency had been withdrawn as soon as its negative features came out prominently and our struggle against the excesses widened and intensified, our party would not have lost so heavily. Though our entire party supported the Emergency at its outset, comrades at various levels began to express doubts …[But] the central leadership continued the wrong course in a dogmatic way … Though our policy, as stated in the Party Congress documents, was to build the unity of Left and democratic parties and progressive sections of the Congress, in practice it was ultimately reduced to Congress–CPI unity'.[48]

The CPI(M) charted out its own course, especially after the end of 1976, and allied in the post-Emergency national elections with the newly formed Janata Party, itself an amalgam of various currents, including centre-right elements from the Congress, the socialists, and the Hindu-communal Jana Sangh. It also allied with the Janata Party in most states where assembly elections were held, barring West Bengal, where negotiations for seat sharing collapsed.[49] Although the CPI(M), unlike the socialists, did not actively fight the Emergency regime—leave alone take it on in the streets[50]—it was seen as a force of opposition to the Congress and reaped handsome dividends from this perception and from its alliances.

In many respects, the CPI(M)'s alliance with and support for the Janata Party mimicked the CPI's relationship with the Congress, and was fraught with similar problems. Janata Party could lay claim to being more 'democratic' and respectful of constitutional freedoms, but it was by no means a left-leaning or progressive party. The CPI(M) adopted an ambivalent, even confused, stand on the Janata Party.[51] The party's progressive socialist component had naively accepted the merger of the Jana Sangh into the Janata Party, mediated by Narayan, who bestowed unprecedented legitimacy upon the Sangh Parivar, until then regarded as an interloper, even a pariah. But the socialists were soon outmanoeuvred by the Hindu Right, which captured some key positions in the Central government led by Morarji Desai, and started toppling Janata Party–led state governments which it did not dominate.

The socialists belatedly confronted the Jana Sanghis by questioning them on the issue of their primary loyalty to the Rashtriya Swayamsevak Sangh, precipitating what came to be known as India's own 'July crisis', leading to a disastrous split in the Janata Party and fall of its government—and eventually the return of the Congress to power after it toppled the caretaker Charan Singh government. The CPI(M)'s decision to vote against Desai's government during the 'July crisis' was bitterly contested within the party, especially in its West Bengal unit, and produced a pretty serious internal crisis in the run-up to the 1982 Vijayawada congress. But the issues at stake were never resolved through open and candid debate; rather, the organizational doctrine of 'democratic centralism' was invoked to suppress democratic debate.

Centralism, Not Democracy

This unfortunate part of the organizational practice of the communist movement ensured that there would be no serious inner-party debate on critical issues, including most vitally, the nature and composition of the ruling class and its relationship to different political parties, the 'weak links' in the prevailing chain of power and the opportunities that these create for the working people to advance their interests. In the absence of such deliberation and debate within and across the left parties, there was very little clarity about where their priorities lay and how they would develop coherent political strategies to achieve their goals. There was even less clarity and transparency about the basis of mutual cooperation and common fronts between them.

A new era began in Indian politics when the Janata Party disintegrated, with the Jana Sangh mutating into the Bharatiya Janata Party under the tutelage of the RSS, and the socialists dividing and redividing themselves into factions and groupuscules until they almost ceased to have a significant organizational expression. From now on, the Indian Left would be denuded of its socialist component, and the mutually beneficial relationship of tension and cooperation which they had with the communists, especially in states like Bihar and Maharashtra. This was a historic loss.

The Congress regained national power in the 1980 elections, but found its support rapidly eroding owing to various economic and political factors and the outbreak of a separatist insurgency in Punjab. Soon Indira Gandhi took to using Hindu religious symbolism to shore up her base. This proved futile. As did her devious tactics to divide and contain the Sikh militancy. She finally launched a massive military operation at the Golden Temple in Amritsar against the militants, provoking a terrible backlash which finally led to her assassination in October 1984. Earlier that year, the Sangh Parivar re-mobilized a movement aimed at demolishing the Babri mosque at Ayodhya and building a Ram temple at the site.

In the first half of the 1980s, the Left was called upon to oppose Indira Gandhi and fight the Punjab extremists, as well as to take a stand against the Ramjanmabhoomi agitation. The CPI and the CPI(M) largely reconciled their tactical–political differences in 1978–79, and acquitted themselves reasonably well on these two issues. The CPI in particular courageously combated the extremists in Punjab. But while opposing Sikh separatism, both parties veered towards nationalism. Indeed, they increasingly presented themselves as the main legatees of the Nehruvian tradition of nationalism, coupled with foreign policy independence via non-alignment. This was itself part of their claim to the inheritance of 'the old Nehruvian consensus—the social-democratic vision of a strongly secular, welfarist and non-aligned, yet capitalist India'.[52]

This nationalist bias translated not just into opposition to Western imperialism, but also into support for India's first nuclear weapons test in May 1974, which the Gandhi government disingenuously termed a 'peaceful nuclear explosion'. The term was calculated to disguise the major break that India made from a position of de facto nuclear abstinence to the acquisition of a nuclear weapons capability. It was also meant to protect New Delhi against embarrassing possible litigation under international law for having breached the commitments it made to the US and Canadian governments while accepting their contribution to the design and construction of a so-called research reactor—in reality, an efficient plutonium producer—at Trombay, called CIRUS (Canada–India Research Reactor–US). After pledging that the reactor would only be used for 'peaceful purposes', India's Department of Atomic Energy (DAE) started reprocessing its spent fuel to extract plutonium, which was used in the 1974 blast.

The Left, like all other parties, congratulated the DAE on this fake 'scientific achievement' and became complicit in dangerous nuclear deception.[53] Two decades later, the Left would display similar nuclear nationalism on the issue of the Comprehensive Test Ban Treaty (CTBT), prohibiting test explosions of nuclear weapons. India had pioneered the CTBT way back in 1954, and for long years upheld it as the exemplar of a worthy international agreement that is equal, universal and non-discriminatory.

But just before the CTBT came up for negotiation at the UN Conference on Disarmament in 1995–96, the Indian government reversed its stand because it wanted to keep open the option to test nuclear weapons, which it did in 1998. It condemned the CTBT as an unequal and discriminatory treaty which would not lead to global nuclear disarmament, and termed it 'a façade'. The Left strongly supported the government's stand and demanded that it must not accede to the CTBT.[54]

Opposition to the CTBT significantly changed the climate of opinion in favour of openly crossing the nuclear threshold. Neither the

Narasimha Rao government nor the National Front regime that followed it did anything to counter the growing influence of nuclear hawks on public opinion or official policy. Later, when the BJP-led National Democratic Alliance came to power in 1998, it conducted the Pokharan-II nuclear tests on 11 and 13 May—a decision to which the Rashtriya Swayamsevak Sangh, but not the entire Vajpayee cabinet, was a party.

To their credit, the Left parties, after some initial hesitation, condemned the Pokharan-II tests and corrected their nuclear-nationalist position. A major role was played in bringing about this change of stand by India's fledgling peace movement organized under the banner of the Movement in India for Nuclear Disarmament (MIND), which later merged into the Coalition for Nuclear Disarmament and Peace (CNDP).[55]

Meanwhile, in the 1980s, the Sangh Parivar–led Ayodhya movement grew from strength to strength, but there was no mass counter-mobilization against it, in which the Left could have played a valuable role. A major obstacle here was the Left's growing confinement to West Bengal and Kerala, and its weakness in the Hindi belt. But the Left did not muster the will even to attempt to build a sustained national-level campaign against the Sangh Parivar based on the working class and other toiling people, which would address a broad range of issues. It confined itself largely to localized middle-class-oriented interventions or to organizing one-day bandhs, processions and token protests.

Left as Kingmaker

The Congress won a massive victory in the 1984 elections under Rajiv Gandhi, but soon went on the defensive in the face of the Ayodhya movement. Gandhi opened the gates of the Babri mosque to Hindu worshippers in 1985. The following year, he indulged in a parallel act of 'appeasement' of Muslim obscurantists by diluting the effect of a Supreme Court ruling in the Shah Bano case, which greatly strengthened the Parivar mobilization. Meanwhile, the Bofors scandal broke out over bribery in the purchase of Swedish guns, which V.P. Singh turned into the centrepiece of a nationwide agitation after resigning from the government and the Congress. Following a report by the Comptroller and Auditor General of India on the scandal, seventy-three opposition party MPs resigned their Lok Sabha seats on 15 August 1989, precipitating an election, in which Gandhi lost power.

The era of single-party majority government had ended. The 1989 election produced a fractured verdict, necessitating the formation of a coalition government, in which the Left would play a major role. The Left parties soon gained prominence and high visibility in national politics, not merely as important allies, but as kingmakers—something they had not even dreamed of earlier.

For the next two decades, the Left parties would become a force to reckon with for all governments in India. They would catalyse and influence the formation of non-BJP regimes and approve or veto their policies on major issues. This role was thrust upon them *before* they had theorized a strategic response to the new epoch of coalition politics. The CPI(M) did not seriously revisit its 'twin danger' theory which entailed equidistance from the Congress and the BJP. At its Trivandrum congress of December 1989, for instance, the CPI(M) softened its stance on Rajiv Gandhi and stressed its affinity with the Congress in foreign policy matters. It soon veered around to an altogether different view. These policy shifts would have consequences.

V.P. Singh's National Front government came to power in December 1989, led by the 143-strong Janata Dal (in a 545-member Lok Sabha). This loose and weak coalition, backed by two opposite forces—the BJP (eighty-five seats), and the Left (fifty-three seats)—seemed doomed to fail from the start, not least because of the BJP's higher weight and its narrow agenda of keeping the Congress out of power. Some Left leaders made a distinction between the BJP, the political party, and its 'more fanatical' associates like the VHP and Bajrang Dal, and appealed to the BJP to drop the Ram temple issue, in particular L.K. Advani's 1990 rathyatra from Somnath to Ayodhya, in the 'national interest'. The BJP predictably refused. Advani warned of dire consequences if the yatra were stopped.

As soon as the yatra was halted, on 23 October 1990, the BJP withdrew support to Singh, whose government collapsed on 9 November. Four days earlier, Chandrashekhar and Devi Lal had split the Janata Dal and constituted a new party with sixty-four MPs. This formed a minority government on 10 November. It survived briefly, but only because the Congress supported it for opportunistic reasons. Chandrashekhar resigned in March 1991 when the Congress withdrew support. The Congress failed to win a Lok Sabha majority in the election that followed despite the sympathy it gained from Rajiv Gandhi's assassination in May 1991. But it formed a government under P.V. Narasimha Rao, who inaugurated a policy of liberalization, privatization and globalization with Manmohan Singh as his finance minister.

The Left was in a quandary. It was tempted to extend support to the Rao government, primarily to counter the BJP's aggressive bid for power. Yet it could not but pick up the economic policy gauntlet that Rao and Singh had thrown down. It also faced the Congress as its main adversary in its strongholds of West Bengal, Kerala and Tripura. It ended up lending the Rao government issue-based support while opposing liberalization, at least rhetorically.

Retreat from Ambitious Goals

The Left by this time had become preoccupied with state power, and working through its institutions, processes and dynamics. It placed a low priority on or detached itself from mass mobilization on issues which would place the focus sharply on society and raise the consciousness of the working people in order to confront or influence the state and push it leftwards.[56] Instead of plebeian mobilizations, the Left parties concentrated their efforts on a much more limited and defensive agenda: that of fighting the growing menace of Hindu communalism, and after 1991, combating the policy of economic neo-liberalism—largely by parliamentary means.

The erosion of the Congress party, itself part of the process of its long-term decline, on the one hand, and the limited strength of the BJP until the late 1990s, on the other, created a sizeable space in national politics for the Left and the regional parties. The Left could have conceivably expanded that space through working class and peasant struggles on issues such as minimum wages, better working conditions, access to food at affordable prices, enhanced old-age pensions and other social security programmes, and defence of rural livelihoods threatened by a growing agrarian crisis, which would soon drive hundreds of thousands of farmers to suicide. Such struggles would have immensely strengthened the Left parties' own base and political influence, and brought people's pressure to bear on the Central government.

However, that was not to be under the changed trajectory that the Left parties chose. By the mid-1990s, if not earlier, they themselves began to embrace conservative industrial policies to attract private investment and promote GDP growth, which to some extent blunted their criticism of the Centre or lowered its credibility. This was especially true of West Bengal, where the Jyoti Basu government brought in a new industrial policy in 1994 through the back door, without discussion in the Left Front. This differed sharply from the previous (1978) policy: it recognized 'the importance and key role of the private sector in providing accelerated growth' and welcomed 'foreign technology and investments, as may be appropriate, or mutually advantageous ...'[57]

The Left Front government by then had already appointed representatives from two major chambers of commerce to the board of the state-owned West Bengal Industrial Development Corporation (WBIDC). It now inducted Somnath Chatterjee, a highly influential CPI(M) leader and high-profile lawyer,[58] as WBIDC chairman. In 1995, the Indian Chamber of Commerce and the WBIDC commissioned the global consultancy Pricewaterhouse Coopers to help promote West Bengal as an investment target for international companies.[59] The government accepted most of its pro-corporate recommendations and implemented them. But these measures did not create an industrial boom.

According to an analyst, the West Bengal government's industrial policy had a 'demoralizing effect' on the 'political elites in other states', but its impact on national CPI(M) representatives was 'perhaps even worse'.[60] He cites an instance from 1995: 'The CPI-M's parliamentary leader, Somnath Chatterjee, was greeted with derisive laughter from all sides when he launched a broadside on the floor of the Lok Sabha against "the government's total surrender to the IMF and World Bank".'[61]

The Left Front government 'quickly developed close ties with the business community and made specific policy initiatives to placate business'. But 'in its labour policy, the government also ... sought to institute a class compromise around a tripartite arrangement in the labour market similar to those corporatist or social partnership arrangements known from the experiences of small European states dominated by social-democratic parties'. The number of strikes declined dramatically from the 1980s onwards. Employers took the lead 'as initiators of industrial strife' and lockouts increased. Soon, the state's legacy of labour militancy was replaced by 'employer's militancy'. 'This situation has left labour unions, and in particular the dominant unions affiliated with the CPI(M), in a quandary'. [62]

The Left's shift in West Bengal towards conservatism was itself part of the larger process of its de-radicalization at the national level amidst the shock delivered by the collapse of the Soviet Union and a generalized rightward drift in Indian society. The Left got more and more alienated from the trade union movement (which itself entered a period of relative decline) and other forms of mass mobilization, pursued increasingly conservative agrarian agendas, failed to pay heed to growing mass protests on issues related to environment and natural resources as well as on gender justice and anti-caste agendas, and stopped projecting a perspective of radical social change, backed by concrete policies and programmes.

The Indian Left parties' trajectory now resembled that of many mass communist parties in Europe, 'which went from Stalinism to Euro-communism to ultimate subordination their Euro-socialist competitors';[63] except that the CPI(M) and the CPI increasingly became 'the main social-democratic force in Indian politics' in practice while still largely adhering to Stalinism in theory and strategy, as well as organizational culture. At the same time, the Left parties increasingly adopted a relatively unambitious, non-hegemonic perspective narrowly concentrated on the state and parliamentary politics. Their links with mass organizations got weakened. Both these factors limited their horizons and the scope for intervening in social and political processes.

Mandal and Mandir

In the 1990s, the Left parties were confronted with two major developments which were to reshape Indian society and politics: V.P. Singh's August 1990 announcement of the implementation of the

Mandal Commission report on the OBCs (Other Backward Classes, or the middle and non-Dalit low castes) which recommended reservations for them in Central government jobs; and the Ayodhya movement, leading to the demolition of the Babri mosque (1992) and the wave of anti-Muslim violence that followed. These were formidable new challenges for the Left.

The Left traditionally did not favour reserving government jobs for the OBCs,[64] as distinct from the SCs and STs, although it supported some forms of affirmative action. It rightly questioned the view that the OBCs form a unified group that was historically subjected to severe forms of social discrimination. But when Singh made his surprise reservations announcement—largely for reasons of political survival, which was threatened by the Ayodhya agitation—the Left responded in a contradictory manner.

The CPI supported reservations without serious qualification, but the CPI(M) was divided on the issue along regional lines, with the West Bengal unit opposing the move, and the Kerala party backing it. The CPI(M) vacillated on the issue for two weeks before finally supporting OBC reservations.[65] Both parties however strongly condemned the explicitly upper-caste-supremacist and violent anti-Mandal agitation that had broken out. Yet, when the Supreme Court later rejected wholesale reservations for the OBCs and ordered that 'the creamy layer' among them be excluded, the Left by and large welcomed the verdict.

Merits of OBC reservations apart, this seemingly sudden turn from class- to caste-based politics caused a great deal of confusion in the Left's ranks, and attracted the charge that outside its strongholds, and in national politics in general, the Left had 'virtually resigned itself to playing second fiddle to the Janata Dal' and made its planned expansion in the Hindi belt, talked about since the CPI(M)'s 1978 Salkia Plenum, conditional upon alliances with the Dal and kindred parties.[66]

Stopping Advani's Chariot

The CPI in particular suffered major erosion in its bases in Bihar and Uttar Pradesh. In Bihar, a significant number of upper-caste Bhumihars, an important component of the party membership, deserted the CPI. In

UP, a large number of OBC leaders quit the party to join, or rather were poached by, the Samajwadi Party, which they saw as Mandal's 'A-Team', rather than stay with its derivative supporters on the Left. Many left leaders continued to warn against the use of the Mandal platform to perpetuate casteism[67] and entered other reservations too while generally upholding OBC quotas. But the Left Front in West Bengal was itself tardy in implementing such quotas in higher education until as late as 2009.[68] At any rate, the Left did not have, or develop, an independent agenda-setting position on the OBC issue, as opposed to a reactive one. This, as Chapter 8 argues, was related to its ambivalent stance on core social policies and agendas.

The Sangh Parivar's mobilization against the Babri mosque introduced new and virulent forms of Hindu communalism in society. With the repeated failure of the Central government to bring it to heel, the movement gathered momentum, especially after Rajiv Gandhi allowed shilanyas (a ground-breaking ceremony) for a Ram temple at a site close to the mosque in 1989. On 20 September 1990, barely six weeks after the OBC reservations were announced, L.K. Advani launched his rathyatra, partly to counter the Mandal agenda with a Mandir mobilization.

The 10,000-kilometre yatra, which was scheduled to reach Ayodhya on 30 October traversed several states, arousing vicious anti-Muslim sentiment and leaving a trail of blood in its wake. The Left condemned the yatra and warned against its destructive potential, besides questioning its legality. It however did nothing to halt Advani in his tracks, whether in West Bengal or elsewhere. Advani's yatra was finally stopped by Laloo Prasad on 23 October at Samastipur in Bihar.

Similarly, the Left mainly confined its anti-communal activities in the early 1990s to public education, signature campaigns by eminent personalities, art exhibitions and cultural performances largely targeting elite audiences through organizations like Sahmat (Safdar Hashmi Memorial Trust, formed in 1989 in Delhi), which invoked India's syncretic bhakti and Sufi traditions. Worthy as this contribution was, it did not develop into large-scale mobilization of citizens that could offer an effective moral–political challenge to the Parivar before the demolition of the Babri mosque.

Nor did groups like Sahmat deal with the demolition's aftermath by, for instance, forming mohalla committees in vulnerable or affected areas. These could have created—as they did in a few cities, under the leadership of independent non-Left groups—plebeian structures of secular solidarity, and held the police's feet to the fire in abiding by its duty to protect the right to life and elementary liberties of all citizens without fear or favour.

True, the Left parties were not strong in some of the states where the worst anti-Muslim violence occurred after 6 December 1992. But they did not treat the violence as a *national* issue, which would leave deep scars on its victims, damage the cause of secularism (not least through the state's brazen partisanship of the Hindutva forces), deeply communalize society, and change the face of Indian politics. They underrated the moral–political stature of their own leaders and the scope for influencing public and official perceptions through the power of personal initiative.

If Morarji Desai could succeed in 1974 in getting Gujarat's Chimanbhai Patel government dismissed for corruption during the Navnirman movement by sitting on a fast, the Left's leaders could similarly have exercised serious pressure on the Centre to act against the perpetrators of communal violence which would eventually result in the killing of thousands of innocent citizens.

After the demolition of the Babri mosque, and the spate of communal riots that erupted all over India in its wake, the Left got actively involved in anti-communal mobilizations. In particular, the CPI(M) took the initiative to call a national convention on 19 December 1992 which included a large number of secular opposition parties. Out of the convention emerged the Rashtriya Ekta Abhiyan (campaign for national unity) which conducted a mass campaign between January and April 1993. This included taking a mass pledge on 30 January, the anniversary of Gandhi's assassination, a major signature campaign, state-level rallies, and a national rally on 14 April.

According to the Left parties, some twenty million people participated in the 26 January 1993 'human chain' in West Bengal, and 7.5 million signatures were gathered nationally and submitted to the president of India. These were no doubt worthy initiatives. But the turning point of 6 December had already been passed in Indian politics. Indian secularism would pay heavily for its aftermath.

The mid-1990s witnessed a major restructuring of Indian politics: the regional parties grew substantially, while the Congress continued to decline and the BJP's parliamentary strength steadily rose: in 1996, the BJP became India's single largest party in the Lok Sabha with 161 MPs. It formed a minority government which was hopelessly isolated because of its stand on the three controversial, but core-Hindutva, issues (Article 370 on Kashmir, a Ram temple at Ayodhya, and a Uniform Civil Code targeting Muslim personal law). It lasted all of thirteen days before it badly lost a no-confidence motion.

'Historic Blunder'

The ignominious fall of the Vajpayee government in 1996 galvanized the forces of a non-Congress-non-BJP 'Third Front', in which the communist parties would play a pivotal role. CPI(M) general secretary Harkishan Singh Surjeet made the formation of a new United Front his mission. (It was then still called the National Front, like in 1989, but would soon rename itself). This alliance would include a dozen regional outfits such as the Samajwadi Party, Telugu Desam Party, the Dravida Munnetra Kazhagam (DMK), and Laloo Prasad's faction of the Janata Dal. But even with the Left's backing, it would still need the support of the Congress to stitch together a majority in the Lok Sabha. It was imperative that the Front's prime ministerial candidate be acceptable to all of these parties, including the Left and the Congress.

A clear unanimity emerged in favour of Jyoti Basu, the Left's best-known face, chief minister of West Bengal for almost two decades and a leader with unparalleled moral authority, whose political acumen and statesmanship were universally respected.[69] The UF was apparently not the first, or only, group to have offered the prime minister's post to Basu. A former senior police official has recently claimed that Rajiv Gandhi did so twice, in 1990 and 1991.[70] A host of non-BJP leaders mounted a powerful and concerted effort in 1996 to persuade the CPI(M) to join and lead the government.

Basu was better placed than any other leader to lend credibility and prestige to the United Front despite his communist ideological commitment. However, the choice of accepting the prime minister's post lay not with Basu, who was in favour of it, but with the CPI(M), which now became the nation's most wooed party. The CPI(M) politbureau met on 11 May to deliberate over the unique opportunity that had come the party's way. It reportedly decided by majority vote in favour of participating in the government.[71] But the final decision lay with the central committee, itself dominated by members from West Bengal and Kerala, where the Congress was the party's main opponent, and from where a majority of the CPI(M)'s MPs came.

The central committee met on 13 May for a prolonged debate. It overruled the politbureau and rejected the offer, thus sorely disappointing the Front's leaders who had pinned great hopes on Basu's leadership. A number of leaders—including Surjeet, Basu, CPI general secretary A.B. Bardhan, former prime minister V.P. Singh and National Front stalwarts like Mulayam Singh Yadav, Chandrababu Naidu, Ram Vilas Paswan and M. Karunanidhi—went into a huddle at New Bihar Bhavan in New Delhi. They decided to appeal to the CPI(M) central committee to reconsider its decision.

The central committee met again the next day and reiterated its earlier decision, supported reportedly, by twenty-seven votes to twenty-two.[72] But the committee did not state on what grounds it had rejected the offer, whether the reasons involved were strategic or tactical in nature, and under what conditions or circumstances it might reconsider such a decision. A long silence followed till the CPI(M)'s highest decision-making body, the party congress, debated the issue when it was convened for the first time after the May 1996 crisis—at Calcutta in October 1998.

The congress allowed the proponents of both minority and majority positions to state their views on the participation question. But these deliberations, to which the congress documents devoted more than twenty pages, were astonishingly opaque, and reproduced 'first-principles' statements by both sides couched in shopworn party jargon, which did not clarify the basis or rationale of the majority decision. The documents effectively occluded the central issue. The central committee's decision was reportedly put to the vote at the congress. Basu's line was trounced by 441 votes to 198.[73]

Losing by Default?

Speculation reigned in the media over the rationale of the central committee's (and later the Calcutta congress's) decision. Many journalists attributed it to the fact that the CPI(M) had contested the Lok Sabha election on the plank of the 'twin danger' represented by the Congress and the BJP, especially in West Bengal and Kerala; it would be unacceptable for a majority of the committee's members to run a government dependent on the Congress's support. There was speculation too over the lines of division in the central committee. The two main protagonists of participation, Surjeet and Basu, it was reported, were backed by Buddhadeb Bhattacharjee, Hannan Mollah and M.A. Baby; ranged on the other side were Prakash Karat, Biman Bose, Anil Biswas, E.K. Nayanar and V.S. Achuthanandan[74].

Meanwhile, an unusual development occurred on 14 May. A number of Left supporters, including some CPI(M) members and activists associated with progressive cultural organizations, gathered in a demonstration in front of A.K. Gopalan Bhavan in New Delhi, the CPI(M)'s national headquarters, to urge the central committee to reconsider its decision. A signature campaign got under way, supported by 'a broad cross-section of the country's Left-wing intelligentsia, including some of its leading figures', as well as some signatories 'who were known to be at least very close to CPI(M)'.[75] It was soon widely publicized. This is perhaps the first time that supporters of a Left party made such a public intervention or issued an open appeal to its leadership on a crucial policy matter.

The campaign statement said: 'The decision of the CPI(M) not to participate in a new government … runs counter to the entire effort of the CPI(M) to forge a third front, an effort whose logical culmination had to be participation in government.… The Left forces led by the CPI(M) have an essential role to play not only in keeping BJP out of power, but more importantly in eliminating the very causes behind the BJP's recent success. Their vision and their wit are needed for putting into practice a socio-economic programme of relief for the common people which would overcome apathy and cynicism, and enthuse the people into finally transcending the era of "scams" and "rathyatras". What is needed is a bold initiative for a new beginning; and the Left can provide it ...This is not the time for misgivings. The fear that participation in government would expose the Party to Congress pressures is best met by substituting "open politics" for behind-the-scenes manoeuvres'.[76] The central committee remained unmoved by this appeal, and stuck to its decision.

In January 1997, Basu famously called the decision a 'historic blunder'[77] and reiterated this view until his death in 2010. The issue was fiercely debated within the CPI(M) and the CPI—which joined the UF government, with Indrajit Gupta as home minister and Chaturanan Mishra as agriculture minister—as well as outside the party Left. Three kinds of argument were offered in defence of the CPI(M)'s decision, besides the formalistic one, internal to the party, namely, that article 112 of the CPI(M)'s party programme of 1964 only mandates it to participate in state governments, not the Central government, in order to provide 'immediate relief to the people' and afford opportunities to 'educate' them on the need to replace 'the present bourgeois-landlord state' and help 'strengthen the mass movement', but without fundamentally solving the nation's 'economic and political problems'.

The first of the three arguments maintained that the Left, specifically the CPI(M), would not be able to lay down or control the policy agenda of the UF government, and even influence it sufficiently, given the Left's own low parliamentary representation (fifty-three MPs in a 540-plus-strong Lok Sabha) at the time. The Left would be outmanoeuvred by the regional parties and the Congress—all slaves to neo-liberal policies and compromised with communalism in various ways—and forced into diluting its programmes and policies; the Left would thus earn discredit rather than gain from participation.

The second line of reasoning was that the CPI(M) would face such powerful opposition from a hostile Sangh Parivar, and the police–bureaucracy establishment in general, that its nominated leader would not be invited to form the next government; even if he heads the government, that would soon prove unviable, especially if the Parivar resorts to violent means aimed at destabilising it. Worse, some of the CPI(M)'s own allies and supporting parties would desert it, and it would court unpopularity by having to use repressive measures against its opponents.

The third line of argument was that communist parties are essentially cadre parties, whose strength ultimately depends on their grass-roots workers' morale and their faith in the leadership's fidelity to their professed ideology and programmes and policies; any retreat from these for 'pragmatic' considerations would demoralize the cadre and effectively demobilize left politics. This posed a far greater danger than the imminent likelihood of 'fascist' forces growing in case the BJP comes to power in place of the UF—a hazard greatly exaggerated by the votaries of participation. So it would be prudent, according to all three lines of argument, to reject participation in, leave alone, leadership of, the UF, and instead concentrate on building up the Left's parliamentary strength until such time as it can make a credible bid for national power based on its own agendas.[78]

Inflexion Point

However, such reasoning ignores, as many analysts have argued, the specific, even unique, nature of the conjuncture in 1996, in which the Left's leadership with its tremendous moral authority could have played an agenda-setting or transformatory role, much in the way constituent assemblies do in situations of historic or systemic transitions by laying down new ground rules. Radical parties do not always wait for majority support to accrete to them gradually; they can create conditions where they can command it through the power of example and initiative, without violating the majority test.

The year 1996 was probably such an inflexion point, where the people's aspirations for social change, frustrated by successive regimes, were still not defeated and were amenable to incorporation in imaginative left-of-centre programmes and policies—especially if they were coupled with mass-mobilization strategies, and backed by the Left's announcement of its intent to run specific mass campaigns on issues with progressive content and popular appeal.

Such programmes and their acceptance by a broad coalition like the UF would, of course, be a matter of negotiation and hard bargaining. But that was no reason for the Left to fight shy of pressing a strong radical stand in such bargaining, based on a larger, coherent, holistic perspective which the Left was best placed to articulate, given its ideological–theoretical equipment and its far richer intellectual resources in relation to all other parties.

The Left could at least have tried to push the policy envelope and secured some major concessions from the UF parties as part of its price for leading them. It did not try. Nor did the Left deploy its analytical resources to produce an alternative policy package as the prime criterion to decide whether it would accept or reject the UF's offer. Even in the event of rejection, that alternative would have brought some clarity to the debate; it would have minimally served as a future benchmark.

The second argument seems based on a first-principles-style rejection of the idea of exploring and testing the limits of the existing political system. These are not forever given in advance. They can be pushed back through creative political initiatives and mass movements. That is what cutting-edge, or rather, close-to-the-barricades, politics is about, which inevitably entails experimentation and taking some risk, provided that is prudent and reasonable. Fear of failure should not make a Left party so totally risk-averse that it altogether loses or squanders an opportunity to breathe fresh life into the governance system and policy regime and thus to shift the balance of political forces.

As for the cadre-party argument, it became less and less relevant over the years because the Left itself reorganized its internal structures and allowed large-scale induction of ideologically uninspired members into its ranks.[79] Besides, no dividing line of 'purity' separates a communist cadre party from a mass party which practises parliamentary politics and devotes considerable energies to electoral mobilization and post-election alliance formation. Cadres accustomed to such mobilization can understand the rationale of making reasonable compromises and adjustments.

After all, the Indian communist parties had a long history of making alliances with parties which are ideologically dissimilar to them; and yet, they could push through progressive policies and programmes with reasonable success, as they did in Kerala and West Bengal. In 1996, the cadres were left totally confused by the CPI(M)'s refusal to explain the rationale of its decision; they could at best speculate and guess.

Lessons: Negative and Positive

At any rate, India's communist movement, which had earned the unique distinction of coming to power through democratic elections in a sizeable region or province anywhere in the world (in Kerala, in 1957), spurned the opportunity that arose for the first time anywhere to have one of its members elected to head a national government, that too in the world's second most populous country. What a morale-booster that would have been for the international working class movement in the decade the Soviet Union collapsed, when the dominant trend in the former socialist countries favoured rabidly anti-Marxist ex-communists being put in power by desperate and exhausted electorates in deeply flawed nominal democracies!

Many hypotheses can potentially explain why the CPI(M) rejected or squandered this extraordinary opportunity: unflinching adherence to ideological–political principle or 'purity' to the point of self-abnegation or sacrifice; diffidence about sharing power in arrangements which the party does not dominate or fully control, especially as regards the policy agenda; 'pragmatic' privileging of narrow regional (Bengal- and Kerala-specific) considerations over national and international ones; excessive reluctance to grow out of the ideological cocoon of orthodox Stalinism to embrace social democracy both in practice (as it had already done) and in theory; absence of clarity about the alternative policy agenda the party would fight for in a ruling coalition; or less charitably, sheer political timidity or pusillanimity and unwillingness to think national, think big.

Which, or which combination, of these factors prevailed is not simply an academic question, but a very material issue which would point to the likely direction of evolution of communist politics in India, to which we return later.

However one judges the CPI(M)'s fateful decision of May 1996, a more interesting and productive question can be asked as to what lessons can be drawn from the whole episode and whether these would stand the Left as a whole in good stead in the future. A negative lesson, which the CPI(M) did not draw, is that a narrow preoccupation with local or regional issues is liable to detract from real engagement with national challenges, and grand challenges at that. To the extent that state-level considerations played a role, as they might have (especially in respect of West Bengal, which seems plausible, as we shall see later) they would exercise an unwholesome influence on decision making.

A big positive lesson, one which the CPI(M) did draw, is that resilience is crucial in deciding on joining governments. It soon amended its 1967 party programme to allow for participation in the Central government.[80] This showed recognition of the possibility that 'the requirements of a rapidly changing political situation' could include communist participation in national power structures—although it did not define the precise basis, purpose, duration or limits of such participation.

The resolutions adopted in subsequent party congresses and central committee meetings (for example, the 1998 Calcutta congress and the 2002 Hyderabad congress) also underscored the prevalence of a situation of political flux and intense instability, which would throw up opportunities for the formation of a 'Left and Democratic Front' or governments, but not necessarily at a time of the communists' choosing; such governments would by definition include non-communist parties.

This too showed resilience. But the 'Left and Democratic Front' formulation was later diluted to a 'Third Force', then a 'Third Front', and later still, a 'Third Alternative', all defined rather vaguely and negatively as a non-BJP non-Congress entity. This could facilitate potentially opportunistic alliances with all kinds of parties, unless the criteria and conditions for building alliances were clearly defined. They were not.

The 'Third Front' or 'LDF' formulation could thus be subjected to all kinds of interpretation. In 1994, shortly after the Babri mosque demolition, Namboodiripad argued on its basis for an alliance with a breakaway faction of the Indian Union Muslim League. In 1996, the CPI(M) central committee determined that in the context of the new situation in the Lok Sabha with the BJP emerging as the leading party, and in view of the very serious prospect of a reactionary communal party coming to power at the Centre, it was necessary to strive to bring into existence a broad-based non-Congress secular government which could be supported by the Congress from outside. This led to the formation of the United Front, which the party would support but not join.

Yet, the precise programmatic foundation on which such different fronts might be formed was not defined; the criteria for inclusion or exclusion of various parties from them remained unstated; and the communists' own red lines were not clearly drawn. All this might have made for tactical flexibility, but it also left open the possibility of sealing shaky, unviable or unprincipled power-oriented alliances. Severed from grass-roots work, such alliance building can only get the Left tied up with or locked into a series of unstable Third Force or Third Front–based arrangements that were liable to weaken its distinctive independent character and lower its credibility.

The Left started its life in independent India with great promise, indeed with gloriously exuberant hope. It seemed set to play a strong national role by combining mass mobilization and parliamentary politics. It made historic gains in Kerala. But it did not develop a coherent all-India political strategy that could have sustained its forward march. The Left's links with mass organizations got weakened and it became a movement of fragmented parties with a regional focus and a relatively narrow agenda, especially in West Bengal. It survived the collapse of international socialism with some aplomb. But it squandered a historic opportunity in 1996. Soon, its promise faded. Whether the Left can regain the initiative is discussed in Chapters 9 and 10.

4

Into Power in Red Bengal

Land Reforms, Panchayati Raj, Party Control

The Left Front, comprising the mainstream communist parties and their allies in West Bengal led by the Communist Party of India (Marxist), remains unparalleled for its staggering record of ruling the state for an uninterrupted thirty-four years beginning 1977—the longest such tenure in power yet in a state for a party or alliance, whether communist or bourgeois, in any electoral democracy in the world. The Left Front accomplished something that few other parties have done in India, viz., to penetrate the countryside without relying primarily on privileged landed interests, as used to be the case in most states until then. It also restored a modicum of law and order and politically stabilized West Bengal which had long been torn by turmoil and violence, and did so relatively quickly.

These achievements were, however, unevenly matched by the Front's performance: significant reform of agrarian relations and decentralization of power through panchayati raj in the first decade, which raised the hope that a new model of radical, if gradual, social change would soon crystallize; followed in the next decade by slow progress and stagnation, leading to slippages in social development indices and to bureaucratization and ossification of state structures, in particular village panchayats; and a drift thereafter into increasingly conservative economic policies and outright betrayal of the original promise, leading to an ignominious exit from power.

The Left Front initiated what became India's largest tenancy registration and protection programme, but did not pursue it into actual large-scale transfer of landownership to the tenants. Its constituents sank roots among the lower peasantry, but soon allowed the rural panchayats to be dominated by the middle and upper layers, which weakened their radical potential.

The Front, in particular the CPI(M), mastered the art of winning elections—seven assembly elections in a row—but without substantially radicalizing and expanding its plebeian support base, consistently altering the balance of class forces in favour of the underprivileged, or acquiring commanding political superiority over its rivals, leave alone hegemony. Well before its exit from power in 2011, the Front had become a far less radical entity than it used to be in the 1980s.

Janata's Error, Left's Triumph?

It is an irony of history that the Left Front, which proved so remarkably durable, came to power in West Bengal in June 1977 on somewhat shaky foundations and at least partly as a result of its political opponents' mistakes. The six-party alliance—then comprising the CPI(M), Forward Bloc, Revolutionary Socialist Party, Revolutionary Communist Party of India (RCPI), Forward Bloc (Marxist) (FBM) and Biplabi Bangla Congress (BBC)—emerged triumphant in 231 of the state assembly's 294 seats, up from less than twenty in the 1972 elections. Staggering as this victory was, it was probably attributable as much to a division in the non-Left vote between the newly formed Janata Party and the Indian National Congress, as to the Left Front's own voter support based on its distinctive programmes and policies, which did not figure prominently in the election campaign.

The Front's success rested on a relatively thin margin: a vote share of 45.8 per cent of the total, and less than three percentage points higher than that of the Congress (23 per cent) and the Janata Party (20 per cent) combined. But given India's first-past-the-post system, the three-way contest ensured that these two parties ended up only winning twenty and twenty-nine seats respectively.[1]

The result would have been dramatically different had the Left Front succeeded in sealing a mutual alliance with the Janata Party for the assembly elections, which the two were negotiating. This would be similar to the arrangement they had reached for the Lok Sabha polls held in March, which yielded handsome dividends: the Front won twenty-three of West Bengal's total of forty-two seats, to the Janata Party's fifteen. Despite its superior performance in March, the rather diffident Left Front was keen to become the Janata Party's junior partner in the assembly. In the event, the Janata Party grossly overestimated its strength and tried to drive an unrealistic bargain. The alliance talks broke down.

The Janata Party–Left Front differences over seat sharing concerned an unbelievably small number of constituencies, just 4 per cent of the assembly's total. The Front, 'for the sake of anti-Congress unity', as it itself put it, offered the Janata Party 153 constituencies (or 52 per cent of the assembly's 294 seats) for contest. The Janata Party first demanded 200 (or 68 per cent) seats. Eventually, it lowered its demand to 165 seats (56 per cent). This was not acceptable to the Left, and the talks collapsed. The Left Front contested the elections separately.[2] The Janata Party's error became the Front's triumph.

Had a Left Front–Janata Party alliance come about, the Front would probably have become a much smaller component of an altogether different centre-left ruling coalition in 1977, and the Left parties' future trajectory might have been dramatically different, possibly similar to that of the two United Fronts (1967–70) discussed below.

In 1977, the CPI(M) contested from 224 constituencies and won 178 seats, an absolute majority in the assembly, with a 35.5 per cent vote share (see table after the end of this chapter). The party could have formed a government on its own, but it perspicaciously included its smaller partners in the ministry, assigned important portfolios to some of them and thus helped consolidate the Left Front. Soon, the Communist Party of India (CPI), which was not with the Front in 1977—and had ended up with 2.6 per cent of the vote and just two assembly seats—also joined the Front.

West Bengal's Left parties were now placed on an altogether new footing, unlike in 1967 or in 1969. In March 1967, the Congress, which had ruled the state since 1947, failed to win a majority in the assembly, and was replaced by a fourteen-party coalition called the United Front (UF). The UF had significant representation from the CPI(M), CPI and Forward Bloc, but it also included centre-right parties like the Bangla Congress, a state-level party formed by a dissident group of the Indian Nation Congress, which nominated the chief minister and the finance minister. The first United Front, riven by internal differences, and buffeted by social turmoil, including the eruption of the Naxalbari uprising, did not last beyond November 1967.

In the elections held in February 1969, after a period of president's rule, the same coalition returned to power, but with a much larger number of seats and a more prominent role for the communist parties. The second UF government was also dismissed early, in April 1970. The Left parties had by then been recognized as the major political force in West Bengal, but not big enough to come to power on their own. They were subjected to severe repression during 1970–71, and particularly after the Congress won an almost three-fourths majority in the 1972 elections by massively rigging them. The CPI(M), which won fourteen seats in the elections, boycotted the assembly for five years.

In 1977, the Left parties emerged from one of the darkest periods in West Bengal's history. In the preceding years, their cadres had been systematically hounded out of trade unions, ousted from their living quarters, prevented from holding public meetings, and subjected to all manner of harassment. During the reign of intimidation and terror unleashed by Chief Minister Siddhartha Shankar Ray of the Congress during 1972–77, thousands of Far Left and Left activists were arrested or physically liquidated. Even liberal journalists were not spared. West Bengal had one of the highest rates among all Indian states of detention under the Maintenance of Internal Security Act during the national state of Emergency (1975–77). Its political prisoners alone were estimated to number up to 40,000.[3]

The Left Front parties went into hibernation and largely lost touch with their constituents during this phase.[4] So it is hard to attribute their handsome victory in 1977 to active or courageous resistance on their part, or to a systematic campaign to mobilize the masses on a radical or progressive agenda. Rather, it is explained by popular disgust with the Ray regime and the Emergency, with all their abominable excesses, as well as a degree of sympathy for the Left among the poorer strata of society.

It is a tribute to the CPI(M)'s political acumen that it led the Left Front in seizing the opportunity to build on this sympathy by underscoring an ideological commitment to economic equity and to improving the position of the poor, especially in the rural areas, as a matter of priority. The new government launched a series of reforms in governance and in agrarian relations, including restoration of law and order, freeing of political prisoners, resumption of normal processes of social and wage negotiation, registering tenant-cultivators, and devolving power to local government based on village panchayats. These reforms, combined with the CPI(M)'s formidable alliance-building skills, succeeded in quickly consolidating the Left Front both politically and electorally.

A strengthened Front would now hold its own and halt the Congress's electoral advance in West Bengal after that party returned to national power in 1980 with a two-thirds majority following the splintering of the Janata Party. In the 1982 assembly elections in West Bengal, the Congress's vote share fell below the CPI(M)'s 38.5 per cent by almost three percentage points. The Congress won just forty-nine seats to the CPI(M)'s 174 and the Left Front's 238 seats (see table at the end of this chapter).

The Left Front mastered and repeatedly deployed the electoral tactic of using India's first-past-the-post system to win a convincing two-thirds or even higher majority of seats in the West Bengal assembly with a much smaller share of the vote, usually under 50 per cent. The Front crossed the halfway vote-share mark only three times: in 1982, 1987 and 2006 (see table at the end of this chapter).[5]

The Left parties' victory march—through nine Lok Sabha elections, seven assembly contests and seven elections to the three-tier panchayats[6] in a row—was halted only with the Lok Sabha election of 2009. This saw their West Bengal seat tally plummet from thirty-five to fifteen, followed by their complete rout in the assembly elections of 2011 and in the panchayat elections two years later.

The Left parties' spectacular success owed itself in no small measure to their mass mobilization methods and campaigning style based on an energetic cadre, itself part of a tight organizational structure, for which the CPI(M) has been especially noteworthy. But it was also based on some substance: the reforms launched by Front's government had the potential to change the balance of political power in favour of disadvantaged classes and groups. This allowed the Front's constituents to expand their urban and more so their rural constituency.

Explaining Early Success in Bengal

However, there is a historical context to this, which needs some explaining, however brief. Why did left-leaning politics take early roots in West Bengal and what explains the relative success of the Left parties there in the years preceding 1977? The short answer to this question, which has engaged the attention of many scholars and activists, lies in the peculiarities of the class–caste structure of Bengal during the colonial period; its status as a major centre of early industrialization; and the unique importance that the landed bhadralok (literally, 'respectable people') elite came to acquire in Bengal's social life and in what has been called its 'cultural renaissance'. Reinforcing these factors are the relative weakness of the Congress right since the beginning of the twentieth century; the two partitions of Bengal (1905 and 1947); and the growing attraction of communism for the elite in a context of social turmoil, the Great Famine of 1943, and the Tebhaga sharecropper movement of the 1940s.

Through the Permanent Settlement of 1793, the colonial state created a uniquely powerful class of zamindars in Bengal drawn from a privileged minority of the three upper castes (Brahmins, Kayasthas and Vaidyas). This 'leisure' class took to modern education, occupied key professional and clerical positions and pursued literary, artistic, scientific and political interests. Extremely jealous of their privilege, proud of their language, history and culture, and adept at maintaining integration as a community through kinship networks, the bhadralok claimed and were generally accorded superiority in social status.[7]

Cleavages soon developed within the bhadralok. Its more radical sections initially took to revolutionary terrorism through the Anushilan Samity and Jugantar, founded early in the twentieth century. Soon, jute workers' unions—among the first unions in India—and kisan agitations attracted more young educated people. Although small, these movements created a relatively radical context which affected both the then emerging Congress party and the, predominantly Muslim, Krishak Praja Party (KPP) and, in particular, limited the Congress's influence. In keeping with their own disdain for commerce, the radicals among the bhadralok developed a loathing towards the Marwari business community, which exerted a powerful influence on the Congress through heavyweights like G.D. Birla.

Bengal was partitioned in 1905 for political reasons. This weakened these emerging radical groups. Bengal's reunification led to the shifting of British India's capital to Delhi. This marginalized the bhadralok and caused a loss of their control over institutional life in Bengal.[8] The rise of Subhas and Sarat Bose in the Congress further limited Gandhi's influence over the party in Bengal. His veto against a Congress–KPP alliance isolated the party from Muslim peasants, and generally, the broad masses. Gandhi never gained acceptance or popularity in Bengal which was remotely comparable to what he enjoyed in the Hindi belt. Subhas Bose's expulsion from the Congress in 1939 after his democratic election as president brought further opprobrium to the party in Bengal.

The situation was now ripe for the embrace of Marxism by a number of Bengali bhadralok radical politicians. They were drawn to communism's promise of liberation from the rule of both colonial and indigenous capital and its opposition to the Congress. They too had an affinity for an enlightened modernity in which intellectuals and artistes would have a role. The bhadralok radicals also shared the communists' aesthetic aversion to traders and banias, whom they considered philistines.

In the 1930s, the Communist Party of India was recruiting members furiously, not least in the jails of Bengal. Its membership in pre-Independence Bengal rose sharply from thirty-seven in 1934 to more than 1,000 in 1942 and nearly 20,000 in 1947.[9] The CPI's exemplary mobilization of relief during the Bengal Famine of 1943—when it made full use of the lifting of the ban placed on it by the colonial state—and the Tebhaga movement greatly helped the party grow to a substantial size.

More Left parties were also founded in Bengal in the 1930s and 1940s, including the Revolutionary Communist Party of India, the

Bolshevik Party, the Revolutionary Socialist Party and the Forward Bloc. These further restricted the influence of the Congress and were later to lend more heft to the Left Front and kindred alliances.

Partition brought a large number of Hindu refugees from East Pakistan into urban West Bengal, many of them educated, but penniless and robbed of their property under the Enemy Properties Act. The Left parties helped them with resettlement and rehabilitation and won their allegiance. East Bengal refugees, whose numbers swelled considerably after the Bangladesh war of 1971, were to become the staunchest supporters of the Left, the CPI(M) in particular.

At Independence, the Left parties became a force to reckon with in West Bengal's trade union, peasant and student movements. As an ensemble, they emerged as a sizeable opposition in the legislative assembly too, winning close to 18 per cent of the popular vote in the first election (1951–52) and well over 20 per cent in 1957. After the food and land movements of the 1960s, in which they mobilized millions of people, they became a formidable force. Their vote share climbed steadily, and reached 47 per cent in 1971, when they overtook the Congress in the number of seats won in the assembly.

Euphoric Hopes, Modest Solutions

To return to 1977, the Left Front's rise to power kindled unprecedented hope and euphoric expectations. In a famous broadcast from the Calcutta station of All India Radio on 22 June, Chief Minister Jyoti Basu promised the people of West Bengal 'a new future' and sought their 'cooperation in abundance' to fulfil the tasks of the new government. Basu said the government 'shall not be guided by a bureaucratic outlook. We shall try to move with the active cooperation of the common people and their organizations. This government will not put down democratic movements through repressive measures, but will help them advance.'[10]

Basu said the new cabinet's very first meeting had decided to grant a general amnesty to all political prisoners: 'It is the sincere desire of the Left Front government that new horizons will open up with regard to the movements of the democratic masses…. Let me tell you that this government is your own. You have installed it in office, and it is for you to give it [the] necessary direction and guidance ... We shall do our best to serve the interests of people in the political, economic and social spheres ...'[11]

Ashok Mitra, an eminent economist who became West Bengal's finance minister (1977–87), expressed the exuberant hope which many Left Front supporters then cherished, when he wrote: 'Suddenly the people of West Bengal find themselves in a position where they can act as pace-setters for the rest of the nation ...'[12] The Left Front, he wrote, 'embodies a corpus of dreams and hopes'. Its victory is 'reflective of the mood and emotions for majority of the West Bengal electorate, particularly those in the countryside and in areas where the working classes predominate ...'

This opportunity, wrote Mitra, 'has to be converted into a challenge'—that of 'making the most effective use of the transitional time, which need not last long'. The Left Front government must 'seize the initiative ... and give a push to the forces of social transformation.... The modest adventure in West Bengal, its proponents hope, would act as a great persuader; by its example, it would captivate the imagination of the millions who constitute India's exploited majority and pulsate them into an all-compassing drive for social revolution.'[13]

This hope was not unfounded. On coming to power on a thirty-six-point common minimum programme in June 1977, the Left Front government (LF government) rolled out reform measures to bring about moderate but progressive change in the state's social relations and agrarian economy. Such change in a large, populous, and strategically located state like West Bengal, it was then expected by many, would have an impact on India's eastern region as a whole, and on Bihar, Odisha and Assam in particular. Nationally, it would greatly strengthen the forces of the Left, and would be a litmus test for the feasibility of a parliamentary road to socialism in India, then contested by the more radical sections of the Left, which advocated a non-parliamentary path including armed struggle.

The Left Front government faced daunting challenges when it came to power following a long period of social unrest, political strife, agitation and violence, including politically motivated killings. West Bengal was seething with discontent rooted in stagnation in agriculture, industrial decline,[14] high and rising demographic pressure, growing land hunger, dizzying levels of unemployment, especially among educated urban youth, and extreme rural poverty. A climate ruled by Naxalite violence and state counter-violence prevailed amidst bloody clashes over land and harvest. Added to this was a sizeable refugee influx beginning with the Bangladesh crisis and war of 1971, which continued well into the next decade, adding to the demographic pressure and lowering wage rates. Social scientists warned of 'a crisis of governability'.[15]

In 1977, West Bengal's headcount poverty ratio, which measures the proportion of people with incomes (or expenditures) below the poverty line, was about 75 per cent, the highest among all Indian states.[16] The incidence of rural landlessness in the state was among the highest in India. The 1970–71 Agricultural Census categorized 35 per cent of its rural households as 'agricultural workers'. Its land to person ratio, long among the lowest in the country, fell from 0.44 acres in 1961 to just 0.32 acres in 1971.[17]

This speaks of great land hunger and large-scale dependence of the poor on wage labour. The village economy left a large section of the population without any rights in land, and led to a greater preponderance of small and tiny peasant holdings than in the rest of India, as well as a higher incidence of sharecropping.[18] At the same time, there was much greater resort to extensive cultivation in West Bengal: almost two-thirds of its entire geographical area was under cultivation, compared to just over 45 per cent in India as a whole.

Zamindari, created by the Permanent Settlement imposed by the colonial state in 1793, was abolished through the Estates Acquisition Act, 1953. The zamindars' power, curtailed further with the law's actual enforcement, was partly replaced by a heterogeneous class of landowners called jotedars, many of whom had earlier been subordinated to them. Nevertheless, multiple layers of rack-renting prevailed through 'sub-infeudation' to numerous categories of jotedars. But the jotedars were not numerous, they were regionally dispersed, and they lacked a coherent state-level leadership.

West Bengal's agrarian structure in the 1970s was marked primarily by a smallholding peasant economy, with a tiny number of big landlords at the top, a middling number of independent owner-cultivators in the median, and a very large number of landless and semi-landless people at the bottom. The relative weakness of big landlords, and the peculiar balance of class forces, as we shall see below, is one reason for the success of the Left Front's land reform programme.

Even in the 1950s, the average size of landholdings in West Bengal (barely 3 acres) was less than half the national average. More than 54 per cent of cultivated land in Bengal was in holdings of five acres or less (Indian average, 16 per cent). Holdings above 15 acres constituted only 2.6 per cent of the total cultivated land in the state, as compared to 52.5 per cent nationally.[19]

By 1971, only 2 per cent of West Bengal's holdings were larger than 4 hectares (10 acres), compared to 11 per cent for India as a whole. The 10-acre-plus holdings accounted for only 15 per cent of the state's total cropped area, compared to 53 per cent for India as a whole. The state's 'agrarian structure was thus characterized by a relatively high incidence of landlessness on the one hand, and the relatively equal distribution of landholdings (among those with land), on the other.'[20]

Many among the land-poor and landless group were tenant-farmers, called bargadars (sharecroppers), bound in a long-established subordinate relationship and multiple forms of tenancy to jotedars and other big landowners. Sharecropping was practised widely, and included both independent tenants and those tied or bonded in different ways to landowners. Bargadar families were variously estimated in 1981 to number between 1.5 and three million[21]—equivalent to a quarter or more of all rural households.

The Left Front's land reform programme had another backdrop: a rich history of militant peasant mobilization going back to the famous Tebhaga movement of the mid- and late 1940s for a two-thirds share of the crop for the tenant-cultivator. Even more important was the change in class relations that took place in the late 1960s during the two United Front ministries in rural West Bengal, which was a defining moment for radical politics in the state.

This change was broadly in keeping with the national trend set by the general elections of 1967, which saw the 'beginning of a new configuration of forces in Indian politics', based on the rise and growing domination 'by the newly refurbished rich peasant and middle peasant landowning classes ... that arose from the members of a vanishing class species of absentee landlords'.[22]

In West Bengal, this change was mainly expressed in two ways. One was the Naxalbari armed uprising of June 1967, which delivered a seismic shock to the Indian political system, besides causing a split in the CPI(M). Another manifestation was a broad-based peasant and landless labourer mobilization during 1967–69 to identify, occupy and redistribute lands in excess of the legal ceiling declared in 1953, but poorly enforced by the state. Termed the 'land grab' movement by the mainstream media, this was a hugely successful mobilization, supported by all the left parties and factions. It still remains the greatest, and the most radical and far-reaching land reform movement based at the grass roots, in the state's history, as we shall see below.

The two United Front governments (1967 and 1969–70), in which the CPI(M) held pivotal importance, played a major role in this mobilization. These governments, reflecting a shift in power away from absentee landlords towards middle and rich peasants, were determined to acquire ceiling-surplus land from those with large landholdings. Although their efforts were initially resisted by the bureaucracy and the police, they eventually succeeded in effecting a significant change in the structure of control over land.[23] This was carried over into the post-1977 agrarian reforms, albeit in a milder form.

The Left Front launched its land and governance reform programmes in 1978 amidst high expectations. The agrarian reform had as many as ten components. Two were particularly important. First, resumption of the takeover and redistribution of land which exceeded the ceiling imposed by laws enacted in 1953, and amended by the two United Front governments of 1967–70, but since left largely unimplemented. The ceiling was set at 5 to 7 hectares (12.5 to 17.5 acres).[24] Second, the government launched tenancy reform under Operation Barga, which would register bargadars (sharecroppers), give them security of tenure, plug legal loopholes which allowed for their eviction, and raise their share of the cultivated crop.

Landless and Women Neglected

The Left's land reform in West Bengal was modest not just in comparison with Kerala's (discussed in Chapter 6), but also in relation to its potential, given Bengal's specific circumstances. The 5-ha–7-ha ceiling was significantly higher than that advocated by CPI(M) kisan sabha leader Benoy Krishna Choudhury, who became the land reforms and land revenue minister. Just before the 1977 assembly elections, he argued for the complete confiscation of all holdings over 4 ha (10 acres).[25]

Owned by only 4.2 per cent of all households, these holdings accounted for one-third of all arable land. Their takeover would enable the redistribution of 1.5 acres to each of the estimated 3.75 million landless and marginal farmer households. Anything less, Choudhury held, would end up as a farce, without enough land to distribute.[26] Judged by this criterion, the land redistribution programme proved inadequate, if not paltry. The average area transferred to each beneficiary family was well under an acre, not enough for its subsistence needs. Indeed, it shrank to 0.30 acres in the 1977–83 period.[27]

The LF government did not bring about a mass-scale transfer of landownership or titles in keeping with the classical Left slogan 'land to the tiller'; indeed, it did not even attempt to do so. Nor did it even consider promoting the collectivization or 'co-operativization' of agriculture which might have been appropriate given growing landlessness and the puny size of most holdings in the state.

The Left Front's land reform, including both redistribution of ceiling-surplus land and Operation Barga, nevertheless resulted in direct benefits in the form of land rights or security of tenure for perhaps one-third of West Bengal's rural households, a significant proportion of whom were landless or land-poor. Estimates vary of the extent of the arable land these gains covered, but it would be reasonable to say that redistribution and Operation Barga each accounted for about 7 to 8 per cent of the state's arable land. These benefits are by no means negligible, although under a more ambitious programme, they could have been greater.

The other main plank of the LF government, related to governance reform, was a programme of revitalization of three-tier local government—panchayats (village councils)—through regular elections, devolution of powers, and bringing about their involvement in various social sector programmes. West Bengal became the first Indian state to allow elections to panchayats along party lines. The Left Front had a more consistent record of holding elections without interruption than most other states, including some (e.g., Karnataka) which also took early initiatives towards such devolution.

To return to the ten-point agrarian reform programme, it also included identifying and acquiring more ceiling-surplus land; giving landless workers titles to small plots of homestead land; restoring to poor farmers land lost through distress sales; providing small-scale irrigation and cash subsidies to encourage high-value multiple cropping; a food-for-work programme to develop the rural infrastructure; providing institutional credit to bargadars and beneficiaries of land redistribution to break the hold of moneylenders and usurers; and the abrogation of the old revenue system of the zamindari era, with exemption for small and marginal farmers from land revenue payment. The last two elements were new; the others had been tried out earlier with varying degrees of success or failure.

Progressive as these reform measures were, they were marked by five deficiencies or flaws in conception or implementation. First, they wholly excluded agricultural workers, undoubtedly the poorest and most deprived section of the population and were silent on the enforcement (leave alone raising) of a statutory minimum wage. Second, the ceiling-surplus land was not fully identified and taken over ('vested' in the state) for long years. Third, there was a major lag between the vesting of land and its actual redistribution to targeted groups like the landless. Fourth, Operation Barga succeeded only partially in registering tenants and raising their share of the cultivated crop. And finally, the land reform programme was largely insensitive to women and their rights.

West Bengal witnessed rising landlessness after the 1950s thanks to growing subdivision of tiny plots, and rising input prices and interest costs, leading to distress sales. The number of agricultural workers' households increased from 1.8 million to 3.2 million between 1961 and 1971; by the late 1970s, they were estimated at four million—clearly higher than the number of bargadars. Besides, unlike many bargadars, who owned significant amounts of land and hired seasonal labour, the agricultural workers tended to be landless and poorer, and hence more deserving of support.

Economist Ashok Rudra argued that the exclusion of agricultural workers from the purview of agrarian reform, which aimed to build a 'common front' of all the landowning sections barring the big landlords, would 'in the ultimate analysis betray the most exploited and the most oppressed sections of the rural masses'.[28] The statutory minimum wage for farm labour had been fixed in 1975 at Rs 8.10 a day and was not revised by the Left Front government despite the inflation that had occurred in the intervening years.

Although the government claimed that the prevalent wage rates had improved from a daily average Rs 5.65 in 1976–77 to Rs 6.75 in 1979–80, they remained well under the minimum even four years on.[29] Rudra found on the basis of a 1979 survey of 110 randomly selected villages that some wage increase had taken place in about a third of the villages as a result of the activities of Left party workers. Yet, the actual wage rate 'was distributed around a mode of Rs 5 per day'. He attributed this to the Left Front's partisanship of middle and rich peasants who employ agricultural labour, and the impossibility of harmonizing the interests of these disparate groups with the landless in an alliance that constitutes 'the overwhelming majority of the agricultural population'.[30]

The situation was hardly remedied by the rather meagre food-for-work programme, which annually created just 17.5 additional days of work per agricultural labourer against the official requirement of 210 days.[31] Besides, this relief measure, 'inherited from the British days', paid the workers a near-starvation daily wage of Re 1 and 2 kg of wheat for manual work, usually road construction.[32]

Land redistribution, based on the state's takeover of lands above the legal ceiling, took place in West Bengal mainly in two phases: in the late 1960s, under the tenure of the two United Front governments lasting a total of thirteen months; and under the post-1977 Left Front regime. Efforts to enforce the land ceiling laws were thwarted by landlords through benami transactions, i.e., fraudulent transfer of property into the names of relatives, friends and even unwitting tenants in order to evade its surrender to the state.

However, beginning in 1965–66, village committees of poor peasants and landless labourers launched a campaign to identify such lands and redistribute them. This 'land grab' movement was partially inspired by the general radicalization of West Bengal society under the rising influence of the Far Left, which itself found an armed expression in Naxalbari in 1967. It helped galvanize support for the parties of the United Front, which fought and won the 1967 assembly election on the slogan of locating and redistributing benami lands and lowering the legal ceiling.

Such ceiling-surplus lands were identified and redistributed through direct action on the part of the landless and poor peasants working under the guidance of Kisan Sabhas and political parties. The legal granting of titles (pattas) usually followed the takeover or 'land grab', after the legal acquisition ('vesting') of the ceiling-surplus land by the state and its redistribution.

Thanks to the mobilization of the landless and land-poor, about twice as much land was vested with the state between 1967 and 1970 under the two United Front ministries as had been vested during the entire period since the zamindari abolition in 1953. The role of the UF's land and land revenue minister Hare Krishna Konar was pivotal in this. Konar, a legendary peasant leader with the energy of a tornado, set out to implement the land reform programme, but within the four corners of the Indian Constitution.

'The Konar Recipe'

On the one hand, Konar strongly affirmed the constitutional rights to form associations and unions and to assemble peacefully, and applied them to peasant organizations. On the other, he used the Indian Evidence Act and Section 110 of the Criminal Procedure Code to establish reliable oral evidence against benami owners on the testimony of local agricultural workers and bargadars, who had by now gathered the courage to expose and denounce their 'masters'. This was in no small measure due to their experience of struggle under the krishak sabhas (peasant assemblies).

This was the 'Konar recipe', as the director of land records and surveys in the late 1960s, D. Bandyopadhyay, terms it. It combined legal land reforms with popular participation.[33] Such participation was critically important to the multistage process involved in vesting land in excess of the ceiling: including identifying families suspected of possessing benami land, locating and identifying all such plots, tracing the fraudulent or fictitious transactions involved and initiating the necessary quasi-judicial process after gathering strong evidence which would stand legal scrutiny.

The process of identification of benami lands was originally launched in 1967 and guided from above, but 'soon turned into a voluntary deluge of evidence coming from organized and often not-so-organized peasants and peasant groups'.[34] By 1970, nearly one million acres of land was vested in the state through legal processes which withstood the scrutiny of the appeal courts. This 'broke the backbone of the economic power and social dominance of the landed aristocracy of West Bengal'.[35]

However, says Bandyopadhyay, 'an ugly feature of this magnificent effort was a fierce internecine fight among the UF partners for the occupation of vested land. Konar, who was so insistent on the legality of vesting, took a completely different line so far as [the] distribution of vested land was concerned. Instead of going through any established procedure, he encouraged extra-legal occupation by peasant groups. This resulted in competition among the UF partners to occupy vested lands, which caused bloodshed among the partners and ultimately the second UF cracked under internal pressure.'[36] Despite his sectarianism, however, 'Konar succeeded in weaning away the poor peasantry from the Naxalite movement.'[37] The movement also disproportionately benefited the supporters of the CPI(M) at the expense of other Left parties.

Yet, by the time the first phase of the land agitation ended, a real *breakthrough* had occurred in land redistribution. When the Left Front government came to power in 1977, over 625,000 acres had already been redistributed. The government merely institutionalized this process. It placed the distribution mechanism in the hands of local-body governments although peasant and political organizations remained involved in it. The process continued well into the 1990s and beyond.

However, thanks to the power wielded by landlords over the bureaucracy, there always remained a huge gap between the land area estimated or claimed to be above the ceiling and the acreage so declared and vested. For instance, going by the Krishak Sabha's estimates, 30 per cent of West Bengal's cultivated land would have been in excess of the legal ceiling by the late 1970s. This would amount to a substantial forty lakh acres, and would be broadly in line with former chief minister B.C. Roy's estimate of the late 1950s that 20–22 lakh acres were above the ceiling. But of this forty lakh, only 11.8 lakh acres were officially declared surplus.[38] Even if the peasant movement's estimate was somewhat excessive, the disproportion was surely glaring.

The Left Front government itself admitted that 'there is further scope for vesting land in the state' by removing 'the deficiencies in the law'. The report of the Third Workshop on Land Reforms held by the state Board of Revenue in September 1980 stated: 'A very large quantity of ceiling-surplus land was retained by the intermediaries by (sic) clandestine manner ... [through] creation of the sham and fake tenancies, trusts and endowments... '[39]. It said there is a need to 'pay further attention to this matter at the field level and to speed up the vesting of surplus land ...'[40]

The redistribution of this vested land was a painfully slow process. Of the 12.12 lakh acres vested by the end of 1980, 1.79 lakh acres were tied up in injunction orders from the courts, reducing the land available for distribution to 10.32 lakh acres. But of this, only 6.73 lakh acres (or 65 per cent) were actually handed over to the designated beneficiaries, numbering a little over a million.[41] In other words, some 3.59 lakh acres had not been redistributed.[42] This speaks more of the power of the landed classes and lack of political will in the LF than of mere bureaucratic lethargy.

Peasant unions were to be involved in helping to detect surplus land, but they could take possession of it only after 'quasi-judicial and administrative processes' were completed. West Bengal land reforms minister Benoy Choudhury admitted: 'The achievement in the matter of distribution of vested land has not been satisfactory though [the] highest priority was assigned to the job.'[43] Besides, much of the redistributed land was of low quality and too small in extent to make a significant difference to the possibility of increasing agricultural output and help the beneficiaries.[44]

At any rate, by the end of 1983, over 1.45 million households, or nearly a quarter of the state's rural total, were estimated to have been direct recipients of the land redistribution programme; by 1991, their number reached almost two million (1,993,616 to be precise).[45,46] Each of them received on average a tiny plot of land, measuring just 0.46 acre. The extent of land redistributed to them until 1992 was estimated by the Union rural development ministry at just under a million acres: to be precise, 936,000 acres, or 6.72 per cent of the state's operated agricultural area.[47,48]

While low in absolute magnitude, this compares favourably, indeed impressively, with the abysmal average national land redistribution ratio of a mere 1.24 per cent to the total cultivated area. Put differently, West Bengal, with a 3 per cent share of India's crop area, accounted by the end of 1991 for about one-fifth of all cultivable land redistributed under agrarian reforms in the country, and for more than 40 per cent of the total number of beneficiaries from such reforms.[49,50]

The modest or moderate success of the Left Front's land reforms in West Bengal—depending on the criterion one uses—is partly explained by a certain relationship of class forces, 'where big landowning interests were in a relatively weaker position, and where pressure of the landless and land-poor was further strengthened by the refugee influx, and also where the metropolitan elite who held political power had smaller stakes in rural land'.[51]

Among the factors limiting the extent of the reform were: the dominance of middle and rich peasants in the kisan sabhas, who could successfully press the Front's political parties and the government not to unearth some of their benami holdings and 'vest' and redistribute them quickly enough; collusion between landlords and the bureaucracy to weaken the legal cases against so-called land injunctions and to legally challenge their illegitimate transfer to other uses like fisheries; and the weak influence of landless labourers within the agrarian economy and political system.

The Left in Bengal, in contrast to Kerala, proved persistently reluctant to grant titles to tiny homestead plots to the landless or near-landless, including agricultural labourers, rural artisans and fisherfolk. The government was to give possession of homestead lands to them under a Central Act of 1975. By September 1980, a little over 54,000 beneficiaries had received such land.[52] The precise number of households who were entitled to homestead plots is not known. But going by official figures of landlessness, it obviously ran at least into a few million. Yet, only 200,000 families received homestead plots by the time the Left Front exited.[53]

This casts doubt over the claim that the Left Front continually pressed against what Ashok Mitra—in an interview with Atul Kohli (1987), fn98—called 'the feasibility frontier' in a hostile political environment, and was successful in using its broad power base to benefit poor rural people, albeit within a framework of modest reformism.

This is not to belittle the Left Front government's contribution or achievements. But it bears noting that a great deal of land transfer had taken place *before* it assumed office, during the 'land grab' movement of the late 1960s. The amount of land redistributed before 1977 accounted for a high 81.7 per cent of the cumulative area distributed even by 1983. The average area distributed per beneficiary household had more than halved from 0.26 hectares in the pre-1977 period to 0.12 hectares, which represents a marginal or below-subsistence holding.[54]

Going by the latest available figures, the number of beneficiary households had risen in cumulative terms by 2003 to a little over 2.74 million and the cropped area redistributed to 439,585 hectares.[55] But this is still barely two-fifths (to be precise, 42.3 per cent) of the area redistributed before the Left Front came to power in 1977.

Gender Blindness

Another major flaw in West Bengal's land redistribution programme was its gender blindness. Issuing land titles to women would have been a major means of empowering them. The Left Front government started issuing joint pattas (land titles) to the husband and wife only in 1994–95, by which time it was too late: the land redistribution process had been almost completed. Thus, only 9.7 per cent of all pattas issued by 1999 were in favour of joint names. And an even smaller 5.9 per cent of the total were issued to single-female households.[56] A precious opportunity was thus lost.

The West Bengal Human Development Report 2004 admits: 'The issue of ownership or titles to assets is ... very significant for women ...' who are denied rights to land or control over other important assets.

It says West Bengal's land redistribution programme was 'much less effective in terms of reducing gender discrimination: indeed ... the allocation of pattas tended to reinforce existing gender inequalities ... West Bengal tends to have lower-than-average recorded work participation of women in agriculture and in the rural areas generally... The pattern of land redistribution has been even more discriminatory in terms of the relative exclusion of women from land titles.'[57]

A positive feature of the land redistribution programme was that by the late 1970s, 57 per cent of the beneficiaries were from the Scheduled Caste and Scheduled Tribe groups[58], which gained only partly because they constituted a majority of the state's landless and land-poor people.[59]

In retrospect, the stipulation of a relatively high land ceiling, and absence of clarity over 'land to the tiller', would seem to have compromised the LF's agenda. Earlier, the CPI(M) central committee had advocated more radical positions in *Tasks on the Kisan Front* (1967) and *On Certain Agrarian Issues* (1973), including a campaign for ownership rights for tenant-cultivators. Former party general secretary P. Sundarayya was even more explicit in his emphasis on building a base among rural landless labourers and poor peasants.[60]

The kisan sabha leader Hare Krishna Konar also reiterated that 'the old practice of building peasant unity based on the middle peasants is not useful for an agrarian revolution, but that old outlook still holds the activists of the peasant movement back'. He also laid 'particular emphasis' on 'the task of organizing the agricultural labourers and poor peasants and making them conscious'.[61]

There was a major hiatus between this emphasis and actual practice. Critics commented that the CPI(M)'s 'central leadership wanted to abandon political action that would polarize the rich and middle peasants on the one hand and the poor and marginal peasants and landless workers on the other'; therefore, they practically abandoned 'meaningful struggle for land reforms'.[62] Another study noted: 'In their eagerness to preserve all-peasant unity in rural West Bengal, the government is probably shifting away from potentially the most active agents of agrarian reorganization',[63] namely agricultural labourers and poor peasants.

Operation Barga was by design a limited initiative to register sharecroppers and give them security of tenure; it never grew into a programme of transfer of land titles to the tenant-cultivators. Bargadars were not a 'pure class', but a 'mixed' or 'intermediate' group, with rich and middle peasants at the upper end, who outnumbered landless sharecroppers. In the 1970s, about one-fifth of West Bengal's land was cultivated by sharecroppers, only 3.2 per cent of whom were landless. Most bargadars owned more than half the land they tilled; about one-fifth were better off than landowners in some districts; and the richer cultivator-sharecroppers 'partially belong to the capitalist class'.[64]

Typically, bargadars were much better off and had a higher status and landed interest than agricultural labourers, who were tied to landlords through employment, debt and various social obligations and who sometimes owned too little land to be able to make a living. Agricultural labourers are the countryside's most exploited class, and the most difficult to organize. But the communists did not put a higher priority on organizing them than on mobilizing sharecroppers—despite Sundarayya's admonitions.

Bargadars were part of the complex systems of tenancy, including 'reverse tenancy', and variable crop/produce-sharing arrangements. Sometimes, the poorest of smallholders would lease their lands to the better-off bargadars because of their inability to work in the fields owing to old age or compulsion to seek urban employment.[65] Registered bargadars tended to be privileged as compared to unregistered ones. But before Operation Barga, very few sharecroppers were registered, crop shares were well below the legal minimum and tenure was widely seen as insecure.[66]

Operation Barga was in many ways the culmination of various peasant movements in West Bengal which demanded higher crop shares for tenants and security of tenure (including the right to inherit tenancy), especially the celebrated Tebhaga movement of the 1940s under the leadership of the Communist Party of India. The Left Front government amended tenancy laws to plug loopholes for the eviction of tenants, make tenancy inheritable, and to raise the bargadar's crop share to three-fourths of the total (where the tenant bears the entire cost of production) and to 50 per cent (where the landlord meets all costs barring labour). Operation Barga identified the recording of tenants and giving them greater rights as a necessary condition for the legislation to work.

Launched under Benoy Choudhury in September 1978, the operation first evoked a rather muted response from the peasantry. The CPI(M), the dominant partner of the LF, also adopted a cautious tactical line, keeping in view its experience with the two UF governments. As a sympathetic observer-participant put it: 'Quite probably, in order to deny the Central government any excuse to intervene, the LF government eschewed the line of mass mobilization which the CPI(M) had consciously followed on the earlier occasion ... political prudence dictated that to avoid ugly and self-destructive inter-party clashes ... it would be desirable to hand over the initiative to the administrative machinery and provide it with support from below, whilst at the same time applying pressure from above.'[67]

The Left Front government adopted a method developed by the National Labour Institute, New Delhi, during the Emergency (1975–77) as part of the implementation of Indira Gandhi's first twenty-point programme: that of holding rural workers' camps to 'conscientize' them (in Paulo Freire's words).[68] A three-day camp was held in the presence of the minister of land reforms in Hooghly district, attended by 35–40 sharecroppers/landless peasants, which turned out to be a great success. This led to the abandonment of the traditional revenue court approach, which demanded the engagement of lawyers and documentary evidence, which most sharecroppers did not possess because the vast majority of tenancy leases were oral.

The new method depended heavily upon sharecroppers' group action to identify and verify their tenancy of particular plots. 'The quality of verification in the fields was of a very high order. One could hardly get away with a lie in public and cases were disposed of at a considerable speed. The new procedure enabled the sharecroppers to overcome their fear and significantly reduced the possibility of severe reprisals by landowners because they knew that they would have to face organized resistance against any such attempt.'[69]

Operation Barga Slows Down

Operation Barga was meant to be completed in a year. Its deadline was repeatedly extended.[70] By April 1980, it resulted in the recording of 8.55

lakh sharecroppers and within three years twelve lakh of them. On one view, 'it was the crowning achievement of Benoy Choudhury as the land reforms minister ... It would be wrong to presume that Operation Barga was a cakewalk. There were problems galore, but Benoy Choudhury, by very deftly and adroitly removing all the hindrances, never allowed the speed to slow down.'[71]

This assessment was questioned by some others,[72] who argued that the average rate of recording bargadars increased by 300 per cent per month in the initial period, but soon slowed down. 'The highest monthly figure was attained in January 1979, when 32,000 bargadars were recorded by the special OB [Operation Barga] camps ... [B]etween September 1978 and July 1979, 732,955 bargadars could be identified and recorded. But the overall success was not satisfactory ...' Only 50 per cent of all bargadars were recorded, assuming their total number was two million. If the total was higher, as seems plausible, the achievement would be proportionately lower.

Choudhury also drafted major amendments to the West Bengal Land Reforms Act by removing the distinction between agricultural and non-agricultural land and imposing a single ceiling. He provided for consolidation of holdings of marginal and small farmers below 1 hectare, and for mutual self-help cooperative societies for the beneficiaries. 'The Central government held up the [amendment] Bill for several years. But even after it was cleared with minor changes, Benoy Choudhury could not do much to implement the provisions of the Act. Perhaps by that time the LF's interest in land reforms had waned and it had started its courtship with industry to re-industrialize the state.'[73] Choudhury quit the Left Front government in 1996 and died an unhappy man.

Operation Barga did succeed in recording a substantial number of sharecroppers, although the number of those *not* registered remains unclear and disputed, as do the reasons for non-registration, including the fear/risk of being evicted or receiving a lower share of the crop, especially among landless, marginal or small farmers.[74] Because political activism and peasant organizations played a major role in implementing the programme, 'its success varied from district to district according to the strength of the political machinery involved'.[75]

By the mid-1980s, the pace of the programme had greatly slackened and it was increasingly implemented by the administrative bureaucracy without much attention to sharecroppers' rights: 'over time, this issue [bargadar recording] has become much less of a concern among district officials, panchayats and peasant organizations ...' and 'the registration appears to have become very routine, and therefore very sparse in terms of numbers ...'[76]

By 2000, Operation Barga had recorded 1.68 million households (or 20.2 per cent of the state's agricultural households), and covered 1.1 million acres or 8.2 per cent of West Bengal's arable land.[77] There was tremendous variation across districts, with registration rates exceeding 35 per cent (as a proportion of all cultivators) in Bardhaman, Birbhum and Howrah, but dipping to a low of under 3 per cent in Bankura, one of the poorest districts of the state, indeed of India.

While West Bengal's tenancy reform performance was better than that of many states, it was far from exemplary or spectacular. Besides, the bargadar often did not get to keep the stipulated crop share—75 per cent for self-cultivation with his own inputs and a maximum of 50 per cent if the landlord contributed to all inputs other than labour. Early surveys found that the higher share was reportedly 'rarely given' or confined to only one-third of bargadar households in villages surveyed in Birbhum district, an LF stronghold. Yet another survey found that the prevalent share in certain areas was as low as 40 per cent, compared to the mandatory 75 per cent, although higher than the traditional 33 per cent.[78]

A more comprehensive and updated survey, by the West Bengal State Institute of Panchayats and Rural Development,[79] found that nearly 19 per cent of bargadars deliver 50 per cent of the crop share to landowners while another 13 per cent yield 40 per cent of the cultivated crop—way above the highest share (25 per cent) the landowner can demand under the law. This is the case despite the presence of Kisan Sabhas, which regrettably, 'are often dominated by the middle peasantry'.[80] There was often a trade-off between security of tenure and higher crop shares. Many registered bargadars settled for security while accepting a 50 per cent, rather than a 75 per cent, crop share. Similarly, some of the vested land was not distributed because it was declared 'unfit' for cultivation.[81]

Operation Barga did not have a positive effect on improving the status of the girl child either. A study[82] found 'a strong exacerbating effect of increased tenancy security on land on son-bias in parents to help investments among Hindu children'. Infant mortality declined by 1.5–1.6 percentage points in districts where 50 per cent or more of sharecroppers were registered. In non-Hindu families, both sons and daughters experienced reduced neonatal mortality of 2.8–3.1 percentage points; but in Hindu families, only the sons benefited and daughters showed largely unchanged mortality risk.

Operation Barga, like land redistribution, definitely benefited Dalits and adivasis (Scheduled Caste and Scheduled Tribe groups). Although they were not specifically targeted, the two groups respectively formed 30.5 and 11 per cent of all beneficiaries, suggesting that they were favoured in practice.[83] But the extent of the land which their registration covered is not known.

However, at least some of the benefits of the land reforms proved short-lived for a significant number of households. Beginning with the mid-1980s and especially in the 1990s, some of the recorded bargadars started getting evicted as landlords forcibly took over lands and resistance from kisan sabhas and the state proved inadequate. By 2001, the number of evicted tenants exceeded 14 per cent of the total. Similarly, more than 13 per cent of the pattadars who had benefited from land redistribution had lost possession.[84] These numbers were not small. They represent retrogression.

Another less-known aspect of land reforms under the Left Front deserves attention. This was the Restoration of Alienated Lands Act, which was meant to give back lands to the peasants who had sold them in distress. The number of such pending cases was officially estimated at more than two lakhs. But the Third Workshop on Land Reforms (1980) noted that the rate of disposal of such cases was 'not satisfactory' and 'a comparatively large number' of claims were being rejected, especially in area with tribal concentration.[85]

Overall then, the objectives of the Left Front's land reform programme were achieved 'at least partially', or 'at best partially', depending on one's point of view. The Human Development Report 2004 contends that 'the economic, social and political domination of landlords in rural West Bengal has declined, and that the more traditional forms of oppression by landed groups, which are still found in other parts of eastern India, are no longer prevalent in this state'. But the same report admits that 'other, more complex class configurations have emerged, as there has been the emergence of a "new rich" category in rural areas of the state, with salaried groups and traders emerging along with surplus farmers, and becoming more economically and politically influential.'[86]

Landlessness Grows

The land reform programme was to be followed by supplementary measures to help the beneficiaries through the provision of institutional credit, assistance of Rs 500 per hectare for land development and minor irrigation by dug wells, bamboo tube wells or ring wells. Institutional credit was a major need of the poor in the West Bengal countryside, where short-term production and consumption loans from private moneylenders typically bore an interest rate 'ranging from 150 to 300 per cent per annum'.[87]

Of the Rs 450 crore of credit needed, institutional credit accounted for a little less than Rs 150 crore. The Left Front government in 1979 launched a scheme under which 80,000 sharecroppers and beneficiaries of redistributed land would get credit from the nationalized banks. The panchayats were to identify and select these households. But in 1979, they could only identify 52,000. In 1980, the banks agreed to advance credit to 1.59 lakh households, but the panchayats could only sponsor 41,000 names. The other two schemes performed rather poorly.[88]

Nor were West Bengal's land reforms reinforced adequately by anti-poverty programmes, which would have helped the less privileged amongst their beneficiaries 'to come out of the poverty trap permanently'. Thus, 73.1 per cent of pattadars and 77.5 per cent of bargadars were outside the purview of any anti-poverty programme. Similarly, only 14.6 per cent of pattadars and 21 per cent of bargadars were found to be members of primary agricultural credit societies.[89]

'A very disturbing feature' of the more recent past, says the West Bengal Human Development Report 2004, is 'the rapid increase in landlessness among rural households ... NSS [National Sample Survey] data indicate that the proportion of landless rural households in West

Bengal increased from 39.6 per cent in 1987-88 to 41.6 per cent in 1993-94, to as much as 49.8 per cent in 1999-2000. In other words, by the end of the decade, nearly half the rural households in West Bengal were landless. (This compares with 41 per cent for rural India as a whole)'.[90]

Such high landlessness spells acute deprivation, if not near-destitution, for half the rural population and should be considered unacceptable. The reasons for this are no doubt complex and related to the diversification of rural employment patterns and rising importance of non-agricultural activities. But it is hard to argue that the lot of West Bengal's poor and dispossessed improved dramatically or consistently as a result of three decades of land reforms and agrarian change or 'transformation'.

In fact, evidence of stagnation in the standards of living in rural West Bengal accumulated within barely a decade of the LF coming to power. An analysis spread over a series of articles,[91] based on the twenty-seventh and twenty-eighth rounds of the National Sample Survey (1972–73 and 1973–74) and a resurvey in 1985–86 in three West Bengal districts, showed that there was little change in household and per capita food consumption, and only 'a mild' improvement in non-food consumption.

Absolute household consumption remained 'nearly as dismal in 1985–86 as 1972–73'. There was 'considerable improvement' in access to drinking water, but unremarkable change in access to health and educational facilities and to roads. There was substantial deterioration in the availability and quality of housing, 'some improvement in the stocks of some consumer durables but little improvement in the use of clothing and footwear' by rural households.[92]

This should have set alarm bells ringing in both Writers' Building, the seat of the state government, and Alimuddin Street, the West Bengal CPI(M)'s headquarters, but it did not. As we shall see in Chapter 5, their complacency grew even as social development indices, including access to health care and education, rapidly deteriorated in subsequent years.

Meanwhile, an ominous trend was consolidated: malign neglect of the landless, and stagnation or a fall in the real wages of agricultural labour in West Bengal relative to many other states. Thus the index of real wages for male agricultural labourers declined between 1977–78 and 1984–85 by 6 per cent in West Bengal, but rose significantly in most other major states barring Punjab, Karnataka, Rajasthan and Haryana. The index rose impressively not just in Tamil Nadu, Andhra Pradesh and Maharashtra, but also in traditionally backward states like Uttar Pradesh (31 per cent), Bihar (18 per cent), Madhya Pradesh (32 per cent) and Odisha (22 per cent).[93]

To take another comparison, wages under the Minimum Wages Act remained unchanged in West Bengal between 1978 and 1983, while they rose much more impressively in some other, poorer, states like Assam, Madhya Pradesh and Uttar Pradesh, with no claims to 'progressive' governments. Over the following decade, nominal wages rose by a multiple of 3.72 in West Bengal, but by higher factors in some other states (5.0 in Odisha, 4.1 in Assam and 5.6 in Madhya Pradesh). The state did only marginally better than Uttar Pradesh (3.1) and Bihar (3.7).[94]

A likely explanation for this is the weakness of agricultural labourers' unions in West Bengal, and the CPI(M)'s aversion to building an organization representing them that is separate from the Kisan Sabha, discussed elsewhere in the book. This does not argue that agricultural workers in West Bengal failed altogether to improve their bargaining power after 1977, but only that they deserved to do far better under a progressive government.

Panchayati Raj

In a landmark move, the Left Front in 1978 decided to revive the three-tier panchayat system, which had been dormant for fourteen years without an election being held. This would have a far-reaching impact on rural society and power structures in West Bengal for three decades. On 4 June 1978 direct elections were held under the West Bengal Panchayat Act 1973 to choose some 56,000 representatives to 3,242 gram panchayats, 324 panchayat samitis and 15 zilla parishads.[95]

The Act was passed under a Congress government but bore the strong imprint of a bill formulated by the second United Front government, which amended the original Act. 'The ... fundamental criticism of the initial pachayati raj programme came from the parties of the Left. They argued that panchayats could never be genuine institutions for popular participation and a means through which the vast majority of rural population could have a role in policy determination and implementation while the existing rural class structure, rooted in land relations remained untouched.'[96]

After it came to power, the Left Front was extremely keen, indeed in a hurry, to revitalize the panchayats for a number of reasons. It had taken office just after the Emergency and amidst extremely fraught Centre–state relations, with a history of discrimination against the two United Front governments, both of which had been dismissed by New Delhi. There was serious apprehension within the Left Front that the Centre might at some point of time cause problems for its government and even dismiss it.

The panchayats would help the Left parties, in particular the CPI(M), create a protective armour through the building of an alternative rural base which they then largely lacked. This would help the Left create and maintain influence at the grass-roots level which could possibly survive and outlast a predatory intervention by the Centre and loss of power at the state level—a sort of insurance or 'anticipatory bail against the onslaught of centralized intervention'.[97]

However, legitimate as this strategic consideration was, the devolution of power to the panchayats was not purely an instrument for the retention of power by the Left. It was also integrated into the Left's agrarian reform programme, which the panchayats were to spearhead. This programme aimed at breaking the stranglehold of old jotedars or big landowners and help reduce the dependence of the landless and the land-poor on them for credit. Revitalizing and strengthening the panchayats would meet the ideological objective of altering the rural structures of political power, and lay the foundation for other pro-poor measures.

The LF government took a major step in allowing direct elections to all three panchayat tiers on a party basis, and another in altering the prevalent relationship between locally elected politicians and the bureaucracy, under which the latter were real decision makers and advisers.[98]

The CPI(M), then without a strong rural base, and with a membership of only about 30,000 concentrated primarily in Calcutta and other urban industrial centres, was suddenly called upon to put up nearly 60,000 candidates along with its allies. 'The middle and upper peasantry, now free from the social and economic yoke of the landed gentry, seized the opportunity. En masse, they moved in to offer themselves as candidates of the LF. They came in and not for any ideological consideration but to protect their own interests. So long as the CPI(M) was against the zamindars and aristocracy, they had nothing to fear … The party also welcomed them because they formed the much-needed rural base which it did not have. It was a win–win situation for both sides.'[99]

In 1978, the CPI(M) won an impressive 60 per cent of all gram panchayat seats, 66 per cent of panchayat samiti seats and 75 per cent of zilla parishad seats. Its performance declined somewhat in 1983, with victories in respectively 53, 60 and 66 per cent of seats in the three tiers, but improved in 1988 to 65, 72 and 85 per cent of seats. The government made panchayats responsible for implementing a variety of rural development schemes and placed substantial resources at their disposal. This strengthened the hold of the party and its rural cadres over the panchayats.

However, the new panchayats were dominated by intermediate social layers, such as middle peasants or owner-cultivators and schoolteachers, and largely excluded the landless and small sharecroppers.[100] The skewed class composition of the panchayats was revealed in a survey of 100 such bodies by the West Bengal Development and Planning Department in 1978. Owner-cultivators accounted for 50.7 per cent of their members and the landless only 4.8 per cent, and sharecroppers just 1.8 per cent. As many as 14 per cent were teachers. Another survey of 200 panchayats conducted in 1983 showed that the owner-cultivators' proportion had risen to 51.8 per cent and teachers' to 15.3 per cent, but the shares of the landless and sharecroppers remained negligible at respectively 3.3 and 2.2 per cent.

Domination by Middle Layers

Another study, from Bankura district (1980) concluded that little change has taken place in the power structure in the villages through the panchayat election. The poor peasants and agricultural labourers, in reality, do not play any role in organizing the programmes of the panchayats, nor in organizing the so-called Left movement in the locality. If the objective of the CPI(M) is to change the basis of the united peasant movement from jotedar and rich peasants to poor peasants and agricultural labourers, that has not yet been realized.

Other studies too noted a gradual deterioration in the work of the panchayats, which had initially 'helped to generate social and political awareness among the people and facilitated the development of new leadership ...That initial zest started fading after 1983 when the second panchayats were elected. And with the coming of the third panchayats in 1988, it seems to have all but disappeared. The innovative spirit of early years is hardly to be seen. The panchayats have become overly engrossed in routine work... [and tended] to run out of steam...'[101] The prescription offered for recovery was to move 'beyond development to self-government'. But this did not happen.

In an important comparative study, political scientist Amrita Basu found that 'the panchayats embody many of the undemocratic and inegalitarian features of larger society', including overrepresentation of landowning cultivators and members with a middle class social background. 'The underrepresentation of agricultural labourers and sharecroppers may in turn contribute to the panchayats' laxity in enforcing minimum wage laws and ensuring sharecropper registration'.[102]

'The panchayats are also unrepresentative in another respect: given their inability to formulate policies, they enable the state government to penetrate down to the village level but scarcely enable villagers to communicate their grievances back to Calcutta.' She also argues that 'non-agriculturalists and owner-cultivators are likely to be more numerous, while sharecroppers and landless labourers are likely to be fewer in the panchayat samitis and zilla parishads'.[103]

Basu concludes: 'The CPI(M) has pursued a strategy of class conciliation to encourage rural entrepreneurship. Since obtaining power in 1977, it has distinguished between jotedars, whom it regards as "class enemies" and rich peasants, whom it regards as allies. Thus by 1981, Promode Dasgupta, the former state secretary of the West Bengal CPI(M) could comment: "We do not regard the big farmer as a representative of feudal monopoly interests. Our class struggle is against the landed jotedars ..." To appease rich peasants, CPI(M) has not levied a centrally sanctioned agricultural income tax. It has demanded higher procurement prices for agricultural commodities that would primarily benefit middle and rich peasants ...'[104]

In 1981, an exclusive organization for agricultural labourers was formed within the All India Kisan Sabha whose membership reached 1.5 million by 1989. But in West Bengal, the AIKS refused to set up such a union. In fact, the West Bengal unit of the CPI(M) consciously decided 'not to form such a union in the state in the interest of broad "peasant unity"'.[105,106]

Unequal Partnership

The background and rationale for this was laid by the CPI(M)'s keenness to gain political acceptance in a competitive democracy by altering its programmatic perspectives. 'Of particular importance is the issue of "peasant unity", which played a key role in the party's rural mobilizations. For the CPI(M) and the Krishak Sabha, "unity" was far from an aggregation of demands, whereby all sections of the peasants (barring the non-cultivating landlords) could be given equal space and a uniform stake so as to strike a neat balance. On the contrary, such unity was presented as a necessary item in the agenda for "peasant struggle".'[107]

This struggle came to be identified by the early 1980s with an emphasis on rich and middle peasants. At the 1982 Medinipur session of the All India Kisan Sabha, Harkishan Singh Surjeet (who later became the CPI(M) general secretary) enunciated a 'new orientation' based on the awareness 'that without raising the demands of the peasantry as a whole, including the rich and the middle peasants, and without merging the different currents into one, we can neither advance towards the agrarian revolution, nor will we be able to raise the movement to the level of land occupation'.[108]

The 'new orientation' was duly endorsed by the West Bengal AIKS, which declared after the LF's return to power in the 1982 assembly elections that 'but for the support of an influential section of the middle peasants, this victory would never have been possible'.[109]

The West Bengal Pradeshik Krishak Sabha rhetorically laid emphasis on organizing the poorer sections of rural society. In 1986, it claimed that about three-fourths of its primary members were agricultural labourers. 'The reality, however, was quite different. Between 1982 and 1989, the Sabha held three state conferences in which, of all those attending, less than 9 per cent were agricultural labourers and less than 24 per cent poor peasants. A similar pattern was discerned (at the all-India level) as well in the 26th conference of the AIKS ...' Here the proportion of agricultural labourers present was only 4.85 per cent and that the poor peasants 24.28 per cent.[110]

Several analysts have commented on the skewed nature of class relations in rural Bengal and their institutionalization in the panchayat system, as well as the adverse effects on agricultural wages.[111] Some argue that 'keeping agricultural wages down has been one of the main instruments of containing class conflict in rural areas and thereby keeping the multi-class alliance of [the Left Front government's] social base intact. Since a substantial portion of the agricultural workers are hired by the middle peasantry, increasing wages would naturally be opposed by them. The fact that employers and employees are almost always members of the same party—the CPI(M)— means that to keep both under its wings, the party would need to not only negotiate between the two classes but also sacrifice the interests of one for the benefit of the other. And the class that has had to always sacrifice its interests at the altar of the Left Front government has been the landless labourers!'[112]

Although agricultural wage workers in West Bengal numbered five million according to the 1991 census (or one-quarter of the total rural and urban workforce put together), there has been 'no effective regulation regarding the terms and conditions of agricultural employment ... and no direct action to ensure minimum wages—certainly not with anything like the vigour put into land redistribution and registration of tenants.'[113] Yet, paradoxically, large numbers of agricultural workers probably did not vote as strongly against the Left Front as many other rural classes did, including middle/rich farmers, sharecroppers and skilled/semi-skilled workers until the 2009 Lok Sabha elections.[114]

Many scholars tried to explain this by referring to various kinds of patron–client relationships between the CPI(M) and agricultural workers, changing caste relations and crossover into different cultural–economic categories, and manipulative management of local conflicts and labour relations by party cadres, who enjoy a great deal of flexibility and autonomy within an otherwise highly centralized party.[115] Crucial to the cadres' exertions was the 'almost exclusive concern' of the CPI(M) with 'the politics of winning elections'.[116]

By the late 1990s, if not earlier, it became clear that the Left Front's main agenda or prime concern had changed: from generating a political movement for change, however moderate, to developing a limited strategy with the sole goal of getting itself re-elected to power—even if that meant abandoning its original goals, with the risk of alienating its support base, creating widespread disillusionment, and inevitably losing power. By the time the Singur and Nandigram crises occurred, the fall of the Left Front was within the realm of the possible, if not the probable, as many of its critics from the Left predicted.

West Bengal's record on panchayats, like that on land reforms, then, is mixed. Although it greatly helped the middle peasants and sections of landowning bargadars, it did so at the cost of the poorest layers of the population, women and other marginalized groups.

The following pages of this chapter present a table detailing the election performances of the Left Front (with constituency-wise break-up) vis-à-vis other political parties in the state assembly elections from 1977 to 2001. This will help interested readers in better understanding the dramatic rise and the expected fall of the Left parties in West Bengal electoral performances.

Year	West Bengal: Performance of Left Parties in Assembly Elections			
		Seats Contested	Seats Won	Vote (%)
1977	**Left**	**294**	**231**	**45.84**
	CPI(M)	224	178	35.46
	RSP	23	20	3.74
	Forward Bloc	36	25	5.24
	RCPI	3	2	0.37
	FBM	2	2	0.23
	BBC	3	1	0.25
	Independent (Left Supported)	3	3	0.55
	Congress	290	20	23.02
	CPI	63	2	2.62
	Janata Party	289	29	20.02
	Muslim League	32	1	0.38
	SUCI	29	4	1.48
	Independent	566	7	6.37
	Other Parties	9	–	0.27
	Total	**1572**	**294**	**100.00**
1982	**Left**	**294**	**238**	**52.77**
	CPI	12	7	1.81
	CPI(M)	209	174	38.49
	RSP	23	19	4.01
	Forward Bloc	34	28	5.90
	Independent (Left Supported)	16	10	2.56
	Congress	249	49	35.69
	Indian Congress (Socialist) ICS	28	4	3.94
	BJP	52	–	0.58
	SUCI	34	2	1.03
	Independents	432	1	4.47
	Other Parties	115	–	1.52
	Total	**1204**	**294**	**100.00**

West Bengal: Performance of Left Parties in Assembly Elections				
Year		Seats Contested	Seats Won	Vote (%)
1987	Left	294	251	52.96
	CPI	12	11	1.92
	CPI(M)	213	187	39.30
	RSP	23	18	3.94
	Forward Bloc	34	26	5.84
	Independent (Left Supported)	12	9	1.96
	Congress	294	40	41.81
	BJP	57	–	0.51
	Muslim League	36	1	0.62
	SUCI	46	2	0.90
	Independents and Others	770	–	3.20
	Total	1497	294	100.00
1991	Left	294	246	48.88
	CPI	11	5	1.54
	CPI(M)	213	189	36.87
	RSP	23	18	3.47
	Forward Bloc	34	29	5.51
	Janata Dal	8	1	0.67
	GNLF*	2	2	0.35
	RCPI(RB)**	2	1	0.30
	DSP***	1	1	0.17
	Congress	284	43	35.12
	BJP	291	–	11.34
	Jharkhand Party (JKP)	5	1	0.33
	Independents	634	4	2.66
	Other Parties	395	–	1.67
	Total	1903	294	100.00

* Gorkha National Liberation Front
** Revolutionary Communist Party of India
*** Democratic Socialist Party

Year	West Bengal: Performance of Left Parties in Assembly Elections			
		Seats Contested	Seats Won	Vote (%)
1996	**Left**	**294**	**203**	**49.33**
	CPI	12	6	1.75
	CPI(M)	217	157	37.92
	RSP	23	18	3.72
	Forward Bloc	34	21	5.20
	Janata Dal	5	–	0.29
	RCPI(RB)	2	–	0.29
	Independent (Left Supported)	1	1	0.16
	Congress	288	82	39.48
	BJP	292	–	6.45
	GNLF	3	3	0.44
	Forward Block (Socialist) (FBS)	20	1	0.34
	Jharkhand Party (Naren) JKP(N)	8	1	0.40
	Independents	842	4	2.44
	Other Parties	288	–	1.12
	Total	**2035**	**294**	**100.00**
2001	**Left**	**294**	**199**	**48.98**
	CPI	13	7	1.79
	CPI(M)	211	143	36.59
	RSP	23	17	3.43
	Forward Bloc	34	25	5.65
	Janata Dal (Secular)	2	–	0.08
	Rastriya Janata Dal	2	–	0.07
	RCPI(RB)	2	–	0.13
	West Bengal Socialist Party	4	4	0.67
	Independent (Left Supported)	3	3	0.57
	Congress and allies	**294**	**89**	**39.37**

West Bengal: Performance of Left Parties in Assembly Elections				
Year		Seats Contested	Seats Won	Vote (%)
	Congress	60	26	7.98
	Trinamool Congress	226	60	30.66
	GNLF	5	3	0.52
	Independent (Supported)	3	–	0.22
	BJP	266	–	5.19
	Independents	518	6	4.26
	Other Parties	304	–	2.20
	Total	1676	294	100.00
2006	Left	294	235	50.18
	CPI	13	8	1.91
	CPI(M)	212	176	37.13
	RSP	23	20	3.71
	Forward Bloc	34	23	5.66
	NCP*	2	–	0.19
	RJD	2	1	0.08
	WBSP	4	4	0.71
	DSP	2	1	0.36
	Independent (Left Supported)	2	2	0.43
	Congress and allies	292	24	15.59
	Congress	262	21	14.71
	PDS**	9	–	0.09
	JMM***	5	–	0.13
	GNLF	3	3	0.46
	Independent (Congress Supported)	13	–	0.20

* Nationalist Congress Party
** Party of Democratic Socialism
*** Jharkhand Mukti Morcha

	West Bengal: Performance of Left Parties in Assembly Elections			
Year		Seats Contested	Seats Won	Vote (%)
	NDA	**294**	**31**	**29.09**
	BJP	29	–	1.93
	Trinamool Congress (TMC)	257	30	26.64
	Independent (NDA Supported)	8	1	0.52
	JKP(N)	4	1	0.26
	Independents	501	3	3.07
	Other Parties	269	–	1.81
	Total	1654	294	100.00
2011	**Left**	**294**	**62**	**41.05**
	CPI	14	2	1.84
	CPI(M)	213	40	30.08
	RSP	23	7	2.96
	Forward Bloc	34	11	4.80
	Samajwadi Party	5	1	0.74
	RCPI(R)*	2	–	0.23
	DSP(P)**	2	1	0.35
	RJD	1	–	0.05
	Trinamool Congress Alliance	**294**	**227**	**48.35**
	Congress	65	42	9.08
	Trinamool Congress	226	184	38.93
	NCP	1	–	0.03
	SUCI (TMC supported)	2	1	0.31
	BJP	289	–	4.06
	GOJAM***	3	3	0.72

* Revolutionary Communist Party of India
** Democratic Socialist Party (Probodh Chandra)
*** Gorkha Jana Mukti Morcha

West Bengal: Performance of Left Parties in Assembly Elections				
Year		Seats Contested	Seats Won	Vote (%)
	SUCI*	30	–	0.44
	Independents	400	2	3.13
	Other Parties	482	–	2.25
	Total	**1792**	**294**	**100.00**

* Socialist Unity Centre of India

5

Crisis and Exit in West Bengal

*Faltering Social Development, Governance Slippages,
Into the Quagmire*

A number of factors explain why the Left Front lost power in West Bengal in 2011 after a generation-length tenure of thirty-four years, itself a record probably unmatched in a large region, province or city in any democracy. The Front's tenure can be divided into three broad chronological phases.

The first phase, from the late 1970s to around 1990, was marked by worthy, if modest, social welfare and land reform measures delivered through administrative means, combined with limited people's participation. The second phase broadly covered the decade of the 1990s. It saw popular demobilization and a turning away from redistributive policies, leading to alienation of the poorer strata. The last phase, beginning early in the twenty-first century, was marked by a further rightward shift and embrace of neo-liberalism, with predatory land acquisition and industrialization policies. Grass-roots opposition to these was a major factor that dislodged the Front from power.

The Front came to power on a wave of popular mobilization that it helped organize, and greatly benefited from. It presented itself as a partisan of the underprivileged. This early radical phase soon gave way to a contest between two different objectives: consolidating the Left, in particular the CPI(M), in power, and creating a progressive political and development model for West Bengal. The first objective prevailed.

Party structures were re-engineered to win elections. The Front's response to the challenges posed by the Central government's shift to neo-liberalism in the early 1990s proved lame, even imitative, eroding its plebeian support base. But the culture of the Left, mired in bhadralok ways of thinking, and 'democratic centralism', prevented it from taking corrective steps.

Early Promise Wilts

The Left Front's ascent to power raised high expectations of improved governance and social welfare. It initially fulfilled many of them, especially through limited land reforms and devolution of power to elected village panchayats. The reforms were modest on purpose because the Front, fearing a hostile Central response, as with the United Fronts of the 1960s, adopted a cautious stance. But they helped it build and consolidate a rural base—no mean achievement for parties whose leadership was overwhelmingly drawn from the bhadralok urban elite. Yet, precisely because the reforms were of a limited—and not power-transforming—nature, they did not impart enough social heft or political power to their beneficiaries and limited the potential for more radical change.

Within a decade or so, the Left's, in particular the CPI(M)'s, priorities shifted towards consolidating its power through a patronage system in the panchayats by relying on middle and rich peasants, besides state employees and a shrinking trade union base in the cities. Party structures got heavily bureaucratized. The LF government's social development performance started faltering. Its policies turned increasingly conservative. Yet, the formidable electoral machine that the CPI(M) built repeatedly produced handsome victories for the Left parties disproportionate to their vote shares.

This bred complacency and political hubris especially as agricultural production grew thanks largely to the adoption of conventional Green Revolution techniques. Increased rural incomes, and a softer posture towards West Bengal by the Centre, broadened the Left Front's economic policy options. But its leaders did not use these imaginatively to create a radical people-centred development model, fearing that this would run up against 'the feasibility frontier'[1] in the given national political environment. Meanwhile, the state's health, education and employment indices stagnated or sank. Nepotism and cronyism became deeply entrenched in the administration and educational system.

Soon after the Centre embraced economic liberalization and globalization in the early 1990s, the Left Front more or less adopted the same course, its pessimism about radical alternatives no doubt reinforced by the collapse of the USSR and the apparent success of Deng Xiaoping's pro-market policies in China. The Front courted Bengal's consumerist neo-liberal elite and fervently promoted private- capital-driven industrialization, while evicting poor people from city centres to 'beautify' them. By the end of the decade, all progressive content had been drained out of Left Front politics.

From here it was but a short step to the practice of Beijing-style policies of appropriating people's land, and using coercion, even thuggish tactics, against dissidents, critics and opponents. The Front's violent confrontations with peasants and adivasis, leading to gross human rights violations, alienated it from these strata and the progressive intelligentsia. Its failure to redress the grievances of the religious and ethnic minorities, which gained prominence in public discourse, further eroded its legitimacy and its social support. The Front refused to acknowledge any of this. It suppressed internal debate and failed to take remedial measures until it was too late.

This chapter begins by analysing the Left Front's record on social development. Between the late 1970s and early 1990s, West Bengal witnessed significant improvements in people's lives as measured by many indices. But this performance was not sustained. West Bengal soon became a laggard in human development in relation to many other states. In general, the Left Front over three decades betrayed the early promise of empowering the exploited and oppressed classes, promoting equity and human security, and infusing substantive content into formal democracy.

When the Left Front came to power in 1977, West Bengal had the highest poverty headcount ratio (HCR) in India.[2] At about 75 per cent, it was similar to the ratio prevalent in other backward eastern states like Bihar and Odisha. By 1983, its HCR had improved in relation to Bihar, and by 1987, in comparison with both Bihar and Odisha.[3] In 1993–94, West Bengal's HCR fell to 40.8 per cent and in 1999–2000 further to 31.9 per cent.[4]

There was a marked reduction in the state's infant mortality and maternal mortality rates between 1977 and the late 1980s. Literacy rates in rural West Bengal for the five-plus population group rose from 48.6 per cent in 1981 to 57.7 per cent in 1991. The Left promoted an even greater advance by reducing West Bengal's rate of population growth from 24.7 per cent during 1981–91 to 17.8 per cent (compared to the national average of 21.2 per cent) during 1991–2001.[5] These gains were fairly impressive.

Early Social Gains Taper Off

However, some of these improvements soon began to taper off in relation to the rest of India. By the end of the 1990s, 56.2 per cent of West Bengal's rural population lived below the poverty line, compared to 36.5 per cent for India as a whole.[6] West Bengal lagged behind many other states in human development indicators and especially in the quality of health care, child nutrition, literacy and education. As we shall see below, its record on other issues, including labour relations, human rights, gender, treatment of the religious minorities (especially Muslims), provision of basic services such as safe drinking water, sanitation and domestic electric supply, ranges from poor to middling.

On issues such as environmental protection, preserving ecological diversity, pollution control and promoting ecologically sound urban planning and development, West Bengal under the Left Front performed poorly. And on agendas such as public distribution system for food, the Integrated Child Development Services (ICDS), the midday meal scheme for schoolchildren and the Mahatma Gandhi National Rural Employment Guarantee Act (MGNREGA), its performance was worse than that of most major states.

After nearly two decades of relative stagnation, agricultural production in West Bengal took off in the late 1970s, its growth averaging 3.4 per cent over the following decade.[7] For the entire period from 1978 to 1991, West Bengal's growth rate in foodgrains output was

4.6 per cent, compared with 2.8 per cent for India. There was a robust debate over the factors responsible for West Bengal's rapid agricultural growth in the 1980s, in particular the part played by the agrarian reforms and by other factors such as groundwater irrigation leading to higher cropping intensities, adoption of higher-yielding crop varieties and increased consumption of fertilizers.[8]

Land reforms, however, appear to have played a secondary role in triggering GDP growth.[9] And higher growth did not generate 'a substantial wage premium' despite greater labour organization, strikes, panchayat-mediated wage settlements, and Left leadership of the state in general.[10] Between 1980 and 1991, wages did rise in West Bengal. But this was in keeping with the national trend, and broadly in conformity with the state's overall growth rate. The early big gains in income on account of land redistribution and Operation Barga probably eroded at a rapid pace.

Historically, West Bengal had relatively better health conditions in the rural areas in spite of its generally low per capita income levels. For instance, in the 1981–83 period, the infant mortality rate (IMR, a key index of health status) was 95 per 1,000 live births for rural West Bengal. This was far superior to the IMR for Bihar and Odisha (respectively, 114 and 136), which had similar poverty levels.[11] Bengal's IMR fell further to 75 in 1990, but its rate of decline slowed down compared to many other states, including Uttar Pradesh, Bihar, Tamil Nadu, Gujarat and Punjab.[12] By the end of the 1990s, West Bengal ranked eleventh among all states, with an IMR of 48.7, compared to 16.3 for Kerala.[13]

In child nutrition, West Bengal presented a mixed picture in the late 1980s, which further deteriorated later, relative to other states.[14] Strong evidence of the poor nutritional status of the state's children and women emerges from National Family Health Surveys (NFHS). In 1998–99, a high 78 per cent of its children (and 82 per cent of its rural children) were anaemic, compared to the national average of 74 per cent.

This put West Bengal at the nineteenth rank amongst twenty-five states. In consumption of various items of food across age groups, 'the most deprived group consists of children between 1–3 years of age'.[15] The ICDS scheme in West Bengal did not do enough to relieve this situation of undernourishment among children below six.[16]

The nutritional status of women in West Bengal at the end of the 1990s was appalling. Measured by important indicators, it was considerably worse than the Indian average: the eighth lowest among nine states in chronic energy deficiency; number nineteen among twenty-five states in respect of anaemia; and an abysmal twenty-fourth among twenty-five states in respect of an abnormally low Body Mass Index (BMI). The relevant data compiled from NFHS website is presented in the table below:[17]

Nutritional Status of Women and Children in West Bengal		
	NFHS III (2005–06)	NFHS II (1998–99)
Children under 3 who are stunted (%)	33	41.5
Children under 3 who are wasted (%)	19	13.6
Children under 3 who are underweight (%)	43.5	48.7
Women whose Body Mass Index is below normal (%)	37.7	43.7
Children aged 6–35 months who are anaemic (%)	69.4	78.3
Married women aged 15–49 who are anaemic (%)	63.8	62.7
Pregnant women aged 14–49 who are anaemic (%)	62.6	56.9

Source: Compiled from NFHS website: http://www.rchiips.org/nfhs/, accessed on 14 May 2014.

Apathy Towards Health Care

Despite some improvement between the late 1970s and late 1990s, West Bengal has an embarrassing record as regards sanitation. For much of the Left Front's tenure, more than half its households had no toilets. As late as in 2001, 56.3 per cent of them had no toilets. In the rural areas, this ratio was 73.1 per cent.[18] Even a decade later, the two ratios still remained as high as 38.6 and 53.3 per cent.[19]

West Bengal in general fared poorly in access to three basic amenities: toilets, piped drinking water and domestic electricity supply. In 2011, the percentage of households which had none of the three facilities was a high 25.2.[20] Only 15.5 per cent of West Bengal's households reported having all three facilities, compared to 18.3 per cent nationally.[21]

A different problem but one related to sanitation and health is the poor quality of West Bengal's groundwater. It is contaminated with arsenic and fluoride, which are extremely harmful to health. The contamination has got aggravated in recent years, and now affects 29 per cent of the state's rural population. The causes, suspected to be related to groundwater overuse, remain largely unaddressed. Fluoride contamination, first detected in 1996, spread to forty-five blocks in nine districts by 2003.[22] The growing contamination speaks of the state government's apathy towards major health issues.

Health care facilities in West Bengal have long been unsatisfactory. The LF government did very little to improve them. The average population served by an allopathic doctor in the state sector was as high as 14,064 in comparison with 9,095 in Kerala and 7,718 in Tamil Nadu in 2006. The number of hospitals in the state rose fivefold to over 2,000 between 1994–95 and 2006–07, but that was largely because of the spread of private hospitals, facilitated by the state. A better indication is the increase in the total number of hospital beds, which was a modest 49 per cent during this long period.[23]

More tellingly, the Left Front government was extraordinarily negligent in building primary health centres (PHCs) and sub-centres, the mainstay of the rural health care system. The number of PHCs did not grow at all for more than two decades until 2006–07.[24] During the last eight years of its rule, the Left Front did not add a single sub-centre to this paltry stock[25]. This is a shocking comment on its commitment to health care, especially for the rural population.

No wonder West Bengal ranked among the lowest-performing states in India in respect of the staff, infrastructure and supply of drugs index in a 2008 survey by the Voluntary Health Association of India (VHAI). It was in the same league as Bihar, Madhya Pradesh, Chhattisgarh and Odisha, with 83 per cent of its districts falling in the 'Red' category, which calls for 'urgent action'.[26]

The West Bengal government's Human Development Report 2004 (WBHDR) admitted to the inadequacy of the physical health care infrastructure in the state. However, it attributed this in significant measure to 'the very large responsibility and coverage' thrust upon the public health system, reflected in the fact that '76 per cent of the health institutes in West Bengal are run by the government, compared to less than 40 per cent elsewhere in India'. But this constitutes a strong case for building up and reforming the public sector rather than emphasizing the role of private health care provision.

The WBHDR also minimized the magnitude of the persistent shortage of allopathic doctors in West Bengal's PHCs by saying that 'non-allopathic and traditional systems of medicine (such as ayurvedic, homoeopathic and Kabiraji [local herbal-based] systems) are widely used in the state'. But this is true of much of India. Yet, several large states (Tamil Nadu, Maharashtra, Andhra Pradesh, Karnataka, and even Madhya Pradesh and Rajasthan), not to speak of Kerala, have achieved a substantial increase in the number of allopathic doctors and coverage of PHCs through conscious efforts.[27]

Literacy and Education

West Bengal historically had higher literacy and educational indices than many other states with comparable poverty ratios. Building on these, the Left Front government made significant progress in reducing illiteracy, increasing student enrolment, establishing new primary schools and appointing teachers. But it fell short of the promise made in the manifesto for the 1977 assembly elections, which raised high expectations by pledging to implement 'concrete and effective programmes, including legislative and administrative measures backed by popular efforts, for eradication of illiteracy'. This has not been achieved: according to the 2011 census, the state's overall literacy rate still remains 76.26 per cent, and a wide differential persists between male and female literacy.

Nor did the Left Front attempt to promote, or even explore the development of, a common school system, in which all children would go to a neighbourhood school and follow a common curriculum. Such a system would have greatly helped universalization of education—until then absent—with equal access for all, and prevented privatization, while laying the basis for non-elitist educational development. The

Left's indifference to the common school agenda issue too speaks of its leadership's lack of imagination and insufficient commitment to equity.

Between 1981 and 1991, West Bengal's overall literacy rate improved from 43.6 per cent to 57.7 per cent, putting its national rank at number six. Although this figure was higher than the Indian average (52.1 per cent), it was below the rates for Kerala (90.6) or even Tamil Nadu (63.7). In female literacy, the state's rank remained unchanged between 1981 and 1991 at number seven.[28]

The Total Literacy Campaign (TLC), launched in 1988 with the objective of raising India's literacy rate to 75 per cent by 2007, offered West Bengal an opportunity to raise its literacy by roping in volunteers to work among the 15–35 age group. The Left Front leadership was initially indifferent to the TLC; the state joined the campaign only in 1991. Although the panchayats played an active role in it, West Bengal's overall TLC performance was far from impressive, and marked by high dropout rates.[29]

By 2001, West Bengal had firmly exited the group of nine states/Union territories which had achieved literacy rates of 80 per cent or more. While higher than the national average (65.4 per cent), West Bengal's 69.2 per cent literacy rate placed it at an unflattering fourth position from the bottom among the twenty-two states which exceeded the national threshold—way below established high achievers like Kerala, Goa and Delhi, but also large states like Maharashtra, Tamil Nadu, Gujarat and Punjab.[30]

In 1991, the LF government set up a commission under former finance minister Ashok Mitra to look into the state of education. The commission noted that primary school enrolment had expanded by 80 per cent between 1977 and 1992, and numerous improvements had occurred.[31] But it also noted several flaws, including high dropout rates, little improvement in the quality of teaching, high teacher absenteeism, poor accountability and collapse of the school inspections system.[32]

West Bengal's education-development indicators slid in relative terms during the second half of the Left Front's tenure. In literacy, inter-group differentials widened. Compared to the overall literacy rate of 69 per cent, women, adivasis, Muslims and Dalits had lower rates (respectively, 59, 43, 57 and 59 per cent), and women among the latter three groups even lower rates (29, 49 and 47 per cent respectively). The three account for 54 per cent of the total population, but form a nearly two-thirds share of West Bengal's illiterates.[33]

Among those who documented this are researchers belonging to the Pratichi (India) Trust, set up by Amartya Sen, which produced two major reports in 2002 and 2009 on education and related issues.[34] These showed that despite greater enrolment, almost 15 per cent of children in the age group 6–11 were out of school in 1997–98. There were on and average 2.98 teachers per school, and a student: teacher ratio of 54:1, which is far higher than the declared official norm (40:1). West Bengal at the end of the 1990s still stood at a dismal eighteenth position in literacy rates among thirty-five Indian states and Union territories. The rate of literacy among the Scheduled Castes remained as low as 42.2 per cent.

In 1999, the LF government launched Shishu Shiksha Kendras (SSKs) to bring the underprivileged into the primary schooling system. These were more poorly funded than regular primary schools, often staffed with untrained and underpaid teachers, and not covered by programmes for nutrition and free textbooks. They were marked by greater caste, ethnic and gender discrimination.[35]

In general, said the Pratichi reports, schools in West Bengal remain afflicted by high student absenteeism (as high as 54 and 64 per cent) and low quality of teaching: the state has '… a long way to go' in improving 'the qualitative aspect of the delivery of primary education …'[36]

The Pratichi report also highlighted the proportion of schools without basic amenities, and the dismal state of midday meal (MDM) programmes.[37] Thus, 11 per cent of the total of 50,255 primary schools in the state had no toilets in 2008–09, and 7 per cent no drinking water. The state's MDM scheme served food on only 60 per cent of all the days for which allocations were made, and used only 55 per cent of the grain quota.[38] The report comments that the state government's 'political commitment'—which plays 'a pivotal role in the delivery of primary education'—is 'mixed'.

The Pratichi team noted low enrolment of girls, a disproportionately low share of female teachers (just one-fourth of the total), high teacher absenteeism especially in schools attended mainly by Scheduled Caste and Scheduled Tribe children, lack of attention to children from particularly disadvantaged backgrounds, absence of inspections, significant levels of dissatisfaction among parents about the quality of teaching, growing dependence on private tuition (among more than half the pupils),[39] and denigration of SSK teachers to 'sahayaks' (assistants/ helpers) or para-teachers.

The Pratichi reports made a number of detailed and thoughtful suggestions, including some about involving teachers' unions in addressing issues of quality, paying greater attention to social discrimination in the classroom, and improving the physical infrastructure and MDM coverage. Many of these were ignored or received scant attention.

The general decline in West Bengal's school education indicators continued into the first decade of the twenty-first century.[40] Teacher: pupil ratios worsened.[41] School infrastructure further deteriorated in relation to other states.[42] Later in that decade, West Bengal's gross enrolment ratios for all groups of schoolchildren in Classes I–VIII fell below the national average for both boys and girls.[43] In literacy and school education, then, communist-ruled West Bengal performed no better than, and in some respects fared definitely worse than, many states under right-wing or centrist parties' rule.

MGNREGA and Food Security

If the Left Front government largely betrayed its promise on health and education, it did not do much better in respect of job creation under the Mahatma Gandhi National Rural Employment Guarantee Act (MGNREGA) scheme,[44] said to be the largest job creation programme in the world, which guarantees employment to each rural household for 100 days a year on minimum wages.

Between 2006–07 and 2011–12, a period which covers the last five-and-a-half years of the Left Front's tenure, West Bengal generated only eight person-days of employment per enlisted household per year under MGNREGA, compared to 14.8 days nationally, and 49.8 days in Rajasthan, 22.8 days in Tamil Nadu, and 32.8 days in Madhya Pradesh. It lagged behind most major states including Uttar Pradesh.

West Bengal generated only ten person-days per job card between 2008–09 and 2011–12, compared to 16.8 nationally, and much lower than the better-performing states like Rajasthan (31.5 person-days), Andhra (26), or Tamil Nadu (24.8). It performed worse than relatively backward Uttar Pradesh (18), Jharkhand (17.3) and Madhya Pradesh (13.5), although it did better than Bihar (5).

The state's record was better as regards the proportion of Scheduled Castes (SCs) and Scheduled Tribes (STs) in total person-days, which was 43.9 per cent. But even here it lagged behind the national average of 45.6 per cent, and stood well below top-scorer Rajasthan (73.2), and states with high SC and ST populations such as Odisha (61.1) and Chhattisgarh (51.4) although it did marginally better than Madhya Pradesh (43).[45]

Women's share of MGNREGA employment in West Bengal was an average of 30.9 per cent between 2008–09 and 2011–12, also below the national average of 47.3, and way below that of Kerala (89.3 per cent), easily the top-scorer, and also below the proportions for most major states barring Bihar. This record is of a piece with the low wages earned by agricultural labourers in West Bengal, 95 per cent of whom receive less than the national statutory minimum of Rs 66 a day.[46]

Even worse, and persistently so, was the Left Front's record on food security. This is a sour irony because the 'Food Movements' of 1959–60 and 1966–67, which demanded affordable and adequate quantities of food, had played a major role in grass-roots mobilization by the communists in West Bengal, and were the key to the Left's ascent to power in the United Front governments of the late 1960s.

Yet, on assuming power, the Left Front neglected the food security issue, in particular reaching affordable food to the poor through controlled-price or ration shops. In fact, between 1980 and 2011, the number of such shops in West Bengal under the so-called 'urban PDS' decreased from about 2,700 to under 2,300, while the number of 'modified ration shops' established in all districts declined between 2000 and 2011 after registering 20 per cent growth between 1980 and 2000.

The state under the LF had an abysmally poor public distribution system (PDS), with an offtake rate that is about one-fourth or one-fifth of the national average. More than 70 per cent of the foodgrains which should be available for purchase were 'diverted' (pilfered or sold on the black market by using 'ghost' ration cards) between 2001–02 and 2007–08.[47]

After West Bengal moved over to the 'targeted PDS', with the focus confined to the below-poverty-line (BPL) people, it recorded one of the highest 'exclusion errors' (not covering BPL families) in India (32 per cent), even exceeding the proportion in the BIMARU (Bihar, Madhya Pradesh, Rajasthan, and Uttar Pradesh) states. The new food procurement system largely benefited big corporates which entered the market in West Bengal, such as Reliance, Godrej, Mahindra, and Cargill.[48]

Food prices rose sharply in 2006 in West Bengal, and anti-ration-shop riots broke out in Bankura district where the CPI(M) had scored big victories in that year's assembly election. There were mass protests against corruption in the PDS in 2007, and violence in the countryside, especially in backward tribal areas, against ration shop dealers, which reflected anger against the ruling coalition. These food-related protests were part of, and were strengthened by, the dissent and defiance that swept West Bengal from Singur to Nandigram.[49]

In August 2007, Left leaders addressed a rally of All-India Fair-Price Dealers' Federation in Delhi and said that the attack on the dealers was an attack on the PDS itself.[50] This pointed to mutual collusion and earned the ruling Left Front much antipathy.

Overall Assessment

To sum up, West Bengal's overall social development record under the Left Front turned out to be indifferent or middling, and in some respects poor. In sectors like sanitation and food security, its performance was always below par. On some indices, like reducing infant mortality or population growth, and spreading literacy and primary education, the Left Front government did not start out badly. But its record deteriorated after the late 1980s as it increasingly failed to address issues such as quality, funding, equity and intra-group discrimination along class, caste, gender and religious lines. It also became unresponsive to popular aspirations for better delivery of social services.

The Left Front's performance in its first decade or so pointed to the redistributive possibilities that existed within India's bourgeois democracy and how they could be exploited to bring about modest reforms. But in later years the Front largely failed to use these possibilities, although the climate and scope for doing so improved as the Indian state itself launched limited social welfare measures (described later in this chapter). More important, the prospect of the Centre taking punitive measures against a Left-reformist state government had greatly receded. By the late 1980s, the 'feasibility frontier'[51] had shifted outwards, and the national political environment was no longer as hostile as earlier assumed.

The Left's failure is all the more problematic and disappointing because it involved wilful neglect of the social sector in spite of warnings by well-wishers (like Pratichi) and refusal or inability to learn from past experience and incorporate the lessons into more radical but practicable alternatives. A likely underlying cause is the lack of radical power-transforming land reform in West Bengal, noted earlier, which limited the social power of the underprivileged and poor to demand and secure better services, including sanitation, health care and primary education, from the state.[52]

The failure also testifies to the Left's retreat from the classical agendas of fighting discrimination and iniquities, into sheer political callousness and bureaucratic woodenness. What else, but this retreat, and preference for elitist policies which favour privatized health care, can explain the Front's refusal to open new primary health centres for long years? Again, it is not so much lack of funds as pure apathy that ensured that the primary education infrastructure would remain starved of vital support and that the grain allocation for midday meals in schools would be underutilized.

It is hard to believe that the Front's leadership could not have found ways of maintaining and generalizing its early success in some of these social agendas if it really wanted to do so and had invested its energies in the effort. A more logical explanation is that its basic political priorities had turned conservative, especially in the 1990s, if not earlier. The Left increasingly retreated from the discourse of expanded rights for the labouring poor and was no longer as concerned as in the past to build a relationship of solidarity with them—although the existence of many groups in the informal sector became more and more precarious with predatory capital intruding into the economy.

The Left did not face intense pressure from below to act on social sector agendas, as it once did on the land question, which is more immediate and tangible. In any case, the constituencies that might have pressed for health care, education and other reforms in the second half of the Front's tenure were far more atomized and dispersed than the organized peasant groups active in the first half.

The Left's post-1990 social sector failures stand out because they cannot be attributed to a tight resource constraint. By the 1980s, several Centrally-sponsored schemes (Jawahar Rozgar Yojana, Integrated Rural Development Programme, Integrated Child Development Services, etc.,) had been launched, which reduced the states' burden of financing social programmes. These were followed by the extension of other Centrally-funded schemes like Sarva Shiksha Abhiyan and midday meals.

Earlier, the Left Front did face a constraint because of the Centre's 'obstructionist' attitude towards opposition-ruled states and its animus towards the LF government, which delayed power and petrochemicals projects. But things changed after the Sarkaria Commission report on Centre–state relations (1988) and the abolition of the 'freight equalization' policy[53] for steel, coal, etc., which the CPI(M) had demanded for long years as part of its campaign for greater federalism. By 1990, the campaign had succeeded, and more financial power was devolved to the states. Besides, as West Bengal's growth picked up to 8 per cent a year, its revenues increased. But these were spent more on creating the infrastructure and incentives to attract private investment than on people's welfare.

Politics of 'Middleness'

Meanwhile, the Left parties, in particular the CPI(M), built and steadily relied on party-sponsored or -controlled panchayat institutions to implement social sector programmes and act as intermediaries between the local people and the state bureaucracy. The panchayats became increasingly detached from genuine mass-level political mobilization, and were dominated by influential interest groups. They became a source of patronage and corruption, especially in rural works programmes, primary education and contracts for construction and maintenance, etc. Panchayat leaders sometimes played a questionable role in securing the eviction of bargadars from their patta lands and in facilitating coercive land acquisition for industrial and service-sector projects.[54]

Landlessness and fragmentation of landholdings continued to grow in West Bengal,[55] further changing the balance of class forces in favour of the privileged peasantry. As the gains of Operation Barga started vanishing, petty agricultural producers became the prey of traders and rice millers, whose economic power was left largely unaffected by the Left Front.[56] Only a tiny minority of the small producers were members of primary credit societies;[57] the rest were dependent on moneylenders for credit needed to meet rising costs of inputs like fertilizer. The kisan sabhas, which would earlier hear their grievances, came to be dominated increasingly by rich and middle peasants, a process that advanced throughout the 1990s.[58]

The panchayats, which gained prominence and power as a result of decentralization, became sources of organized quasi-centralized patronage,[59] and came under the control of the local committees (LCs) usually of the CPI(M). The LC gradually became the main power broker in the village or small town, feared as much as respected as the arbiter of all development-related decisions. No contract would be negotiated, leave alone approved, without its say-so. Soon, a collusive arrangement got consolidated, which some analysts have termed 'party society'.[60]

This patronage network was based on a form of substitutionism, what is known in Bengali as the system of *paiye debar rajneeti*—politics based on delivering services or favours to putative clients, or 'getting things done' on their behalf.[61] Such patronage treats the beneficiaries as passive receptacles, discourages their proactive involvement and makes the party apparatchik's role irreplaceable. It probably leads to waste and inefficiency in service delivery, reduces the impact and effectiveness of social programmes and weakens collective organizations such as trade unions and kisan sabhas. But it strengthens 'the Party'— as the CPI(M) widely came to be known even among unlettered people.

Paiye debar rajneeti in a context where the Left was the entrenched ruling party meant that the 'services to which people are entitled became favours that the party conferred in exchange for loyalty'.[62] Thus, this form of politics 'was a mode of mass mobilization that turned people profoundly apolitical in their choices. It also obliterated all distinction between party and government'.[63]

The institutionalization of paiye debar rajneeti in rural West Bengal meant that social sector schemes, typically drawn up without popular consultation as to their design and implementation, acquired an essentially top-down and bureaucratic character. This made for projects which were inappropriate to or unrelated to people's needs, in particular those of the poor, who lacked representation, social influence or access to political power. The panchayats were not amenable to their influence. Panchayat-approved projects would be largely irrelevant to them or exclude them altogether.

Thus crystallized what has been called the 'politics of middleness' in West Bengal,[64] based on the exclusion of the top and bottom extremes of the rural population. This in particular entails the explicit and overt exclusion of agricultural workers from the krishak sabhas, and their capture by the dominant proprietary peasant groups. Such politics would strongly favour compromises between the latter and subordinate groups, including stage-managed wage strikes by landless labourers,[65] whose outcome was determined in advance. Schoolteachers, whose unions were affiliated to the CPI(M)-controlled CITU became important intermediary players in this, as discussed in Chapter 3. The 'politics of middleness' took over the functioning of the entire panchayat system. In addition, there was the phenomenon of 'clientelism' and elite capture of institutions,[66] which perverted the purpose of public service provision and social programmes, and alienated the Left from its original social base, especially in rural areas.

This patronage network was replicated at the urban level in municipal and higher-level bodies, mediated by special agencies and interest groups which acquired their power through political connections with state leaders. A crucial link was furnished here by the CPI(M)'s district committees, run by powerful party officials, increasingly as their fiefdoms. Their bosses sported a luxurious lifestyle, in contrast to the relative austerity practised by LF ministers. A good example is Lakshman Seth, the former CPI(M) boss of East Medinipur district and chairman of the Haldia Development Authority, who played a pivotal, if deplorable, role during the Nandigram crisis.

In the urban context, paiye debar rajneeti played a major role in the trade unions in the jute and engineering industries, and among white-collar employees of the government, banks and other service sector industries, transport and municipal workers, and so on. Coupled with economism (or excessive preoccupation with short-term wage-related demands), it encouraged collusion between party apparatchiks and private or state employers aimed at delivering small wage increases to employees, typically negotiated on terms favourable to the employer.

The party-linked union bosses would take credit for these minor gains, which were premised on the absence of self-activity and militancy on the workers' part and their passive acceptance of deals reached through collaboration with private or state employers, mediated by the party's influence. Workers would be reduced to virtual supplicants; in no case would they get politicized or radicalized.

At the same time, monetary and political corruption, based on buying and selling patronage, sank deep roots in the administration and party apparatuses. In 1993, Buddhadeb Bhattacharjee, then a minister under Jyoti Basu, dramatically resigned from his cabinet in protest against corruption. Two years later, venerated CPI(M) politbureau member and former Tripura chief minister Nripen Chakraborty accused Basu, no less, of corruption.[67] Corruption grew to monstrous proportions after the mid-1990s as LF functionaries offered sweetheart deals to businessmen at every level.

By the late 1980s or so, the Left Front had acquired notoriety for creating its own version of a nomenklatura in state institutions, the economy and civil society. Appointments were made to key positions in the administration, public undertakings, municipalities and the health and education sectors, primarily on the criterion of loyalty to the CPI(M), although the smaller partners also got some crumbs.[68] Through this, a large petty–bourgeois population was tied to the party. So were musclemen who would help party apparatchiks push through contracts and appointments by coercive means. Racketeers strengthened their control over midday meal and ICDS schemes, and over issuance of MGNREGA job cards.

From cadre parties inspired by high ideals, the Left Front's constituents, especially the CPI(M) and the Forward Bloc, degenerated into groups representing vested interests and parochial agendas. Their venality and cynicism infected the parties' younger members, 90 per cent of whom had joined them after the Front came to power. The exigencies of practical politics, based on preserving and expanding the patronage system that kept the LF in power, meant that cadre education was severely neglected. Tens of thousands of candidate members, who did not have even a passing acquaintance with the party programme, leave alone Marxism, were given full membership and important posts. This further prevented corrective action.

No matter which explanation or combination of explanations one opts for, the truth is that the Left Front denied these flaws or failed to take cognisance of them and initiate corrective action in time. It became complacent and thus lost a unique opportunity offered by its thirty-four-year-long tenure in power—and its initial reform programmes—to bring about exemplary social development based upon popular participation.

Alimuddin Street

At the top of this elaborate structure of patronage run by the nomenklatura stood the state leadership of the CPI(M) headquartered in Alimuddin Street, Calcutta. The entire architecture was fashioned by the state party secretary Promode Dasgupta, and secondarily by Chief Minister Jyoti Basu, into a gigantic electoral machine as well as the hegemon of the Left Front. The sequencing of the state assembly, Lok Sabha and panchayat/municipal elections was such that there would rarely be a gap of more than two years between one election and the next one.

The electoral machine, trained in careful micromanagement of polling booths and wards, would forever be in a state of readiness. As would party managers and state and district committee members who would calculate how best to extract the maximum advantage from the first-past-the-post election system without winning a clear majority of votes. One method of doing so was to mobilize voters and take them to polling booths, reflected in a dramatic increase in voter turnout—from under 66 per cent in the 1970s to 78 per cent in the late 1990s.

Dasgupta, a former member of the Anushilan Samity, a revolutionary terrorist organization—as such groups were then called in a non-derogatory manner—had long experience of underground organizing, bomb making and other secret work, and was known to be a stern disciplinarian not averse to using strong-arm tactics.[69] He took over the CPI organization in the 1950s and became state secretary in 1961. He remained in that post through the CPI–CPI(M) split until his death in 1982. During the United Front period in the late 1960s, Dasgupta crafted what came to be known as the 'Promode (or Promode Dasgupta) Formula' for ticket allocation among coalition parties.

Under the formula, the Front parties would not run against one another, but fight elections on their own individual manifesto. They would retain the seats they had won; where none of them had won a specific seat, the runner-up would be nominated. The formula actually owes its origin to E.M.S. Namboodiripad who successfully applied it to consolidate a seven-party alliance in Kerala on the eve of the 1967 elections. But Namboodiripad was flexible in applying the formula.[70] Dasgupta was not.

This meant that the ticket shares of the non-CPI(M) parties that came together to form the Left Front in 1977—mainly the Forward Bloc and the Revolutionary Socialist Party—the CPI was not part of the alliance then—remained more or less frozen. The CPI, which had only won two assembly seats in 1977, got a raw deal when it joined the LF later. The arrangement was heavily skewed in favour of the CPI(M), which won 178 seats in 1977, to the FB's twenty-five and the RSP's twenty. It remained that way.

It speaks rather poorly of the CPI(M)'s allies in the Left Front that they meekly accepted this seat-sharing formula for expedient and opportunist reasons—wholly related to winning a limited number of seats which would bring them the loaves and fishes of office. They got locked into this arrangement primarily because winning elections became their topmost priority too, as it did for the CPI(M). Everything else, including the CPI's work among public sector workers and intellectuals, or the RSP's trade union activities among the tea-garden workers in north Bengal, would be subordinated to that paramount goal.

At any rate, the CPI(M) for decades faced no competition from within the Left Front or from outside it, thanks to its mastery of the first-past-the-post system. It stood well placed to exploit the divisions that opened up within the opposition especially after Mamata Banerjee walked out of the Congress in 1996. Its leadership was under no compulsion to acknowledge the ossification of the party and the rot that had spread in the patronage system—leave alone take corrective measures.

This allowed the CPI(M) to become complacent and arrogant. Unlike in Kerala, it was never kept on a tight leash in Bengal. Its leaders deluded themselves by the late 1980s that the party had become so widely or universally popular as to be invincible. Many of them persisted with the delusion until 2008, when the LF got its first jolt in the panchayat elections. Some did so right until 2011.

In reality, despite land reforms, panchayati raj and other social measures, the CPI(M)'s own vote share improved from 35.5 per cent in 1977 to 38.5 per cent 1982 and only marginally thereafter. It peaked at 39.3 per cent in 1987. The CPI(M)'s vote share roughly equalled, and was sometimes lower than, the Congress/Congress–TMC's, which never dropped below 35 per cent after 1982 (see table at the end of the chapter). But the distribution of the party's vote, especially its concentration in certain regions, helped the CPI(M) disproportionately until 2011. In that election, it became a victim of the 'winner takes all' phenomenon that had helped it in the past: with just a five percentage point drop in its vote share, its seats tally plummeted from 176 to forty.

Yet, the ground for the 2011 debacle had been prepared much earlier. By the mid- or late 1990s, the Left Front came to preside over a huge empire, with more than a quarter-million members, based on patronage and mediation between divergent classes, and driven by desperate efforts to draw in private capital investment into various industries and services, no matter what the cost. This required, among other things, infiltrating, capturing and corrupting all manner of institutions, administrative, educational and cultural, in a comprehensive manner to promote parochial agendas.

Appointments of schoolteachers would be determined primarily by party affiliation: after all, they played a major role in the panchayats and would be roped into election-related party work. New projects in construction or road building would be used to promote and strengthen the patronage network. Positions in literary academies, universities and other institutions of learning would be increasingly given to party supporters or sympathizers, regardless of merit.[71]

Novelists, playwrights and film-makers who dared to criticize 'the Party' would face social boycott and censorship or physical harassment. Independent feminists who exposed cases of sexual violence by party cadres were ignored by Left-affiliated women's organizations, or vilified outright. Intellectual freedom suffered. Bangladeshi writer Taslima Nasreen, who had taken refuge in Kolkata, saw her books banned. She was hounded out of Kolkata in 2007 by a small Muslim communal organization which paralysed, or was allowed to paralyse, the city.

Under the CPI(M)'s domination, the richly pluralistic, enlightened and vibrant intellectual culture with which the communist movement was traditionally identified, suffered great impoverishment. The undivided CPI was known as a party of intellectuals and artists. The CPI(M) came to be known for its suspicion of them. In the last decade of the Left's tenure, intolerance towards dissidence became the norm. Philistinism prevailed in numerous institutions. This had a corrosive impact on artistic production. It demoralized good scholars and fine writers and led to the flight of talented young people from Kolkata in large numbers. This further culturally impoverished a city which many of its inhabitants still regard, somewhat quaintly, as 'the cultural capital of India'.

During its thirty-four years in power, the Left did not launch a single journal of ideas or a publication that could claim or even aspire to a national stature. It did not build any worthy institution in the field of art and culture—including literature, music, theatre and cinema, for which Bengal was long known—that made a lasting contribution. Civil society organizations always remained weak in West Bengal, unlike in Kerala and in numerous other states. The people's science movement did not put down deep roots in the state. Nor did environmentalism or alternative lifestyle movements.

At the ground level, a new party-linked web of coercion, extortion and intimidation was created by inducting goondas and shady business operators who would demand baksheesh or kickbacks for rendering all kinds of services, from evicting unwanted tenants, to encroaching on protected wetlands, to securing school or college admissions, or arranging medical treatment for a person in dire need of it. Running such operations needed some help from pliant police officers, who would be duly sought out and appointed—and rewarded if and when necessary.

None of this argues that other parties or governments are not guilty of similar venal practices and causing institutional corrosion or corruption, or that West Bengal would have been better off had Congress rule continued in some form. The Trinamool Congress is doing all this, and more, on a larger scale. But the bar has to be higher for the Left if only because it aspires to something loftier than the TMC or the BJP, and because it started with far greater promise in West Bengal.

By the early years of the new century, the Left Front's leaders had run out of all ideas of a socialist, even social democratic, nature and embraced the perspective of Deng Xiaoping–style neo-liberal developmentalism. Their prime task would to be to industrialize West Bengal at any cost by drawing in corporate capital and allowing it to set the terms for investment. That would be the only way to progress and the growth of 'the productive forces' since agriculture has reached a plateau: so Industrialize or Perish! Industrialization, or rather reindustrialization, would bring back the glory of Bengal, once India's most advanced province in which the capital of British India used to be located.

Among the priority projects of the government were real estate development and private housing construction, information technology parks, shopping malls, industrial infrastructure, and highways and roads. The large tracts of land needed for these would have to be acquired from peasants living close to Kolkata and other cities—if necessary, by force.

That is how the Rajarhat New Town project was launched as the Left's own answer to Bidhan Chandra Roy's Salt Lake development. Rajarhat would turn out an urban-ecological nightmare[72] which would displace large numbers of people while destroying natural drainage in the Kolkata conurbation, thus compounding the damage already done to East Calcutta Wetlands, a Ramsar Convention site.[73] But Rajarhat was planned, and land acquisition for it began, years before Singur and Nandigram were even conceived of. Scores of other smaller projects, primarily in real estate development, were similarly launched from the mid-1990s onwards. Many of these also involved coercive land acquisition and razing of poor people's homes.

Singur and Nandigram, discussed briefly in Chapter 1, are instances of the state using brutal violence against peasants to crush their resistance to land acquisition for predatory projects, and of a Left party not only becoming complicit in the violence, but launching punitive attack on the protesters. That is what happened especially in Nandigram, which saw fourteen people being killed in April 2007 in a police firing. The government was compelled to put land acquisition in Nandigram on hold under protests from the CPI, RSP and Forward Bloc. But CPI(M) cadres were bent on avenging their 'humiliation' and launched an armed assault in November to 'recapture' the village. An orgy of murder, rape and arson followed, which produced widespread revulsion all over India and beyond.

Another crisis erupted in November 2008 at tribal Lalgarh in West Medinipur district, when Maoist guerrillas tried to bomb a convoy in which Chief Minister Buddhadeb Bhattacharjee was travelling. The state police unleashed virulent attacks on innocent villagers. Massive local-level protests broke out which the state government tried to crush with indiscriminate force along with Central paramilitary troops as part of anti-Naxal 'Operation Greenhunt'. Thousands of people were besieged and driven to near-starvation. The operation severely damaged the Left Front's political credibility.

The operation continued for ten months, in which several Maoists and sympathizers were killed in 'fake encounters'. Civil society organizations in Kolkata and elsewhere responded with huge demonstrations against the police excesses. During part of this period, Mamata Banerjee too joined hands with the protesters. But when she assumed power in May 2011, she too used the same military means and completed the task of crushing the Maoists, and with them innocent villagers of the area.

Singur and Nandigram were part of the pathology of the Left Front's industrial policy: its refusal to secure the consent of people whose land is being acquired, its contempt for the rights of the poor, its embrace of the agenda of merely managing capitalism, and the conservatism that lay at the core of its politics. Lalgarh showed its visceral hatred of the Maoists, its willingness to use indiscriminate force against non-combatants, and its profoundly despotic approach towards legitimate protest.

These episodes brought literally hundreds of thousands of citizens on to the streets of Kolkata in spontaneous protests repeatedly between 2006 and 2009. The discrediting of the Left Front in their eyes was the prelude to its defeat in the Lok Sabha elections of 2009. Several signs had appeared from 2006 onwards of a shift in the Left's social base form the rural poor to rich and middle layers, erosion of its advantage among women voters, and its decline in the industrial belt (with a 5 per cent decrease in vote share and a loss of seventeen seats from fifty seven).[74]

The Front's leaders chose to ignore the signs in the street. At the CPI(M) state conference in January 2008, many spoke of the crucial importance of building capitalism. Jyoti Basu reportedly declared: 'Socialism is not possible now ... capitalism will continue to be the compulsion for the future ...' Buddhadeb Bhattacharjee said: 'Let industry grow on its own momentum.... There is no need for any political interference in the process of industrialization.... The only sphere in which the party's involvement is needed is to ensure that corporate social responsibility is being carried out properly ...'[75]

Besides the loss of the intelligentsia, the Left also suffered a depletion of support from two different groups or traditional 'vote banks': Hindu refugees from East Bengal and Muslims who form more than a quarter of the state's population. The first group was affected in recent years in no small measure by the rise of Hindutva politics nationally and the expansion of the BJP's influence in West Bengal. In earlier years, when they were disenfranchised and unemployed, they supported the Left which took up their cause and helped them resettle. Now that they have been that rehabilitated, some of them nurse a grievance against Muslims.[76]

This itself is related to the West Bengal Left's refusal to pursue a combative agenda against the slow process of spread of Hindutva-style communalism under way since the 1980s, and in particular to fight it ideologically and politically rather than through symbolic events like commemorating the 6 December 1992 demolition of the Babri mosque in Ayodhya, or periodically calling for Hindu–Muslim unity in the abstract. The CPI(M) rarely educated its cadres on Hindutva, its political history and the nature of the danger it presents today. Nor did it desegregate Muslims living in Kolkata's ghettos and try and culturally integrate them and its own Hindu supporters on an equal basis.

At the same time, the Trinamool Congress was able to wean away a large chunk of Muslims from the Left. They had traditionally voted for the Left because it gave them minimal physical security against communal violence. But the Left had treated Muslims as if they had no identity other than a purely religious one, and as if they had no aspirations as secular-minded citizens to modern education and jobs; they would remain content with Islamic religious instruction alone. Their religious identity was frozen and totally subordinated to other identities and aspirations, including secular ones related to modern education and jobs. It also cultivated orthodox clerics and subsidized madrasa education.

Muslim perceptions of Left politics changed dramatically after the publication of the Sachar Committee report (2006), which highlighted the terrible disadvantages and discrimination, including exclusion from government jobs, which West Bengal's Muslims faced, even in comparison with a communalized Gujarat. Then came the Rizwanur Rahman scandal of 2007, in which a young Muslim graphic designer was declared by the police to have committed suicide, without even the mandatory post-mortem examination being completed to determine the cause of his death.

It was widely believed that Rahman was victimized for his relationship with a Hindu woman from a business family, and that top police officers close to the LF leadership were complicit in this sordid episode.[77] This proved the last straw for many Muslims. In the 2009 Lok Sabha elections, the Left Front's Muslim vote was estimated to have fallen to 36 per cent from 47 per cent in 2004, while the TMC–Congress share rose from 24 to 58 per cent. By 2011, Trinamool had 50 per cent of the Muslim vote and the Left was left with 42 per cent—a big differential given the concentration of Muslim votes in certain pockets.[78]

The Left Front's electoral base shifted more and more rightwards after 2009. In the 2014 Lok Sabha elections, a higher proportion of 'the rich' (42 per cent) were estimated to have voted for it than the 'poor' or 'lower' classes (respectively 36 and 27 per cent) who preferred the Trinamool Congress (37 and 43 per cent). More upper-caste people voted for the Left than the BJP, and a higher proportion of 'business' and 'salaried' classes preferred the Left to the other two parties.[79]

The Left lost multiple opportunities in West Bengal—instituting ambitious land reform, radicalizing the decentralization and devolution agenda, reinvigorating numerous social development sectors, conceptualizing new and different models of agricultural growth, industrialization and urbanization, and building a participatory, non-clientelist relationship with its support base. It proved far too timid and pusillanimous on certain radical agendas, and far too rigid and orthodox in its industrialization and organizational policies. By the end of its first two decades in power, it had become disconnected from the people and immune to criticism from within and without. Its exit from power was a surprise only to some of its own leaders.

It will not be easy for the Left Front to recover in West Bengal unless it candidly acknowledges its many policy blunders and the causes of its alienation from the workers and peasants who were once part of its base, thoroughly revamps its leadership, and embarks on a new course that re-establishes its relationship with the people. As of now, there are few signs of this happening.

Seats and Vote Share (in per cent) of Major Parties in West Bengal Assembly 1951–2011

Parties	CPI		CPI(M)		Forward Bloc		RSP		Congress		TMC	
Years	Seats	%	Seats	%	Seats	%	Seats	%	Seats	%	Seats	%
2011	2	1.8	40	30.1	11	4.8	7	3.0	42	9.9	184	38.9
2006	8	1.9	176	37.1	23	5.7	20	4.8	21	14.7	30	26.6
2001	7	1.8	143	36.5	25	5.7	17	3.4	26	8.0	60	30.6
1996	6	1.8	157	37.9	21	5.2	18	3.7	43	39.5		
1991	5	1.5	189	36.8	29	5.5	18	3.5	43	35.1		
1987	11	1.9	187	39.3	26	5.8	18	3.9	40	41.8		
1982	7	1.8	174	38.5	28	5.9	19	4.0	49	35.7		
1977	2	2.6	178	35.5	25	5.2	20	3.7	20	23.0		
1972	35	8.3	14	27.5	0	2.5	3	2.1	216	49.1		
1971	13	8.4	113	32.8	3	2.9	3	2.1	105	29.2		
1969	30	7.0	80	20.0	21	5.0	12	2.7	55	41.3		
1967	16	6.5	43	18.1	13	4.4	6	2.1	127	41.1		
1962	50	24.9	-		13	4.6	9	2.5	157	47.3		
1957	46	17.8	-		8	3.8	3	1.2	152	46.1		
1951	28	10.7	-		11	5.3	0	0.8	150	38.8		

6

Historic Triumph in Kerala

Mass Mobilization, Electoral Victory, Land Reform, the 'Kerala Model'

The history of the rise of the Left in Kerala, as colourful and fascinating as the state itself, is a story of multiple mobilizations—for social and religious reform, against caste oppression, for literacy, education and culture, for independence from British rule, against landlord oppression, autocracy and monarchy, for the state's linguistic reorganization and unification, for far-reaching land reforms, for women's rights to education and work in salaried jobs, for the empowerment of workers and peasants through expanded rights, and for measures of social protection of vulnerable groups. These movements deeply politicized Kerala society, and radically changed its complexion.

The importance and singular nature of Kerala's transformation simply cannot be overstated. At the beginning of the twentieth century, Kerala was the most hierarchy-bound and caste-ridden region of India. But by the middle of the century, it had made dramatic progress in fighting hierarchy and achieving social cohesion, moved towards substantially improving the quality of life of the mass of its population, and become the first Indian state to embrace progressive politics by voting in a communist government.

This transformative change was brought about by social reform measures from above (such as promotion of education by princely rulers) and people's movements from below for equal rights. These movements also gave rise to the Left. The Left in turn was pivotal in shaping them and enriching and carrying forward their agendas.

This interplay between social movements and left-wing politics holds the key to understanding the celebrated Kerala Model of development, or the state's achievement of high levels of social and human development decades ahead of the rest of India, despite Kerala's relatively sluggish economic growth and low per capita income until the 1970s. Notwithstanding its inadequacies, and its many recent problems—or as some analysts put it, its 'grave crisis'[1]—the social gains delivered by this model remain unparalleled in India, indeed in most of the Third World, including fast-growing economies like China's. Kerala is India's only state to have reached literacy, infant mortality and life expectancy rates, and not least, female: male sex ratios, close to those prevalent in the First World.

Social Reform and Left Politics

Kerala is also the site where the Left made its greatest advance in India in bringing about radical changes in society, agrarian structures, class relations, education, culture, status of women, and in public discourse and politics—by democratizing politics and making it more participatory. In Kerala, the Left came closest to creating a relatively egalitarian society, with enlightened intellectual and literary traditions, and strong civic organizations and vigorous associational life, indeed to creating a new civic culture. These achievements were greater, more deep-rooted and more emancipatory in nature than the Left's long-term gains in any other state, including West Bengal, which is three times more populous.

These advancements transformed, as in no other Indian state, the very texture of social intercourse in Kerala, generated mass political awareness, and instilled a wholly new kind of self-confidence and assertiveness among plebeian social strata, which were once noted for their docility and obeisance to rigid social hierarchy[2]. This was a historic achievement.

Today, when the Left in Kerala seems politically deadlocked against its opponents and not quite on the upswing, some of these gains may appear to be in jeopardy. But it is vitally important to understand the reasons for the Left's past successes and its strengths and weaknesses, to inquire as to what extent its achievements can be replicated elsewhere in India, and to ask if and how it can rejuvenate itself and regain leadership in the state.

To return to the origins of the Left in Kerala, it is impossible to comprehend these in isolation from two phenomena: Kerala's history, which influenced its cultural traditions and set its special socio-economic context; and second, the intellectual–social renaissance of the late nineteenth and early twentieth century, expressed through multiple movements against casteism and for social reform.

Many geographical, demographic and economic factors set Kerala apart from other Indian states. These include a remarkably mixed religious composition, with a roughly 60:20:20 distribution between Hindus, Muslims and Christians, not found anywhere else in India; the absence of one of the four basic varnas (Vaishya) in Hindu society, and the weak presence of another varna (Kshatriya;) [3] and the prevalence of matriliny among numerically large groups like the Nairs and (significant sections of the) Ezhavas.

There was also a 2,000-year-long history of trade and external contact with the outside world through seafaring merchants, which 'may have helped condition Kerala's people to respond easily to outside influences';[4] the special ecology of this densely populated yet very rural state, marked by 'demographic vigour of the countryside', and a 'ribbon- even cobweb-like' pattern of settlement,[5] which facilitates easy and close contact among people and communities.

This set the context for the birth and growth of movements against casteism and for social reform among different groups, facilitated by the spread of education and rise of modernist progressive literary movements. The most important of these were mobilizations of the low-caste or 'outcaste'[6] Ezhavas by leaders such as Sree Narayana Guru and Kumaran Asan, organized under the Sree Narayana Dharma Paripalana Yogam (SNDP Yogam, founded in 1903), and a major rights-based 'self-respect' movement among the Pulayas, a Dalit caste, inspired and led by Sree Ayyankali. There were reform movements too among the upper-caste Nairs and Namboodiri Brahmins. Among the Namboodiris, the reform initiative took the form of the progressive Namboodiri Yogakshema Mahasabha (established 1908), of which the legendary communist leader E.M.S. Namboodiripad later became president.[7]

These movements struggled against some of the vilest forms of casteism and untouchability (indeed unseeability) known in India: Kerala's Hindu society extended 'the concept of pollution from touch to sight. The lowly Pulaya must remain not less than ninety-six feet from the Brahmin, sixty-four feet from a Nair and thirty feet from an Ezhava ...'[8] The reformers also powerfully critiqued superstition, oppressive customs and obscurantist traditions; promoted education; argued for enlightened rationality; and embraced modernity in its most progressive features while sinking roots amongst the masses.

The social reform movements took up other agendas like reform of family organization, marriage and inheritance rules, internal caste practices, access to public roads and entry into temples denied to low-caste Hindus,[9] and inter-caste sharing of meals. At even more radical political levels, they inspired or organized agrarian mobilizations: the SNDP Yogam mobilized cultivating peasants and the landless, and Ayyankali, the great Dalit leader, organized one of the first strikes of agricultural labourers.[10]

Equally important was the phenomenon of early proletarianization in Kerala, attributable to the development of a rudimentary factory-based working class, based on the processing of cash crops like coir and cashew nut. All these factors taken together, especially the ecology and emergence of the working class, facilitated solidarity and collective action, which inspired many political activists who took up plebeian causes with remarkable vigour and some early successes.

'However, by 1930s and 1940s the first stage of the Kerala renaissance led by the great socio-religious reform movements had run out of steam and the energy for continuation of the renaissance traditions came from a new source, the socialist and communist tendencies that had crystallized within the national movement in Malabar'.[11] Many radical intellectuals and activists who participated in or were influenced by these reform movements became organizers of mass political mobilizations in Kerala, which fused with or joined the Congress, the Congress Socialist Party, and later, the Communist Party of India. Similarly, there was rich interaction between litterateurs and new-generation writers, and the organizers of radical mass movements, which enriched the Left.

Social scientist Robin Jeffrey, who has researched Kerala's history, advances a deeper explanation for the origins of Kerala's radical political tradition. He calls it 'a unique river formed of two tributaries. The first grew out of the generation of educated, uprooted, caste-Hindu youths drawn into politics by the dissolution of the matrilineal joint family between 1900 and 1950. The second tributary came from the lower-caste activists of the same period who confronted the most rigid, demeaning and absurd system of caste in India. The two streams met, mingled and found sustenance in Marxist ideas that promise to build a new world out of a degenerate old one.'[12]

Education: Early Progress

Kerala stands out in India in the first half of the twentieth century for its achievements in literacy, which Daniel Lerner termed more than fifty years ago as 'the basic personal skill that underlies the whole modernising sequence',[13] and holds the key to progress. In 1941, overall literacy rates in Travancore and Cochin were respectively 47 and 41 per cent, about three times higher than India's figure of 15 per cent. Female literacy was proportionately even higher.[14] The early spread of literacy and elementary education in Kerala played a key role in raising public awareness, opening up avenues of mobility and employment, empowering women, and breaking down hierarchical social structures. Modernization contributed to radicalization and spurred the growth of the Left.

The political activists who later became the most energetic drivers of the movements for universal access to education built on the foundations laid by the early initiatives of the princely states (especially of Travancore, and to a certain extent, Cochin), as well as Roman Catholic and Protestant Christian missionaries, to promote elementary schools and in particular education for girls.

Modern schooling was introduced in Kerala in the first half of the nineteenth century. Earlier, between the sixteenth and the eighteenth century, literacy grew in Kerala and education spread beyond the traditionally literate Brahmins to reach 'almost all of the socially and economically privileged sections of society'.[15] But it was only in the nineteenth century that primary education in Travancore received state grants, expanded and 'acquired the characteristics of a "modern" system'.[16]

The first English school was established in 1834 in Trivandrum. A committee was set up to write textbooks in Malayalam, and education was linked to employment in state jobs. The Travancore maharaja famously declared in 1883: 'No civilised government can be oblivious to the great advantages of popular education … for … a government which has to deal with an educated population is by far stronger than one which has to control ignorant and disorderly masses. Hence education is a twice-blessed thing—it benefits those who give it and those who receive it'.[17]

Nevertheless, despite all the progress in education policy, 'there was no mass literacy at the end of the 19th century'. 'Even in Travancore— where Christian missionaries were most active and where the 19th century state was most interventionist—less than a quarter of all males and less than 5 per cent of all females were literate'.[18] Mass literacy had to wait until an 'official environment of support for education' was created through the promotion of female education by the state and organized movements developed to spread literacy among the subaltern classes. Crucial to this process was female literacy. As Jeffrey put it, it is women who made Kerala literate: 'literate men have literate sons; literate women have literate children'.[19]

Before we turn to the emergence and institution of the Kerala Model, it would be relevant to take a look at the growth of radical political mobilizations in the state. Among the first of these was a movement of coir workers in Travancore state in the south in the early and mid-1920s, organized by the pioneering trade unionist P. Krishna Pillai, who would soon become 'the undisputed leader of the early Communist Party in Kerala'.[20] Another high point was the mobilization of the severely exploited tenant-cultivators of the relatively backward Malabar region in the north (part of the Madras Presidency until 1956), which earlier witnessed the famous Moplah Rebellion of 1921. The two movements were later knit together by the 700-kilometre-long marches called jathas undertaken by communist leaders like Krishna Pillai and A.K. Gopalan from Malabar to Travancore.

Anti-Caste Agitations

By the late 1920s, the activists who were later to join the Congress had been involved in various mass agitations against British rule, against caste-Hindu oppression, and for workers' and peasants' rights. They also came into contact with 'revolutionary terrorists' from Bengal gaoled by the colonial government in Cannanore (Kannur), who introduced them to left-wing ideas, made them aware of the anti-imperialist struggles under way elsewhere in India, and broadened their horizons.[21]

The temple entry satyagraha (1924) at Vaikom near Kottayam, and the Congress-inspired civil disobedience movements of 1930 and 1932, were landmarks in the development of radical activism in Kerala. Even more important were the formation of the Travancore Labour Association and the organization of the first Kerala Workers' Conference at Calicut (Kozhikode) in 1935, followed by the second conference in Trichur (Thrissur) in 1937, as well as the creation of several peasant associations in Malabar in the mid-1930s.

These early gains were impressive. Kerala's newly formed unions demonstrated their vigour both in numbers and in intensity of activism, which won their members higher wages and better working conditions. In the period from 1935 to 1940, 'the All-Malabar Karshaka Sangham (peasants' union or kisan sabha) had a paid-up membership of 5,000 in Kasargod, and 10,000 in Chirakkal ... The Shertellai Coir Factory Workers' Union in 1946 had 98 per cent of the workers as members. Six other unions in the area had above 80 per cent membership ... Similar concentrations existed in recent years for toddy-tappers in Thrissur ... and agricultural labourers in Kuttanad and Palakkad.'[22] Their struggles had a salutary impact on the general public, as shown in the growth of political activism via the Congress party.

By the early or mid-1930s, a large number of radical activists thrown up by workers' and peasants' mobilizations entered the Congress. The party was then an important broad-church centrist ['broad church' means open to multiple currents of thought and faith, ecumenical, etc; but the party was primarily centrist] platform for anti-colonial struggles which also accommodated some social agendas. The activists included future communist leaders who would become well-known names in Kerala or national politics, such as K. Damodaran, C.H. Kanaran, K.C. George, K.P.R. Gopalan, M.N. Govindan Nair, C. Achutha Menon and T.V. Thomas. They could now legitimately use the Congress party's identity and win wider public acceptance. They could also influence its policy and strategy at the provincial level.

The Congress underwent a split in 1932 because of its decision to picket the Guruvayoor temple (located in Malabar) to secure the entry of low-caste Hindus, leading to the exit of many higher-caste leaders from the party. The Congress as it existed then was described as 'an empty shell, a table, chair and almirah' in the corner of a newspaper office in Calicut, and 'serviced by a staff of "Sunday Congressmen" drawn chiefly from the legal community of Calicut. It was ripe for a takeover.'[23] The Congress's weakness in Kerala, especially in Malabar, became the proto-communists' strength because it furnished an opportunity to them to control the party organization.

The 'takeover' came not through subterfuge, but overtly and legitimately, via the Congress Socialist Party, formed as a left-wing group within the parent organization in Bombay in 1934. Krishna Pillai was among those who attended the CSP's founding conference. Two other major future communist leaders, E.M.S. Namboodiripad and A.K. Gopalan, were active in the CSP's formation in Kerala, which was joined by some 'moderate' Congressmen as well.

The CSP in 1934 won six out of nine places on the Kerala Provincial Congress Committee (KPCC) and five out of the eight Kerala seats on the All-India Congress Committee and became the dominant force within the Congress in Kerala. It pushed through a series of left-wing resolutions, including an explicit rejection of Gandhian methods at the KPCC meeting in October 1934. 'In December, E.M.S. Namboodiripad became joint national secretary of the CSP, an early recognition of his stature and a reflection of the progress made by the Kerala unit of the CSP'.[24]

However, this was not a palace coup. The CSP had worked hard at the grass roots against the Malabar landlords' efforts to extract extortionate rent from the peasantry, and also won support among unemployed youth. By 1935, 'the CSP activists had established a "Congress" committee in almost every village in Malabar outside the Moplah zone, backed by reading rooms where local activists taught the illiterate to read socialist books and pamphlets and conducted study classes'.[25]

CSP workers also performed socialist plays, including K. Damodaran's highly popular and influential *Rent Arrears* and *Drinking of Blood*. They joined labour leaders to form the All-Kerala Trade Union Congress, and launched a party paper (*Prabhatham*) in 1935. The party, and with it, the Congress, expanded rapidly[26] because it undertook energetic mobilization 'on all fronts of mass activity'.[27]

A real breakthrough came when the CSP organized successful jathas against prominent landowners and built strong peasant unions, especially in Malabar. It garnered tremendous influence in rural Kerala partly on account of growing public disillusionment with the Congress both nationally and in the Madras province. The CSP also gained by cooperating with nationalist Muslims in Malabar against the caste-Hindu Right. In 1938, Namboodiripad was elected general secretary of the Kerala CSP, winning the contest by one vote.

From CSP to CPI

Meanwhile, formal contacts grew between the CPI's national leadership and the Kerala CSP leaders. In 1935, Krishna Pillai and Namboodiripad had a detailed exchange of views with P. Sundarayya, the Andhra communist leader, who would become the CPI's general secretary. The exchange was followed by a visit to Kerala by S.A. Dange and Sundarayya. In 1937, S.V. Ghate, general secretary of the CPI, formed a five-person party faction in Calicut, with Krishna Pillai as its secretary.[28] In 1938, a communist cell became active in Ernakulam on the labour front. In October 1939, the Kerala CSP, now controlled firmly by the communists, secretly joined the CPI en masse, but announced this only on 26 January 1940, which had been declared Independence Day ten years earlier.[29]

The formation of the CPI in Kerala was quickly followed by the arrest of its members on account of the party's opposition to World War II, which it characterized as an 'imperialist' war. By mid-1941, almost all its key leaders barring Namboodiripad had been arrested. Yet, the CPI managed to keep its organization going by involving itself in distress relief work in areas recently hit by a cyclone, and in committees formed to fight famine conditions in 1942–43. As a critical analyst notes: 'On the eve of the German invasion of the Soviet Union, and the transformation of the communist conception of the war from an "imperialist war" to a "people's war", the Kerala party could claim to have played a difficult hand remarkably well'.[30]

A majority of the Kerala communists, who first heard of the invasion of the Soviet Union in jail, resisted the new party line asking them to abandon their opposition to the war. According to a remarkable account by K. Damodaran, many CPI members supported his view calling for intensifying anti-imperialist activity—at least until a party circular reached them.[31] The CPI, of course, paid a price for this through its isolation from the mainstream nationalist movement, especially during the Quit India agitation of 1942, and the rise of rival unions and organizations of workers, peasants and students. Some of the leaders of these organizations were later to form the Revolutionary Socialist Party and the Kerala Socialist Party. This rivalry would impede the CPI's future expansion in the trade union movement.

However, after 1943, the CPI made a remarkable recovery in membership, flow of funds, and quality of cadres; its membership tripled between 1940–41 and 1945 to 600.[32] It took full advantage of its now-legalized status to work in the Grow More Food campaign, ostensibly to help the war effort, and to use anti-fascist meetings to propagate the cause of establishing an independent national government. As a Madras government official noted, 'the Malabar comrades were 10 per cent anti-Nazi and 90 per cent anti-British government …Collectors generally find them intolerable friends of the government'.[33]

A rash of labour disputes erupted in Kerala during 1943–45, in which the CPI played a leading role. A major development was the Punnapra–Vayalar Rising of 1946, which saw the CPI get into an all-out confrontation with the Travancore state, leading to martial law and the killing of 300 peasants. Meanwhile, with the end of the war, new uncertainty arose about the future of the princely states, including Travancore, which wanted, like Hyderabad, to proclaim independence once British paramountcy lapsed. The CPI first opposed this and argued for the incorporation of the princely states into the Indian Union. It demanded full independence in place of the Mountbatten Award.[34]

However, the inner-party debate on the tactics to be adopted in the anti-imperialist, anti-feudal struggle soon became infructuous with the adoption by the CPI's national leadership of the 'Ranadive Line' at its Calcutta congress in 1948. This dismissed Indian independence as a chimera and called for an armed insurrection against the Nehru government. The attempted insurrection, of course, failed to overthrow the government, and cost the party hundreds of lives.

In Kerala, the Ranadive line invited a great deal of state repression against communist activists, including mass arrests and prolonged detentions, and led to a loss of the party's influence in trade unions and peasant organizations. The party later condemned it as 'adventurist'. Yet, the communists 'earned respect in Kerala for suffering selflessly for a cause'—unlike Congressmen, who 'seemed intent on scrabbling for the spoils of office'.[35]

The CPI recovered relatively quickly from these setbacks, thanks to its spirited opposition to the Travancore dewan, its strong involvement in working class and peasant agitations, the corruption of the provincial Congress government leading to its discrediting, the high reputation of the communist leadership attributable to its honesty, austere lifestyles and its distance from communal forces, and not least, its growing involvement in the Aikya Keralam movement for a unified Kerala based on language.[36] By the time provincial elections were held in 1951–52, the CPI was 'stronger than ever'.[37] It would soon make further advances in District Board elections in Malabar, and go on to win the state 1957 assembly elections, the first to be held in a unified Kerala.

Library Movement

The point of recapitulating the evolution of the CPI in Kerala in its multiple dimensions at such length is to stress its deep roots in Malayali society, its cultural life and its public sphere. The early communists were closely associated with subaltern mobilizations against casteism and social reform movements for literacy and women's education. They did much to shape Kerala's public culture based on meetings, rallies and oratory, which made politics the 'national sport of the Malayalis'.[38]

The communists spread the reading habit among the poorer classes, so that 'by the 1950s it was the proud—and not unjustified—boast of the Malayalis that even the poor in their teashops had read a daily paper by tiffin (lunch) time'.[39] In 1961, Kerala had a circulation of thirty-two daily newspapers per 1,000 speakers, compared to only eleven in all Indian languages. The Kerala figure further rose to sixty-one in 1989, compared to twenty-eight in all Indian languages.[40]

The communists were an integral component of Kerala's cultural renaissance movement, whose writers commanded a wide audience thanks to the rapid spread of literacy, and established a strong literary tradition marked by social realist writing. This led to rich modern literature, much of it from the Progressive Writers' Association, whose members included formidable figures like P. Kesavadev, Thakazhi Sivasankara Pillai, K. Kumar Pillai, Vaikom Mohammed Basheer and Joseph Mundassery.

The titles of some of their famous and popular novels 'speak for themselves: P. Kesavadev's *From the Gutter* (1942), and Thakazhi's *Scavenger's Son* (1947) and *Two Measures of Rice* (1948). Namboodiripad estimated that in 1951 alone no fewer than 2,000 poems and short stories dealing with aspects of the struggle for a United People's Democratic Kerala were published in left-wing magazines.'[41] The CPI, committed both to Kerala culture and to socialism, was a major beneficiary of this growing literary movement. In turn, it encouraged the movement through village reading rooms and 'study classes in the evenings and school holidays', in which teachers and student volunteers would 'teach the rudiments of Marxism in a manner relevant to the environment ...'[42]

This raises a question of a counterfactual nature: Could the communists, with their uniquely intimate relationship to Kerala's social reform initiatives and to its cultural, literary and anti-caste movements, have built another kind of party, indeed another kind of politics, with a broader agenda than the conventional Marxist one? Could the objectives of achieving independence and socialism have been combined with a Dalit–Bahujan orientation, with Ayyankali and Sree Narayana Guru, besides Marx, as the sources of its inspiration?

The answer to this, as answers to all such questions, must of necessity be speculative. But it seems plausible that the Kerala communists could have developed a broader 'socialism-plus' orientation and a more inclusive appeal had they delved analytically deeper into the roots of their own success, and reconceptualized the socialist agenda with specific reference to the Indian (and Kerala) context, with caste, gender and ethnic–cultural identities woven into it, or at least broadened the scope of that agenda to include these concerns.

Put crudely, Kerala's communist pioneers denied themselves an opportunity to do so by what might be called theoretical self-abnegation, or precluding the possibility of deep reflection and original thinking. Many of them were strongly activist and practically minded in their orientation, in sharp contrast to the doctrinaire theory-driven or -obsessed image of the typical Marxist intellectual. They were also too modest (or timid?) to believe they could produce and defend an alternative 'socialism-plus' perspective with regard to caste and class, or gender, culture or ethnicity. This is true even of Kerala's best-known communist leader and social theorist, E.M.S. Namboodiripad.

Namboodiripad, who exercised unrivalled influence on Kerala's public life for six long decades, did not have an early exposure to Marxist literature.[43] As a student, he 'had read Laski and Fabian literature, and in jail in 1932-33 he encountered the works of Lenin and Stalin in stray pamphlets smuggled into the prison. EMS describes his "education in socialism" [quotes within the original quote of Hardgrave] as beginning with Jayaprakash Narayan's book, *Why Socialism?*, published in 1934. Although Marx was available in Malayalam … it was only in 1935 that EMS began his study of Marx starting with the *Communist Manifesto*. It was not through socialist theory, says EMS, but in practical political work that he and others in Kerala were drawn towards socialism.'[44]

EMS later wrote: 'Our understanding about the socialist idea was incomplete and hazy. But we tried to spread what we knew among the people using the propaganda machinery then available … [without] … substantial knowledge … [of the] basic tenets of socialism. But we knew that Soviet Union was a living symbol of all that.'[45] At any rate, Kerala's communists got drawn into intense mass agitation and fervent party-building activity from the mid-1930s onwards and never grappled with the broader theoretical agenda.

The Kerala CPI remained relatively aloof from the concerns of the party's national leadership and its positions on international issues.[46] It was deeply rooted in the provincial Congress, and after 1934, in the Congress Socialist Party; nearly all its early leaders occupied important positions in these in the pre-1947 period. It acquired enviably rich experience in organizing mass movements. It established the All-Kerala Trade Union Congress and the provincial Karshaka Sangham (kisan sabha), and had an exceptionally active presence in the peasant movement, including its most vigorous agitations such as the militant 1938–39 campaign against the levies paid by tenant-farmers to landlords.

Thus, *Mathrubhoomi*, a leading Malayalam daily, which traditionally supported the Congress party, assessed the CPI in Kerala as follows: 'Deep-rooted in the soil of Kerala and tended by the constant care and attention of its activists is the Communist Party ...   In every remote village there are communist activists who are closest to the most downtrodden of the people and who have identified themselves with these sections ... [I]n his village, [the communist] ... keeps daily contact with all individuals. And he takes the message of the party to every heart. He has an objective which keeps him inspired. And to achieve that objective he devotes his self-sacrificing endeavours ... The better tomorrow may perhaps be a mirage, but to him it is the complete truth. And the means to achieve his aims he finds in the Communist Party. The party is his body and soul'.[47]

The CPI, along with the socialists, remained wedded to the promotion of a Malayali identity, culture and statehood, 'in the achievement of which the efflorescence of Malayali writing was a powerful factor. By 1947 almost every village had had its reading room containing newspapers, novelettes, and copies of sacred texts and famous Malayalam literature ...'[48] Communist party members and sympathizers looked after many of these reading rooms. The CPI also regularly published pamphlets and leaflets, as well as weekly and daily newspapers. In 1942, its weekly paper was the largest circulated periodical in Kerala. All this bestowed unique prestige on the Kerala communists.

Long March to Power

The CSP, and later the CPI, were crucial components and participants in the Malabar-to-Travancore long marches, and the formation of village-based organizations which wrought major changes in society and political culture of the state. No less important was the CPI's work among students and youth, especially from working class and poor peasant families. The party 'treated the neglected youngsters of the economically and socially backward communities as if they mattered. These teenagers of 1947 were to be the electors of 1957'.[49]

The stage for the CPI's participation in the 1957 state assembly elections was set by the so-called Palghat Line, adopted at the party's fourth congress in 1956. This largely conformed to the 'Centrist' position of 'unity and struggle' with the Congress, to which Namboodiripad adhered[50]—in contradistinction both to the right standpoint which advocated collaboration with the Congress, in keeping with the USSR's now-friendly disposition towards the Nehru regime on account of its foreign policy, and to the left tendency's implacable hostility to the regime given its class character and its domestic policies.[51] The 'unity and struggle' approach yielded rich dividends.

The Palghat Line 'stressed that the continuance of the democratic front tactic of ad hoc alliances with the Left did not imply anti-Congressism'.[52] It also recommended fighting for the 'extension of the rights and powers of the people's elected organs such as 'panchayats, district boards, etc.,'—the 'etc.' implicitly covering the provincial assemblies.

The Kerala CPI followed up on the Palghat congress with its provincial conference at Trichur in June 1956, which produced a 'Communist Proposal for Building a Democratic and Prosperous Kerala'. This included a special appeal to the Praja Socialist Party (PSP) to reconsider its recent decision to reject alliances with the communists and a minimum programme aimed at political stability, social justice and economic reconstruction.

This programme found expression in the CPI's 1957 election manifesto, the thrust of which resembled that of India's just-launched Second Five-Year Plan and had a broadly social-democratic, not a hard-line communist, orientation. The manifesto promised a 130 per cent increase in Kerala's plan allocation, establishment of new industries, development of cooperatives in the small industrial sector, creation of new job opportunities, 25 per cent higher wages and a further bonus of up to 12.5 per cent for workers. It pledged increased food production, a large-scale housing development plan, a thorough reform of education, administrative decentralization, an impartial police policy, nationalization of foreign plantations, and an end to eviction of tenant-cultivators. Most important, it promised a comprehensive Agrarian Relations Bill, including protection of tenants and transfer of land titles to them, imposition of ceilings on landholding, and redistribution of surplus land.[53]

In 1957, the CPI contested 100 of the total of 126 assembly seats, and won sixty of them, with a 35.3 per cent share of the state's vote. Together with the five seats (and 5.5 per cent vote) won by party-supported independents, it secured an overall majority in the assembly. The Congress contested 124 seats, and won only forty-three, with a 37.8 per cent vote. The Praja Socialist Party won nine seats with a 10.8 per cent vote, and the Muslim League eight seats with a 4.7 per cent vote. The CPI would now form independent India's first non-Congress government and demonstrate that communists could come to power by peaceful means in a free and fair election in a bourgeois democracy.

Historic Triumph

The CPI's triumph was an achievement of world-historic proportions for the international communist movement, its first victory outside Europe and China, and pregnant with rich possibilities. Not only was the CPI's victory unprecedented in its long-term domestic import, it also pointed to a potential way forward for left-wing politics in the newly decolonized countries, which were now coming into their own on the global stage.

Progressive political leaders, parties and intellectuals in India and abroad exuberantly welcomed the CPI's historic victory. Conservatives, especially those with cold war mindsets, expectedly deplored or rued it, and expressed their apprehension that Kerala would become the 'Yenan of India', the title of a book typical of the historiography of the period dealing with the 'Red menace'.

Yet, seen from within a broader framework, communism's rise to power in Kerala would have been a huge achievement for India's bourgeois democratic system itself if it could prove to have become inclusive and expansive enough to accommodate an oppositional or anti-establishment current which enjoyed popular support. That would signify that democracy need not remain procedural, but could acquire a radical transformative potential. Alas, the accommodation did not last long.

The CPI won in Kerala primarily because it was the only party with a credible, coherent and equitable vision of the state's future and commanded support among its poor and underprivileged. A number of other factors have been cited for the CPI's victory.[54] Among them were the poor, divided state of the provincial Congress, which had earned widespread ignominy because of its inability to deliver a stable government in Travancore–Cochin for the first decade of Independence despite having had ten opportunities to do so; the failure of the PSP to offer an alternative to the well-organized and cohesive CPI; the merger of communist-inclined 'Red Malabar' into Kerala; and the alignment of some high-caste Hindu groups behind the CPI, besides help from a number of enthusiastic non-party volunteers.

Some of these factors undoubtedly played a role in determining the quantitative aspects of the CPI's victory, but none of them would have had much impact in the absence of the tremendous credibility and moral prestige that accrued to the party because of the clarity of its vision and the base it had built among Kerala's workers and peasants. The CPI's credibility was also enhanced by its new line of 'moderation' and support for the Second Five-Year Plan. This probably convinced sections of the middle classes that the CPI in Kerala was far better placed to realize Nehru's new goal of a 'socialistic pattern of society' than the effete Congress.

CPI general secretary Ajoy Ghosh also reiterated the theme of moderation when he said in April 1957 that the party's aim in Kerala was merely to fulfil 'the hitherto unfulfilled promises of the Congress party made at its Karachi and Faizpur sessions and in its election manifestos'.[55] It bears stating that these promises represented the strongest component of the reformist agenda adopted by the pre-Independence Congress, partly in response to pressures from below, discussed in Chapter 1.

The Congress itself never pursued the 1931 Karachi session's agrarian agenda or the recommendations of the Congress Agrarian Reform Committee, commonly known as the Kumarappa Committee, of 1949. Nevertheless, an emphasis on continuity with the Congress's programme had its own impact. Chief Minister Namboodiripad also took care to stress at the swearing-in ceremony of the new cabinet that his ministry would follow a policy of giving effect to the election programme of the party within the limits of the Indian Constitution.[56]

Immediately after assuming office on 5 April, the CPI government set about fulfilling its election promises. 'Within six days of its swearing-in, it banned evictions of cultivating tenants and introduced land reform legislation which, though hardly revolutionary, was the most far-reaching in India. It instructed the police not to interfere on the side of capitalists in labour disputes ... And in September 1957 it passed legislation to nationalize primary education and bring private high schools and colleges receiving public grants under greater government control'.[57]

The government also commuted all death sentences and released all political prisoners convicted of offences during the 1948–50 insurgency—which frightened and outraged Congress politicians. It raised the salaries and allowances of village officers, set up an anti-corruption department, reformed the jail system, and constituted an Administrative Reforms Committee to review the state's administrative machinery and recommend measures to improve its efficiency.

The most important legislative reform attempted by the communist government was the Agrarian Relations Bill, which aimed to transform agrarian relations in Kerala by abolishing its old land tenure system, 'frequently called the most bewildering in India'[58] given its maze of intermediary rights and 'esoteric' mortgage tenures. Namboodiripad regarded this Bill as his first ministry's greatest achievement.[59] The land reform closely followed the policy model advocated by the 1949 report of the Kumarappa Committee of the Congress party, which abandoned it in practice. In a sour irony, the Congress became a fierce opponent of the land reform in Kerala and eventually brought about the communist ministry's dismissal.

Land Reform at Last

Kerala's land reform laws, drafted by the ministries headed by Namboodiripad in 1957–59 and 1967–69 and implemented in the latter period, had three major components: tenancy reform, homestead plots for the poor, and imposition of ceilings on landownership and redistribution of surplus land to the landless. The first sought to provide security of tenure to tenants, prohibit evictions, take over the rights of the jenmis (traditional landlords) and their intermediaries to vest them in the government, and stop rent payments.

The land reform's most important component was to give land to the tiller—not by expropriating the landlord without compensation, as the CPI had originally promised, but by allowing the tiller to purchase land by paying twelve times the 'fair' rent, fixed at between one-fourth and one-twelfth of the value of the gross produce, itself a wide margin. The landlords would be compensated on a graduated scale. 'The terms of payment were favourable to the tenant, and the purchase price was treated as a debt to the government, with no forfeiture of ownership rights in case of default.'[60]

The land-to-the-tiller reform fell roughly midway within the radical-to-moderate continuum, perhaps closer to the moderate end of the reform spectrum. It clearly made a compromise as far as compensating landlords was concerned. Staunch defenders of the reform later argued that paying compensation was partly necessitated by 'legal requirements related to the constitutional "right" to property'.[61] But the content and limits of the 'right' had not been put to the test then. It is more plausible to argue that political caution rather than legal considerations impelled the CPI to opt for a compromise. It was new to office and unfamiliar with what 'working within the system' meant. In retrospect, the caution was probably justified, but this was still a grey area in 1957.

The land-to-the-tiller measure made no distinction between different classes or groups of tenants; it did not privilege the poorer among them, and thus risked creating a class of 'petit-bourgeois agrarians' (as Lenin called it) and promoting embourgeoisement. It has been argued that 'vesting land in the tenants was the only possible response to the long-standing popular demands and decades of agitations on the part of the peasantry (particularly in Malabar) and was central to the strategic requirements of eliminating the feudal residues of parasitic landlordism'.[62] Yet a different approach, more partisan to poor tenants, was seemingly feasible, and could have been debated within the CPI. Regrettably, going by available published accounts, there was no such debate.

The second component of the reform gave ownership rights to the homestead land (kudikidappu) occupied by the rural poor. The size of the plot to be allotted varied from 0.03 acres in a town or city to 0.10 acres in a village and could be purchased at 25 per cent of the market rate, and half of that if the owner had land above the ceiling'.[63] The government subsidized half the purchase price; the rest was to be paid in instalments. The occupancy rights were made secure and inheritable. This would reduce 'the abject dependence of the totally landless on landowners', but the plots distributed would be far below the 'economic' level.[64]

The third component of the reform 'concerned the imposition of limits on landownership and distribution of land identified as surplus to the landless. The land ceiling in Kerala, which was imposed on household landholdings, varied with the size of household',[65] subject to a maximum of 25 acres. This was extremely, perhaps unconscionably, generous given that the average size of operated holdings in Kerala was as low as 1.25 acres.[66] The plantation sector was totally exempted from the ceiling, contrary to the manifesto's pledge to expropriate foreign plantations altogether through nationalization.

The land reforms were limited, or as some would say, moderate in nature.[67] But they were fiercely opposed by a coalition of right-wing groups, including landlords, the Catholic Church, caste organizations like the Nair Service Society (NSS)—ironically, a traditional rival of the Church—and various entrenched interests working through the Congress party. The coalition was joined and reinforced by representatives of the private sector in education, especially church institutions, which opposed the education reform bill. The bill sought to regulate the appointment and conditions of service of teachers, maintain proper records, reduce corrupt practices, eradicate communal biases, and establish local educational authorities with tiers of elected, official and nominated members.

CIA–Congress Collusion

The communist government was trying 'to beard two lions in the same den'. The combined opposition of the two coalitions became fierce as they launched a violent campaign of disruption in the state, called the 'liberation struggle'. There is some evidence that the government tactically mishandled the agitation, aggravating resentment against itself. At any rate, the agitators were not concerned beyond a point with scuttling specific land and education-related legislations. Their express objective was to topple the Namboodiripad ministry itself.

The Central government led by Jawaharlal Nehru on 31 July 1959 dismissed the Kerala government apparently under the goading of his daughter (and then Congress president) Indira Gandhi, the home ministry and various hawks in the New Delhi establishment. It invoked Article 356 of the Constitution, which empowers the Centre to dismiss a state government which fails to rule in conformity with the statute. By doing so for patently parochial and self-serving political reasons, it set an egregious precedent for the Article's future abuse on more than 100 occasions.

Nehru's controversial role in this has been critically discussed—not least because he, unlike Indira Gandhi, was thought not to bear a visceral antipathy towards the communists, pledged adherence to constitutional rectitude and democratic values, and repeatedly discounted the counsel of intelligence agencies and some of his own advisers in favour of dismissing the elected communist ministry. A charitable view is that Nehru was weak and indecisive at this point of time, and that after resisting it for some months, he eventually succumbed to the combined pressure from the Intelligence Bureau, the home ministry, senior Congress leaders and his own daughter.[68]

On a balanced assessment, a combination of factors, domestic and external, and political as well as economic, would seem to have resulted in this momentous decision. There was, of course, heavy pressure on Nehru from the Congress party, which was loath to see a challenge arise to its monopoly over state power, especially from the Left. The Congress in Kerala was badly divided and in disarray: defections from the party, leading to its possible disintegration there, would have national consequences. Going by her public statements, Indira Gandhi seems to have had a strong aversion towards the communists during this period.[69] Besides, R. Sankar, a thoroughly opportunist Ezhava leader, became the president of the Congress's Kerala unit in April 1959. He was eager to break what was generally perceived as a strong link between his community and the CPI.

The Congress's antipathy towards the CPI government was shared by, and probably reinforced by, the intense, ideologically driven cold war anti-communism of the United States government, acting through the Central Intelligence Agency (CIA). The two colluded extensively and consciously to oppose and dislodge the Namboodiripad government. Some aspects of the CIA's role and its collaboration with the Congress have been public knowledge since 1972, when former IB director B.N. Mullick published his memoir[70].

However, new and more detailed evidence of CIA–Congress collaboration has since emerged through the memoirs or biographies of two former US ambassadors to India, Ellsworth Bunker (1956–61) and Daniel Patrick Moynihan (1973–75), and via recently declassified official US and British documents.[71] From these, it is clear that the CIA funded and supported anti-CPI activities in Kerala in multiple ways and over a period of years. These included not only Congress efforts aimed at preventing a communist victory in 1957,[72] as previously thought, but also support for the Congress's participation in the 'liberation struggle' of 1959 to topple the Namboodiripad ministry.[73]

The CIA secretly channelled funds to Congress office-bearers and labour leaders to foment industrial unrest and political turmoil.[74]

EMS Ministry Dismissed

There is simply no doubt that US covert activity to subvert the Left played a major role in both these anti-CPI campaigns, although the CIA used different individuals and means over a period of time. Bunker states that the main intermediary for the funds transferred by the CIA to the

Congress was the Bombay-based right-wing party operator S.K. Patil, notorious for his corporate links and corrupt ways, and his later role in the Syndicate Congress faction opposing Indira Gandhi. But Moynihan identifies the intermediary as Gandhi, then Congress president herself, no less.

These narratives are mutually compatible and complementary. Gandhi and Patil probably both collaborated with the CIA over different time frames in trying to preclude the formation of a CPI government in Kerala, and failing that, to topple it two years on. The central fact of CIA interference remains indisputable.

Added to this sordid Congress–CIA collusion was energetic lobbying against the CPI and its government by British tea plantation owners in Kerala, then a powerful interest group which probably had access to Nehru.[75] The CPI had demanded nationalization of all foreign-owned plantations, but chose to exempt plantation land in Kerala from the Agrarian Relations Bill of 1957 owing to political opposition from the Congress. The conflict between the planters and communist-led trade unions, however, remained unresolved. In October 1958, the unions organized a major strike on working conditions, wages and bonuses at the huge Kanan Devan tea estates, owned by James Finlay. The management refused to concede the workers' demands.

The Nehru government, lobbied by the British high commission and Kanan Devan's representatives, 'pressurized' the CPI into calling off the strike on humiliating terms.[76] Encouraged by this, Kanan Devan's managers joined forces with the 'liberation struggle'. Using the offices of the United Planters' Association of South India, two of the managers approached Nehru, and 'convinced the Central government that Namboodiripad's government must be terminated'. After it was dismissed, Finlay's general manger W.S.S. Mackay triumphantly declared: '...it was here (in the High Ranges) that Namboodiripad met "his Waterloo".'[77] The claim that the Kanan Devan managers 'convinced' Nehru is probably boastful and extravagant, but it is indisputable and significant that Nehru was accessible to them and open to their lobbying.

At any rate, the Congress, already a part of the 'liberation struggle' against the CPI government, became hyperactive in it especially when its 'civil disobedience' phase, directed at all government activities, was launched on 12 June 1959. Soon afterwards, a stream of senior Congress leaders visited Kerala. Party secretary Sadiq Ali (17 June) was followed by Nehru himself (22–25 June),[78] and later by another secretary, Sucheta Kripalani. They all made public their hostility to the state government. Kripalani met Governor B. Ramakrishna Rao and told him to write a report to President Rajendra Prasad recommending the ministry's dismissal. Rao resisted on the ground that he had not yet heard from Nehru. But the resistance would not last.[79]

On 23 July, Intelligence Bureau chief B.N. Mullick and law minister A.K. Sen prepared a 'chargesheet' against the state government, based on an earlier note written by Mullick under the orders of the home ministry, to justify Namboodiripad's dismissal. This was flown the same day to Governor Rao in Trivandrum. 'With the necessary document in hand, and Sucheta Kripalani on his doorstep, the Governor drafted a report for the President of India'.[80] Rao was asked to rush the report to the capital, where it reached on 29 July. President's rule was imposed on Kerala on 31 July 1959.[81]

The Namboodiripad ministry's dismissal paved the way for a Congress-led government in Kerala, which proceeded to dilute the Agrarian Relations Bill severely and introduced new exemptions from land transfers. Even this legislation was struck down by the Kerala High Court and the Supreme Court. In 1964, another Act was passed which placed the subject outside the purview of the courts.

Finally, in 1967, a second Namboodiripad ministry took office, led by the CPI(M), which had split three years earlier from the CPI and become the larger of the two parties.[82] This ministry introduced the Kerala Land Reforms Bill. This set the stage for the legislations enabling the reforms that took place in the 1970s. Land reforms in Kerala were always a struggle, one not concluded even thirty years after the communists introduced the Agrarian Relations Bill in 1957. The reforms came about as much through pressure from below as through state policy, resulting in the laws of the 1960s, which an analyst has termed 'a standing monument to the irrepressible spirit and untiring efforts of the peasantry'.[83]

What was the final result of the land reforms? By February 1981, the implementation of the first two components—tenancy reform and transfer of homestead land—was 'virtually complete' according to Kerala Land Board records. This proved relatively successful (especially in respect of the first), but implementation of the third scheme (of identification and distribution of ceiling-surplus land) did not. Under tenancy reform, land measuring about 1.97 million acres was transferred by 1991 to 1.23 million tenants—an average of 1.6 acres per household. The beneficiaries constituted a little over 40 per cent of Kerala's agricultural households. No less impressive was the proportion of the land transferred to the net sown area—36.5 per cent, and as much as 42.9 per cent, if plantation crops are excluded.[84]

A much smaller area (just 21,500 acres) was transferred under the homestead scheme to 270,000 households, or an average of 0.08 acres, less than one-tenth of an acre.[85] But under the third scheme, only about 77,000 acres were taken over, of the 115,000 acres declared surplus in 1964; and just about 50,000 acres were distributed among 81,000 households, or a paltry average of 0.62 acres.[86]

This last figure, amounting to just 1 per cent of the total operated area, is explained by the partitioning of holdings by landlords among their kith and kin, and bogus land transfers including conversion into plantations. This was facilitated by the decade-long delay in the passage of the land reform law after the landlords saw the 'danger signal' from the communists' ascent to power in 1957, which gave them plenty of opportunities to circumvent the ceiling law.[87]

Tenants Gain, Not Workers

The land transfers continued over many years. By 1993, economist Prabhat Patnaik, who later became the Kerala State Planning Board's deputy chairperson, estimates that '1.5 million tenants in the state had benefited from tenancy legislation … In addition 5.28 lakh agricultural labourers had been provided house-sites'.[88]

On the whole, Kerala's land reform was fairly impressive in altering tenancy relations and covered two-fifths of all agricultural households and land area—a much higher proportion than in any other state, with the exception of Jammu and Kashmir.[89] It was modestly to moderately successful in respect of transferring homestead plots to the landless, and largely a failure in the redistribution of ceiling-surplus land. But the biggest component, tenancy abolition, was not without blemish. While it had 'positive consequences such as the abolition of landlordism, at least in its traditional sense, and the emancipation of the tenants from their socio-economic subservience to the landlord class', it did not usher in 'an era of equality and social justice in land ownership'.[90]

Glaring inequalities persisted in Kerala's agrarian structure, in particular in the ownership and control of land. Clear differentiation became visible between 'at least three distinct agrarian groups':[91] a small number of rich farmers who displaced jenmi landlords at the top; a large number of agricultural labourers—two-fifths of Kerala's agricultural households in 1951—with shrinking employment opportunities and the prospect of pauperization, at the bottom; and a huge number of poor and marginal farmers in the middle, who were small tenants before the reforms.

According to an analysis of a statewide sample survey by the Indian School of Social Sciences, the primary beneficiaries of the tenancy reform were the rich peasants: they constituted 13.3 per cent of the households but received 38.7 per cent of the land transferred. Households possessing less than 5 acres formed 84.2 per cent of the sample, but received only 36.2 per cent of the transferred area. The smallest peasants, holding less than an acre, were 16.6 per cent of the sample, but received only 0.9 per cent of the land. In contrast, those holding over 5 acres (15.8 per cent of the sample) gained 63.8 per cent of the transferred acreage.[92]

These limitations were serious and must not be minimized. Yet, Kerala's land reform succeeded in ending rentier landlordism and the jenmi system, in reducing extreme concentration in land ownership and income inequalities, and in undermining at least a part of the material foundation of caste and class oppression (with all the extra-economic coercion and subjugation that comes with it). It led to the virtual disappearance of 'landlords in the true sense, lords of the land'. It stirred up rural society, to some extent improved the bargaining power of the landless who got house sites, and altered the overall balance of class power in a positive direction, although not radically.

These were moderate gains. But the reform was not meant to be radical. It was not designed to abolish the privilege of obtaining income from owning land without having to labour on it—but only to transfer that privilege. Rich peasants and capitalist landowners, not poor peasants or agricultural labourers, were the greatest beneficiaries of the abolition of landlordism and the system of rent. Thus the reform fell well short of giving 'land to the tiller', the real cultivator, as is often claimed. Indeed, the truly landless, the rural proletariat, were virtually excluded.[93]

Although the land reform was reasonably well implemented, it produced a less-than-satisfactory result in terms of equity because of the flaws in the way it was conceived and designed. First, it treated tenancy as a homogeneous production relation, when it was a form of property compatible with various configurations of production relations, including capitalist farming.[94] Secondly, the reform fixed an excessively high land ceiling (25 acres), which meant that large landholders, with several nuclear families per household, not only could retain their land, but could even increase their holdings by claiming ownership of leased-in lands under tenancy provisions.[95]

The Kerala reform, then, transferred land largely to the immediate proprietor. It did not result in a shift in 'agrarian power to agricultural labourers and poor peasants, and did not end capitalist landlordism. It did not lead to the establishment of production cooperatives or collectives or to other post-capitalist forms of agrarian production organization .... [It] was not followed by substantial increases in crop production ... nor were there substantial increases in rural employment.'[96]

Yet, the land reform responded to pressures from below in two ways. First, it 'represented the expressed demands of the agrarian movement in the state (dominated, as elsewhere in India historically, by pucca tenants of higher social status rather than by sharecroppers and labourers)'.[97] Second, it stimulated and was accompanied by specific measures by the communist government to create new rights for landless agricultural labourers and empower them—as if in recompense.

Movements Drive the 'Model'

Thus the Kerala Agricultural Workers Act, in force since 1975, remains a model charter for India's rural workers, and the only law of its kind which legislates minimum wages, working hours and conditions, job security, and retirement benefits (through a provident fund to which both workers and employers contribute); it also creates a system for registering agricultural workers and arbitration boards for settling labour disputes. Kerala's agricultural workers have made the highest gains in real wages in India since the early 1970s,[98] and benefited from state-level schemes for unemployment insurance and labour pensions, launched in the early 1980s—again pioneered by Kerala in India.

Several other disadvantaged groups such as construction labourers and domestic workers have also gained over the past four decades from the policy measures introduced by the communist parties organized within the Left Democratic Front, which has tended to alternate in power with the Congress-led United Democratic Front. Kerala's electorate—in particular, increasingly vocal groups representing women, subaltern castes and ethnic identities, as well as traditionally well-represented class interests—has kept the LDF on a tight leash by periodically voting it out of power, and demanding improved performance on a variety of divergent agendas.

But despite these internal differences and divergent gender-, caste- and class-related priorities, the electorate never rejected the basic policy orientation set by the Left on major public-service or redistributive programmes. The UDF did not find it politically feasible to dismantle these, despite the state's precarious financial position and lack of Central support.[99] The 'basic' orientation may well represent the lowest common denominator of what is easily doable, which excludes more radical options within the realm of the feasible. But it still demarcates Kerala from most other states.

The remarkable continuity in Kerala's social policy regime from the late 1960s onwards resulted in the institution and crystallization, whether by design or otherwise, of what has been termed and lauded worldwide as the Kerala Model.[100] The Model is not a combination or package of policies, but depicts or captures a certain pattern of social progress: relatively high achievements in people's well-being, and improvements in their social, political and cultural conditions, even at low levels of income, with a degree of equity and wealth redistribution, accompanied by public politics and people's participation.[101]

Indeed, important as they were, progressive state policies alone did not result in these outcomes. Critical to bringing them about was another kind of public action, namely, popular movements which exercised great pressure on the state and impelled it to implement social development programmes. During the 1970s and 1980s, 'the dynamism of social policies ... was matched by societal activism, which fostered an efficient and well-utilized network of public goods. While Left mobilization was also an important contributory factor, a strong identification with their state was critical in generating a high degree of political consciousness among the people of Kerala.'[102]

Political consciousness triggered and sustained exceptionally high rates of unionization across both the formal and informal sectors of the economy, and countless popular mobilizations devoted to a variety of causes. 'Kerala's movements have often contained very large numbers of members ... In 1957 the membership of the Kerala Karshaka Sangham [kisan sabha] reached 190,000.... With just 3.5 per cent of India's people, Kerala had 20 per cent of all the unions in the country (7,836) in 1984. Kerala's union membership accounted for 7.5 per cent of total Indian union membership ... In 1983, 44 per cent of workers in Kerala's factory sector were trade union members ... In 1988 ... CPM-organized events in Alleppey involved 750,000 participants ...The 1989-91 Total Literacy Campaign recruited 350,000 volunteer teachers ...'[103]

Kerala came to be marked by an exceptionally high density of civil society organizations and vigour of associational life, with the most extensive network of cooperative societies, as well as numerous non-government organizations, networks of private and semi-private educational institutions, and caste self-help groups and social upliftment societies with a long history of active civil engagement.[104]

Popular movements often held the state's feet to the fire, enforcing accountability. 'The combination of top-down state policies and bottom-up social activism has generated remarkable social gains in Kerala'— through public vigilance, for instance, by ensuring 'one of the lowest rates of teacher absenteeism' in state-run schools, and regular attendance on the part of health centre staff. Perhaps no state but Kerala has seen public demonstrations prompted by the absence of a physician from a health centre or action to demand humane treatment of people in pain.[105]

John Kurien, who has studied Kerala's social and political movements in depth, observes that the 'politicization and awareness' generated by popular struggles inspired yet other movements: 'The [early] success of agricultural labour in safeguarding their rights and enhancing their social welfare had a very strong demonstration effect among other occupational groupings both in the agrarian and traditional industrial sectors,' including toddy tappers, cashew and coir workers, and beedi rollers, and inspired them to take 'collaborative and/or adversarial collective action'.[106]

Therefore, says Kurien, 'the higher quality of life in Kerala is thus not merely the result of provisioning of services by the state in the form of physical facilities: schools, health centres, fair price shops, metalled roads, post offices, public transportation, etc. It is equally important to recognize the growth of awareness among the masses and collective action by them to ensure that these facilities are utilized fully and well ... It really does not matter which comes first—the facilities or the collective action. The point is that without the latter, even radical and committed action by the state alone will remain a sterile challenge. For those who wish to emulate the "Kerala model", we consider this to be the main insight ...'[107]

Rising Social Indices

Many of Kerala's social indices showed steady improvement year after year. Take literacy, in which Kerala established an early lead, almost a century ago. The Left not only laid great emphasis on literacy; it made it a cornerstone of Kerala's political culture. By 1981, Kerala's overall literacy rate (78.1 per cent) was almost twice the Indian average (42.9), and its female literacy was almost two-and-a-half times greater. By 1991, Kerala's literacy rate for those above seven years of age had risen to 90.6 per cent compared with India's 52.1 per cent; and the rate for females above seven to 87 per cent, more than double the rate for Indian females (39.4 per cent).[108]

One of the reasons for Kerala's noteworthy success in this field was the Total Literacy Campaign, pioneered by the Kerala Sasthra Sahithya Parishad (KSSP), and later emulated in the rest of India through a Central government–led programme. The KSSP launched this first in late 1988 in Ernakulam district, which includes Cochin City, with some 50,000 volunteers who tracked down its 175,000 illiterates. The KSSP mobilized 20,000 volunteer tutors to impart literacy skills to them.

Thirteen months later, on 4 February 1990, Prime Minister V.P. Singh declared Ernakulam India's first totally literate district. On 18 April 1991, Kerala became India's first state to be declared totally literate.[109] Similar achievements registered by Kerala in respect of health, poverty alleviation, education and other social sector areas between the 1970s and 1990s were collectively identified by social scientists and development practitioners as constituting what came to be popularly known as the Kerala Model.

The Model was first definitively documented and rigorously analysed in 1975 by the Centre for Development Studies (CDS), Trivandrum, in a study published by the UN Department of Economic and Social Affairs, which however did not use that famous term.[110] This 'addressed issues relevant to mass poverty and unemployment and ... examined the evolution and working of several redistributive policies.... It looked at the development process as a complex whole within which both economic and social factors play important roles', including 'measures meant to reduce inequalities', instead of depending on 'trickle-down' effects.[111]

The CDS–UN study showed that Kerala's social achievements, such as expansion of education, provision of affordable health care, food security and access to many other amenities, were not the result of an inspired plan quickly implemented with success, but truly 'a product of Kerala's unique development history ...' The study considerably demystified the Kerala experience and 'led to much academic research work later that demonstrated how, apart from leftist parties in power or in opposition, several other agencies led to the advancement of an egalitarian society. The study ... has thus undoubtedly contributed to the elaboration of concepts such as "public action" and "human development" ... in recent economic literature.'[112]

The Kerala Model came to be recognized through an ensemble of outstanding social indices: high life expectancy (ten or more years greater than India's average); low infant mortality (almost one-fifth the national average), high immunization rates, and massive improvements in women's health status; India's highest female: male sex ratio (greater than 1020:1000 for most of the past century) and the country's lowest birth and death rates; and remarkably high literacy and high female literacy.

The model also captured other related achievements in Kerala: India's most radical land reform outside Kashmir; major progress in abolishing untouchability; India's best public distribution system for food; narrowing of regional and urban–rural development gaps; high levels of public awareness, reflected in India's topmost figures of per capita newspaper circulation, among other things; a tradition of lively public debate; and greater popular participation in local decision making.

To this must be added the legacy of Kerala's robust civic culture which created a space in which writers, academics and intellectuals could make forceful interventions on major issues of the day. Kerala's tradition of political meetings, mass rallies and public oratory encouraged this. The library movement, film societies, and theatre or music performances by travelling troupes thrived in the state. The sheer vigour of literary and artistic activity and the creativity of Malayali theatre and cinema earned Kerala a reputation as a major centre of culture disproportionate to its size.

By the early 1980s, the Kerala Model began to attract the attention of international scholars, and health, education and development specialists. Many in the world marvelled at how Kerala achieved this despite being one of 'the most densely crowded places on earth—the population of California squeezed into a state [the] size of Switzerland.'[113] Kerala's Physical Quality of Life Index (PQLI), rated 82 in 1981 on a scale of 1 to 100, exceeded the score of all of Africa, and all but three countries of Asia (much richer Japan, Taiwan and South Korea). By 1989, its PQLI had reached 88.[114]

In 1985, Kerala, along with Costa Rica, Cuba, Sri Lanka and China, was held up to the world as a model of 'good health at low cost' at a conference held in Bellagio, Italy, under the auspices of the Rockefeller Foundation. An ecologist lavished praise on Kerala's frugal use of natural resources, and termed it 'the Kerala Exception': 'The Malayalam-speaking people of South India offer an example for the whole Earth. Extraordinary efficiencies in the use of the Earth's resources characterize the lifestyles of the 29 million citizens of Kerala. Following the Kerala leadership we can see our way to prudent human behaviour maintaining high life quality through the twenty-first century.'[115]

Missed Opportunities?

Among the first to shower encomiums on the Kerala Model were unorthodox economists and radical social scientists. To them, Kerala not only disproved conventional economic wisdom—which held that the standard of living of the masses would generally improve only after agriculture and industry have developed—but also offered tantalizing possibilities of new policy approaches. But soon, the Model got 'mainstreamed'. The orthodox establishment too acknowledged its achievements. Why, even the World Bank honoured it with fulsome praise.

Ironically, just as high praise was being lavished upon the Kerala Model, ground reality was gradually changing. Beginning with the late 1970s, agricultural output shrank and GDP growth slowed down. With a decrease in the growth of the state's revenues, financial support for health and education began to decline, and privatization started creeping in, especially in tertiary health care. Most important, unemployment increased, including unemployment among women. Emigration rose sharply, especially to the oil-rich Persian Gulf countries.

These processes were gradual. But as the next chapter shows, their direction was unmistakable. They got accelerated in the 1980s when GDP growth fell in Kerala to just one-fourth of its national rate and public expenditure in the social sector declined in real terms. Perceptive observers increasingly recognized that it would be hard for Kerala to sustain its social progress at the old rates given the state of its economy. By the late 1980s policymakers and development specialists would start talking of 'the crisis' of the Kerala Model. Soon, the phrase became part of public discourse.

The early 1990s witnessed a debate within Kerala's intelligentsia on the need to stimulate the state's economy without following the neo-liberal approach led by private capital that the Central government had just embraced. But no easy solutions emerged. The political leadership too groped for answers, without much success.

The crisis of the Kerala Model warrants some reflection on the frailties and flaws in the manner in which it was constructed. Three considerations are pertinent here. First, many policies associated with the model were adopted without clarity about whether they were chosen because they were intrinsically progressive or radical and normatively desirable, or because they were expedient and necessitated by the prevalent balance of political forces. But all policies have an opportunity cost. Alternative policies, especially more radical and equitable ones, are rejected as choices are made in favour of a specific reform package.

Some of these choices were made for 'pragmatic' reasons, but also proved normatively ideal and worthy, as if by accident. This is true in the case of the Kerala Agricultural Workers Act. But the opposite could also be true. For instance, the tenancy reform led to an increase in the power of rich farmers, which adversely affected the interests of the poor in the long run. Going by my interviews with left leaders and intellectuals, such issues and the challenges they pose—of creating countervailing forces and taking corrective steps—were not fully deliberated within the LDF or the communist parties. The appropriate lessons were not fed into the formulation of future policy.

Second, some progressive changes for which Kerala is known, such as abolition of untouchability or narrowing of regional and urban–rural disparities, occurred not as a result of conscious state policy, but of voluntary activities and social processes in which the state played little role. That, of course, is natural and unexceptionable. The question is whether the LDF's political leadership developed an analytical understanding of these processes, of ways of revitalizing them if they slacken, and of their potential for replication in different situations. The answer would seem to be largely negative.

Third, some of the inadequacies, flaws and weaknesses of the Kerala Model were not understood or acknowledged until much later—early or mid-1990s. These included exclusion of certain social groups, poor equity outcomes, relatively high ecological costs, imbalances between different economic sectors and so on, which are discussed at length in the next chapter. By the time the Model's crisis was recognized, some of these problems had become chronic, some almost intractable. There was too much complacency about high female : male sex ratios and women's employment, and not enough acknowledgement of the growth on the ground of new forms of gender discrimination, sexual harassment and insecurity among women.

Over and above these considerations stands out yet another deficit: lack of serious and continual deliberation within the Left parties on these issues and the virtual absence of a debate on alternative policies and approaches about the paths not taken. There was nothing preordained about the Kerala Model; nor was it the only possible one. It could have been improved to deliver more desirable outcomes, especially after it was recognized by the mid-1990s that it had run into a crisis and needed to be reformed.

On available evidence, there seems to have been little debate on this either in individual Left parties or between them, both in Kerala and nationally. Party-affiliated intellectuals were deeply involved in these debates, and senior party officials would often participate in them. But the ideas such interactions generated were rarely transmitted into inner-party deliberations and debates.

Similarly, there has been very little discussion within the national Left about learning from the Kerala experience. This applies to 'positive' lessons on fighting casteism (which Kerala did far more successfully in the first half of the twentieth century than most other states,[116]) or bringing about a close relationship and coordination between the Left parties and social reform movements. It also holds true of 'negative' lessons from Kerala's land reforms, which could have been integrated into the West Bengal agrarian programme or kisan sabha agendas in numerous other states. Surprisingly, there was very little sustained dialogue within and between the Left parties on such issues, as distinct from, say, electoral alliances—a sign of their parliamentary preoccupations.

The next chapter looks at the crisis of the Kerala Model and the search for future solutions which are rooted in radical alternative frameworks. A debate on such solutions is imperative if the Left's spectacular achievements in the early period are not to become a mere relic of history.

The following pages present a table showing the comparative performances of the LDF and UDF in the Kerala assembly elections from 1977 to 2011. It may be interesting to note—and may also enthuse social scientists to conduct additional research on it—that in contrast to the uninterrupted rule of the Left Front in West Bengal over this thirty-four-years-long period, neither the LDF nor the UDF has ever won two consecutive assembly election in Kerala from 1977 onwards. Perhaps the developments in Kerala owe a lot to this particular aspect of the mindset of the electorate.

Year		Seats Contested	Seats Won	Vote (%)
1977	**LDF**	140	29	43.26
	CPI(M)	68	17	22.18
	Kerala Congress (Pillai group) (KCP)	15	2	4.53
	Bharatiya Lok Dal	26	6	7.86
	All-India Muslim League (AIML)	16	3	4.45
	Independent (LDF Supported)	15	1	4.24
	UDF	140	111	52.93
	Congress	54	38	20.02
	Indian Union Muslim League (IUML)	16	13	6.66
	RSP	11	9	4.20
	CPI	27	23	9.94
	Kerala Congress (KEC)	22	20	8.38
	Independent (UDF Supported)	10	8	3.73
	Independents and Other parties	289	0	3.81
	Total	569	140	100.00
1980	**LDF**	140	93	50.68
	CPI	22	17	7.80
	CPI(M)	50	35	19.35
	RSP	8	6	3.02
	Indian National Congress (Urs) INC(U)	30	21	10.95
	KEC	17	8	5.25
	AIML	11	5	3.51
	KCP	2	1	0.80
	UDF	140	45	43.69
	Congress	53	17	17.03
	IUML	21	14	7.18
	Kerla Congress Joseph (KCJ)	15	6	4.61
	Janata Party (JNP)	27	5	7.60

Kerala: Performance of UDF and LDF Parties in Assembly Elections

Kerala: Performance of UDF and LDF Parties in Assembly Elections				
Year		Seats Contested	Seats Won	Vote (%)
	Independent (UDF Supported)	24	3	7.27
	Independents (Rest)	305	2	4.81
	Other Parties	17	–	0.82
	Total	**602**	**140**	**100.00**
1982	**LDF**	**140**	**64**	**47.12**
	CPI	25	13	8.42
	CPI(M)	51	26	18.80
	AIML	12	4	3.25
	RSP	8	4	2.76
	Indian National Congress (Socialist) (ICS)	15	5	4.81
	JNP	13	4	4.04
	Independent (LDF Supported)	16	8	5.04
	UDF	**140**	**76**	**48.18**
	Congress	35	20	11.89
	Muslim League	18	14	6.17
	KEC	17	6	5.86
	KCJ	12	8	4.55
	National Democratic Party (NDP)	5	2	1.67
	Independent (UDF Supported)	53	26	18.04
	BJP	69	–	2.75
	Independents (Rest)	350	–	1.95
	Total	**699**	**140**	**100.00**
1987	**LDF**	**140**	**77**	**44.99**
	CPI	25	16	8.07
	CPI(M)	70	38	22.84
	RSP	6	5	2.07
	ICS	14	6	4.01
	JNP	12	7	3.78
	Lok Dal	2	1	0.61

Kerala: Performance of UDF and LDF Parties in Assembly Elections				
Year		Seats Contested	Seats Won	Vote (%)
	Independent (LDF Supported)	11	4	3.61
	UDF	**140**	**62**	**44.15**
	Congress	76	33	24.81
	IUML	23	15	7.72
	KEC	14	5	3.54
	Independent (UDF Supported)	27	9	8.08
	BJP	116	–	5.63
	Independents (Rest)	858	1	5.23
	Total	**1254**	**140**	**100.00**
1991	**LDF**	**140**	**50**	**45.59**
	CPI	24	12	8.26
	CPI(M)	65	29	22.08
	RSP	6	2	1.73
	Janata Dal	13	3	4.04
	KEC	10	1	2.99
	ICS	12	2	3.47
	Independent (LDF Supported)	10	1	3.02
	UDF	**140**	**90**	**47.80**
	Congress	91	55	32.07
	IUML	22	19	7.37
	Kerla Congress (Mani) KCM	13	10	4.32
	Communist Marxist Party of India CPM(K)	4	1	1.18
	NDP	3	2	0.93
	Independent (UDF Supported)	7	3	1.93
	BJP	137	–	4.76
	Independents and Other parties	392	–	1.85
	Total	**809**	**140**	**100.00**

Kerala: Performance of UDF and LDF Parties in Assembly Elections				
Year		Seats Contested	Seats Won	Vote (%)
1996	**LDF**	**140**	**80**	**45.67**
	CPI	22	18	7.62
	CPI(M)	62	40	21.59
	RSP	6	5	2.07
	Janata Dal	13	4	4.12
	KEC	10	6	3.10
	ICS	9	3	2.49
	Independent (LDF Supported)	18	4	4.68
	UDF	**140**	**59**	**44.84**
	Congress	94	37	30.43
	IUML	22	13	7.19
	KCM	10	5	3.18
	CPM(K)	2	–	0.49
	Janadhipathiya Samrekshana Samiti (JPSS)	4	1	1.28
	Kerla Congress (Balakrishna Pallai)KEC(B)	2	1	0.64
	KCJ	4	2	1.14
	Independent (UDF Supported)	2	–	0.49
	BJP	127	–	5.48
	Independents (Rest)	634	1	2.51
	Other parties	160	–	1.50
	Total	**1201**	**140**	**100.00**
2001	**LDF**	140	40	43.69
	CPI	22	7	7.25
	CPI(M)	65	23	21.36
	NCP	9	2	2.60
	JD(S)	10	3	2.94
	RSP	6	2	1.71
	KEC	10	2	2.90
	Indian National League (INL)	1	–	0.29

Year		Seats Contested	Seats Won	Vote (%)
	Kerala: Performance of UDF and LDF Parties in Assembly Elections			
	Independent (LDF Supported)	17	1	4.64
	UDF	**140**	**99**	**49.07**
	Congress	88	62	31.40
	Muslim League	21	16	7.59
	KCM	11	9	3.54
	CPM(K)	2	1	0.61
	JPSS	5	4	1.78
	KEC(B)	2	2	0.72
	Revolutionary Socialist Party of Kerla – Bolshevik RSPK(B)	4	2	1.37
	KCJ	3	2	0.97
	Independent (UDF Supported)	4	1	1.09
	BJP	123	–	5.02
	Independents (Rest)	235	1	2.14
	Other parties	38	–	0.08
	Total	**676**	**140**	**100.00**
2006	**LDF**	**140**	**98**	48.63
	CPI	24	17	8.09
	CPI(M)	85	61	30.45
	NCP	2	1	0.64
	JD(S)	8	5	2.44
	RSP	4	3	1.44
	INL	3	1	0.90
	KEC	6	4	1.75
	Kerla Congress Secular (KCS)	1	1	0.31
	Congress (S)	1	1	0.47
	Independent (LDF Supported)	6	4	2.14
	UDF	**140**	**42**	**42.63**
	Congress	77	24	24.09

Year		Seats Contested	Seats Won	Vote (%)
	IUML	21	7	7.30
	Democratic Indira Congress (DIC)	17	1	4.27
	KCM	11	7	3.26
	JPSS	5	1	1.51
	CPM(K)	3	–	0.81
	KEC(B)	2	1	0.62
	RSP(B)	1	–	0.01
	Independent (UDF Supported)	3	1	0.76
	BJP	136	–	4.75
	Independents and other parties	515	–	3.99
	Total	**931**	**140**	**100.00**
2011	**LDF**	**140**	**68**	**44.94**
	CPI	27	13	8.72
	CPI(M)	84	45	28.18
	NCP	4	2	1.24
	Janata Dal (Secular)	5	4	1.52
	RSP	4	2	1.31
	KC(AM)	2	–	0.51
	INL	2	–	0.24
	Independent (LDF Supported)	12	2	3.22
	UDF	**140**	**72**	**45.84**
	Congress	81	38	26.40
	Muslim League	23	20	7.92
	KCM	15	9	4.94
	Socialist Janata (Democratic) SJD	6	2	1.65
	CPM(K)	2	–	0.65
	JPSS	4	–	1.31
	KEC(B)	2	1	0.72

Kerala: Performance of UDF and LDF Parties in Assembly Elections

Kerala: Performance of UDF and LDF Parties in Assembly Elections				
Year		Seats Contested	Seats Won	Vote (%)
	KCJ	3	1	0.91
	Kerala Revolutionary Socialist Party (Baby John)	1	1	0.37
	Independent (UDF Supported)	3	–	0.97
	BJP	138	–	6.03
	Independents and Other parties	553	–	3.19
	Total	971	140	100.00

7

Cracks in the Kerala Edifice

Factionalism, 'People's Plan', Shifting Social Base,
Opportunities for Revitalization

B y the 1970s, the Kerala communists had two huge achievements that they could boast of. They came to power for the first time in a sizeable province in a free and fair election in a democracy anywhere in the world. And they initiated and were largely responsible for what became famous as the Kerala Model, of reaching First World standards of social development even at low levels of income and growth, accompanied by a degree of social cohesion and high public awareness, civic engagement, and popular participation. The Left Democratic Front (LDF) government, led by the Communist Party of India (Marxist) [CPI(M)], was commended the world over for the success of the Kerala Model.

Kerala still continues to boast some of the best human development indices anywhere, especially in longevity, health, literacy and education. But there have been slippages and regressions, followed by recovery and improvement, and yet more ups and downs. This chapter surveys this record, especially since the early 1980s, looks at the major social, economic and political changes that have occurred, and analyses how well the Left adapted to these, and what its near-term prospect might be.

To summarize the results, Kerala's agriculture and traditional industries declined and growth slowed down for about a decade, producing a fiscal crisis. This affected employment and reduced public social-sector spending, eroding Kerala's lead in some indices and spurring privatization in health care. Emigrants' remittances and other factors rather than state intervention revived the economy, but created distortions by promoting consumption-led growth driven by construction, thus aggravating class inequalities and ecological destruction. This accelerated social retrogression and had a negative impact on the Left.

The People's Plan Campaign (1996), a radical decentralization programme, attempted to reverse this, but met with internal opposition and was abandoned. Issues of equity continued to be neglected and Kerala society moved rightwards. The Left's old social base has steadily eroded and its leadership has been de-radicalized. The Bharatiya Janata Party has recently made inroads into Kerala. The Left can regain lost ground only if it undertakes radical course correction.

Low Growth, High Unemployment

Weaknesses became apparent in the Kerala Model beginning with the mid-1980s or so, with noticeable stagnation in 'the spheres of employment and material production'. With its agriculture in crisis, and the government unable to resolve the crisis, Kerala became dependent for its food needs on other states. Industrial growth did not take off.[1] There was large-scale emigration to other parts of India and, beginning in the mid-1970s, to the Gulf. Employment was badly affected. Because of falling public spending, 'even the much acclaimed progress in education and health' looked 'vulnerable'.[2] These sectors underwent partial privatization.[3]

Between the 1970s and the late 1980s, Kerala's GDP growth rate decreased from 2.3 per cent to less than 1.2 per cent, compared to 4.1 per cent for the national economy.[4] Its overall industrial performance from the mid-1970s to the early 1990s was dismal, and the share of manufacturing in the state economy declined. Kerala's traditional industries like coir, cashew and handloom cloth experienced a decline in output and employment 'due to scarcity and escalation of prices of raw materials and increased competition'.[5]

Meanwhile, the fiscal crisis of the state worsened owing to economic stagnation, rising social expenditure and growing burden from subsidies, which the Centre passed on to the states. Kerala's revenue account deficit steadily increased. The mismatch between high social spending by the state, and low growth accompanied by a falling capacity of the state to finance its expenditure, raised questions about the sustainability of the Kerala Model. Talk of the 'crisis of the Kerala Model' soon entered mainstream discourse. Kerala earned 'the dubious distinction' of being the only state in India whose social expenditure decreased in real terms during the period between 1985–86 and 1991–92, compared to the decade from 1974–75 to 1984–85.[6]

This set alarm bells ringing. E.M.S. Namboodiripad, no less, warned that 'the praise that scholars shower on Kerala for its achievements' should not be allowed to 'divert attention from the intense economic crisis that we face. We are behind [the] other states of India in respect of economic growth, and a solution to this crisis brooks no delay. We can ignore our backwardness in respect of employment and production only at our own peril'.[7] The Model's 'crisis' demanded urgent solutions.

Yet, the fiscal crisis and falling social spending did not generate a vigorous debate on how the state could take remedial action by stimulating the economy, mobilizing more resources, improving efficiency in the delivery of public services, and reducing waste in its own unproductive expenditure even while strengthening a commitment to equity and inclusion of vulnerable groups. Rather, there was an unhealthy shift in policy discourse away from equity to raising GDP growth. This prolonged the stagnation that had set in in some of Kerala's human development indices—although they still remained far ahead of the rest of India, and could have improved with a little help from the state.

The economic crisis was initially camouflaged by the inflow of emigrants' remittances from the Persian Gulf region. 'Fortunately for Kerala, the migration to the Gulf began to pick up from mid-1970s—precisely the period when the downward trend in the regional economy became visible ... At the peak, the remittance inflows constituted as much as a quarter of the state domestic product'.[8] Remittances boosted Kerala's per capita income above the national average, but also led to a construction boom based on imports from other states.

The sphere that suffered the most under the slowdown was employment. The number of job seekers registered in employment exchanges, roughly three-fifths of whom were educated, rose almost tenfold between 1971 and 1991. During the 1980s, the number of the jobless spurted from 1.90 million (13 per cent of the labour force) to 3.64 million (20 per cent of the workforce).[9] In the early 1990s, Kerala's unemployment rate was about three times higher than the national average.[10]

Eminent economist K.P. Kannan analysed the dismal situation thus: '[The] unemployment rate is higher among the educated particularly those with middle level ... [education] ... Unemployment is higher in rural areas than in urban areas and it is acute among the younger generation ... As the general education level of the population increased over time, the problem of unemployment has tended to become one of educated unemployment ...Women have higher rates of unemployment with rural, young, school-educated women showing the highest incidence.'[11]

This meant that the gains Kerala's women had famously made in securing jobs were rapidly wiped out, the gap between male and female employment further widened, and women's labour force participation rates soon fell to levels that were among the lowest in India.[12] Women's employment got increasingly concentrated in low-paid, unskilled and casual jobs, with a strong tendency towards the feminization of poverty and an increase in the number of female-headed poor households.[13]

High unemployment led to rising withdrawal of women from public life. Despite higher levels of education and participation in grass-roots movements, women 'were conspicuously absent in the higher levels of decision-making'. Even in mass organizations where membership is predominantly of women, their representation in the leadership was 'marginal'. In the recent period, 'there are visible and disturbing signs of erosion of progressive attitudes to gender issues, like the spread of the dowry system, purdah amongst Muslims, degrading depiction of women in the mass media, sexual harassment and violence'.[14] These were all symptoms, as many commentators have noted, of deplorable slippages and regressions from past achievements.

The 1994 International Congress on Kerala Studies[15] discussed these. One of its sessions, on the social construction of gender, 'revealed several constituents of patriarchal ideology that have been deeply embedded in Kerala society and political culture. They called for a re-evaluation of the movements, institutions, customs and traditions from a gender perspective and development of a thoroughgoing critique of the patriarchal ideology from the positions of the left. Similarly the economic marginalization of women ... calls for a re-examination of development policies.'[16]

Many Groups Left Out

Women were not the sole group to have been left out as the Kerala Model went into a crisis. Many others suffered the same fate, including agricultural labourers (the number of days of employment for whom shrank,)[17] fisherfolk, coir workers, female domestic servants, female stone cutters, tribal people, migrant workers from Tamil Nadu and many head-load workers and other casual labourers, comprising 'up to 15 per cent of Kerala's people'.[18] This proportion was by no means negligible.

Although Dalits were relatively better off in Kerala than in the rest of India, their 'relative backwardness' persisted.[19] Two communities totally failed to gain benefits from Kerala's social development and welfare programmes: 'the tribals in the hills on the high eastern fringes of the state and the fishing communities on the coastal front along the western fringe'.[20]

'In the case of the fishing communities—particularly the Muslim and Catholic among them—the control of religious interests and the economic domination by merchants and middlemen from within the communities, who in turn had considerable influence over organized religious affairs, gave credibility to the perception held by political parties in the state that fishing communities were "vote banks" to be wooed only at election time.'[21] In 1991, infant mortality among fisherfolk was an alarming *five times higher* than for Kerala as a whole, and the community's population growth rate was 2.3 per cent, compared to 1.9 per cent for Kerala.[22] Fisherfolk deprivation has proved persistent.

The Kerala Model's crisis went hand in hand with another crisis: that of environmental destruction and degradation, 'which threatens the quality of life and reduces the resource base that must be tapped to sustain the main elements of the Model'.[23] Loss of high-quality forest cover resulted in soil erosion in the highlands and waterlogging of lowland areas. Kerala's environmental problems include water and air pollution, and 'possible overfishing of some offshore regions',[24] not to speak of the growing chemicalization of agriculture.

No wonder Kerala witnessed a series of conflicts over environmental issues, ranging from dams, access to land and water, energy projects, and pollution. These increasingly pitted local communities and environmental activists, including those of the Left-inclined people's science movement Kerala Sasthra Sahitya Parishad (KSSP), against state policies and private interests.

Better known—and more successful—among these was the confrontation over the Silent Valley hydroelectricity project, which would have destroyed a pristine rainforest. The project was eventually cancelled, a great victory for the KSSP.[25] There were many other struggles too: against a highly polluting rayon factory of Grasim Industries in Kozhikode (Calicut) on the Chaliyar river, which discharged cancer-causing chemicals as well as highly toxic mercury and lead, and against a planned nuclear power plant at Peringome in Kannur in 1991 (which led to its cancellation).[26]

By the mid-1980s, 'serious doubts were being expressed as to the desirability of the Kerala "model" in health', wrote a health expert, who pointed to Kerala's high and growing morbidity patterns.[27] He cited a pioneering study,[28] and its corroboration by a statewide KSSP survey and various micro-studies,[29] to argue that despite Kerala's impressive health indices, there was '... no conscious policy effort to create an equitable health system which would offer health security to all. What was described as the Kerala "model" in health is a demographic transition that occurred faster than in many other parts of the world, bringing down death and birth rates within the span of a single generation. This was the result of a political environment that emphasized rights, and a policy thrust that ensured rights in education and health.'[30]

Like health, education in Kerala too did not present an edifying picture from the 1980s onwards. In contrast to Kerala's historic achievements in literacy, and its success in enrolling and retaining students in elementary and middle schools, some 'qualitative aspects' of its primary education system were described as 'distressing': studies showed that Kerala ranked low among its learning achievement. About 30 per cent of the children who complete primary school 'do not reach the necessary achievement levels in literacy and numeracy'. Kerala's middle schools reported high dropout rates among Dalit and adivasi students.[31]

In higher education, a study found that Kerala was a laggard with respect to many states in the 1980s, with a gross enrolment ratio in the relevant age group of under 4 per cent, compared to the national ratio of 6 per cent, with only eighty institutions of higher education (national average ninety-nine) per one lakh population, and with a preponderance of private colleges (over 80 per cent of the total).[32]

The crisis of the Kerala Model came under critical scrutiny in several seminars and conferences, including an International Conference on Kerala's Development Experience (organized by the Institute of Social Sciences in New Delhi in 1996),[33] besides a number of papers in academic journals. The crisis 'paved the way for an ideological backlash against the Left. The dominance of the Left in the state was alleged to be the stumbling block for economic progress. Trade unions and strikes for higher wages were blamed for the economic retardation, land reforms for agricultural stagnation, education for high unemployment, and social welfare expenditure for the fiscal crisis. Equity in Kerala, it was argued, was achieved at the cost of future economic progress.'[34]

New Challenges

Some of these arguments are questionable, if not altogether specious, because they hold that growth and equity can never be complementary, they are always mutually incompatible.[35] Apart from being rooted in neoclassical dogma, this proposition is ahistorical and disproved by Kerala's own experience for three decades after Independence. However, there could be little doubt about the reality of economic stagnation, the crisis of petty production, the fiscal crisis of the state, and growing unemployment in the 1980s.

The consequences, in particular growing unemployment, converted reservations in jobs for Dalits and backward castes 'into a hotly contested issue and a cause for casteist mobilization'. Stagnation in productivity became 'a major factor in the accentuation of the conflict between petty producers and wage labourers'.[36] Yet regrettably, there seems to have been very little discussion among LDF policymakers in the late 1980s or early 1990s on revitalizing Kerala's economy along non-conventional lines—for instance, by creating avenues in which foreign remittances could be productively invested, and by finding new pathways to agricultural and industrial growth.

To their credit, progressive intellectuals, many of them unaffiliated to the Left parties, but some party members too, suggested some alternative approaches. One such informal proposal was to break the agrarian impasse not by reviving conventional cereal production, but by promoting high-value alternatives like medicinal plants, vanilla beans, herbs, flowers, etc., besides encouraging collective farming. Another was to set up industrial cooperatives and joint sector companies in fields where Kerala enjoyed a natural advantage related to skills or natural resources, such as modern fisheries or 'sunrise' sectors like electronics and information technology.[37] Regrettably, these did not result in concrete policy packages or well-rounded plans of action.[38]

Such proposals did not evoke much resonance from within the LDF, and certainly found no expression in its policies. There was little discussion within the LDF—when it was in power from 1987 to 1991, or after 1996, when it returned to office—on ways of strengthening the equitable distribution of the fruits of growth by focusing on the marginalized or strengthening social security measures.[39]

For reasons which had little to do with state intervention, Kerala's economy turned around in the late 1980s, and its GDP growth rate rose to the all-India level, close to 6 per cent a year. By the early 1990s, Kerala's growth rate (about 9 per cent) and per capita income had surpassed the national average.[40] It also resumed its lead over the rest of India in human development indicators.

By the beginning of the present century, Kerala's life expectancy at birth was 73.3 years, which compared well with Asian countries such as South Korea, Malaysia, China and Indonesia, which achieved high levels of per capita income in recent years. With a Human Development Index value of 0.790, Kerala belongs, along with Cuba and Uruguay, to the top quarter of the UN Development Programme's high-HDI group, way above India's rank of 134 among 187 countries, which places it in the bottom quarter of the 'medium development' group.

Kerala's female-to-male ratio, which is 1.058, is similar to that of Europe and North America, and substantially higher than the figures for China (0.94) or the rest of India (0.93). The infant mortality rate is only thirteen per thousand live births. Besides the fact that there is no female disadvantage on any of the indicators related to health status, the relative advantage seems to have increased over time.

For instance, women in Kerala, who used to live only a year longer than men in the 1950s, were expected to live 5.5 years longer in the 1990s, whereas in India as a whole, women were expected to live only 1.2 years longer than men. Kerala is well ahead of other major Indian states in achieving the goal of universalizing elementary education, which is reflected in its literacy rate of over 90 per cent, and almost universal enrolment and very low dropout rates at the primary and middle level.[41]

However, beneath these commendable achievements lie serious problems and challenges, some of which are the consequences of the Kerala Model's early success, followed by its faltering during the 1980s. As K.P. Kannan puts it: 'Kerala has gone "beyond the basics", signifying its transcendence of the first threshold of the development challenge. It now has to grapple with the second-generation challenges,' whose 'meaning and content are also undergoing deep changes'. But Kerala's 'otherwise active public domain' is 'yet to absorb the full significance' of the 'remarkable transformations' that have occurred during the last two decades 'so as to prepare itself for meeting' these challenges.[42]

The Left has not yet fully comprehended these new challenges or developed solutions to them. For instance, demographic change has resulted in a total fertility rate (average number of children per couple) of 1.7, below the replacement rate of around two, and also reduced inter-religious disparities and gender biases. The challenge is how to take 'care of an ageing population whose share [in the total] is twice the national average'. Kerala has not devised a comprehensive policy for doing this.

The health transition has both positive and negative features. On the positive side of the balance sheet is steady improvement in many health and nutrition indices. For instance, Kerala's women now report India's lowest incidence of anaemia, and its Muslim women are the least anaemic among women belonging to four broad groups (SC/ST, OBCs, Muslims and Others) across all the states.

Privatization of Health Care

However, on the negative side, Kerala's health care system faces the onslaught of privatization. The number of beds in public hospitals increased by a mere 5.5 per cent between 1986 and 1996 to about 38,000, whereas the number in private institutions rose by almost 40 per cent to 67,500.[43] The pace of privatization further rose, 'making way for a new breed of highly commercialized and explicitly profit-seeking institutions. Large-scale privatization of health created a big market in health-related goods and services, many of them unproven and perhaps even unnecessary.'[44]

Kerala's public expenditure on health and family welfare fell both as a percentage of total state expenditure (from 9.34 per cent in 1990–91 to 4.74 per cent in 2007–08) and as a percentage of its domestic product (from 1.75 to 0.9 per cent). Quality of service in the public sector deteriorated due to inadequate supply of equipment, drugs and service personnel: 'Some 70 per cent of the poor now rely on the private sector ... [and are] forced to spend as much as 40 per cent of their income on healthcare as against 2.4 per cent by the rich.'[45] High health spending on account of treating major illnesses has become a significant factor in pushing people below the poverty line.[46]

Overemphasis on curative care in the private sector meant that public health and related issues were neglected in doctors' training; and 'medical specialization was over-emphasized, leading to a health sector dominated by specialists and procedures, but woefully lacking skills in meeting basic public health functions'.[47] By 2005, 'more than two-thirds of the curative aspects of healthcare' were 'in the private sector without government support'.[48]

Kerala's educational transition 'is manifested in the size and structure of the student population, the prominent role of girls ... the demand for higher education, the migration of students in search of quality education and the impact of education ... Consequently, from a peak of 59 lakh students in schools (from class one to ten) in 1991, the number declined to 51 lakh in 2001 and to 43 lakh in 2011...'[49] It is set to decline further, below the level warranted by demographic factors.

There is growing 'feminization of higher education, with girls currently constituting ... 76 per cent at the undergraduate level and 74 per cent at the postgraduate level. They are certainly catching up with boys in technical education with 62 per cent in industrial training institutions, 27 per cent in polytechnics and 32 per cent in engineering degree courses.' This is partly because young males face greater compulsion to work at an early stage than do young women.[50]

At the same time, a survey showed that 3.1 lakh students from Kerala were studying outside the state in 2011, mostly in undergraduate and postgraduate courses, of whom 40 per cent were girls—in contrast to Kerala's total enrolment in higher education of just around 2.5 lakh. Very few students from other states come to Kerala because of its poor or mediocre higher education system.[51]

Kerala has made a transition from an agrarian to a non-agrarian economy. The latter now accounts for 74 per cent of the state domestic product and 68 per cent of total employment, in contrast to about 40 per cent for India. This change has proved extremely problematic. Its prime driving force has been construction and services, financed primarily by remittances from emigrants, predominantly in the Gulf. Such migration, now equivalent to 17 per cent of Kerala's labour force, contributes about 30 per cent to the state's income—'historically unprecedented for any economy'.[52]

Emigrants' remittances are typically invested in real estate in the cities. This has led to unprecedented urbanization—Kerala's urban population is now 48 per cent of the total, according to the 2011 census—disrupting a well-established urban–rural continuum, and engendering a runaway construction boom, which generates enormous quantities of solid waste. Municipal bodies are singularly ill-prepared to manage this. Waste disposal is precipitating a social conflict as educated and highly conscious villagers openly revolt against the dumping of urban waste in their backyards.[53]

The construction boom has spawned the growth of haphazard quarrying and sand mining which has fractured and literally mutilated river beds all over the state. Sand mining yields huge profits, which allow the emerging sand mafia to circumvent regulations, 'often in connivance with the local political and bureaucratic class'. Wetlands, mangroves, forests and paddy fields are under the threat of numerous mafias. Digging for soil to fill up low-lying areas, including rice fields, is destroying natural hydrology. Vulnerable ecosystems are being undermined to construct tourist resorts and 'theme parks' in the name of 'boosting economic growth' via private profit. In recent years, such ecologically destructive activities have gathered enormous momentum.[54]

Lapsing into Illiteracy

Under the impact of these processes, and the social disruptions they bring in their wake, Kerala has become 'a fast-globalizing regional economy under a national dispensation of a neo-liberal policy regime that has elevated "growth at any cost" as a paramount national objective. Instead of graduating to an expected higher threshold of social welfare and human development with equity as a core value,' Kerala now presents 'a picture of uninhibited prosperity for some, resulting in sharply rising economic inequality with its expected social correlates…' This is bound to have 'unanticipated and adverse consequences'.[55]

These recently manifested themselves in a partial reversal of Kerala's historic gains in literacy. Kerala was declared India's first 'wholly literate' state in 1991, when Chelakkodan Ayesha, a Muslim woman from a remote village in Malappuram district, read out a Quranic verse to a 100,000-strong crowd in Kozhikode city. By 2002, she reportedly lapsed back into illiteracy—like twelve lakh others in Kerala, according to an estimate by the Centre for Development Studies.[56] Kerala's literacy rate was estimated in the early years of the twenty-first century to have fallen to 'around 80 to 85 per cent instead of the 95 per cent' that was achieved through the Total Literacy Campaign; it now probably ranks number four in India.[57]

Once known for a degree of social cohesion and solidarity, Kerala is increasingly marked by social discontent, anomie and disequilibrium. It has India's highest rate of suicides (9,000 reported suicide deaths a year, and 80,000 attempts), alcoholism (liquor consumption three times higher than India's average), and crime (306.1 per 1,000 people per year, almost double the national rate of 176.7).[58]

For long decades, Kerala rightly boasted India's highest overall sex ratio, with more than 1,040 females per 1,000 males. But it witnessed a distressing decline in the ratio for young girls in the zero-to-six age group: from 976 girls per 1,000 boys in 1971, to 962 in 2001, to 959 in 2011. There were about 100 ultrasound centres in the state a decade ago, now there are close to 850. Although it is difficult to prove this conclusively, a part of this increase probably indicates a sharp rise in sex-selective abortions or incidence of female feticide, which was until recently unknown in Kerala.[59]

Kerala has become notorious for violence against women (reported by 23 per cent of them), and large-scale prevalence of sexual harassment: 71 per cent of women in an interview-based survey by six women journalists said that travel in Kerala is unsafe for women.[60] Several recent cases of rape and sexual violence against women became a cause for concern not only because of the brutality involved, but also because of their deplorable sensationalization in the media.

One of the worst of these was the Suryanelli case of 1996, involving a high-school student from Idukki district, who was reportedly handed over to a prostitution ring and sexually assaulted over forty days by forty-two men, including politicians and influential professionals. The episode itself, the way the media reported it, the judgments passed by the higher judiciary, and the treatment of the case in cinema, all point to a terrible coarsening of Kerala's public discourse, and its appetite for voyeurism and tolerance of vicious gender- and caste-based prejudice.[61]

This is part of the process of corrosion and degradation of Kerala's public culture which has been in evidence especially since the early 1990s. The grand traditions of collectivist thought and practice that prevailed earlier have given way to tawdry forms of individualism and consumerism. Left initiatives like the library movement, film societies, and theatre and music performances by travelling troupes have become virtually extinct; the traditions of political meetings, mass rallies and public oratory have more or less collapsed; gaudy display of wealth is considered normal and acceptable in Kerala's public spaces,[62] as is aggressive strutting by testosterone-driven alpha males.

Kerala's public discourse used to be marked by forceful interventions on major issues by writers, academics and intellectuals, who would vociferously protest against infractions of political decency and decorum and violations of human rights. Today, few intellectuals protest even against the sexual harassment of women in the streets, display of rank communal bigotry, mindless violence, hate crimes, assassinations of political leaders, or inter-party vendettas leading to multiple murders and revenge killings, as happens in north Malabar with sickening frequency.[63]

One of the more egregious recent 'political' murders was the assassination in May 2012 of a CPI(M) rebel leader, T.P. Chandrasekharan, who set up an independent Left party called the Revolutionary Communist Party. Chandrasekharan was barbarically hacked to death. A senior CPI(M) leader from another district brazenly justified the killing. In January 2014, a special sessions court convicted twelve of the accused, including three CPI(M) leaders, for the murder.[64] Astonishingly, this revolting episode evoked only very feeble protests from traditional supporters of the Left within the otherwise vocal intelligentsia. But as we see below, the murder had a significant political impact.

All these deficits, slippages and retrogressions pointed with urgency to a huge agenda of corrective actions, which could only be drawn up on the basis of serious and honest introspection on Kerala's growing social, cultural, economic and political crises and their causes. Kerala's progressive intellectuals, including some senior leaders of the Left parties, engaged in such much-needed introspection in the mid-1990s. They tried to analyse the implications for the state of the neo-liberal policy course taken by the Central government earlier, which was clearly biased against the poor and underprivileged, but which the Kerala government was under pressure to adopt as well.

People's Plan Campaign

Some of these intellectuals were preoccupied with economic matters. They were convinced that to avoid getting discredited, the Left in Kerala would have to adopt a coherent alternative to neo-liberalism. They debated a few options, including further decentralization of development-related decision making and related measures to create what might be called a 'new' Kerala Model, which could help rebuild the Left parties' links with the plebeian classes and rejuvenate radical politics.

A strong sentiment emerged among them, especially economists, in favour of radical devolution of powers to village panchayats. When the Left Democratic Front returned to power in 1996 after a hiatus of five years, it adopted an ambitious new policy: of devolving as much as 35–40 per cent of its Ninth Five-Year Plan outlay to local self-government bodies for projects and programmes to be formulated by them, based on thorough, bottom-up, people's participation.

A mobilization was then launched, called People's Campaign for Decentralized Planning—more informally, People's Plan Campaign (PPC)—to help the local bodies prepare their development plans. Funds would be transferred to finance the plans without waiting for the local administrative capacity to build up. According to T.M. Thomas Isaac, the campaign's main architect, and a member of the State Planning Board, the PPC sought to transform 'existing state institutions into empowered deliberative bodies'[65]—an ambitious goal indeed.

The CPI(M)'s adoption of the PPC surprised many analysts who rightly noted the party's traditional aversion to decentralization and its preference for top-down command structures. Some of them suggested that the reasons lay in the CPI(M)'s recognition of the limits of its own electoral appeal amidst an exhaustion of the 'redistributive capacities of the developmental state' and failures of dirigisme; hence it saw the need for 'de-bureaucratised government and sustainable development', with a greater role for civil society.[66]

A more mundane reason might be that Namboodiripad, Kerala's tallest communist, endorsed the PPC and became the chairperson of the High-Level Guidance Council of the People's Campaign. He underlined his commitment to decentralization: 'Our greatest assets are our mass organizations and the democratic consciousness of our people. The combined strength of all mass organizations in the state is about ten million. Besides, there is a vast network of cooperative organizations ... such as ... the library and literacy movements ... I feel that one big question that we face is whether the organized strength and political consciousness of our people can be used to increase production and productivity. I want to answer in the affirmative. But there is a precondition: the government and the ruling classes must change their attitude to the organizations of the people and their demands ... I must emphasize the importance of democratic decentralization in this context'[67].

Decentralized planning of the PPC variety had never been attempted before in India—'or perhaps anywhere else in the world. It involved an extraordinary mobilization of volunteers and several rounds of intensive training of large numbers of people, on a scale that has probably never been matched anywhere.'[68] The activities involved the mobilization of huge numbers of people in grama sabha (village council) meetings and local development seminars, and in forming task forces to address complex issues.

An estimated 1.8 million people took part in grama sabha deliberations in each of the first two years; in the first year more than 300,000 people attended local development seminars for training purposes. These are huge numbers indeed, comparable to those mobilized, for instance, in the 'participatory budgeting' campaigns of Latin America, in particular the initiative launched by the Workers' Party in Brazil in its more radical phase under Luiz Inacio Lula da Silva. But there seems to have been little dialogue or cross-fertilization between these campaigns, from which they would have mutually gained a good deal.

The KSSP did most of the groundwork for PPC activities, especially identification of local needs and resources, drafting of project proposals and preparation of training programmes. The KSSP based itself on practical knowledge and ideas drawn from a twenty-five-year repertoire of local-level initiatives and planning experiments, which included local resource mapping[69] to develop a database on human and natural resources, and raise people's environmental consciousness; experiments in group farming and vegetable cultivation with organic fertilizers and bio-pesticides; small-scale hydroelectricity production; developing smokeless cooking stoves; building artificial reefs; and rejuvenating public health, literacy and education programmes through popular involvement.[70.]

The most important experiment was from Kalliasseri in Kannur district, which had a long history of CPI(M) and KSSP activism. This included producing vegetables and eggs locally—the area's 30,000 people daily consumed 20,000 eggs, but produced none—cleaning up canals and building new canals and roads with voluntary labour, raising energy efficiency, improving drainage, and so on. This created a strong base of local ecological zone-based planning spread over twenty-five panchayats.

The State Planning Board, which designed the PPC, drew on this knowledge and the CPI(M) and KSSP's experience. The PPC was conducted in six phases: galvanising grama sabhas; preparation of panchayat development reports for discussion at development seminars; formation of task forces to translate seminar proposals into actual projects; formulation of plans, with a further round of training; integration of block and district panchayat plans; and finally, appraisal of the plans by a Voluntary Technical Corps—partly recruited from retired government officials and skilled volunteers, itself impressive in strength, with 3,000 members.[71]

The achievements of the PPC were significant in scale and numbers. But above all, they lay in the political change it brought about by devolving funds and establishing a participatory process in the face of opposition and resistance from a number of sources including the bureaucracy, commercial banks and party leaders, and an avalanche of criticism from sections of the media. For instance, say Issac and Franke, some newspapers ran such a hostile campaign against the PPC just before the 1998 local body elections as would drain 'the optimism of even the best enthusiasts'.[72]

'Forcing Its Own Hand'

Despite this, by adopting the PPC, the government did something unusual, say Issac and Franke: 'In a sense, [it] launched a movement to force its own hand radically to restructure the mode of governance.'[73]

Among the great merits of the People's Plan was that it promoted participatory programmes like local resource mapping: community-based surveys of natural resources in a village, and an assessment of its people's needs for food, water, energy, transportation, etc., leading to the collective determination of the best ways of marrying the two in cost-effective, equitable and environmentally sound ways.

The PPC experimented with new activities like dairying and ran modest but significant projects for Sangha Krishi or collective farming through pooling and sharing of resources, including labour. It also brought about greater coordination between different institutions such as the State Planning Board, KSSP, Kerala Agriculture University, Centre for Earth Science Studies and so on.

Yet, the PPC's achievements were not sustained for long and should not be overemphasized. The claim by its architects that it was creating 'a new civic culture' deserves to be interrogated. Its implementation was tardy because it followed an extremely complicated multistage process, with numerous seminars, training programmes, and village- and higher-level meetings, which did not conform to the planning schedules and the tight timelines that were set. As its architects themselves admit: 'There was lack of proper planning in the implementation of developmental works and a strict time-schedule was seldom adhered to ... Rather than initiating the works at the commencement of a fiscal year, the entire exercise ... was rushed through towards the fag end with the result that their very purpose was defeated in most cases.'[74.] At the end of the first year, the panchayats could only spend one-tenth of the earmarked funds. Levels of non-utilization remained high through the PPC's first four years.

The grama sabhas and other local bodies were charged not only with setting the overall development goals and priorities, which was their legitimate function, but also with onerous technical and administrative tasks that they were simply not capable of handling. There were very few innovative projects. Allocations to productive sectors were way below the recommended levels. And many programmes were gender-insensitive or simply failed to involve women.[75]

The PPC, some critics said, was launched without proper delineation and devolution of authority, both administrative and operational. 'The whole exercise came to rest in the hands of people with no experience of the planning process.... Used to measly allotments of a few lakhs, these local bodies found themselves wallowing in money. Lacking expertise to make [the] best use of this money, they opted for the conventional route of expenditure. Invariably, the funds were spent not so much on asset creation as for patronage ...'[76] In the initial years a good chunk of money was used to distribute cows, sheep and goats and so on—schemes reminiscent of Congress-sponsored 'loan melas'.[77]

'The real damage' lay in the choice of beneficiaries, which 'smacked of partisan politics'. Non-beneficiaries distanced themselves from the whole process; many stopped attending grama sabha meetings. LDF partners, especially the CPI, were uneasy with the setting up of expert committees to scrutinize and vet development plans. 'Their main objection was that, conceptually, the expert committee went against the grain of [the PPC] in that a non-elective, quasi-official body was given the power to scrutinise and even scuttle plans and programmes passed by elected representatives.'[78.]

'Open Warfare'

Independent but sympathetic social scientists also expressed their scepticism about some of the assumptions underlying the PPC. For instance, while reviewing Isaac and Franke's book, Robin Jeffrey interrogates their claim that 'democracy in Kerala has so far been linked to redistribution, but Kerala now seeks to link it to increasing production', and asks: 'But will the two—can the two—be linked in practice? Is it not just as likely that 900 panchayats will spend money in uncoordinated and unproductive ways, concerned to build a toilet block here and a piped water supply there, but with no overall plans for investment that will lead to sustain production and employment?'[79]

Several weaknesses, imbalances and flaws in the conceptualization and execution of the People's Plan, as well as its strengths and benefits, were analysed in a Planning Commission report.[80] The flaws include a narrow overemphasis on roads and bridges, neglect of agriculture, lack of a watershed-based approach, uneven participation at different levels of decision making, lack of involvement of educated youth, absence of links between discrete projects and state plans, and 'information failure' which impedes attendance by SC/ST villagers, etc.

An even more basic criticism comes from social scientist Rajan Gurukkal, who argues that the PPC largely remained 'a constitutional reform of development administration stabilising the status quo, rather than leading to alternate institutional development' and the rise of a 'people-centred politics and the entailing empowerment-oriented praxis' which should trigger 'struggles over access to, and distribution of, critical resources, and initiating structural changes in the local power relations'.[81]

'What has been attempted in Kerala so far', says Gurukkal, 'is decentralised planning, which involved transfer of several tasks and responsibilities from the state-level authorities and bureaucracy to local public bodies or government-controlled institutions … Nevertheless, this transfer of power is being impeded both by the conflicts between the ruling front and the opposition as well as the cleavage in the government between "centralisers", represented by bureaucrats and "decentralisers", represented by left politicians. On the whole the decentralised planning has been working generally as a state-induced administrative reform from above'—despite 'some indications of empowerment of civil institutions and organizations at the local level'.[82]

Politically, the PPC proved extremely divisive. The Congress-led United Democratic Front saw it as a politically partisan programme and criticized it. Worse, the PPC met with resistance from within the CPI(M). 'Open warfare' broke out between a section of the party leadership and its trade union wing, the Centre of Indian Trade Unions (CITU), which was opposed to large-scale devolution of power to local bodies. This is 'said to have contributed hugely' to the party's poor performance in the local panchayat polls and the 1998 Lok Sabha elections, and also affected the PPC. A number of party members who worked hard for the success of the People's Plan were refused tickets as candidates. Some rebelled and fought as independents. This too damaged the LDF electorally.[83]

Many senior CPI(M) leaders, including Chief Minister E.K. Nayanar, were uncomfortable with the PPC. 'Barring EMS none of the top leaders' was seen as committed to the idea of decentralization concept and the PPC—unlike the Total Literacy Campaign earlier.[84]

They did not raise their voice against the PPC because Namboodiripad had endorsed it. But they did not put their heart into it. Nor did many leaders see it as part of a strategy to unite people at the grass-roots level, to empower them to shape the way they fulfil their aspirations for a better life through 'their own plans', to raise their consciousness and politicize their struggles.[85]

Eventually, the PPC was abandoned mainly because it was opposed from within the CPI(M). It also had rather limited acceptance outside political circles. Says the highly regarded political analyst B.R.P. Bhaskar: 'Most of the non-party experts who were associated with the People's Plan programme became disillusioned with it as they felt it was used to promote party interests. In many places the panchayat process got discredited as a result of partisanship. Thanks to politicization, people were disillusioned and did not attend the mandatory grama sabhas. In the absence of a quorum, meetings were often not held. Yet, fictitious records of meetings were created within minutes'.[86]

To sum up the discussion so far, the LDF initiated the Kerala Model, which despite its weaknesses, produced India's best human development record. This still remains unsurpassed. When the model ran into a crisis in the early 1980s, very little was done to address the underlying causes, which were rooted in cutting public spending on the social sector. Market forces and spontaneous economic processes, including migration, remittances and speculative activities, relieved pressure on the state. But a decade on, policy discourse had moved away from equity to GDP growth. Distortions had crept into the economy and society, and privatization had sunk roots in health care and education. A new, radical alternative has not replaced the old model. The PPC was no substitute for a new model.

The ADB Loan Issue

From the 1990s onwards, the Kerala Left came perilously close to adopting market-friendly economic approaches, although it never embraced neo-liberalism the way the Left Front in West Bengal did. For instance, the LDF government initiated talks with the Asian Development Bank (ADB) in 1996 and 1998 for a 'project and policy' loan to turn the state's finances around and boost economic growth; LDF leaders did so without discussing the matter in the CPI(M) state secretariat or with the Front's coalition partners.[87]

The loan agreement was later signed under a UDF government for three sets of 'reforms': a 'modernising government programme' and fiscal reform; power sector reforms; and a 'sustainable urban development, environmental improvement and poverty reduction programme'. The agreement imposed familiar conditions such as fiscal adjustment, adherence to 'market principles', and levying of increased taxes in education, health and water, and higher tariffs in the power sector.

The linking of state finances and governance in Kerala with the ADB was strongly opposed by various groups such as trade unions, socially concerned scholars, women's organizations, environmentalists and student activists. In May 2002, protest demonstrations broke out under the banner of the 'ADB-Quit Kerala' campaign. The Left parties too joined these under public pressure and pledged that they would not repay the ADB loan if they came to power. Yet, when the LDF did come to power in May 2006, it went back on its earlier stand and began to catalyse the full implementation of the ADB package.[88]

A fight broke out between the CPI and the CPI(M), and between two factions of the latter, over who was responsible for signing the deal, in particular the requirement to meter public water taps under the third 'reform'.[89] Public opposition mounted. Eventually, Chief Minister V.S. Achuthanandan weighed in strongly against continuing with the agreement. And finance minister T.M. Thomas Isaac succeeded in not implementing the first two components of it, without paying a penalty.[90]

However, there was another questionable project, on piped drinking water supply, launched by the UDF and financed by the World Bank, to which the LDF offered very little resistance. The Kerala Rural Water Supply and Sanitation Agency set up in 1996 was not a high-profile affair. It was limited to four districts. But under this scheme driven by demand and beneficiary group, a silent shift took place from a 'right to water' approach, to treating water as an 'economic good' or 'commodity', with a considerable increase in capital costs and user charges.[91]

The economic and social processes set in motion in the late 1970s inevitably made their impact felt in Kerala politics two decades on, with a gradual weakening of the appeal of the LDF and the old agendas identified with it, and a general drift towards right-wing ideas. The PPC did not have enough political impact to stem this trend. The LDF lost the 2001 assembly elections to the Congress-led United Democratic Front. The UDF did not jettison the PPC altogether, but renamed and recast it to deny credit to the LDF.

When the LDF returned to power in 2006 after another five-year break, it did not consider it necessary to revive or restore the People's Plan or some of the other worthy initiatives that accompanied it, such as local resource mapping. Instead, the LDF promoted another flagship programme: the Kudumbashree Poverty Alleviation Mission, a revised and expanded form of the Centre's self-help group programme, combined with devolution of powers to the panchayats. This is a far tamer reform, but it too has attracted charges of politicization, and a powerful feminist critique of some of its patriarchal premises.[92]

Nevertheless, Kudumbashree has achieved significant success in promoting women's participation and political mobilization and created opportunities for innovative schemes for local development and governance, making Kerala one of India's top performers in panchayati raj programmes. Women account for a high 52 per cent of the panchayats' elected members, and play a major role in the implementation of Kudumbashree services and schemes.[93]

A 'Hindu' Party?

The LDF narrowly lost the 2011 Assembly election, and did not rise to expectations in the 2014 Lok Sabha election, winning just eight of the twenty seats despite the UDF's vulnerability on account of various corruption scandals. The CPI(M) took a unilateral decision in 2014 to field politbureau member M.A. Baby from Kollam, a constituency held prior to 1999 by the RSP, which had been demanding its return from the CPI(M). When the CPI(M) refused to stand Baby down, the RSP walked out of the LDF, and its candidate N.K. Premachandran won the seat.[94]

In 2014, the BJP polled close to 11 per cent of the vote, and surpassed the LDF in many assembly segments (for example, in four of the seven segments that fall in the Thiruvananthapuram Lok Sabha constituency). Hindu communalism represents a grave new and growing danger in Kerala, which until recently was seemingly inhospitable to it. The BJP is electorally targeting specific caste groups like the Nairs and Ezhavas through their opportunist caste leaders, with some success. Sections of the Ezhavas, the communists' traditional support base, are gravitating towards the BJP, although the LDF parties still command close to majority support among them.[95]

Despite its secular ideology, the CPI(M) carries a major burden on the communalism–secularism question in Kerala because of its past alliances with communal parties and individuals. In the 1967 assembly elections, it roped in the Indian Union Muslim League (IUML) and the Karshaka (peasant) Thozhilali (worker) Party (KTP) (formed by Father Joseph Vadakkan to protect the interests of forest encroachers) into a winning seven-party alliance.[96] This bestowed respectability on these communal organizations and whitewashed their record of joining the Congress-led campaign to overthrow the first communist ministry. It tainted the CPI(M) as a party partial to minority communalism.

For a variety of reasons, the very opposite has happened in recent years. The Kerala CPI(M) is increasingly seen as a 'Hindu' party, or at least as a party dependent on a predominantly Hindu voter base,[97] in contrast to its opponents in the UDF, who are strongly supported by Muslims and Christians (probably for parochial–communal reasons).

Muslims and Christians account for respectively 24.7 and 19.0 per cent of Kerala's population,[98] but their share in the CPI(M)'s membership in Kerala is much lower: just under 10 per cent in the case of Muslims, and probably even lower for Christians.[99] Hindus constitute 90 per cent of the membership of party committees at different levels, and of affiliate organizations like the Students' Federation of India and the Democratic Youth Federation. Their non-Hindu members, unlike the Hindu communists, 'are often disowned by their communities as having no relation with the Church or the Muslim religious establishments', according to Ninan Koshy.[100] This was not always so.[101]

Among the reasons for the CPI(M)'s unflattering image in this regard is that it has not tried to draw Muslim and Christian youth into its activities on the basis of a principled, uncompromisingly secular programme and a universal appeal cutting across communities, so much as by approaching them through their 'community' identities and through their religious leaders whom it placates.[102] Koshy holds that 'the approach of the CPI(M) to the minorities is not very different from that of the Congress: [one of] treating them as a vote bank. You can hear party leaders declaring that they will protect "minority rights" and "minority interests". The fact is that in Kerala (as far as Christians are concerned) minority rights are used for the elite in the community and minority interests are the interests of the Christian establishment … When campaigning in the elections and when in power their interlocutors are the bishops and [the] hierarchy. There is no discussion with secular Christians who support the Left even on the so-called minority matters …'[103]

Like its counterpart in West Bengal, the CPI(M) in Kerala too has failed to educate its cadres and supporters on the question of secularism by stressing its centrality to a democratic, pluralist and non-parochial conception of socialism, or by developing and propagating a foundational critique of Hindutva based on ideological, sociocultural and political grounds. Nor has it promoted active citizen solidarity across religious communities on issues that go beyond confessional identities.

Both the CPI(M) and CPI allied with the Indian Union Muslim League in the past. By doing so, they lost a precious opportunity to build an independent following among the Moplah peasantry and sharecroppers of Malabar and take on the peasants' oppressors who are strongly represented in the conservative Muslim League. Coupled with the Left's failure to start a fruitful secular conversation across different religious groups, this is one of the main reasons for the persistence of Kerala's rigidly community- and caste-based pattern of electoral politics. Despite the roots that progressive and radical ideas have sunk into Kerala's soil over decades, the Left has failed to break this pattern.

The CPI(M) will find it hard to counter the BJP and will have to cede ground to it unless it itself pursues a radically different, credible agenda which has a secular, universal, popular, trans-community appeal akin to its past programmes of agrarian and educational reform or its social security policies. It is not clear if the party or its allies can summon up the will to do so.

The People's Plan Campaign, despite all its limitations, was the last major policy initiative taken by the LDF. Since 2001, the Front has been too preoccupied with internal problems, and its constituents have been too divided, to get its act together and return to creative political activism. One reason for this is factionalism within the CPI(M): an unbridged rift between former state party secretary Pinarayi Vijayan and former chief minister V.S. Achuthanandan, who remains the party's most popular leader.

This has had serious consequences: Achuthanandan's suspension, and later expulsion, from the politbureau, open confrontations between competing CPI(M) factions and leaders, and paralysis of its local and district units. Vijayan completed his three terms as the state secretary and was replaced in March 2015 by Kodiyeri Balakrishnan, who has had a less antagonistic relationship with Achuthanandan. Whether that reduces factionalism in the CPI(M) remains to be seen: Achuthanandan has been removed from the politbureau and is only a decorative invitee to the party's central committee.

However, the leadership crisis has another dimension and that has to do with understanding the processes at work deep down in society and economy and the way they impact social perceptions, class, caste and group behaviour, and hence political choices. It is only on the basis of such understanding that appropriate political strategies and tactics can drawn up. There are few leaders now in the Kerala Left who have the intellectual calibre of an E.M.S. Namboodiripad, K. Damodaran, C. Achutha Menon, P.K. Vasudevan Nair or C.K. Chadrappan, who can grapple with these issues on their own, or engage in fruitful conversation on them with non-party academics and analysts. The tradition of intellectual debate and interaction across party divides has greatly weakened. The production of new analysis and fresh ideas has slowed down.

Grappling with New Issues

Among the issues in question are the emergence and crystallization of a services-based economy in Kerala, in which foreign remittances form nearly a third of total income. These no longer come from migrant labour in the Persian Gulf alone, but also from more prosperous professionals based in North America and Europe.[104] Dependence on remittances has had some extremely negative effects, whose existence is well known, but whose full magnitude is often not understood.

Take the real estate boom, for instance. Kerala is estimated to need a total of about ninety lakh dwelling units, including small independent houses, apartments, cottages, etc. It already has an estimated inventory of 110 to 115 lakh units, but is furiously building more.[105] Most of these are meant to be sold and bought—only to be resold at a premium.

Apart from the colossal financial speculation it needs and encourages, the construction boom is wreaking environmental havoc through various processes: degradation of the Western Ghats via deforestation and plunder of other biomass, soil, etc.; erosion of fragile coastal areas; flooding of paddy fields and blocking of natural drainage; quarrying for construction material; sand mining on river beds; and pollution and urban waste, especially non-biodegradable plastic used in packaging material to wrap everything from fresh vegetables to groceries to industrial products.

Stemming and reversing such damage calls for drastic remedies and multiple state and civil society interventions, some of which are bound to antagonize the affluent and middle classes in the short run. The bourgeois parties would be understandably loath to do that, but this offers the Left a great opportunity not just to demand (and organize people around) corrective measures that promote the common good and public welfare, but also to create new forms of radical solidarity among citizens based on collective action to defend their shared natural heritage and habitat.

The Left had the organizing ability, knowledge resources and institutions needed to provide some practical alternatives to runaway urbanization. These last include the Integrated Rural Technology Centre (IRTC) in Palakkad (Palghat) set up in 1990 by the KSSP, and the Centre of Science and Technology for Rural Development known as COSTFORD (established 1985) in Trichur. IRTC's specialization is micro-level land and water management; efficient use of energy and development of renewable energy sources; and developing new agronomic models. COSTFORD's core activity lies in designing, developing and propagating cost-effective building construction, using, as far as possible, locally available, low-energy-intensity materials such as mud bricks following the philosophy and practice of the famed British architect-humanist Laurie Baker who settled in Kerala.

Regrettably, the Left has failed to address this agenda. It has instead adopted an ultraconservative stand on habitat, urban planning and environmental matters. This is nowhere more evident than in its position on conserving the Western Ghats, an extremely sensitive, gravely threatened ecosystem, which covers over 160,000 sq. km across six states, including Kerala. The Left rejected a thoughtful report (the Gadgil Committee) on the issue.[106] It sided with prosperous farmers who have encroached on the slopes of the Ghats. To start with, it did so entirely for opportunistic, election-related reasons, but has now hardened its stance. This has pitted the Left against not just grass-roots environmentalists,[107] but the KSSP too, which is running a 'Save Western Ghats' campaign.[108]

To take another example, one of reasons for the Left's loss of influence in the cities is its own past success in unionizing white-collar workers. Coupled with a disproportionately rapid growth in employment opportunities in government and in the fast-expanding education, insurance and banking sectors, this has led to a burgeoning of the middle class. Being unionized, these middle strata could secure large increases in salaries. The boom in construction, trade and health services further expanded employment and income opportunities for them.

Consumerist Elite Takes Over

The culture of social solidarity the Left once promoted, but which has been enfeebled in recent years, had no appeal for these upwardly mobile privileged strata. They moved rightwards and became the main drivers of crass consumerism. Their fast-rising incomes flowed into bank deposits and purchase of jewellery and all manner of luxury goods. Kerala became a highly consumerist society much before the emergence of the new, globalizing malls.[109]

To paraphrase K.T. Rammohan,[110] Kerala has since the 1970s witnessed a large-scale process of embourgeoisement which excludes only its most marginalized people. Thus not only white-collar employees, but even manual workers, have seen their wages rise owing to increased money in circulation, growing unionization, and labour scarcity caused by emigration and increased local preference for non-manual employment following a rise in the levels of education.

Even the relatively low class of head-load workers have tended to gain—if not through direct wage increases, then at least through the practice of nokkukooli (literally, looking-on wage, collected by union members for work done by persons who are not union members).[111] No wonder the head-load workers' union membership card, which can be passed on from father to son, has become a 'dowry item', a part of the assets to be counted while paying off the bridegroom's family. The pernicious practice of dowry did not exist in Kerala until a few decades ago, but has now become ubiquitous.

Kerala's overall class composition has dramatically changed over the past two to three decades. The small peasantry is more scattered than earlier and more difficult to organize. The size of the agricultural working class has shrunk owing to declining rice cultivation. Workers in declining traditional industries like coir, toddy tapping, handloom weaving, cashew processing and beedi rolling now form a minuscule share of the population. But there are few large-scale industries and hence only a tiny modern working class. The service sector has massively expanded, but many workers in services (e.g., private bus transport and autorickshaws) have no common worksite; the nature of their work is individuated and their working hours are uncertain.[112] This makes it difficult for them to develop a collective consciousness.

The sole sector which has witnessed a substantial growth of demand for manual workers is construction. However, thanks to emigration and reduced preference for manual work among local educated youth, this demand has largely been filled by labourers from other states: it is now rare to find a Malayalee working at a road construction or repair site, or in housing construction. The number of workers' struggles has dwindled and their vigour has declined.

In Kerala, embourgeoisement has been accompanied by crime and lumpenization, based on multiple channels of illegitimate movement and accumulation of capital. The cut-throat competition for prime urban sites that drove the construction boom entailed bypassing and sabotaging building byelaws and zoning regulations through bribery. Enormous volumes of sand were removed from river beds, violating licensing and control conditions. A nexus of sand miners, transport operators, local panchayat officials, the police, legislators and even trade unionists soon emerged all across the state. The same pattern is replicated in other businesses such as quarrying granite, smuggling liquor or reclaiming ecologically fragile land for tourist resorts.

Under the impact of these processes—including growing individualism, rampant lumpenization, and entropy of the public culture in which the Left thrived—social attitudes and mores have changed. Kerala is now being transformed into an altogether different entity from what the Left helped to make it until the 1970s or 1980s: the virtual opposite of a relatively egalitarian society proud of its high literacy, women's education, health indices, and enlightened intellectual and literary traditions.

Party Mirrors Society

Even the Left, in particular the CPI(M), is not spared by the mighty tide of the new economic processes. Under their impact, the size and political weight of the working class has decreased in the larger society. The party now mirrors this decline. Thus a key recent development is the 'convergence' between two tendencies: a smaller proportion of the traditional working class is politically conscious and active; and secondly, its growing lack of participation in the CPI(M) means that it influences the party's politics less and less. In the absence of substantive political struggles, the role of the working class in CPI(M) politics is mostly reduced to sustaining the CITU and participating in rallies held at the time of party conferences and elections.

This has had a telling effect on the character of the middle- and high-ranking leadership of LDF constituents. But now their core social base is itself being shaken: traditional support groups like the Ezhavas, Dalits and adivasis, on the one hand, and coir and cashew factory workers, and municipal and state government employees, on the other, are moving away from the LDF parties and their student unions and youth organizations. New social groups are not filling the gap.

Since the 1990s, a massive transformation has occurred in the CPI(M), especially in northern Kerala: a shift 'from cooperatives to corporations'.[113] The CPI(M) started small 'as an economic entity'. It set up primary credit cooperatives, headed by local party officials, which prioritized credit flow to the cadre and the fellow-travelling middle class. A host of handloom-weaving cooperatives and a beedi-rolling cooperative were also established to provide bare sustenance to the poorer party workers and sympathizers, and to advance the ideology of communism among the rural masses. The party was run almost entirely on members' levies and small contributions from well-wishers.

However, with money pouring in from migrants, and increasingly from labour-export contractors and other dubious sources, the party set up a wholly different category of enterprises: multi-speciality hospitals, TV channels, tourist resorts, and IT and amusement parks. 'Party offices began to wear the look of corporate cabins, and party officials enjoying a range of perks—like vehicles on command, governance of economic undertakings, networking with the moneyed elite and regular foreign tours to raise funds from the global migrants. Thus, losing an official position was like losing a plush job, whether in government, a bank, a university or elsewhere.'[114]

The party leadership also developed cosy relations with property speculators, lottery operators and shady businessmen. It made a special effort to woo affluent emigrants, who by and large retain their traditional party loyalties, by regularly sending fund collectors to the Gulf States to raise resources. All this has had harmful social, political, strategic and organizational consequences in de-radicalizing the Left, ideologically pushing it in a right-wing direction and alienating it further from poor and underprivileged workers and peasants.

The character of the CPI(M) has changed to such an extent that its nineteenth congress, held at Kozhikode in April 2012, was organized not by party cadres or volunteers, but by a corporate event management company, with a reported budget of Rs 5 crore—unheard of in the history of India's communist movement which used to take pride in the spartan lifestyle and simplicity that befits a party of poor working people.

Meanwhile, environmental protection, pollution and the urban waste management crisis—every city in once spotlessly clean Kerala now stinks because garbage is not cleared for days—have gained importance in public discourse. The dumping or incineration of urban wastes in nearby villages has become an extremely contentious issue, and acquired a confrontational character at Vilappilsala village near Thiruvananthapuram amidst vigorous protests by the local community. A new campaign is attracting public attention all over Kerala: for 'zero-waste' lifestyles, 'zero-garbage' cities, and so on.

Relating to New Struggles

Kerala has witnessed powerful environmental struggles in recent years: for banning endosulfan, an extremely toxic pesticide used in cashew plantations; against scores of sand-mining and quarrying operations; against a Coca-Cola plant at Plachimada in Palakkad district for appropriating large quantities of water and lowering the water table;[115] against planned motorways and airports, which would destroy trees, natural drainage and paddy lands, to mention only part of the likely damage.

Many of these struggles are led by grass-roots panchayat leaders, urban and rural casual workers and youth affiliated to no political party. They often attract women and adivasi and Dalit youth. But most political party leaders, including those of the Left, do not engage with them; some oppose them outright. There are notable exceptions like Achuthanandan who has supported or joined such agitations. He won a great deal of goodwill in recent years by expressing solidarity with a prolonged and spirited agitation against the Koodankulam nuclear power project near the southern end of Tamil Nadu, which is right next door to the Kerala border. Achuthanandan defied the apex CPI(M) leadership when he decided to visit the nuclear plant site in September 2012, but was stopped at the border and sent back by the Tamil Nadu police.

Despite its society's rightward shift in recent years, Kerala shows many signs of heightened awareness among oppressed groups and new forms of radicalism especially among low-caste and tribal youth. Young women are becoming self-confident and assertive as never before because of the decisive lead they have taken in higher education through its 'feminization'.[116]

Kerala's more than a million 'Gulf wives' (married women whose husbands work and live in the Gulf) have had to learn how to manage bank accounts, property transactions and small businesses, besides organizing school admissions for their children—among other tasks typically performed by men. This has raised their social status and made them aware of the larger world. Even poor women are no longer happy merely with 'work', or paid labour alone; they aspire to what they regard as 'jobs', including employment under MGNREGA.

Young people in Kerala tend to protest spontaneously and in new ways at social regimentation and what has come to be called 'moral policing'. This is right-wing vigilantism against public conduct that is branded as offensive, including even innocuous activities like young men and women holding hands, sharing a meal in a cafe, or exchanging Valentine's Day greetings. In October–November 2014, a campaign broke out in Kerala against moral policing, called 'Kiss of Love', which triggered solidarity movements in other cities including Hyderabad, Mumbai and Delhi. Young people, angry at what they saw as the criminalization of affection, contacted one another through the Internet and social media and organized public protests outside college campuses to hug and 'kiss' one another (usually with their mouths suitably covered with cloth).

The 'Kiss of Love' protests drew sizeable numbers, were often colourful and had public visibility. The Right, including the BJP-controlled Akhil Bharatiya Vidyarthi Parishad (ABVP), predictably condemned them but did not gather the gumption to physically attack the protesters. Left- and Congress-led student unions took an ambivalent stand. Some SFI activists expressed sympathy and support for the campaign, but some others deplored it as 'apolitical' and 'anarchic'. CPI(M) leaders were deeply uncomfortable with it, and deplored it.[117]

This exposed not just the generation gap between the party leadership and youth, but also the social and political distance that separates them. Another innovative public action initiative that has gained popularity among Kerala's young people is a voluntary movement to look after old people and provide palliative care to those in acute distress.[118] The Left has not engaged with this with the seriousness it deserves. This does not bode well for the long-term future of the Left.

Meanwhile, Kerala's electoral politics remains firmly stuck in the mould of community- and caste-based voting. The LDF has not been able to break that mould or win over the support of Muslims and Christians on a significant scale—although both the Congress party and the Kerala Congress (which mainly represents the Christians) are in gradual decline. The fortunes of the LDF and the UDF are often decided by wafer-thin margins, such as one or two per cent of the total vote.

T.P. Chandrasekharan's assassination probably contributed to thinning the margin further to the LDF's disadvantage in the 2014 election—not least because Achuthanandan called on his widow and expressed sympathy for her. The UDF lost its vote share by almost six percentage points, but the LDF could only gain 0.3 percentage points of this, with the BJP taking a 4.5 percentage-point lead. 'Public awareness about scams and scandals',[119] including Chandrasekharan's killing, was probably important in contributing to the tilt against the Left.

Chandrasekharan's murder commands the highest degree of such 'public awareness', at more than 90 per cent of the sample. More than two-thirds of all respondents surveyed supported the UDF government's decision to hand over the investigation of the murder to the Central Bureau of Investigation (CBI), as demanded by his widow and Achuthanandan. Evidently, the CPI(M) underestimated the impact of this terrible act of violence.

The LDF's image has suffered in recent years on various counts. As B.R.P. Bhaskar puts it, 'The contest in Kerala is now between a debilitated UDF and a debilitated LDF, more precisely between a debilitated Congress and a debilitated CPI(M).'[120] The BJP seems best placed to gain from this. That could prove a huge setback for the Left not just electorally, but in its medium- and long-term socio-political impact too. If Kerala's rightward drift continues, and if the LDF does not reinvent itself through innovative politics and mobilizations on issues of contemporary relevance and public concern, the Left could find the ground slipping ever further from under its feet.

This is by no means inevitable. There are grass-roots struggles that the Left must relate to.[121] There is a whole agenda of analysis, strategizing, education, organizing and action waiting to be taken up. As the Kerala Sasthra Sahitya Parishad's new slogan says, 'A Different Kerala is Possible.' The Left has a role, and a stake, in reinventing this alternative in contemporary terms and fighting for it.

8

Social Policy Challenges

Caste, Gender, Religion, Ecology, Human Rights

The Left's claim to be an agency of progressive change—which leads to freedom from exploitation, the full development of people's true human potential and, eventually, to social emancipation and socialism—hinges on its comprehension of, and practices pertaining to, what might broadly be called social policy or the social agenda. This encompasses a range of issues such as caste; religion, secularism and communalism; patriarchy and gender equality; environmental protection; the rights of ethnic, religious, and linguistic minorities; respect for civil and political liberties; promotion of economic and social rights; an expansive and inclusive view of culture; and a compassionate approach to the dispossessed and underprivileged. Clear positions on these are necessary to inspire a spirited effort at evolving an alternative model of an egalitarian non-hierarchical community based on caring and sharing and social solidarity.

These issues fall outside the template of the conventional Marxist focus on class exploitation, but should rank high on an agenda for radical change, especially in a society like India with its distinctive features of 'uneven and combined development'[1] characteristic of backward capitalism. These include caste oppression, extreme forms of patriarchy, a history of divisive religion-based politics, coexistence of vastly different economic forms and relations, immense ethnic, linguistic and cultural diversity, a myriad inequalities and hierarchies, and an imperfect, over-centralized system of democracy which readily compromises with ultra-nationalism, authoritarianism and militarism.

Historically, the Left has acknowledged the importance of these issues. It has by and large adopted a far more progressive stand on them than most political parties and firmly rejected narrow, parochial or sectarian views on social policy. But as we shall see below, it no longer plays a leading or enlightening role in this sphere; it is often as much a part of the problem as part of the solution.

The Left for many decades was able to attract and inspire some of the most talented and creative among India's intellectuals, artists, practitioners of different scholarly disciplines, and men and women of exceptional intelligence and commitment from a wide cross section of classes, groups and communities, because of the apparent plausibility of its claim to a progressive social perspective. It served as a magnet, and a 'natural', if not unique, destination at least at the level of ideas, for many people inclined towards an unconventional, uncynical, enlightened and forward-looking view of the world, who yearned for a critique of, and a way out of, the social status quo.

However, the Left's avant-garde social appeal has declined in recent years. It continues to fade as society changes and new challenges arise from more radical critiques of the social order and from autonomous movements focused on discrete issues like caste, gender, tribe and ecological justice.

Historically, the Left did not analyse social policy issues specific to India sharply or consistently by developing a theoretical–ideological framework which would accommodate them adequately. For instance, the communist Left has always been weak on understanding the question of caste in Indian society, the multiple forms of exploitation and oppression of which it is a part, and the political functions it performs.

The Caste Question

The communist Left early on tended to view caste as a mere 'remnant' or hangover from feudal or pre-capitalist social formations,[2] the implicit assumption being that capitalism would eventually abolish caste or make it irrelevant as a form of 'social organization'. Later, in its revised

(2000) programme, the CPI(M) stated: 'Capitalist development in Indian agriculture is not based on a resolute destruction of older forms, but has been superimposed on a swamp of pre-capitalist production relations and forms of social organization,' which include 'old forms of landlordism and tenancy and archaic forms of labour service, servitude and bondage', which still 'play an important part in agrarian relations' in certain regions of India.[3]

But the 'bourgeois–landlord system', it said, has 'failed to put an end to caste oppression'. Indian society 'under capitalist development has compromised with the existing caste system. The Indian bourgeoisie itself fosters caste prejudices. Working class unity presupposes unity against the caste system and the oppression of Dalits, since the vast majority of the Dalit population are part of the labouring classes. To fight for the abolition of the caste system and all forms of social oppression through a social reform movement is an important part of the democratic revolution. The fight against caste oppression is interlinked with the struggle against class exploitation.'[4]

This recognition of the amalgam of capitalist and pre-capitalist forms of social organization and exploitation is important, and the emphasis on social reform welcome.[5] Yet, the Left parties largely remain fixated on class. They have never taken on board the scholarly insights on the caste–class relationship provided by non-party Marxist historians such as D.D. Kosambi or other independent anthropologists and sociologists. Nor have they adequately theorized caste as a specific relation of social exploitation which is integrated into *contemporary* capitalism in India— similar to the way racism played a key role in shaping capitalism in the United States, both in the North and South, and was incorporated into southern capitalist agriculture in the eighteenth and nineteenth century, and in a different form, into contemporary capitalism in the US.

The Left parties have not analytically explored the complex, but well-mediated and culturally–politically articulated connections of caste with class as a social category in today's India, and the changes these have undergone since the rise of the Dalit movement and the 'Forward March of the Backwards', or the growing assertiveness of the middle castes (Other Backward Classes—OBCs) for the past half-century. They also do not theorize the changing political role of caste.[6]

In recent years, the Left parties have paid greater attention to Dalit issues, and launched or participated in temple entry movements, for instance in Tamil Nadu, besides organizing national conventions on Dalit issues.[7] But they are rarely in the forefront of solidarity campaigns or protest movements that erupt when anti-Dalit atrocities are committed. The communist Left largely views caste as a phenomenon that divides the class(es) it regards as the agency of revolutionary change. It does not emphasize the importance of, and is uncomfortable with, the autonomous self-organization of the Dalits. Such organization is necessary because Dalit oppression—historically unique, and sanctioned or legitimized by the scriptures and custom—is a central and integral component of the relations of social bondage on which the system of power is founded in India.

Dalits organized qua Dalits must have a pivotal role in overthrowing the system. The Left, which too is committed to radical systemic change, must work wherever possible with them and share joint platforms with them. The Left also does not accommodate within its theory or practice the forms of disadvantage, deprivation and oppression—themselves qualitatively different from those heaped upon Dalits—suffered by severely underprivileged groups like the most backward OBCs (or MBCs).

In part, this is because Indian communists tended to think and conceptualize matters within a rigid, often mechanical, wholly class-based Marxist framework, and simply could not accommodate caste as an agent of history or even as a functional category relevant to understanding and shaping social and political processes. The presumption was that if capitalism did not get rid of the 'feudal remnants' of casteism, they would finally be swept away by the socialist revolution anyway.

In part, the communist Left's failure to theorize caste and recognize its salience is also attributable to its fraught past relationship with the Bahujan Samaj–Dalit movement of Phule–Shahu Maharaj–Ambedkar in Maharashtra and with Periyar's 'self-respect' movement in Tamil Nadu, to which they never related positively. The communists saw Ambedkar as an adversary who reminded them of their own complicity in casteist practices, including untouchability, which was rampant in the Bombay textile mills where their Girni Kamgar Union was based. Ambedkar confronted them in 1928 on the issue of debarring 'polluting' Dalits from employment in better-paying departments such as weaving—a widely prevalent practice, which the communists did not oppose.[8]

The CPI had no sympathy for Ambedkar's Independent Labour Party (ILP) (founded in 1938) although it advocated socialism and 'state management and state ownership of industry whenever it may become necessary in the interests of the people', besides other progressive agendas.[9] Communist hostility to Ambedkar[10] became more pronounced when he served as labour member in the Viceroy's Executive Council (1942–46). The CPI was similarly indifferent to Bengal's Dalit leader Jogendranath Mandal,[11] and did not take the issue of Dalit oppression on board until much later.

This contrasts the communists with the socialists, who had a far better comprehension of caste as a living social reality and a relationship or condition of existence that must be fought, along with class exploitation, to achieve anything approaching freedom and social equality.[12] The socialists may have overemphasized the importance of caste oppression within the upper-caste- or savarna-dominated hierarchy, to the point of losing sight of internal differentiation within the OBCs and the OBCs' oppressive relationship with the Dalits. But they seriously engaged with caste as a fundamental fault line in Indian society, and also as a basis of political organization for radical change.

Yet, despite differences, there was political cooperation and fruitful dialogue on caste, land reforms and social issues between the communists and socialists in the 1960s and 1970s, especially in Bihar. Many communists in the state had high regard for Lohia and Jayaprakash Narayan (JP), whose book *Why Socialism?* had influenced them in their younger days. When the CPI's Indrajeet Singh became revenue minister in Bihar's first non-Congress government in 1967, he appointed a land reforms committee with JP as chairman and veteran communist Jagannath Sarkar as a member.[13] Unfortunately, the dialogue that took place between these two major currents of the Left ceased with the organizational disintegration of the socialists.

The communists were consistent supporters of affirmative action for Dalits, in the form of reservations in jobs and education, but had a markedly different position on reservations in respect of the OBCs and the Mandal Commission (appointed in 1979). Thus, the Left Front government in West Bengal adopted an antagonistic position towards the Mandal Commission and caste-based reservation, which it viewed as an obstacle to class consciousness. The government 'in fact refused to answer the Mandal Commission queries and identify OBCs on the basis of caste, arguing that poverty and low standards of living were better indicators of backwardness than caste...'[14]

According to another researcher, 'a committee set up by the West Bengal government to look into the question of caste backwardness in August 1980 maintained that "poverty and low levels of living standards rather than caste should, in our opinion, be the most important criteria for identifying backwardness"... This enabled the chief minister of West Bengal to remark before the Mandal Commission that in the state there were only two castes—the rich and the poor!'[15]

It is only later, beginning with 1990, when the upper-caste-led violent and self-evidently reactionary anti-Mandal movement erupted, that the CPI(M) came to terms with the self-assertion of the OBCs and lent support to the Mandal scheme of reservations for them, which led to the setting up of the West Bengal Commission for Backward Classes in 1993.

Bhadralok Domination

The communist parties have remained largely insensitive to caste divisions in their own organization, particularly in the national leadership, which is dominated by the savarna castes.[16] While they did attempt and achieve a relatively high representation of low castes, especially the Ezhavas, in their organizations in Kerala, they conspicuously failed to do so in West Bengal, where the Left's leadership has been heavily dominated by the three Bhadralok upper-caste groups: Brahmins, Kayasthas and Vaidyas, who form about one-tenth of the population. No Dalit was included in the first two ministries of the Left Front, which came to power in 1977.

Defying the trend in much of the country, and in the Hindi belt— where the proportion of upper-caste MPs to the total decreased from over 40 per cent in 1989 to 33 per cent in 2004[17]—West Bengal continued to have a high proportion of upper-caste legislators throughout the

Left Front's tenure. In 1977, when the Front came to power, the upper castes accounted for 46 per cent of all MLAs in the state, compared to an average of 39 per cent in the previous three assemblies. This ratio was grossly disproportionate to their share of the population. But it rose even further to 49 per cent in 1996 (although it fell to 37 per cent in 2001).[18]

The share of CPI(M) and CPI upper-caste MLAs among their parties' legislators was similarly high, fluctuating between 42 and 45 per cent between 1977 and 1996, but falling to 34 per cent in 2001. Between 1977 and 1996, the two parties accounted for 49 to 62 per cent of the assembly's upper-caste members, a ratio that fell to 43 per cent in 2001.[19]

In contrast, Muslims were under-represented among the MLAs belonging to the CPI (M) and CPI, accounting for 12 per cent of their total, or half their share in the population. The intermediate castes accounted for 35 per cent of the state's population in 1991, but their share of MLAs to the total was meagre, falling from 8.4 per cent in 1977 to 5 per cent in 1996.

The dominance of the upper castes in West Bengal cabinets remained embarrassingly high throughout the Left Front's thirty-four-year tenure. It peaked at an incredible 81.8 per cent in 1982, and fell in later years, but still exceeded 51 per cent in 2001.[20] By contrast, not a single Dalit or adivasi—communities which respectively form 24 and 6 per cent of the population (according to the 1991 census)—found a place in the first two Left Front governments. Adivasis were altogether absent from LF cabinets between 1977 and 1996—although these two groups' share rose in 2001.[21]

One reason for the Left Front's appalling record on inclusion in respect of caste is the prevalent myth that 'caste is irrelevant in West Bengal politics', which is shared across the state's political spectrum, including the Left. 'It can indeed be observed in situ that politicians—party cadres, elected representatives—pretend not to know the caste of their colleagues, nor even their own, beyond categories such as upper castes or Scheduled Castes.'[22] In reality, caste identities and divisions, and caste-based forms of discrimination and oppression, have, of course, long been part of West Bengal society and daily life, as numerous ethnographers, sociologists and historians have shown.[23]

When confronted in 2013 with questions about the persistent savarna-biased composition of the Left's leadership, CPI(M) politbureau member Sitaram Yechury responded by asserting that the Left's lower-level committees and student unions are dominated by the subaltern castes (whose influence would soon percolate upwards), and then by pleading innocence on caste issues: 'We don't believe in symbolic change, where one face is projected and the reality remains unchanged. This is a serious problem in the sense that we don't have this in our consciousness ...' Yechury spoke disparagingly about the communist parties being forced to 'stoop' to 'the level' of the founder leader of the Bahujan Samaj Party Kanshi Ram[24]—as if their own lack of caste awareness were a state of bliss and a mark of fidelity to true Marxism.

Religion and Public Life

On the issue of religion and religious belief too, India's communist parties have been ambivalent. Ideologically, and in party education, their cadres are coached to follow and propagate atheism, religion being 'the opium of the people'. But in spite of being chided and maligned as 'godless communists' by non-secular parties and religious leaders, many of them rarely take an atheist or even agnostic stand in public life; their personal and family affairs, including life-cycle rituals or ceremonies, are usually conducted in 'traditional' or 'conventional' (that is, religious and caste-determined) ways. This is no different from the practices followed by pious, unthinking believers.[25]

In respect of their individual members, the left parties often treat religious belief as an intimate personal matter, but discourage them from publicly expressing their religious sentiments or participating in religious ceremonies. This is at best an awkward compromise in a deeply religious society where there are more temples than schools, where faith and superstition are hard to separate, and where religion-based identities have long been harnessed to political agendas and exploited to incite violence to serve extremely divisive ends, including Partition.

Every now and then, individual members of the communist parties go public with their pieties and personal religious beliefs or their view of the inherent 'superiority' of Hinduism over other faiths, especially those based on the Book, on account of Hinduism's tradition of 'tolerance' and 'polycentrism'. (This is an extremely dubious claim, given the adherence to dogma and unquestioning faith, indeed crass intolerance of dissenting opinion, which is demanded by most religions. Polytheism does not equal polycentrism, and neither represents or entails tolerance in the modern sense.)

In the past, such utterances would attract censure from the party. Censure would act as a (weak) deterrent against voicing religious sentiments, although it would not prevent it altogether. In recent years, even party leaders have become indulgent towards public expression or advocacy of faith. For instance, West Bengal's former transport minister, the late Subhas Chakraborty, known to be close to Jyoti Basu, made a well-publicized visit to a Kali temple in 2006 and made a statement saying his primary identity is that of a Hindu and a Brahmin first, and that he is a communist only secondarily.[26] Chakraborty was let off with a mild reprimand.

In Kerala too, the CPI(M) 'has not been able to lift a finger to reprimand—let alone punish—the "religious-minded" legislators, Aisha Potti, the Marxist-ruled state's first Brahmin woman MLA, and M.M. Monayi, a practising Christian' who had both taken their oath as MLAs 'in the name of God'.[27] "We don't censure any party leaders for their ignorance or backward consciousness. We try to indoctrinate them into the Marxist way of thinking,"' said Kerala education minister M.A. Baby',[28] then a CPI(M) central committee member, now also in the politbureau.

For the most part, the compromise involving silence on religion has not worked—certainly not to the Left's benefit. Rather, it has hobbled the Left in various ways. It prevents it from frontally addressing the issues of religion, ethnicity and faith-based identity, and hence communalism or the politicization of religion. In the past, the Left parties would use the medium of culture and folk idiom to question piety and blind faith while arguing for secularism, or at the minimum, for a principled distance between religion and politics.

Left-wing activists in the arts and theatre would deploy satire and parody to demolish the moral claims of devotees of Ram, including the Kshatriya prince's upholding of customary casteist dogmas and practices such as beheading a Shudra for committing the crime of reading the Vedas, or driving Sita to self-destruction in defence of male-supremacist prejudice. They would pour scorn on religion and self-styled swamis. They rarely do so now. They are more content to sing paeans to India's (steadily weakening) syncretic traditions and interfaith 'unity'—an exercise not just in futility, but in utter pusillanimity in the face of the recent ferocious offensive launched by Hindu-communal forces.

The Left has effectively withdrawn from the arena of combating religion, faith, and denominational politics to retreat to an insipid, bloodless agenda of 'national integration' and 'communal harmony'. This cannot even generate the kind of creative anti-communal initiatives—mohalla committees in working class neighbourhoods, joint patrolling by citizens and trade union activists, relief and rehabilitation operations cutting across communities, collective advocacy and lobbying with the police, and public interest litigation—witnessed after the Babri mosque demolition.

These initiatives not only saved thousands of lives, but also rekindled the hope that India could have a secular future based on equal rights for all its citizens. The Left's retreat here is all the more tragic because it has been the most vocal supporter among all political parties of 'principled' secularism, and has an ideology that militates against promoting religious community-based politics of any kind.

The Left in recent years has ignored the growing phenomenon of segregation between Hindus and Muslims and the ghettoization of Muslims, now starkly evident in every Indian city under the impact of Hindutva prejudice.[29] Such ghettoes are starved of schools, milk booths, government dispensaries, banks, municipal amenities, civic infrastructure and transportation, and typically boycotted by chemists, pizza-delivery boys and grocers. Muslims are forced to create or move into ghettoes by insecurity and threat or perpetration of communal violence, and the refusal of landlords or builders to sell or rent them accommodation in 'Hindu-only' areas or apartment houses.

Segregation excludes Muslims from civic life and, effectively, from citizenship altogether. This is as unacceptable and egregious as segregation in the American South until the 1960s. Segregation of 'social and cultural spaces', says the Kundu Committee, 'fuels a deep sense of insecurity … subdues the democratic voice, and discourages active citizenship among minorities'.[30] The Left should have been in the forefront of the struggle against such segregation and taken the initiative to formulate a law against discrimination based on religion, caste, disability, sex, and so on, in both state and non-state spheres. Sadly, its response has been passive, or largely confined to press releases.

As discussed earlier, the Left did not attempt to fight Hindutva through a popular counter-mobilization. It did not analyse the rise of communalism, especially its dominant Hindu version and its various recent mutations, in relation to economic policies and processes and to changing class, caste, regional and cultural equations, which would help define a clear strategy to combat it.[31] Nor did it develop a critique of Muslim communalism in its contemporary forms.

Rise of New Hindutva

In particular, the Left has not paid adequate attention to Hindutva's resurgence with the rise to dominance of a belligerent form of 'Mera Bharat Mahan' nationalism, celebration of nuclear-weapon status and militarism, and the increasingly Islamophobic terms in which the Indian state conceives 'terrorism' and fashions its battles against it by military and harsh police means without acknowledging or addressing the root causes of the discontent underlying Islamist extremism. These causes are located in the systemic discrimination faced by Muslims (documented by the National Commission on Minorities and by the Sachar Committee),[32] the persecution of young Muslims suspected to be involved in violent activities, and the state's coddling of the Hindu Right, among other factors.

The Left has paid scant attention to recent changes in the composition[33] and political preferences of the Indian bourgeoisie, which explain its support for authoritarian–majoritarian forms of rule which combine crass neo-liberalism with Hindutva—a combination best exemplified in the 'Gujarat model' of development.[34] This shift prepared the ideological basis and political ground for Narendra Modi's nomination as the bourgeoisie's and later the BJP's prime ministerial candidate long before the 2014 Lok Sabha election. Modi took control of the BJP and severely refashioned and reorganized it, forcing the Sangh Parivar to follow his diktat on strategic matters, as well as campaigning tactics.

All these changes are part of a tectonic, if glacially slow, shift that has been under way in Indian society for the past decade or more. This shift consists in growing differentiation within the OBCs, Dalits and other subaltern groups and the emergence of new, upwardly mobile or 'aspirational' elite or middle-class strata among them which have no compunctions about breaking ranks with their underprivileged peers and joining social and political coalitions dominated by upper-caste–upper-class groups that seek to perpetuate their power and privilege.

This shift may or may not last, but the coalitions and alliances that it facilitated allowed a new, more aggressive, more corporatized BJP to emerge as the spokesperson or forum of these elite strata among subaltern groups, and hence to polarize classes, castes and communities as never before, especially in northern and central-western India. The Left did not develop a specific, conjuncture-based analysis of these trends, or anticipate the transition under way to new forms of communalism. Its analysis was no sharper or better than the guesswork-based common sense on communalism prevalent among most Indian parties. It paid heavily for this weakness nationally, and in West Bengal and Kerala.

At the same time, the Left has not done enough to demarcate itself consistently from Muslim communal elements and political parties, allying with whom brought it short-term electoral dividends from time to time. For instance, in Kerala, it allied with the Indian Union Muslim League in 1967–69, which it later said was a 'mistake'. But it again allied with a breakaway faction of the League called the All-India Muslim League (AIML) in 1977–85. Since then, the Left, especially the CPI(M), has made repeated overtures to Muslim-denominational parties in Kerala, in 1996 and again in 2000[35].

In West Bengal, the Left Front government placated Muslim conservatives by banning a book by Taslima Nasreen, and became complicit in 2007 in chasing her out of Kolkata after violent protests broke out against her 'anti-Islamic' writings. This raises uncomfortable questions about the Left's commitment to secularism, precisely when it is vital to demonstrate it exemplarily in practice.

In 2014, the Left parties in Kerala also sealed an understanding with conservative elements in the Church who lead a coalition of interests which include medium and small farmers, a majority of them Christians, who have encroached upon the Western Ghats. The coalition predictably opposes proposals for conservation of the Ghats, contained in the Gadgil report, discussed below. To reap benefits from the deal, the Left Democratic Front fielded four Christians as independent candidates in the Lok Sabha elections, none of whom was a seasoned party member comparable to M.M. Lawrence, M.A. Baby or T.M. Thomas Isaac, or associated with the Left through work or conviction.

Shortly after the Sachar Committee report was published in 2006, the Left Front government of West Bengal attracted a great deal of criticism for its less-than-honourable record on addressing the problems of poverty and backwardness among the state's Muslims who form more than 25 per cent of its population. The committee showed that Muslims record the second highest incidence of poverty, with 31 per cent below the poverty line, following the SCs and STs (35 per cent). Literacy among them was far below the national average in 2001, and the rate of decline in illiteracy much lower than among SC/STs. A quarter of Muslim children in the 6–14 age group either never went to school or else dropped out at some stage.[36]

West Bengal recorded some of the lowest shares of Muslims in state government employment in India—respectively 4.7 and 1.8 per cent in 'higher' and 'lower' positions, compared to the corresponding national aggregates of 5.7 and 5.6 per cent. Even Gujarat, where 9 per cent of the population is Muslim, had a better record: 3.4 and 5.5 per cent. This provoked anger and sullen disillusionment among young Muslims. Even more galling to many of them was the iniquitous manner in which electoral representation was gerrymandered by designating at least ten Muslim-majority or -plurality constituencies as reserved for the SCs in the West Bengal Legislative Assembly.[37]

The Left Front steadily lost support among Muslims after 2007, a loss reflected in its electoral performance at various levels, including panchayats in the rural areas, where Muslims in West Bengal tend to be concentrated, unlike in most other states. In February 2010, the government announced that it would provide 10 per cent reservation in government jobs to economically, socially and educationally backward Muslims. This was a desperate measure, calculated to recover lost Muslim support ahead of the assembly elections the following year.[38] But it was taken without due regard to criteria for determining backwardness, and therefore might well fall foul of the higher judiciary.[39]

The measure claimed to cover 85 per cent of Muslims in the state, and would raise the OBC quota in West Bengal to 17 per cent, including 7 per cent for non-Muslim OBCs.[40] 'The additional groups of backward Muslims to be included in the OBCs would be identified by a panel comprising representatives from a number of state commissions and would exclude the creamy layer, identified as persons from families with an income of Rs 4.5 lakh per annum.'[41] In the event, this move did not help the Left Front much in the election; it suffered a rout.

The Left parties have tried over the years to raise the proportion of Muslims and Christians in their membership, but have succeeded only partially, and in a few states like West Bengal. At the all-India level, just 9.6 per cent of the CPI(M)'s members in 2011 were Muslims, and a more respectable 4.8 per cent were Christians. The proportion of Muslims in party membership ranged from roughly 10 per cent in Kerala to 12 per cent in Uttar Pradesh to 15 per cent in West Bengal—well below their shares of the population in the three states (respectively, 27, 18 and 27 per cent).[42] Kerala reported a drop of 1.78 percentage point in the share of Christians in its membership between the Calcutta (1998) and Hyderabad (2002) congresses, leading to exhortations to the Kerala unit to 'pay more attention' to recruiting more members from the minorities.[43]

Ambivalence on Feminism

In the 1970s, the Left was confronted with the rise of a women's movement in various parts of India, focused on a wide spectrum of issues ranging from high prices of the necessities of life like food and milk, low female participation in the workforce, unequal wages even in the organized sector, rape and sexual violence and, more broadly, the systemic discrimination faced by women in education, homes, streets and workplaces. Some of these issues were highlighted in the landmark report of the government-appointed Committee on the Status of Women in India, *Towards Equality*, published in 1975 in the wake of the International Decade of Women.

At this time, only the CPI and the socialists had women's organizations (respectively, the National Federation of Indian Women (NFIW), established in 1954, and Samajwadi Mahila Sabha, formed in the 1960s), which functioned as their auxiliaries. They joined hands with independent women's groups in Bombay in the Anti-Price Rise Movement (APRM) during 1972–75, which saw remarkable activism, with women marching holding rolling pins,[44] inspecting ration shops and raiding hoarders. The APRM developed new methods of struggle, participatory structures and novel forms of democratic organization, whose vibrancy took even the Left parties by surprise.

Soon, other increasingly autonomous groups sprang up in cities like Hyderabad (Progressive Organization of Women, with some 5,000 members in 1974). 'In 1975 a conference in Bombay brought together eight hundred women, mainly working-class, but the proceedings were boycotted by the traditional left parties ... A further important development was the formation of an autonomous Socialist Women's Group in Bombay in 1977.'[45] This was followed by the publication of the group's newsletter, *Feminist Network*, in July 1978, the creation of a Women's Liberation Coordinating Committee, which tried to bring together women's groups and mass organizations, and the launching of *Manushi*, India's first non-commercial feminist journal, in January 1979.

A turning point was the custodial rape of a fourteen-year-old tribal (Mathura) in 1978 near Nagpur, followed by a perverse Supreme Court judgment,[46] which led to the formation of the Forum against Oppression of Women in 1980. 'Even the official communist parties placed themselves under its banner for the anti-rape campaign, and on 8 March 1981, International Women's Day, its principal demands gained great resonance on the Left. In its first year of existence, the Forum could count on sixty regular women activists ...'[47]

Meanwhile, in 1975, a conference backed by the Communist Party of India (Marxist) was held on women's issues in Trivandrum. *Social Scientist*, a journal run by individuals close to the CPI(M) or part of it, published a special issue on the occasion, to which E.M.S.

Namboodiripad contributed an article. In this, he supported the cause of women's emancipation but linked it to the struggle against 'the oppression and exploitation to which the working people as a whole—men as well as women—are subjected'.[48] Namboodiripad advocated 'a relentless struggle as much against bourgeois and petty-bourgeois "feminism" as against male chauvinism'. Because 'it adopts a "Leftist" and "revolutionary" garb', he said, this variety of feminism is 'even more dangerous to the integration of the women's movement for their equality with men, and the common movement of the working people for ending all forms of pre-capitalist exploitation and, along with it, liquidating capitalism'.[49]

This defined the line that would be adopted by the CPI(M)-sponsored All India Democratic Women's Association (AIDWA) formed in 1981, which does not describe itself as feminist. AIDWA, like NFIW, works and cooperates with non-party and autonomous feminist groups from time to time, but maintains its own party-linked special identity. It continues to be described routinely by the CPI(M) as its 'women's front'.[50]

Similarly, Vimla Farooqui, a leading veteran of NFIW, told an interviewer: 'We are not a feminist organization, we are not anti-men. We are not the only ones who are exploited, Harijan men are no less exploited, of course, their woman are doubly exploited. Since 1971 in the CPI, the two women-specific points of debate have been: (1) how to draw/attract, more women to our struggle/movement, and (2) how to change the attitudes of male comrades to encourage women to join the political struggle/the party. One has to be a good, sympathetic husband to allow [a] woman to join the struggle ...'[51]

Tensions between feminist and party-linked groups became apparent early on. In 1990, when the autonomous women's movement held its fourth all-India conference at Kozhikode, part of the CPI(M)'s heartland in north Kerala, it faced stiff opposition from AIDWA and the party, including a 'smear campaign', which alleged that it 'was organized by foreign-funded groups and CIA agents, and concentrated on the urban elite'.[52] Senior party leader Susheela Gopalan warned women against joining these 'separatist' groups, and another CPI(M) leader Bhargavi Thankappan called them 'vulgar feminists' who aspired to a 'free life'.[53]

Several analysts have documented the differences between party-linked women's organizations like AIDWA and NFIW, on the one hand, and autonomous feminist groups, on the other, such as the Forum Against Oppression of Women and the Women's Centre in Bombay, Nari Mukti Sanghatana, Samagra Mahila Aghadi, Stree Adhikar Sampark Samiti and Shramik Stree Mukti Dal elsewhere in Maharashtra, Sachetana in Calcutta, Stree Shakti Sanghatana in Telangana, Mahila Mukti Morcha in Chhattisgarh, Pennurimari Iyakkam in Tamil Nadu, Anweshi in Andhra Pradesh, to mention only some of the organizations formed in the early period.[54]

Ideologically, the party-affiliated women's groups typically base themselves on *The Origins of the Family, Private Property, and the State* by Engels, which says all these emerged simultaneously; the autonomous feminists usually argue that 'women's oppression and subjugation began much before the generation of surplus, the emergence of private property and class'.[55] Politically, the two define their goals and functions divergently: the first, through its connection with the larger movement for the emancipation of workers and peasants; the second, in relation to patriarchy and its control over women's labour, fertility and sexuality.[56]

AIDWA activists, says a researcher, 'support the argument that the women's question is incorporated into the social question and the class struggle, and not distinguished as an individual aspect of gender relations. The group's main concern is the emancipation of Indian women but [it] refuses to be labelled feminist. For AIDWA, the women's question is interlinked with social and economic conditions, and only a change in the general conditions can bring a change for women and their status within the society.'[57] Party-linked organizations tend to be relatively conservative in family matters while autonomous groups confront questions of domestic violence, cultural values and ways of controlling women's sexuality, including their reproduction.[58]

These organizations struggle to maintain their autonomy from the parent body, but do not always succeed.[59] In many cases, their leaders and activists pursue a highly conservative agenda, including legitimation of a questionable notion of 'respectability',[60] projection of women as the protectors of 'national purity', endorsement of upper-caste gender norms, and defence of the Hindu joint family. Thus in her excellent study, Basu observed a strong connection between the democratic centralism of the CPI(M) and the ethos of the Bengali Hindu joint family which 'mystifies ... inequality and projects itself as a solidaristic unit whose members share identical interests'.[61]

To be fair, the Left's position on women's issues has not remained totally unchanged or unresponsive to new realities.[62] In December 2005, the CPI(M) central committee produced a 13,000-word document, which modified the party's earlier positions by accommodating a critique of patriarchy, linking women's exploitation to the co-optation of 'male supremacism' by capital, and discussing at length the condition of women in the Indian context.[63]

This marks a definite advance. But the resolution nevertheless reverts to the stand that it was 'class society that gave birth to patriarchal ideologies and the subordination of women. In contrast to current feminist theories, Marxism does not see patriarchy as an autonomous system, unconnected to the basic economic organization of a given society[64] ... It is only in a socialist society when the means of production are socially owned that the material conditions are created for women's emancipation through the introduction of the mass of women into the sphere of socially productive labour on an equal footing with men.'[65]

Meanwhile, AIDWA has registered spectacular growth. Its membership has increased more than tenfold over the last three decades, and an extraordinarily dynamic leadership has emerged, which courageously took up issues like fighting the khap panchayats, which most political parties (including, it needs stating, the Aam Aadmi Party), had shied away from. AIDWA's success is probably attributable more to its engagement with livelihood issues—through thrift societies, microcredit groups, and women's cooperatives—than to addressing core feminist concerns. It is nevertheless remarkable, and would have been amplified if the party had joined hands with AIDWA.

Leaving aside these debates, there is no doubt that the Left remains, at least in its stated positions, the staunchest supporter within the Indian political spectrum of women's equality and empowerment. But three important questions arise. Has the Left promoted gender equality in its own ranks, its leadership and among its legislators? Has it done enough to implement its long-standing and consistent demand for reserving 33 per cent of all seats in legislatures for women where it can do so, namely, in the states where it has been in power? Third, has it raised the priority accorded to the struggle for women's equality within its programme and its work on the ground?

The answer to the first question is that the communist Left has performed better than many other parties—and especially the former socialists, who have emerged as the strongest opponents of gender equality[66]—but that it still has a long way to go in giving women adequate representation in its own organization. Women's representation in the CPI(M)'s overall membership increased from under 5 per cent in the late 1980s/early 1990s, to 12 per cent in 2007, and stood at just 14 per cent in 2011.[67] Only two of its new politbureau's sixteen members are women: the first of them was elected in 2005,[68] and the second in 2015.[69] Just thirteen women sit on its ninety-one-strong central committee. Women are better represented in the CPI's membership, accounting for 17 per cent of it, but their situation is not much better in the leadership: only one of the party's nine central secretariat members is a woman; just two of its thirty central executive members are women; and women account for only eight per cent of its 124-strong national council.

Equally important is the poor representation of women among the delegates to party congresses. For instance, women accounted for between just 6 and 11 per cent of all delegates at the CPI(M)'s recent congresses.[70] AIDWA's reported all-India membership rose dramatically: it more than tripled between 1981 and 1990 to 31.2 lakhs, further doubled to 63.3 lakhs by 2001, and reached a peak of 121 lakhs in 2010, but declined to 107 lakhs in 2011.[71] But this rise was not reflected in increased women's representation in CPI(M) forums, despite AIDWA being called the party's 'front'.

Women were severely under-represented in the assemblies in the Left's former strongholds. In West Bengal, they accounted during the half-century 1952–2001 for less than 7 per cent of the MLAs of all parties.[72] The exception was the Gorkha National Liberation Front, for which the ratio was 25 per cent. Women's share of the CPI(M)'s legislators was no better than the all-party average: just 6 per cent; the CPI's corresponding share was 4 per cent. Even the Trinamool Congress's share was slightly higher (6.7 per cent).[73] Kerala, which early on achieved higher rates of women's literacy, health and education than most Indian states, has remained a laggard in women's participation in politics and government, except at the panchayat level.

The Left parties made a strong and commendable pitch for one-third reservation for women in parliament, and the highly regarded CPI MP Geeta Mukherjee put in a great deal of energy into trying to evolve a consensus around this. But when that effort repeatedly failed, the Left could have introduced reservation bills in state assemblies, especially those where pro-reservation parties had a majority, including the Congress. It could certainly have done so in West Bengal, Kerala and Tripura. By doing this, the Left could have creatively generated pressure on the Centre—just as it had earlier done by allowing party-based elections to the West Bengal panchayats. But it did not.

Finally, nothing suggests that the Left parties have raised the priority given to women's equality in their programmatic agenda, party educational activity or day-to-day work. AIDWA and NFIW may be getting more play in society and the media. But the parent parties have not taken up women's issues with enthusiasm—by joining or initiating demonstrations and campaigns against sexual harassment and violence or 'Love Jihad' and moral policing; by educating their cadres on patriarchy or the importance of sexual freedom; or even by pursuing demands for equal wages for women in state-run programmes and legislation. They did not play a prominent role in lobbying for the recently passed domestic violence bill either.

The Left has been relatively passive on gender issues even in Kerala, where women face growing and terrible forms of harassment in the street, at the workplace and at home, comparable to those prevalent in the semi-literate social cesspools of the north.[74] This, of course, is not the Left's fault. But the Left has not paid this issue the kind of attention it demands—and deserves—from a political current which is keen to create a new 'Kerala model' worthy of emulation.

Ecological Conservatism

On yet another pivotal issue, that of ecology and the environment, the Left has moved from a severely productionist stance, which regards the development of the productive forces as the central criterion of all social progress, to a partial, grudging recognition of the importance of environmental protection. Until fairly recently, it saw environmentalists fighting against destructive 'development' projects such as high dams, river diversion schemes, gigantic mining ventures, highways cutting through rainforests, and highly polluting chemical and metallurgical industries or coal-fired power stations, in largely adversarial terms, as enemies of 'development'.

The Left shared Nehru's early vision of the 'Temples of Modern India'. It counterposed environmental protection to development, and branded ecological activists Luddites and irrational opponents of progress, who are more concerned with saving a handful of 'monkeys' (such as the gravely threatened lion-tailed macaque found only in Kerala) than with providing electricity to the energy-poor masses. The Left also ignored the social costs of 'development', including the displacement of millions of people, many of them vulnerable.[75]

In the 1970s and 1980s, the Left entered into a confrontation with people's mobilizations, often led by groups that were sometimes called 'non-party political formations', against numerous 'development' projects and proposals. These included the Silent Valley hydroelectric dam in Kerala, the Sardar Sarovar projects on the Narmada in Gujarat and Madhya Pradesh, the Tehri high dam in a seismically ultra-hazardous region in the central Himalayas, nuclear power plants in various states, and countless coal-mining projects and coal-fired power plants everywhere.

In the early 1980s, CPI(M) ideologue Prakash Karat, who later became general secretary of the party, added a strongly sectarian ideological dimension to the Left parties' suspicion of and opposition to such movements by writing a major article entitled 'Action Groups/ Voluntary Organizations: a Factor in Imperialist Strategy'.[76] This identified civil society groups and 'non-party political formations', many of them foreign-funded, as a new instrument used by the forces of 'imperialism' to work through 'academic outfits' and penetrate groups of landless people, adivasis, women, slum dwellers and unorganized labour to influence the 'course of development' and counter the Left.

Sometimes, the Left treated its own sympathizers and associates as its worst adversaries, such as those in the Kerala Sasthra Sahitya Parishad. This became evident in the Silent Valley case and later the Peringome nuclear project, both cancelled under the pressure of public opinion generated through the KSSP's educational campaigns and grass-roots mobilizations.

In the late 1990s, as gigantic mining, metallurgical, chemical and power generation projects proliferated in various parts of India—which were often promoted by multinational corporations and have been extremely predatory on natural resources and people's livelihoods—the Left conditionally supported mobilizations opposing them. But it did so mainly on account of the displacement they would cause, not on foundational ecological grounds, such as their consequences in terms of deforestation and destruction of natural watersheds, hydrological imbalances, increased greenhouse gas emissions, or large-scale pollution of land, water and air. The Left rarely showed any recognition of the irreversible character of such destruction, and the long-term effects of the loss it would entail of biodiversity and the finer balances of nature. The Left parties never reconciled their notions of development and environmental conservation or protection, in theory or practice; even some of the most powerful movements against destructive projects were led by activists who are their own members—as in the case of the giant Posco steel plant in Odisha.

A major confrontation is now under way between the CPI(M) leadership and environmentalists, including the KSSP, on the issue of conservation of the Western Ghats, which have been called the Water Tower of peninsular India and a unique treasure trove of biodiversity.[77] The party lacks serious comprehension of how ecologically fragile the Ghats are and what their further degradation would entail for the monsoon system and water availability. It rejects the report of the Western Ghats Ecology Expert Panel headed by Madhav Gadgil,[78] which would lead to the creation of Ecologically Sensitive Area zones where no polluting industries, mining or plantation-related activities would be permitted.[79] It opposes the report for entirely short-term considerations, namely, protecting those who have encroached on the Ghats or are planning major destructive projects there. This is likely to be one of the great fault lines in India for ecological conflicts involving the fate of millions of people.

The Left parties used to be ardent, and uncritical, advocates of nuclear energy, and saw it both as an exemplar of modern science and advanced technology and as the key to India's energy sovereignty—at least until the US–India nuclear deal was signed in 2005. They were as vocal as the bourgeois parties in condemning the (rather mild) restrictions[80] imposed by the West on nuclear trade and cooperation with India following the 1974 atomic explosion, and in linking these with 'imperialist designs' against India's ambitions for endogenous, self-reliant development— much like the most paranoid elements in the establishment, who saw a US-led 'conspiracy' in this 'technology denial', ignoring India's own disgraceful record of nuclear duplicity and disingenuousness.[81]

The Left did little to counter the malicious propaganda launched by the Department of Atomic Energy, and its stooges in the media, against all those who dared to question its always overstated power generation targets and extravagant technological claims, and even more vitally, its poor safety record, replete with accidents and negligent practices.[82] Nor did the Left show much concern for radiation health hazards and other safety issues—in keeping with its virtual technocratic blindness to these, and the faith that all hazards would always be assuredly overcome with yet more technology. Not even the Chernobyl meltdown (1986) shook the Left out of its uncritical admiration for nuclear power. And the still-continuing disaster at Fukushima, which began in 2011, has not yet led it to reject nuclear power as unacceptably risky and unsafe.[83]

Two considerations fed into, and reinforced, the Left's rosy, if uninformed, view of matters atomic and environmental. First, the keen, large-scale pursuit of nuclear energy and other ecologically unsound technologies by the Soviet Union, and later China, the sole models of 'socialism' for the Indian communist parties, whose cadres were coached to defend them at least until the Soviet Union's collapse. And second, many Left leaders turned especially hostile to environmentalists, civil society groups and local activists who extended their ecological opposition to a nuclear power project at Haripur in East Medinipur, which the Left Front supported.[84]

The Left's dogma-driven approach to ecological questions dispensed with the need to engage in concrete, issue-specific, well-reasoned arguments about the appropriateness or relevance of nuclear power and other high-risk technologies for India, their economic costs and generic safety problems, or India's embarrassingly poor record on assessing their risks and regulating them.

In recent years, however, the Left has become selectively critical of such technologies and acknowledged the need for environmental protection. Although the CPI remains silent on environmental issues in its draft party programme (2012), it too speaks of 'environmental pollution' as a consequence of capitalism's 'mad drive for profits and ever greater profits'.[85] It is also becoming far more critical of nuclear power generation for its hazards and high costs.

The CPI(M) since 1998 has included ecological issues in its congresses' political resolutions and stressed the links between environmental destruction/degradation, caused by 'deforestation, soil erosion, pollution of air and water resources', and its 'adverse effects on the well-being of the people'.[86] In 2008, the CPI(M) explicitly stated: 'Environmental problems in India have been worsening and are reaching crisis proportions ... with serious impact on livelihoods, living conditions and health of the people, especially the poor and marginalized ... These problems have been exacerbated by the policies of liberalization and globalization, by commercialization of common resources, and by the failures of government to regulate these sectors'.[87]

Since 2008, the CPI(M) has also paid attention to climate change, caused primarily by greenhouse gas emissions. But it has largely adopted a 'climate nationalist' position in the international context, blaming 'global capitalism' and the developed countries for causing the climate crisis, which 'affects the people in the developing world most adversely'.[88] In the domestic context, the party emphasizes rich–poor inequalities in consumption and access to energy, and criticizes the elite's profligate energy use and high per capita greenhouse emissions.[89]

If the Left is genuinely concerned about climate change in the domestic context, it should logically oppose power generation based on coal, the dirtiest fossil fuel, which accounts for 70 per cent of India's electrical capacity, itself the biggest contributor to the country's greenhouse gas emissions. But the Left does not oppose the rampant growth of coal-based power in India or demand that, to mitigate climate change, India must rapidly move away from fossil fuels towards renewable energy.

The time to do so could not be more opportune, now that a renewable energy revolution is under way the world over.[90] The Left has paid little attention to renewables, to energy conservation and efficiency, and to other 'green' measures. Nor does it have a position on adaptation to climate change, based on innovative ways of promoting low-energy-intensity agriculture, afforestation, water and coastline conservation, and so on.

Although there has been definite progress in the Left's perspective on ecology and a positive transition away from its past hostility towards environmentalism, it has still not developed a *radical ecological critique* of capitalism and the paradigm of limitless growth. Such a critique must view the process of capital accumulation—and not just neo-liberal capitalism—as inevitably entailing the predatory appropriation of natural resources and destruction of nature. The Left does not base itself on the key concepts of entropy and 'the metabolic rift' that capitalism causes, disrupting the link between humans and the rest of the natural world, to the detriment of both.[91]

Consequently, the Indian Left does not advance a concept of socialism as an order based not just on a different relationship between classes, or between state and society, but on a qualitatively new relationship between production, consumption and nature. Communism cannot be the society of unlimited material abundance that some of Marx's writings suggest it would be. Material consumption must be finite and limited in a world with finite resources.

Human Rights: Spotty Record

The Indian Left has historically been a vocal champion of democracy and citizens' civil and political liberties, as well as their economic and social rights. Its own ability to function openly and without fear of repression or victimization—which it could not take for granted for the first half of its existence—is conditional on such rights and their enrichment. The Indian Left, typically the underdog in society, therefore has a straightforward stake in defending human rights. But this does not always hold true when it is in power, or when it faces opposition from the Far Left.

The Left's record on human rights and tolerance of violence is distressing, particularly in West Bengal. To take just one staggering figure, there were an average of four 'political murders' a day during the first two decades of the Left Front's rule in West Bengal, according to its former home minister and later chief minister Buddhadeb Bhattacharjee.[92]

The Left in West Bengal was born in a climate of great social unrest and violence. It faced severe repression under Congress regimes right until it first came to power in the United Front government in 1967, and again during the Emergency. The violence got aggravated with the Naxalite insurgency of 1967, which sometimes targeted cadres of the parliamentary Left parties, which in turn retaliated with great ferocity. The violence prevalent in the state was always extremely brutal and often barbaric in form. Extrajudicial executions of political opponents, Naxalites or suspected police informers were not uncommon; nor was mutilation of the dead bodies of 'enemies'.

Between 1970 and 1976, the state witnessed the liquidation of literally hundreds of Naxalites and CPI(M) and CPI activists at the hands of Congress goons, with police complicity, including the gruesome Baranagar killings in north-western Calcutta.[93] A particularly bloody period was 1971, during the Bangladesh war, when the Central government took over the state's anti-Naxalite operations. 'The Indian Army and Central Reserve Police undertook a "cleansing operation" in the countryside, flushing out the Maoist peasant guerrilla bases as well as the CPM peasant bases'.[94]

The Left parties, and the CPI(M) in particular, built self-defence squads to cope with state repression and attacks by political opponents. Some of these squads mutated into bands composed of men who would use strong-arm tactics to extort money or impose 'the party's diktat. Some evolved into virtual militias like the 'Harmad sena' (derived from the Portuguese term for armadas) for which West Bengal became known, especially during the Singur and Nandigram episodes.

It was difficult for the Left in the 1970s not to internalize some of the culture of violence which it inherited, and which was part of the food agitations and 'land-grab' movements that it launched in the 1960s. Some key leaders of the CPI(M), such as Promode Dasgupta, themselves came from former revolutionary terrorist groups and practised organizational tactics based on secrecy and despotic intolerance of dissent. This reinforced the culture of violence and resulted in periodic intimidation of and attacks on political opponents.

The West Bengal police by the early 1970s had become notorious for its harsh methods, including unreported detentions, arbitrary arrests, torture and cavalier resort to firing on unarmed protesters, as well as collusion in the killing of Left cadres, especially Naxalites. Upon coming to power in 1977, the Left Front government to its credit released thousands of political prisoners and pledged never to use draconian laws like the Maintenance of Internal Security Act and Essential Services Maintenance Act. But it retained most police officers who were guilty of past crimes, and never addressed the issue of police reform. The police had a free run. By 1981, West Bengal's share of the 751 cases of police firing resulting in 337 deaths recorded in India was 248 firings and 62 deaths.[95]

Massacre at Morichjhanpi

The Left Front's human rights record,[96] documented by civil society groups like Nagarik Mancha, People's Union of Civil Liberties and Association for the Protection of Democratic Rights, was unflattering. While it was far better than that of the Congress in West Bengal, it was marked by arbitrary arrests, forced eviction of poor people like street hawkers, police intimidation of and brutality towards ordinary citizens, land acquisition by violent methods, persistent violence against women, and custodial deaths.[97] Its thirty-four-year tenure in power witnessed several episodes of violence.

One of the earliest major incidents of violence was directed not against the Left's opponents, but against poor, mostly Dalit,[98] refugees from Bangladesh. This was the massacre at Morichjhanpi, an island in the northern-most forested part of the West Bengal Sundarbans, in which thousands of people are believed to have perished. They were part of the influx of refugees of the post-1971 period, whom the Central government under the Congress forcibly resettled in Dandakaranya, comprising parts of Chhattisgarh, Andhra Pradesh and Odisha—a move then denounced by the Left which promised to settle them in West Bengal, probably on an island in the Sundarbans.[99]

When the LF came to power, some 30,000 of the refugees returned to West Bengal and set up a settlement at Morichjhanpi, which by then had been declared part of a reserve for the Royal Bengal Tiger. The West Bengal police started forcibly evicting them. On 31 January 1979 the police opened fire killing thirty-six people. The area was soon declared out of bounds for journalists, and an economic blockade (announced on Republic Day) was imposed in May. When that failed, thirty police launches encircled the island, depriving the settlers of food and water; 'they were also tear-gassed, their huts razed, their boats sunk, their fisheries and tube-wells destroyed, and those who tried to cross the river were shot at. To fetch water, the settlers had now to venture after dark and deep into the forested portion of the island and forced to eat wild grass. Several hundred men, women and children were believed to have died during that time …'[100]

Researcher Ross Mallick—who interviewed several people in the area, and quotes a report by three MPs appointed by Prime Minister Morarji Desai to visit the site before the evictions—estimates that of the 14,388 families who left Dandakaranya for West Bengal, as many as 4,128 families 'perished in transit, died of starvation, exhaustion', or drowned when their boats were scuttled by the police and were shot dead in firings.[101] 'How many of these deaths actually occurred in Morichjhanpi we shall never know. However, what we do know is that no criminal charges were laid against any of the officials or politicians involved. Even then Prime Minister Desai, wishing to maintain the support of the communists for his government, decided not to pursue the matter.'[102]

Despite its scale and brutality, Morichjhanpi never entered public consciousness or debate in a big way—unlike Nandigram or Singur three decades later—although Amitav Ghosh wrote about it in his novel *The Hungry Tide*.[103] At any rate, according to Mallick, the CPI(M) leadership 'congratulated its participant members on their successful operation ... and made their refugee policy reversal explicit stating that "there was no possibility of giving shelter to these large number of refugees under any circumstances in the State" ... Within the CPM there was some dissatisfaction with the way the party leadership had handled the question. Many CPM cadre felt the leadership had dealt with the problem in a "bureaucratic way"... In a final twist to the episode, the CPM settled its own supporters in Morichjhanpi, occupying and utilizing the facilities left by the evicted refugees ...'[104]

There was dissension within the LF cabinet over the settlement decision. The Revolutionary Socialist Party, 'which had a political base in the Sundarbans ... opposed the decision, as did other Left Front supporters. The RSP minister, Debabrata Bandyopadhyay, was not given a new portfolio after the subsequent election ... His exclusion ... was attributed to his efforts to eradicate corruption in CPM-controlled village councils, though his opposition ... to the eviction may have been a contributing factor.'[105]

In another instance of gruesome violence, seventeen followers of the Ananda Marg cult were dragged out of taxis in broad daylight in Ballygunge, and burned alive on 30 April 1982. It was rumoured that they were 'child-lifters' who became victims of spontaneous 'popular anger'. The Ananda Marg has always blamed the CPI(M) for the savagery, but who perpetrated it remains a mystery to this day.

Nothing suggests that such cases of extreme violence have been debated inside the CPI(M) with any seriousness, or that it has ever admitted to having committed blunders on the issue. Yet, many of the party's leaders and cadres have been charged with grave offences including murder and rape, such as the Sainbari case in Bardhaman (1970) involving two politbureau members, the Birati rape episode and the Bantala rape and murder (both 1990), the Suchapur massacre in Birbhum (2000), where eleven agricultural workers were killed, Keshpur and Garbeta (West Medinipur), which have seen a vendetta between the CPI(M) and Trinamool Congress for more than a decade since 1998, with dozens of casualties, Chhoto Angaria (West Medinipur, 2001), Singur and Nandigram (2006 and 2007), and the Netai (Lalgarh) gunning down of nine people in 2011.[106]

The official figures for 'political murders' between 1977 and 1996 are staggering: 28,000, according to former chief minister Buddhadeb Bhattacharjee.[107] This works out to a daily average of four murders committed with a political motive. Nothing suggests that this level of violence has declined since then; it is only likely to have increased with the rise of the Trinamool Congress to power.[108]

In recent years, the Left parties have rightly condemned draconian laws which violate or endanger civil and political liberties, and which give the police and army extraordinary powers and, worse, impunity from prosecution. India is estimated to have scores of such laws in different states.[109] However, the Left parties have not been averse to using some of these laws when in power. An example is the Unlawful Activities Prevention Act (UAPA), under which Chakradhar Mahato, a leader of People's Committee against Police Atrocities spearheading the Lalgarh agitation in West Bengal, was arrested and abducted in September 2009. Even worse, in Left-ruled Tripura, the Armed Forces Special Powers Act[110] was in force from February 1979 until May 2015.

It is impossible not to deplore the attitude adopted by senior Left Front functionaries towards their political opponents in the recent past, and their open encouragement to the police to shoot first and ask questions later—as happened in 2000, shortly after Bhattacharjee became chief minister, when he told the police: 'Those who roam the roads with arms cannot enjoy human rights. Just shoot them and leave me to handle the repercussion.'[111] Such statements mock the rule of law.

Chandrasekharan's Shadow

Kerala's political culture is much less violent than West Bengal's, but violence exists there too in the form of inter-party feuds and murderous punishment delivered to those who leave existing parties and set up rebel organizations. There is also intimidation of the public by party-linked mafias connected with the real estate business and extraction of natural resources like water and sand. North Kerala, in particular Kannur district, has long been notorious for cyclical violence between the CPI(M) and the RSS–BJP, which has resulted in the killing and maiming of scores of their cadres.

Since 1980, nearly 180 of their members have lost their lives in political vendettas in Kannur, some of them triggered by attempts to poach each other's members. The latest instance, after a five-year lull, was the 1 September 2014 killing of the RSS's E. Manoj, allegedly by CPI(M) members. Manoj in turn was among the accused in the stabbing of CPI(M) district secretary P. Jayarajan in 1999.[112] Both sides take pride in their masculine muscle-flexing abilities, glorify 'martyrdom', and invest violence with a dangerous form of self-esteem.[113]

A 2012 incident, in which CPI(M) rebel leader T.P. Chandrasekharan was hacked to death at Onchiyam, Kozhikode district, produced widespread public revulsion. 'As many as 12 people, including three CPI(M) leaders, were convicted in the murder case.'[114] The killing caused deep divisions in the CPI(M), with former chief minister V.S. Achuthanandan publicly expressing sympathy for Chandrasekharan's widow.[115]

Ultimately, however, even Chandrasekharan's killing did not lead to serious rethinking in the party or the Left Democratic Front on the issue of violence—although the LDF paid a heavy price for the murder through a loss of credibility and electoral support.[116] The Left's social policy deficit on the issue of human rights remains glaring nationally, as well as in Kerala and West Bengal.

Unimpressive Agenda

The Left's overall balance sheet on the social policy agenda, although far better than that of most other political parties, is unimpressive, and in places, tainted. Its record has improved on the caste question and to an extent on gender issues at least in acknowledging the existence of its deficits, although not in bridging them in theory or practice. The Left is the last force in Indian politics that would countenance cohabiting with the BJP. Reassuring as that might be, the Left's record on actively, practically, combating communalism is patchy and full of vacillation. It falls conceptually and politically short of what is needed at a time when Hindutva gravely threatens Indian democracy.

As for the environment, the Left parties have still not freed themselves from the straitjacket of developmentalism or recognized the intimate connections between the accumulation of capital, ecological destruction and undermining of people's access to natural resources and their livelihoods. Nor do they acknowledge the crucial importance of protecting irreplaceable natural resources, including the climate system or the Western Ghats.

On human rights, some attitudes of the Left to violence are deplorable and deeply rooted in its Stalinist organizational culture. Unless it reforms its perception of human rights, the Left cannot become a beacon of hope to citizens, particularly from underprivileged sections like the Dalits, who are becoming increasing aware of social issues and concerns. The Left is not an inspiring influence or a reliable ally for progressive grass-roots movements active on such issues; it can sometimes even be an adversary. The Left, with its baggage of suspicion of radical civil society groups and people's movements—whom it derisively terms NGOs—finds it difficult to work with them in joint campaigns on an equal footing.

For a decade or so after the mid-1990s, the Left seemed to have shed some of its inhibitions and started interacting with radical people's movements and the progressive intelligentsia in a positive manner, to the point of participating in the World Social Forum process. That dialogue was interrupted when the Singur–Nandigram crises broke out. It has not been properly resumed yet. Still, the Left should know after its recent debacles that it must open up to other radical currents and join people's mobilizations in a spirit of humility and mutually beneficial interaction.

9

Lost Opportunities

Parliamentary Pinnacle, Nuclear Deal Fiasco, 2014 Debacle

Less than a decade after the Left parties committed a 'historic blunder' by turning down an offer to head India's Central government, another grand opportunity came their way. In May 2004 the Bharatiya Janata Party–led National Democratic Alliance lost the Lok Sabha elections after six years in power. The Left parties, having notched up their highest-ever tally of Lok Sabha seats, became indispensable to the formation of a Centre-Left government that would keep the increasingly aggressive and importunate BJP at bay. The arithmetic overwhelmingly favoured the Left as a balancer. The Congress, which won 145 of the Lok Sabha's 543 seats, drew in more than fifteen regional parties to constitute the United Progressive Alliance. The UPA, with 221 seats, still fell short of a majority and would need the support or participation of the Left, with its sixty-one seats.

There were broadly two ways of looking at the 2004 conjuncture: as a unique *parliamentary* opportunity to bring into being a strongly secular left-leaning government with progressive policies, which would offer a welcome respite from communal strife and divisive, regressive politics; and as a unique *strategic* opportunity to reorient, revitalize and reinvent the Left politically, as a movement as well as a parliamentary entity, and at the same time, to try to force a further shift in the overall balance of class forces, not just in parliament, but in the larger society.

The first approach would emphasize the importance of establishing a government which catalyses further progressive change. This would centrally involve tactics of manoeuvring and bargaining over policies, programmes and placement of personnel in key positions. Many Left politicians had by now become consummate practitioners of such tactics, but they were nevertheless confronted with a formidable challenge—that of countering the strong neo-liberal orientation of many Congress leaders, and especially of Manmohan Singh, party president Sonia Gandhi's prime ministerial nominee. The key questions here would be how to maximize the Left's tactical advantage in what could often turn into a war of nerves or a contest of wills over economic and social policies, and to find ways of combating the communal forces and reaffirming the secular character of the state.

The second, seemingly more ambitious, perspective would take into account both the Left's strengths and weaknesses. It would acknowledge the disproportion between the Left's parliamentary numbers and its real political power based on support among underprivileged groups, and seek to improve this support through extra-parliamentary popular mobilizations from the ground up and left-leaning policies from the top. These mobilizations would serve to mount pressure on the government and influence its programmes. By adopting this approach, the Left would set far larger objectives than the short-term goal, itself worthy, of establishing a secular left-leaning government.

The two approaches would entail divergent priorities and different patterns of commitment of the Left's energies to parliamentary and non-parliamentary efforts. In the event, the Left parties chose the first approach—by default though, not after a thorough debate. Following a debate, it might have been perfectly legitimate to conclude that the second approach was excessively ambitious and fraught with a high risk of failure in the short run and losses for the Left in the long run; it would be prudent to stick to the straight and narrow. Yet, the absence of a debate itself points to the low-ambition goals that the Left's leadership instinctively set itself—in keeping with its 'modest parliamentary mandate'.[1]

Compromise Without a Fight?

This chapter argues that the Left did not play its hand particularly adroitly even in the parliamentary game. It did not bargain hard enough on many policy issues and did not exercise its veto against some of the UPA's decisions, although it could have legitimately done so. It compromised much too quickly on some progressive or radical measures and allowed the UPA to ride roughshod over it on economic and foreign policy matters and on security issues when it could have offered resistance. Among the tangible, if rather modest, benefits the Left received in the shape of a few personnel appointments was the post of the Speaker of the Lok Sabha, to which it nominated the veteran lawyer Somnath Chatterjee.

In 2004, unlike in 1996, the question of the Left parties' participation in government was not keenly or fractiously debated within Left circles or their periphery. But more than 200 progressive intellectuals, artistes, theatre and film personalities and social activists made an appeal to the Left parties to participate in the government as part of a 'creative and constructive initiative' to impart 'an entirely new direction' to economic policies and dismantle 'the ideological structure created by communalism'.[2]

Individual leaders of the Left, especially of the CPI and other smaller parties in the Left Front, but also some in the CPI(M), favoured participation, although not strongly. But the proposal was shot down by the CPI(M)'s top leadership even before it came up for formal discussion. The Left parties opted for supporting the government from the outside. Such support would be based on a Common Minimum Programme (CMP), whose formulation they could negotiate and influence.

Negotiations began in right earnest in the third week of May on eighteen points drawn up by the Left, covering a range of issues including a reaffirmation of secularism, progressive policies in agriculture and industry, increased spending on health and education, an employment guarantee programme and foreign policy and security matters.[3] Logically, the Left's leaders should have prepared the initial draft to be discussed. But the Congress party seized the initiative and thus established a head-start. The Left parties insisted, among other things, on the inclusion of social sector programmes, opposed privatization of public sector enterprises, called for more balanced Centre–state relations and demanded an independent and progressive foreign policy, which stressed improved relations with India's neighbours, and opposed unilateralism in international relations.

The UPA made concessions and accommodated some of these demands. For instance, it agreed to pass a National Employment Guarantee Act, to 'provide a legal guarantee for at least 100 days of employment, to begin with, on asset-creating public works programmes every year at minimum wages for at least one able-bodied person in every rural, urban poor and lower-middle class household'. It also pledged to launch 'a massive food-for-work programme', raise public spending on health and education, and set up a national commission on labour in the unorganized sector. And it promised to 'take immediate steps to reverse the trend of communalization of education' that had set in under the NDA. But the UPA refused to budge on several crucial economic policy issues.

Eventually, a compromise agreement was reached on the CMP and announced on 27 May, which broadly reflected the UPA's 'abiding commitment' to (it bears stating, neo-liberal) 'economic reforms with a human face', which 'stimulates growth, investment and employment'. The CMP said that 'generally', profit-making public sector companies would not be privatized. 'All privatization will be considered on a transparent and consultative case-by-case basis. The UPA will retain existing "navaratna"[4] companies in the public sector, while these companies raise resources from the capital market'; foreign direct investment 'will continue to be encouraged and actively sought, particularly in areas of infrastructure, high technology and exports … The country needs and can easily absorb at least two to three times the present level of FDI inflows.'[5]

The CMP promised to pursue 'an independent foreign policy, keeping in mind its past traditions' (presumably meaning Nehruvian non-alignment), which would 'promote multi-polarity in world relations and oppose all attempts at unilateralism'. India, it said, would maintain 'a credible nuclear weapons programme' while taking 'demonstrable and verifiable confidence-building measures with [India's] nuclear neighbours. It will take a leadership role in promoting universal nuclear disarmament and working for a nuclear weapons-free world'.

The CMP covered twelve of the eighteen listed points; the rest were left in abeyance or encapsulated in anodyne formulations. This itself represented an unexplained and undebated retreat on the Left's part. Arguably, the Left could have bargained harder. It could have drawn sharper red lines, as many left-of-centre parties in Europe routinely do when forming coalition governments with ideologically dissimilar parties. The Left could have listed some issues explicitly as potential deal breakers. Given its own courageous stand against the 1998 nuclear tests and its demand that India and Pakistan roll back their nuclear weapons programmes, it could have at the minimum insisted on a nuclear freeze instead of acquiescing in a 'credible nuclear weapons programme'—which would legitimize and perpetuate these weapons of mass destruction and make nonsense of its original demand.

The Left could have demanded and possibly secured active measures of nuclear restraint such as separation of nuclear warheads from delivery vehicles, and a moratorium on missile test flights and fissile material production by India and Pakistan. It could have insisted on negotiations for more arms control measures and improved relations with Pakistan, and on demilitarization of India's policy towards its neighbours. It could have explicitly stated its reservations and written dissenting notes on a number of other issues too. And it could have gone public with these. Of course, India's mainstream media, among the most right-wing in the world, would have maligned the Left for such 'irresponsible' and reckless 'populism', but that should not have deterred the Left. Its primary constituency lay not in the media but somewhere else.

The Left did not drive a hard bargain on many issues. What emerged was a compromise whose content the UPA further diluted—for instance, by limiting the employment guarantee Act only to rural areas instead of the whole country, and implementing it in phases. The UPA continued to deregulate the economy and delicense industries; it curtailed the public sector, cut back public investment and squeezed the flow of resources to the state governments.[6] The commission on unorganized labour became a commission on 'enterprises in the unorganized sector'. The vague pledges to raise public spending on health and education never got translated into real numbers.

The government used various loopholes and voids in the CMP to drive its own foreign and security policy agendas, including strengthening the 'strategic partnership' with the United States and entering into the US–India civilian nuclear cooperation deal in 2005. This last caused intense friction between the UPA and the Left and eventually led to the withdrawal of the Left's support to the government in 2008.

Lending a Progressive Thrust

None of this belittles the Left's contribution in giving the CMP a positive or progressive thrust in its social sector programmes—e.g., the Mahatma Gandhi National Rural Employment Guarantee Act (MGNREGA), the Scheduled Tribes and Other Traditional Forest Dwellers (Recognition of Forest Rights) Act, 2006 (popularly called the Forest Rights Act or FRA, which grants to forest-dwellers rights to cultivate lands and usufruct rights to minor forest produce, etc.), enforcement and enrichment of the Right to Information Act, lobbying for a right to food legislation, and not least, in pushing through a creative interpretation of the amended Patents Act, which restricts monopolies in pharmaceuticals production and prevents the 'evergreening' of patented molecules and is yet compatible with the intellectual property rights regime under the World Trade Organization (WTO).[7]

Similarly, the Left also succeeded to an extent in restraining the UPA from going the whole hog in privatizing the public sector. It resisted the unbridled entry of foreign direct investment (FDI) in retail trade, the insurance sector and pension funds, and large-scale implementation of Special Economic Zones (SEZs) which threaten peasant livelihoods and offer undeserved concessions to private entrepreneurs, while creating opportunities to grab land.[8] Without the Left, the outcome of the UPA's economic policies would arguably have been far worse.

The Left also played a moderating or sobering role on some foreign policy issues. Although it could not prevent a close strategic relationship between India and the US or a steady shift towards Israel on the Palestinian nationhood issue, its opposition to sending Indian troops to

Iraq did make a difference. On Nepal, the Left, in particular the CPI(M) politburo member Sitaram Yechury, joined a major and welcome initiative to bring the Maoists overground and into the mainstream, and thus helped the cause of republican democracy there. In general, the Left's pleas for a more cooperative relationship with India's neighbours, including Pakistan and Bangladesh, could not be entirely ignored.

However, three qualifications or caveats are in order. First, the Left succeeded best when it supplemented or joined initiatives launched by civil society movements and progressive sections of the intelligentsia. This is especially true of the MGNREGA, a campaign for which was first launched by the Rozgar Adhikar Abhiyan, a civil society initiative, on whose foundation the Left parties later built through their participation and parliamentary intervention. This also holds true for the FRA, Right to Information Act, Food Security Act and the patents initiative. The Left parties cannot claim to have initiated any of these campaigns, which produced tangible gains especially for the poor.

Second, a clear dissonance or disjunction emerged within the Left, which weakened its credibility in proposing progressive changes or opposing the UPA's right-wing moves. For instance, West Bengal chief minister Buddhadeb Bhattacharjee violated the CPI(M)'s stated policies when he chose to invite Wal-Mart into retail trade, made deals with multinational seeds and food companies like Cargill, welcomed World Bank and Asian Development Bank advice and loans and zealously campaigned for SEZs. The party's national leadership opposed such moves, but only rhetorically.

Third, the Left did not reinforce its parliamentary interventions with, or bring pressure to bear on the UPA through, popular mobilizations. It confined itself largely to media statements and 'palace politics' interventions, with a tiny, limited demonstration thrown in here and there, perhaps too small to be effective. After Singur and Nandigram, the Left's moral authority collapsed, its internal crisis greatly worsened and its capacity to sustain the practice of mobilizing large numbers of people on their rights, needs and aspirations—and hence crucial to furthering radical social agendas—substantially decreased.

On a less charitable view, even the Left's will to do so weakened: it had begun to see politics in far more limited terms, detached from mobilizations in which the masses have agency. By the late 1990s, much of the top leadership of the CPI(M), the leading Left party, came from middle class and students union leaders, with little exposure to working class or peasant movements, unlike in the past. This had an impact on the importance it attached to people's mobilizations.

As for the US–India nuclear deal, it would have been difficult at the best of times for the Left to educate and mobilize the public on this extremely complex issue. Doing this would require a sophisticated understanding of geopolitics and a specialized grasp of the nature of the global nuclear order, and the abstruse processes of negotiating its modification through national and multilateral organizations. Yet the Left chose to focus on the nuclear deal and turn it into a litmus test for its relations with the UPA. In India, no foreign or security policy question has become the centre of public attention to the point of being the fulcrum around which critical political choices are made. This would be even truer of a relatively esoteric issue like the nuclear deal.

Nuclear–Nationalist Trap

The US–India civilian nuclear cooperation agreement, inked in 2005 and finalized in 2008, made a one-time exception for India in the global nuclear commerce regime by permitting the sale and transfer of nuclear materials to India for its civilian programme although India is not a signatory to the Nuclear Non-Proliferation Treaty (NPT) or any other nuclear restraint agreement. The special waiver was rationalized on the ground that India is 'a responsible state with advanced nuclear technology', with which the US sought to forge a 'global partnership'.

This followed an agreement called the 'New Framework for the US–India Defence Relationship', under which the two countries would undertake greater military collaboration and cooperate on ballistic missile defence and other advanced technologies, thus forging the basis of a long-term alliance. Such cooperation led to India's participation in large-scale US-sponsored military exercises with Japan, Australia and Singapore. India was also 'coerced' by the US into voting against Iran at the International Atomic Energy Agency (IAEA) twice, in September 2005 and February 2006.[9]

Under the nuclear deal, India agreed to separate its civilian and military facilities and place some but not all of its civilian reactors under IAEA 'safeguards' (inspections to ensure that no nuclear materials are diverted to military use). In effect, the deal accorded recognition and legitimacy, although not a de jure status, to India's nuclear weapons. Internationally, it expectedly provoked controversy and was opposed vigorously and openly by Pakistan, and covertly and diplomatically by China and some other countries. But it was eventually approved in 2008 by the IAEA and the Nuclear Suppliers' Group (NSG), a voluntary grouping of forty-odd states,[10] which jointly monitors and regulates trade in nuclear materials. The deal's stated rationale was to help India build up its nuclear power generation several-fold with imported uranium and especially imported reactors. Yet, seven years on, not a single commercial contract for imported reactors has been finalized.

The Left parties pilloried the nuclear deal on a number of grounds: it would further consolidate the US–India 'strategic partnership', making India Washington's subordinate ally; it would interfere with India's sovereign decision making in nuclear matters, including programmes linked to the production of plutonium and other weapons-related materials; it would not ensure full civilian nuclear cooperation or guarantee uninterrupted fuel supply on the part of the US, as promised; it would impose extraneous 'non-nuclear' conditions on India, such as a commitment to support a Fissile Material Cutoff Treaty at the UN Conference on Disarmament. Besides, the legal agreements and US legislation that the deal involved would not be compatible with Indian 'self-reliance in the nuclear sector'. Thus, in all these ways, the deal would violate 'the national interest'.[11]

The Left was virtually silent on the deal's impact in weakening the global non-proliferation regime thanks to the special exception it made for India, which set a dangerous precedent. The Left also did not question the safety and ecological sustainability of nuclear power generation as such,[12] although expanding it was officially presented as the key to India's energy security and 'decarbonization' of its energy economy. The Left primarily confined itself here to commenting adversely on the high costs of imported reactors, while arguing for 'indigenous' reactors—in reality, pressurized heavy water reactors designed by Canada—and rationalizing the fantasy of India's 'three-stage' nuclear power programme, with thermal or normal uranium-fuelled reactors in the first stage, fast-breeder reactors in the second stage, and eventually, thorium-fuelled reactors.[13]

The central thrust of the Left's attack on the US–India deal was founded on unrefined nationalism, which made decision making in respect of nuclear weapons the litmus test of national sovereignty—contrary to the classical socialist stand which vests sovereignty in the people, and holds that there is no such thing as 'the national interest' which can be separated from the interests of the dominant or ruling class.[14] This stance pushed the Left into the arms of the hawks within the nuclear establishment, typically former officials of the Department of Atomic Energy (DAE), which is in charge of both the military and the civilian nuclear programmes.

Some of the hawks opposed the deal either out of blatantly national-chauvinist considerations, or because it would drive the Indian government towards a policy of nuclear restraint, a prospect they loathed.[15] Yet others opposed the original terms of the deal (for instance, on bringing India's fast-breeder reactors under the purview of the civilian programme and hence IAEA inspections), but only because they wanted to drive a better or stronger bargain on the civilian power front.[16] Most of them did not share the Left's strategic rationale for opposing the deal (namely, that it would bring about a US–India strategic alliance, and compromise Indian sovereignty).

Yet, the Left joined hands with them, as also did the BJP from time to time. (The BJP ultimately voted against the deal, out of the purely opportunistic tactical calculation of toppling the UPA government; on coming to power in 2014, it enthusiastically supported the deal.) At the very least, the Left's crude nuclear nationalism eclipsed, if it did not practically undermine, the contribution it had itself made to the cause of peace and social sanity in 1998 by opposing and condemning India's nuclear tests and demanding that its nuclear arsenal be dismantled.

A word is in order here about why nuclear weapons must be unconditionally opposed, as the international Left has traditionally done, without caving in to crude nationalism which separates sovereignty from the people and vests it in military preparedness and armaments. Nuclear weapons are instruments of mass annihilation, which are quintessentially meant to be used against non-combatant civilians; they kill massively, indiscriminately and cruelly; and they violate the rules of just war. Nuclear arms are not weapons of defence. The doctrine of nuclear deterrence, which rationalizes them, is morally unacceptable and provides the illusion of security. Deterrence has proved perilously unreliable on countless occasions. Nuclear weapons are extremely costly and can become ruinously so if there is an arms race—in keeping with their logic.[17]

In India (and Pakistan), where half the population remains deprived of the basic necessities of life, there are even stronger moral, economic and social arguments against nuclear weapons. Support for nuclear weapons is intimately connected with militarist, belligerent nationalism and has been appropriated by Hindutva supporters, with harmful political consequences.

At any rate, the Left's nationalist stance did not evoke a strong popular response. Leave alone large numbers of the general public, the Left could not mobilize even sympathetic middle-class intellectuals on a significant scale on the nuclear deal issue. The Left parties, with their parliamentary leverage, however succeeded in persuading the UPA to set up a joint committee to look into their objections to the nuclear deal. A key player in the committee was the then foreign minister, Pranab Mukherjee, who had a line of communication open with the Bengal leaders of the CPI(M). The committee held nine meetings between September 2007 and June 2008, which failed to resolve UPA–Left differences. Eventually, the UPA stuck to its guns and even refused to hand over to the Left a copy of the draft of the safeguards agreement to be signed with the IAEA: it only presented a brief note on the agreement's salient features and took it back.[18]

The November 2007 Cop-out

Initially, the UPA was reluctant to confront the Left on the deal and lose its support in the Lok Sabha. But the situation changed after the violence in Nandigram in West Bengal's East Medinipur district over land acquisition for a chemicals complex ('hub') in April 2007, when fourteen protesters organized under the Bhoomi Uchchhed Pratirodh Committee

(BUPC) (committee to resist land acquisition) were killed in a police firing. This led to a huge public outcry. Unprecedented demonstrations broke out against the Left Front's action, led by some of its own constituents (especially the RSP and the Forward Bloc), by its supporters within the intelligentsia and by a wide array of civil society groups,[19] besides the political opposition led by the Trinamool Congress (TMC).

Following the protests, the Left Front government announced in September 2007 that it would shift the chemical hub to another site. But in November, the CPI(M)'s cadres unleashed punitive violence against the BUPC to 'recapture' Nandigram, from where the police was withdrawn. The CPI(M)'s state secretary described the operation as 'a new dawn' and Chief Minister Bhattacharjee justified it as a way of 'paying [the protesters] back in their own coin'.[20] This provoked widespread outrage. Singur and Nandigram became household words all over the country and beyond, signifying a Left party's violence against its own popular base.

Thanks to the Nandigram episode, the Left lost a great deal of its moral authority and was politically put on the defensive.[21] The nuclear deal had to clear one more obstacle, however: getting the Left to agree that it be sent to the IAEA for negotiation of safeguards (inspections); once the IAEA approved a safeguards agreement, the deal would be on 'auto-pilot', effectively out of the Left's influence or reach. The Left publicly said, firmly, categorically and repeatedly, that it would oppose any move by the government to take the deal to the IAEA in Vienna. This was the Left's final bargaining counter, its trump card, against the UPA.

However, the Left's resolve soon crumbled. This became starkly clear at the 16 November 2007 meeting of the UPA–Left joint committee on the nuclear issue. The committee agreed that the government would go ahead and negotiate the safeguards agreement with the IAEA secretariat, but that 'the outcome will be presented to the committee for its consideration before it finalizes its findings. The findings of the committee will be taken into account before the operationalization of the India–US Civil Nuclear Cooperation Agreement.' Politically weakened and diffident, the Left had in effect surrendered its trump card, if not beaten a retreat without firing a shot.[22]

The UPA, in particular Prime Minister Manmohan Singh and

Foreign Minister Mukherjee, took full advantage of the Left's weakened position and fashioned a confrontationist strategy in the succeeding months. Eventually, in July 2008, soon after Singh met US president George W. Bush at the Hokkaido G-8+5 summit in Japan, the UPA government approached the IAEA to finalize the deal. Singh by then had decided to push it through in the teeth of opposition from the Left, whose stand against it he described as irrational and reactionary. He staked the survival of his government on the issue and threatened to resign if the deal was not approved by parliament.

CPI(M) general secretary Prakash Karat declared that the Left would withdraw support to the UPA. The Congress taunted the Left for collaborating with the BJP, which too opposed the deal, albeit for unconvincing and opportunistic reasons. Karat rebutted this by saying the Congress had no right to 'point fingers' at the Left, and it had itself 'conspired' and voted with the BJP to topple the 'secular governments' of V.P. Singh, H.D. Deve Gowda and I.K. Gujral in the 1990s.[23]

The crunch came on 22 July. The UPA demanded a vote on a confidence motion in its favour in the Lok Sabha, during which the Left found itself on the same side as the BJP. The UPA won by 275 to 256 votes thanks largely to support from Mulayam Singh Yadav's Samajwadi Party, a former CPI(M) ally. This was a murky episode, with charges of bribery, revealed through a 'sting operation' by a TV channel,[24] the display in the Lok Sabha of bundles of cash reportedly offered to buy votes, and cross-voting by twenty-eight MPs, including some belonging to the BJP.

At any rate, the UPA won the confidence vote and the deal-related legislation went through in the Lok Sabha. In August, the IAEA board of governors approved it, and in September, the forty-five-member NSG granted India a waiver from the prevalent nuclear commerce rules, ignoring the misgivings expressed by Austria, Ireland and New Zealand.

The Left was humiliated, but won little sympathy even from its own supporters, leave alone the larger public. On 23 July the CPI(M) expelled from the party Somnath Chatterjee, the Lok Sabha Speaker nominated by it, 'for seriously compromising the position of the party', without stating the reasons in detail. Chatterjee, a party member for four decades, had decided not to vote with the Left and the BJP; nor did he agree to the party's demand that he step down as Speaker before the vote.

An immediate consequence of the stance adopted by Left parties' national leaders on the nuclear deal was the alienation of their state units, especially in West Bengal, which feared that the collapse of the UPA government would help the Congress and the Trinamool Congress seal an alliance in the state in future elections, which would inflict serious damage on the Left. West Bengal state secretariat member Subhas Chakraborty and some other senior state party leaders publicly criticized the central leadership of the CPI(M) for expelling Chatterjee.[25]

On 27 July Chief Minister Bhattacharjee snubbed Karat, then on a visit to Kolkata, by boycotting a meeting addressed by him at the state party headquarters. But Bhattacharjee made it a point to call on Pranab Mukherjee, then also in the city.[26] The CPI(M)'s national leadership later rationalized the decision to withdraw support to the UPA. But to placate the Bengal unit, it said the decision's timing was wrong; it should have withdrawn support earlier and not waited till July 2008.

Expedient Federalism

Well before the July confidence vote, a new power equation had got consolidated in the CPI(M), which determined the course of Left party politics as a whole. This was a peculiar form of expedient 'federalism' inconsistent with the nature of the party and its belief in unitarian central authority. The 'federalism' consisted in a division of labour (rather authority) between the CPI(M)'s national leadership and the two big states where the party held power. This was true with a vengeance of the party's West Bengal unit.

West Bengal leaders Buddhadeb Bhattacharjee and Biman Bose had no interest whatever in national politics, leave alone international matters.[27] They would support the CPI(M)'s central leadership on the nuclear deal regardless of its merits or demerits—provided they were left to their own devices on state-level policies, however retrograde and incompatible these might be with the stated positions of the national leadership. The latter, in turn, would limit its criticism of neo-liberal policies, being pursued as zealously and mindlessly as Bhattacharjee alone could do, to the level of rhetoric.

The CPI(M) national leadership's own stature and authority on policy matters was badly compromised when it supported the UPA on the Special Economic Zones Bill in 2005. It also campaigned feverishly against foreign investment in retail trade, while keeping silent on the entry of domestic big business into the sector, which would be equally predatory as far as the livelihoods of petty shopkeepers, small farmers and above all informal sector workers are concerned. It could hardly reprimand the Bengal comrades for pursuing the same line.

Under this new 'federalism', the CPI(M)'s state units failed to evolve coordinated strategies or mutually compatible positions. The Kerala CPI(M) opposed water abuse by a Coca-Cola bottling plant at Plachimada in Palakkad, thanks to the moral pressure of popular mobilization and V.S. Achuthanandan's support to it. The West Bengal unit had no compunctions in inviting similar predators to the state. The two units did not harmonize their positions even on parliamentary matters. When the railway budget was presented in 2008, the Kerala MPs walked out in protest against the 'raw deal' meted out to the state. The Bengal MPs did not.

The West Bengal CPI(M) had developed a soft spot for Manmohan Singh's policies. Singh made no secret of his admiration of Bhattacharjee's 'pragmatic' approach. Pranab Mukherjee was always at hand to broker agreements in case of disputes between the UPA and the CPI(M)'s national leaders.

The growing divergence in policies and priorities between the West Bengal and Kerala units soon got reflected within the apex of the national leadership. The former got increasingly identified with Sitaram Yechury who represented the state in the Rajya Sabha; the latter, albeit less obviously, with Prakash Karat. While this was by no means a factional divide of the kind that exists in bourgeois parties, the divergence or rift nevertheless brought (and even now brings) no credit to the CPI(M); it is a party whose internal differences are supposed to be decided on ideological and programmatic grounds, not on the basis of regional loyalties or state-specific concerns.

The Left parties would soon practise the politics of unadulterated expediency geared to fighting elections. Thus began their secular slide after the 'freak' West Bengal victory of 2006: the 2009 Lok Sabha elections, followed by the Bengal rout of 2011, the defeat (albeit by a narrow margin) suffered by the Left Democratic Front in the Kerala assembly elections the same year, the Left Front's defeat in the West Bengal panchayat elections in 2013, and finally, the Lok Sabha election debacle of 2014.

The collapse of the UPA–Left arrangement in 2008 led the Left to attempt to put together a rickety non-Congress, non-BJP Third Front or 'third alternative' with all manner of regional parties, including the Bahujan Samaj Party (BSP), Biju Janata Dal (BJD), Telugu Desam Party (TDP), Janata Dal (Secular) [JD(S)] and All-India Anna Dravida Munnetra Kazhagam (AIADMK), and even Om Prakash Chautala's Indian National Lok Dal (INLD). A majority of these parties had allied with the BJP in the past and could not be remotely credited with progressive policy agendas. The Front was for all intents and purposes a non-starter. But the Left would not abandon its Front-centric strategy.

'Third Alternative' Falls Apart

The Left's leading party, the CPI(M), continued with minor variations to adhere to the 'political line' formulated at the sixteenth congress held in 1998 at Calcutta, which laid stress on the formation of a 'third alternative', as a transitional or interim step towards building a 'left and democratic front'.[28] The seventeenth congress (Hyderabad, 2002) added the need for a common programme for 'the third alternative' and specifically targeted the BJP.

Since then, the 'third alternative' has gone through various tactical interpretations. The CPI(M)'s eighteenth congress (New Delhi, 2005) committed the party to 'build on the success of dislodging the BJP from the Centre' by extending 'support to the UPA government' and pressing it 'to see that the positive features in the CMP are implemented and carried forward', by 'bringing into play' the pressure of mass movements and struggles. It also said that the process of formation of 'a third alternative', as distinct from reaching a mere electoral understanding with sundry regional parties, 'must begin by drawing the non-Congress secular bourgeois parties and other democratic forces into campaigns and struggles on common issues'. Such struggles never took place.

The CPI(M)'s nineteenth congress (Coimbatore, 2008) differentiated 'between the BJP and the Congress, considering the latter as a secular bourgeois party, though it often vacillates when the communal forces take the offensive. The party will continue to adopt tactics for isolating and defeating the BJP. It will not enter into any alliance or united front with the Congress.' It would however 'maintain relations with all the non–Congress secular parties for developing united struggles and joint actions issues', to build 'a third alternative'. It would 'project the Left and Democratic' front by 'taking up the issues' of 'workers, poor peasants, agricultural workers, artisans and other sections of the working people'.

Such issue-based mobilization never happened. But the Left parties continued to advocate the same strategic and political–tactical line. Not even the results of the 2009 national elections, which saw the Left parties' Lok Sabha strength plummet from sixty-one to twenty-four seats, impelled them to reconsider this line. By then, the CPI, the RSP and Forward Bloc had surrendered their policy independence to the CPI(M).

The twentieth congress of the CPI(M) held in 2012 at Kozhikode returned the party to the policy of 'equidistance' between the 'twin evils': it would 'politically fight the Congress and the BJP', both of which 'represent the big bourgeois–landlord order which perpetuates class exploitation and is responsible for the social oppression of various sections of the people. They pursue neo-liberal policies and advocate a pro-US foreign policy. Defeating the Congress and the UPA government is imperative given the crushing burden of price rise, unemployment, suffering of the farmers and workers on the one hand and the brazen corruption and big sops to big business and the wealthy sections. Isolating the BJP and countering its communal and right-wing agenda is necessary and important for the advance of the left, democratic and secular forces.'

The political resolution passed at the congress said: 'Only a Left and Democratic platform can be the alternative to bourgeois–landlord rule;' this 'needs to be built up through a process of movements and struggles … In the course of these efforts, it may be necessary to rally those non-Congress, non-BJP forces which can play a role in defence of democracy, national sovereignty, secularism, federalism and defence of the people's livelihood and rights ... In the present situation we should strive for joint actions with the non-Congress secular parties on issues so that the movements can be widened. On specific policy matters and people's issues, there can be cooperation in Parliament with these parties. As and when required, there can be electoral understandings with some of these parties.'

This could be interpreted to rationalize all manner of alliances and understandings with parties which have nothing in common with the Left, and which might walk out of such arrangements for short-term electoral gains. Harkishan Singh Surjeet, who was general secretary of the CPI(M) between 1992 and 2005, had already legitimized such arbitrary interpretation way back in 2002, when he invested the tactical line with unlimited resilience.[29]

To sum up, in 2004, just before its own decline accelerated visibly in West Bengal, the Left was offered another special opportunity to influence national politics. The Left, the CPI(M) in particular, did not refine its old, vague, 'political-tactical line' and ignored mass mobilization. It did not identify the issues and ideas which could have served as the appropriate 'pressure points' in its interaction with the UPA. It compromised too easily on economic policy issues and foreign policy and security matters, and did not press home the advantage it enjoyed on social policy issues such as health care and education. It did not generate extra-parliamentary pressure to back up its negotiating stances.

The Left wrongly focused on the esoteric and technically complex, indeed arcane, issue of the US–Indian nuclear deal, on which to confront the UPA in its final stand-off. It made the wrong alliances with nuclear hawks and undermined its own sound stand against nuclear weapons. In criticizing the nuclear deal on strategic grounds, it overestimated the strength of the sentiment critical or independent of the US in the middle-class and the mainstream media. It committed an almost inexplicable tactical blunder by allowing the UPA to take the deal to the IAEA for safeguards negotiations in 2007. It banked on unreliable parties like the Samajwadi Party in the 2008 confidence vote. It compounded its mistakes by expelling Somnath Chatterjee from the party. Its poor performance in the 2009 Lok Sabha elections was a foregone conclusion.

The CPI(M) had played Big Brother to the other parties in the Left Front and Left Democratic Front, especially since the mid-1990s, and in the process damaged the prospect of consensual democratic decision making and collective action based on mutual trust. It seriously weakened 'Left unity' by deciding to support former finance and defence minister Pranab Mukherjee in the presidential election of July 2012—in contrast to the other Left parties which opposed Mukherjee on account of his right-wing economic and security policies and his close links with powerful but shady business houses. This not only pitched the CPI(M) on the same side as its adversaries like Trinamool Congress, but also led to a rift between the party and a section of the Students' Federation of India.[30]

The Debacle of 2014

Disaster struck the 'third alternative' just before the 2014 Lok Sabha elections. In February, the four Left parties under the CPI(M)'s leadership stitched together an eleven-party front, including the Samajwadi Party, Janata Dal (United), AIADMK, Asom Gana Parishad (AGP), Jharkhand Vikas Morcha (JVM), Janata Dal (Secular) and Biju Janata Dal. The parties resolved to defeat both the Congress and the BJP, but said they would not form a national-level alliance. They issued a vaguely worded joint declaration which said the people should have an alternative to the Congress and BJP, 'an alternative which has a democratic, secular, federal and pro-people development agenda'. This was widely seen as a precursor to an electoral alliance or understanding of sorts, and created much confusion.

Two of the parties (AGP and BJD) did not even attend the 25 February meeting of this grouping. Prakash Karat was at pains to deny that this is a 'front',[31] and called it an 'alternative'. At any rate, the grouping disintegrated within weeks after holding three meetings. If the Left thought it would at least gain a few tickets from the regional parties in their home states, that hope proved illusory. The SP refused to give any tickets to the Left parties in Uttar Pradesh, and even the Tamil Nadu–based electoral alliance between the AIADMK, CPI(M) and CPI broke down ahead of the elections.

The 2014 Lok Sabha elections produced the worst ever verdict for the Left parties: their tally nosedived from twenty-four to just ten seats (twelve seats, if the two Left-backed independents who won from Kerala are counted); and their national vote shrank from the traditional 7–10 per cent to 4.5 per cent.

The results delivered a seismic shock to the Left parties. Their first response was denial, and accusations of widespread rigging in West Bengal.[32] The next response was: 'the verdict of the people ... has been clear and decisive. There has been an anti-Congress wave ... The BJP has gained from this anti-Congress wave resulting in a big victory for the BJP and the NDA ... The results for the CPI(M) and the left parties have been disappointing ...'[33] It is only much later that the party admitted that the 'primary responsibility for the failure' lies with its central leadership. But it did not link the failure to the leadership's political strategy or its election-related alliance-building tactics.[34]

At any rate, the CPI(M) was reduced in the Lok Sabha from sixteen seats in 2009 to nine in 2014. It won only two of the forty-two Lok Sabha seats in West Bengal—the same number as the BJP, and even lower than the CPI(M)'s score of five seats in 1967, the first election after its 1964 split from the much larger CPI.

The CPI could win only one seat in the latest election, from Kerala. This compares poorly with its four-seat tally in 2009, including two from West Bengal, and one each from Tamil Nadu and Odisha. The Forward Bloc drew a blank. The RSP won one seat, from Kerala, where it walked out of the Left Democratic Front in March on being denied a nomination to a constituency long regarded as its stronghold. The RSP joined Kerala's ruling United Democratic Front.

In West Bengal, the Left Front's vote plummeted to 29.6 per cent from 43.3 per cent in the 2009 Lok Sabha election and 41.1 per cent in the 2011 assembly election—its poorest showing since 1977. If elections are held to the 294-strong state assembly now, and votes are cast in the same way as they were for the Lok Sabha, the Left's strength would fall from sixty-two seats to just twenty-nine, and the Mamata Banerjee–led Trinamool Congress would win a crushing 217 seats compared to the 185 it holds now.

Of Kerala's total of twenty Lok Sabha seats, the LDF in 2014 won only eight against the UDF's twelve. The CPI appears to be a declining force in Kerala, and the CPI(M) was long riven with factional strife between its former state secretary Pinarayi Vijayan, a conservative, and former chief minister V.S. Achuthanandan, the party's most popular leader. Vijayan has stepped down, but the factionalism issue is still not settled. Some CPI(M) leaders also stand charged with plotting the 2012 assassination of dissenting leader T.P. Chandrasekharan who formed a rival party.

The handful of CPI(M) leaders who offered to resign after the 2014 results came in were told not to do so: unlike 'bourgeois' parties, Marxists believe in 'collective', not 'individual' responsibility. This is cruelly ironic. The logic actually points in the opposite direction: the entire leadership should resign! Party ideologues argued that communist leaders do not resign on the basis of election results: these are far less important than a failure to expand the party's 'mass base' which, of course, their strategy did not even remotely promote. But this denies that flesh-and-blood individuals' decisions have huge political consequences: Buddhadeb Bhattacharjee's industrialization-at-any-cost policy, at work in Singur and Nandigram, ravaged the CPI(M)'s shrinking 'mass base' in Bengal, and Vijayan's narrow-minded pro-neo-liberal conservatism has visited devastation upon the Kerala party, whose chances of winning the 2011 assembly elections he had all but sabotaged.

For all their periodic talk of supplementing their electoral work with 'mass struggles' on issues of importance to the working people, the Left parties have invested virtually no energy in building such movements— even after their Lok Sabha rout underscored that imperative.

Post-2014: Limited Rethinking

The initial shock delivered by the 2014 Lok Sabha election results soon gave way to somewhat more sober reflection, though not radical rethinking, within the CPI(M) and the CPI. The CPI was particularly scathing in criticizing the Left parties for withdrawing support to the United Progressive Alliance government on the India–US nuclear deal issue in 2008, and in projecting a ragtag combination including themselves and assorted regional parties as a 'third alternative' both in the 2009 and 2014 elections.

In the run-up to its twenty-second party congress held at Puducherry (Pondicherry) in March 2015, the CPI emphasized the need for 'reactivating and rejuvenating [the] party organisation from the grass-roots level by concentrating on result-oriented mass struggles on local issues of the people' and urged a reunification of the communist movement 'on a principled basis'.[35] The congress itself witnessed lively interventions by delegates from Kerala, Tamil Nadu, Bihar, Odisha, Punjab, Chhattisgarh and Uttar Pradesh, which highlighted the need for independent mass mobilizations and for a concerted campaign against the Sangh Parivar. The CPI re-elected S. Sudhakar Reddy as general secretary and also appointed Gurudas Dasgupta, a militant trade union leader, as deputy general secretary. A recurring theme at the congress was CPI–CPI(M) reunification.

The CPI(M) witnessed more important developments, including a leadership change. Its central committee in its 2014 Lok Sabha election review admitted that 'the party has been unable to advance for some time'; 'this was reflected' in its poor electoral performance. Its draft political–organizational report presented to its twenty-first congress at Visakhapatnam in April 2015—parts of which found their way into the media—says the 'inescapable conclusion is that there is a decline in the mass-base of the party ... [It has failed] to expand its political influence, increase its organizational strength and develop its mass base, especially among the basic classes.' It also says: 'The party has been able to rally only a small section of party members ... Enough effort was not made to reach wider sections and rally them in programmes. Propaganda work organized among the people was very weak.'[36]

The political–organizational report also notes a high rate of membership depletion, attributable to 'organizational weaknesses such as loose recruitment, inactivity of the party members and branches, low political–ideological level, weaknesses in educating party member[s], etc'. It comments on the 'ageing of party membership': one-half of CPI(M) members belong to the 32–50 age group; only 20 per cent are under thirty-one; but 27 per cent are in the 50–70 group.[37] These and other organizational issues would be taken up at a special plenum, a forum larger than the central committee—similar to the Salkia plenum of 1978—to be held by the end of 2015.

In contrast to the introspective tone of this national report stands the celebratory account of the thirty-four years of Left Front rule in West Bengal, contained in a document[38] adopted by the state committee of the CPI(M) in February 2015, before the state conference preceding the Visakhapatnam congress. This trumpets the Left Front government's achievements, with little explanation of why the Front and the party suffered serious erosion of support even before Singur and Nandigram (2006–07), setting off a series of reversals, which have since continued unabated.

The document uncritically praises all the policies of the LF government, including those on land, agriculture and panchayats, and also on employment and industry, which achieved 'positive results'. All it concedes by way of weakness is this: 'But on the issue of land acquisition, the two exceptions of Singur and Nandigram halted our industrial progress. There was an adverse reaction among a section of the people of the state.' It does not even mention the killing of fourteen people in a firing in Nandigram.

Paralysing Blow in Bengal

The Left Front's failures and shortcomings in West Bengal were rooted, as discussed in previous chapters, in its lack of radicalism, organizational ossification, poor commitment to social development, embracing of neo-liberal policies and growing alienation from the underprivileged. But they are explained away by its state leaders by citing factors such as (the presumably inherent) 'limitations and weaknesses in running a state government', and 'continuous attacks, counter-publicity and conspiracy (sic) from the ruling classes'. The factor the leadership now emphasizes the most is the 'reign of terror' unleashed by the Trinamool Congress against its cadres, rigging of elections, etc.

This minimizes, indeed trivializes, the paralysing blow suffered by the West Bengal CPI(M), which has lost 40,000 members since 2011 and the morale of whose cadres is so abysmal that they cannot summon up the will to resist threats and physical intimidation. Hundreds have defected to the BJP, besides the TMC.

Since losing power in West Bengal in 2011, the CPI(M) has become a mere shadow of its former self. The party has faced major setbacks in its work among industrial workers, peasants and urban youth, and a rout in all significant elections, including the panchayat elections of 2013, and the municipal elections of April 2015.[39] The TMC's sweep of the municipalities gave the lie to the wishful thinking that its base is mainly rural and confined, in the cities, to fringe or lumpen elements, as distinct from the middle class, which still retains some loyalty to the Left. In January 2015, the CPI(M)-led Students' Federation of India did not even file nominations for elections to the 600-strong students' union in Calcutta University, which it had dominated for thirty-two years until 2010–11.[40]

The sole consolation for the Left in West Bengal at the time of writing seems to be that the prospect of the BJP emerging as the number two party in the state in place of the CPI(M) has dimmed significantly with the wearing thin of the Narendra Modi 'novelty factor' nationally and the BJP's poor performance in the municipal elections.

The rift between the CPI(M)'s national and state-level leaders came into prominence at its Visakhapatnam congress, in particular in the election of a new party general secretary who would take over from Prakash Karat who served his three terms, the maximum that the party's recently amended constitution permits. In the politburo, there were reportedly two contenders for the post: Sitaram Yechury (62), the party's best-known parliamentarian and multilingual leader with contacts and acceptability across the political spectrum; and the quiet, virtually unknown, much older S. Ramachandran Pillai (77). Yechury was long aligned with the West Bengal leadership, and Pillai reportedly enjoyed the confidence of the just retired long-serving Kerala state secretary Pinarayi Vijayan, besides Karat.

In the politburo, which normally proposes the name of the general secretary to the newly elected central committee, the scales were originally tipped in Pillai's favour, according to media reports. The politburo debated the issue late into the night of 18 April, the penultimate day of the congress. Yet Yechury, strongly backed by the West Bengal party unit, eventually prevailed[41]. A major role in bringing about this change was reportedly played by former West Bengal party secretary

Biman Bose. Bose spoke for himself and on behalf of Buddhadeb Bhattacharjee and Nirupam Sen, members of the outgoing politburo who could not attend the party congress owing to poor health, but whose opinion in favour of 'a younger face' could not be ignored.[42]

Pillai reportedly withdrew from the contest. On the morning of 19 April, Karat proposed Yechury's name. Yechury, flanked by Karat and Pillai, was declared elected 'unanimously', with all sixteen members of the new politburo holding up one another's hands on the congress dais. The episode revealed some of the CPI(M)'s internal differences. Yechury's election was resented in the Kerala party and in the media sympathetic to Vijayan. The CPI(M)'s Kerala party organ did not carry an editorial-page article introducing the new general secretary, as is customary.[43] The election also testified to the party leadership's anxiety to appear united and cohesive. And yet it proved that the communists have far more democratic organizational structures than most Indian parties.

New General Secretary

How Yechury deals with internal differences will influence the future of the party's political line and organizational trajectory in no small way. In the popular media, Yechury is portrayed as a 'networker' in the style of Harkishan Singh Surjeet—a leader who is generally affable, consensus-oriented and accessible, but 'soft' on the Congress party. Karat is depicted as distant, doctrinaire and anti-Congress, which he regards as the main party of the ruling class, which the Left must oppose. Karat is considered the prime architect of the 1996 'historic blunder'.

These labels probably distort and exaggerate the differences between the two best-known CPI(M) leaders of the day. Yet, there is little doubt that the two have found themselves backing different shades of opinion within the party—for instance, on West Bengal's land acquisition policies or withdrawal of support to the UPA on the India–US nuclear deal.

More pertinently, Yechury recently wrote a sixteen-page note of dissent on the draft of one of the two important documents adopted at Visakhapatnam: the 'Review Report on the Political–Tactical Line', the other being the 'Political Resolution'.[44] The 'Review Report', discussed at a CPI(M) central committee meeting in October 2014, and adopted by it in January 2015, called for a re-examination of the tactical line the party has pursued since the tenth congress at Jalandhar in 1978, namely, building a 'left and democratic front'.

The Report argues that the party had failed to form such a front at the national level, and instead forged short-term 'secular alternatives' to the Congress, and later to the BJP, and then formed alliances for a 'third alternative'. In the process, the party 'relegated the "left and democratic front" to a propaganda slogan'; it failed to build 'the independent strength of the party' necessary to rally other parties. The Report urges the formulation of an 'effective' tactical line that would restore 'the primacy' of the 'left and democratic front' and rallying the right combination of classes behind it, with an emphasis on 'mass struggles' to fight both neo-liberal capitalism and communalism.

Yechury's note[45] argues that there is nothing wrong or inadequate about the political–tactical line (P–TL) adopted since 1978, the 'left and democratic front' notion remains valid, and there is no need to 'undertake the current exercise for "the formulation of a fresh P–TL"': 'What requires to be thoroughly examined, therefore, is … why has our organizational political strength not grown to achieve this objective? If in the process of implementation this objective got deflected, the concrete reasons for this must be identified and corrected. This demands of us to address persisting organizational weaknesses and repeated tactical mistakes that have been committed … The current exercise only serves to divert [the] party's attention away from overcoming these weaknesses' and from making 'the necessary corrections' in the implementation of the political–tactical line.

Yechury then goes on to identify some of the reasons for the 'uneven' growth and 'decline' of the party, attributes them (among other factors) to 'the dangerous growth of subjectivism within the party, particularly amongst the leadership' as regards 'overestimations' of the party's strength and its electoral assessments, as well as to the poor education of cadres, non-implementation of resolutions on mass organizations, failure to rectify 'deviations' such as factionalism and 'parliamentary illusions'. He calls for mainly organizational solutions to these problems, and proposes 'an organizational plenum', to be 'convened soon after the twenty-first congress … to clinch these issues'.

Neither the main Report nor Yechury's note deals centrally or up front with the question of mass struggles and a return to grassroots level organizing on issues of gut-level importance to the poor and underprivileged, which alone can invest real meaning in a 'left and democratic front'. Neither advocates a decisive shift away from parliamentarism to a perspective of rebuilding live links with people's movements.

Merits apart, a delegates' majority won the battle on the political–tactical line at Visakhapatnam, with minor modifications. Yechury is now called upon to implement the same Review Report that he disagreed with, besides setting up an organizational plenum by the end of 2015. He has been publicly reminded by another politburo member that he is bound by the Visakhapatnam Political Resolution to oppose both the Congress and the BJP and simultaneously fight 'the twin assaults, of neo-liberal economic policies and Hindutva forces'; since there is 'no difference' between the Congress and the BJP on economic policies, 'any alliance or front with the Congress in the name of fighting Hindutva is ruled out'.[46]

None of this has prevented Yechury from articulating in various interviews his view, with varying emphases or qualifications, that his party would work with the Congress on specific issues without forming an alliance with it. Immediately after his election, he exhorted the Congress and other non-NDA parties to join together 'to safeguard India's secular, democratic foundation ... [W]e are not seeking their support to secure our future. We appeal to the Congress and other parties to come together on different issues to secure the future of the country ...'[47] The Congress in turn said it hopes that 'Yechury will try to change Karat's policies which were impractical and not in favour of secular forces'.[48]

Yechury also said the BJP and the Congress 'follow the same neo-liberal policies in relation to the economy. But, of course, there is a difference between the two parties on systematic (sic) threat to secularism and democracy'. Yet, the CPI(M) must always respond to 'the main challenge before the Indian people in a concrete situation'; as examples, he cited its support for the first UPA government to counter communalism, and earlier, its joining the anti-Emergency struggle without becoming part of the JP movement. More explicitly, he said the CPI(M) 'is prepared to work with the Congress and other secular and democratic parties in parliament on three issues'.[49]

Congress of the Future?

On the issue of CPI–CPI(M) reunification, for which the CPI leadership has pleaded since 1989, and which it again emphasized at the Puducherry congress, Yechury is no different from his predecessors. On 21 April 2015, when CPI general secretary S. Sudhakar Reddy called on him and reiterated his party's 'desire for reunification', Yechury publicly said that a merger cannot take place on the basis of 'tactical' considerations, and would not be possible until the ideological and programmatic differences that led to the split of 1964 were 'resolved in the first place'; what is on the agenda is 'working together' on people's issues.[50]

The CPI(M) has inducted a second woman member into its sixteen-strong politburo, and also elected a Dalit and two new women to its ninety-one-member central committee, a belated but welcome move. It has, however, dropped V.S. Achuthanandan from the politburo—not on account of ill health, as with Buddhadeb Bhattacharjee and Nirupam Sen—but like them, it has given him the decorative post of a 'special invitee' to the central committee.[51]

Before Visakhapatnam, the party's Kerala and West Bengal secretaries (Vijayan and Bose), who had completed three terms, were replaced by Kodiyeri Balakrishnan and Surjya Kanta Mishra respectively, and some changes were executed in the composition of many district and state committees too, but largely retaining continuity. This does not add up to a cleansing or refurbishing of the party apparatus, with large-scale induction of young, new leaders drawn from popular movements.

Nevertheless, Yechury's election has generated cautious hope within CPI(M), the Left and civil society circles. It has been widely welcomed by the political class and the media, sections of which were predictably quick to advise him to adopt an unabashedly social democratic course. More encouragingly, many CPI(M) members were reportedly palpably enthused[52] by Yechury's opening remarks at the conclusion of the Visakhapatnam congress: 'This is the congress of the future for the party and it will form the basis for strengthening our independent identity.'

Party leaders have spoken in the past also of the need for 'mass struggles' against neo-liberalism and communalism, and for building the party's independent strength. All Left party congress resolutions stress struggles, but these have not materialized for at least a quarter-century or more. The Left has led no mass mobilization on any issue for a long time. It will not be easy for the Left parties to re-establish the organic links that they traditionally had with workers' and peasants' movements. These have been substantially weakened, and in some respects qualitatively transformed.

For instance, the composition of the peasantry has changed, with increasing inter-generational division and parcellization of land, growing landlessness, and a rise in contract farming (or leasing of land to rich peasants or corporations). India's agrarian crisis has become so acute that it is virtually impossible for smallholders to subsist on farming. Yet demanding higher output prices does not work in the interest of the really poor who are net consumers, not producers, of food.

This confronts the Left with the complex challenge of making graded and highly region-specific demands, which primarily focus on the poorest rural layers, the landless workers, but which are also relevant for marginal farmers. It has to work seriously on the land question by opposing the transfer of agricultural land to industry and the real-estate business. This has already become a burning issue.

So far as trade unions are concerned, the Left-affiliated federations still command membership in the millions or more, but they no longer seem to enjoy the edge they long had over some other unions.[53] They are strongest in the public sector, including the railways, where employment has largely remained frozen for long years. But Left-affiliated unions are growing in new areas, sectors and categories such as contract workers in a range of industries, small-scale transport, rural employment schemes and health sector workers, and especially the 1.2 million-plus anganwadis connected with the Integrated Child Development Services.[54]

There is also rising and sometimes unpredictable militancy, often driven by desperation and harsh condition of work, among workers in new, expanding and technology-intensive industries like automobiles.[55] The Left has not found it easy to deal with this phenomenon; indeed no unions have. But the Left has a major battle ahead in terms of offering resistance to the government's plans to dilute and liquidate labour laws so as to remove all existing protections against retrenchment and making unionization itself difficult. It simply cannot afford to compromise on these rights.

All this demands creative new forms of thinking, as does meeting the greatest challenge of them all: to unionize scattered and atomized workers in tiny industries and sweatshops, create schemes to protect domestic servants and home-based workers, and to bring into the ambit of minimum wage laws sectors traditionally excluded from them, and so on.

These challenges have arisen just when the Left is at its nadir, indeed at a make-or-break moment in its history. Yet it is not inevitable that the Left must go down the abyss. Whether the Left parties can rejuvenate themselves will depend primarily on whether they seriously rethink their ideology, strategy, political programmes and organizational practices. Equally vitally, it will be determined by the passion and tenacity with which they rebuild their links with the working people on the basis of grass-roots movements and struggles in which the self-activity of the masses plays a prominent role.

10

Towards a New Left

Rethinking Ideology, Returning to Grass Roots,
Re-imagining Counter-hegemony

If analogies make any sense in historical explanation, India's parliamentary communist parties today stand between two fateful moments: the collapse of the Berlin Wall, and the demise of international socialism. The Wall's brick-by-brick dismantling by people disgusted with a putrefied system was more than a warning signal, even more than the final alarm before the shipwreck. Similarly, the communist Left's debacle in the 2014 Lok Sabha elections is a cataclysm which marks the end of an epoch spanning almost a century. Even if the Left can somehow revive itself and recover partially, it will probably not be the same social and political entity it was twenty years, even ten years, ago.

This is a tragic moment for all those who yearn for radical anti-capitalist change and a socialist future—even if they have been unsparingly critical of the existing Left—in the same way that many Marxists belonging to the Far Left mourned the disintegration of the Soviet Union—not because they believed in that variety of 'actually existing socialism', but because its collapse set back a hundred different causes.

Historic Setback

India's mainstream Left parties not only suffered their worst-ever rout in parliamentary elections in 2014, which has reduced them to a marginal presence in the Lok Sabha, but they were also delivered a comprehensive moral–political defeat which puts a question mark over the viability of the entire political project that they espoused for nine decades. The prospect of further decline into irrelevance now stares them in the face. The defeat comes on top of a series of setbacks in state assembly and panchayat elections, a fall in the membership and level of activity of their mass organizations, including the Kisan Sabhas and women's associations and, equally important, a visible collapse of the political strategy and tactics based on the idea of a Third Front or Third Alternative, which they have pursued for more than a quarter-century.

Yet, the Left leadership's response to the catastrophe has been virtually supine—particularly from the CPI(M) and the CPI, not to speak of the smaller parties of the Left Front like the Revolutionary Socialist Party or Forward Bloc. The two communist parties have not even produced a class-based and social-group-based structural analysis of the election results and their conjunctural context; indeed, they have not ventured beyond number-counting and vague generalities.

The Left parties have no explanation to offer for the dramatic victory of the Bharatiya Janata Party under Narendra Modi and the BJP's emergence as the biggest force and central point of reference in national politics, or its huge gains in West Bengal and Kerala, where it won respectively 17 and 11 per cent of the vote. They are silent on the reasons for the RSP's exit from the Left Democratic Front in Kerala, which was a blow to the idea of 'Left unity' which they espouse.

Even after the CPI's and CPI(M)'s party congresses, respectively in March and April 2015, there are few signs that the Left is about to engage in serious stocktaking and undertake the cruelly honest and even painful introspection that is called for—indeed, that it even has the will to do so. This has produced even greater dismay, disappointment and disillusionment among radicals and progressives, including sympathizers of the Left parties.

The Left has not analysed why the maverick Aam Aadmi Party (AAP), which many had dismissed as a merely passing challenge to the Bharatiya Janata Party in Delhi, broke the BJP's victory run there by winning an astounding sixty-seven of seventy assembly seats in February 2015; and what lessons the Left parties should themselves draw from AAP's politics, its methods of campaigning, and its ability to attract and inspire the poor and underprivileged to vote for it with such unprecedented enthusiasm. If, as some analysts believe, AAP used slogans and methods which communists themselves used to deploy in the past to attract the poor, the Left showed no recognition of this, nor learnt any lessons from it.

Amidst all this stands out the Left's failure to analyse the magnitude, quality and causes of its own electoral rout. The CPI(M), for instance, first practised outright denial by alleging 'large-scale rigging' of the elections, then admitted to its 'poor' showing, and finally accepted its central leaders' 'primary responsibility for the failure', but without identifying precisely where this responsibility lay and what were the causal connections between the leadership's strategies and tactics and the setbacks the party suffered. The causes do not lie in this or that tactical error related to alliance building or election-related choices, or the mistakes committed by particular leaders, although these may have contributed to the magnitude of the defeat.

The deeper causes must be traced back to multiple layers of the Left's ideological, strategic and programmatic inadequacies and failures. As argued earlier, especially in Chapter 2, the Left failed to forge an uncompromisingly radical yet resilient strategic framework for transformative or revolutionary change. It worked largely within a theoretical–ideological framework inherited from the Communist International ninety years ago, with its rigid, formulaic understanding of the 'stages' of revolution, 'fronts' based on multi-class alliances, and 'unity and struggle' tactics.

The mainstream Indian Left did not develop the notion of building a counter-hegemonic alternative to the bourgeois democratic system through anti-capitalist popular mobilizations even while exploiting all the possibilities available in the system, both electoral and non-electoral, for advancing the interests of workers and other toilers. Instead, it neglected mass mobilization, succumbed to parliamentarism and allowed the system to co-opt it.

The Left embraced a notion of socialism which led it to regard the Soviet Union, and later China, as models, which they are not. It has long failed to define a coherent project of socialism for the twenty-first century, and to identify possible pathways that might connect it to the present. The Left did not develop an India-specific understanding of caste, gender, tribal and ethnic identities in relation to class, nor a political strategy that could help translate that understanding into a realizable, practical project. At another level, it lacked an analysis of the specificities of Indian capitalism, the nature of the state, and the character of the ruling class, especially since the early 1990s.

Parliamentary Obsession

The Left did not fashion programmes and policies that are based on working people's aspirations and yet are connected to larger strategies of progressive change. It remained stuck with old slogans like 'land to the tiller' even where there is little land to be distributed. It followed industrialization and land acquisition policies which are predatory on people's livelihoods and on natural resources. Along with the Left's failure to oppose environmental destruction comprehensively and to make it a central component of the struggle against the present bourgeois order, these policies put it on the wrong side of the ecological barrier.

After the early 1980s, the Left parties got increasingly de-radicalized and preoccupied with winning elections. They neglected work in trade unions and Kisan Sabhas. This disconnect continued to grow both nationally and in the states where they were in power or were serious contenders for it. The patronage system that the Left built through the panchayats in West Bengal masked its real weakness and allowed it to retain power for three decades, but all radical content had been hollowed out of its politics. Yet, the Left continued to adhere to outmoded 'vanguardist' notions of leadership.

Bereft of independent strength and radical identity, and yet keen on winning elections, the Left made all manner of questionable alliances. In many states, it became almost indistinguishable from the bourgeois or centrist parties with which it allied for unconvincing reasons. Meanwhile, it continued to get more and more alienated from the exploited and oppressed masses it claimed to represent. The Left's organizational practice of 'democratic centralism' stifled free and open debate and prevented it from acknowledging and learning from its past mistakes.

The political defeat the Left has suffered is thus the result not just of a passing electoral–political crisis, but an existential crisis, with multiple dimensions: ideological–theoretical, programmatic and organizational. The Left must acknowledge this and revisit the foundational premises of its politics. Unless it does so, and evolves visions, policy perspectives and political mobilization strategies and tactics appropriate to Indian conditions, it cannot hope to stem or reverse its precipitate decline, leave alone rejuvenate itself and rebuild its links with the working people.

It might appear logical to some that the best forum to address these issues would be a platform or conclave organized on the basis of 'Left unity',[1] itself an attractive slogan for many communists both inside and outside the parties; that would at least help the Left parties overcome disunity, one of their major weaknesses. This proposition, understood in purely political-party terms, is somewhat naive. It severely underestimates the asymmetrical nature of the existing Left Front in West Bengal and the Left Democratic Front in Kerala.

Not only are these Fronts heavily dominated by the CPI(M); they have also historically served as organs of power, not forums of debate. They can easily stifle the voices of the smaller parties,[2] not to speak of non-party organizations and people's movement groups. That apart, it stretches credulity to think that the Left parties will suddenly reach a consensual, but brutally honest, accurate and illuminating understanding of the causes of their crisis through debates in a common 'Left unity' forum, when they manifestly and repeatedly failed to do so after the 2009 and 2011 electoral setbacks. The appropriate forum must be more broad-based and evolve through debate as well as action.

One must hope that the parliamentary Left parties analyse the crises that confront them with the utmost sincerity and candour. Whether they do so or not, at least a part of that task has fallen to progressive currents outside these parties' formal structures. There are many such currents. India has seen an eruption of popular movements for the defence of livelihoods and access to natural resources, for extension and deepening of democratic rights, and in protest against countless injustices and iniquities. These have drawn in vast numbers of people acting spontaneously or through what have been termed New Social Movements or 'people's movement' structures,[3] as distinct from conventional non-governmental organizations (NGOs).

Not all such groups are amenable to working with a broad cross section of Left-party and non-party organizations on a genuinely egalitarian agenda. They must not be glamorized. Some of them differ politically, or have their own biases, personal prejudices, class- or caste-based sectarian concerns and political conceits. But there is a considerable number and large variety of them who could be as productively brought into a process of dialogue as can many big and small parties of the Left.

Among them are India's rights-based movements pertaining to agitations for and realization of the Right to Information (RTI), Right to Education (RTE), right to employment via MGNREGA, Right to Food Security, Forest Rights Act, and in a few states, Right to Public Services. These movements were born during the era of neo-liberalism and have made impressive, at times spectacular, gains against heavy odds—precisely because they fought hard to secure the rights on which they focus; these were not gifted to them as doles or charity. Neither the Congress-led United Progressive Alliance in its worst phase nor the BJP-led National Democratic Alliance under Narendra Modi was able to neutralize, undermine or eliminate them, despite trying.[4] Such rights-based approaches must be extended to other sectors like health care, shelter and social security.

For a People's Charter

Amazing as it might seem, an estimated eight to ten million RTI applications continue to be filed every year across the country, mostly by individuals, but some by movement-based groups. Some of the applications have resulted in huge social gains—for instance, exposure of corruption in MGNREGA, and the dismantling of plans to privatize water in Delhi, one of the successful campaigns in which Arvind Kejriwal was involved, many years before he joined the Anna Hazare agitation and later formed the Aam Aadmi Party.[5]

The currents that must carry the mantle of the old Left include, besides the Left parties themselves, independent Marxist and Left–socialist groups, radical non-party political formations, trade unionists, organizers of agricultural workers and marginal farmers, Dalit networks, feminist groups, anti-communal campaigners and environmental activists. They also include health and education rights campaigners, civil society groups devoted to defending people's livelihoods, movements that seek to deepen and enrich democracy, the radical intelligentsia and all those non-affiliated groups and individuals who believe in a post-capitalist future. A component of the last is what might be called the 'social' or 'cultural' Left, including writers, artists and cultural activists.

All such currents—diverse as they might be, with some of them sharply focused and well grounded on single issues, and others with a broader horizon but a diffused focus—have a vital stake in engaging in critical introspection. Such introspection is necessary to prevent further disillusionment and demoralization in the broad constituency of the political–social Left, whose causes and arenas of work are bound to suffer under the growing influence of the Right in society and politics. The organized parliamentary Left is no longer in a position to counter that influence adequately.

These currents, which themselves form a rainbow coalition of sorts, must explore the possibilities of working with the broadest possible range of progressive parties and organizations—including the Left Front parties and the trade unions, kisan sabhas and women's associations affiliated to them—on issues of common concern and resistance to the NDA's policies. They must start a conversation with all left-leaning organizations and groupings, and keep it going.

Indeed, such a conversation, often at a low-key level, has been in progress for the past few years and has picked momentum since mid-2014. Various grass-roots 'people's movement' groups and kindred currents have held dozens of meetings, colloquia and seminars in different cities and towns on the central agenda of understanding the causes of the decline of the Left as a movement and finding ways to rejuvenate it. The places where they held these meetings are as diverse as Dhinkia (Odisha), Panvel (Maharashtra), Rewa (Madhya Pradesh) and Sonebhadra (Uttar Pradesh), besides Dehradun, Ranchi, Nagpur, Hyderabad, Kolkata, Thiruvananthapuram, Bengaluru, Mumbai, Chennai and Delhi.

In the more recent past, these groups have jointly and vigorously campaigned against the NDA land acquisition Bill/Ordinance, and tried to broaden the land issue to extend it to the notion of people's sovereignty over land. This issue, and the demand to restrict the state's powers to acquire land for industry, mining and urban development, promises to be a major pivot of popular mobilization as projects like the Delhi–Mumbai Industrial Corridor are promoted.

Some of these 'people's movement' groups have been debating issues pertaining to the Left's multiple crises, their own predicaments, and solutions to them, on the basis of their long experience of working on land, water, forest and environment-related questions. They have also been active participants in recent campaigns for the right to social security and numerous other progressive policies. What follows is based on interaction with some of the key people involved in the process.[6]

The topmost priority, as many of these currents see it, would be to launch a process of deep, collective reflection and analysis, which alone can produce what might be called a *People's Charter*. In essence, this would be a thorough, comprehensive critique of the present social and political order and its pathologies. This critique would form the basis of and aim at developing the essentials of a common perspective for emancipatory anti-capitalist social change, outline the political and mobilizational strategies needed to achieve its principal objectives, and identify some of the agencies and instruments that can best express and advance such strategies.

It is not easy to decide how and through what procedure such collective reflection might be organized. But a few suggestions, which have emerged from recent interactions between grass-roots activist groups including cadres of the Left, might be worth considering. Such introspection could best happen through semi-informal but personal face-to-face interaction between activists, in keeping with their past tradition and oral culture—i.e., a series of meetings in the states and important centres of activism. But it must be accompanied by written interventions which lead to precise formulations and greater clarity. Such interaction is best initiated by civil society groups and party or non-party political leaders with wide appeal and acceptance, of whom there are many.

There is every reason to invite the parliamentary Left to join such an effort, but none at all to make it dependent or conditional upon its participation or its agreement to play a central role. Going by past experience, the Left may or may not want to seize the initiative for such a dialogue with non-party or independent groupings and individuals. But any response by the Left to the People's Charter process, and to the proposals the document makes as it evolves, should be welcomed.

The central task of such collective introspection would be to develop a broad, principled and common—but by no means excessively general and shallowly non-specific—analysis of the present conjuncture, based on the exchanging and pooling together of the experiences and insights of diverse groupings, in order to generate the elements of a programmatic perspective on how to advance the cause of India's socialist transformation. This exercise would be more limited than a large-scale effort to produce a full-fledged programme or manifesto.

Such an initiative needs to be taken along *five axes* simultaneously:[7] one, defining the broad vision, goals and long-term tasks of a socialist or social liberation agenda specific to India while critiquing conventional Left approaches; two, identifying the key demands for building and radicalizing popular struggles and deepening democracy; three, evolving sector-based or micro-level alternatives on day-to-day issues of vital concern to the poor and underprivileged; four, conceptualizing a non-vanguardist relationship between the people and political parties, and between and within parties, based on democratic principles; and five, evolving a critique of chauvinist nationalism in India, and developing new forms of international solidarity among working people.

This task might seem forbiddingly ambitious, but it need not be. Rather, it is useful to see it as a relatively modest proposal for a 'research and activism'-style agenda, which restates certain principles and underscores several issues which are relevant for the rejuvenation of mainstream Left parties, but which they have not taken up as seriously as they deserve to be.

To illustrate, the *first axis* of the proposed dialogue initiative focuses on basic strategic issues outlined above, such as building a counter-hegemonic alternative to the bourgeois democratic system through anti-capitalist popular mobilizations even while exploiting all possibilities available in the system. It links these to India-specific characteristics of the long-term social liberation agenda. Such characteristics must at the minimum include class (with its Indian peculiarities related to a capitalism not centred on manufacturing and to the dominance of the unorganized sector), caste (especially Dalit oppression), gender (uniquely Indian features of patriarchy), secularism and communalism (especially Hindutva), and protecting the environment against neo-liberalism's fierce onslaught, including an agenda to combat climate change to which India is especially vulnerable.

This is not an arbitrary wish list; all these characteristic issues or agendas are at the very core of the bourgeois system of power in India. Any radical transformation of that structure of power must grapple with them. As discussed in Chapter 8, the Left in India fudges these issues at least partly because it cannot accommodate them in its rigid, schematic and class-obsessed analytical framework. This makes it all the more necessary to stress both the centrality of these issues and their mutual interrelationships, and to integrate them into the core agenda of socialism in the Indian context.

Dalit Emancipation and Other Issues

Socialism in India, defined on the minimalist criterion of basic equality of citizens, would make no sense without Dalit emancipation. Dalit emancipation must not remain the empty slogan it has long been. All progressive forces must acknowledge the historic injustice inflicted on the Dalits, in which they have been complicit through their own failure to see the pivotal importance of caste oppression, by not organizing joint campaigns with Dalits on an equal footing, and in not proactively promoting Dalit leadership in their own organizations. Left-wing activists must be the first to reach the spot whenever a case of anti-Dalit discrimination or violence breaks out, whether in cities or tiny hamlets.

In India, women's liberation from patriarchal tyranny is an elementary but urgent agenda. The Left ought be in the forefront not just of initiatives to demand reservations for women in legislatures, but also lead systematic efforts to educate the public and its own cadres on patriarchy and the gross discrimination that the female child faces, and in campaigns against male-supremacist khap panchayats, selective sex abortion and 'honour killings'. It should aim to be identified as a feminist, unabashedly pro-women current.

Democracy would be turned into a majoritarian nightmare under the influence of communalism. As emphasized in Chapter 8, progressive forces must fight communalism in its more insidious forms—such as segregation of Muslims, their stereotyping in textbooks as fanatical, and their demonization in public discourse as 'anti-national'—as well as in its violent manifestations. This is a sorely neglected agenda. An immediate priority is to start an agitation on making the 'Post-Sachar Evaluation Committee' (Kundu Committee) report public, and demand its full implementation.

There can be no socialism without a qualitatively different relationship being established between natural resources, production and consumption, which is different from the predatory one that capitalism has always entailed. Neo-liberal capitalism is worse. It is especially destructive of nature and the fine balances that have long sustained the climate system—because it promotes runaway increases in greenhouse gas emissions which warm the planet and disrupt those balances irreversibly.

This entails demanding that India rapidly phase out fossil fuels and make a transition to renewable energy; use low-energy- and low-water-intensive techniques in agriculture; discourage and tightly regulate private transport; protect vulnerable ecosystems such as the Western Ghats, the coastline, fisheries and biodiversity hot spots by banning predatory industries, mines, dams and construction; effectively prevent forest destruction and degradation; reorganize the urban environment through ecologically sound planning; and undertake ambitious emissions reduction combined with extensive adaptation to climate change.

Analysis along the first axis must also clarify that there is no historical or present model of socialism which India (or for that matter any country) can emulate. The Soviet Union, a bureaucratized anti-democratic system, was a disaster after the late 1920s, if not earlier, despite the progressive role it continued to play globally in some respects. 'Socialism in one country' was a perverse doctrine, calculated as much to ensure the subordination of the international communist movement to Stalin's Russia as to rationalize the failure of the European revolution in the 1920s and the isolation of the USSR, with all its terrible consequences. Today's China, profoundly undemocratic, and addicted to neo-liberalism and climate-threatening growth, is even less of a model.

The socialist project's future vision for India should be organically linked to the actual experience of the struggles of workers, peasants and artisans, of Dalits and adivasis, of men and women committed to building an open, forward-looking, non-hierarchical society, free of ignorance and superstition, which respects diverse non-consumerist ways of relating to natural resources and cooperative, not competitive, relationships between communities and people.

Its charter should stress the need to develop a state- and region-specific understanding of the class–caste relationship, and act on it through a minimum programme of empowering Dalits, adivasis and perhaps the most backward OBCs (MBCs) through affirmative action rather than quotas and reservations. The charter's signatories must also commit themselves to raising the representation of these groups, and of women, in their own organizations' leadership to their proportion in the membership.[8] They must lead by example—by deeds, not just words.

The new Left must respect the principle of autonomy of the feminist and Dalit movements, and not treat them and their organizations as appendages, wings or auxiliaries of political parties.[9] It must seek as many avenues as possible of working with the feminist movement in solidarity campaigns, protests against rape, sexual violence and harassment, issues of women workers in the unorganized sector, and so on. It must build a special relationship of solidaristic affinity with the Dalit emancipation movement even as it conducts a serious dialogue with them on theoretical and practical issues pertaining to class and caste within a broad framework that recognizes the Phule–Ambedkar legacy.

The *second axis* explores what needs to be incorporated into a radical movement's medium- or long-term demands. These include deepening and extending issues like agrarian reform, the right to work, the right to education, old-age pensions, minimal food security, forest rights, and so on. Some of these are being currently agitated, often with remarkable success, but not without stiff resistance from the state and other entrenched interests. People's movements, including prolonged struggles on discrete issues, have succeeded in forcing the state to recognize some of these rights and incorporate them into laws—itself a signal achievement. These rights-based approaches need to be extended to health care, access to old-age care, affordable housing, and different forms of social security, including unemployment allowances and pensions.

Collectivism in Agriculture

People's movements to reclaim lands seized or confiscated from them by the state have registered impressive successes from Chengara in Kerala to Rewa in Madhya Pradesh to Sonebhadra in Uttar Pradesh. Tens of thousands of acres have been reclaimed. One of the central issues now is how to make their occupation equitable and sustainable on a *collective* or cooperative basis while using innovative and ecologically sound farming methods. It is just not enough that individuals get de facto cultivation rights or legal pattas; these reclaimed spaces must become exemplars of viable collective initiatives worthy of emulation. A second issue is how other mass movements can lend support to them or participate in efforts to win them wider recognition and legitimacy.

The charter must be extended to include other issues such as legally enforceable rights to homestead land, safe drinking water, universal access to health care (financed by tax revenues, not insurance), and affordable public housing—which has fallen off the Indian policymaker's radar for decades. Equally important is the agenda of promoting good-quality education based on a common schooling system with a secular–humanist curriculum. This must do justice to the Dalit struggle's legacy, should not mince words about the multiple forms of oppression women have always suffered, must abjure and criticize a national–chauvinist approach, and should promote respect and tolerance for diverse cultures and civilizations. The curriculum should respect regional and ethnic linguistic variety and not impose 'standard' official languages on adivasis and speakers of so-called dialects.[10]

Needless to say, this cannot happen without purposive, well-targeted state action, which can only come about as a result of people's struggles. Such struggles exist today in atomized forms; they need to be brought together with a concentrated focus as part of a broad political agenda.

The longer-term perspectives in such a People's Charter must deal with sustainable livelihood questions in a context where agriculture has become unviable in many parts of India, and more than a quarter-million farmers have committed suicide over the past one-and-a-half decades.[11] There is simply not enough cultivable land left in most parts of the country which can enable the average rural household to earn a half-way decent living.

This calls for a widespread campaign by kisan sabhas and other mass organizations for *collective farming* based on sharing labour and other inputs and resources in agricultural production and in operations such as processing, packaging and transportation, as well as marketing of produce—the traditional method. The old bourgeois slogans such as 'land to the tiller', aimed at the petty proprietor, will not work and must make way for collectivist proto-'socialist' demands.

The rural economy can no longer be sustained on the strength of conventional agriculture alone, based on cereals and pulses, etc. It must be regenerated through innovations in horticulture, silviculture, pasture and animal breeding, and cultivation of herbs, supplemented by handicrafts production and small enterprises based on local resources, including micro-hydroelectric and solar and wind power generation. Cooperatives could play a central role in such an effort. Of vital importance here would be *local resource mapping*,[12] which makes people aware of their natural resource endowments and allows them to draw up plans to meet their basic community needs in equitable, economically efficient and environmentally sustainable ways.

The basic objective of such initiatives would be to establish and expand sectors of the economy which are not driven by corporations, whether private or state-owned, but by diverse collective and cooperative ventures which pool together resources, skills and small amounts of capital to produce material goods for local consumption.

Such sectors could probably offer the most practical, and yet the most equitable, route to sustainable livelihoods at a decent level of income to large numbers of unemployed educated rural youth who have little hope of finding a productive job—and many of whom are attracted by the illusory promise of 'development' based on the 'Gujarat model' that Narendra Modi trumpets.

An Incomes Policy

The *second-axis* agenda must also take up demands for far-reaching structural reforms which can evoke strong popular resonance and yet have the potential for radicalizing people's struggles in an anti-capitalist direction. Take the issue of income and wealth inequalities, which have acquired grotesque proportions in India, but which do not figure in the agenda of a single political party. It is imperative to return to a classical demand of the socialist and workers' movement: *an incomes policy*, which raises (and enforces) minimum wages to a standard of living compatible with human dignity, and imposes ceilings on the salaries and perquisites of the super-rich both by setting absolute limits and by substantially raising top-bracket income tax rates, which in India are among the world's lowest.[13]

India, to its shame, abolished the estate duty (also called death duty or inheritance tax) in 1985. This runs against elementary considerations of ethics and unjustly favours those who have not earned but merely inherited their wealth. This is doubly obscene in a society marked by extreme disparities of wealth. Even capitalist countries levy such taxes, and at rates such as 40 per cent or higher. A movement that aims to transcend capitalism must do more and better. Indeed, that is how it can show the pathway to the future. The People's Charter must lay stress on a public campaign to compel the Indian government to impose the estate duty at high rates.

It is important to learn from people's movement experiences from India's past and present, and from other countries in respect of decision making in macroeconomics and developmental and habitat planning. These experiences include participatory budgeting in Brazil and other Latin American countries, re-municipalization of (privatized) water in more than thirty countries,[14] group housing in Uruguay and some central European countries, distribution and marketing cooperatives in parts of Africa, the 'transition towns' in the United Kingdom, and workers' cooperatives in Spain and workers' self-management councils in the former Yugoslavia (besides Kanan Devan in Kerala).

Equally relevant is the repertory of experience based on experiments like Cuba's urban farming, 'communities of peace' in Colombia,[15] collective decision making through town-hall meetings recently seen in Greece and Spain, and the kind of 'mohalla (neighbourhood) democracy' that AAP practised for a while in Delhi before and during the 2015 elections, including the very imaginative idea of separate micro-manifestoes for each of Delhi's seventy constituencies, which focused on their specific problems—an idea relevant for a region (population, twenty-five million) which is the size of a country.

It is also vital to incorporate into these narratives lessons in greater transparency in corporate bookkeeping to facilitate workers' scrutiny as an input in wage bargaining, direct shop-floor democracy which demands a say in the labour process, and experiments in workers' control of industries. Such experiences need to be carefully documented and analysed to build up a case for a workers' sector in the larger economy which points to the future even if in an embryonic manner. All of these can contribute to developing what have been termed 'anti-capitalist structural reforms'.

A new socialist charter must lay heavy emphasis on workers in the unorganized sector, who account for more than 90 per cent of India's workforce and most of whom are subject to unspeakably rapacious exploitation. It is notoriously difficult, although not impossible, to organize and unionize these workers. But they, rather than Marx's collective or mass workers in giant factories, are the present and future working class, or the bulk of it. It is in organizing them that the new Left will have to invest its best energies and imagination.

Unorganized Workers: New Approach

So far, two approaches have been tried out, both state-centric. One is to create special boards for different categories of unorganized workers, e.g., in construction, beedi rolling, brick kilns, garment manufacture, etc., and make it mandatory for their employers to be registered with the boards before they can apply for contracts—so that they can be made to conform to certain standards. The second, and weaker, approach consists in legislating minimum wages, working conditions, pensions and welfare funds for workers in the unorganized sector.

Neither approach has worked satisfactorily. But by now their conceptual and implementation flaws have been documented and analysed. Insights gained from such analysis can be used to forge a better strategy, which might consist in creating associations or cooperatives of workers in the unorganized sector, which are treated favourably in respect of government contracts and credit through an explicit affirmative action programme. The rationale for such treatment is incontrovertible: if Dalits, OBCs or ethnic and religious minorities are entitled to concessional credit from the banking system, so should workers' cooperatives be.

Equally important is the evolution of global standards for labour, to be implemented through governmental and intergovernmental organizations and multilateral bodies. Civil society initiatives based on lobbying commodity traders and regulatory boards (for instance, those dealing with garment importers in First World countries) have proved effective in some Third World societies.

Some civil society groups have developed labour standards that meet the criteria of 'decent work' and have the capacity to monitor and implement these. Involving them in efforts to improve labour conditions in India is part of an international solidarity programme. This process needs to be extended to a range of products beyond garments and to regional and international organizations. The old Left neglected these crucial agendas, which is one reason why it became irrelevant for the emerging working class. The new Left cannot afford to neglect them.

Similarly, there must be a campaign to demand substantial social security provision for old people, the unemployed and the disabled, and other vulnerable groups such as households headed by single women[16]. If states like Kerala and Tamil Nadu could institute these provisions and increase the benefits over the years to almost half the level of a living wage, there is no reason why other states, and the Centre, cannot be compelled to do so. This must be pursued as part of the national-level radical social reform agenda that is central to the second axis.

The economic burden that air and water pollution, along with deforestation, imposes on India, including health damage, disability years lost to illness, and the costs of medical treatment, has been estimated by the World Bank at 5.7 per cent of GDP,[17] close to the entire annual addition to the national income in recent years. This is completely unacceptable. There is an urgent need to strengthen environmental regulations and the environmental impact assessment process, which is being scuttled.

It is vitally important to demand statutory changes in the way in which industry, mining, and water and power projects are granted clearances by various advisory and expert appraisal committees set up by the environment and tribal affairs ministries, and by the controlling ministries themselves. Many of these committees have been packed with pro-corporate interests, including the statutory Forest Advisory Committee, whose composition was recently altered in violation of public interest. Interventions that demand representation for project-affected people (PAP) and independent experts, and greater transparency and accountability, are crucial to the transition which popular movements are called upon to make from single-issue campaigns to building a counter-hegemonic thrust.

The *third axis* must grapple with local-level, sectoral or 'micro' issues, which are of immediate concern to the people, especially the underprivileged—from municipal governance to urban and rural air and water pollution and waste disposal; and from affordable, clean and safe public transport to the provision of clean drinking water; and from locally accessible and affordable health care facilities to decent school education.

Micro-sectoral Planning

Such sectoral plans are an integral part of a *counter-hegemonic* plan, one that is designed to mobilize—and is potentially capable of mobilizing—a broad popular coalition. The old Left could never define or articulate such a coherent alternative vision. For instance, it had no conception of urban spaces and cities which are designed to be friendly to people—and not meant to displace them and deprive them of basic civic amenities. The new Left must make this a critical part of its urban agenda.[18]

Here, a great deal can be learned from Latin America's and southern Africa's successful movements to reclaim public water and electricity. Similarly, the Right to Education campaign, which seeks to implement a new constitutional amendment guaranteeing underprivileged children admission to neighbourhood schools, must be integrated into an agenda of equity and universal access, with the involvement of their parents and neighbourhood councils. All neighbourhood schools must have libraries and recruit volunteers to inculcate the reading habit among children—and adults too.

Equally important is the launching and sustenance of a movement to reclaim urban road space for pedestrians from private cars and two-wheelers. These vehicles today grab more than half of the road space but account for only 10 to 15 per cent of all passenger or commuter trips. Yet they contribute two-thirds of the urban air pollution burden. They are unfairly granted huge fuel subsidies; they also benefit from gigantic amounts of public funding which goes into the construction of roads, bridges and flyovers for the exclusive use of private vehicles. Systematic, legally enforceable, programmes to prevent and reduce pollution, including urban waste, must be integrated into urban planning, in which the local population must have a say.

Aggressive promotion of safe, efficient and affordable public transport is an important component of any rational plan to improve the quality of urban life. This cannot be done merely through expensive, capital-intensive systems like the metro (subway), which has become the darling of the middle classes because of its high-technology image and gleaming air-conditioned coaches. The metro becomes viable only at high volumes of traffic[19], which many corridors in Indian cities cannot generate. It therefore inevitably needs huge subsidies despite which it is compelled to charge exorbitantly high fares—simply because its capital costs are ten to thirty times higher than the costs of road construction.

A far superior alternative, which also promotes the equitable use of road space, is Bus Rapid Transit (BRT) which reserves special lanes on existing roads for buses which deliver 40 per cent or more of all commuter trips. The automobile industry lobby has joined hands with affluent car owners and the police to sabotage the BRT in many Indian cities, including Delhi. This must be resisted through street-level campaigns in which underprivileged people demand a fair share of road space for the public transport that they use. Pedestrianization, or reclaiming road space for people to walk freely, is a vital part of the urban democratization agenda. It needs to be pursued seriously.

Private hospitals are mushrooming in every Indian city, fattened by subsidies in land and water rates, exemptions from zoning regulations, and outright grants. They typically cater only to the elite. Many of them are given generous land or high floor-space allowances on the condition that a certain proportion (typically one-fifth) of their patients, who are poor, would be treated free of cost. Corporate hospitals brazenly violate this condition and plead that they cannot 'afford' the free treatment that the poor are entitled to. There must be a sustained public agitation against these malpractices, as well as legal and legislative intervention, to hold their feet to the fire.

It is only through the development of such sectoral micro-level plans—including provision of shelter to the homeless, setting up good free public libraries, creating safe playgrounds and leisure spaces, conserving pavements for pedestrian use by preventing encroachment of cars, encouragement of non-fossil-fuel transport, creation of exclusive bicycle lanes, making inhabitants feel welcomed in their own cities, and rendering them safe especially for women—that the Left will be able to build new neighbourhood solidarities and initiatives that contribute to a counter-hegemonic force or movement which has an alternative plebeian vision to offer.

Grand macro-level national visions and programmes and policies are, of course, important; indeed there is no substitute for them. But they must be translated, in the manner of a Shankar Guha Niyogi,[20] into ground-level popular initiatives amenable to grass-roots control and accountability. This can only be done by civil society movements working jointly with neighbourhood or mohalla committees and people's representatives.

Against Vanguardism

The *fourth axis* must focus on conceptualizing a non-vanguardist relationship between the people and political parties, and between and within parties, based on democratic principles. One of the great lessons from the bureaucratic degeneration of the Russian Revolution, the rise to dominance of Stalinism in the Soviet party and the Communist International, and eventually, the collapse of the Soviet Union, is that a party that claims to be the 'natural' vanguard of the working class and of the people will be eventually rejected by them.[21] This is true with a vengeance of the contemporary epoch, marked by democratization, even if partial, of public culture and politics, and the communications revolution.

Any politics based on a claim to vanguardist pre-eminence becomes simply unviable although it may survive for a time on the basis of a patron–client relationship rather than genuine legitimacy and moral authority. This is exactly what happened to the Left Front, in particular the CPI(M), in West Bengal. It started losing support in its core base well before a series of electoral reverses set in, culminating in its ouster from power. To be sustainable, any claim to leadership within a competitive political environment can only be based on the ability of a party to articulate programmes and policies that are relevant to substantial sections of the people, and deliver on its promises. Coercive methods may delay the expression of popular disapprobation for a period of time, but not forever.

As noted earlier, India in recent decades has seen an eruption of popular movements on livelihood issues, democratic rights and social justice questions. These have drawn in vast numbers of people acting spontaneously or through civil society mobilizations and 'people's movement' structures, as distinct from NGOs. The old Left for the most part kept away from these movements, and often deplored them as a 'diversion' from 'the real issues', or half-heartedly participated in them only if it was assured of leadership and control over them.

This proved counterproductive and isolated the Left from some of the most energetic popular mobilizations witnessed in India on issues of long-term relevance to the Left's own cause[22]. Bereft of new activists and fresh ideas, the Left's leaders resorted to outright coercion to push through neo-liberal agendas such as Singur and Nandigram in West Bengal and entertainment parks in Kerala.

As popular discontent mounted, and with it inner-party dissension, the Left's leadership suppressed debate by invoking the organizational 'principle' of 'democratic centralism', which mandates that members follow the official line once it is set by party congresses or conferences held every three years or so, during which they are free in theory to debate policies and other matters, but are forbidden from expressing dissenting views in the interim.

Unlike many Left or centre-left parties in Europe or Latin America, however, the Indian Left parties do not allow the formation of inner-party tendencies or factions, based on different strategic or tactical positions, which are free to express their views and circulate their literature, and indeed get financial support to enable them to do so.

In practice, 'democratic centralism' has worked as a blunt instrument of censorship or suppression of debate even when the need for the airing of differences is palpably urgent. This too is linked to the Left's vanguardism. Nothing could be more self-destructive at a time when the CPI(M), for example, is in a shambles especially in West Bengal. Hundreds of its members, under attack from Trinamool Congress goons—against which the once mighty party can no longer defend them—are quitting the CPI(M) to join the BJP, and are yet barred from debating the party 'line'.

Unless the Left makes a decisive break with 'democratic centralism', embraces a tolerant approach to dissent and inner-party debate, and allows its members to go public with their views without fear of being reprimanded or expelled, its organizational crisis will only worsen.

There is a larger lesson in this for all of those who wish to create the embryo of a new Left. They too must start with a clear enunciation of openness and tolerance of difference and dissent, with full freedom for all to go public with their views especially on policy matters.[23] This is essential to create not just a new inner-party or organizational culture, but a new culture of politics itself, based on active citizenship.

It is crucial here to understand the role that rights-based movements can play in raising issues that go to the heart of governance and the existing power structures. When people use rights-based laws to claim land, for instance, they become active subjects. They assert their agency and their role as part of the process of determining land use which is no longer left to government officials. They thus create or fashion a space for future struggles over entitlement to other resources too.

As for the *fifth* and last axis, what is needed today is a reaffirmation of internationalism in two senses of the term: rejection of narrow nationalism as a parochial and retrograde agenda; and solidarity amongst working people across the world against their exploiters and oppressors, who are bound together by their struggle against the global capitalist economy. A rejuvenated Left in India must adopt a critical stance vis-á-vis the aggressive, threatening, masculine nationalism that is growing in the country; indeed, it must fight it in a spirited way.

Fighting National Chauvinism

Chauvinistic nationalism domestically fosters parochial forms of patriotic hubris, promotes irrational notions of Indian exceptionalism, celebrates obscurantist notions of India's uniquely glorious past, and breeds contempt for 'other' cultures, civilizations and values as inferior. It also reinforces militant Hindutva. Such nationalism furnishes a fertile ground in which Islamophobic approaches to 'terrorism' can flourish and rationalize immense brutality and blatant violations of civil and political liberties and human rights on the part of the state, especially directed against the religious minorities.

In the neighbourhood, militant Indian nationalism entails aggressive posturing against the smaller countries and, at times, covert or overt interventions in them, as has repeatedly happened in the case of Bangladesh, Nepal, Sri Lanka and the Maldives. It also sustains dangerous India–Pakistan hostility. Unlike the old Left, which often tailed the Indian state in South Asian policy, the new Left must condemn the state's arrogant and imperial behaviour in the neighbourhood. It should be equally unsparing of the Indian government's policy and conduct on the Kashmir issue and the brutal repression it has practised through the Armed Forces Special Powers Act and other means in the north-east, where India's military and paramilitary troops are seen as an occupying force.

The conduct of all arms of the government in these regions—as well as in the tribal heartland where it is waging war on its own citizens in the name of fighting an 'internal security threat' in the shape of Maoism—exposes the seamy, ugly, unacceptable side of the Indian state and the travesty of its claim to being a democracy based on the rule of law.

The solidarity-based internationalism that is necessary today is different from the kind of 'internationalism' that India's mainstream Left parties practised for decades within their nationally limited 'socialism in one country' frameworks. This was based on fraternal relations with kindred parties in communist regimes, including despotic ones as in North Korea, Romania and other eastern European states within the Soviet sphere of influence, and of course China. This involved sending observers or greetings to each other's party congresses, periodic visits and sometimes special meetings, but little genuine engagement at the ideological level, joint activity at the political level, or even practical acts of solidarity.[24]

The new internationalism could usefully involve exchange of experience, collaborative analytical work, preparation of common alternative policy papers (Left parties in some of the BRICS [Brazil, Russia, India, China and South Africa] countries could do so), and active participation in joint campaigns—for instance, on climate change issues, on labour standards, on trade and intellectual property issues and on human rights, in respect of which progressive movements differ strongly with 'their' national governments.

This list of issues and subjects can be greatly expanded once the dialogue on reinventing the Left acquires momentum and produces results in the form of platforms of ideas and programmatic understandings that could go into the proposed People's Charter. It would be prudent to wait for that to happen rather than anticipate the outcome. One can only hope that this chapter makes a contribution, however modest, to that much needed process.

Lessons from the Aam Aadmi Party

A final question, one that is often asked by people within the Left and its well-wishers both in India and abroad is: What about the Aam Aadmi Party, which has made such a dramatic entry into Indian politics and halted the Modi juggernaut, itself a historic achievement? How best can AAP be evaluated as a new movement or a novel kind of politics, and what future does it have? How should the Left relate to it? What can the New Left learn from AAP? Can AAP make a genuine contribution to the agendas discussed above, and help rejuvenate the Left?

AAP is indeed a qualitatively new phenomenon, born both of hope and of popular disillusionment and exhaustion with conventional politics and with self-serving, corrupt and cynical leaders who lack legitimacy and credibility because they are as far removed as they can be from the agenda of popular welfare. AAP has successfully energized, inspired and mobilized the urban poor in Delhi, but it is not a left-wing party. It has a dual base: on the one hand, workers and self-employed people in the informal sector, most of whom are indigent but have strong aspirations for a better life; and on the other, middle-class- and upper-middle-class-strata, including relatively affluent professionals.

It is expedient for AAP to claim that it follows no particular ideology, philosophy or political doctrine—partly because that appeals to the second part of its constituency, which is inclined to be 'post-ideological', has very little sympathy for left-leaning ideas or any notion of egalitarianism, and is not instinctively anti-communal or secular. This layer is impressed by AAP's, in particular, Arvind Kejriwal's, 'solutions-oriented' technocratic approach to social problems. It likes him because he is clean, he is a 'doer', and also very much like themselves: upper caste, educated at an Indian Institute of Technology (he could have been an MBA or an accountant), and not steeped in liberal values.

However, AAP's committed support, and the bulk of its votes,[25] comes from the poor and the lower middle class, which it mobilized through its promise of removing petty corruption (a form of harassment they face every day), 'regularizing' their supposedly illegal colonies and providing municipal services more reliably and cheaply. AAP's novel methods of campaigning, based on door-to-door canvassing, use of autorickshaws and attractive lyrics, and backed by very little money power, also played a major role in drawing out the poor.

For them, Kejriwal is/was a hero because he is unconventional, rebellious and speaks the language of entitlements and rights of the poor, without being aggressive in Narendra Modi's boastful '56-inch chest' way. He seems to have tapped to some extent into the disillusionment with Modi that set in early. Whatever the reason, breaking the BJP's victory run under Modi was a contribution to secular politics that far exceeds Laloo Prasad's halting of L.K. Advani's rath yatra in 1990.

The Left has a good deal to learn from AAP, especially its emphasis on grass-roots consultation, its promise (not always fulfilled) of popular participation in decision making on civic matters, and its localized involvement of mohalla committees in referendum-style votes. AAP has also found and institutionalized ways of raising funds through small individual donations (although questions have been raised about some large anonymous donations), from which the Left can learn.

Above all, it is AAP's preference for grappling with municipal issues by making local officials accountable to slum dwellers and neighbourhood committees that inspires people and instils confidence in them about their own agency, rights and power as citizens. Here too, the Left has something to take away.

However, AAP has failed to institutionalize itself and create an internal structure of democratic consultation and decision making, based on fair representation and accountable procedures. It remains too individual-centric, in ways that carry wholly negative messages for the Left. The shoddy manner in which Yogendra Yadav and Prashant Bhushan were treated and hounded out of the party brought little credit to Kejriwal. True, they had their own ambitions (by no means illegitimate) and genuine differences with Kejriwal on the priorities for AAP in contesting elections outside Delhi. He saw these as proof of disloyalty and betrayal. AAP could and probably will grow and expand, but as a less radical, open and democratic party than it was before its spectacular victory in Delhi.

Kejriwal's autocratic methods and organizational practices cannot help the cause of rejuvenating a robustly democratic Left which has agendas that are not parochial either in their regional scope or their ideological reach and content. Ideology, clarity of strategy and democracy must provide to the Left the oxygen it needs to introspect, correct course and regroup. AAP-type short cuts are no substitute.

Appendix 1
The Mode of Production Debate

Beginning in the late 1960s, a passionate debate raged for one-and-a-half decades among Indian and foreign scholars of a broadly Marxist persuasion on the mode of production prevalent in Indian agriculture (or more generally, in India), or the extent to which capitalist relations of production had penetrated it, and where the future direction of evolution of agrarian relations lay.

The participants included redoubtable names in the world of social science scholarship on India, including Ashok Rudra, Amit Bhaduri, Utsa Patnaik, John Harriss, Jairus Banaji, Paresh Chattopadhyay, Kathleen Gough, Pradhan H. Prasad, Nirmal Chandra, Amiya K. Bagchi, Ranjit Sau, Joan P. Mencher, Hamza Alavi and Gail Omvedt, to mention only some. A major early contributor was the pioneering agrarian economist Daniel Thorner, a refugee from McCarthyism in the United States settled in France, but deeply engaged with India.

The debate raised a series of questions: What are the distinguishing features of the dominant production relations in Indian agriculture? Are they 'capitalist', 'pre-capitalist' or 'semi-feudal'? Are 'semi-feudal' relations a fetter on the productive forces, unlike (supposedly) capitalist relations? Are landlordism, sharecropping, tenancy, rent extraction and unfree labour necessarily semi-feudal? How did colonialism impact agrarian relations and land property regimes? Is petty commodity production in agriculture evolving towards capitalism? Which are the main rural classes and the principal lines of conflict between them today? What do the answers imply for the Left's class-alliance strategies?

As economists developed mathematical models, sociologists gathered fresh field data, and historians struggled with analysing past patterns of the transition to capitalism elsewhere, yet others raised conceptual issues related to understanding relations of production in the complex landholding and labour-hiring systems prevalent in different parts of India. Sharp lines of division emerged between the proponents of the 'capitalist', 'semi-feudal', 'pre-capitalist', 'colonial'/post-colonial and 'composite' or 'dual' modes of production.

This exchange built upon the foundations laid by an earlier, and very lively, debate (beginning in 1950) on the transition from feudalism to capitalism between Paul Sweezy and Maurice Dobb, with later interventions by Kohachiro Takahashi, Rodney Hilton, Christopher Hill and others, which was itself a landmark in Marxist scholarship in economic history.[1]

Although the participants in the India debate were scholars and activists who explored various themes in Marxist agrarian political economy and the history of transition to capitalism in the countryside, and the discussion itself took place mainly in the pages of the *Economic and Political Weekly*, *Frontier* and *Social Scientist*, its backdrop was provided by the radical political mobilizations of the mid-1960s onwards, including the Naxalite upsurge, the 'land-grab' movements in West Bengal and Bihar, and agrarian struggles in the southern and western states, especially among the landless.

The mode of production debate had significant implications for an analysis of the evolution of class relations and contradictions in the Indian countryside, different views about the persistence of 'semi-feudal' relations, or alternatively, their weakening under capitalism, and hence the nature of agrarian struggles in the context of the recently launched Green Revolution. Although the debate did not directly result in changes in the strategies and tactics of the Left parties, it was influenced by their agendas and approaches. It would in turn generate long-term inputs for a discussion of the Indian road to socialism, in particular, the relevance of a protracted agrarian people's war, with the countryside surrounding the cities (advocated by the Naxalites), vis-á-vis different strategies based on radical rural (and urban) mobilizations, within the existing 'democratic' system. The discussion remains relevant to this day.

The debate had rich empirical, conceptual, analytical and historical dimensions. It occurred at different levels, ranging from individual farms (or groups of them), to agriculture in specific geographical regions/sub-regions, to the entire economy of a region or of India as a whole, and went on to raise questions about the impact of colonialism on India and the economy's relationship with the more advanced capitalist countries. But its focus remained on the specificity of India's agricultural economy, class relations, and the potential for the development of agrarian capitalism.

The mode of production debate was preceded by the empirical work of several scholars, some of it going back to the late 1940s to the mid-1960s, including Kathleen Gough (south India), Jan Breman (Gujarat), Daniel Thorner (seven different states in five regions), and Ashwani Saith–Ajay Tankha and Sulekh Gupta (both Uttar Pradesh). All of them reported a strong spread of capitalist relations in agriculture, based on the use of hired or commodified labour, growing production for the market, appropriation of the surplus through mercantile profit and interest on credit, and accumulation of capital through rising investments in new technologies and modern methods of production. Ironically, the debate proper did not refer to most of this work.

The mode of production debate, summarized below along thematic rather than chronological lines, was inaugurated in 1969 by Ashok Rudra with a sample survey of villages in Punjab, which contended that there had been no significant growth in capitalist farming even in this relatively prosperous region: the category of 'capitalist farmers', who cultivate their land with a higher proportion of hired workers than their own labour, market an important share of their produce, use farm machinery, and seek a high return on investment, could not be statistically proved to exist.[2]

Rudra was strongly challenged by Utsa Patnaik on methodological grounds for using 'unhistorical' categories. Patnaik insisted that the use of wage labour to produce surplus value, and significant production for the market, are not enough to define genuine capitalism; also indispensable is 'capital intensification', or accumulation and reinvestment of surplus value on an ever-increasing scale. 'Ex-colonial countries like India', she held, 'are characterized precisely by a limited and distorted development of capitalism which does not revolutionize the mode of production'.[3]

Patnaik at this point was not arguing against Rudra's substantive position, but criticized him for holding that farm size is a criterion for categorizing groups of farmers. Patnaik also argued that bourgeois property relations could develop with functioning markets in land and labour without the development of capitalist relations of production. Chattopadhyay intervened to argue that this was impossible since property relations are only the juridical expression of relations of production.[4]

Varied themes entered into the ensuing debate: the nature of 'semi-feudalism' and the role of rent, usury, and trading profits in subjugating the peasantry, which demarcate it from capitalism; the relationship between Indian agriculture and the world economy in the context of colonialism; and rural class structures, the process of class differentiation and its likely direction. We deal here primarily with the first theme, although the class structure issue is discussed briefly.

The starting point of the semi-feudal thesis is what Daniel Thorner (1956) had described (without using the S-word) as 'a built-in depressor', produced by the 'legal, economic and social relations uniquely typical of the Indian countryside', with highly skewed landholding, landlord domination through tenancy, sharecroppers' dependence on subsistence crop loans at usurious rates of interest, and the landlord's appropriation of high trading profits from selling produce on the market. This left the landlord with no incentive to invest and raise productivity through technological change; at the same time, the peasant-cultivator was too impoverished and dependent to be able to invest. The 'depressor' would ensure agrarian stagnation and low productivity.[5]

Amit Bhaduri, basing himself on a survey of twenty-six West Bengal villages in 1970, built an elegant model of such agrarian relations and argued that the 'dominant character of existing production relations' could 'best be described' as semi-feudal in that they 'have more in common with classic feudalism of the master–serf type than with industrial capitalism'. He listed four prominent features of these semi-feudal relations: share-cropping; perpetual indebtedness of the small tenants; concentration of two modes of exploitation, namely usury and landownership in the hands of the same economic class; and lack of accessibility to the market for the small tenant or kisan.[6]

Bhaduri notes that the kisan is compelled to borrow consumption loans at rates of interest as high as 25 to 200 per cent over about four months. He argues that since 'usury as an important mode of exploitation depends largely on the kisan's having to borrow regularly for consumption, the continuation of the system requires that the available balance of paddy of the kisan must always fall short of his consumption requirement. Consequently, technological improvements, which raise the productivity level of the kisan, become undesirable to the landowner to the extent that they increase the kisan's available balance of paddy in relation to his consumption level so as to reduce his requirement for consumption loans. For it weakens the system of semi-feudalism, where economic and political power of the landowner is largely based on his being able to keep the kisan constantly indebted to him.

'Further, since the semi-feudal landowner derives his income both from property right to land and usury, he will be discouraged from introducing any technological improvement so long as his gain in income from increased productivity brought about by technological change falls short of his loss in income from usury due to a reduction (or complete elimination) in the level of consumption-loan required by the kisan ... This also gives a precise form to Marx's general idea that the relations of production may become a constraining factor on the release of the "forces of production" and, according to any materialistic interpretation of history, such a situation is ripe for historical change'.[7]

Pradhan H. Prasad and Nirmal K. Chandra reinforce Bhaduri's conclusions based on their empirical studies from Bihar and West Bengal. Prasad holds that big landowners oppose the introduction of improved agricultural practices which might serve eventually to free their tenants from their 'semi-feudal' bondage. 'This results in semi-servile conditions of living and a low level of consumption ... low productivity of land and labour ... under-utilization of resources and almost negligible net investment in the agricultural sector.'[8] He later concludes, on the basis of various sample surveys during 1951–71 that his 'semi-feudal model (but for variations in details) is, by and large, valid for the most part of rural India'.[9]

Chandra argues on the basis of state government surveys that India 'has not been going through a capitalist transformation at all, and that there are important socio-economic forces impeding such a transformation', the 'biggest single obstacle' being British colonial rule, which 'greatly strengthened feudal or semi-feudal elements in the countryside that are primarily responsible for the indifferent progress in the post-colonial era'. Chandra emphasizes 'massive unemployment in the countryside', and contends that a 'labour surplus on a scale that is probably unparalleled in human history is perpetuating the semi-feudal set-up'.[10] Further, given the extreme weakness of industrial capitalism in India, says Chandra, 'We cannot envisage how ... things might radically improve on the industrial front or in respect of surplus labour ...[or] ... visualize when productive capital will dominate over usury capital in our agriculture or when the pre-capitalist crop-sharing system will disappear.'[11]

He later argues that the replacement of domination by old zamindars (non-cultivating landlords) by jotedars (former tenants with occupancy rights over large blocks of land, which they get cultivated by sharecroppers or by hired agricultural labour) has not qualitatively altered the agrarian situation. Usury continued unabated, with the landlord making a profit of 'up to 300 per cent' on his wage advances by exploiting the difference in grain prices between different agricultural seasons. Evictions of tenants increased over the preceding decade: 'nearly two-thirds' of tenant households had been evicted. The top eight to ten families in each survey village constitute 'the main bottlenecks to the development of [the] productive forces' and hence to the growth of capitalism.[12]

Ranjit Sau shares Chandra's 'characterization of the mode of production in Indian agriculture as semi-feudal', but supplements this with the argument that small peasants continue to cultivate land despite meagre returns because of 'the absence of alternative job opportunities in industry'—to the point of reducing their own consumption to 'an unbelievable minimum'. Thus, irrespective of returns to scale, 'capitalist farmers would face insuperable barriers' in ousting small tenants.[13]

Rudra, in 1974, executes a radical shift in his stand and contends on the basis of his 'direct first-hand knowledge of conditions prevailing in West Bengal' that there is no landowning class 'that finds it more in its economic and social power interests to resort to usury rather than capital investments'; on the contrary, many landowners 'are very much engaged in capital investments in the form of irrigation, fertilizers and high-yielding variety seeds'.[14] Against Chandra, he also finds a trend towards a concentration of landholding 'as a result of investments on land' by large landowners.

Similarly, while poor tenants, farm servants and casual labourers typically borrow loans for consumption, such loans are interest-free 'when taken by a tenant from the landowner from whom he has leased in land or by a farm servant from the landowner for whom he works'. Contrary to Chandra's thesis of a labour surplus, Rudra argues that in many parts of West Bengal, there exists 'a scarcity of actual labour supply in relation to demand during the peak periods'—despite a great deal of unemployment during the lean season.

So contrary to his own original position in 1969, in which he failed to discern capitalism among farmers in Punjab, Rudra concludes: 'If generation of surplus through the employment of wage labour, appropriation of that surplus by the owners of capital and reinvestment of that surplus for the purpose of expansion of that capital be a characteristic feature of capitalism, then there are indeed increasing manifestations of such capitalistic feature in West Bengal agriculture.'[15]

Rudra would further develop his new stand in a three-part article in the *Economic and Political Weekly*.[16] The shift was not as sudden or drastic as might seem. Rudra earlier questioned, with Aparajita Chakravarty, the widespread view that tenancy is not only detrimental to welfare but also inimical to growth, thanks to a lack of security of tenure and of sufficient incentives for and returns from investment. Rudra and Chakravarty's analysis of farm management studies found no major 'marked differences in the input–output patterns of owner-operated farms and tenant-operated farms'.[17]

More important, there occurred a huge conceptual–theoretical shift in the understanding among scholars, both Indian and foreign, including Rudra, of the Marxian concept of modes of production; the complex relationship between empirically observed, 'mixed' or 'contingent' phenomena such as class relations and forms of exploitation on the one hand, and modes of production in their 'essential' form on the other; the question of free labour as an indispensable ingredient of capitalism; and the many ways in which the metropolitan–periphery circuit of capital drained surplus value out of India for one-and-a-half centuries and left its impact even after Independence.

Crucial here are the interventions of scholars like Jairus Banaji, Ashok Rudra, Kathleen Gough and Gail Omvedt. Banaji in particular takes issue with analysts like Bhaduri and Patnaik who hold a 'conception of capitalist relations of production' which is incompatible with the relations of 'bondage' between the landlord-cum-moneylender and the sharecropper-cum-small producer who is tied to him through land leases, rent, and usurious loans, and 'who bears no direct relationship to the market', because the former 'intervenes in the process of production to realize the surplus-labour extorted from him on the market'.[18]

Banaji argues for a critical distinction: that between two forms of what Marx called 'subsumption of labour into capital' in the historic process of the subordination of the small producer—i.e., 'in the long-term evolution of the bourgeois mode of production'—namely, 'formal' and 'real' subsumption. 'Both forms imply capitalist relations of exploitation', i.e., 'the extortion of surplus-labour as *surplus-value*. However, the *formal* subordination of labour to capital presupposes a process of labour that is "technologically" continuous with earlier modes of labour. It is the form that crystallizes when capital confronts the small producer, invades his process of production and "takes it over" without subjecting it to technical transformation. These relations ... do not presuppose the bourgeois mode of production in its advanced or developed form, under which labour is subordinated to capital no longer merely "formally", but "really"....'[19]

Yet, contends Banaji: 'The formal subsumption of labour into capital implies that ... "the process of production has become the process of capital itself", i.e., of the self-expansion of value, of the conversion of money into capital ... This in turn implies that capital is here "the immediate owner of the process of production" and that the immediate producer is merely "a factor in the production process and dependent on the capitalist directing it".'[20]

Banaji goes on to draw a 'very important conclusion', namely, that 'there might be historical situations where in the absence of a specifically capitalist mode of production on the national scale, capitalist relations of exploitation may nonetheless be widespread and dominant'. He cites the case of the Deccan, with its history of expanding production of cotton and groundnut for export, and of sugar, foodgrains and garden crops for the growing population of Bombay and Poona cities during 1850–90. Growing commodity production based on conversion of labour power led to the impoverishment and proletarianization of the peasantry. Droughts and famines seemingly played an immediate and decisive role in the proletarianization, but this became possible 'only because of the already exhausted and decrepit condition of the Deccan small-production economy'.[21]

Capitalist exploitation operated in the Deccan both through the 'widespread' capital–wage labour relationship and through the subsistence loans advanced by merchant-moneylenders to small peasants. The 'purely capitalist nature of relationship between the peasant and moneylenders', says Banaji, was concealed by the fact that the *'surplus-value* extorted from the small producer would be called "interest"'.[22] Banaji criticizes the 'widespread tendency' to identify labour arrangements like sharecropping and other forms of tenancy with pre-capitalist or 'semi-feudal' production relations.

'Now big peasants of the sort that we encountered in the nineteenth century Deccan would be "capitalist entrepreneurs in agriculture who as a rule employ several hired labourers" (Lenin) but who do not necessarily confine themselves to labour-arrangements involving only day-workers or casual labour.' They might maintain a reserve of permanent farm labour or base themselves 'on one of several types of tenancy'.[23] But that does not affect the 'social character or content of the production relations' these arrangements embody. Similarly, 'indebtedness, as such, is not a hallmark of "pre-capitalist" relations, if only because it is precisely through the *power of money* that the *despotism of capital* is initially established'.[24]

Banaji argues that in the late nineteenth-century Deccan, 'capitalist relations of exploitation signifying the less developed forms of capitalist production had emerged ... and were widespread and in some districts dominant'. But for India as a whole 'the bourgeois mode of production in its developed or "adequate" structure was neither dominant nor widespread'. The specific form of capitalist production which evolved in the Deccan constituted 'a *subordinate and transitional system* within the bourgeois mode of production in its *world* extension'.[25]

Banaji extends his analysis to the contemporary period and argues that 'the struggle against capitalist forms of exploitation has already begun' in the countryside which should be 'conducted on the basis of its character', i.e., on 'a programme for the abolition of *the system of wage-slavery*'.[26] Although Banaji's characterization of the Deccan in these terms was contested, his discussion of the formal subsumption of labour into capital and the evolution of agrarian capitalism proved extremely influential.

Hamza Alavi and Gough reach broadly similar conclusions. Alavi holds that peasant farming continued in India on the basis of largely unchanged techniques; it was nonetheless subject to formal subsumption of labour by capital, and at a later stage, by 'real subsumption', with a rise in the 'organic composition of capital'. Peasants, he argues, are more resilient than urban petty commodity producers because they need not depend on the market for their food and shelter, and desperately hold on to their tiny plots of land. But their conditions are progressively undermined by the 'dynamics of peripheral capitalist development'.[27]

Gough argues, on the basis of her analysis of Thanjavur district of Tamil Nadu, that 'the capitalist mode of production was dominant' there in the late nineteenth and early twentieth century despite the persistence of certain pre-capitalist features, including 'traditional gifts', caste discrimination, and infliction of corporal punishment on labourers. In the period 1947–80, Thanjavur saw greater production for export and a transformation of farming through the use of chemical fertilizers, hybrid high-yielding seeds, pesticides, tractors, tube wells and electric irrigation pumps. Gough noted that 'there is a continuing rise in the organic composition of capital' especially on the larger farms. Correspondingly, 'the extraction of relative surplus value has greatly increased'.[28]

Omvedt and Rudra bring in the issue of caste oppression and 'social, cultural and religious institutions' to argue for the need to fight both social oppression and caste exploitation simultaneously. Omvedt holds that capitalism is dominant in Indian agriculture now, unlike at Independence, because over half of the rural population depends upon wages; generalized commodity production, including the sale of labour power, prevails; all cultivators are forced to sell to some extent in the market, and their production is governed by the laws of the market; the means of production in agriculture are to a large extent produced industrially and acquired through the market; there has been a substantial growth in the use of capital inputs such as fertilizers and oil engines; there has been a genuine, if halting, growth in agricultural production; and the primary aspect of the relationship of the rural rich with the rural poor is as exploiters of labour power.[29]

Rudra makes a foray into history to argue that the proponents of an Indian feudalism like R.S. Sharma and B.N.S. Yadava were comprehensively wrong. He holds that 'the struggle against the reactionary elements of the Brahmanic ideology' should constitute an important element 'in any struggle for progress in this country'[30].

The debate is greatly enriched empirically by a discussion of the rural class structure in its interplay with caste by Mencher, Chandra, Patnaik, Rudra, Prasad and Bardhan, among others. This engages with issues of labour exploitation, the complex and changing relationships between different strata of the peasantry, the 'hybridity' of the class of big landowners ('part-feudal, part-capitalist'), and the growing or 'emerging contradiction' between the landlords and big peasantry on the one hand and the poor peasantry and landless labourers on the other. Further insights are provided by Breman in his work on different forms of labour bondage and their compatibility with capitalism, and the historical analysis of landlordism in Bengal by Rajat and Ratna Ray.[31]

Also explored in the discussion is the emergent bonding between different class and caste groups in the Hindi belt: the changing power balances between the 'traditionally dominant' upper castes and the 'rising' middle castes (Other Backward Classes in officialese), a phenomenon that would soon lead to 'the Forward March of the Backwards' and the Mandal scheme of reservations for the OBCs.

The 'majority opinion'[32] here (for want of a better term) is that the most important contradiction in the countryside is that between the big landowners (including rich peasants) and labourers (landed or landless)—although there are differences on the role of the middle peasant, and other issues.[33]

At the end of one-and-a-half decades of this debate, concludes Alice Thorner, 'There would no longer appear to be any doubt that capitalism today dominates Indian agriculture as it already was generally seen to dominate industry at the time the discussion began. Does this mean that the mode of production which prevails in contemporary India is capitalist, and subject to the Marxist laws of motion of capitalist development? Here, the answer is less evident, since India's capitalism has emerged in a particular colonial setting, markedly different from the conditions in the metropolitan countries where capitalism was born.'[34]

Yet, argues Thorner: 'It has been abundantly shown that the existence of widespread tenancy and/or share-cropping does not necessarily indicate the presence of feudal relations of production; nor does the concentration of landholding together with cultivation of small units by large numbers of peasants. By the same token, the use of wage labour cannot by itself be taken as a sure sign of capitalist relations. Yet the shift from exploitation through tenants to large-scale or intensive farming by means of hired labour is significant.'[35]

Further, says Thorner: 'The growth of capitalist farming in India has been accompanied by, in fact amounts to, a transformation of relations of production and forms of exploitation. Servile, debt-bonded, and/or traditionally tied labour has been largely supplanted by free, relatively mobile, wage labour, paid (if meagrely) for the most part in cash. Investment in modern, scientific agriculture has enormously expanded, and has resulted, on the whole, in enhanced production, at least of certain crops in certain areas. Tenancy and share-cropping arrangements have in many regions been adapted to the new economic and technical requirements.'[36] Nevertheless, 'there is agreement that capitalism in agriculture cannot be depended upon to solve the crucial problems of access to land and to food of the whole rural population'.[37]

Rudra (with Chakravarty) reaches an important political conclusion: 'The orthodox Left standpoint in this country has been that the main enemy (of progress) in the rural sector is feudalism. Certain feudal elements are supposed to be the exploiters of all the other classes defined as landless labourers, poor peasants, middle peasants and rich peasants. Feudalism being the only enemy, the orthodox Left parties have treated—whether or not in theory, certainly in practice—all the remaining classes, from landless labourers to rich peasants as possible allies. Feudalism being the only force of reaction in the countryside, emerging capitalism in agriculture tends to be regarded as progressive ... Anti-feudalism has therefore taken the form of demands for conferment of ownership rights to tenants. However ... it would seem that leasing in and out of agricultural land may not necessarily be any more feudal or any less capitalistic a transaction than say the renting of a building by a business concern for setting up its office ...'[38]

Rudra, who started the entire mode of production debate, has the last word on its political significance: 'In the meanwhile, the political interests of the landless labourers and poor peasants have gone by default. That is bound to happen whenever attempts are made to build a united front of all the non-feudal rural classes against a phantom feudalism. The orthodox Left parties have thus ended up by supporting the emergent forces of agrarian capitalism to the hilt in the name of fighting feudalism.'[39] This comment was doubtless eloquent and acerbic, even vitriolic. But it drew virtually no response from the 'orthodox' parties at which it was directed.

Appendix 2: Electoral Performances of Parties and Groups over the Years

Performance of the Left Parties in Lok Sabha Elections				
Year		Seats Contested	Seats Won	Vote (%)
1977	Congress	492	154	34.52
	Bharatiya Lok Dal (BLD)*	387	280	39.32
	Left	**87**	**45**	**7.84**
	CPI(M)	53	22	4.29
	BLD(Left supported)	18	15	2.01
	RSP	4	4	0.45
	Forward Bloc	4	3	0.34
	Kerala Congress (Pillai group)	3	0	0.28
	All India Muslim League (AIML)	2	0	0.17
	Independent (Left Supported)	3	1	0.30
	Independents and Other parties	1473	63	18.32
	Total	**2439**	**542**	**100.00**
1980[1]	Congress	492	353	42.69
	Janata Party (Secular) JNP(S)	294	41	9.41
	Janata Party (JNP)	432	31	18.95
	Left	**149**	**58**	**10.82**
	CPI	47	10	2.49

* The Janata Party used the symbol allotted to the BLD

Performance of the Left Parties in Lok Sabha Elections				
Year		Seats Contested	Seats Won	Vote (%)
	CPI(M)	64	37	6.24
	RSP	8	4	0.65
	Forward Bloc	21	3	0.51
	INC(U) [Left supported]	6	3	0.65
	KEC	2	1	0.18
	Muslim League Opposition	1	–	0.10
	Independents and Other parties	3262	46	18.13
	Total	**4629**	**529**	**100.00**
1984	Congress	517	415	48.01
	BJP	229	2	7.40
	Left	**145**	**34**	**9.76**
	CPI	66	6	2.70
	CPI(M)	64	22	5.72
	RSP	4	3	0.47
	Forward Bloc	5	2	0.42
	IUML '	1	–	0.09
	ICS(Left supported)	2	1	0.19
	Lok Dal	1	–	0.07
	Independent (Left Supported)	2	–	0.10
	Independents and Other parties	4602	91	34.83
	Total	**5493**	**542**	**100.00**
1989[2]	Congress	510	197	39.53
	BJP	225	85	11.36
	Janata Dal	243	143	17.70
	BSP	245	3	2.07
	Left	**134**	**53**	**10.72**
	CPI	50	12	2.57
	CPI(M)	64	33	6.55
	RSP	6	4	0.62
	Forward Bloc	8	3	0.42
	Janata Dal (Left supported)	1	–	0.09

Performance of the Left Parties in Lok Sabha Elections				
Year		Seats Contested	Seats Won	Vote (%)
	ICS (Left supported)	1	1	0.12
	KEC	1	–	0.02
	Independent (Left Supported)	3	–	0.33
	Independents and Other parties	4803	48	18.62
	Total	**6160**	**529**	**100.00**
1991[3]	Congress	505	244	36.64
	BJP	478	121	20.04
	Janata Dal	310	60	11.64
	BSP	243	3	1.80
	Left	**142**	**57**	**10.47**
	CPI	43	14	2.48
	CPI(M)	63	35	6.14
	RSP	9	4	0.63
	Forward Bloc	19	3	0.41
	Janata Dal (Left supported)	4	–	0.35
	KEC	1	–	0.11
	ICS (Left supported)	1	1	0.14
	Independent (Left Supported)	2	–	0.21
	Independents and Other parties	7075	52	19.41
	Total	**8753**	**537**	**100.00**
1996	Congress	529	140	28.80
	BJP	471	161	20.29
	Janata Dal	193	45	7.85
	BSP	210	11	4.02
	Left	**145**	**53**	**9.61**
	CPI	43	12	1.97
	CPI(M)	75	32	6.12
	RSP	5	5	0.63
	Forward Bloc	16	3	0.38
	Janata Dal (Left supported)	2	–	0.13
	KEC	1	–	0.10

Performance of the Left Parties in Lok Sabha Elections				
Year		Seats Contested	Seats Won	Vote (%)
	ICS(Left supported)	1	–	0.10
	Independent (Left Supported)	2	1	0.18
	Independents and Other parties	12404	133	29.43
	Total	**13952**	**543**	**100.00**
1998	Congress	477	141	25.82
	BJP	388	182	25.59
	Janata Dal	189	6	3.08
	BSP	251	5	4.67
	Left	**144**	**48**	**8.30**
	CPI	58	9	1.75
	CPI(M)	71	32	5.16
	RSP	5	5	0.55
	Forward Bloc	4	2	0.33
	Janata Dal (Left supported)	2	–	0.16
	KEC	1	–	0.09
	Independent (Left Supported)	3	–	0.26
	Independents and Other parties	3301	161	32.54
	Total	**4750**	**543**	**100.00**
1999	Congress	453	114	28.30
	BJP	339	182	23.75
	Janata Dal (United)	60	21	3.10
	BSP	225	14	4.16
	Left	**150**	**43**	**7.68**
	CPI	54	4	1.18
	CPI(M)	72	33	5.40
	RSP	5	3	0.41
	Forward Bloc	15	2	0.35
	KEC	1	1	0.10
	JD(Secular) [Left supported]	1	–	0.09
	Independent (Left Supported)	2	–	0.15

Performance of the Left Parties in Lok Sabha Elections				
Year		Seats Contested	Seats Won	Vote (%)
	Independents and Other parties	3421	169	33.01
	Total	**4648**	**543**	**100.00**
2004	Congress	414	145	26.44
	BJP	364	138	22.16
	Janata Dal (United)	33	8	1.95
	BSP	435	19	5.33
	Left	**112**	**61**	**8.02**
	CPI	33	9	1.32
	CPI(M)	69	43	5.66
	RSP	4	3	0.43
	Forward Bloc	3	3	0.35
	KEC	1	1	0.09
	JD(S) [Left supported]	1	1	0.09
	Independent (Left Supported)	1	1	0.08
	Independents and Other parties	4077	172	36.10
	Total	**5435**	**543**	**100.00**
2009	Congress	440	206	28.55
	BJP	433	116	18.80
	Janata Dal (United)	27	20	1.42
	BSP	500	21	6.17
	Left	**179**	**24**	**7.61**
	CPI	56	4	1.43
	CPI(M)	82	16	5.33
	RSP	17	2	0.38
	Forward Bloc	22	2	0.32
	KEC	1	–	0.08
	Independent (Left Supported)	1	–	0.07
	Independents and Other parties	6491	156	37.45
	Total	**8070**	**543**	**100.00**

Performance of the Left Parties in Lok Sabha Elections				
Year		Seats Contested	Seats Won	Vote (%)
2014	Congress	464	44	19.31
	BJP	428	282	31.00
	BSP	503	–	4.14
	Left	**210**	**12**	**4.83**
	CPI	67	1	0.78
	CPI(M)	93	9	3.25
	RSP	5	–	0.23
	Forward Bloc	39	–	0.22
	JD(S) (Left Supported)	1	–	0.05
	Independent (Left Supported)	5	2	0.30
	None of the above (NOTA)	543	–	1.08
	Independents and Other parties	4113	205	39.64
	Total	**6261**	**543**	**100.00**

West Bengal: Performance of Left Parties in Lok Sabha Elections			
Year		Seats Contested	Seats Won	Vote (%)
1977	**Left**	**42**	**39**	**57.03**
	CPI(M)	20	17	26.15
	Janata Party on BLD symbol	15	15	21.46
	RSP	3	3	3.94
	Forward Bloc	3	3	4.30
	Independent (Left Supported)	1	1	1.18
	Congress Allies	**42**	**3**	**35.86**
	Congress	34	3	29.37
	CPI	8	–	6.49
	Independents and Other parties	87	–	7.11
	Total	**171**	**42**	**100.00**
1980	**Left**	**42**	**38**	**53.97**
	CPI	3	3	4.28
	CPI(M)	31	28	39.91
	RSP	4	4	5.22
	Forward Bloc	4	3	4.56
	Congress	41	4	36.51
	Janta Party	35	–	4.53
	Independents and Other parties	167	–	4.99
	Total	**285**	**42**	**100.00**
1984	**Left**	**42**	**26**	**48.43**
	CPI	3	3	3.76
	CPI(M)	31	18	35.92
	RSP	4	3	4.62
	Forward Bloc	4	2	4.13
	Congress	42	16	48.16
	BJP	9	–	0.40
	SUCI	9	–	0.71
	Independents and Other parties	146	–	2.30
	Total	**248**	**42**	**100.00**

Year	West Bengal: Performance of Left Parties in Lok Sabha Elections	Seats Contested	Seats Won	Vote (%)
1989	Left	42	37	51.44
	CPI	3	3	3.90
	CPI(M)	31	27	38.38
	RSP	4	4	4.69
	Forward Bloc	3	3	3.95
	Janata Dal	1	–	0.52
	Congress	41	4	41.38
	GNLF	1	1	1.37
	Independents and Other parties	252	–	5.81
	Total	336	42	100.00
1991	Left	42	37	48.13
	CPI	3	3	3.69
	CPI(M)	30	27	35.19
	RSP	4	4	4.51
	Forward Bloc	3	3	3.65
	Janata Dal	2	–	1.09
	Congress	41	5	36.21
	BJP	42	–	11.67
	Independents and Other parties	268	–	3.99
	Total	393	42	100.00
1996	Left	42	33	49.09
	CPI	3	3	3.81
	CPI(M)	31	23	36.70
	RSP	4	4	4.76
	Forward Bloc	3	3	3.42
	Janata Dal	1	0	0.40
	Congress	42	9	40.09
	BJP	42	–	6.88
	Independents and Other parties	271	–	3.94
	Total	397	42	100.00

West Bengal: Performance of Left Parties in Lok Sabha Elections				
Year		Seats Contested	Seats Won	Vote (%)
1998	**Left**	**42**	**33**	**46.83**
	CPI	3	3	3.64
	CPI(M)	32	24	35.41
	RSP	4	4	4.48
	Forward Bloc	3	2	3.30
	Congress	39	1	15.20
	All-India Trinamool Congress (AITC)	29	7	24.43
	BJP	14	1	10.20
	Independents and Other parties	148	–	3.34
	Total	**272**	**42**	**100.00**
1999	**Left**	**42**	**29**	**46.74**
	CPI	3	3	3.47
	CPI(M)	32	21	35.57
	RSP	4	3	4.25
	Forward Bloc	3	2	3.45
	AITC Alliance	**42**	**10**	**37.95**
	AITC	28	8	26.04
	BJP	13	2	11.13
	Independent (BJP Supported)	1	–	0.78
	Congress	41	3	13.29
	Independents and Other parties	184	–	2.02
	Total	**309**	**42**	**100.00**
2004	**Left**	**42**	**35**	**50.72**
	CPI	3	3	4.01
	CPI(M)	32	26	38.57
	RSP	4	3	4.48
	Forward Bloc	3	3	3.66
	UPA	**42**	**6**	**14.99**
	Congress	37	6	14.56
	Jharkhand Mukti Morcha (JMM)	2	–	0.15

Year		Seats Contested	Seats Won	Vote (%)
	West Bengal: Performance of Left Parties in Lok Sabha Elections			
	Republican Party of India (RPI)	1	–	0.06
	PDS	2	0	0.22
	NDA	**42**	**1**	**29.11**
	BJP	13	–	8.07
	(All India Trinamool Congress) AITC	29	1	21.04
	Independents and Other parties	229	–	5.18
	Total	**355**	**42**	**100.00**
2009	**Left**	**42**	**15**	**43.33**
	CPI	3	2	3.60
	CPI(M)	32	9	33.13
	RSP	4	2	3.56
	Forward Bloc	3	2	3.04
	UPA	**41**	**25**	**44.63**
	AITC	27	19	31.18
	Congress	14	6	13.45
	BJP	42	1	6.14
	Independents	116	1	3.08
	Other Parties	127	–	2.82
	Total	**368**	**42**	**100.00**
2014	**Left**	**42**	**2**	**29.61**
	CPI	3	–	2.33
	CPI(M)	32	2	22.71
	RSP	4	–	2.43
	Forward Bloc	3	–	2.14
	Janata Dal			
	Congress	42	4	9.58
	BJP	42	2	16.84
	AITC	42	34	39.35
	Independents and Other parties	346	–	4.62
	Total	**514**	**42**	**100.00**

Kerala: Performance of UDF Parties in Lok Sabha Elections				
Year		Seats Contested	Seats Won	Vote (%)
1977	**UDF**	**20**	**19**	**58.89**
	Congress	11	11	29.13
	CPI	4	4	10.38
	Indian Union Muslim League (IUML)	2	2	6.03
	Kerala Congress (KEC)	2	2	5.55
	Independent (UDF Supported)	1	–	1.80
	LDF	**20**	**1**	**44.70**
	CPI(M)	9	–	20.33
	Kerala Congress (Pillai group)	3	–	5.95
	RSP	1	1	3.08
	BLD	3	–	7.20
	All India Muslim League (AIML)	2	–	3.60
	Independent (LDF Supported)	2	–	4.54
	Independents and Other parties	23	–	3.59
	Total	**63**	**20**	**100.00**
1980	**UDF**	**20**	**8**	**40.41**
	Congress	11	5	26.32
	IUML	2	2	5.56
	Independent (UDF Supported)	7	1	8.53
	LDF	**20**	**12**	**50.51**
	CPI	2	1	4.13
	CPI(M)	8	7	21.48
	RSP	1	–	2.27
	Indian National Congress (Urs) (INC(U))	6	3	15.85
	KEC	2	1	4.37
	AIML	1	–	2.41
	Janata Party	4	–	6.70
	Independents and Other parties	49	–	2.38
	Total	**93**	**20**	**100.00**

Kerala: Performance of UDF Parties in Lok Sabha Elections

Year		Seats Contested	Seats Won	Vote (%)
1984	**UDF**	**20**	**17**	**50.92**
	Congress	13	13	33.27
	Muslim League	2	2	5.29
	KEC	1	–	2.37
	Kerla Congress (Joseph)	2	2	5.49
	Independent (UDF Supported)	2	–	4.50
	LDF	**20**	**3**	**42.29**
	CPI	4	–	7.37
	CPI(M)	10	1	22.27
	IUML	1	–	2.06
	ICS	2	1	4.38
	Lok Dal	1	–	1.71
	Independent (LDF Supported)	2	1	4.50
	BJP	5	–	1.75
	Independents and Other parties	106	–	5.04
	Total	**151**	**20**	**100.00**
1989	**UDF**	**20**	**17**	**49.29**
	Congress	17	14	41.70
	IUML	2	2	5.23
	Kerala Congress (Mani) KCM	1	1	2.36
	LDF	**20**	**3**	**42.48**
	CPI	3	–	6.20
	CPI(M)	10	2	22.87
	RSP	1	–	2.41
	Janata Dal	1	–	1.86
	ICS	1	1	2.48
	Independent (LDF Supported)	4	–	8.59
	BJP	20	–	4.51
	Independents and Other parties	158	–	3.72
	Total	**218**	**20**	**100.00**

Kerala: Performance of UDF Parties in Lok Sabha Elections				
Year		Seats Contested	Seats Won	Vote (%)
1991	**UDF**	**20**	**16**	**49.14**
	Congress	16	13	38.77
	IUML	2	2	5.02
	KCM	1	1	2.70
	Independent (UDF Supported)	1	–	2.65
	LDF	**20**	**4**	**44.78**
	CPI	4	–	8.12
	CPI(M)	9	3	20.71
	RSP	1	–	2.41
	Janata Dal	2	–	4.51
	KEC	1	–	2.24
	ICS	1	1	2.77
	Independent (LDF Supported)	2	–	4.02
	BJP	19	–	4.61
	Independents and Other parties	120	–	1.47
	Total	**179**	**–**	**100.00**
1996	**UDF**	**20**	**10**	**45.75**
	Congress	17	7	38.01
	IUML	2	2	5.08
	KCM	1	1	2.66
	LDF	**20**	**10**	**44.96**
	CPI	4	2	8.22
	CPI(M)	9	5	21.16
	RSP	1	1	2.50
	Janata Dal	2	1	4.40
	KEC	1	–	2.23
	ICS	1	–	2.31
	Independent (LDF Supported)	2	1	4.14
	BJP	18	–	5.61
	Independents and Other parties	174	–	3.68
	Total	**232**	**20**	**100.00**

Kerala: Performance of UDF Parties in Lok Sabha Elections			
Year		Seats Contested	Seats Won	Vote (%)
1998	**UDF**	**20**	**11**	**46.08**
	Congress	17	8	38.67
	IUML	2	2	5.01
	KCM	1	1	2.40
	LDF	**20**	**9**	**44.60**
	CPI	4	2	8.32
	CPI(M)	9	6	21.00
	RSP	1	1	2.67
	Janata Dal	2	–	3.90
	KEC	1	–	2.20
	Independent (LDF Supported)	3	–	6.51
	BJP	20	–	8.02
	Independents and Other parties	60	–	1.30
	Total	120	20	100.00
1999	**UDF**	**20**	**11**	**46.94**
	Congress	17	8	39.35
	IUML	2	2	5.27
	KCM	1	1	2.32
	LDF	**20**	**9**	**43.66**
	CPI	4	–	7.57
	CPI(M)	12	8	27.90
	Janata Dal (Secular)	1	–	2.17
	KEC	1	1	2.38
	Independent (LDF Supported)	2	–	3.64
	BJP	14	–	6.56
	Independents and Other parties	88	–	2.84
	Total	142	–	100.00

Kerala: Performance of UDF Parties in Lok Sabha Elections				
Year		Seats Contested	Seats Won	Vote (%)
2004	**UDF**	**20**	**1**	**38.38**
	Congress	17	–	32.13
	IUML	2	1	4.86
	KCM	1	–	1.39
	LDF	**20**	**18**	**46.15**
	CPI	4	3	7.89
	CPI(M)	13	12	31.52
	JD(S)	1	1	2.25
	KEC	1	1	2.34
	Independent (LDF Supported)	1	1	2.14
	NDA	**20**	**1**	**12.08**
	BJP	19	–	10.38
	Indian Federal Democratic Party (IFDP)	1	1	1.70
	Independents and Other parties	117	–	3.39
	Total	**177**	**20**	**100.00**
2009	**UDF**	**20**	**16**	**47.73**
	Congress	17	13	40.13
	IUML	2	2	5.07
	KC(M)	1	1	2.53
	LDF	**20**	**4**	**41.90**
	CPI	4	–	7.44
	CPI(M)	14	4	30.48
	KEC	1	–	2.08
	Independent (LDF Supported)	1	–	1.90
	BJP	19	–	6.31
	Independents and Other parties	158	–	4.06
	Total	**217**	**20**	**100.00**

Kerala: Performance of UDF Parties in Lok Sabha Elections			
Year		Seats Contested	Seats Won	Vote (%)
2014	**UDF**	**20**	**12**	**41.98**
	Congress	15	8	31.10
	Muslim League	2	2	4.54
	Socialist Janata (Democratic)	1	–	1.71
	RSP	1	1	2.27
	KC(M)	1	1	2.36
	LDF	**20**	**8**	**40.12**
	CPI	4	1	7.59
	CPI(M)	10	5	21.59
	JD(S)	1	–	1.69
	Independent (LDF Supported)	5	2	9.25
	NDA	**20**	**–**	**10.82**
	BJP	18	–	10.33
	RSPK(B)	1	–	0.24
	Independent (NDA Supported)	1	–	0.25
	Independents and Other parties	226	–	7.08
	Total	**286**	**20**	**100.00**

Appendix 3: Seventh Term in Tripura

Tribal Question, Clean Government, Full Literacy,
Limited Vision on Equity

Tripura, located in the north-east, is India's second smallest state, with a population of 3.7 million. It is probably one of the few regions of the world, and the only one in India, where communist influence has been sustained among an indigenous tribal (adivasi) population for more than half a century.[1] In 2013, Tripura's electorate returned the CPI(M)-led Left Front to power for the seventh time (five of them consecutively), a record matched solely by West Bengal in a democracy anywhere in the world. The Tripura Left seems far better placed at the time of writing to be elected to an eighth term than the Left Front in West Bengal was at a comparable moment.[2]

Tripura is the only state where Indian communists have had to confront ethnic identity as a pivotal issue head-on—that too in a fraught, and often violent, situation where the indigenous population was overrun by migrants from East Pakistan/Bangladesh. The proportion of adivasis in the total fell from 50 per cent in 1941 to 31.5 in 1961 and further to 28.4 per cent in 1981.[3] It now stands at 31.8 per cent. But much of the tribals' land has been appropriated by Bengali settlers or the state. The Left Front's record on the issue of restoring the land to the adivasis is poor, as we shall see below, despite its very high score in overall governance.

Tripura has many distinctions to its credit. It has often been described as India's least corrupt state under a leader (Manik Sarkar) who is probably the poorest of all the chief ministers in the country.[4] More important, Tripura is all set to emerge as India's first state with full, 100 per cent, literacy. In September 2013, the Tripura government reported that thanks to special drive, it had achieved a literacy rate of 95.16 per cent, up from 87.75 per cent in 2011. The new rate surpassed those recorded in Kerala (94 per cent), Mizoram (91.58) and Goa (88.7) in 2011.[5]

This is a stupendous achievement for a state with a per capita income below the Indian average, and only half of whose people were literate in 1981 and barely 60 per cent in 1991. The recent increase was brought about through the involvement of local government bodies, gram panchayats, NGOs and local 'youth clubs' under the supervision of the State Literacy Mission Authority headed by the chief minister.

Tripura has similarly registered impressive improvements in human development indicators, including life expectancy at birth (seventy-one and seventy-four years for males and females, higher than sixty-one and sixty-three years respectively for India in 2001), health, nutrition, education, employment, human security and democratic decentralization. Tripura's sex ratio (961 females to 1,000 males) is higher that India's (940), its infant mortality per thousand births is twenty-eight (India, forty-two). Eighty-six per cent of the population has a toilet at home (India, forty-seven), and 68.4 per cent uses electricity as the main source of lighting. Seventy-nine per cent of Tripura's people use banking services, compared to 58.7 per cent in India.

Between 1991 and 2001, Tripura registered greater improvements in the human development and gender development indices than India as a whole.[6] Tripura's implementation of the Mahatma Gandhi National Rural Employment Guarantee Act (MGNERGA) is among the best in Indian states and so is its performance in respect of the Forest Rights Act. Until June 2013, it distributed more than 120,000 titles to forest land, accounting for almost two-thirds of all claims. Between 2004–05 and 2009–10, rural and urban poverty fell by respectively 24.7 and 12.5 percentage points.

Tripura recently discovered natural gas reserves, and built a 726 MW gas-fired power station, which has made it a power-surplus state. It is selling 100 MW to Bangladesh and building a cooperative economic and trade relationship with it. Under the Left Front, Tripura has launched a number of initiatives in agriculture, horticulture, dairying and so on. It is running a government competently, purposively and with serious commitment to public welfare.

How did the Left get implanted in the soil of Tripura? The roots go back to movements in the 1930s against the ruling royal family of Tripuri ethnicity by tiny groups of Bengalis—Bengalis were invited into Tripura by the monarchy which was in awe of Bengali culture—radicalized by 'terrorists' of the Anusilan Samity variety, and indigenous tribals, especially those belonging to non-Tripuri groups such as the Reang, Jamatia, Chakma and Halam. A turning point was the Reang rebellion (1943–45), followed by the formation of Jana Mangal Samity (popular welfare association),[7] and attempts to unionize workers in the tea gardens that were being set up.

However, the real breakthrough happened in the late 1940s during the 'Ranadive period', when the tribal autonomist entity Gana Mukti Parishad (GMP) launched an armed struggle against the autocratic rule of the Tripura princely family. (Tripura formally merged into the Indian Union only in October 1949.) The communists had a small base in this period. The GMP, led by Aghore Devbarma, a Tripuri, and Biren Dutta, a Bengali, became almost synonymous with the Communist Party of India, and soon merged with it. The two GMP leaders were soon joined by other Tripuris, most prominently, Dasarath Devbarma (or Dasarath Deb), who became communism's most important tribal face in Tripura, and later its chief minister.

The GMP must be one of the most remarkable and radical movements in modern India. It undertook armed raids against landlords who had seized tribal land through usurious moneylending. When repression followed, it declared the local Congress government illegal and started redistributing land. During 1949–52, it ran an 'undeclared parallel government' in large parts of Tripura, covering a population of 400,000, based on Shanti Senas (peace brigades) and people's committees at several different levels.

The GMP campaigned for social reform including abolition of child marriage, dowry, polygamy and untouchability practised against non-

Tripuri tea workers, and against superstition. It also demanded land ceilings and higher wages. It lowered the interest rates on loans advanced by moneylenders, and seized a part of their land and redistributed it among landless tribals and tea workers. By 1951, the GMP had a membership of 300,000 in Tripura's population of 700,000—a truly amazing feat!

However, a major change occurred in the early 1950s in the GMP–CPI relationship when the CPI adopted the Rajeswara Rao line eschewing armed struggle. The GMP was not dissolved, as some CPI members wanted, but placed under the CPI's control. The CPI sent Bengali comrades to help build the party in Tripura, including Nripen Chakraborty, who later became Tripura's first communist chief minister. Soon after his arrival in August 1950, Chakraborty accused the GMP leadership of following a 'bourgeois ideology' and succumbing to 'nationalism, sectarianism, opportunism', charges which were motivated by his intent to legitimize the subordination of the GMP to the CPI.[8]

According to another commentator, 'The course of Tripura communism during 1951–52 was changed on the basis of two important inner-party documents: one prepared by Nripen Chakraborty in 1951 and the other by Dasarath Deb in 1952. The Chakraborty document was intended to orient the CPI to the newly emerging political situation in the country involving participation in parliamentary politics. The Deb document prepared after the first general election in Tripura (1952) was intended to explain the integration of Tripura communism with all-India communism.'[9]

Very little material is available on this period in Tripura's politics and the CPI's internal debate. One can at best speculate on the consequences had the Deb line prevailed. At any rate, given the historical weakness of the Congress in Tripura, as in many other princely states, the CPI performed well even in electoral politics.

The CPI emerged as the largest single party in the 1952 assembly elections, winning 43 per cent of the popular vote—higher than in Kerala, where it would win 38 per cent of the vote in 1957. This, says Harihar Bhattacharyya, 'entitles them to claim to have preempted the Kerala comrades' 1957 achievement' in forming the world's first democratically elected government (barring the case of the minuscule

Italian principality of San Marino in 1946–47). But despite winning the election, the Tripura communists could not take office 'in the absence of an appropriate political–constitutional setup'.[10]

The CPI grew rapidly in Tripura between 1952 and 1963 and was firmly anchored among both the adivasis and the Bengalis. It played a balancing role between the two and fought hard battles to keep parochialism at bay. After the CPI split of 1964, the CPI(M) became the dominant faction, and by 1971–72 the state's second largest party. After the Janata Party's victory in the general elections of 1977, the Congress in Tripura went into disarray, the biggest beneficiary of which was the CPI(M). It formed two short-lived coalition ministries before calling an assembly election in December 1977.

By mobilizing its tribal and Bengali peasant base, the CPI(M) won an overwhelming fifty of the sixty assembly seats with 49 per cent of the vote. In 1978, the CPI(M)-led Left Front came to power. Biren Dutta, the founder of the Tripura communist movement, pleaded with the CPI(M) state committee and the party's top leadership to install Dasarath Deb as the chief minister. But the party's observer Promode Dasgupta, who was a member of the politburo, 'pushed Nripen Chakraborty to the top job, on grounds that he was a more experienced administrator and the state was a Bengali majority state. This, in Dutta's opinion, was the "one big mistake by our party in Tripura".'[11] The Left Front went on to win the 1983 assembly elections too, albeit with a reduced majority.

Meanwhile, the question of restoring land to the adivasis was still unresolved. The Congress, which teamed up with the ultra-chauvinist Amra Bangali, virulently opposed the implementation of the Restoration of Alienated Lands Act, 1976, which it had itself passed. The CPI(M) tried to substitute tribal autonomy for land. In 1979, it moved a bill in the Tripura assembly for the formation of a Tripura Tribal Areas Autonomous District Council. The assembly passed a resolution in March 1982 and again in February 1983, urging the Central government to apply the provisions of the Sixth Schedule of the Constitution to the tribal areas of Tripura. The Centre brought a constitutional amendment to enable this in 1984. This was handled clumsily and produced 'a bloody Bengali backlash'.[12]

The fundamental problem in Tripura was restoration of illegally transferred land in the absence of any record of sharecropper rights and the presence of politically powerful Bengali interests. The CPI(M) recognized this, but failed to find a remedy. There were two references in the CPI(M)'s 1985 party congress, which 'report the redistribution of land to 100,000 landless ... [or apologetic] restoration of alienated land to the tribal people "to the extent possible"...'[13]

The land reforms minister, Biren Dutta of the CPI(M), was disillusioned with the government's achievement of its agrarian aims and resigned on health grounds. He later stated: 'The record of rights of sharecroppers is far below the expectations of the exploited.' He added that in 'my whole career as land reforms minister, I could not get Agricultural Workers Act passed because of fears all around the party of losing the middle classes and absentee landlords' support'.[14]

Meanwhile, the refugee/migrant influx continued and so did the displacement of huge numbers of people, mainly adivasis. Between 1947 and 1971, more than 600,000 Bengalis entered Tripura.[15] After the 1971 Bangladesh crisis, Tripura sheltered more than 1.7 million refugees when her own population was under 1.6 million.[16]

Tribal insurgent groups emerged in Tripura in response to this influx of Bengalis. A full-scale violent insurgency erupted in 1980, when nearly 350 Bengalis were killed in a single night at Mandai. More than 5,000 Bengalis have reportedly died in violence perpetrated by different rebel groups in the last twenty years. 'The US Committee for Refugees estimated the internal displacement of Bengalis in various parts of Tripura at more than 200,000 at the peak of tribal militancy between 1995 and 2000 ... Towards the end of 1999, the Bengalis started hitting back. ... A Bengali militia vigilante group called the United Bengal Liberation Front (UBLF), bombed vehicles carrying tribals and markets frequented by them, killing more than 20...'[17]

All manner of insurgent groups wreaked havoc in Tripura between 1996 and 2004: ranging from the Tripura Upajati Juba Samiti (TUJS), the Tripura National Volunteers (TNV), the National Liberation Front of Tripura (NLFT), and All Tripura Tiger Force (ATTF). Several links were formed between the underground organizations and political parties in the north-east. The Tribal National Volunteers, resurrected by B.K.

Hrangkhawl, was one of the most violent groups. The Left Front lost the state assembly elections in 1988 amidst massive violence unleashed on Bengali settlers by the TNV, which left 117 people dead in a month.

Within four months of the Left's defeat, the TNV walked out of the jungles and signed an accord with Delhi. The Left Front returned to power in 1993, and Tripura got its first tribal chief minister in Dasarath Deb. But the ground situation did not improve.

The Left Front responded to the insurgency in two ways: by trying to settle tribals practising shifting jhum (slash-and-burn) cultivation by promoting rubber plantations and other 'development' schemes; and by raising the Tripura State Rifles (TSR) as a counter-insurgency force from the mid-1980s, while using strong-arm tactics. A whole new class of cultivators and others from the middle class became rubber planters: an estimated 50,000 families were pulled out of poverty.[18] Tripura has now become India's second largest producer of rubber. Rubber provided jobs and created some interlocking economic relationships between entrepreneurs from indigenous tribes and Bengali-speaking settlers who run rubber-processing firms.

In the late 1990s, the emphasis shifted to the second, military, approach. Massive counter-insurgency operations were launched by the Indian Army and Central paramilitary forces. The draconian Armed Forces Special Powers Act (AFSPA) was enforced in Tripura in 1997. Beginning 2000, Tripura got police and intelligence officers who were known for their unorthodox approach, including one who had already made a name in anti-rebel operations for his 'alleged involvement in the so-called secret killings'[19] (assassination of relatives and kinsmen of top United Liberation Front of Asom leaders using surrendered militants). He used a vastly improved police structure to conduct routine 'area domination' operations using the TSR, which was regarded by the tribal people as 'an essentially pro-Bengali force, with a frequent tendency to carry out depredations against the tribals ...[20]

More important, the police initiated a series of 'trans-border attacks on rebel bases and safe houses as far as Dhaka where NLFT and ATTF leaders used to stay, using a combination of surrendered militants and Bangladeshi mafia lords'. In these operations, which sometimes used 'hired killers'[21], the police was ably supported by local Border Security

Force (BSF) commanders, local intelligence agency station chiefs and military intelligence officers. The Union home ministry under L.K. Advani was fully complicit in the raids. Many of them were kept a secret not only from the prying eyes of Bangladesh intelligence and the rebel scouts but also from the sleuths who report to Delhi.[22]

Whether these operations finally brought the Tripura insurgency to heel, or some other reasons or processes did, will remain a subject of debate. But they certainly violated the rights of many innocent people, promoted a culture of cynicism which would tolerate anything from torture to killing suspects first and asking questions later, and left the original cause of adivasi resentment—land alienation—unresolved.

Relative peace returned to Tripura following a long-drawn-out counter-insurgency campaign. On 28 May 2015, Tripura revoked the draconian Armed Forces Special Powers Act, which had been in force in the state since February 1997.[23] The Act had to be extended every six months. Revoking it was a persistent demand of opposition parties like the Indigenous Nationalist Party of Tripura (INPT) and the Indigenous People's Front of Tripura (IPFT), which claimed it had been selectively used to suppress Adivasi aspirations.

Why Manik Sarkar revoked AFSPA after eighteen years is probably partly due to a decline in insurgent activity. The Left Front vote had just suffered a decline of nine percentage points in the Tribal Areas Autonomous District Council elections held weeks earlier. And this, it was speculated, might have been Sarkar's way of neutralizing his opponents and recouping the loss.[24]

Meanwhile, the LF launched a number of development programmes, including dairying, horticulture, poultry and piggeries. Tripura has moved to SRI (system of rice intensification) in a big way, and is now producing, besides rubber, substantial quantities of potatoes, fruits (including pineapple, limes, jackfruit, bananas), nuts and spices like back cardamom. The government also recently reconstituted its planning board, with a view to providing 'a clear direction to policy formulation and planning process for all-round development of the state'.[25] The document visualizes considerable devolution of powers and functions to local bodies, in order to 'enhance people's participation' and is similar to the 2006 People's Plan initiative in Kerala, with grass-roots planning based on participatory resource mapping.

These initiatives are welcome. But they do not address the problem of restoring land alienated from tribals, which continues to rankle. As does the marginalization of Kokborok, the principal tribal language, which is nominally declared an 'official' language but has hardly displaced the use of Bengali. Many tribals want Kokborok to be written in the Roman script, which will facilitate a transition to English. But there is resistance to this from the Bengali majority.

Tripura could make substantial progress in overcoming adivasi alienation and resentment in three ways. First, it could promote collective and cooperative farming and other common activities cutting across ethnic communities on the basis of equity, which give the tribals a sense of participation and ownership of land and land-based resources that goes beyond individual possession and creates a sense of community and caring and sharing. Second, the government could find a way of reclaiming land given for suboptimal use and hand it over to the adivasis; this would be a big symbolic gesture, but perhaps more than that. And third, the Left Front, the CPI(M) in particular, could create a new composition and line of succession in its leadership which indicates that it is prepared to move towards a tribal leadership decisively.

All three are within the realm of the possible. Given the small size of most farms in Tripura, it makes perfect sense for small farmers to pool their resources together with some support from the state, including outright cash subsidy, concessional credit, leasing of farm equipment and marketing facilities at concessional rates, and other ways of promoting collectivism. When I put this to Sarkar, he flinched, saying, 'All these programmes belong to the stage of socialism; we are still at the bourgeois stage.'[26] Such initiatives are simply not on the party's horizon.

This is part of a larger problem. The Left is into good governance in Tripura—responsible, clean governance, but not into *equity*, into radical collectivist programmes that build on the advantages of a semi-tribal society, which can make the transition to a post-capitalist order that much faster. This is evident in the way Tripura is doing its urban planning, based on private housing and transport and (middle class) individual mobility, its education (welcoming private profit-oriented schools and colleges), or its cultural institutions. It is following the same dualistic elite- or middle-class-oriented development model that most states in India do, but with better welfare programmes for the poor. It is not creating a radically different alternative model, as it could do.

Second, thoughtful suggestions have been made about how land committed to wasteful use can be recovered. An instance is the 30-metre high Gumti hydroelectric dam, commissioned in 1976, which produces a paltry seven MW of power but has displaced an estimated 8,000 to 10,000 families.[27] If the dam is decommissioned, argues Subir Bhaumik, 45 sq. km of land can be reclaimed and huge fertile tracts of flatland would be opened up for farming and resettlement of the landless tribal peasantry of the state. 'At least 30,000 tribal families, perhaps the whole of its landless population, can be gainfully resettled in this fertile tract,'[28] each being given a viable plot of one hectare. This is definitely an idea worth exploring seriously.

Third, chief minister Sarkar is highly regarded. But so is his former deputy Jitendra Chowdhury, a tribal who is widely considered his possible successor, and certainly a desirable one, according to many adivasi professionals I spoke to. But Chowdhury has since May 2014 been a Lok Sabha MP and effectively isolated from the party and administration in Tripura. Many party leaders think it would be wise for the CPI(M) to create and publicize a line of succession that represents a fair balance between the indigenous tribals and migrant Bengalis. Will the leadership summons up the imagination to do so is a big question.

For the benefit of the serious and interested readers, a table is presented on the next page showing the vote percentage and the number of seats (out of sixty) in the elections to the Tripura state assembly from 1972 (after it attained full statehood) till 2013. It may be seen that barring the very first election (after statehood) in 1972 and the one in 1988 the CPI(M)-led Left Front won all the seven elections. This shows how deep-rooted the party is in the state and how the people have reposed their faith in the party.

Vote Percentage of Parties in Tripura

Year	CPI(M)	CPI	Congress	TUJS/INPT	Ind	FB	RSP	Amra Bangali	LF*
1972	39.66 (16)	3.04 (1)	44.83 (41)	7.44	11.92 (2)	8.55			
1977	47.00 (51)	0.84	17.76	7.93 (4)	4.11 (2)	1.04 (1)	1.66 (2)		50.54
1983	46.78 (37)	0.83	30.51 (12)	10.47 (6)	8.89 (3)	0.71	1.64 (2)		49.96
1988	45.82 (26)	0.82	37.33 (25)	10.52 (7)	2.98	0.67	1.6 (2)		48.91
1993	44.78 (44)	1.35	32.73 (10)	7.52 (1)	6.15	0.8 (1)	1.58 (2)	1.46	48.51
1998	45.49 (38)	1.38 (1)	33.96 (13)	7.19 (4)	3.29 (2)	0.56	1.65 (2)	0.32	49.08
2003	46.82 (38)	1.54 (1)	32.84 (13)	12.46 (6)	0.84	0.65	1.89 (2)	0.45	50.90
2008	48.01 (46)	1.48(1)	36.38 (10)	6.21 (1)	3.21	0.16	1.69(2)	0.31	51.34
2013	48.11 (49)	1.57 (1)	36.53 (10)	7.59	0.96	0.7	1.95	0.25	52.33

Source: Election Commission of India

*In 1972, Forward Block was not a part of the Left Front
Figures in brackets indicate number of seats won

Courtesy: Subhanil Chowdhury and Gorky Chakraborty

Notes

Preface

1   A large number of books and articles have appeared on the Indian Maoist movement, written by journalists, scholars and activists. Among the recent books are Rahul Pandita (2011): *Hello Bastar: The Untold Story of India's Maoist Movement*, New Delhi, Tranquebar Books; Robin Jeffrey, Ronojoy Sen and Pratima Sen (eds) (2012): *More Than Maoism: Politics and Policies of Insurgency in South Asia*, New Delhi, Manohar Publishers; Anuradha M. Chenoy and Kamal A. Mitra Chenoy (2010): *Maoist and Other Armed Conflicts*, New Delhi, Penguin Books; Shubhranshu Choudhary (2012): *Let's Call Him Vasu: With The Maoists in Chhattisgarh*, New Delhi, Penguin Books; Dilip Simeon (2010): *Revolution Highway*, New Delhi, Penguin Books; Sudeep Chakravarti (2008): *Red Sun: Travels in Naxalite Country*, New Delhi, Penguin Books; Anand Swaroop Varma (2001): *Maoist Movement in Nepal*, New Delhi, Samkaleen Teesri Duniya; Neelesh Misra and Rahul Pandita (2010): *The Absent State: Insurgency as an Excuse for Misgovernance*, New Delhi, Hachette India; Alpa Shah and Judith Pettigrew (eds.) (2012): *Windows into a Revolution: Ethnographies of Maoism in India and Nepal*, New Delhi, Social Science Press and Orient BlackSwan; Prakash Louis (2002): *People

Power: The Naxalite Movement in Central Bihar, Delhi, Wordsmiths. As far as articles go, one of the finest analyses is to be found in Jairus Banaji (2010): 'The Ironies of Indian Maoism', *International Socialism*, Issue 128, 15 October. Also see Arundhati Roy (2010): 'Walking with the Comrades', *Outlook*, 29 March, and (2010): 'The Trickledown Revolution', *Outlook*, 20 September; Gautam Navlakha (2010): 'Days and Nights in the Maoist Heartland', *Economic and Political Weekly*, 17 April; Santosh Rana (2009): 'A People's Uprising Destroyed by the Maoists', *Kafila*, 23 August, http://kafila.org/2009/08/23/a-peoples-uprising-destroyed-by-the-maoists-santosh-rana/; K. Balagopal (2006): 'Maoist Movement in Andhra Pradesh', *Economic and Political Weekly*, 22 July, and 'Chhattisgarh: Physiognomy of Violence', *Economic and Political Weekly*, 3 June; Sumanta Banerjee (2003): 'Naxalites: Time for Introspection', *Economic and Political Weekly*, 1 November; Bela Bhatia (2005): 'The Naxalite Movement in Central Bihar', *Economic and Political Weekly*, 9 April;, Dipankar Bhattacharya (2006): 'Trail Blazed by Naxalbari Uprising, *Economic and Political Weekly*, 16 December; Independent Citizens' Initiative (2006): 'Open Letters to Government and Maoists', *Economic and Political Weekly*, 8 July; Ganapathi (2007): 'Open Reply to Independent Citizens' Initiative on Dantewada', *Economic and Political Weekly*, 6 January; Nandini Sundar (2006): 'Bastar, Maoism and Salwa Judum', *Economic and Political Weekly*, 22 July; Manoranjan Mohanty (2006): 'Challenges of Revolutionary Violence: The Naxalite Movement in Perspective', *Economic and Political Weekly*, 22 July. There are of course the old 'classics' like Mohan Ram (1970): *Indian Communism: Split Within Split*, Delhi, Vikas, and (1971): *Maoism in India*, Delhi, Vikas; Manoranjan Mohanty (1977): *Revolutionary Violence: A Study of the Maoist Movement in India*, New Delhi, Sterling Publishers; and Sumanta Banerjee (1980): *In the Wake of Naxalbari: A History of the Naxalite Movement in India*, Calcutta, Subarnarekha.

2   Many of these deal with West Bengal and, to a limited extent, Kerala, Assam and Maharashtra. There are of course several compilations of articles and booklets on specific issues connected with the Left's policies and performance, including the Nandigram–Singur crises, the Left–Dalit dialogue, and the Left and communalism. But there is nothing comparable to the studies that appeared from the 1950s to

the 1980s on the mainstream national communist movement. Many of these were inspired by the anti-communism typical of Western cold-war scholarship, but some were also written from the opposite point of view. At any rate, they contained valuable empirical material and rich insights.

Chapter 1: The Rise and Decline of the Left

1 The CPI(M)'s official website cites a party membership figure of 1,065,406 for 2013. (http://www.cpim.org/about-us, updated on 5 January 2015, accessed on 6 January 2015). The CPI's Organisation Report adopted at its 21st Congress (27–31 March 2012) at Patna gives the figure of 644,656 members.(http://xxicongress.communistparty.in/, accessed on 6 January 2015).

2 The two parties claim that the mass organizations affiliated to them, not counting student and youth associations, have more that fifty million members. The CPI(M) alone claims to have over 5.1 million members in affiliated trade unions, nearly 22.5 million kisan sabha members, and 10.7 million members in the All-India Democratic Women's Association. (CPI(M), Political-Organizational Report, adopted at the 20th Congress, Kozhikode, 4–9 April 2012).

3 Different dates are cited for the founding of the CPI, including 1913–14 (when the nationalist, proto-communist Ghadar Party was formed), 1920 (when an 'émigré' CPI was set up at Tashkent), and 1925. (See http://cpim.org/history/formation-communist-party-india-tashkent-1920, accessed on 4 February 2015). But the most commonly accepted year, on which India's communist parties agree, is 1925, when the first conference of the Communist Party of India was held in Kanpur.

4 Much of this factual information is derived from Gene D. Overstreet and Marshall Windmiller (1959): *Communism in India*, Berkeley, University of California Press.

5 This spelt out the 'third period' line. The Comintern proclaimed that the world capitalist system was entering the period of final collapse and therefore all communist parties should adopt a highly aggressive, militant, ultra-left stance and treat social-democratic or moderate Left-wing parties as 'social fascists'. Indian communists were asked

to adopt a harsh line towards the Left wing within the Congress. For more on the Sixth Congress, see Duncan Hallas (1985): *The Comintern*, London, Bookmarks. For greater detail, see the monumental work by Jane Degras (1971): *Communist International: Documents 1919-1943* (in three volumes) London, Routledge, now also available at www.marxists.org

6 As distinct from the early Russian, Soviet and East European traditions. See Perry Anderson (1976): *Considerations on Western Marxism*, London, Verso.

7 Rather sketchy information is available on the RSD from rashtra-seva-dal.blogspot.in/2009_08_01_archive.html; and lohiatoday.com/SocialistMovement/SOCIALISTOrganisation.pdf (both accessed on 2 April 2014). But branches of the Dal continue to be active in Maharashtra.

8 Sonal Shah (1994): *Indian Socialists: Search for Identity*, Bombay, Popular Prakashan, p. xiii.

9 For an extended discussion, see Rai Chowdhuri (2011).

10 Half-Indian-half-Swedish, Palme Dutt (1896–1974) was a founder-member of the CPGB. Long based in Cambridge, he was an extraordinarily dogmatic Stalinist whom Eric Hobsbawm described as 'an instinctive hardliner'. He spoke several languages fluently, including Russian.

11 John Patrick Haithcox (1971): *Communism and Nationalism in India*, Bombay, Oxford University Press, pp. 97–108.

12 However, a large number of individual communist cadres at the provincial and local level actively participated in the movement and used the relaxed restrictions on their freedom to organize anti-war struggles. This has been documented at length in, among other sources, M.N.V. Nair and Praful Bidwai (eds) (2005): *Labour Movement in India: Documents 1941–1947*, New Delhi, Pragati Publication/Indian Council of Historical Research. These are vols 23 and 24 of a series of which the general editor was A.R. Desai.

13 Interview with CPI founding member S.S. Mirajkar, cited in A.G. Noorani (2012): 'Making of a Thesis', *Frontline* (21 May–4 April), available at frontline.in/static/html/fl2908/stories/20120504290809900.htm, accessed on 15 May 2014.

14 www.sacw.net/IMG/pdf/CPI-Adhikari-Pakistan-1942-53pages.pdf, accessed on 15 May 2014.

15 This duly followed Stalin's view, expressed in a speech made in 1925, and 'often cited by the Indian communists ever since', that India is a country with many nationalities, 'each with its own distinctive culture'. Cited in Selig S. Harrison (1959): 'Communism in India: The Dilemma of the CPI', *Problems of Communism*, No. 8 (March–April 1959): pp. 27–35.

16 Ibid.

17 www.sacw.net/IMG/pdf/CPI-Adhikari-Pakistan-1942-53pages.pdf, accessed on 15 May 2014.

18 The memorandum said: 'The provisional government should be charged with the task of setting up a boundary commission to redraw boundaries on the basis of natural ancient homelands of every people. The people of each such unit should have the unfettered right of self-determination … Delegates elected from each national unit shall decide by a majority whether they will join the all-India constituent assembly to form an Indian union, or remain out and form a separate sovereign state by themselves, or join another Indian union.' Cited in Harrison (1959).

19 M.B. Rao (ed.) (1976): *Documents of the History of the Communist Party of India, Vol. VII: 1948-1950*, New Delhi, People's Publishing House, p. viii.

20 Rakhshanda Jalil (2014): p. 362.

21 Jalil (2014): pp. 372–73.

22 Ahmed (2009): p. 152.

23 www.sacw.net/IMG/pdf/CPP1948_0-1to18.pdf, accessed on 15 May 2014.

24 So called after B.T. Ranadive, the general secretary of the party from February–March 1948 to January 1950, which advocated what was later repudiated as a 'Left-adventurist line', declaring India's independence to be a chimera, and holding that the country was ripe for an armed revolution.

25 'Review of the Second Congress of the CPI', cited in Rao (1976): pp. 200–02.

26 www.sacw.net/IMG/pdf/CPP1948_0-1to18.pdf, accessed on 15 May 2014.

27 This first appeared in the journal *Crossroads* of 6 January 1950, and was reprinted as a pamphlet. www.sacw.net/article5453.html, accessed 6 June 2014.

28 Ibid.

29 This shift formally occurred at the third congress of the CPI at Madurai (December 1953), where the then general secretary Ajoy Ghosh regretted that 'in the past, many a time we scoffed at the concept of Indian unity and glorified separatism' and described this as a 'deviation'. The shift coincided with a major change in the Soviet attitude towards Nehru: by 1955, *Pravda* was describing India as a 'peace-loving state upholding its national independence' and praising Nehru for his 'outstanding statesmanship'. Cited in Harrison (1959).

30 It rose to over 15,000 compared to 5,000 in 1942. Overstreet and Windmiller (1959): p. 357.

31 For details, see Overstreet and Windmiller (1959); Ram (1969): *Indian Communism: Split within a Split*, Delhi, Vikas Publications; Bhabani Sen Gupta (1973): 'India's Rival Communist Models', *Problems of Communism*, January; John H. Kautsky (1982): *Moscow and the Communist Party of India: A Study in the Postwar Evolution of International Communist Strategy*, Westport, CT, Greenwood Press.

32 Strictly speaking, Kerala was the second subnational region/province to elect a communist party. The first was the tiny Italian principality or micro-state of San Marino (population 31,000). See T.J. Nossiter (1982): *Communism in Kerala: A Study in Political Adaptation*, Bombay, Oxford University Press, p. 1.

33 Its president is Bhai Vaidya. (www.spi.org.in) This is distinct from the Samajwadi Party led by Mulayam Singh Yadav.

34 These are not non-governmental organisations (NGOs) of the conventional type. Rather, groupings such as the National Alliance of People's Movements, led by Medha Patkar among others, or All-India Union of Forest Working People or National Fishworkers' Forum describe themselves as 'people's movements' and have activities and structures that distinguish them from NGOs. This is also true of the Mazdoor Kisan Shakti Sangathan, which calls itself a 'non-party people's organisation'.

35 See, for instance, the early work of the constitutional expert H.M. Seervai, and the recent vigorous debate around the argument

advanced by Perry Anderson (2012): *The Indian Ideology*, Gurgaon, Three Essays Collective.

36 Some of these were highlighted in recent debates over Francis Fukuyama's book, *The End of History and the Last Man*, and the contributions of Marxist scholars such as Juergen Habermas, Jacques Derrida and Frederic Jameson, which argue contra Fukuyama that the classical world-historic contentions noted by Marx over the content of freedom, democracy and justice have not become obsolete or irrelevant.

37 This is partly related to their embrace of the strategic perspective of a 'two-stage' revolution, with a 'democratic' (or bourgeois) first stage, followed by socialism in the second, and is discussed in Chapter 2. Thus, they effectively accepted the inevitability of managing capitalism for the present period, rather than transforming or overthrowing it.

38 I owe this to Achin Vanaik.

39 The same sources as note 3 above.

40 The Third International, an association of communist parties, emerged in 1919 from a three-way split in the Socialist or Second International over the question of support to World War I. Lenin opposed support to national governments based on patriotism and called for their defeat through social revolution—unlike a majority of socialist parties. (See http://www.britannica.com/EBchecked/topic/290606/Third-International, accessed on 12 December 2014)

41 Germany, western Europe's largest country, has a population of less than eighty-three million.

42 This is not to deny that the Soviet Union played a largely, and often irreplaceably, progressive role in world affairs. It acted as a beacon of socialism and its very existence posited an alternative to capitalism. It was crucial to the defeat of Nazism and fascism. The USSR provided a counterweight to and exerted a 'civilizing' influence on capitalism, which helped to create the welfare state and some of the greatest gains for the working people in bourgeois society. It accelerated decolonization, and politically, materially and militarily aided a number of revolutionary and progressive movements in different parts of the world, including Vietnam, Cuba and parts of Africa even during its declining phase. Yet the Soviet system was in deep internal crisis well before the advent of Gorbachev. For an analysis of the Soviet

system's flaws and its terminal crisis and collapse, see Eric Hobsbawm (1995): *Age of Extremes: The Short Twentieth Century, 1914–1991*, London, Abacus; Robin Blackburn (ed.) (1991): *After the Fall: The Failure of Communism and the Future of Socialism*, London, Verso; Alec Nove (1993): *An Economic History of the USSR: 1917–1991*, Harmondsworth, Penguin Books; (1964): *Was Stalin Really Necessary?: Some Problems of Soviet Economic Policy*, London, Routledge; (1988): *Stalinism and After: The Road to Gorbachev*, London, Taylor and Francis; (2003): *The Economics of Feasible Socialism Revisited*, London, Routledge; Catherine Samary (1992): *Plan, Market and Democracy: The Experience of the So-called Socialist Countries*, Ahmedabad, C.G. Shah Trust; Ralph Miliband (1994): *Socialism for a Sceptical Age*, Cambridge, Polity Press; Ernest Mandel (1992): *Power and Money: A Marxist Theory of Bureaucracy*, London, Verso; Moshe Lewin (2005): *The Soviet Century*, London, Verso; Mike Haynes (2002): *Russia: Class and Power, 1917–2000*, London, Bookmarks; Richard D. Wolff (2002): *Class Theory and History: Capitalism and Communism in the USSR*, New York, Routledge. The paragraphs that follow owe a great deal to these accounts and analyses.

43 Their critique was by and large limited to the terrain defined by the ideological disputes between the USSR and other socialist states, especially China, and to an extent, Yugoslavia and Cuba.

44 This had a strong redistributive focus and respected the autonomy of the mass mobilizations. See, for instance, James Petras (1999): *The Left Strikes Back: Class Conflict in Latin America in the Age of Neoliberalism*, Boulder, Westview Press; Patrick Barrett, Daniel Chavez and Cesar Rodriguez-Garavito (eds) (2008): *The New Latin American Left: Utopia Reborn*, London/Amsterdam, Pluto Press/Transnational Institute; Marta Harnecker (2007): *Rebuilding the Left*, London, Zed Books; and numerous articles in recent issues of *The Socialist Register* and *Monthly Review*.

45 Hasrat Mohani (1875–1951), a founding member of the CPI who addressed its first conference at Kanpur in 1925, wanted to move a resolution in the Congress party as early as in 1921 defining Swaraj as 'complete independence' from foreign control. It was rejected in the Ahmedabad session of the Congress. This was eight years before the Congress adopted the Purna Swaraj demand at the Lahore

session. Mohani is also credited with having coined the slogan *Inquilab Zindabad!* (Long Live the Revolution!) during a labour rally in Calcutta in 1928. This has since become the battle cry of the oppressed across all regions of India, no matter what the cause of oppression. Rakhshanda Jalil (2014): *Liking Progress, Loving Change: A Literary History of the Progressive Writers' Movement in Urdu,* New Delhi, Oxford University Press, pp. 70–71.

46 H.L. Mitra (ed.) (1990): *The Indian Annual Register 1928,* New Delhi, Gyan Publishing House, pp. 354–56.

47 For a detailed account of the role of the CPI in the freedom struggle, see *Documents of the History of the Communist Party of India* in eight volumes covering the period 1917 to 1956, a project initiated by the party's national council under the general editorship of Gangadhar Adhikari, and published between 1971 and 1977 by People's Publishing House, New Delhi. For a discussion of the contribution of the communists and the Congress socialists to shaping the anti-colonial struggle, see Sarkar (1983): *Modern India,* New Delhi, Macmillan, and Satyabrata Rai Chowdhuri (2011): *Leftism in India, 1917–1947,* New Delhi, Macmillan.

48 Granville Austin (1966): *The Indian Constitution: Cornerstone of a Nation,* Oxford, Clarendon Press, p. 76. On the influence of socialism on the Constitution, also see pp. 41–43, 59–60 and 77–78. Austin, the great constitutional historian of India, sees the Directive Principles as the highest expression of the goal of 'social revolution' fostered by the Constitution.

49 See for instance Jalil (2014); Sudhi Pradhan (ed.) (1979): *Marxist Cultural Movements in India: Chronicles and Documents (1936-47),* 2 vols, Calcutta, National Book Agency; Talat Ahmed (2009): *Literature and Politics in the Age of Nationalism,* New Delhi, Routledge; Kalpana Sahni and P.C. Joshi (2012): *Balraj and Bhisham Sahni: Brothers in Political Theatre,* New Delhi, Sahmat; Priyamvada Gopal (2005): *Literary Radicalism in India: Gender, Nation and the Transition to Independence,* London, Routledge; and Ralph Russell (1977): 'Leadership in the All-India Progressive Writers' Movement, 1935–1947', in B.N. Pandey (ed.), *Leadership in South Asia,* New Delhi, Vikas Publishing House.

50 They were not always consistent or unanimous in this regard. For instance, in the 1940s and 1950s, many individual communists would

privately defend homosexuality, while senior party leaders would publicly oppose it as 'unnatural'.

51 The British Marxist historian Victor Kiernan, who spent many years in India, describes a commune in which 'were crowded a growing number of men, and a sprinkling of women, from all over India, veterans and beginners, plebeians and aristocrats, Hindus and Muslims ... Ordinarily behaviour was easy and informal; people came and went unchallenged ... Living and working among them was ... the most exhilarating experience of my life. ...' (Victor G. Kiernan, 'Some Reminiscences of India and the CPI,' 15 March 2009 on www. sacw.net, accessed on 14 March 2014).

52 I acknowledge with gratitude Ania Loomba's personal email based on her notes for a talk delivered at the P.C. Joshi Archives on Contemporary History at Jawaharlal Nehru University in Delhi on 30 January 2014, on 'Indian Girls in Search of the Party or the Lost Worlds of Indian Communism'.

53 The Left has consistently assailed the US for lending uncritical support to Israel's occupation of Palestine and to numerous authoritarian regimes. The Left remains a fierce critic of NATO and the US system of strategic alliances and its 'war on terror'. Although the Left may not have mobilized people on a large scale on these issues, or succeeded in preventing the Indian government's pro-US strategic tilt, it has maintained its opposition at the level of ideas and political discourse.

54 However, as independent Marxist scholars such as D.D. Kosambi pointed out long ago, the contributions of thinkers and writers unaffiliated to the communist parties were often not recognized or appreciated by party intellectuals. He termed them 'Official Marxists', who are distinguished by their 'theological emphasis on the inviolable sanctity of the current party line, or irrelevant quotations from the classics'. See 'Introduction' in D.D. Kosambi (1957): *Exasperating Essays*, New Delhi, People's Publishing House.

55 The CPI and the Revolutionary Socialist Party stood reduced to near-irrelevance, having only won one seat each nationally. The Forward Bloc was completely wiped out. Worse, all of these four parties lost not just votes, but chunks of their social base, to the BJP.

56 The number rises to twelve if the two independents who won, backed by the Left in Kerala, are counted.

57 When the 2014 election results were announced, the Left's leaders showed little comprehension of the magnitude, quality and causes of the crisis they faced. Instead of acknowledging the debacle as the result of deep-rooted flaws in its programmes and strategies, a massive leadership failure, and its alienation from the people, the CPI(M) first practised denial by alleging large-scale rigging of the elections, then admitted that its showing was 'poor', and finally accepted its central leaders' 'primary responsibility for the failure'. But it refused to acknowledge the culpability of specific individuals in positions of power for the debacle and cited the principle of 'collective responsibility'—in contrast to the 'bourgeois parties' notion of 'individual responsibility'. By that logic, the entire top leadership should have resigned. Yet, the CPI(M) leaders who reportedly offered to resign their posts after the election results were told not to do so, including two politbureau members. A detailed analysis of the causes of the election rout was postponed to future central leadership meetings. All that the Left promised is a review of its 'political line and organisational functioning ... to take corrective measures', and forging 'close links with the masses' to 'conduct struggles' to defend their 'livelihood interests', 'secularism and democratic rights', and so on.

Chapter 2: Search for a Strategic Framework

1 Achin Vanaik (1986): 'The Indian Left', *New Left Review*, I/159, September–October.

2 Vanaik (1986). This writer's analysis in the next section largely agrees with the thrust of Vanaik's argument. The CPI's membership rose rather sluggishly to 150 by 1934 and then far more rapidly to 5,000 in 1942. It increased sharply to 15,563 by the time the CPI held its first party congress in Bombay in 1943. It is only in 1946 that its membership crossed the 50,000 mark. It was estimated to be 60,000 at the time of Independence. Gene D. Overstreet and Marshall Windmiller (1959): *Communism in India*, Berkeley, University of California Press, p. 357. These numbers should not be taken directly

to represent the level of activity or political strength and influence of the party.

3 Barrington Moore Jr in his classic (1966): *Social Origins of Democracy and Dictatorship* (Boston, Beacon Press) argues that this was a key element in India's successful transition to democracy, as opposed to descent into authoritarian or military rule, as happened in many former colonies.

4 Many historians have noted this, including Sumit Sarkar, and the Subaltern School's Ranajit Guha, Partha Chatterjee, Gyanendra Pandey and Shahid Amin.

5 Vanaik (1986).

6 Ibid.

7 Sumit Sarkar (1983): *Modern India*, New Delhi, Macmillan, pp. 269–74.

8 See note 17 in Chapter 1.

9 As Vanaik puts it: 'This missed opportunity was of considerable consequence, as Gandhi now had free rein to co-opt and maintain control of the Congress in the campaign of non-cooperation with the British. Only in 1932 did the Comintern leadership take the first steps to review its policy and to suggest that the CPI might "cooperate with" or "infiltrate" mass reformist organizations such as the Congress.' Vanaik (1986).

10 Sarkar (1983): pp. 312–13.

11 Ibid., p. 381.

12 'From the Sundarlal Report', *Frontline*, 3 March 2001; also A.G. Noorani, 'Of a Massacre Untold', in the same issue. The report was long suppressed, but is now available at the Nehru Memorial Museum and Library, New Delhi.

13 According to Mohit Sen (2003): *A Traveller and the Road: the Journey of an Indian Communist*, New Delhi, Rupa & Co., pp. 124–26, Stalin advised CPI leaders at his February 1951 Moscow meeting that the struggle be called off. Nehru did not initially restrain the army, but once he got to know that the CPI had withdrawn the insurrection, he 'did all he could to see that communists were released or that lighter sentences were passed on them'. Many CPI leaders, says Sen, saw this as 'a cunning manoeuvre' on Nehru's part to 'emasculate the communists', and some others as a way of bringing them into the

national 'mainstream'. For a participant's account of the Telangana struggle, see Ravi Narayan Reddy (2011): *Heroic Telangana: Reminiscences and Experiences* (2nd edition), New Delhi, People's Publishing House; also see P. Sundarayya (1972): *Telengana People's Struggle and its Lessons*, Delhi, Foundation Books; Mohit Sen (2003): especially chapters 5 and 7; and Rao (1976).

14 Sarkar (1983), pp. 381–82.

15 Rao (1976), p. xi.

16 Overstreet and Windmiller (1959), p. 357.

17 See, for instance, Sen (2003), p. 82.

18 The draft of the CPI's agrarian reforms bill, like its election manifesto, followed the framework suggested by the Congress's Agrarian Reform Committee of 1949. T.J. Nossiter (1982): *Communism in Kerala: A Study in Political Adaptation*, Delhi, Oxford University Press, p. 150.

19 The Revolutionary Socialist Party, a constituent of the Left Front in West Bengal and Tripura, never accepted the 'semi-feudal' or 'two-stage' revolution formulation. It had its origins in the so-called revolutionary terrorist group called Anushilan Samity in colonial Bengal. Like small Trotskyist groups such as the Bolshevik–Leninist Party of India, and later affiliates of the Fourth International, the RSP rejected Stalin's 'socialism in one country' thesis. It has been sharply critical of Stalinism, but has never embraced Trotskyism. The RSP characterizes India as a capitalist society with some pre-capitalist remnants, and stands for a socialist revolution. It opposes any alliance with any section of the bourgeoisie. See RSP (2011): *A Positive Programme for the Indian Revolution*, 2nd ed., Kolkata, Lokayata Sahitya Chakra, . The RSP in Kerala walked out of the Left Democratic Front on the eve of the Lok Sabha election in March 2014.

20 A number of pertinent issues are discussed in various chapters and sections here: on the mode of production in agriculture, agrarian reform, caste, culture, industrialization, and the character of the state, which set India apart from 'semi-feudal semi-colonial' societies.

21 The programmes of both the 'National Democratic Revolution' and the 'People's Democratic Revolution' are derived from the tradition of the Communist International 1919–1943 (Comintern), and the strategic perspective of the Communist Party of China, which

advocated a Four-Class Alliance or Bloc in 1949, comprising the working class, the peasantry, the urban petit bourgeoisie and the national bourgeoisie, which would establish a 'people's democratic dictatorship' against the 'landlord class' and the 'bureaucratic-bourgeoisie' (sometimes called compradors, i.e., agents of foreign imperialist interests). www.marxists.org/glossary/terms/b/l.htm

22 The CPI's programme closely follows the formulations of the 'Statement of 81 Communist and Workers Parties' Meeting in Moscow, 1960', which said: 'The urgent tasks of national rebirth facing the countries that have shaken off the colonial yoke cannot be effectively accomplished unless a determined struggle is waged against imperialism and the remnants of feudalism by all the patriotic forces of the nations united in a single national-democratic front. The national democratic tasks on the basis of which the progressive forces of the nation can and do unite in the countries which have won their freedom, are: the consolidation of political independence, the carrying out of agrarian reforms in the interest of the peasantry, elimination of the survivals of feudalism, the uprooting of imperialist economic domination, the restriction of foreign monopolies and their expulsion from the national economy, the creation and development of a national industry, improvement of the living standard, the democratization of social life, the pursuance of an independent and peaceful foreign policy, and the development of economic and cultural co-operation with the socialist and other friendly countries.' It added: 'In present conditions, the national bourgeoisie of the colonial and dependent countries unconnected with imperialist circles, is objectively interested in the principal tasks of anti-imperialist, anti-feudal revolution, and therefore retains the capacity of participating in the revolutionary struggle against imperialism and feudalism. In that sense it is progressive. But it is unstable; though progressive, it is inclined to compromise with imperialism and feudalism. Owing to its dual nature, the extent to which the national bourgeoisie participates in revolution differs from country to country. This depends on concrete conditions, on changes in the relationship of class forces, on the sharpness of the contradictions between imperialism, feudalism, and the people, and on the depth of the contradictions between imperialism, feudalism and the national bourgeoisie.'

www.marxists.org/history/international/comintern/sino-soviet-split/other/1960statement.htm, accessed on 12 June 2014.

23 'Draft Programme of the CPI(M)', 1964, pp. 31–47. This closely follows the perspective outlined in certain documents of the East European workers' parties summarized in *The Great Soviet Encyclopedia* (1978): 'The distinguishing characteristic of a people's democratic revolution is the composition of its motive forces. The motive forces of a bourgeois democratic revolution of the old type were classes headed by the bourgeoisie, and the motive force of a socialist revolution is the alliance of the proletariat with all the working people and the exploited under the leadership of the proletariat. The people's democratic revolutions are different in this respect. Their motive force is the broad popular front of the proletariat, the peasantry, the petite bourgeoisie, and various strata from different classes (for example, the middle or national bourgeoisie). The broad popular front is based on an alliance between the proletariat and the peasantry and is led by the proletariat headed by a Marxist-Leninist party ... The most important distinguishing feature of a people's democratic revolution is the character of the state power it establishes: a revolutionary democratic dictatorship of the revolutionary classes led by the proletariat. This power is primarily charged with implementing democratic transformations, while preserving to a certain extent the private capitalist ownership of the means of production. Unlike the bourgeois democracy, which is a government of the minority, the revolutionary democratic dictatorship of the revolutionary classes is the government of the overwhelming majority, in whose interests it carries out profound socioeconomic transformations.' (http://encyclopedia2.thefreedictionary.com/People%27s+Democratic+Revolution)

24 The succeeding paragraphs are quoted verbatim from 'Record of the Discussions of J.V. Stalin with the Representatives of the C.C. of the Communist Party of India Comrades, Rao, Dange, Ghosh and Punnaiah', www.revolutionarydemocracy.org/rdv12n2/cpi2.htm#2, accessed on 6 June 2014.

25 For instance, Mohit Sen (2003), p. 126.

26 www.revolutionarydemocracy.org/rdv12n2/cpi2.htm#2

27 'Programme of the Communist Party of India', the 'Tactical Line', and the 'Statement of Policy of the Communist Party of India', in

Mohit Sen (1977): *Documents of the History of the Communist Party of India*, Volume VIII: 1951–1956, New Delhi, People's Publishing House. The Programme was formally approved by the third congress of the CPI at Madurai during December 1953–January 1954.

28   The debate was summarized by Alice Thorner in the *Economic and Political Weekly (*4, 11 and 18 December 1982): and later by Utsa Patnaik (ed.) (1990): *Agrarian Relations and Accumulation: The 'Mode of Production' Debate in India*, Delhi, Oxford University Press. Several articles in a special number of the *Journal of Agrarian Change* (Vol. 13, No. 3, July 2013) have since revisited the debate.

29   Brenner showed that tenant farmers who leased in land from big landlords in late medieval England to produce for the market were under constant pressure to reduce costs and raise profits. This, and competition among tenants for extending leases, drove the process of raising productivity and capital accumulation. The tenants became capitalist farmers themselves. Thus, there is no contradiction between tenancy and growth of capitalist agrarian relations. Brenner (1977): 'The Origins of Capitalist Development: a Critique of Neo-Smithian Marxism', *New Left Review*, 104, July–August. Brenner's thesis remains the focal point of contemporary Marxist debate, which has transcended the Sweezy–Dobb debate discussed in Appendix 1.

30   See note 25 in Chapter 1.

31   Palme Dutt travelled to India to cover the Cabinet Mission's visit of 1946 for the CPGB's *Daily Worker*. See Marcus Franda (1971): *Radical Politics in West Bengal*, Cambridge (Mass.), The MIT Press, p. 30.

32   In a somewhat harsh judgement, a well-known analyst of Indian communism argues that 'the communist movement in pre-Independence India was a colonial adjunct of the CPGB, which in turn was suborned to Moscow'. Mohan Ram (1969), p. 1. Some scholars have identified such dependence on external sources as the prime cause of the failures and flaws of the Indian communist movement. This view is one-sided: Indian communists often sought the intervention of foreigners because they needed such assistance owing to their own theoretical and practical inadequacies in devising a revolutionary strategy for India. The dependence was an effect and a symptom of their weakness and failure, not their cause.

33 Even E.M.S. Namboodiripad, one of India's tallest communist intellectuals, confessed that he had no early access or exposure to Marxism; it was only in 1935 that he began his study of Marx starting with the *Manifesto.*

34 Marcus Franda notes that West Bengal's Western-educated 'gentleman communists', as the Marxists were described by the intellectual community in Calcutta, are 'people who are well read; most of them have friends in communist, socialist, and labour movements in Great Britain, and many of them have travelled to the Soviet Union and Eastern Europe. Very few members of the older generation of Marxist scholars in Bengal have ever studied Marx himself in any depth, and most of them confess to great difficulty in getting through *Das Kapital* or other highly theoretical works ... Party members are the first to admit that the communist movement in Bengal has never been able to boast a truly original Marxist theoretician, despite the presence of many brilliant scholars in the party'. Marcus Franda (1971): *Radical Politics in West Bengal,* Cambridge (Mass.), The MIT Press, pp. 30–31.

35 Mohit Sen and M.B. Rao (eds) (1968): *Das Kapital: Centenary Volume,* Delhi, People's Publishing House, pp. 228–229.

36 It was translated by Pius Dasgupta and published by Baniprakash, Calcutta. Personal email communication from Nupur Dasgupta, the translator's daughter-in-law, 13 February 2015.

37 In recent years, the CPI and the CPI(M), especially the CPI, have both acknowledged the development of capitalist relations in agriculture, although they emphasize that 'landlordism', archaic forms of labour 'bondage', and 'old feudal relations' continue to exist in different regions of India. But the CPI (Maoist) remains stuck in the 'semi-feudal' formulation. All three parties however share the view that abolition of 'landlordism' would form the core of their agrarian reform agenda for the present stage of the revolution.

38 The terms 'rich', 'middle', 'poor', etc., are not income or size categories, but are defined according to their landholding and relations of production within a specific context in the rural economy, as in Kautsky and Lenin, and other Marxist theorists of the agrarian economy.

39 E.M.S. Namboodiripad (1952): *On the Agrarian Question in India*, Bombay, People's Publishing House, pp. 27, 49, 61.

40 Sahajanand Saraswati, the founder president of the All 'India Kisan Sabha, was Bihar's pre-eminent peasant leader of the 1930s and 1940s. For more information on him, see Walter Hauser (ed.) (2003): *Religion, Politics and the Peasants: A Memoir of India's Freedom Movement*, Delhi, Manohar Publishers, and (ed.) (2005): *Sahajanand on Agricultural Labour and the Rural Poor*, Delhi, Manohar Publishers.

41 See A.R. Desai (ed.) (1986): *Agrarian Struggles in India*, New Delhi, Oxford University Press.

42 Barbara Harriss-White has highlighted the influence wielded by West Bengal's rice millers even during the Left Front's rule. See Harriss-White (2008): *Rural Commercial Capital: Agricultural Markets in West Bengal*, New Delhi, Oxford University Press.

43 This was the stand adopted in the late 1960s by a section within the Lal Nishan Party, a militant Marxist organization in Maharashtra which was particularly active in the trade unions, including those of Bombay's textile millworkers. It split from the CPI in 1942 over the party's 'People's War' line and built its own working class base.

44 http://peoplesdemocracy.in/2014/0810_pd/eighth-all-india-conference-all-india-agricultural-workers-union

45 This was justified as follows: 'Questions were raised whether this was permissible. At the 12th Congress of the party in December 1985, the matter was discussed. B.T. Ranadive summed up the discussions by stating that West Bengal under Left Front rule has been facing an economic blockade from the Centre. West Bengal was discriminated against on a class basis because it is run by a Left-led government. It is in the class interests of the working class to break this blockade. Industrialisation is necessary for West Bengal to generate employment … Within the existing capitalist system and the parameters set out by the big bourgeoisie-led government at the Centre, it was not possible to develop industries in West Bengal with the limited resources of the state government … West Bengal government cannot by itself break from this … system. So the petro-chemical project with private sector participation is a tactical necessity …' 'Part II of the political-organisation report of the 19th Congress of the CPI(M)', *The Marxist*, Volume XXIV, No. 2, April–June 2008.

46 'On Certain Ideological Issues, Resolution Adopted in the 14th Party Congress,' www.cpim.org/documents/1992-14-Cong--ideological-issues.pdf, accessed on 22 January 2015.

47 The subsidies were estimated at Rs 850 crore in Mitra (2007): 'Santa Claus Visits the Tatas: Freebies from a Debt-Ridden Government', *The Telegraph*, 30 March 2007; the cost of developing the Nano car, 'including the cost of the plant that will build it' was reported at Rs 1,700 crore. www.business-standard.com/article/management/what-drives-tata-motors-108012201043_1.html, accessed on 22 December 2014.

48 Interview with Nirupam Sen, the former commerce and industries minister in the Left From Government, Kolkata, 25 February 2013.

49 See Ratna Sen (1986): 'Experiment in Workers Management: Sonali Tea Garden, 1973–1981', *Economic and Political Weekly*, 30 August, M-74 to M-80. Also Sharit K. Bhowmik (1995): 'Worker Cooperatives', *Seminar*, May. The CPI-led AITUC, to which the Sonali union was affiliated, reportedly disowned it.

50 The mill was locked out in 1993 and forcibly occupied by workers who tried to restart production through a workers' cooperative. The CPI(M)-led Centre of Indian Trade Unions (CITU) did little to support them. But other organizations emerged such as the Sangrami Sramik Union, whose nucleus consisted of the workers responsible for occupying the mill. See www.outlookindia.com/printarticle. aspx?234197, www.revolutionarydemocracy.org/rdv9n1/westbengal1. htm, and www.epw.in/system/files/pdf/1994_29/1-/commentary_ labour_under_left_front_ii_kanoria_jute_workers_historic_struggle. pdf, all accessed on 2 January 2015. Also A.K. Roy (1994): 'Kamani to Kanoria: Marxists and Workers' Cooperatives', *Economic and Political Weekly*, 24 September. In another case, involving New Central Jute Mills, the Left unions formed a joint front with other unions in setting up a cooperative in 1989, but they did not take the lead.

51 Kanan Devan continues to operate as a successful employee-owned cooperative and sells several varieties of tea under the brand name 'Ripple'. See http://kdhptea.com

52 Sharit K. Bhowmik (1989): 'Workers Take Over Kamani Tubes', *Economic and Political Weekly*, 23 January, pp. 124–27; B Srinivas (1993): *Worker Takeover in Industry: The Kamani Tubes Experiment*,

New Delhi, Sage Publications; also http://www.pria.org/docs/The_ Takeover.pdf. The factory finally shut down not because it failed to keep pace with changes in technology and market conditions, but because public sector banks and financial institutions refused to loan working capital to it. (Interview with D. Thankappan, former working president of the Kamani Workers' Union, Mumbai, 21 March 2013). It is plausible, indeed likely, that a united effort by Left-wing unions, with fresh infusion of managerial expertise, could have enabled Kamani Tubes to survive and flourish. My discussions during that period with Bombay's left leaders suggest that 'two-stage' inhibitions apart, the idea of a workers' takeover had virtually no space in their political imagination. Nevertheless, the Kamani Tubes example proved inspiring and resulted in the establishment of the Workers' Solidarity Centre Against Job Losses and Industrial Closures in Bombay and the Centre for Workers' Management in Delhi. These initiatives produced some outstanding material, most of which is, alas, not easily traceable.

53   Interview with D. Thankappan, Mumbai, 21 March 2013.

54   I was astonished by the frequency with which this stock argument was used by communist leaders, especially in West Bengal and Tripura, to dismiss proposals even for experimenting with cooperative/collective altarnatives.

55   See   www.mondragon-corporation.com/eng/,   also   www.bbc. co.uk/news/world-europe-19213425,   and   www.theguardian.com/ world/2013/mar/07/mondragon-spains-giant-cooperative,   www. counterpunch.org/2014/04/30/the-case-of-mondragon/

56   This is a widely accepted figure and is cited by several official reports (e.g.   www.moef.nic.in/downloads/public-information/FRA%20 COMMITTEE%20REPORT_FINAL%20Dec%202010.pdf. It is primarily based on Hari Mohan Mathur (2008): 'Development and Displacement: Introduction and Overview', *India Social Development Report 2008*, New Delhi, Council for Social Development/Oxford University Press. Also see infochangeindia.org/Agenda/Migration-Displacement/Paying-the-price-for-someone-else%E2%80%99s-displacement.html, accessed on 1 March 2015.

57   The title of Nehru's famous speech of 14–15 August 1947.

58 For a critical discussion of Indian exceptionalism, see Praful Bidwai and Achin Vanaik (2000): *South Asia on a Short Fuse: Nuclear Politics and the Future of Disarmament*, New Delhi, Oxord University Press, especially Chapters 5, 6 and 9.

59 This crisis was ably analysed early on by scholars like Rajni Kothari, Francine Frankel and T.V. Sathyamurthy.

60 www.newageweekly.com/2012/03/eleventh-party-congress.html see also: http://www.sacw.net/article7850.html

61 Such was the CPI(M)'s animus towards Indira Gandhi during this period that some of its members reportedly chanted the slogan 'Indira Yahya *ek hai*' at the height of the Bangladesh crisis in 1971, equating her 'dictatorship' over West Bengal with the brutal subjugation of Bangladesh by the Pakistani military ruler Yahya Khan, and asserting the state's right to 'liberate' itself from her. Profulla Roy Chowdhury (1985): *Left Experiment in West Bengal*, New Delhi, Patriot Publishers, pp. 15 and 132.

62 Paragraph 72, 'Programme of the CPI(M)', adopted at the Seventh Congress of the Communist Party of India, Calcutta, 31 October to 7 November 1964, New Delhi, CPI(M), 1967.

63 Paragraph 113, 'Programme of the CPI(M)'.

64 Paragraph 112, 'Programme of the CPI(M)'.

65 This is discussed further in Chapter 3.

66 Interview with M.J. Akbar (1997): *The Asian Age*, New Delhi, 1 January 1997.

Chapter 3: Forward March in National Politics

1 '… though obviously still incomparably weaker' than either. Sumit Sarkar (1983): *Modern India*, New Delhi, Macmillan, pp. 412–32.

2 This, says Sarkar, brought the communists perilously close to 'accepting the Pakistan demand'. Sarkar (1983), p. 412. Also see Gangadhar Adhikari (ed.) (1942): *Pakistan and National Unity*, Bombay, People's Publishing House. PDF version at http://sacw.net/article5487.html, accessed on 4 March 2014. Perry Anderson takes a somewhat different view: With the publication of Adhikari's thesis, 'the CPI came out with a clear position on the legitimacy—as distinct from desirability—of a demand for Pakistan, and more generally of

rights to self-determination in the subcontinent'. Anderson (2012): *The Indian Ideology*, Gurgaon, Three Essays Collective, p. 90.

3   The two splits are discussed extremely briefly here primarily because abundant material is available on them in a number of party and independent sources.

4   Sarkar (1983): pp. 412–32.

5   Figures from Gene D. Overstreet and Marshall Windmiller (1959): *Communism in India*, Berkeley, University of California Press, and from CPI party congress documents.

6   Led by the legendary leader Godavari Parulekar, and documented by her in her semi-autobiographical book (1975): *Adivasis Revolt*, Calcutta, National Book Agency.

7   'The decisions and actions of leaders, British or Indian, cannot really be understood without the counterpoint provided by pressures from below. Popular action, above all, made continuance of British rule untenable; fear of popular "excesses" made Congress leaders cling to the path of negotiation and compromise, and eventually even accept Partition as a necessary price; and the limits of popular anti-imperialist movements made the truncated settlement of August 1947 possible.' Sarkar (1983), p. 415. Also Amit Kumar Gupta (1987) (ed.), *Myth and Reality: The Struggle for Freedom in India, 1945–47*, New Delhi, Nehru Memorial Museum and Library/Manohar Publishers.

8   Javeed Alam (1991): 'State and the Making of Communist Politics in India, 1947-57', *Economic and Political Weekly*, 9 November, pp. 2573–83.

9   See 'Stalin's Advice on the Agrarian Revolution' in Chapter 2 pp. 64–66.

10 This is borne out by the accounts of Jolly Mohan Kaul (2010): *In Search of a Better World*, Calcutta, Samya; K. Damodaran (1975): 'Memoir of an Indian Communist', *New Left Review*, September–October; E.M.S. Namboodiripad (1987): *Reminiscences of an Indian Communist*, New Delhi, National Book Centre; and Mohit Sen (2003): *A Traveller and the Road: The Journey of an Indian Communist*, New Delhi, Rupa and Co., and (2007): *An Autobiography*, New Delhi, National Book Trust. It is corroborated by this author's discussions with communist leaders including B.T. Ranadive and G. Adhikari over many decades. Even as well-regarded a communist as S.A. Dange

did not consider it necessary to go beyond limited textual references and study specific features of India's past while describing the course of Indian history from 'primitive communism to slavery' and beyond. Learning by rote was the norm among most Indian communists, as was a schematic linear characterization of history through various 'stages' defined by modes of production and the development of the productive forces.

11   Although this line was reversed by the Seventh Congress (1935), which called for 'united front' tactics, the original influence remained strongly ingrained and was reflected in the CPI's organizational culture.

12   As Alam (1991, p. 2574) put it: 'One important but curious feature within the nationalist movement in India visible right up to 1948-49, which the communists at that time never really comprehended, was that the popular upsurges and agitations in which people took massive initiative and went in for large-scale self-mobilizations went far beyond the limits set by the nationalist leadership; and yet when the Congress leadership moved in to contain them, the people, disappointed with the Congress party for putting the brakes, continued to repose in an overall sense faith in the Congress as the leader of the national movement. The complexity really was that the people were ready to go far beyond in struggle than the Congress wanted and this superficially brought them closer to radical positions but were not prepared to politically move over into the Left political parties. This discrepancy, or paradox, between people's struggling propensities and their stable political allegiance was the crucial factor during that period. Failure to grasp this deflected the political understanding of the CPI into illusory revolutionary visions while the Congress became the biggest beneficiary of the great popular upheavals'. P. 2574.

13   This came after an editorial appeared in the organ of the Communist Information Bureau advocating that line's rejection.

14   For details, see Alam (1991) and Mohan Ram (1969): *Indian Communism: Split within a Split*, New Delhi, Vikas Publications. Before the 1951 programme emerged there was an intervention through the 'Three P's' document (September 1950) prepared by Ajoy Ghosh (pseudonym Prabodh Chandra), S.A. Dange (Prabhakar) and

S.V. Ghate (Purushottam). This debunked both the Chinese and the Russian paths, advocated 'all forms of partial struggles' to combat the people's deep-rooted illusions about the Nehru government, and stressed that the CPI was weak both organizationally and in its influence. The document produced a deadlock, to resolve which it was 'decided to seek "fraternal" international advice'. A delegation of four, including two of its authors, Ghosh and Dange, and two members of the politbureau, C. Rajeswara Rao and M. Basavapunniah, were sent to Moscow. Alam (1991): pp. 2575–76. Their discussion with Stalin is summarized in Chapter 2.

15 Sarkar (1983): p. 419.

16 Some CPI leaders underline that the Samyukta Maharashtra objective was tied up with the demand for a 'socialist' Maharashtra, which gave this progressive cause a great deal of exposure and popular acceptance, and even regard the 1956–60 period as the CPI's 'golden age' in Maharashtra, especially Bombay city. Interview with Prakash Reddy, secretary of the Mumbai CPI, 12 May 2013.

17 Cited in Gyan Prakash (2010): *Mumbai Fables*, New Delhi, HarperCollins, p. 242. Adds Prakash: 'Three months later, the Sena activists attacked the CPI's Dalvi Building office in Parel. They burned files and threw out the furniture. It was an audacious attack, brazenly carried out to strike at the very heart of the enemy. What was the communist response? Nothing.' For more on the Shiv Sena, see Mary Fainsod Katzenstein (1979): *Ethnicity and Equality: The Shiv Sena Party and Preferential Policies in Bombay*, Ithaca and London, Cornell University Press; Jayant Lele (1995): *Hindutva: The Emergence of the Right*, Madras, Earthworm Books; Ashok Dhawale (2000): *The Shiv Sena: Semi-Fascism in Action*, New Delhi, CPI(M) Publications; Shuddhabrata Sengupta (2012): 'Ek Tha Tiger: Death ends Bal Kesav Thackeray', *Kafila*, 20 November.

18 The author was personally present at Dadar and a witness to the events of the day.

19 See Saroj Giri (2012): 'Bal Thackeray, or, Why the Communists Did Nothing', http://sanhati.com/excerpted/5823, accessed on 4 May 2014.

20 At its 1992 party congress, the CPI(M) reiterated its support for 'just Centre–state relations' and 'the principles of a federal Union', but did not define what it meant by federalism.

21 CPI(M) (1972): *National Question in India*, Calcutta, National Book Agency. Prakash Karat also argued that unlike czarist Russia, which was 'a prison-house of nationalities and subject to oppression' by one dominant nationality, India is 'a multinational country where there is no oppression by one or a group of nationalities over the others. Secondly, the ruling class in India ... is a composite one drawn from various linguistic nationalities.' See http://peoplesdemocracy.in/content/mb-ideological-warrior-cpim, accessed on 14 June 2014.

22 Underlying the CPI(M)'s discomfort with further division of states seems to have been its fierce opposition to a separate Gorkhaland state to be created out of the hilly regions of West Bengal—an idea that the bhadralok, with its attachment to Darjeeling as a summer destination, utterly loathes.

23 The CPI(M) strongly opposed a separate Telangana, but came around to accepting it once it became imminent.

24 Arvind N. Das (1997): 'Swami and Friends: Sahajanand Saraswati and Those Who Refuse to Let the Past of Bihar's Peasant Movements Become History', paper for the Peasant Symposium, University Of Virginia, Charlottesville, Virginia, May. Also see Brass's chapter 'Radical Politics of the Left in Bihar', in Paul M. Brass and Marcus Franda (1973): *Radical Politics in South Asia*, Cambridge (Mass.), MIT Press; Jagannath Sarkar (2011): 'The Decline of Communist Mass Base in Bihar', http://kafila.org/2011/09/25/the-decline-of-communist-mass-base-in-bihar-jagannath-sarkar/, accessed on 1 March 2014.

25 Madhu Limaye (1990): *Indian Polity in Transition*, New Delhi, Radiant Publishers, p. 130.

26 Dasgupta had a secret society background and was a tough disciplinarian. He was associated with what was called the left-wing of the CPI(M), in contrast to the centrist current to which Jyoti Basu belonged. For more on Dasgupta, see the chapters on West Bengal.

27 http://kisanmaharashtra.blogspot.in/, accessed on 1 March 2014.

28 Shaji Joseph (2006): 'Power of the People: Political Mobilization and Guaranteed Employment', *Economic and Political Weekly*, 16 December.

29 Punyabrata Gun (2011): 'Looking Back at Shaheed Hospital', *Frontier*, Vol. 44, No. 8, 4–10 September. Also email to the author, 24 August 2014.

30 Sen was implicated in a number of cases in Chhattisgarh and falsely charged with treason and conspiring with the Maoists. His victimization produced an international solidarity campaign supported by forty-eight Nobel laureates, apart from scores of Indian civil society organizations.

31 'His was the lone voice stalling the Rajiv Gandhi proposal for increasing the salary and perks of MPs in the Lok Sabha'. See http://www.thehindu.com/2004/04/17/stories/2004041702451200.htm, accessed on 1 May 2014.

32 Disclosure of interest: I was associated with the Sanghatana in 1971–72.

33 The pivotal figures in URG were Jairus Banaji and Rohini Hensman, but many others including Sujata Gothoskar, Ram Puniyani, Raju Damle, Jagdish Parikh and Girish Vaidya played a significant role in its work. Harsh Kapoor, a former non-Bombay URG associate, has digitized several URG documents, including its bulletins, which can be accessed at http://www.sacw.net/rubrique35.html

34 Discussed in Chapter 2.

35 The CPI was not united in its opposition to the JP movement. S.A. Dange, followed by C. Achutha Menon, M.N. Govindan Nair, G. Adhikari and N. Rajsekhar Reddy, strongly condemned it as 'counter-revolutionary' while defending the Congress. But C. Rajeswara Rao, N.K. Krishnan, Yogendra Sharma, Bhupesh Gupta and Indrajit Gupta were of view that the CPI and the Left should oppose this movement by demonstrating that they were 'the real opponent[s] of the Indira Gandhi government and the system that it defended'. Mohit Sen (2007): *An Autobiography*, New Delhi, National Book Trust, pp. 277–79.

36 It had some reservations about Fernandes's 'plan to disrupt the entire railway system by sabotage if necessary'. Ibid.

37 For a powerful critique of the JP movement, see Ghanshyam Shah (1977): 'Revolution, Reform or Protest? A Study of the Bihar Movement', *Economic and Political Weekly*, 9, 16, and 23 April, later reproduced in his (1977): *Protest Movements in Two Indian States*, Delhi, Ajanta Books International, and also his 1979 review, 'Ideology of Jayaprakash Narayan', *Economic and Political Weekly*, 3 March.

38 Ross Mallick (1994): *Indian Communism: Opposition, Collaboration and Institutionalisation*, Delhi, Oxford University Press, pp. 159–62. Noting that there were 'several big movements', former West Bengal secretary and politbureau member Anil Biswas, said: 'The CPI(M) was self-critical about its inability to take part in the anti-Congress movements across the country … After meeting with Jayaprakash Narayan in Delhi and Kolkata, the CPI(M) … proposed joint, parallel, or coordinated movements.' http://politicalaffairs.net/india-role-of-the-communists-in-the-restoration-of-democracy/, accessed on 14 March 2013.

39 The CPI(M) leadership has never made public Sundarayya's dissenting views and the inner-party debate. The precise reasons for his resignation as party general secretary remain shrouded in mystery. In 1991, six years after his death, a pro-Maoist group published what it claimed was the text of Sundarayya's resignation letter (www.revolutionarydemocracy.org/archive/resig.htm, accessed on 22 August 2014. But it is difficult to establish its authenticity.

40 Mallick (1994) also says: 'For some this represented a failure of the CPM to act as a revolutionary communist party and break with the parliamentary tradition, which at the time of the Emergency … had proved to be defunct'.

41 Mallick (1994), pp. 159–62, observes: 'With thousands of members dead or driven away on threat of death from their place of work and residence, the party was preoccupied, for much of the period, in assisting its whole-timers and supporters financially, and relocating them in safe areas in Bengal and elsewhere'.

42 According to Ray's former secretary, the state government 'took note of the mixed feelings of this party (CPM) and the lack of any plan on their part to take active steps against the Emergency. Therefore, this state did not take action against the ageing leadership of the state cadre but took limited action against the ground-level activists only as [a] prophylactic measure and insurance against the future.' An intelligence report indicated that if 'this party goes underground then [its] compulsion … to go to extremism will be very strong'. Saroj Chakrabarty, *With Bengal Chief Ministers*, cited in Mallick (1994): pp. 159–62.

43 Ibid.

44 Noted by the Salkia Plenum of the CPI(M) in December 1978. CPI(M) 1979: *Report and Resolution on Organization*, adopted at the Salkia Plenum, New Delhi, Communist Party of India (Marxist), p.12.

45 Jyoti Basu was quoted by a newspaper as saying: 'We have no manpower, nor organization. For the first time in ten months we have been allowed to hold public meetings. We are …[in a]… terrific disadvantageous position, but we have received tremendous response from the people of all walks of life.' *Business Standard*, 23 February 1977, cited in Mallick (1994): pp. 159–62.

46 Cited in Norman D. Palmer (1977): 'India in 1976: The Politics of the Depoliticisation', *Asian Survey*, Vol. 17, No. 2, February, p. 171.

47 The CPI(M) by contrast won 22 Lok Sabha seats in 1977 (compared to 25 in 1971), but its vote share fell from 5.12 per cent to 4.29 per cent. Source: Election Commission of India.

48 'Political Review Report' in (1978): *Documents of the Eleventh Congress of the Communist Party of India*, New Delhi, Communist Party of India, pp. 66–68.

49 This is discussed at greater length in Chapter 4.

50 Contrary to claims, the CPI(M) adopted a generally cautious and defensive policy and sent many of its leaders and cadres underground. Its claims attracted acerbic criticism from the CPI: 'Where were the struggles against the Emergency and action calling for it to be lifted conducted by the CPM? What and where did it do anything against sterilization and the savage demolition operations aimed at the urban poor? What it did [sic] to battle against the caucus and the repulsive Sanjay build up campaign? What is its answer to P.C. Sen's public statement that the CPM turned down his proposal to launch a satyagraha against the Emergency in West Bengal? The one minor battlefield it found was in the "safe state" of Kerala where the ministry headed by Achutha Menon was in power! Not exactly a shining record of struggle against the tyranny of the Emergency. And yet it has the cheek to accuse the CPI of cowardice ….' Mohit Sen and Bhupesh Gupta (1978): *CPM's Politics X-Rayed*, New Delhi, Communist Party of India, March, p. 8. This is substantially corroborated by Madhu Limaye (1991): *Socialist Communist Interaction in India*, Delhi, Ajanta

Publications, especially Chapters 19, 20, 22 and 26; see in particular pp. 274–86.

51 For a critical analysis of CPI(M)'s 1978 Jalandhar congress line, see Ajit Roy (1978): 'CPI(M)'s Draft Political Resolution', *Economic and Political Weekly*, 25 February.

52 Achin Vanaik (2011): 'Subcontinental Strategies', *New Left Review* 70, July–August 2011.

53 The 'achievement' was fake because once India had full, unimpeded access to the reactor's spent fuel, it only required elementary chemistry to dump it into nitric acid and separate the plutonium from the solution and convert and forge it into an explosive assembly.

54 For a fuller discussion of the evolution of India's nuclear policy, the 1974 test, the CTBT, and the Left's position on nuclear weapons, see Praful Bidwai and Achin Vanaik (2000): *South Asia on a Short Fuse: Nuclear Politics and the Future of Global Disarmament*, New Delhi, Oxford University Press. Also see Bidwai and Vanaik (1997): 'An Open Letter to the Left' in 'Nuclear Notebook', *Economic and Political Weekly*, 18 January; and Bidwai and Vanaik (1998): 'Why India Should Sign the CTBT: Returning to Our Own Agenda', *Economic and Political Weekly*, 19 September.

55 On 9 June 1998 a Convention against Nuclear Weapons was organized in New Delhi, in which the general secretaries of the CPI(M) and CPI and senior office-bearers of other left parties participated, along with peace activists, trade unionists, people's science movement activists and public intellectuals, which condemned the tests and called for a dismantling of India's and Pakistan's nuclear arsenals. The Convention resolved: nuclearization 'has diverted attention from the grave problems facing the country—hunger, poverty, ill health, illiteracy and lack of basic infrastructure. It is deeply ironic that instead of making serious efforts to rise above the bottom 50 countries of the world in human development, India and Pakistan should want to join the club of the nuclear five.' See http://www.hrsolidarity.net/mainfile. php/1998vol08no09/1627/ accessed on 30 August 2014; and N. Ram (1999): *Riding the Nuclear Tiger*, New Delhi, Leftword Books, p. 13. This marked a turning point for the Left. Also see Bidwai and Vanaik (2000); M.V. Ramana and C. Rammanohar Reddy (eds) (2003): *Prisoners of the Nuclear Dream*, New Delhi, Orient Longman; and

Smitu Kothari and Zia Mian (eds) (2001): *Out of the Nuclear Shadow*, New Delhi, Lokayan and Rainbow Publishers. For more on the CNDP, visit www.cndpindia.org.

56 Javeed Alam argues that two assumptions underlie this rather conservative or non-radical conception of politics: 'first, that to get at the bourgeois state it is sufficient that the state is brought under siege of the exploited and allied classes and that, secondly, this class-based mobilization directed against the state is enough to transform the outlook of toiling people into revolutionary consciousness'. Alam (1991): p. 2573. Alam further contends: 'The error involved in looking at revolutionary politics in this manner leads to a condition of non-hegemonic conquest; that is, the people who come under communist rule or influence for long spells may not acquire a socialist consciousness and may, as they get out of it, ... revert back to earlier modes of thinking and political behaviour.' Ibid.

57 Cited in Jurgen Dige Pedersen (2001): 'India's Industrial Dilemmas in West Bengal', *Asian Survey*, July/August, pp. 646–68.

58 He would become Speaker of the Lok Sabha in 2004.

59 Pedersen (2001).

60 Rob Jenkins (1999): *Democratic Politics and Economic Reform in India*, Cambridge, UK, Cambridge University Press, p. 144.

61 Cited from *Hindustan Times*, 27 April 1995 by Jenkins, who also contends that the voices of some critics who were 'ideologically opposed to liberalization' became 'almost indistinguishable' in the mid-1990s 'from the laments of neo-liberal advocates who complained that each new reform measure was too little, not radical enough, a half-measure'. He adds: 'This view was elaborated forcefully by Biplab Dasgupta, an academic economist and CPI-M MP, in seminars and informal discussion at the Institute of Development Studies, University of Sussex, during the autumn of 1994. Almost three years later, he voiced similar opinions at a seminar on Indian development policy at Birkbeck College, University of London, 10 October 1997'. Jenkins (1999): p. 12.

62 Pedersen (2001).

63 Vanaik (2011).

64 See Chapter 8 for the CPI(M)'s contradictory stand on this issue.

65 http://indiatoday.intoday.in/story/mandal-commission-

political-parties-polarised-along-caste-lines-states-rocked-by-violence/1/315657.html, accessed on 4 June 2015.

66 See, for instance, Vinod Mishra (1991): 'The Fall of VP Singh and After', *Liberation*, January, available at https://www.marxists.org/reference/archive/mishra/1991/01/x01.htm., accessed on 1 May 2014. Also Aditya Nigam (1990): 'Mandal Commission and the Left', *Economic and Political Weekly*, 1–8 December.

67 For instance, CPI(M) general secretary Harkishan Singh Surjeet (1995) said: '… certain political forces, however, who in reflecting the demand of the OBCs are distorting it to perpetuate the caste division among the toiling people. This will prove very dangerous, because it not only disrupts the unity of the toiling people, but also because all those belonging to the upper castes are not well off. They include poor sections as well … The party congress warned against perpetuation of caste divisions and disruption of the democratic movement'. 'CPI(M)'s Fifteenth Congress', *The Marxist*, April–June.

68 See, for instance, http://archive.indianexpress.com/news/cpm-govt-sleeps-on-obc-quota-centre-not-happy/434393/0, accessed on 26 May 2015.

69 This writer has more than once witnessed industrial magnates in the entire Business Class of an airplane rising spontaneously in deference to Basu's presence on the flight; on two occasions, he received a standing ovation when he acknowledged them. For some businessmen, this was a tribute to someone who had done much to 'mainstream' the Left by tempering its opposition to liberalization.

70 Former Central Bureau of Investigation director and West Bengal director general of police Arun Prasad Mukherjee, who later became special secretary in the Central home ministry, and adviser to Home Minister Indrajit Gupta, claimed in his book *Unknown Facets of Rajiv Gandhi, Jyoti Basu, Indrajit Gupta* that in October 1990, Gandhi informally asked him to arrange a meeting with Basu where the prime ministerial offer would be made. Basu said 'it was not his call' and only the CPI(M)'s central committee and politburo could take such a decision. The party vetoed the proposal, and Chandrashekhar became the prime minister with Congress support. 'In 1991, when "Chandrashekhar turned out to be a failure", Gandhi again approached Basu but he … referred the matter to his party leadership,

which turned it down.' Cited in *The Times of India*, 26 November 2013.

71   Smita Gupta (1996): 'V.P. Proposes Basu as NF–LF Stakes its Claim: CPM to Convene Meeting Today', *The Times of India*, 14 May.

72   Monobina Gupta (2010): *Left Politics in Bengal: Time Travels among Bhadralok Marxists*, New Delhi, Orient BlackSwan, p. 83. She does not give the details of the first vote of 13 May but Jyoti Basu later said in an interview: 'So we called an emergency meeting of the central committee and there, by a majority—I don't know how many votes, 35 to 20 or something like that—the decision was made (to keep out). I was in the minority. Surjeet (Harkishan Singh Surjeet) was also in the minority ... [But the UF leaders] were not convinced. They said, you please discuss again. I said that already eight central committee members have left town ... I know who voted for who since I was presiding, so we reconvened the meeting. I told the committee, we have come back to you. We counted, some few people changed their minds, but even then we were in a minority.' Interview with M.J. Akbar (1997): *The Asian Age*, 2 January, available at www.jyotibasu. net/?q=node/34, accessed on 25 August 2014.

73   'Confusion Manifesto', *India Today*, 26 October 1998.

74   Gupta (2010): pp. 83–84.

75   Aijaz Ahmad (1996): 'In the Eye of the Storm: the Left Chooses', *Economic and Political Weekly*, 1 June, p. 1340.

76   Parts of the statement cited in Ahmad (1996): p. 1341.

77   Interview with M.J. Akbar (1997).

78   For the record, this writer offered a totally different argument. In an article written before 13 May 1996 (probably on 11 May), but published later, he proposed that the Left support from the outside a 'non-BJP government centred around the Congress', rather than the National Front. His logic was that the Front lacked 'a strong programmatic basis', and did not know how to do 'purposive coalition politics'. The Left and its progressive Front allies would be better advised to consolidate their own base and launch what has been 'missing' from their recent activities—'a mass mobilization campaign on issues that concern the people'. Praful Bidwai (1996): 'Why Staying Out May Be Better for NF–LF', *The Times of India*, 15 May. I would probably have changed this position after 13 May in view

of the course that events took. In retrospect, I strongly believe the CPI(M) should have allowed Basu to accept the UF's offer.

79   In 1994, 'new' members formed 80 per cent of the CPI(M)'s membership in West Bengal; these are defined as members who were recruited after the party came to power in 1977 in the state (more accurately, who were counted at the 1978 Salkia Plenum). Computed from the political–organizational reports of the fourteenth (Madras) and the fifteenth (Chandigarh) congresses of the CPI(M).

80   The pertinent section of the new article (7.17) of the revised party programme of 2000 reads: 'The Party, therefore, will continue to educate the mass of the people on the need for replacing the present bourgeois-landlord state and government headed by the big bourgeoisie even while utilising opportunities for forming such governments in the states or the Centre, depending on the concrete situation…'

Chapter 4: Into Power in Red Bengal

1   Election Commission of India, results for 1977 from http://eci.nic. in/ (accessed on 12 March 2013).

2   For an account of this, see www.cpimwb.org.in/lf_govt_details.php?lf_ id=28, and Biman Bose, 'How the Left Front and Its Government Emerged' in www.cpimwb.org.in/history_details.php?history_id=7, both accessed 20 January 2014.

3   There are innumerable accounts of this period. Among the best is Sumanta Banerjee (1980): *In the Wake of Naxalbari: A History of the Naxalite Movement in India*, Calcutta, Subarnarekha.

4   'As is well known, and as these [Left] parties themselves have not ceased repeating by way of protest, these parties were totally inactive during the last five years …', Ashok Rudra (1977): 'The Left Front Government', *Economic and Political Weekly*, 3 September, p. 1563.

5   Election Commission of India results, various years from http://eci. nic.in/, accessed on 12 March 2013.

6   The Left Front won an overall victory in the last of these panchayat elections, in 2008, but with significantly depleted scores in relation to 2003. It won thirteen of the seventeen apex-level zilla parishads, winning 519, or almost 70 per cent, of the 748 seats. It won a little

over 57 per cent of the panchayat samitis (2003 total, 85 per cent) and 51 per cent of the gram panchayats (compared to 72 per cent in 2003). But it suffered major setbacks in zilla parishads in three districts, East Medinipur, South 24 Parganas and North Dinajpur, considered its strongholds. For the opposition, the result was the best in thirty years despite divisions between the Trinamool Congress and the Congress party. See www.frontline.in/static/html/fl2512/stories/20080620251203300.htm, accessed 20 January 2014.

7   John H. Broomfield (1968): *Elite Conflict in a Plural Society: Twentieth Century Bengal*, Berkeley, University of California Press, pp. 5–6. Broomfield adds that the bhadralok were 'distinguished by many aspects of the behaviour—their deportment, their speech, their dress, their style of housing, their eating habits, their occupations and their associations—and quite as fundamentally by their cultural values and their sense of social propriety'. See also the work of the Subaltern School, in particular Ranajit Guha (1999): *A Rule of Property for Bengal: an Essay on the Idea of Permanent Settlement*, Durham, Duke University Press; and (1983): *Elementary Aspects of Peasant Insurgency in Colonial India*, Delhi, Oxford University Press; Sumit Sarkar (1973): *The Swadeshi Movement in Bengal 1903-1908*, New Delhi, People's Publishing House; and David Kopf (1969): *British Orientalism and the Bengal Renaissance*, Berkeley, University of California Press.

8   Marcus F. Franda (1971): *Radical Politics in West Bengal*, Cambridge (Mass.), The MIT Press, pp.10–12.

9   Cited in Franda (1971): p. 13.

10 www.cpimwb.org.in/lf_govt_details.php?lf_id=20, accessed on 20 January 2014.

11 Ibid.

12 Ashok Mitra (1978): 'This Opportunity Has to Be Converted into a Challenge', *Social Scientist*, Vol. 6, No. 6/7, Special Number on West Bengal (January–February), pp. 3–8. The excerpts that follow are all taken from this source.

13 Ibid.

14 West Bengal was one of the first regions of India to see early industrial development and accounted for nearly 23 per cent of national industrial output in 1960–61. Thanks to a number of factors, including lack of industrial modernization, preponderance of sunset industries, poor

infrastructure, new investment opportunities elsewhere, and growing social and political strife and labour unrest in the mid-1960s onwards, this proportion fell to about 10 per cent in 1980–81, and to less than 7 per cent by the late 1980s.

15 For instance, see Atul Kohli (1987): *The State and Poverty in India: the Politics of Reform*, Cambridge, UK, Cambridge University Press.

16 Sunil Sengupta and Haris Gazdar, 'Agrarian Politics and Rural Development in West Bengal', in Jean Dreze and Amartya Sen (eds) (1997): *Indian Development: Selected Regional Perspectives*, Delhi, Oxford University Press, p. 170.

17 Cited in Ross Mallick (1993): *Development Policy of a communist Government: West Bengal since 1977*, Cambridge, UK, Cambridge University Press, p. 30.

18 By 1971–72, 11 per cent of all rural households were totally landless and another 67 per cent owned less than one hectare (2.5 acres) of land. Between them, these 78 per cent owned less than 28 per cent of the land. The situation worsened during the decade of the 1970s with further parcelling out of land and growing landlessness. See Kalyan Dutt (1977): 'Changes in Land Relations in West Bengal', *Economic and Political Weekly*, 31 December, Review of Agriculture; Utsa Patnaik (1976): 'Class Differentiation Within the Peasantry', *Economic and Political Weekly*, 25 September, pp. A-82–A-101. There is a rich debate on classes and agrarian relations in the 'Farm Management Studies' series and in the work of Daniel Thorner.

19 Sunil Sengupta (1981):'West Bengal Land Reforms and the Agrarian Scene', *Economic and Political Weekly*, 20 June, pp. A-69–A-70.

20 Sengupta and Gazdar (1997), pp. 139–41.

21 The higher estimate has been attributed to land reforms minister Benoy Krishna Choudhury. Cited in Profulla Roy Choudhury (1985): *Left Experiment in West Bengal*, New Delhi, Patriot Publishers, p. 159.

22 T.V. Sathyamurthy (ed.) (1996): *Class Formation and Political Transformation in Post-Colonial India*, Delhi, Oxford University Press, pp. 438–41.

23 A. E. Ruud (1994): 'Land and Power: the Marxist Conquest of West Bengal', *Modern Asian Studies*, Vol. 28 No. 2, pp. 372–74.

24 The previous ceiling, effective from 1955, was as high as 10 hectares (25 acres) per person. The United Front government lowered it to 5

'standard' hectares (ha) per household of five members for irrigated land and 7 ha for unirrigated land for a family, with half a hectare per additional family member, subject to a maximum of 7 ha.

25 Cited in Mallick (1993), pp. 39–40.

26 Ibid.

27 Sengupta and Gazdar (1997), p. 144.

28 Ashok Rudra (1981): 'One Step Forward, Two Steps Backward', *Economic and Political Weekly*, 20–27 June, pp. A-61–A-68.

29 This is conceded even by Buddhadeb Bose in his critique of Rudra and defence of the Left Front, citing official figures. Bose (1981): 'Agrarian Programme of Left Front Government in West Bengal', *Economic and Political Weekly*, 12 December, p. 2057.

30 Rudra (1981).

31 Based on the government's 1979 publication, *An Evaluation of a Pledge*, cited in P. Roy Choudhury (1980): 'Land Reforms: Promise and Fulfilment', *Economic and Political Weekly*, 27 December, p. 2173.

32 Rudra (1981), pp. A-65–A-67.

33 D. Bandyopadhyay (2000): 'Land Reform in West Bengal: Remembering Hare Krishna Konar and Benoy Choudhury', *Economic and Political Weekly*, 27 May, pp. 1795–97.

34 Ibid., p. 1796.

35 Ibid.

36 Ibid.

37 Ibid.

38 P. Roy Choudhury (1980), pp. 2172–73.

39 Cited in P. Roy Choudhury, (1980).

40 Ibid.

41 Government of West Bengal, *Land Reforms in West Bengal: Statistical Report—V,* cited in Nripen Bandyopadhyaya, *Economic and Political Weekly*, Review of Agriculture, June 1981, p. A-39.

42 P. Roy Choudhury (1980), p. 2172, estimates the figure at a higher 3.74 lakh acres, which would earn an income of Rs 14 crore a year for those clandestinely possessing this. The Third Workshop report observed: 'It was found that progress made ... [in distribution of vested land] was rather tardy and unsatisfactory in almost all the districts.' Government of West Bengal, *Land Reforms in West Bengal: Statistical Report—VI*, cited in Mallick (1993), p. 48. The Workshop

noted that the elected rural institutions described some of these lands as 'unfit for agriculture'. D. Bandyopadhyay later questioned this assessment on the ground that 'with modern technology and diversified agriculture, there is hardly any land "unfit" for agriculture, including allied activities.' Basing himself on a joint report with former cabinet secretary Nirmal Mukarji, Bandyopadhyay also called the legal injunctions on land 'a bogey which is being carefully nurtured for years together', and attributed the failure of distribution to the rise of 'a new class in the rural areas' which derives privilege from the exclusion of the genuinely landless and land-poor peasantry. Nirmal Mukarji and D. Bandyopadhyay (1993): *New Horizons for West Bengal's Panchayats: A Report for the Government of West Bengal,* Calcutta, Government of West Bengal.

43 Government of West Bengal, *Land Reforms in West Bengal: Statistical Report—VI,* cited in Mallick, (1993), p. 48.

44 Mukarji and Bandyopadhyay (1993).

45 Sengupta and Gazdar (1997), p. 144.

46 The same authors estimate, basing themselves on the 1981 census, that the number of households relying mainly on agricultural labour for their livelihoods was about four million (p. 138).

47 P.S. Appu (1996): *Land Reforms in India,* Delhi, Vikas Publishing House, Appendix IV.3.

48 D. Bandyopadhyay, former land reforms commissioner of West Bengal, estimates the land redistributed at 8 per cent of the state's cultivable area. D. Bandyopadhyay (2000): p. 1797.

49 Government of India, Ministry of Rural Development, *Annual Report 1991–92,* New Delhi, 1992.

50 This is contested vigorously by Ross Mallick on the ground that a little over one million acres (or 85 per cent) of the land assumed, or claimed by the Left Front, to have been redistributed by 1982 fell under the Estates Acquisition Act, itself part of the zamindari abolition programme. Mallick (1993): pp.44–45. I am unable, despite serious effort, to get an unambiguous factual confirmation on this. Mallick also argues, on the basis of Ministry of Rural Development reports, that the area redistributed under the Land Reforms Act proper was only 80,639 acres, or 0.55 per cent of the total arable area of West Bengal; this figure alone is comparable with land redistributed

in other states. If this measure is used, West Bengal compares poorly with many other states including Kerala, Andhra Pradesh, and even Bihar, Madhya Pradesh and Assam. Mallick (1993), p. 46. This is plausible, and probably correct. However, D. Bandyopadhyay argues that Mallick is confusing the post–Land Reforms Act numbers with the land actually redistributed *before* the Left Front came to power. (Telephone conversation, 18 March 2015.)

51 Sunil Sengupta (1981), p. A-72.

52 Ibid.

53 'The Left Front Government in West Bengal: Evaluation of an Experience', review report adopted on the 29th Session, CPI(M) West Bengal State Committee, 23–24 February 2015.

54 Sengupta and Gazdar (1997), p. 144.

55 Government of West Bengal, *Economic Review 2003-04*, Calcutta.

56 Government of West Bengal, *West Bengal Human Development Report 2004*, pp. 35–36.

57 Ibid., p. 35

58 Ibid.

59 In many cases, says D. Bandyopadhyay, this had become a fait accompli before the pattas were given; the SC and ST groups were in de facto possession of the land prior to the transfer. (Telephone conversation, 18 March 2015.)

60 Sundarayya presented a powerful critique of the West Bengal party position on the land reform issue in his *Explanatory Note* to the 1973 resolution: 'Some comrades in West Bengal argue that the ownership rights to the tenants should not be campaigned for now … as it would antagonize' the landlords and 'they would go away from the democratic alliance'. These critics, he said, had gone to the 'extremely ridiculous position' of hesitating to raise popular demands. 'This attitude, if logically extended, would mean that we should formulate and advance the demands of tenants in such a way as would be acceptable to the landlords.' Sundarayya reminded the party that its central committee itself had earlier admitted that its notion of peasant unity was erroneously 'based upon the middle and rich peasantry, instead of building it around the rural labour and the poor … And organizing these sections as the main backbone are (sic) driving force of the movement.' This task would not be easy as

the rich and middle peasant orientation was 'deep-rooted and long accumulated' and because 'the bulk of our leading kisan activists, [is] from the rich and middle peasant' class, rather than poor peasants and agricultural labour. Cited in Mallick (1993): pp. 40–41.

61 Hare Krishna Konar (1977): *Agrarian Problems of India*, Calcutta, Gaur Sabha, p. 47.

62 Ranjit Kumar Lahiri, 'Land Reforms in West Bengal—Some Implications' in Manjula Bose (ed.), *Land Reforms in Eastern India*, Calcutta, Planning Forum, Jadavpur University, 1981, cited in Mallick (1993), p. 42.

63 B.K. Sarkar and R.K. Prasannan, *What Happened to the Vested Land?*, Calcutta, Directorate of Land Records and Surveys, West Bengal, March 1976, p. 6.

64 Cited in Mallick (1993): pp. 51–52 quoting, among other sources, a study by Ashok Rudra and National Sample Survey figures.

65 A study based on a large survey of 110 villages in West Bengal reported the existence of as many as eleven different proportions in which the produce is shared. Pranab Bardhan and Ashok Rudra (1980): 'Terms and Conditions of Sharecropping Contracts: An Analysis of Village Survey Data in India', *The Journal of Development Studies*, Vol. 16, No. 3, pp. 287–302. Also see Pranab Bardhan (1976): 'Variations in Extent and Forms of Agricultural Tenancy', *Economic and Political Weekly*, 11 and 18 September.

66 Bardhan and Rudra (1980).

67 Bandyopadhyay (2000) p. 1796.

68 'Conscientization' is defined as: 'The process of developing a critical awareness of one's social reality through reflection and action. Action is fundamental because it is the process of changing the reality.' www.freire.org/component/easytagcloud/%20conscientization,   accessed on 12 January 2015.

69 Bandyopadhyay (2000), p. 1797.

70 P. Roy Choudhury (1980), p. 2172.

71 Bandyopadhyay (2000), p. 1797.

72 For instance, Ratan Khasnabis (1981): 'Operation Barga: Limits to Social Democratic Reformism', *Economic and Political Weekly*, 20 June, 'Review of Agriculture', pp. A-43–A-48.

73 Bandyopadhyay (2000), p. 1797.

74 A wider survey of six villages, cited in Sengupta and Gazdar (1997): p. 150, found that about a third of all tenants were not recorded. Khasnabis's survey of forty-six villages found that 73 per cent of tenants did not register their rights as bargadars. Khasnabis (1981), p. A-45.

75 West Bengal Human Development Report (WBHDR) 2004, p. 31.

76 Ibid., p. 32.

77 Ibid., p. 33.

78 Sengupta and Gazdar, (1997): pp. 50–51. Also Kirsten Westergaard (1986), 'People's Participation, Local Government and Rural Development: the Case of West Bengal, India', Centre for Development Research, Report No. 8, Copenhagen, March 1986.

79 Anil K. Chakraborti, et al. (2003): *Beneficiaries of Land Reforms: The West Bengal Scenario*, Government of West Bengal, Spandan, Kolkata, 2003.

80 D. Bandyopadhyay (2003): 'Unfinished Tasks', *Economic and Political Weekly*, 5 July, pp. 2841–42.

81 Ibid.

82 https://editorialexpress.com/cgi-bin/conference/download.cgi?db_name=NEUDC2013&paper_id=304, conducted by University of Essex researchers Sonia Bhalotra and Abhishek Chakravarty.

83 Human Development Report 2004, p. 35. Also see note 59 above.

84 Ibid., pp. 40–41.

85 P. Roy Choudhury (1980), p. 2173.

86 WBHDR, pp. 36–37.

87 Third Workshop on Land Reforms, cited in P. Roy Choudhury (1980): p. 2172.

88 Ibid.

89 D. Bandyopadhyay (2003): 'Unfinished Tasks', p. 2842.

90 WBHDR 2004: p. 39.

91 Nikhilesh Bhattacharya, Manabendu Mukhopadhyay and Ashok Rudra (1987): 'Changes in Level of Living in Rural West Bengal', *Economic and Political Weekly*, 11 July, 15 August, 5 September, 31 October, 28 November.

92 Ibid.

93 Tables 10A and 10B in A.V. Jose (1988): 'Agricultural Wages in India', *Economic and Political Weekly*, 25 June, pp. A-46–A-58. In 1984–85,

real wages in West Bengal were almost 8 per cent lower than those prevalent in 1956–57, whereas wage rates in most other major states rose significantly over that period, doubling in Uttar Pradesh, Andhra Pradesh and rising by 80 per cent or more in Kerala and Gujarat. Also Rohini Nayyar (1991): *Rural Poverty in India*, Delhi, Oxford University Press.

94 G. Parthasarathy, 'Minimum Wages in Agriculture: A Review of Indian Experience', in Radhakrishna and Sharma (eds) (1998): *Empowering Rural Labour in India*, Institute for Human Development, cited in Dipankar Basu (2001): 'Political Economy of "Middleness",' *Economic and Political Weekly*, 21 April, p. 1337.

95 The gram panchayat or village council constitutes the lowest electoral unit comprising 1–12 villages. The block-level panchayat samiti extends to an average of 115 villages. And at the district level, the zilla parishad is at the apex of the system and is headed by an elected sabhadhipati, who presides over all administrative and development affairs, and to whom the district magistrate plays a secondary or subordinate role.

96 Neil Webster (1992): *Panchayati Raj and the Decentralisation of Development Planning in West Bengal*, Calcutta, K.P. Bagchi, pp. 22–24.

97 D. Bandyopadhyay repeated this observation to this writer in an interview in New Delhi on 20 October 2013. Webster makes a similar point: 'The panchayti raj programme in West Bengal is a central element in CPI(M)'s strategy to entrench its political position within the state of West Bengal so that, even if it should lose state power, it will retain both its organization and the mass support of substantial sections of the rural population who have benefited from the programme.' Webster (1992), p. 110.

98 As Webster noted, both these 'required the strong political will of the Left Front to be successfully implemented in the face of vested interests and they have both facilitated the subsequent changes in [the] politics of rural Bengal.... Electoral politics of the new panchayats required an organizational basis and it is this which made introduction of parties into panchayat elections from 1978 so significant. This introduced party machineries into panchayat elections process... The legislation had laid grounds for a cooperative relationship between the

panchayats and their committees but in reality there was considerable tension and hostility. After 1978 ... the powerful Block Development officer (BDO) and the District Magistrate ... could no longer exercise [their ultimate authority] in the same way. The influence wielded by party mass fronts over members sometimes ran overshod (sic) over the panchayat decision-making processes.' Webster (1992), p. 110.

99 D. Bandyopadhyay (2003a): 'Land Reforms and Agriculture: the West Bengal Experience', *Economic and Political Weekly*, 1 March, p. 882.

100 As the Mukarji–Bandyopadhyay committee noted: 'The panchayats brought in a middle category of society into key positions, many of them schoolteachers ... However, power has yet to travel down the lower levels. SCs and STs have been elected but do not hold key positions. The poor in general have not been elected. The middle category thus remains in firm control of the panchayats.... Panchayats packed with well-intentioned "middle" are no substitute for fair representation from both "middle" and "lowers", for the "lowers" surely know best what is good for them.' A college lecturer, who was a senior panchayat functionary told the committee that 'caste or class composition is not as relevant as what those occupying important positions do for the people, and by this test the present occupants have done well'. It was 'taken aback to hear an argument reminiscent of the "white man's burden" from an elected functionary'.

101 Mukarji and Bandyopadhyay (1993). They also said: 'On the conceptual side, there is lack of clarity about objectives of the panchayats, especially about the implications of their becoming institutions of self-government. On programmes, the virtual exit of land reform from their agenda has left the panchayats with a feeling that there is nothing worthwhile left to do...'

102 Amrita Basu (1992): *Two Faces of Protest: Contrasting Modes of Women's Activism in India*, Berkeley, University of California Press, pp. 37–41.

103 Ibid.

104 Ibid. Basu adds: 'The CPI(M) has compromised the interests of poorest rural groups by continually appeasing middle and rich peasants. It has shied away from conferring landownership rights on tenants ... For years it resisted organizing agricultural labourers

separately from landowning peasants. The All India Agricultural Labourers Union it recently formed is not yet active in West Bengal.'

105 Ibid.

106 Another scholar argues, on the basis of several AIKS and state Krishak Sabha documents: 'In West Bengal, however, the CPI(M) forged no separate organization for the agricultural labourer. Nevertheless, talk of such an organization "to protect and safeguard the interests of agricultural workers"... and to draw them "into the movement and wean away from the influence of the bourgeois-landlord parties"... filled the air...Paradoxically, and this is important, the real (though seldom articulated) objective was to protect the interests of the rural middle classes, and not of the agricultural labourer. In one of the conferences of the Pradeshik Krishak Sabha it was felt that the lack of suitable organization for agricultural labourers made it difficult for the middle class to express its opinion without inhibition ... A similar concern to preserve the domain of middle-class influence was expressed at an AIKS conference which discussed the issue at length ... Middle-class domination in the Krishak Sabha was, therefore programmatically indefensible but pragmatically fortified.' Dwaipayan Bhattacharyya, 'Politics of Middleness: the Changing Character of the CPI(M) in Rural West Bengal 1977–90' in Ben Rogaly, Barbara Harriss-White and Sugata Bose (eds) (1999): *Sonar Bangla: Agricultural Growth and Agrarian Change in West Bengal and Bangladesh*, New Delhi, Sage Publications, pp. 289–90.

107 Bhattacharyya (1999), pp. 284–85.

108 AIKS, *Proceedings and Resolutions, 24th Conference*, 8–11 November 1982, pp. 28–29.

109 Cited in Bhattacharyya (1999), p. 285, who adds: 'The "new orientation" was perceived as less divisive, more inclusive and, indeed, electorally more promising ... It was the electoral exigency to unite various peasant classes which consequently prevailed over most other considerations.'

110 Bhattacharyya (1999), pp. 289 and 297.

111 They include: Ratan Ghosh (1981): 'Agrarian Programme of Left Front Government', *Economic and Political Weekly*, 20 June; John Harriss (1993): 'What is Happening in Rural West Bengal: Agrarian Reform, Growth and Distribution', *Economic and Political Weekly*, 12

June; Arild Engelsen Ruud (1994): 'Land and Power: The Marxist Conquest of Rural Bengal', *Modern Asian Studies*, Vol. 28, No. 2, May; Ratan Khasnabis (1981): 'Operation Barga: Limits to Social Democratic Reformism', *Economic and Political Weekly*, 20 June; D. Bandyopadhyay (1997): 'Not a Gramscian Pantomime', *Economic and Political Weekly*, 22 March; Maitreesh Ghatak and Maitreya Ghatak (2002): 'Recent Reforms in the Panchayat System in West Bengal', *Economic and Political Weekly*, 5 January.

112   Dipankar Basu (2001), pp. 1333–44.

113   Ben Rogaly (1998): 'Containing Conflict and Reaping Votes', *Economic and Political Weekly*, 17–24 October, p. 2729.

114   Jyotiprasad Chatterjee and Suprio Basu (2009): 'West Bengal: Mandate for Change', *Economic and Political Weekly*, 26 September. Based on a Centre for the Study of Developing Societies (CSDS)–Lokniti study, the authors estimate that 46 per cent of rural agricultural workers voted for the Left, compared to 41 per cent for the Congress and allies including the TMC. There was only a 2 per cent shift in the agricultural workers' vote against the Left, compared to a 26 per cent shift among farmers. An estimated 53 per cent of marginal farmers and bargadars, and as many as 65 per cent of other farmers, voted for the Congress–TMC alliance.

115   See in particular, Bhattacharyya (1999), Ruud (1994) and Rogaly (1998).

116   Partha Chatterjee (1997): *The Present History of West Bengal: Essays in Political Criticism*, Delhi, Oxford University Press. Sengupta and Gazdar also recall Mukarji and Bandyopadhyay's warning in 1993 that 'with the implementation of agrarian reforms being exhausted, panchayats run the risk of losing their sense of direction …' Sengupta and Gazdar (1997), pp. 161–62.

Chapter 5: Crisis and Exit in West Bengal

1   Former finance minister Ashok Mitra's phrase, cited in Atul Kohli (1987): *The State and Poverty in India: The Politics of Reform*, Cambridge, UK, Cambridge University Press, p. 87fn.

2   HCR measures the proportion of people with incomes (or expenditures) below the poverty line to the total. Much of the

information here and in the following paragraphs paraphrases or is derived from the excellent study: Sunil Sengupta and Haris Gazdar, 'Agrarian Politics and Rural Development in West Bengal', in Jean Dreze and Amartya Sen (eds) (1997): *Indian Development: Selected Regional Perspectives*, Delhi, Oxford University Press.

3   Between 1983–84 and 1987–88, West Bengal registered the highest decline in poverty ratios of all the major Indian states. It also witnessed a significant improvement in income distribution. The Gini coefficient measuring overall distribution of expenditure fell from 0.31 in 1977–78 to 0.29 in 1983 and 0.25 in 1989–90.

4   Planning Commission (2010): *West Bengal Development Report 2010*, New Delhi, Government of India, p. 95.

5   Population growth fell further to 13.8 per cent (national average, 17.7 per cent) between 2001 and 2011. The state also raised its overall sex ratio from 917 (females per 1,000 males) in 1991 to 934 in 2001, and further to 950 a decade later, above the national average of 933. More impressively, it more or less maintained its child sex ratio between 2001 (957) and 2011 (956), whereas the all-India figure for this fell from 927 to 919 in the corresponding period. See http://www.census2011.co.in/sexratio.php

6   Planning Commission (2010), p 95.

7   'Between 1969-70 and 1979-80, total foodgrains production increased at an average rate of 2.5 per cent a year in India as a whole, and at 1.7 per cent per year in West Bengal—lagging far behind rate of increase of population. From 1979-80 and 1989-90, however, West Bengal's foodgrains output grew at an average rate of 3.4 per cent per year compared India's 2.7 per cent.' Sengupta and Gazdar (1997), pp. 163–67.

8   Certain scholars aligned to the Left Front tended to emphasize the role of reforms while more independent scholars, while supportive of the reforms, focused attention on private incentives. With improved rural electricity supply, groundwater irrigation potential grew, with farmers investing in tube wells for their own land and selling water to their neighbours. John Harriss (1993): 'What is Happening in Rural West Bengal?: Agrarian Reform, Growth and Distribution', *Economic and Political Weekly*, 12 June, pp. 137–47.

9 'In short, the main factors behind the agricultural takeoff in West Bengal are shared with other states of the eastern region, with similar agro-economics. West Bengal's particularly strong record may reflect the state's greater agronomic potential than its neighbours … The tendency to seek retrospective validation for trade reforms on efficiency grounds is surprising, since these arguments have been largely incidental to the political mobilization around agrarian issues in West Bengal, which was based squarely in redistributive terms… The more interesting question … is whether and to what extent the poor have been able to participate in the growth that has occurred.' Sengupta and Gazdar (1997), p. 169.

10 Ibid., pp. 172–78.

11 In the early 1980s, seven of the thirteen major states with lower poverty ratios than West Bengal had higher IMRs compared to it. In IMR rankings for fifteen major states in 1981, West Bengal stood the sixth-lowest, nineteen points below the Indian average. Ibid.

12 During the 1980s, the rate of decline in West Bengal's IMR slowed down in relation to other states. The rate was surpassed or at least equalled by Uttar Pradesh, Bihar, Tamil Nadu, Gujarat, Punjab and Kerala. Between 1983–84 and 1987–88, as many as seven states reduced their IMR at a faster pace than West Bengal, including Maharashtra, Gujarat, Punjab, Kerala, Tamil Nadu and even the BIMARU (the group of four states of Bihar, Madhya Pradesh, Rajasthan and Uttar Pradesh in the Hindi heart land) states of Rajasthan and Utter Pradesh—although four of them witnessed an increase or stagnation in their rural poverty HCR in this period. Even this pattern changed in the 1990s and beyond as many other states (e.g., Tamil Nadu, Karnataka and Gujarat) overtook West Bengal in lowering their IMRs in absolute terms. Sengupta and Gazdar (1997), pp. 186–88. In the new century, West Bengal cannot claim to be a good learner with a consistently improving performance in this regard. In 1998–99, West Bengal's overall IMR was 48.7, compared to 16.3 for Kerala, and ranked eleventh among all states; it fell further to 38 by 2005, but this was extremely unevenly spread between rural and urban areas and across districts. This unevenness has proved persistent: Planning Commission (2010).

13 West Bengal Human Development Report 2004 (WBHDR), Calcutta, Government of West Bengal.

14 Sample surveys in five villages by investigators of the World Institute for Development Economics Research (WIDER) found a clear improvement in the nutritional status of children under five (in the two villages for which earlier data was available). Yet, it concluded: 'The overall level of deprivation ... has remained extremely high. In none of the villages was the estimated proportion of undernourished children below three-quarters in 1988-89'; several children were 'disastrously undernourished'. Malnourishment follows an unequal pattern of incidence across gender, caste, tribe and (religious) community lines. Sengupta and Gazdar (1997), pp. 189–90.

15 WBHDR, p. 128. Although West Bengal, by the late 1990s, had a surplus of cereal production, it was still marked by nutritional deprivation, especially amongst children under three. The state had the highest per capita production of vegetables in India (439 gm), but its per capita consumption was only 63 gm per day, ranking number six nationally. A WHO (World Health Organisation) survey found that '94.7 per cent of the people do not eat sufficient vegetables and fruit'. Planning Commission (2010), pp. 123–24.

16 A study found that in 2002, the ICDS budget allocation was woefully inadequate—just 80 paise per child per day. This was raised to Rs 2.00 from 2006, which was still insufficient to meet the 300-calories-a-day target, let alone the actual deficit of 500 calories calculated by National Nutrition Bureau. The supply of basic ingredients like dal and rice remained irregular and inadequate. In the ten projects studied in 2005–06, the deficit was sometimes 73 per cent for rice and 75 per cent for pulses. About 35 per cent of the centres covered had no physical infrastructure of their own and functioned from clubs, mosques, temples or verandas of schools. The quality of the food and staff was poor. Kumar Rana and Santabhanu Sen (2008): 'The ICDS Programme in West Bengal: Scope and Challenges', Paper presented at 'Regional Consultation on the Status of the Young Child', organized by FORCES (Forum for Creche and Child Care Services) in Ranchi, Jharkhand.

17 Low BMI (weight in kilogrammes divided by the square of height in metres) is a crucial indicator of the proportion of adults who are

underweight. The proportion of women in West Bengal with below-normal BMI (18.5) in 2005–06 was as high as 37.7 per cent, a level considered near-alarming. Sixty-three per cent of its ever-married women also suffered from iron-deficiency anaemia, compared to 52 per cent nationally. There was at best relatively modest improvement in some of these indices since the late 1990s; in fact, some of them deteriorated, as in the case of children under three who are wasted, and married/pregnant women in the 14–49 age group. WBHDR, pp. 125–26.

18 Planning Commission (2010), p. 123.

19 mdws.gov.in/hindi/sites/upload_files/ddwshindi/files/pdf/12_fyp_vol_2_MDWS.pdf, accessed on 9 May 2014.

20 This is only slightly lower than the figure for Uttar Pradesh (29.8), and significantly higher than the all-India percentage of 19.5. Census 2011 data. http://censusindia.gov.in/Census_And_You/availability_of_eminities_and_assets.aspx#; also www.downtoearth.org.in/content/no-latrines-and-drinking-water-half-india-finds-survey

21 Ibid.

22 Although 88.5 per cent of West Bengal's population had access to water 'which can roughly be considered as safe for drinking' in 2001, almost 19 per cent of the urban population had to purify the water before drinking. Planning Commission (2010), pp. 123–24. As many as seventy-nine blocks (of the state's total of 341 blocks) spread over nine districts were reported to be affected by excessive arsenic contamination, up from seventy-five in eight districts. The population of these blocks was 16.7 million (2001 census). Reported in WBHDR.

23 Planning Commission (2010), pp. 124–25.

24 During the period between 1994–95 and 2006–07, it remained at less than 1,270. The number of beds in the PHCs increased by a pathetic 11 per cent. Ibid.

25 http://www.wbhealth.gov.in/Health_Stat/2010_2011/6/VI.1.pdf, accessed on 4 May 2014.

26 Ashish Bose and Mithu Adhikary (2008): 'The Independent Commission on Development and Health in India', *Health Status of the Districts of India*, New Delhi, VHAI, available at http://www.vhai.org/ceo/icdhi-publications/Health%20Status%20of%20

The%20Districts%20of%20India.pdf, maps on p. 21 and p. 34. The state ranked somewhat better ('yellow' category) in the performance index, suggesting 'some effort on the part of the state government to overcome their deficiencies'.

27 www.mohfw.nic.in/WriteReadData/l892s/492794502RHS%20 2012.pdf, accessed on 14 March 2014. Such playing down of the flaws and shortcomings in the state's primary health care system suggested complacency and a failure to come to grips with the real problem.

28 These aggregate figures probably hide major and persistent caste and gender differences. For instance, a village-based sample survey conducted by researchers from WIDER found large differences in literacy between caste Hindus, Dalits and tribals (adivasis), as well as men and women in different groups. For 1983–87, it estimated literacy rates at 95 per cent for caste Hindu males (88 per cent for females), but only 58 per cent for Dalit men (30 per cent for women), and 41 per cent for adivasi men (and zero for women). West Bengal's record in promoting literacy among adivasis, an underprivileged group, was unimpressive between 1961 and 1991. Although it was slightly ahead of the national average in male adivasi literacy in 1961, it fell marginally behind it by 1991. Female adivasi literacy in the state improved significantly from a paltry 1.8 per cent (national average 3.2 per cent) in 1961 to 12 per cent by 1991, but it still did not rise to the 14.5 per cent all-India average by that year. Sengupta and Gazdar (1997), pp. 187–88.

29 Educationist Poromesh Acharya, a member of the executive council of the National Literacy Mission (NLM), concluded that the Left Front missed the 'golden opportunity' offered by the TLC: 'In their futile zeal to claim total literacy, the respective Zilla Saksharata Samitis missed the spirit of functional literacy and reduced the campaign into a Laodicean [lukewarm] exercise. It is no wonder that the first district of West Bengal which had claimed to have achieved the goal of total literacy admitted recently that about 50 per cent of neo-literates had reverted to illiteracy.' See Acharya (1993): 'Panchayats and Left Politics in West Bengal', *Economic and Political Weekly*, 29 May, p. 1080. Also see Tushar Mukherjee (1995): 'Total Literacy Campaign in West Bengal: an Appraisal', *Economic and Political Weekly*, 28 October, pp. 2721–24; National Literacy Mission

(1994): *Literacy Campaigns in India*, New Delhi, NLM; Sumanta Banerji (1994): 'Flowers for the Illiterates', *Economic and Political Weekly*, 26 November, pp. 3013–16; and National Literacy Mission (1994a): *Evaluation of Literacy Campaign in India: Report of Expert Group*, New Delhi, NLM. [Disclosure of interest: I was a member of the NLM executive council for a part of the relevant period.]

30 Only the original BIMARU states, besides Karnataka, Andhra Pradesh and Haryana, ranked below West Bengal in 2001. West Bengal's rank among all thirty-five states and Union territories improved only marginally from nineteenth in 1991 to eighteenth in 2001. Historically, West Bengal had a head-start in education owing to its early exposure to colonial rule. But its post-1977 record in education was not outstanding despite the fact that in 1990–91 it spent the highest proportion (26 per cent) of its revenue budget on education of all Indian states, including Kerala, and well above the national average of 20 per cent. Yet, the state's per capita expenditure on education was lower than that of Gujarat or Kerala, and its school enrolment ratio worse than theirs, as well as Tamil Nadu's or Maharashtra's. In part, this reflected lopsided priorities: a higher proportion (18.4 per cent) of the West Bengal revenue budget was spent on higher education than the national average (16.6). V.K. Ramachandran, Madhura Swaminathan and Vikas Rawal (2003): 'Barriers to Expansion of Mass Literacy and Primary Schooling in West Bengal: A Study Based on Primary Data from Selected Villages', Working Paper 345, Thiruvananthapuram, Centre for Development Studies, http://opendocs.ids.ac.uk/opendocs/bitstream/handle/123456789/3040/wp345.pdf?sequence=1, accessed on 12 February 2014.

31 'In opening new schools, the government of West Bengal concentrated on areas where Dalits and Adivasis predominated. Secondly, all school education was made free. Thirdly, the number of teachers increased raising the average number of teachers per primary school to three in 1992. Fourthly, the government improved the conditions of employment of teachers: their salaries, allowances and retirement benefits rose substantially after the Left Front came to power. Fifthly, certain schemes for providing textbooks to school children and uniforms to girl students were begun although their coverage was not universal. Sixthly, there were changes in the administration of

primary education. West Bengal, for example, introduced a system of no-detention or automatic promotion for the first five years of school'. V.K. Ramachandran, Madhura Swaminathan and Vikas Rawal (2003).

32 It said the system 'has in practice become defunct'. Ibid. According to another analyst: 'In calling for substantially higher college fees, in insisting that the teachers be forced to teach—ensuring their accountability to society through inspection and other ways—and in demanding that the widespread malpractice of using school hours and schoolchildren for extracting money in the form of private tuition be ended, the commission had indeed bared the ugly face of academic institutions' in West Bengal. Tapas Majumdar (1993): 'An Education Commission Reports', *Economic and Political Weekly*, 8 May, pp. 919–20.

33 Kumar Rana (2010): *Social Exclusion in and through Elementary Education*, Kolkata, Pratichi (India) Trust, in association with UNICEF.

34 Kumar Rana, Abdur Rafique and Amrita Sengupta (2002): *The Pratichi Education Report*, Number 1, Delhi, TLM Books; and www.pratichi.org/sites/default/files/Pratichi_Education-Report_II.pdf, accessed on 12 February 2014. These were based on a sample survey covering thirty-eight schools and thirty-seven Shishu Shiksha Kendras in thirty-eight villages of six districts. The findings of the first report were summarized in Kumar Rana and Samantak Das, with Amrita Sengupta and Abdur Rafique (2003): 'State of Primary Education in West Bengal', *Economic and Political Weekly*, 31 May, pp. 2159–64.

35 The second report noted 'greater absenteeism (75 per cent) in schools to which a majority of children come from Scheduled Caste and Scheduled Tribe families, compared to other schools (33 per cent). In some schools with children from "lowly" families, the teaching hours are arbitrarily reduced ...' www.pratichi.org/sites/default/files/Pratichi_Education-Report_II.pdf, accessed on 12 February 2014.

36 Kumar Rana, et al. (2003). To be fair, the first Pratichi report documents the 'significant progress' made by the Left Front government in increasing student enrolment, establishing new

primary schools, appointing teachers and in raising the non-plan budget expenditure on education from 12.9 per cent in 1976–77 to 21.1 per cent in 1992–93. The government 'to a large extent achieved success in giving security of services to teachers and employees in all educational institutions', including substantial increases in teachers' salaries, 'making school education free, supplying dry rations of food and free textbooks at the primary level, supplying free uniforms to a substantial number of girl students and so on'. These efforts 'played a positive role in the expansion of primary education in West Bengal'.

37 'The condition of the SSKs also provides evidence of caste and ethnic discrimination. Since most of the SSKs are located in the places inhabited by the Scheduled Caste and Scheduled Tribe communities, whose children have little access to the primary schooling system, it was upsetting to note the condition of the housing arrangements of the SSKs. In most schools we visited, many of the children learn their lessons standing outside. While establishing an SSK in such place is in itself a positive step, the step can be made much more effective if facilities are expanded'. The report also says: 'There is further evidence of caste and ethnic discrimination in the primary schools (and, to a lesser extent, the SSKs). This includes ignoring the presence of children from low-caste backgrounds, making them sit separately … making derogatory remarks about the children of Scheduled Caste and Scheduled Tribe families and assuming that they simply cannot acquire education. This discrimination repels such children from the primary schooling system and forces them into forming the uneducated underclass of society …' www.pratichi.org/sites/default/files/Pratichi_Education-Report_II.pdf, accessed on 12 February 2014.

38 More details are found at www.planningcommission.nic.in/reports/peoreport/peoevalu/peo_cmdm.pdf, and www.righttofoodindia.org/data/mdms_kumarRana_WB.doc, accessed on 22 January 2014.

39 'There has been a real regression, as opposed to progress, on the dependence on private tuition. The proportion of child relying on it has risen to 64 per cent from 57 per cent for the students of standard primary schools, and 58 per cent from 24 per cent for SSK children. Underlying this rise is not only some increase in incomes and the affordability of having private tuition, but also an intensification

of the general conviction among the parents that private tuition is "unavoidable" if it can be at all afforded (78 per cent of the parents now believe it is indeed "unavoidable", up from 62 per cent).' www. pratichi.org/sites/default/files/Pratichi_Education-Report_II.pdf, accessed on 12 February 2014.

40 For instance, its per capita expenditure on the Sarva Shiksha Abhiyan (SSA) programme during the period 2002–07 was Rs 1,438, or 27 per cent lower than the national average, and considerably below the expenditure even of backward states such as Uttar Pradesh (Rs 1,878) and Rajasthan (Rs 2,089), not to speak of communist-ruled Tripura (Rs 3,622). Government of India, XII Five-Year Plan, 2008. According to an 'RTE (Right to Education) Watch' report, West Bengal's annual school dropout rate later rose to 6.5 per cent, close to the national average of 6.8 per cent. The state also 'shows dismal rates of RTE implementation otherwise'. 'The percentage of teachers without professional qualifications increased from 34 per cent in 2009-2010 to 41 per cent in 2010-2011. Further, only 33 per cent of schools in West Bengal have boundary walls. There was a three per cent decline in the percentage of schools which have playgrounds from 2009-2010 to 2010-2011. The dearth of teachers in the state is so high that 45 per cent of schools have a pupil-teacher ratio above 30. More than 50 per cent of government schools have a student-classroom ratio "higher than 35".' http://azimpremjiuniversity.edu.in/lgdi/rtewatch/west-bengal-shows-dismal-rates-of-rte-implementation/, accessed on 21 August 2014.

41 The percentage of government primary schools with a high student: classroom ratio (SCR) above thirty is 46.6 for West Bengal and 32.4 for all states; and the corresponding percentages for schools with an even more undesirable SCR (above thirty-five) are 69.2 for West Bengal and 32.8 for all-India. While the percentages of primary government schools with above-thirty pupil-teacher ratios are roughly the same, the percentages for upper-primary government schools with above-thirty-five pupil: teacher ratio are 32.0 for West Bengal and 29.1 for all states. The percentages of regularly employed qualified teachers in all types of primary schools are 51.6 in West Bengal and 78.6 for all India. All figures from Arun C. Mehta, 'Elementary Education in India: Progress towards UEE, Analytical Tables 2012–13', New Delhi,

National University of Educational Planning and Administration, District Information System for Education (DISE), www.dise.in/Downloads/Publications/Documents/Analytical%20Table-12-13.pdf, accessed on 21 August 2014.

42 West Bengal's government and aided schools score better at 66.8 per cent in respect of schools with kitchen sheds, compared to all states' percentage of 60.4. But the percentage of schools with electricity is 39.9 for West Bengal and 49.9 for all states. In respect of schools (all managements) with boys' toilets, West Bengal's performance is much lower at 39.9 per cent than the all-India figure of 67.1 per cent. The corresponding figures for schools with girls' toilets are 74.9 and 88.3 per cent. (DISE).

43 By 2008-09, West Bengal's gross enrolment ratios for all groups of schoolchildren in Classes I–VIII were lower for both boys and girls than the national average (except for girls in Classes VI–VIII). Even Uttar Pradesh recorded higher rates except for children in Classes VI–VIII. The state's performance was particularly poor in Classes I–V, with enrolment rates roughly 5 to 10 percentage points lower than the all-India average for both boys and girls. The state's net enrolment ratios improved between 2000–01 and 2008–09: from 50.1 to 84.5 per cent for primary schools, and from 31.0 to 54.6 per cent for middle schools. But they remained firmly below the national averages of 98.6 per cent and 56.2 per cent for 2008–09. Government of India, Economic Survey, 2008–09.

44 These figures have been compiled by economist and right-to-food activist Reetika Khera from an analysis of the official data from various sources, especially www.nrega.nic.in, corroborated with other data, as part of her ongoing work on MGNREGA. Some of the data was used in a paper by Khera and Dimple Kukreja presented at the annual conference of the Indian Society of Labour Economics, Delhi, December 2013. I am most grateful to her for sharing them with me in advance of her publication, through email communications of 12 and 13 June 2014.

45 West Bengal has also been lackadaisical in ensuring that the holders of job cards open bank or post office accounts, into which their wages can be paid. In 2011–12, the proportion of those with a bank or post office account to the total was 79.4 per cent for the state, compared to

87.2 for the country (and of bank account holders even lower: 37 per cent compared to 56.5 per cent nationally). In some states (Andhra Pradesh, Kerala, even Chhattisgarh), the proportion close to 100 per cent. Reetika Khera, as cited in n .43.

46 Figures pertain to 2004–05. From Table 8.1 of the 'Report on Condition of Work and Promotion of Livelihoods in the Unorganized Sector', New Delhi, National Commission for Enterprises in the Unorganized Sector, 2007, p. 124.

47 Reetika Khera's analysis, http://www.cdedse.org/pdf/work198.pdf, accessed on 22 May 2014.

48 Dwaipayan Bhattacharyya and Kumar Rana (2008): 'Politics of PDS Anger in West Bengal', *Economic and Political Weekly*, 2 February, p. 66.

49 Ibid.

50 Ibid.

51 See note 1 above.

52 This connection has been established by many scholars, including Jean Dreze and Bina Agarwal, in case studies of states like Bihar.

53 This raised transportation costs and negated the natural cost advantage which eastern states like West Bengal and Bihar enjoyed because of their proximity to mines, raw material processing industries and ports.

54 See especially Chapters 6 and 5 in Dayabati Roy (2014): *Rural Politics in India: Political Stratification and Governance in West Bengal*, Delhi, Cambridge University Press.

55 The proportion of households owning no land or less than 2.5 acres increased from 28 per cent of the total in 1980 to 43 per cent in 1995. (West Bengal Agricultural Census, various years). Even more telling, the proportion of landless rural households increased from 39.6 per cent in 1987–88 to as much as 49.8 per cent in 1999–2000. WBHDR, p. 39.

56 Barbara Harriss-White (2008): *Rural Commercial Capital: Agricultural Markets in West Bengal*, New Delhi, Oxford University Press; and (2013): 'West Bengal's Rural Commercial Capital', *International Critical Thought*, Vol. 3, No. 1.

57 Estimated at 15 to 21 per cent. D. Bandyopadhyay (2003): 'Unfinished Tasks', *Economic and Political Weekly*, 5 July.

58 Glyn Williams (2001): 'Understanding "Political Stability": Party Action and Political Discourse in West Bengal', *Third World Quarterly*, Vol. 22, No. 4; and D. Bandyopadhyay (2003a): 'Land Reform and Agriculture', *Economic and Political Weekly*, 1 March.

59 Dipankar Basu (2001): 'Political Economy of "Middleness"', *Economic and Political Weekly*, 21 April.

60 Dwaipayan Bhattacharyya (2009): 'Of Control and Factions: The Changing "Party-Society" in Rural West Bengal', *Economic and Political Weekly*, 28 February.

61 I am grateful to Kolkata-based Left activist and film-maker Sumit Chowdhury for this insight.

62 Conversation with historian Tanika Sarkar (26 March 2015). She adds: 'People began to enter the Front in droves or became supporters from the second term onwards since this was the easiest way of getting undue favours or even services that were their just rights.'

63 Ibid.

64 See Dipankar Basu (2001); 'Neil Webster (1992): *Panchayati Raj and the Decentralisation of Development Planning in West Bengal: A Case Study*, Calcutta, K.P. Bagchi Publishers; Arild Englesen Ruud (1994): 'Land and Power: The Marxist Conquest of Rural Bengal', *Modern Asian Studies*, Vol. 28, No. 2, May; Dwaipayan Bhattacharyya (2004): 'West Bengal: Permanent Incumbency and Political Stability', *Economic and Political Weekly*, 18 December; and also Dwaipayan Bhattacharyya (2009).

65 Noted especially by Webster (1992).

66 This is the Bardhan–Mookherjee thesis. See Pranab Bardhan and Dilip Mookherjee (2004): 'Poverty Alleviation Effort of West Bengal Panchayats', *Economic and Political Weekly*, 28 February; and Pranab Bardhan, Sandip Mitra, Dilip Mookherjee and Abhirup Sarkar (2009): 'Local Democracy and Clientelism: Implications for Political Stability in Rural West Bengal', *Economic and Political Weekly*, 28 February, amongst many version of the argument.

67 Chakraborty was expelled from the party, but later readmitted. See his interview in http://indiatoday.intoday.in/story/i-wont-argue-with-surjeet-he-a-pygmy-nripen-chakraborty/1/288778.html, accessed on 21 January 2015.

68 This has been documented ably by, among others, Monobina Gupta (2010): *Left Politics in Bengal: Time Travels among Bhadralok Marxists*, New Delhi, Orient BlackSwan, especially in Chapters 2, 4 and 5; and Ranabir Samaddar (2013): *Passive Revolution in West Bengal*, New Delhi, Sage Publications. Pranab Bardhan has acerbically commented on the 'all-pervasive and oppressive party control of all aspects of local life. If you want a public hospital bed for your seriously ill family member, you have to be a supplicant with the local party boss; if you want to start a small business or be a street vendor you have to pay protection money to the party dada; if you want to ply a taxi or an autorickshaw you have to pay a tribute to the local party union; if you want a school teacher's job you have to be approved by the "local committee" and pay them an appropriate amount; your children are to go to schools where the union activist teacher is often absent, compelling you to pay good money in sending them to his private coaching classes; if you want to build a house you have to employ party-approved construction workers and buy higher-priced or inferior-quality building materials from party-approved suppliers; if you want to buy land, you have to go through the party-connected "promoter", etc'. Bardhan (2011): 'Avoidable Tragedy of the Left in India-II', *Economic and Political Weekly*, 11 June.

69 Dasgupta was also the architect of the CPI(M)'s anti-Naxalite strategy and violent operations in the early period.

70 Under him, the CPI(M) agreed in Kerala to contest fifty-nine seats than the sixty-five which the formula entailed. Anonymous (1968): 'Travails of United Front', *Economic and Political Weekly*, 4 May.

71 'The party has turned mechanisms of control like disciplining, punishment and surveillance into a fine art to control its members … [its mass] organizations are not only mobilized to win elections but they are used as countervailing powers to control the formal systems of power in any organization. For example, in a university the formal bodies are subverted by these mass organizations … In fact, even vice chancellors (VCs) are elected in Bengal. But what is more interesting is how the electoral college entrusted with the task of choosing the VC is turned into a mere rubber stamp to ratify the name already decided by the education cell of the CPM … the party and its mass organizations subvert what is apparently democratic by eliminating

the deliberative process in so crucial a decision.' Sanjeeb Mukherjee (2007): 'The Use and Abuse of Democracy in West Bengal', *Economic and Political Weekly*, 3 November.

72 See the excellent study of the issue by Ishita Dey, Ranabir Samaddar and Suhit K. Sen (2013): *Beyond Kolkata: Rajarhat and the Dystopia of Urban Imagination*, New Delhi, Routledge.

73 The Convention on Wetlands, signed in 1971, is an intergovernmental treaty that provides the framework for national action and international cooperation for the conservation and wise use of wetlands and their resources. See www.ramsar.org.

74 Pre-poll survey by the Centre for the Study of Developing Societies (CSDS) for *The Hindu*-CNN-IBN. Published in *The Hindu*, 6 April 2006. This showed that support for the Left among the rural poor declined by five percentage points, while support from the rich and middle layers rose by twelve and seventeen percentage points. Support from the urban rich and middle layers rose far more sharply (by sixteen and eighteen percentage points) than from the poor (nine percentage points).

75 Cited in Sumanta Banerjee (2008): 'Goodbye Socialism', *Economic and Political Weekly*, 26 January.

76 This is based 'on the ground that they had been driven out of East Bengal by Muslims'. Soma Marik and Kunal Chattopadhyay (2014): 'The Defeat of the Left Front and the Search for Alternative Leftism', *Radical Socialist*, 15 April.

77 For detailed comments on this, see 'India: Calcutta Murder for Inter-Religious Marriage: Commentary in the Media', 18 October 2007 at http://www.sacw.net/article1040.html, accessed on 4 September 2014.

78 Based on a post-poll sample survey. CSDS (2011): 'Fifteenth Assembly Elections in West Bengal', *Economic and Political Weekly*, 18 June, pp. 142–45.

79 Jyotiprasad Chatterjee and Suprio Basu (2014): 'Bipolarity to Multipolarity: Emerging Political Geometry in West Bengal', *Research Journal Social Sciences*, Vol. 22, No. 2. These figures are based on a post-poll sample survey by CSDS–Lokniti.

Chapter 6: Historic Triumph in Kerala

1   For instance, T.M. Thomas Isaac and P.K. Michael Tharakan (1995): 'Kerala: Towards a New Agenda', *Economic and Political Weekly*, 5–12 August, which summarizes the findings of a huge International Congress on Kerala Studies in August 1994, organized by the AKG Centre for Research and Studies, Trivandrum, and attended by 1,600 people, at which more than 600 papers were read and debated at seventeen venues.

2   Robin Jeffrey, who has done outstanding work on Kerala's social and political history, makes an acute observation: 'Nothing more vividly illustrates the transformation of Kerala in the 20th century than the way people use their hands. In the old Kerala that began to dissolve rapidly in the 1920s, a low-caste man put "his left hand on his breast, and his right over his mouth", if he dared to speak to his superiors, "for fear his breath may pollute the air". By the 1960s, however, it was more likely that men—and increasingly women too—would use their hands differently: as clenched fists, shaken above their heads, as they chanted "Inquilab Zindabad" (victory to revolution) and marched in demonstrations. If gestures of the hands provide a metaphor, in old Kerala they contained and controlled, kept things private and within bounds; in the new Kerala, they asserted, challenged and reached out to a public world and a public political process. And by public world, women have come to occupy a place that is remarkable in India, just as they once enjoyed a notable—though different—autonomy in the contained worlds of old Kerala.' Jeffrey (1993): *Politics, Women and Well-Being: How Kerala Became 'a Model'*, Delhi, Oxford University Press, p. 1.

3   The Nairs partly took the place of the Kshatriyas, but were regarded as Shudras by the Nambooodiri Brahmins. The function of the Vaishyas as traders, businessmen and moneylenders was to some extent performed by Muslims and Syrian Christians, but 'neither has fulfilled the role often attributed' to that varna. T.J. Nossiter (1982): *Communism in Kerala: A Study in Political Adaptation*, Delhi, Oxford University Press, p. 26.

4   Richard W. Franke and Barbara H. Chasin (1994): *Kerala: Radical Reform as Development in an Indian State*, San Francisco, Institute for

Food and Development Policy, available at files.eric.ed.gov/fulltext/ED400149.pdf

5   T.J. Nossiter (1988): *Marxist State Governments in India: Politics, Economics and Society*, London and New York, Pinter Publishers, p. 40, argues that this makes the village 'more of an administrative convenience than a spatially distinct reality'.

6   So considered by the Namboodiri Brahmins.

7   For an account of these movements, see E.M.S. Namboodiripad (1984): *Kerala: Society and Politics; a Historical Survey*, New Delhi, National Book Centre, and (1968): *Kerala: Yesterday, Today and Tomorrow*, Calcutta, National Book Agency; T.M. Thomas Isaac (1985): 'From Caste Consciousness to Class Consciousness: Alleppey Coir Workers during the Inter-War Period', *Economic and Political Weekly*, 26 January; Robin Jeffrey (1974): 'The Social Origins of a Caste Association 1875–1905: the Founding of the SNDP Yogam', *South Asia*, No. 4, October; and (1994): *The Decline of Nair Dominance: Society and Politics in Travancore 1847–1908*, New Delhi, Manohar Publishers; and V.K. Ramachandran (1997): 'On Kerala's Development Achievements', in Jean Dreze and Amartya Sen: *Indian Development: Selected Regional Perspectives*, Delhi, Oxford University Press, to which this section is indebted.

8   T.J. Nossiter (1988), p. 49. Ramachandran (1997) cites the prevalent disjuncture between low caste and high economic status through the case of Alamoottil Channar, 'one of the two owners in Travancore of private automobiles in the 1920s': 'When [his] car got to public roads on which persons of the caste were not permitted, he got out of the car and ran along to a point where he could get back in, to which his Nayar chauffeur drove the car. He also had roads built on this private estate on which to drive his car', p. 307. Swami Vivekananda, the Hindu reformer, who visited south India in 1892, termed Kerala 'a madhouse of caste'. Nossiter (1988), p. 49. Even the privileged upper castes of Kerala nurtured ultra-orthodox prejudices against modern means of communications. In the first decade of the twentieth century, 'a Namboodiri Brahmin was ostracised in Kerala for daring to travel by train and Kerala Brahmins thought their community degraded by taking tea'. This, when Brahmins and other upper castes in Bengal

invested in Western-style hotels and 'took active part in tanneries, wine shops and other business ...' Nossiter (1988), p. 120.

9   For instance, 'Malabar's most famous temple of Guruvayoor, owned by the biggest landowner in the district', denied entry to four-fifths of all Hindus. In 1931, a campaign was launched to open the temple to the entire community. Gandhi intervened to break a protest fast of the campaign 'in exchange for nothing more than an understanding that the temple would be made available to the lower castes after a decent interval ...' Nossiter (1988), p. 47.

10   V. K. Ramachandran (1997), pp. 305–313

11   Isaac and Tharakan (1995), p. 1995.

12   Robin Jeffrey (1994): 'Kerala's Story', *Economic and Political Weekly*, 5 March; Jeffrey (1993); his (1991): 'Matriliny, Women, Development— and a Typographical Error', *Pacific Affairs*, Vol. 63, No. 4 (Fall), pp. 85–89, and his (2004–05): 'Legacies of Matriliny: The Place of Women and the "Kerala Model"', *Pacific Affairs*, Vol. 78, No. 1 (Winter), pp. 647–64. This emphasis on the dissolution of the matrilineal system is questioned by T.J. Nossiter (1982), who argues against any 'simple causal connection' between communist support and socio-economic or ecological factors specific to Kerala. While Nossiter does not dispute that 'the break-up of the joint family system was certainly a factor in the social experience of that generation of young men who provided the leadership of the emergent communist movement in the 1930s', speaking of caste Hindus 'as *deracines* may exaggerate the degree to which the traditional family system has changed ... More important, Jeffrey does not clearly establish that the *deracines* were disproportionately attracted to communism.' Ibid., pp. 66–67. A more comprehensive study, based on multi-causal explanations, is called for, but to this writer's mind, Jeffrey's argument must remain an important component of such an endeavour.

13   Daniel Lerner (1958): *The Passing of Traditional Society*, New York, Free Press, p. 64. I am grateful for this reference to Robin Jeffrey, who too has quoted it approvingly.

14   For instance, in 1921, 'the proportion of literate women in Travancore was nearly eight times greater than that for India as a whole: 15 per cent of all females were literate in Travancore; in India, 1.9 per cent'.

Robin Jeffrey (1987): 'Culture and Governments: How Women Made Kerala Literate', *Pacific Affairs*, Vol. 60, No. 4, (Fall), p. 463.

15 P.K. Michael Tharakan (1984): 'Socio-Economic Factors in Educational Development: Case of 19th-Century Travancore', *Economic and Political Weekly*, 10 and 17 November.

16 Ibid.

17 Cited in Jeffrey (1993), p. 56. This declaration was itself preceded almost seventy years earlier by the Royal Rescript issued on behalf of the rani of Travancore, which said: 'The state should defray the entire cost of the education of its people in order that there might be no backwardness in the spread of enlightenment among them, that by diffusion of education they might become better subjects and public servants and that the reputation of the state may be enhanced thereby.' Cited in Ramachandran (1997), p. 268. However, there was little action on this until much later.

18 Ramachandran (1997), p. 270.

19 Jeffrey (1987), p. 462.

20 Robert L. Hardgrave (1973), 'The Kerala Communists: Contradictions of Power', in Paul Brass and Marcus F. Franda (eds): *Radical Politics in South Asia*, Cambridge (Mass.), The MIT Press, pp. 119–20. According to Hardgrave, Krishna Pillai 'received his early political training in the Indian National Congress' and exercised a 'formative influence' in the growth and development of the communist movement.

21 The CPI(M)-Kerala's historical note on the party's evolution (http://www.cpimkerala.org/eng/history-2.php?n=1) mentions several names of such prisoners such as 'Kiran Chandra Das, brother of Jithendra Das, Kamal Nath Thivari, Sen Gupta, T.N. Chandravarthi and Sarath Chandra Acharya' and quotes E.M.S. Namboodiripad as saying: 'It will not be a big exaggeration to say that seeds of Left, Congress and Congress Socialist movements were sown at Kannur jail …' These prisoners ran 'informal' political education classes for the Kerala activists. Some of the latter, including Krishna Pillai and K.P. Gopalan, were so inspired by them that they formed a branch of 'the Bengal terrorist organization Anushilan Samiti'. T.J. Nossiter (1982), p. 70.

22 Cited in Richard W. Franke and Barbara H. Chasin (2000): 'Is the Kerala Model Sustainable?: Lessons from the Past: Prospects for

the Future' in Govindan Parayil (ed.) (2000), *The Kerala Model of Development: Perspectives on Development and Sustainability*, London, Zed Books, p. 25.

23   Nossiter (1982), p. 71.

24   Ibid., pp. 71–72.

25   Ibid.

26   From just 3,000 in 1934, Congress membership in Kerala reportedly soared to 60,000 in 1938–39. http://www.cpimkerala.org/eng/history-2.php?n=1

27   Nossiter (1982), p. 72.

28   Ibid., pp. 75–76 and 82–83.

29   Ibid., p. 84.

30   Ibid., pp. 84–85.

31   K. Damodaran (1975): 'Memoirs of an Indian Communist', *New Left Review* I/93, September–October.

32   Nossiter (1982), p. 85.

33   Cited in ibid., p. 86. Namboodiripad endorses this assessment in *A Short History of the Peasant Movement in Kerala (1943)* reproduced in his (1985), *Selected Writings*, Vol. 2, Calcutta, National Book Agency.

34   As discussed in Chapters 1 and 2, the CPI's position went through many zigzags later.

35   Robin Jeffrey (1991): 'Jawaharlal Nehru and the Smoking Gun: Who Pulled the Trigger on Kerala's Communist Government in 1959?' *The Journal of Commonwealth and Comparative Politics*, Vol. 29, No. 1, p. 74.

36   The CPI's commitment to linguistic states was underscored by A.K. Gopalan, its leader in the Lok Sabha, in 1952 when he asserted that 'India's most important problem, the communists' No 1 goal' was the formation of linguistic provinces. Although the party dissociated itself from the 'communal and anti-North' slogans of the Dravida parties, its Madurai congress (1953) strongly backed 'wider provincial autonomy' and creation of linguistic states. Cited in Nossiter (1982): p. 119.

37   Ibid., p. 89.

38   Ibid., p. 38.

39   Nossiter (1988), p. 42.

40   Cited in Ramachandran (1997), pp. 260–61.

41   Nossiter (1982): p. 95.

42   Ibid.

43   He was drawn to the Congress Left before he was exposed to Marxist ideas, and attended the Payyanur conference of the provincial Congress in 1928. 'Nehru's socialist leanings within the Indian National Congress had attracted EMS's admiration.' http://www.frontline.in/static/html/fl1507/15070140.htm (accessed 30 July 2014).

44   Hardgrave (1973), p. 122.

45   http://www.cpimkerala.org/eng/history-2.php?n=1

46   It has been said that 'no Indian communist intellectual and leader has a greater "localist" image than does EMS Namboodiripad ... [He] is one of the few Indian communist leaders who have tried to apply Marxism creatively to an interpretation of Indian social realities. A Marxian analysis persuades him that Kerala is riper than most other parts of India for radical social change. To Namboodiripad, the principal distinctive feature of Kerala is the fact that "field cultivation here does not, in a normal year, require artificial irrigation canals and other public works ... centralised government could not develop [in Kerala] "because it had no role in production".' Bhabhani Sen Gupta (1978): *Communism in Indian Politics*, New Delhi, Young Asian Publications, p.173.

47   21 March 1957; cited in Sen Gupta (1978): pp. 178–79.

48   Nossiter (1982): p. 94.

49   Ibid.

50   Namboodiripad 'is said to have played a key role' in the drafting of the report of the CPI central committee to the Palghat congress, which was subtle and ambiguous, 'urgent, but ultimately pragmatic'. Nossiter (1982): pp. 120–21. The report stated: 'Even though the Indian National Congress is a political party of the bourgeoisie having in its fold many landlords there is a large number of democrats in it. It has a democratic anti-imperialist tradition. Our attitude to the Congress Party should be one of strengthening those forces within the Congress, which take comparatively progressive stand. We must exhort them to fight against the monopolist feudalist reactionaries who attempt to tighten their hold on the Congress. In matters like implementation of agrarian reforms and the execution of laws aimed at

the good of the people we must request the members of the Congress to join us in urging the government to expedite. We must also try to make common cause on such issues with Congress committees.' www.firstministry.kerala.gov.in/background.htm, accessed on 30 July 2014.

51 These three tendencies first became clearly evident at the third (Madurai) congress of the CPI, held in 1953. Their interplay would have a major impact on the party's tactical line and its political and organizational cohesion, and eventually result in the CPI–CPI(M) split of 1964.

52 Nossiter (1982): p. 121.

53 Victor M. Fic (1970): *Kerala: Yenan of India*, Bombay, Nachiketa Publications, pp. 67–70. Also Nossiter (1982): pp. 121–22.

54 For instance, by R. Ramakrishnan Nair (1965): *How Communists Came to Power in Kerala*, Trivandrum, Kerala Academy of Political Science.

55 Cited in C.P. Bhambri (2010): *Coalition Politics in India*, Delhi, Shipra Publications, p. 49.

56 Ibid.

57 Jeffrey (1991), pp. 75–76.

58 Ronald J. Herring (1983): *Land to the Tiller: The Political Economy of Agrarian Reform in South Asia*, Delhi, Oxford University Press, p. 157.

59 E.M.S. Namboodiripad (1974): *Conflicts and Crisis: Political India*, Bombay, Orient Longman, p. 54.

60 V.K. Ramachandran (1997), p. 295.

61 Ibid.

62 Herring (1983), p. 170.

63 Ramachandran (1997), p. 295.

64 Herring (1983), p. 167.

65 Ramachandran (1997), p. 295.

66 Reported in an official survey (1966–67): which also reported that almost 84 per cent of households owning 25 acres or more leased out their land, which itself accounted for nearly 64 per cent of their owned area. 'Thus land redistribution in Kerala was primarily *via* the abolition of tenancy, rather than *via* a ceiling reform, and consequently favoured those with a stronger traditional claim on the land—the tenants—than that of agricultural labourers.' Herring

(1980): 'Abolition of Landlordism in Kerala: a Redistribution of Privilege', *Economic and Political Weekly*, Review of Agriculture, 28 June, p. A-65.

67 The possibility of instituting more radical reforms—including transfer of land to tenants with no (or token) compensation to the landlord, special treatment for small tenants, lower land ceilings, and more ambitious redistribution—does not seem to have been debated within the CPI. Nor was the question asked as to whether a more radical course might not have generated more powerful popular support (as well as opposition from landed interests), and on balance might have been preferable. After all, the CPI government was soon dismissed. This was not an academic issue then, as might seem in retrospect.

68 Jeffrey (1991) argues (p. 83) after reviewing the events of 1959 at length: 'The dismissal of the communist government shows a quintessential Nehru: thinking aloud about principles but allowing events to take their course. That course, moreover, was increasingly determined by close associates who attempted to manipulate, rather than persuade, a tiring man.... Who pulled the trigger on the communist government in Kerala? Kerala Congressmen loaded the gun and pointed it; Mrs Gandhi, anti-communists and the Intelligence Bureau in New Delhi cocked the hammer; Nehru happened to be holding it when it went off.' The dismissal revealed a good deal more about the 'Congress system' than about communism. It marked a big shift in the Congress's character and internal dynamics. Jeffrey concludes: Nehru's 'apparent bemusement suggested that the political system, in which he was the leading actor, was changing in ways that his daughter comprehended better than he'.

69 In September 1955 she extensively toured Kerala, where she 'bitterly attacked the communists for betrayal of the national cause during the Quit India movement'. Barely three months after taking over as Congress president in February 1959, Indira Gandhi visited Kerala and declared her dismay at 'the discontent prevailing among the people ... against the communist administration'. Both cited in Jeffrey (1991).

70 Mullick (1972): *My Years with Nehru, 1948–64*, New Delhi, Allied Publishers, pp. 339–40.

71 See Paul M. McGarr (2013): *The Cold War in South Asia: Britain, the United States and the Indian Subcontinent, 1945–1965*, Cambridge, UK, Cambridge University Press, especially Chapter 2.

72 Moynihan disclosed in 1979 that the US deployed CIA funds to try to avert a prospective communist party election victory. He wrote: 'I had pressed the embassy to go back over the whole of our quarter-century in India, to establish just what we had been up to … We had twice, but only twice, interfered in Indian politics to the extent of providing money to a political party. Both times this was done in the face of a prospective communist victory in a state election, once in Kerala and once in West Bengal … Both times the money was given to the Congress party, which had asked for it. Once it was given to Mrs Gandhi herself, who was then a party official.' Moynihan, with Suzanne Weaver (1979): *A Dangerous Place*, Bombay, Allied Publishers, p. 41.

73 A recent biography of Ellsworth Bunker, a veteran US diplomat and ambassador to India in the late 1950s, reveals that the American embassy in New Delhi helped a clandestine operation by the CIA to dislodge the Namboodiripad government. This allegedly 'funded political demonstrations organized by the Congress party and other opposition groups that were designed to create a law and order situation' [in Kerala]. Howard B. Schaffer (2003): *Ellsworth Bunker: Global Troubleshooter, Vietnam Hawk*, Chapel Hill and London, University of North Carolina Press, pp. 67–68. An important Congress minister from Bombay and right-leaning political operator S.K. Patil reportedly acted as the conduit for the funds

74 McGarr (2013): p. 68.

75 This is based on K. Ravi Raman (2010): *Global Capital and Peripheral Labour: the History and Political Economy of Plantation Workers in India*, London, Routledge.

76 Ibid., pp. 147–48.

77 Cited in Ravi Raman (2010): p. 148.

78 On June 25, Nehru told the press that that the Central government would not intervene but he would not forbid the Congress from taking part in civil disobedience. Journalist Taya Zinkin, who was at the press conference, concluded that 'if statesmanship is to pat the

cabbage on the back and tickle the goat at the same time, Nehru is a statesman of genius'. Cited in Jeffrey (1991): p. 79.

79   Ibid.

80   Ibid.

81   This account is corroborated by former Intelligence Bureau chief B.N. Mullick (1972).

82   In 1964, the CPI split nationally, leading to the formation of the CPI(M). In Kerala, the CPI retained much of the undivided party's trade union support, particularly in Alleppey, Quilon and Ernakulam districts, and its middle-class and middle peasant base, as well as 'intermediate, middle-class party leaders and a few upper echelon leaders (M.N. Govindan Nair, C. Achutha Menon, T.V. Thomas and K. Damodaran)'. But the CPI(M) held much of the undivided party's mass base, including the support of small peasants and landless labourers, its trade unions in Malabar, and its best-known popular leaders including E.M.S. Namboodiripad, A.K. Gopalan, and many of its 'early founding members'. Hardgrave (1973): pp. 128–30. The CPI first claimed the support of 11,500 members and estimated that 9,000 members joined the CPI(M), while the CPI(M) figures were 19,000 for itself and 3,000 for the CPI which, says Hardgrave, corresponded 'more closely to reality'. The CPI's influence declined considerably after the split. In the 1965 assembly elections, only three of its seventy-eight candidates won, with 8.2 per cent of the vote, while forty of the seventy-three candidates fielded by the CPI(M) were elected, with 20 per cent of the vote. (Ibid.) However, after facing each other in opposition, and trading charges of making opportunist alliances, the two parties forged a united front in 1967 with five other parties, including the Indian Union Muslim League—a decision that Namboodiripad regretted later.

83   P. Radhakrishnan in a fine historical analysis argues that 'far from being a gift from an enlightened government, the modest reforms that have till now been legislated (though poorly, if at all, implemented) have been the outcome of long and protracted struggles by the peasants ... [E]ven though Kerala has a relatively better record than many other states both in the legislation and implementation of land reform measures, the process is far from complete.' P. Radhakrishnan

(1980): 'Peasant Struggles and Land Reforms in Malabar', *Economic and Political Weekly*, 13 December.

84 Herring (1983): p. 211.

85 Tiny, but probably enough to stave off starvation if planted with coconut, areca nut and other home-garden crops.

86 P. Radhakrishnan (1981): 'Land Reforms in Theory and Practice: the Kerala Experience', *Economic and Political Weekly*, Review of Agriculture, 26 December, pp. A-129–A-137.

87 Thus Radhakrishnan (1981) notes the resultant fall in the official estimates of the available surplus land from 1.75 million acres in 1957, to 115,000 acres in 1964, to less than 80,000 acres in 1970.

88 http://www.firstministry.kerala.gov.in/ptnaik_art.htm, accessed on 30 July 2014. Patnaik further says: 'To be sure, there were important segments of the poor who could not directly benefit much from the land reforms measures, such as the tribal population, fishermen and agricultural labourers (whose gain was confined to house-sites). But even though the task is not complete in this sphere ... what has been achieved is nonetheless quite remarkable.'

89 Mohamed Aslam (1977): 'Land Reforms in Jammu and Kashmir', *Social Scientist*, Vol. 6, No. 4, pp. 59–64.

90 Radhakrishnan (1981), pp. A-129–A-137.

91 Ibid.

92 Herring (1983): p. 211–12.

93 See Herring (1980): p. A-59, especially the introductory abstract.

94 Herring (1980) relates this to 'Kerala's agrarian structure', in which 'the larger holdings contained a high percentage of leased-in land, whereas the poorest, landless tenants had very small holdings'; therefore, 'conferring ownership rights on tenanted lands was certain to benefit relatively rich peasants more than relatively poor ones.... The classes least benefited were those most in need of benefits—the poor peasants and agricultural labourers. The reasons ... are primarily found in the strategy and conceptualization of the reforms, not their implementation.' A basic conceptual problem with the legislation was that it treated tenancy not as a form of property, but 'as a homogeneous type of production relations', abstracted from the labour process and control over land. 'But, to paraphrase Lenin, there are tenants and there are tenants. For historical reasons, some tenants of Kerala

were of relatively high social status and economic power ... typically employing sub-tenants or wage labourers to cultivate their holdings... [Besides] "cultivation" was defined to include supervision of hired labour or other production arrangements, or "simply bearing the risk of cultivation"... Tenancy, functionally was simply a different form of land control, and thus of labour control—control of the labour process and its surplus ...' This argument relates in a fascinating manner to the Mode of Production debate (see Appendix 1). Regrettably, space does not permit further discussion on this.

95 Herring (1980) also comments on how the tenancy provisions in Section 72 of the Land Reforms Act could benefit large landholders. The reform's result was 'the virtual exclusion of the truly landless, those whose claim on the land was more tenuous than that of the tenants'. He adds: 'The political consequences of the Kerala model of reform are important, intriguing and unknown. There would be a certain irony if Lenin's fears about land reform come to pass, if redistribution of land through a process of embourgeoisement converted the formerly radical core of the peasant movement, which has been the heart of left politics in Kerala, into a relatively privileged class of proprietors wedded to the status quo politics of defending their privileges from those less privileged. The evidence on this question is not yet in.'

96 Ramachandran (1997): p. 299, who also quotes Namboodiripad from an April 1992 interview as saying that landlordism 'of the old type' has ceased to exist, but there is still 'landlordism of another type', based on cultivation through wage labour, usury, and dominance in rural trade.

97 Herring (1980) underlines the 'important' constraints imposed by the courts and the Centre and says: 'The framers of the reforms were quite conscious of their limitations and argued explicitly that the reforms necessarily were pro-capitalist, anti-feudal in character, reflecting the primary contradiction of the period.'

98 A.V. Jose (1994) records a 63 per cent increase in real agricultural wages in Kerala between the early 1970s and the late 1980s, the highest for any Indian state, and attributes this to 'social policy ... [and] redistributive transfers [which] effectively complemented labour market interventions'. Jose (1994): 'Social Policy towards Wage Determination: Some Lessons from the Indian States', cited

in Ramachandran (1997), p. 298. An additional factor, no doubt, was emigration to the Gulf, which created labour shortages in Kerala, further raising wage rates. This analysis complements Jose's solidly founded empirical work on agricultural wages in India over the decades. Kerala has consistently held the number one rank in rural wages since the late 1990s. Agricultural labour wages in Kerala have further risen (in 2014) to Rs 350, even Rs 400–450 a day, the highest rate in India.

99 John Kurien attributes this to 'the compulsions of [independent India's] parliamentary democratic system', which 'made political parties anxious to see their efforts at politicization of social causes pay off in the form of votes. As a result, irrespective of their position on the political spectrum all the parties were involved in taking up a variety of causes which focused on the issues in the agrarian and related natural resources sectors and the populations involved therein.' Kurien (1995): 'The Kerala Model: Its Central Tendency and the Outlier', *Social Scientist*, Vol. 23, No. 1/3, January–March, p. 97.

100 The use of the term is of course disputed, among others, by Amartya Sen, who emphasizes the importance of 'enlightened public policy' which provides health care and other social services, but 'in conjunction with social institutions and practices ... The heroic view of the state as a "Lone Ranger" cleaning up the Wild West is as unreal as it is pernicious in trivializing and ignoring positive functions of other social and economic institutions.' Amartya Sen (1990): 'Public Action to Remedy Hunger', Arturo Tanco Memorial Lecture organized by The Hunger Project, New York, 2 August. See also *The New York Review of Books*, 20 December 1990 and 24 October 1990 issues on this.

101 Franke and Chasin, enthusiastic supporters of the Model, especially in its 'sustainable' form, define it as: 'A set of high material quality of life indicators coinciding with low per capita incomes, both distributed across nearly the entire population of Kerala; a set of wealth and resource redistribution programmes that have largely brought about the high material quality of life indicators; and high levels of political participation and activism among ordinary people along with substantial numbers of dedicated leaders at all levels. Kerala's mass activism and committed cadre were able to function

within a largely democratic structure which their activism has served to reinforce'. Franke and Chasin (2000): p. 17.

102 Moni Nag (1989): 'Political Awareness as a Factor in Accessibility of Health Services: A Case Study of Rural Kerala and West Bengal', *Economic and Political Weekly*, 25 February.

103 Franke and Chasin (2000): pp. 24–25.

104 Patrick Heller (1996): 'Social Capital as a Product of Class Mobilization and State Intervention: Industrial Workers in Kerala, India', *World Development*, Vol. 24, No. 6, pp. 1055–71. As he puts it: 'Keralites of all walks of life, it would seem, have an irresistible inclination to combine, associate and organize, and to do so without the outbreaks of violent disorder Huntingtonians might have anticipated. Thus, despite extremely high levels of social mobilization, Kerala has largely been spared the sectarian and casteist violence that has recently been on the upswing throughout most of India.'

105 Prerna Singh (2000): 'We-Ness and Welfare: A Longitudinal Analysis of Social Development in Kerala, India', *World Development*, Vol. 39, No. 2. She cites reports by reputed anthropologists like Joan Mencher and Kathleen Gough of public vigilance, such as 'a massive demonstration' prompted by the absence of a physician at a health centre, and an instance when 'angry neighbours dragged a physician from a cinema and forced him to go to the hospital to deliver the baby of a woman who was in great pain'.

106 Kurien (1995).

107 Ibid.

108 Ramachandran (1997): p. 256.

109 Following UNESCO's criterion, which defines it as a society with more than 85 per cent literacy among the adult population, according to Ramachandran (1997): p. 256. There have been slippages, though, since then.

110 CDS–UN (1975): *Poverty, Unemployment and Development Policy: A Case Study of Selected Issues with Reference to Kerala*, New York, United Nations, and reissued subsequently.

111 N. Krishnaji (2007): 'Kerala Milestones: On the Parliamentary Road to Socialism', *Economic and Political Weekly*, 9 June, pp. 2169–76.

112 Ibid.

113 Bill McKibben (1998): 'What is True Development? The Kerala Model', http://www.ashanet.org/library/articles/kerala.199803.html, accessed on 29 July 2014.

114 Ibid.

115 William M. Alexander (1994): 'Exceptional Kerala: Efficient Use of Resources and Life Quality in a Non-Affluent Society', *Ecological Perspectives* in *Science, Humanities and Economics,* Vol. 3, No. 4, Heidelberg, Spectrum Akademischer Verlag GmbH; cited in Joseph Tharamangalam (1998): 'The Perils of Social Development Without Economic Growth: The Development Debacle of Kerala, India', *Bulletin of Concerned Asian Scholars,* Vol. 30, No. 1, pp. 23–34.

116 Kerala often used innovative methods to fight caste discrimination. For instance, Namboodiri children were granted scholarships, in the 1950s and '60s, to encourage them to attend school and sit with the children of other castes.

Chapter 7: Cracks in the Kerala Edifice

1 Some of these issues and trends were analysed early on by K.P. Kannan and others in two special sections of the *Economic and Political Weekly,* 1 and 15 September 1990 over a total of fourteen articles. See, in particular, Kannan's overview, 'Kerala Economy at the Crossroads', in the first of these, and K.K. George, 'Kerala's Fiscal Crisis: A Diagnosis', in the second issue. The latter formed the basis of George's influential monograph (1993): *Limits to Kerala Model of Development: An Analysis of Fiscal Crisis and Its Implications,* Trivandrum, Centre for Development Studies. Agrarian reform did not lead to increased food production. One reason was that the tenant who benefited from the reform looked upon land as an asset to be used to further the family's middle-class aspirations. He either sold the land to finance the education of his children to ensure their place in the growing middle-class, or switched from food crops to more profitable cash crops. A shortage of farm labourers developed as children from traditional farm workers' families got educated and quit the agricultural sector. High wages made rice cultivation increasingly uneconomical.

2 T.M. Thomas Isaac and P.K. Michael Tharakan (1995): 'Kerala: Towards a New Agenda', *Economic and Political Weekly*, 5–12 August, pp. 1993–2004, which summarizes important proceedings of the August 1994 International Congress on Kerala Studies, and to which this section owes a great deal. For more information on the congress, see Endnote 1 in Chapter 6.

3 In 1984–85, '69.3 per cent of the total number of educational institutions were owned by private agencies. These institutions accounted for 58 per cent of [total] enrolment.' K.K. George and N. Ajith Kumar (1999): Working Paper 3, Kochi, Centre for Socio-Economic and Environmental Studies (Henceforth CSES). Since then, this proportion has greatly risen. The role of the private sector expanded greatly in tertiary health care too. By 1995–96, the National Sample Survey's fifty-second round showed, 59.9 per cent of those who received hospitalized treatment in rural areas, and 61.4 per cent in urban areas, did so in private hospitals.

4 K.K. George (2011): 'Kerala Economy: Growth, Structure, Strength and Weakness', Working Paper 25, Kochi, CSES; and Achin Chakraborty (2005): 'Kerala's Changing Development Narratives', *Economic and Political Weekly*, 5 February. According to George, 'the annual growth rate ... of state income between 1971–72 and 1986–87 was just 1.88 per cent'. Chakraborty states: 'While between 1970–71 and 1980-81 Kerala's NSDP (at 1970–71 prices) grew at 2.27 per cent per annum, between 1980-81 and 1987–88 the growth rate further came down to a mere 1.16 per cent, even though India's NDP grew at 4.71 per cent in the same period.'

5 Isaac and Tharakan (1995).

6 George (1993): p. 133. George wrote: '[T]he Kerala model of development has almost reached the end of its tether. The paradoxical phenomenon of rapid social development unaccompanied by corresponding gains in economic growth has been exhausting itself.' He concluded: 'The state's fiscal crisis and its economic crisis are reinforcing each other. Due to paucity of funds, there has been deceleration in the state's plan expenditure in recent years. This along with other exogenous factors [has] contributed to a slow expansion of the state's resources base. As a result, the own resources of the state are inadequate, despite larger resource mobilization efforts, to meet even its current non-plan commitments.'

7 Cited in Isaac and Tharakan (1995): p. 1994.

8 Isaac and Tharakan (1995): p. 1996.

9 In the 1970s, unemployment had more than tripled as a proportion of the workforce, from 4 to 13 per cent. K.P. Kannan (1998): 'Political Economy of Labour and Development in Kerala: Some Reflections on the Dilemmas of a Socially Transforming Labour Force in a Slow-Growing Economy', Working Paper 284, Trivandrum, Centre for Development Studies.

10 Isaac and Tharakan (1995): p. 1996. After the 1980s, the situation worsened. George added: 'The chronic unemployment problem has been the bane of the state eclipsing all its other achievements. Though there was growth in state income from the late 1980s, it was largely jobless growth ... Unemployment rate in Kerala for rural areas is 15.8 per cent against the national average of 2.5 per cent in 2004-05.... For the urban areas, the rate was 19.9 per cent against the national average of 5.3 per cent ... Unemployment rates for the educated in Kerala are the highest for both rural and urban areas among the major states. The unemployment rate for educated persons in rural areas of Kerala was 29.6 per cent against the all- India figure of 8.5 per cent. The corresponding figures for urban Kerala and India were 29.6 per cent and 8.2 per cent.' George (2011).

11 Kannan (1998).

12 By the end of the 1990s, the work participation rate for women was '22.9 per cent ... one of the lowest in India. This low labour force participation is accompanied by high rates of unemployment. The most tragic failure of development in the state is the acute unemployment of both men and women ... the highest [in India] ... in rural as well as urban areas. The overall unemployment rate in Kerala is 11.4 [per cent], with a wide gender gap of 21.5 per cent for women and 7.4 per cent for men.' Alice Sebastian and K. Navaneetham (undated): 'Gender, Education and Work: Determinants of Women's Employment in Kerala', http://www.isical.ac.in/~wemp/Papers/PaperAliceSebastianAndKNavanitham.doc, accessed on 30 July 2014.

13 Sebastian and Navaneetham added: 'The percentage of women in paid jobs in the state is slightly less than 23 per cent. This is much less than the work participation rate of women in other Indian states with far lower levels of literacy ... the proportion of jobless women in Kerala is

ten times the national average …While the male work participation rates improved in the last two decades, female work participation rates declined … Comparing it with the all-India pattern, while male work participation rate in Kerala is higher than [in] India (1999–2000): the trend is reversed in the case of women. This is paradoxical given the fact that, women in Kerala are believed to enjoy a higher status in terms of educational and health achievements compared to their counterparts elsewhere in the country.' Ibid.

14 Isaac and Tharakan (1995): p. 2001.

15 See note 2.

16 Ibid.

17 Isaac and Tharakan (1995): p. 1993.

18 Richard W. Franke and Barbara H. Chasin (2000): 'Is the Kerala Model Sustainable?: Lessons from the Past: Prospects for the Future', in Govindan Parayil (ed.) (2000): *The Kerala Model of Development: Perspectives on Development and Sustainability*, London, Zed Books.

19 Isaac and Tharakan (1995): p. 1993.

20 John Kurien (1995): 'The Kerala Model: Its Central Tendency and the Outlier', *Social Scientist*, Vol. 23, Nos. 1–3, January–March, p. 87.

21 Ibid.

22 Ibid. Even worse, there was a 'strong gender bias in favour of male children as evidenced in the sex ratio of 972 females to 1000 males', compared to the all-Kerala situation where the ratio was 1032:1000.

23 Franke and Chasin (2000): p. 28. The most telling component of such destruction is loss of good forest cover, with thick (over 70 per cent) canopy, which decreased from 27 per cent in 1965, to 17 per cent in 1973, to 10 per cent in 1983. Cited in K.P. Kannan and N. Pushpangadan (1988): 'Agricultural Stagnation in Kerala: an Exploratory Analysis', *Economic and Political Weekly*, 24 September, pp. A-125–A-126. The best figures for later years for 'dense' or 'very dense' forests available from the Forest Survey of India (http://www. fsi.nic.in) do not suggest a significant improvement, in particular between 1995 and 2013 for which comparable numbers exist. August 2011 'Report of the Western Ghats Ecology Expert Panel' (Madhav Gadgil Committee), http://www.moef.nic.in/downloads/public-information/wg-23052012.pdf, accessed on 2 September 2014.

24 Franke and Chasin (2000): p. 28. The authors add: 'Repairing environmental damage is among the costliest of human endeavours, adding difficulty to a stagnant economy with little surplus to invest in renewal. Kerala's ecological problems are exacerbated by the state's high population density and its intense land use that make it difficult to set aside protected areas. Poverty drives settlers on to hillsides too steep for sustainable cultivation and forces people to cut the dangerously depleted forests for firewood to sell.'

25 This was one of India's earliest great environmental struggles and became a cause célèbre the 1970s.

26 This issue is further discussed below and in Chapter 8.

27 V. Raman Kutty (2012): 'Rethinking the Kerala "Model" in Health', *Seminar*, September, pp. 45–48. Also Raman Kutty (1999): 'Development of Kerala's Health Services', in M.A. Oommen (ed.), *Rethinking Development: Kerala's Development Experience*, Vol. 2, New Delhi, Institute of Social Sciences. Raman Kutty was based at the Achutha Menon Centre for Health Science Studies in Trivandrum.

28 P.G.K. Panikar and C.R. Soman (1985): *Health Status of Kerala: The Paradox of Economic Backwardness and Health Development*, Trivandrum, Centre for Development Studies.

29 [which] 'reported a high prevalence of chronic non-communicable diseases like coronary heart disease and diabetes ... about a third of the deaths were attributable to heart disease, and deaths due to infections were only a small proportion ... Apart from these "lifestyle" diseases, which could be attributed to large-scale transformations in society, Kerala ... also witnessed the reappearance, or even the resurgence, of infectious diseases: epidemics of dengue, chikungunya, rat fever and hepatitis became an annual feature in the state. This indicated large-scale environmental degradation ...' Raman Kutty (2012), p. 46.

30 Ibid., p. 47.

31 K.K. George and N. Ajith Kumar (1999): 'What is Wrong with Kerala's Education System?' CSES Working Paper No 3, Kochi, CSES. The authors say: 'The progress of a sample cohort in schools showed that only 73 per cent of the students joining standard I reach the tenth standard. In the case of SC students, only 59 per cent reach the tenth standard. Sixty per cent of the SC students drop out

by the tenth standard. Another major indicator of the inefficiency of Kerala's school education system is the large-scale failure of the students in the matriculation examination. Only about 50 per cent of the students who appear for the examination get through in spite of liberal valuation and provision of grace marks.'

32 Jandhyala B. G. Tilak (2001): 'Higher Education and Development in Kerala', Working Paper No 5, Kochi, CSES.

33 About thirty of the 150 papers presented at this conference were published in 1999 in two volumes edited by M.A. Oommen under the title *Rethinking Development: Kerala's Development Experience*, New Delhi, Institute of Social Sciences/Concept Publishing Company. Together with the multi-volume compendium produced by the 1994 congress, these contain a rich discussion of the evolution of the Kerala Model, its many problems, and the potential for its sustainability in the future.

34 Isaac and Tharakan (1995): p. 1996. An extreme position was adopted in this regard by Joseph Tharamangalam (1998): 'The Perils of Social Development without Economic Growth: The Development Debacle of Kerala, India', *Bulletin of Concerned Asian Scholars*, Vol. 30, No. 1, January–March, pp. 23–34.

35 As Achin Chakraborty (2005), p. 542, argues that Tharamangalam's view sees the lack of growth 'as inherent in the very pattern of development, which has been heavily welfare-oriented. Even though this line of argument appears to be close to [that of K.K. George], the two are fundamentally different. Those who emphasize fiscal limits to maintenance of high welfare expenditure nevertheless accept the assumption that the relationship between human development and economic growth is one of complementarity; economic growth is indeed needed to generate resources for social development. Tharamangalam's position, however, seems to reject the idea of complementarity itself.'

36 Isaac and Tharakan (1995): p. 1996. 'Many on the Left', they say, 'attributed the LDF's poor electoral performance in the late 1970s, especially in its traditional strongholds like Palakkad and Alappuzha, to such conflicts and divisions' and to the Front's alienation from 'the large body of petty owners'. Ibid.

37 I was first told about these by M.N.V. Nair, a sociologist and old friend, who returned to Kerala after retiring from the Indian Institute of Management, Bangalore, and joined a discussion group in Trivandrum. This was recently confirmed by social scientists Ninan Koshy, K.P. Kannan and K. Ravi Raman and political analyst B.R.P. Bhaskar. All of them, however, said that there was no concerted effort to turn these alternative ideas into concrete implemental proposals. When presented to LDF policymakers, they 'did not make much of an impact'.

38 Telephone conversation with B.R.P. Bhaskar, 30 March 2015.

39 A sharper focus on growth in the policy discourse of the 1980s seems to have edged out concerns about equitable distribution and proactive forms of state interventions in favour of the poor.

40 K.P. Kannan characterized this as a case of 'virtuous cycle of growth' arising out of the initial focus on human development. K.P. Kannan (2007): 'From Human Development to Economic Growth: Kerala's Turnaround in Growth Powered by Human Development, Remittances and Reform', in A. Vaidyanathan, and K.L. Krishna (eds) (2007): *Institutions and Markets in India's Development: Essays for K.N. Raj*, New Delhi, Oxford University Press.

41 The foregoing few paragraphs are paraphrased from Chakraborty (2005) and the *Human Development Report 2005*, prepared for the Kerala government by the Centre for Development Studies, Thiruvanthapuram. Since then Kerala's indices have further improved.

42 K.P. Kannan (2012): 'Transformations and Tribulations', *Seminar*, September, pp. 14–19. Kannan says these transformations are best understood as comprising 'four transitions': in demography, in health, in education and in the economy.

43 V. Raman Kutty (1999), pp. 433–34.

44 To this must be added the impact of growing international tourism in health and marketing of 'Ayurvedic' and 'health-promoting' products. 'Many people in the know allege that the diagnostic imaging and clinical laboratory industry thrived through unethical practices such as cutbacks to referring doctors …' Raman Kutty (2012).

45 Joseph Tharamangalam (2012): 'The Kerala Model of Development in the Era of Neoliberal Reforms: New Contradictions, Old and New Questions', IDS Working Paper, 11/1, 16 September, p. 17.

46 According to Tharamangalam (2012): 14 per cent of rural and 11 per cent of urban people in Kerala incurred 'catastrophic expenses (in excess of 15 per cent of their income) in health expenses ... [which] pushed 3.5 per cent of households in rural and 4.5 per cent in urban Kerala below the poverty line'.

47 Ibid.

48 *Human Development Report 2005*, p. 433.

49 Kannan (2012).

50 Ibid. Kannan adds: 'In 2007, one-third of the boys in the age group of 15–19 were in the labour force, [but two per cent of girls]; for the age group of 20–24, [the ratio] was 85 per cent for young men and only five per cent for young women.'

51 Ibid.

52 Ibid.

53 Interview with environmental activist Anitha Sharma in Thiruvananthapuram, 30 December 2013.

54 K.T. Rammohan (2012): 'Contemporary Politics: Horrors and Hopes', *Seminar*, September, pp. 26–32.

55 Ibid.

56 M.P. Basheer (2002): 'Broken Letters: Kerala's Neo-literates Lapse into Illiteracy', *India Together*, September. http://indiatogether.org/education/articles/brokenletters.htm

57 The report quotes Michael Tharakan, then with CDS, as saying: 'Lakhs of neo-literates have lost their skills and rejoined the ranks of illiterates. A six-month gap between the first and second phases coinciding with a change of government in June 1991 has proved fatal. Lack of political will and non-availability of the Continuing Education Programme (CEP) are the other reasons.'

58 Soma Wadhwa (2004): '...And he can keep it', *Outlook*, 12 July.

59 Wadhwa (2004).

60 Ibid. This is documented and analysed by J. Devika (2007): 'Fears of Contagion: Depoliticisation and Recent Conflicts over Politics in Kerala', *Economic and Political Weekly*, 23 June and by M. Sarita Varma (2012): 'Men, Women and the Fidgety Cat in the Kerala Cupboard', *Seminar* 637 (September), pp. 61–64. Also see J. Devika and Praveena Kodoth (2001): 'Sexual Violence and Predicament of Feminist Politics in Kerala', *Economic and Political Weekly*, 18 August.

61 For an enlightening discussion on this, see Carmel Cristy K.J., (2015): 'The Politics of Sexuality and Caste: Looking through Kerala's Public Space', in Satheese Chandra Bose and Shiju Sam Varughese (eds) (2015): *Kerala Modernity: Ideas, Spaces and Practices in Transition*, New Delhi, Orient BlackSwan.

62 As social scientist K. Saradamoni perceptively puts it: 'Weighed down by gold on every part of the body, brides here nowadays, whether Hindu, Muslim or Christian, can barely walk straight. We had no tradition of dowry, today it's commonplace.' Cited in Wadhwa (2004).

63 Rammohan (2012) provides a passionate yet thoughtful critique of Kerala's public culture and its dominant political practices.

64 http://www.thehindu.com/news/national/kerala/12-held-guilty-of-tp-chandrasekharan-murder/article5605223.ece?ref=relatedNews, accessed on 21 December 2014.

65 T.M. Thomas Isaac with Richard W. Franke (2000): *Local Democracy and Development: People's Campaign for Decentralised Planning in Kerala*, New Delhi, LeftWord Books, p. 6.

66 Patrick Heller (2001): 'Moving the State: The Politics of Democratic Decentralisation in Kerala, South Africa, and Porto Alegre', *Politics and Society*, Vol. 29, No. 1, March.

67 Presidential Address, International Congress on Kerala Studies, Trivandrum, AKG Centre for Research and Studies.

68 John Harriss (2000): 'Renewing Development and Deepening Democracy', *Frontline*, 19 August – 1 September.

69 This noteworthy initiative consists in organizing groups of youth and students to prepare an inventory of the natural resources available in and around a village/district through a systematic survey, as part of a larger exercise to marry them with the local people's needs for food, water, energy, etc., in cost-effective, equitable and environmentally sound ways. Besides promoting popular participation in planning, this has extraordinarily high educational value.

70 Michelle Williams (2008): *The Roots of Participatory Democracy: Democratic communists in South Africa and Kerala, India*, Sandton (South Africa), SG Distributors.

71 For a detailed description of the PPC, see Isaac and Franke (2000): and Williams (2008).

72 Isaac and Franke (2000): p. 256.

73　Isaac and Franke, cited in Harriss (2000).

74　Isaac and Franke (2000): pp. 136–47.

75　The PPC's limitations are discussed at greater length by several writers: M.K. Das (2000): 'Kerala's Decentralised Planning: Foundering Experiment', *Economic and Political Weekly*, 2 December; K.P. Kannan (2000): 'People's Planning, Kerala's Dilemma', *Seminar*, January; Robin Jeffrey (2000): 'Creating New Civic Culture', *Economic and Political Weekly*, 2 December; Rajan Gurukkal (2001): 'When a Coalition of Conflicting Interests Decentralises: A Theoretical Critique of Decentralisation Politics in Kerala', *Social Scientist*, Vol. 29, No. 9/10, September–October; Patrick Heller, K.N. Harilal and Shubham Chaudhuri (2007): 'Building Local Democracy: Evaluating the Impact of Decentralisation in Kerala, India', *World Development*, Vol. 35; No. 4; and K.N. Harilal (2013): 'Confronting Bureaucratic Capture', *Economic and Political Weekly*, 7 September.

76　Das (2000).

77　Ibid.

78　Ibid.

79　Jeffrey (2000). He writes: 'We need to know how all these little plans are intended in practice to add up to something that coheres at the state level … It is commendable that the local plans, calling as they did for more expenditure than there were funds, led to attempts to mobilize other resources … It is difficult to see the needed economic transformation emerging from these political reforms … the evidence to date leaves the big question unanswered: will grassroots political participation, however vigorous and genuine, bring about economic change and meaningful work for Kerala's people?'

80　http://planningcommission.nic.in/reports/peoreport/peoevalu/peo_kerala.pdf, accessed on 31 July 2014.

81　Gurukkal (2001): p. 60.

82　Ibid., p. 70. He argues (pp. 72–73): 'There is no sign of alternate political development anywhere in the state, paving the way for the transition from "representation" to "participation"… [T]he devolution of power to the local-level administration would … involve political empowerment of the poor and facilitate institutional development leading to structural changes in the local society. However, these have not happened to the anticipated extent in Kerala so far.' He concludes:

'This is a paradox but only ostensibly, for theoretically it is true too that a government under capitalist democracy put to decentralised planning cannot lead to structural changes. [F]or the government is a coalition of conflicting interests, incessantly pulled to the Left and Right. Theoretically the government cannot succeed beyond a point in empowering the weak, because it means the government joining the class war in favour of the poor, which is unlikely, as the government is an upper class instrument, ultimately.'

83 Das (2000).

84 Ibid.

85 Social activist I.V. Babu says: 'Had the PPC been propagated and carried out as envisioned by EMS, it would have given some relief to the toiling people while helping to contribute to the larger goal of building a People's Democratic Front. Instead, it was depicted as an alternate programme of revolution, which will create a 4th world. It created a lot of illusions among party activists … Its implementation also led to grassroots-level corruption …' (Email communication to the author, 30 July 2014.)

86 Telephone and email communication with the author, 15 July 2014.

87 K. Ravi Raman (2009): 'Asian Development Bank, Conditionalities, and the Social Democratic Governance: Kerala Model under Pressure', *Review of International Political Economy*, Vol. 16, No. 2, May, pp. 284–308.

88 Ibid.

89 http://archive.indianexpress.com/news/cpi-sees-red-over-kerala-adb-loan/18919/; http://www.downtoearth.org.in/node/5536; http://cadtm.org/IMG/pdf/ProtestAgainstADB_in_Kerala.pdf, all accessed on 2 March 2015.

90 My telephone conversation with Isaac, 3 April 2015. Isaac said the third component of the loan agreement, pertaining to urban development and sanitation was still in progress.

91 See S. Mohammed Irshad (2015): 'The Pipe Dreams of Development: Institutionalising Drinking Water Supply in Kerala', in Bose and Varughese (eds) (2015): pp. 162–78.

92 J. Devika and Binitha V. Thampi (2012): *New Lamps for Old: Gender Paradoxes of Political Decentralisation in Kerala*, New Delhi: Zubaan; (2007): 'Between "Empowerment" and "Liberation":

The Kudumbashree Initiative in Kerala', *Indian Journal of Gender Studies*, Vol. 14, No. 1, pp. 33–60; J Devika, Binitha V. Thampi and S. Anitha (2008): 'Final Report Gendering Governance or Governing Women? Politics, Patriarchy, and Democratic Decentralisation in Kerala State, India', Thiruvananthapuram, Centre for Development Studies, September. Also see, G. Williams, et al. (2011): 'Performing Participatory Citizenship: Politics and Power in Kerala's Kudumbashree Programme', *Journal of Development Studies*, Vol. 47, No. 8.

93 K.P. Kannan (2014): The New Panchayat Raj and its Development Initiatives: Reflections on Kerala's Record and its Successful Cases', Study prepared for the Research Unit in Local Level Development, Centre for Development Studies, Thiruvananthapuram. I am grateful to Kannan for sharing a working draft of this study.

94 Many political observers believe that the RSP's exit from the LDF could have been prevented. It was reportedly willing to accept the Pathanamthitta seat instead of Kollam. But the CPI(M) fielded a Congress defector from Pathanamthitta as an LDF-backed independent. CPI(M) state secretary P. Vijayan also launched a nasty personal attack on Premachandran, a well-regarded leader, which rebounded.

95 According to the Lokniti–CSDS National Election Study, 47 per cent of Ezhavas supported the LDF in the 2014 elections, compared to 23 per cent who voted for the BJP; in 2009, 57 per cent had voted for the LDF. K.M. Sajad Ibrahim (2014): '2014 Lok Sabha Elections in Kerala', *Punjab University Research Journal Social Sciences*, Vol. 22, No. 2, 2014, pp. 261–70.

96 EMS accommodated both parties in his ministry. He later regretted the alliance. But after 1987, the CPI(M) again returned to the policy of accommodating breakaway groups of communal parties. This weakened its claim to principled secularism. The Congress, of course, had no compunctions in joining hands with blatantly communal parties of all kinds.

97 There is no space here to discuss this issue at length, but this view is confirmed by a number of perceptive observers of Kerala politics and society, including the late Ninan Koshy, Bhaskar, Babu and Kannan in email communications with this writer in July 2014. The view is corroborated by Lokniti–CSDS surveys. Ibrahim (2014): pp. 266–67.

98 These are firm figures from the 2001 census. http://censusindia.gov. in/Census_And_You/religion.aspx#, accessed on 11 March 2015. In January 2015, the Modi government released partial figures from the 2011 census, which put Kerala's Muslim population at 26.6 per cent of the total. http://timesofindia.indiatimes.com/ india/Muslim-population-grows-24-slower-than-previous-decade/ articleshow/45972687.cms, accessed on 11 March 2015.

99 CPI(M) (2012): 'Political-Organizational Report' adopted at the twentieth party congress at Kozhikode. No state-wise break-up is given for Christians, but they account for 4.8 per cent of the party's total national membership.

100 Email communication of 12 July 2014. Koshy who died in March 2015, was a highly regarded political thinker, foreign affairs expert, theologian and social analyst, who twice stood for Lok Sabha elections as an independent supported by the LDF. Koshy argues that the CPI(M)'s policy 'towards religious believers' is marked by 'ambivalence and lack of clarity and even differences in acceptance of religious practices of party members at different levels'.

101 The undivided CPI had a number of prominent Christians such as K.C. George, a leading lawyer, T.V. Thomas, who was industries minister in the first EMS ministry, Joseph Mundassery, a major literary figure who became education minister under EMS, and Mathew Kurian, an economist. There were also prominent Muslims like E.K. Imbichi Bava, transport minister in the first EMS ministry. When the party split, says Koshy, very few Christians went over to the CPI(M).

102 The CPI(M), says Bhaskar, 'was making inroads into the Christian and Muslim communities, overcoming the opposition of the clergy, at one time. Once it started making deals with caste/religious organizations for short-term gains, its ability to attract youth from these communities suffered.' Bhaskar, email communication of 15 July 2014.

103 'Christians who move to Left do not want to be labelled as coming from the minorities. They are secular citizens of the country following Christian faith. In politics they don't want any special treatment as minorities. The CPI(M) is still confused on this question.' Koshy: email communication with the author in July 2014.

104 In contrast to the 94 per cent of the emigrants who are based in the Gulf, the latter accounted for just 2.2 per cent of the total in 1998. Their proportion has since tripled. www.cds.edu/wp-content/uploads/2012/11/WP450.pdf, accessed on 3 February 2015 (see pp. 28–30).

105 Estimates by M.P. Parameswaran (2014) of the KSSP, email of 12 August 2014.

106 The Gadgil recommendations (August 2011 'Report of the Western Ghats Ecology Expert Panel', http://www.moef.nic.in/downloads/public-information/wg-23052012.pdf, accessed on 2 September 2014) would lead to the creation of Ecologically Sensitive Areas where no polluting industries, mining or plantation-related activities would be permitted. This would cover 64 per cent of the total area of the Ghats, spread over Gujarat, Maharashtra, Goa, Karnataka, Kerala and Tamil Nadu. The report was badly diluted by the so-called High-Level Working Group headed by K. Kasturirangan, which drastically reduced the Ecologically Sensitive Areas to 37 per cent, and also did away with the process of consultation with local communities. This issue is discussed at greater length in Chapter 8.

107 See J. Devika (2014): 'March to Implement the Gadgil Committee Report in Kerala: An Appeal and Some Dilemmas', kafila.org, 8 January, accessed on 1 May 2014.

108 Paramaeswaran (2014).

109 Not that Kerala has lagged behind India in mall development since the 1990s. Kochi now boasts India's largest malls dedicated to gold and silver, similar to those in Dubai.

110 Rammohan (2012).

111 This is rationalized on the ground that employment of such people results in loss of work and earnings for the union members. Thus if a person moving house packs and loads or unloads her furniture herself, she would still have to pay nokkukooli. This is precisely what happened to a young woman IAS officer in June–July 2014. Her complaint led to the arrest of a local leader of the CITU. http://indianexpress.com/article/india/india-others/citu-leader-arrested-for-threatening-kerala-ias-officer/, accessed on 5 April 2015. In April 2015, American artist Waswo X. Waswo, who had participated in the Kochi–Muziris Biennale, faced the same demand, backed

by intimidation and threats of violence. He protested by publicly destroying his own work. http://www.huffingtonpost.in/2015/04/03/kochi-biennale-protest_n_6998376.html, accessed on 5 April 2015.

112 This paraphrases Rammohan (2012): as do the next few paragraphs.

113 Ibid.

114 Rammohan (2012). He adds: 'Many of the rank and file became small-time contractors, real estate brokers, money lenders and sand miners, and began pursuing varied routes to lumpen accumulation. Further, as a link with power was crucial to the conduct of such activities, many of the new lumpen classes sought party membership, with some even rapidly rising to become local party officials. A change in the composition of the rank and file had the ideological sanction of the state leadership, which also resorted to similar, illegitimate ways of accumulation, the difference being merely of scale ... Often the second generation of the earlier rank and file does join the party, but they are not of the same class as their parents ... Many are employed in the new corporate ventures of the party, even if at lower levels. For them ... allegiance to the party is a prerequisite of economic survival. Dissent involves the threat of ouster, both from employment and from the party .'

115 This was all the more remarkable because it was led by the local panchayat. The Gadgil report (see n. 106) devoted a special section to it (pp. 107–08).

116 Noted by Kannan above (see note 42).

117 In February 2015, CPI(M) politbureau member M.A. Baby released a book by SFI central committee member Chintha Jerome condemning 'Kiss of Love'. This drew protests from the campaign's supporters, one of whom said: 'KOL is Left ideology, if it is not Left then what is it? Dear comrade, please don't think that [the] Left is only CPIM...' http://www.thenewsminute.com/keralas/722, accessed on 30 March 2015.

118 This has been cited as a model worthy of emulation by the Union health ministry because it involves the active participation of community volunteers; this could hold a lot of relevance for the rest of the country. www.thehindu.com/news/cities/Thiruvananthapuram/kerala-a-role-model-in-palliative-care-desiraju/article4914575.ece, accessed on 11 October 2014.

119 Expression used by Lokniti–CSDS researchers in their post-poll survey. It lists five scams, including the infamous recent lottery scam, the 'ice-cream parlour' case, the SNC–Lavalin issue, and a corruption case around a dam. Ibrahim (2014).

120 Email communication with the author, 15 July 2014.

121 Special mention must be made of the Adivasi struggles at Chengara and Arippa to occupy plantation land and cultivate it. This is discussed further in Chapter 8.

Chapter 8: Social Policy Challenges

1 This refers in Marxist literature to the amalgam within the same society of different economic, cultural or social forms, features or practices belonging to 'backward' or older epochs, with those that are more modern or 'advanced'. Their simultaneous coexistence can allow societies to skip linear sequences of development stages over a prolonged period and to telescope or compress development processes within a much shorter span.

2 Thus, the original (1967) programme of the CPI(M) bracketed caste with 'other social systems', and described them as 'remnants of pre-capitalist society' which 'keep the villages tied to age-old backwardness'. It pledged 'sweeping measures' to reform the social system which would supplement 'radical agrarian reforms' aimed at removing 'feudal and semi-feudal fetters' on the productive forces (paragraph 97). The revised, updated programme adopted in 2000 describes 'caste oppression and discrimination' as a problem which 'has a long history and is deeply rooted in the pre-capitalist social system'. CPI(M) (2000): *Programme*, New Delhi, Paragraph 5.12.

3 CPI(M) (2000), paragraphs 5.10 and 5.12.

4 Ibid.

5 The CPI in its 2012 Draft Programme does not make a characterization or analysis of caste, but talks mainly about its effects. It states: 'The social reality in India is the existence of both classes and castes. Even the unity of the working class and the toiling peasantry is difficult to sustain by ignoring their caste differences. Caste has always been a powerful potential and actual weapon in keeping the people divided

and weak in face of any challenge.' CPI (2012): *Draft of the Party Programme*, New Delhi, CPI, Paragraph 7.12, pp. 41–42.

6   There is a rich repertoire of scholarly material on this in the work of Rajni Kothari, D.L. Sheth, Gail Omvedt, James Manor, Jan Breman, Gopal Guru, Valerian Rodriguez, Anand Teltumbde, Sharmila Rege, Satish Deshpande and S.S. Jodhka, among others.

7   See for instance, CPI(M) (2012): *In the Cause of Dalits: Struggle for Social Justice*, New Delhi, CPI(M).

8   See, for instance, Anand Teltumbde (2012a): 'It's not Red vs Blue', *Outlook*, 20 August, and (2012b): 'Ambedkar and communists', http://www.countercurrents.org/teltumbde160812.htm (accessed on 30 August 2014).

9   Eleanor Zelliot (2013): *Ambedkar's World: the Making of Babasaheb and the Dalit Movement*, New Delhi, Navayana, p. 178.

10 The CPI denounced him as an 'opportunist' and an 'imperial stooge'. E.M.S. Namboodiripad characterized Dalit mobilization as 'a great blow to the freedom movement', which led to 'the diversion of the people's attention from the objective of full independence to the mundane cause of the uplift of Harijans'. Namboodiripad (1986): *History of the Indian Freedom Struggle*, Trivandrum, Social Scientist Press, cited in Arundhati Roy's Introduction to Ambedkar (2014): *Annihilation of Caste*, New Delhi, Navayana.

11 See Dwaipayan Sen (2013): 'Representation, Education and Agrarian Reform: Jogendranath Mandal and the Nature of Scheduled Caste Politics, 1937–1943', *Modern Asian Studies*, February, pp. 1–43.

12 See for instance Madhu Limaye (1991): *Socialist-Communist Interaction in India*, Delhi, Ajanta Publications

13 Jagannath Sarkar (2010): *Many Streams: Selected Essays by Jagannath Sarkar*, Patna, Jagannath Sarkar Felicitation Committee, pp. 324–25. Many other articles in this compilation also speak of improved relations between the communists and socialists and a convergence of views although their differences remained. Also see Limaye (1991).

14 Stephanie Tawa Lama-Grewal (2009): 'The Resilient Bhadralok: A Profile of the West Bengal MLAs', in Christophe Jaffrelot and Sanjay Kumar (eds), *Rise of the Plebeians?: The Changing Face of Indian Legislative Assemblies*, New Delhi, Routledge, p. 362.

15 Anjan Ghosh (2001): 'Cast(e) Out in West Bengal', *Seminar* 508 (December). Denial of the reality of casteism has long been characteristic of Bengal, especially on the Left. But as many scholars have pointed out, 'the Bengali Hindu population ... takes its religion, including caste (particularly in matters of marriage) as seriously as the rest of India'. See, for instance, Rabindra Ray (1988): *The Naxalites and Their Ideology*, Delhi, Oxford University Press, p. 58.

16 Thus, at least two-thirds of the CPI(M) politbureau's fifteen members elected at the 2012 congress belong to the upper castes, one is a Christian, and two belong to the intermediate castes. An overwhelming majority of the members inducted into the politbureau in recent years belong to the upper castes, including Brinda Karat, Manik Sarkar, Nirupam Sen and Surjya Kanta Mishra. This pattern changed somewhat at the 2015 congress with the induction of two Muslims and a second woman member into the politbureau.

17 The trend was even stronger at the state level. 'In [the] assemblies of Uttar Pradesh, Madhya Pradesh and Bihar, the proportion of upper caste MLAs has declined from about 40–55 per cent in the 1950s to about 25–35 per cent in the 2000s (sic) while the share of the OBCs grew from 10–20 per cent to about 20–40 per cent.' Vandita Mishra (2010): 'Importance of being an upper caste in Bengal House', *Indian Express*, 2 March 2010.

18 Lama-Grewal (2009), Table 12.2.

19 Ibid., Tables 12.4 and 12.5b.

20 Mishra (2010).

21 Lama-Grewal (2009), p. 390.

22 Ibid., p. 363.

23 See the ongoing debate on the issue since August 2012 in the pages of the *Economic and Political Weekly*, besides the work of Partha Chatterjee, Sumit Sarkar, Sekhar Bandyopadhyay, Dayabati Roy, Ranabir Samaddar, Sudipta Kaviraj, Anjan Ghosh, Dwaipayan Sen and Sarbani Bandyopadhyay, among others.

24 He cited an anecdote: Kanshi Ram once asked him 'why there wasn't a single Dalit minister in the West Bengal government. I was shocked, so I said let me find out. I discovered many Dalits and tribals. Kanti Biswas was the education minister for many years in West Bengal. I had no idea he was a Dalit. We used to travel all across the country in

the same coupe. I did not know he was Dalit till Kanshi Ram asked this. The point was these things were never part of our consciousness. Unfortunately, instead of raising the country's level to mine, where I, a Brahmin, did not even know I am in the same carriage as a Dalit, we had to stoop down to the Kanshi Ram level. We are doing it now.' Interview with Saba Naqvi and Panini Anand, *Outlook*, 22 April 2013.

25　Bhabani Sen Gupta contends that the middle-class intellectuals who joined the CPI in the 1930s and 1940s were not 'very different' from their counterparts in other parties; they were only 'de-classed intellectually (if that)'. 'An inquiry into the lifestyles of thirty leading communists in Bengal, Kerala and Uttar Pradesh I made in 1960 showed that twenty-five of them took part in traditional Hindu festivals, twenty-one had married off their sons and daughters in the traditional religious manner, twenty-two had on more than one occasion consulted astrologers, and none thought it would be "wrong" to perform the prescribed religious rites upon the death of their parents'. Sen Gupta (1978): *Communism in Indian Politics*, New Delhi, Young Asia Publications, p. 13.

26　Cited in *The Indian Express*, 23 September 2006; *The Telegraph*, 24 September 2006; *Outlook*, 2 October 2006. The *Outlook* article added: 'Though not many Calcutta-based or senior state-level leaders practise their religion openly, those in the districts who form a majority in the party do so, and very openly too. In fact, CPI(M) leaders lead religious processions, CITU holds Vishwakarma pujas, teachers' unions affiliated to the CPI(M) hold Saraswati pujas while the party's local units support Durga pujas across the state. It's indeed strange that for a party that puts a premium on discipline, such 'indiscretions' and acts of 'indiscipline' have gone unpunished. However, state secretary Biman Bose has now sent out advisories to members of the CPI(M) state committee, asking them not to associate themselves with community Durga pujas.' This had little effect.

27　Debashis Bhattacharyya (2006): 'In God We Trust', *The Telegraph*, 24 September.

28　Ibid. The Kerala party has come a long way. In the 1980s, E.M.S. Namboodiripad would not let Kerala Congress (Joseph) chief P.J.

Joseph into the Left Democratic Front 'unless he disowned the bishops publicly'.

29 This has been documented in various official reports, including those of the Sachar Committee (see note 32 below), and the Amitabh Kundu committee established to follow up on it, as well as in newspaper articles and books, such as Christopher Jaffrelot and Laurent Gayer (eds) (2012): *Muslims in Indian Cities: Trajectories of Marginalisation*, Noida, UP, HarperCollins.

30 'Post-Sachar Evaluation Committee Report', New Delhi, September 2014, p. 166. The government has not made the report public at the time of writing this.

31 This has been attempted by scholars like Tanika Sarkar, Amrita Basu, Jairus Banaji, Achut Yagnik, Ornit Shani and Nikita Sud, among others. (See note 34 below.)

32 Government of India (2006): 'High-Level Committee on the Social, Economic and Educational Status of the Muslim Community of India: A Report', New Delhi, Cabinet Secretariat. The Committee was headed by Justice Rajinder Sachar, and submitted its report in November 2006. For a detailed discussion of this, see 'Symposium' in *Economic and Political Weekly*, 10 March 2007. The Sachar Committee was followed by the National Commission for Religious and Linguistic Minorities, headed by Justice Ranganath Mishra, to identify the criteria for socially and economically backward classes among the religious and linguistic minorities. Its report was tabled in parliament in December 2009. The recommendations of the two reports have only been partially implemented.

33 See, for instance, Harish Damodaran (2008): *India's New Capitalists: Caste, Business, and Industry in a Modern Nation*, Ranikhet, Permanent Black, which documents a certain blurring of the lines of distinction between the national and regional bourgeoisies.

34 This extremely skewed, inequality-enhancing model of growth has been subjected to a powerful critique in Atul Sood (ed.) (2012): *Poverty Amidst Prosperity: Essays on the Trajectory of Development in Gujarat*, Delhi, Aakar Books; Rohini Hensman (2014): 'The Gujarat Model of Development', *Economic and Political Weekly*, 15 March; Indira Hirway, Amita Shah and Ghanshyam Shah (eds) (2014): *Growth or Development: Which Way is Gujarat Going?*, New Delhi, Oxford

University Press; Ornit Shani (2007): *Communalism, Caste and Hindu Nationalism: The Violence in Gujarat*, Cambridge, UK, Cambridge University Press; Achyut Yagnik and Suchitra Sheth (2005): *The Shaping of Modern Gujarat: Plurality, Hindutva and Beyond*, New Delhi, Penguin books; and Nikita Sud (2012): *Liberalisation, Hindu Nationalism and the State: A Biography of Gujarat*, New Delhi, Oxford University Press. For a discussion of fascism in India, see Jairus Banaji (ed.) (2013): *Fascism: Essays on Europe and India*, Gurgaon, Three Essays Collective. For an analysis of the connections between globalization and the Hindu Right, see Meera Nanda (2011): *The God Market: How Globalisation is Making India More Hindu*, New Delhi, Random House. Also see the late Mukul Sinha's writings in www.truthofgujarat.com. Gujarat's record even on GDP growth and industrialization has been surpassed by other states. However, such is the power of the highly charged propaganda unleashed by the BJP and corporate houses that support it that an astonishingly large proportion (64 per cent) of those polled in a CSDS survey after the 2014 elections named it as India's most developed state—in contrast to Maharashtra (a poor 4 per cent).

35 See, for instance, J. Prabhash (2000): 'CPI(M)'s Muslim League Dilemma', *Economic and Political Weekly*, 19 August.

36 Centre for Equity Studies (2012): 'Promises to Keep: Investigating Government's Response to Sachar Committee Recommendations', New Delhi http://centreforequitystudies.org/wp-content/uploads /2012/08/Sachar-study.pdf

37 Sachar Committee Report (2006): p. 270. http://www.minorityaffairs. gov.in/sites/upload_files/moma/files/pdfs/sachar_comm.pdf, accessed on 2 September 2014.

38 See CPI(M) (2011): 'LF government and Development of Muslim Minorities in West Bengal' CPI(M) Campaign Material, West Bengal Assembly Election, April–May 2011. Available at http://www.cpim. org/documents/2011-minority.development_wb.pdf, accessed on 2 September 2014.

39 A recent judgment of the Andhra Pradesh High Court struck down as unconstitutional the Andhra Pradesh Reservation in Favour of Socially and Educationally Backward Classes of Muslims Act, 2007, which reserved 4 per cent of jobs for backward Muslims.

40   CPI(M) (2011).

41   'Reservations for Muslims', editorial in the *Economic and Political Weekly*, 20 February (2006). This warned: 'If the LF government is not to find its new reservations struck down by the courts, it needs to work towards the identification of only the backward sections among Muslims beyond the 12 sub-groups of Muslims that are already in the OBC list of the state; the framework for this has been provided by the Sachar Committee.'

42   CPI(M) (2012): 'Political–Organizational Report', Twentieth Congress, Kozhikode, April.

43   CPI(M) (2002): 'Documents of the Hyderabad Party Congress', p. 101. More recent figures for membership breakdown are not available.

44   For a detailed account of this, see Nandita Gandhi (1996): *When the Rolling Pins Hit the Streets: Women in the Anti-Price Rise Movement in Maharashtra*, New Delhi, Kali for Women.

45   Vibhuti Patel (1985): 'Women's Liberation in India', *New Left Review*, September–October. This gives a detailed account of the growth of an autonomous women's movement until the mid-1980s.

46   Perverse because it cast suspicion on the victim's 'character', noted her history of sexual activity and suggested that she might have 'incited' the rapists.

47   Patel (1985). Valuable material on the evolution of the feminist movement in the early period is to be found in Radha Kumar (1993): *The History of Doing: An Illustrated Account of Movements for Women's Rights and Feminism in India 1800–1990*, New Delhi, Kali for Women; Ritu Menon (ed.) (2011): *Making a Difference: Memoirs of the Women's Movement in India*, New Delhi, Women Unlimited. See in particular the accounts of Gabriele Dietrich, Nalini Nayak, Vibhuti Patel, Vasanth Kannabiran and Ilina Sen.

48   E.M.S. Namboodiripad (1975): 'Perspective of the Women's Movement', *Social Scientist*, November–December, pp. 1–8.

49   Ibid.

50   That description is found in the documents of all recent congresses of the CPI(M) including Kozhikode in 2012.

51   Cited in Kumari Jayawardena and Govind Kelkar (1989): 'The Left and Feminism', *Economic and Political Weekly*, 23 September, p. 2123. The two authors also quote from a CPI(M)/AIDWA document,

Feminists and Women's Movement ('undated', probably 1987), which says that feminists are 'urban middle class women' who wish to divide the people, particularly the working class; they would like 'women of all classes should come together to fight against men' (p. 3); 'women's organizations, particularly autonomous groups, are responsible for keeping women out of politics and would not like them to join struggle against the state' (pp. 16–17). Another Left theoretician, Vimal Ranadive, is quoted as saying: 'According ... to the feminists, the origins of the exploitation of women' lie in the 'patriarchal system of society ... in India the political and left parties as well as trade unions are "patriarchal", they "subsume" the women's question ... The point to be noted here is [that] these groups would like to keep away the women from the common movement, by taking up only social issues like dowry, etc., under their leadership. They would not like women to be politicized so that they can march ahead in the mainstream of the revolutionaries struggle.' Cited in Ilina Sen (ed.) (1990): *A Space within the Struggle*, New Delhi, Kali for Women, p. 2.

52 'Left Govts Shackle Women's Movement', *The Times of India*, 6 January 1991.

53 Cited in J. Devika and Binitha V. Thampi (2012): *New Lamps for Old*, New Delhi, Zubaan, p. 30.

54 For instance, Neera Desai (1998): *A Decade of Women's Movement in India*, Bombay, Himalaya; Ilina Sen (ed.) (1990); Nandita Gandhi and Nandita Shah (1991): *The Issues at Stake: Theory and Practice in the Contemporary Women's Movement in India*, New Delhi, Kali for Women; Amrita Basu (1992): *Two Faces of Protest: Contrasting Modes of Women's Activism in India*, Berkeley, University Of California Press; Raka Ray (2000): *Fields of Protest: Women's Movements in India*, New Delhi, Kali for Women; besides Ritu Menon (ed.) (2011): and Devika and Thampi (2012).

55 Gandhi and Shah (1991): p. 89.

56 The second group is not homogeneous, but divided between socialist feminists (who locate subjectivity and personal experiences within existing social relations), and others, including radical feminists who reject left-wing politics. In recent years, the socialist feminists' influence has declined in the Indian women's movement. The movement has become more fragmented and ideologically divided.

57 Susanne Kranz (2008): 'Feminism and Marxism in the All India Democratic Women's Association: a Leftist Approach to the Women's Question in Contemporary India', paper presented at the annual conference of the Economic History Society, University of Nottingham. She concludes: 'AIDWA members seem unable to define themselves in relation to feminism; however, there is no necessity to define themselves in relation to feminism and the Western movements ... within the Left-oriented women's movement there is neither a clear set of ideas about feminism nor Marxism. AIDWA is striving to be a unique movement within the contemporary Indian women's movement, but it seems to have difficulties combining the idea of Marxism with the concept of feminism' (p. 5).

58 'Many Marxists typically argue that feminism is at best less important than class conflict and at worst divisive of the working class ... Whilst Marxist analysis provides essential insight into the laws of historical development, and those of capital in particular, the categories of Marxism are sex-blind [...] only a specifically feminist analysis reveals the systematic character of relations between men and women.' Heidi Hartmann (1979): 'The Unhappy Marriage of Marxism and Feminism: Towards a More Progressive Union', *Capital and Class*, No. 8, p.1.

59 AIDWA affiliates sometimes refuse to criticize or act against alleged rapists belonging to their party or its associates. Examples are Dahanu in Maharashtra (1989); and Birati (1990): and Singur and Nandigram (2007) in West Bengal.

60 Documented by Monica Erwer in her 2003 study of women's politics in Kerala, cited in Devika and Thampi (2012): pp. 7 and 30–31. The two authors speak of the case of a woman full-timer 'who managed to gain entry' into a CPI(M)-affiliated trade union's 'upper echelons', but faced serious discrimination from her own colleagues while contesting an assembly election because she was not a graduate— not 'respectable' enough. They observe: 'This notion of respectability clearly leaves the sanctity of the patriarchal family untouched. Indeed, the notion of the family was not so much critiqued as expanded by most AIDWA women we interviewed, in which the party is perceived as the senior-most and most revered guardian' (p. 7). They also cite the case of AIDWA resorting to upper-caste rituals like 'purifying' water

with cow dung at the site of an all-night vigil in solidarity with a Dalit land struggle at Chengara, which it branded as an instance of 'sexual anarchy'. Tanika Sarkar persuasively interrogates another notion, that of the mother woman, in (1991): 'Reflections on Birati Rape Case: Gender Ideology in Bengal', *Economic and Political Weekly*, 2 February.

61 Basu (1992), p. 54; Anisha Datta (2009). Datta argues in 'Syncretic Socialism in Post-Colonial West Bengal: Mobilizing and Disciplining Women for a "Sustha" Nation-State', that the Paschim Banga Ganatantrik Mahila Samity, AIDWA's largest state unit, 'relentlessly fights for women's rights in public life', but 'an examination of its published materials suggests that its ultimate aim to create a sustha (normal) nation-state, a cohesive society and a happy family, which turn these rights into new shackles for women. In particular, through a close reading of its publications—including pedagogical booklets, editorials, essays, poems, travelogues and fictional narratives from the periodical *Eksathe*—the thesis explores how the PBGMS views women instrumentally as reproductive and socializing agents for the supply of future sources of productive labour and as productive beings to act as a reserve force of labour'. Ph.D. thesis, Vancouver, University of British Columbia, p. ii. https://circle.ubc.ca/bitstream/handle/.../ubc_2009_fall_datta_anisha.pdf?, accessed on 20 June 2013.)

62 Some of the changes are reflected in Brinda Karat's newspaper articles and other writings compiled in the very readable book, Karat (2005): *Survival and Emancipation: Notes from Indian Women's Struggles*, Gurgaon: Three Essays Collective.

63 CPI(M) (2005): 'Party's Perspective on Women's Issues and Tasks', New Delhi, CPI(M).

64 Nor do many Indian feminists, especially socialist feminists.

65 This may seem unexceptionable, but the document goes on to cite evidence of women's advancement and liberation in the Soviet bloc countries, and in China, which is dubious.

66 The Janata Dal (United) and Samajwadi Party have repeatedly opposed the women's reservation bill. JD(U) president Sharad Yadav has made egregiously sexist remarks against women, which have embarrassed his own followers.

67 The ratio rose between 1994 and 2011 (the latest year for which the figures are available from the 2012 Kozhikode congress Political–

Organizational Report) by more than 80 per cent each in West Bengal, Kerala and Tripura, but it still remained low at respectively 11 per cent and 14 per cent in the first two states; it exceeded 20 per cent only in Tripura. The Political–Organizational Report for the 2015 congress is not yet public.

68 This is Brinda Karat, who famously refused a second term on the central committee at the Calcutta congress of 1998 and accused 'the party leadership of a gender bias'. *India Today*, 26 October 1998.

69 Former MP Subhashini Ali.

70 Averages pertaining to the congresses of 1992, 1995, 1998, 2005 and 2008, for which figures are available from the corresponding political–organizational reports.

71 Various political–organizational reports of the CPI(M)'s congresses.

72 Which had at least one woman MLA each.

73 Lama-Grewal (2009): p. 385.

74 This is discussed at greater length in Chapter 7.

75 As noted in Chapter 2, as many as sixty million people, roughly equivalent to the population of France or Britain, are estimated to have been displaced since Independence.

76 Published in *The Marxist*, April–June 1984, and in various other versions, including Prakash Karat (1988): *Foreign Funding and the Philosophy of Voluntary Organizations: A Factor in Imperialist Strategy*, New Delhi, National Book Centre.

77 The Western Ghats are critical to the monsoon system and harbour well over a thousand endemic species of flowering plants, fish, frogs, birds and mammals. Their riverine systems drain almost two-fifths of India.

78 Available at www.moef.nic.in/downloads/public-information/wg-23052012.pdf, accessed on 4 May 2014.

79 This would cover 64 per cent of the total area of the Ghats, spread over Gujarat, Maharashtra, Goa, Karnataka, Kerala and Tamil Nadu. The party even rejected the diluted proposals on the issue made by the so-called High-Level Working Group headed by K. Kasturirangan, which drastically reduced the Ecologically Sensitive Area to 37 per cent, and also did away with the process of consultation with local communities. The KSSP defends the core ideas of the Gadgil report, although it finds technical inconsistencies in some of its estimates.

In June 2014, it launched a large-scale public education campaign on the issue. http://www.thehindu.com/todays-paper/tp-national/tp-kerala/retain-core-of-gadgil-report-kssp/article4622254.ece, and http://timesofindia.indiatimes.com/city/kozhikode/Kerala-Sasthra-Sahithya-Parishad-to-revive-campaign-on-Gadgil-report/articleshow/35859029.cms, both accessed on 14 June 2014.

80 For instance, the US did not campaign for choking off the supply of enriched uranium to the Tarapur nuclear plant which it had built for India, as it could have done after 1974. Instead, it got France, and later China, to supply the fuel, which India could not then manufacture.

81 Discussed in Chapter 3.

82 For instance, this writer was branded 'unpatriotic' by the DAE chief in 1984 for exposing the gross failures and underperformance of its heavy water programme in *The Times of India*. Even the mainstream media deplored his remarks, but the Left was not particularly vocal on the issue. The same pattern repeated itself at Koodankulam, where the popular movement opposing the nuclear plant was maligned as 'antinational' and many of its leaders were charged with sedition and 'waging war on the Indian state'. The Left did not defend them strongly, as it should have.

83 Soon after Fukushima, the CPI set up a committee to review its policy on nuclear energy under Sanjay Biswas, a distinguished engineer based at the Indian Institute of Science, Bangalore, and founder president of the All-India Progressive Forum. Unfortunately, Biswas died in April 2013. The committee's report has still not been published.

84 The project was dropped around the middle of the first decade of the current century, but is now reportedly being revived.

85 CPI (2012): 'Political Resolution', twenty-first congress at Patna, March.

86 Political resolution of the eighteenth congress (2005) of the CPI(M), para 2.48.

87 The political resolution of the CPI(M)'s 2008 congress also noted: 'Huge tracts of forest lands are being diverted for mining, industries or commercial plantation at the expense of both the environment and livelihoods of tribals and other traditional forest dwellers. Water resources are being severely depleted due to overexploitation,

contamination and release of untreated industrial waste and urban sewage. Groundwater reserves are particularly threatened … Air pollution is worsening due to reckless promotion of private transportation and neglect of public transport. Unregulated expansion of polluting industries and import of hazardous and toxic wastes for recycling [are] turning India into the garbage dump of developed countries … Instead of strengthening environmental regulation and controls, the state is deliberately loosening them in the name of market forces and in order to promote GDP growth …' CPI(M) (2008): 'Documents of the Nineteenth Congress', New Delhi, CPI(M), pp. 49–51.

88 Ibid., paragraphs 1.22–1.24.

89 'On climate change and greenhouse gases, while it is true that India has almost 1/20th per capita emissions of the US, it should be noted that inequity within India too is pronounced with rural and urban poor availing only a fraction of average Indian energy use. Using the excuse of low per capita emissions, corporates, industrial houses and elite classes in India cannot be allowed to profligate energy consumption and consequent emissions at the expense of the poor and at the cost of the common good …' Ibid., paragraph 2.74.

90 Wind and solar photovoltaic power are both rapidly growing in India too. In April 2015, India had a wind generation capacity exceeding 23,000 MW, almost one-tenth of its total installed electrical capacity, and five times higher than its nuclear energy capacity. Solar power too has been expanding dramatically. Grid-connected solar power is now close to 4,000 MW; the target for 2022 is 100,000 MW.

91 Marx sometimes calls this 'an irreparable break in the coherence of social interchange prescribed by the natural laws of life'. For Marx, 'capitalist production, by collecting the population in great centres, and causing an ever-increasing preponderance of town population, on the one hand concentrates the historical motive power of society; on the other hand, it disturbs the circulation of matter between man and the soil, i.e., prevents the return to the soil of its elements consumed by man in the form of food and clothing; it therefore violates the conditions necessary to lasting fertility of the soil …' For further discussion on this, see John Bellamy Foster (2000): *Marx's Ecology: Materialism and Nature*, New York, Monthly Review Press; and

Paul Burkett (1999): *Marx and Nature: A Red and Green Perspective*, London, Palgrave Macmillan. See also the work of Karl Polanyi, Nicholas Georgescu-Roegen, Kenneth Boulding, Elmar Altvater, James O'Connor, Joan Martinez-Alier and the Ecological Economics School.

92   See note 107.

93   Anonymous (1971): 'The Cossipore-Baranagar Murders', *Economic and Political Weekly*, 28 August; Kalyan Choudhury (1977): '"Law and Order" Killings', *Economic and Political Weekly*, 16 July.

94   Bhabani Sen Gupta (1979): *CPI(M): Promises, Prospects, Problems*, New Delhi, Young Asia Publications, p. 45.

95   Special Correspondent (1982): 'Police under Left Front Government', *Economic and Political Weekly*, 11 December.

96   Numerous articles and reports have analysed and commented on this, including Biren Roy (1994): 'West Bengal: Human Rights Abuse Continues Unchecked', *Economic and Political Weekly*, 1 October; People's Union of Civil Liberties (2006): 'Report on State Repression on Political Opposition in West Bengal', January at http://www.pucl. org/Topics/Human-rights/2006/wb-hr-report.html; Arup Kumar Sen (2011): 'Retelling the Rajarhat Story', *Mainstream*, 2 April.

97   Asian Centre for Human Rights (2011):, '14,231 Custodial Deaths from 2001 to 2010', at http://www.achrweb.org/press/2011/IND07-2011.html

98   Most of them belonged to the Namasudra caste.

99   Annu Jalais (2005): 'Dwelling on Morichjhanpi', *Economic and Political Weekly*, 23 April. According to the author, this article is based on 'nearly two years' fieldwork' in the Sundarbans.

100 Ibid.

101 Ross Mallick (1999): 'Refugee Resettlement in Forest Reserves: West Bengal Policy Reversal and the Marichjhapi Massacre', *The Journal of Asian Studies*, Vol. 58, No. 1, February, pp. 104–25.

102 Jalais (2005).

103 He returned to the subject in another context, that of a proposed tourism complex in the Sundarbans. Amitav Ghosh (2004): 'A Crocodile in the Swamplands', *Outlook*, 18 October.

104 Mallick (1999).

105　Ibid. According to Mallick, 'his successor, the number two CPM Minister, Benoy Chowdhury, years later was not renominated for a party seat after he complained about how corrupt his party had become ...'

106　For more details, see Debabrata Bandyopadhyay (2011): 'West Bengal: Urgent Tasks before the New Government', *Mainstream*, 9 June.

107　Answer to an assembly question in 1997, when he was the home minister. Cited in Debabrata Bandyopadhyay (2010): 'Census of Political Murders in West Bengal during CPI-M Rule—1977–2009', *Mainstream*, 14 August.

108　Bandyopadhyay (2010) makes an estimate of 149 murders a month for the period 1977 to 2009, but this seems to be high because it conflates 'murder' with 'political murder' in the figures extrapolated for 1997–2009.

109　Some have been listed in Prakash Louis and R. Vashum (2002): *Extraordinary Laws in India*, New Delhi, Indian Social Institute.

110　This law, in force in Jammu and Kashmir and parts of north-eastern India is perhaps the worst of its kind. It grants an officer who kills immunity from prosecution without the consent of the defence forces, which is rarely given.

111　'Cops Get CM's Licence to Kill', *The Statesman*, Calcutta, 26 December 2000, cited in D. Bandyopadhyay (2001): 'Licence to Kill?', *Economic and Political Weekly*, 6 January, p. 12.

112　Mohamed Nazeer (2014): 'Trapped in Cyclical Violence', *The Hindu*, 23 September.

113　'The motive of revenge behind incidents of political clashes is an offshoot of a combative political milieu that emerged in the politically volatile parts of the district after the Emergency. The Sangh Parivar started organizing its shakhas in neighbourhoods that have been treated as pocket boroughs of the CPI(M). The legacy of previous political hostilities between the communists and the socialists in some of these areas assumed a new violent form as CPI(M) and BJP–RSS workers started treating their areas of influence as their "party villages".' Ibid.

114　Ibid. K.T. Rammohan, an eminent social scientist, commented on the killing: 'Even more painfully, there is blood in the emerald bowl.

The blood-spill owes not merely to extreme right wing communal forces, but to the state's biggest political organization, the CPI(M). Such is its attitude towards dissent that recently a long-standing activist who had chosen to form a new parliamentary, communist organization, was put to a gruesome death with no less than fifty-one slashes. This horrid act had other frightful dimensions. Apparently, the killer comrades had travelled in a cab that bore a sticker with the Arabic words *Masha Allah* (as God wills) to misdirect the police investigation and to deceive the public. Had the sinister ploy worked, many innocent Muslims would have been taken into police custody or killed in the possible violence set off by the right wing Hindu forces ... In connection with the recent killing, in which some key party officials were allegedly involved in the conspiracy and interrogated, the secretary threatened that the party would turn into a flaming torch if there were more arrests. This was soon followed by the tragicomic intervention of another leader who sought to invoke images of the historic peasant resistance to justify the present intolerance of police investigation. A district secretary ... boasted about the 1980s: "We drew up a list of thirteen men. [He then called out the digits in English] One, two, three, four ... The first three were the first to be killed. One was shot dead, another was beaten to death, the third stabbed to death".' Rammohan adds: 'Most of Kerala's intellectuals, otherwise eloquent, chose to remain silent over the recent killing or were snail-slow to react. Not surprising, considering that the vast majority of this class are 'paid intellectuals' of the party. The silence also owes to the lack of a tradition of inner-party democracy and their servility to the party headquarters. A few years ago, when a primary school teacher, a key organizer of the RSS, was lynched to death in the classroom right in front of little children, a leading intellectual of the party, who had extensively written and spoken on both Marxism and psycho-analysis, justified the killing by noting that the RSS had earlier finished off a comrade in front of his parents ...' Rammohan (2012): 'Contemporary Politics: Horrors and Hope', *Seminar* 637, September, pp. 26–27.

115 In March 2014, Achuthanandan was asked to lead the CPI(M)'s election campaign and came around to formally supporting the party's stand on Chandrasekharan's killing, but only for a while.

K.P.M. Basheer (2014): 'It's no more VS versus CPI(M) in Kerala', *Hindu Business Line*, 29 March. But the issue has still not been settled. Achuthanandan yet again came under attack at the Kerala state party conference in Alappuzha in February 2015. He retaliated by demanding that 'the party members linked to the T.P. Chandrashekharan murder case should be expelled from the party'. http://articles.economictimes. indiatimes.com/2015-02-24/news/59460691_1_vs-achuthanandan-opposition-leader-party-members, accessed on 21 March 2015.

116 See Chapter 7 for the electoral consequences.

Chapter 9: Lost Opportunities

1 These are the words of a senior Left leader, whose identity I am unable to reveal.

2 Among the signatories were social scientists Bipan Chandra, Irfan Habib, K.N. Panikkar, Sumit Sarkar, Tanika Sarkar, Zoya Hasan, Neerja Gopal Jayal and Sukhdev Thorat, theatre figures Habib Tanwir and Kirti Jain, film-makers Saeed Mirza, Shyam Benegal and Anand Patwardhan, actors A.K. Hangal, Shabana Azmi and Nandita Das, activists Nirmala Deshpande, K.G. Kannabiran, Harsh Mander, Shabnam Hashmi, Kavita Srivastava and Javed Anand. The statement is available at http://sacw.net/article9524.html, accessed on 31 August 2014.

3 The author was privy to this information shared with him by two senior Left leaders, who insisted on anonymity.

4 Literally meaning 'nine jewels', the top-performing nine public companies.

5 For the full text of the CMP, see http://nceuis.nic.in/NCMP.htm or www.thehindu.com/2004/05/28/stories/2004052807371200.htm, accessed on 30 August 2014.

6 Some of these issues are listed in various statements by Left party leaders and in the documents of the 2008 congress of the CPI(M) at Coimbatore, available at http://www.cpim.org/content/19th-congress-political-resolution as a pdf file.

7 This last drew upon a January 2003 report of the 'People's Commission on Patent Laws in India', chaired by former Prime Minister I.K. Gujral, with several experts as members.

8 However, the Left itself promoted SEZs, especially in West Bengal, and undermined the credibility of its own opposition to them.

9 Stephen Rademaker, a former US assistant secretary for International Security and Non-Proliferation, said this during a talk at the Institute for Defence Studies and Analyses, New Delhi. http://www.thehindu. com/todays-paper/tp-national/indias-antiiran-votes-were-coerced-says-former-us-official/article1797853.ece, accessed on 2 September 2014.

10 India deprecated this as a cabal and a closed grouping which polices the world. India is now keen to join the NSG.

11 See CPI(M), CPI, RSP and All-India Forward Bloc (2008): *Left Stand on the Nuclear Deal*, New Delhi, published by the CPI(M) on behalf of the Left parties.

12 The Left did not acknowledge the potential of nuclear power generation for catastrophic accidents like Chernobyl or Fukushima and the grave difficulties with storing radioactive waste for centuries. Nor did the Left counter the 'decarbonization' claim by pointing to the extremely limited contribution that nuclear energy can potentially make to reducing carbon emissions and thus mitigating climate change. For this last, see Praful Bidwai (2012): *The Politics of Climate Change and the Global Crisis: Mortgaging Our Future*, New Delhi, Orient BlackSwan, Chapters 9 and 10.

13 For a powerful critique of this fanciful plan drafted by Homi Bhabha, see M.V. Ramana (2012): *The Power of Promise: Examining Nuclear Energy in India*, New Delhi, Penguin Books/Viking. Fast-breeders have not proved viable or safe anywhere. And thorium-fuelled reactors have not been proved on a pilot scale, leave alone industrial scale, anywhere in the world. The plan is based on wishful thinking—primarily because India has abundant reserves of thorium ore, but very limited reserves of uranium.

14 For a critique of the nationalist stance, see Aniket Alam (2008): '"National Interest" not the Issue in Nuclear Deal', *Economic and Political Weekly*, 27 September. Also this author's numerous articles in *Frontline, The Times of India*, InterPress Service, some of which are available at www.prafulbidwai.org and www.tni.org.

15 Some of them, such as P.K. Iyengar, former chairman of the Atomic Energy Commission, publicly demanded that India must conduct yet

another nuclear test explosion to prove its hydrogen-bomb capability because the thermonuclear device, one of the five bombs tested in 1998, failed to produce the expected explosive yield.

16 Some of the key individuals whom the Left treated as its allies or advisers were nuclear hawks who had no sympathy for left-wing or progressive causes. They were neither against nuclear power per se, nor of course against nuclear weapons, least of all India's weapons. They used the Left mainly to demand yet more negotiations on the deal and to secure better terms from the US. As soon as they secured these, they turned against the Left.

17 For further discussion on this, see Praful Bidwai and Achin Vanaik (2000): *South Asia on a Short Fuse: Nuclear Politics and Future of Global Disarmament,* New Delhi, Oxford University Press.

18 CPI(M), CPI, et al (2008): *Left Stand on the Nuclear Deal,* p. 8.

19 The civil society protests on Nandigram were among the largest in the history of West Bengal.

20 http://articles.economictimes.indiatimes.com/2007-11-15/ news/27687226_1_cpm-leader-relief-fund-nandigram, accessed on 30 August 2014.

21 Negative public sentiment towards the Left was soon reflected in the setback it suffered in the panchayat elections of May 2008, when the TMC won thirty-five of fifty-three seats in the East Medinipur zilla parishad, the Left's stronghold for decades, and also emerged victorious in the South 24 Parganas zilla parishad. A month later, the TMC wrested from the CPI(M) three municipalities with a sizeable Muslim population.

22 There were unconfirmed reports that prior to the meeting, top Left leaders were solemnly assured by Congress president Sonia Gandhi that the UPA would abide by its commitment to consult the Left parties before making the next move. It is not clear if Gandhi reneged on her assurance, or the Left shifted its stand, or other developments forced a change in the situation. But Debabrata Biswas, Forward Bloc general secretary, told reporters immediately after the 16 November meeting that 'the deal was now destined to be through'. Prakash Karat had the opposite view. Diptendra Raychaudhuri (2010): *Understanding CPI(M): Will the Indian Left Survive?,* New Delhi, Vitasta, p. 80.

23   *The Telegraph*, 15 July 2008, http://www.telegraphindia.com/1080715/jsp/nation/story_9550826.jsp, accessed on 30 August 2014.

24   These were later corroborated by WikiLeaks. See http://www.ndtv.com/article/india/full-text-of-wikileaks-cable-on-trust-vote-controversy-92301 and http://indiatoday.intoday.in/story/upa-govt-bribed-mps-to-win-trust-vote-in-2008-says-wikileaks/1/132636.html, accessed on 30 August 2014, among numerous other reports.

25   Chakraborty said: 'I am shocked and sad. The expulsion will do damage to the party.' See 'Karat's Kangaroo Court: Somnath Expelled in a Hurry', *The Telegraph*, 24 July 2008.

26   'CM Sips Governance Brew: Prakash at Party Office, Buddha Goes to Meet Pranab', *The Telegraph*, 28 July 2008.

27   I have personally never met a more insular set of communists anywhere else in the country, indeed the world. I must have interviewed or interacted with at least thirty West Bengal CPI(M) leaders over the years, many of whom knew I was working on a book on the Indian Left. None of them, barring two (Ashok Mitra and earlier Jyoti Basu), evinced the faintest interest in national affairs or the state of the Left in India—except for the implications for Bengal.

28   The political–tactical line based on such a front was originally formulated at the tenth congress of the CPI(M) held at Jalandhar in 1978. The 'left and democratic front' would consolidate progressive social forces and bring them into 'an alliance for People's Democracy under the leadership of the working class'.

29   Harkishan Singh Surjeet (2002): 'Significance of the 17th Party Congress of the CPI(M)', *The Marxist*, January–March.

30   The party expelled Prasenjit Bose, one of its most articulate spokespersons, for opposing its decision to back Mukherjee. Bose was one of the few intellectuals to have joined and stayed with the party as a full-timer in recent years. His expulsion led to a major crisis in the SFI unit at Jawaharlal Nehru University.

31   http://www.hardnewsmedia.com/2014/03/6226

32   On 16 May CPI(M) general secretary Prakash Karat termed the results from West Bengal as 'distorted'. Addressing the press, he said that there was widespread rigging and violence during the last three phases of the elections and the entire democratic process was vitiated. 'The results do not reflect the strength and support of the people for

the Left Front in West Bengal.' He termed the drop of over 11 per cent vote since the last assembly elections as 'unacceptable'. 'This does not reflect the true situation,' he said. 'Our immediate concern will be taking our Party and the movement ahead in West Bengal, irrespective of the election results.' About the national-level outcome, Karat said though the party had worked for the rejection of the Congress, it was not happy 'as the main benefit of the anti-Congress mood has gone to the BJP. http://www.cpim.org/content/west-bengal-verdict-distorted, accessed on 25 May 2014.

33 Prakash Karat, quoted in http://www.cpim.org/content/lok-sabha-verdict, accessed on 25 May 2014. He added: 'The people have voted against the policies of the Congress-led UPA government which resulted in price rise, agrarian distress and corruption. They voted for a change and for relief from the problems afflicting them. The CPI(M) will continue to work to defend the interests of the working people and to safeguard the secular democratic framework of the country.'

34 When the CPI(M) politburo met on 18 May, it issued the following statement: 'The Polit Bureau discussed the results of the Lok Sabha elections and the post-election situation. It conducted a preliminary review of the elections and the performance of the Party. It examined the various factors which led to the poor results for the Party and the Left. The Polit Bureau will meet again on June 6 to finalise the election review and the political-organisational steps to be taken in the present political situation. This will be placed before the Central Committee meeting on June 7 and 8 for discussion and adoption. The Polit Bureau condemned the continuing attacks on the CPI(M) and the Left Front workers and supporters in West Bengal.' http://www.cpim.org/content/pb-communique-22. Nothing could have better trivialized the gravity of the message delivered by the election results.

35 http://www.communistparty.in/2015/04/consolidate-through-mass-struggles-cpi.html, accessed on 17 April 2015.

36 Ruhi Tewari (2015): 'CPM Looks Within: "Ageing, not Growing"', *The Indian Express*, 15 April.

37 Ibid.

38 'The Left Front Government in West Bengal: Evaluation of an Experience (Draft)', adopted at the state committee's twenty-ninth session during 23–24 February 2015.

39 The municipal elections saw the Left parties' state-level vote share shrink from 41 per cent (in the Assembly election of 2011) to 30 percent (in the 2014 Lok Sabha election) to an estimated 27 per cent, way behind the TMC's 42 per cent. Their tally of wins in Kolkata wards declined from thirty-two (2010) to fifteen, or barely one-tenth of the total number of wards. In the ninety-one civic bodies elsewhere in West Bengal, their score fell from fifteen to five. By contrast, the TMC won seventy-one of the ninety-two civic bodies (up from the thirty-eight it won in 2010). In Kolkata, it won a crushing 114 of 144 wards (ninety-five in 2010). The Left's main consolation is that it regained its number two status in Kolkata from the BJP. The BJP had led in 2014 in twenty-six wards, compared to the Left's lead in just eleven wards. The BJP's Kolkata tally has now fallen to seven wards, against the Left's fifteen. The Left won an estimated 25 per cent of the vote in Kolkata, compared to the BJP's 15 per cent. (*The Telegraph*, 29 April 2015). Secondarily, the Left won the Siliguri Municipal corporation, the state's second biggest municipality after Kolkata. But the victory there of Ashok Bhattacharya, a former minister and a 'development-friendly' neo-liberal in the Buddhadeb Bhattacharjee mould, is hardly a victory of the Left as an ideological–political force. See Praful Bidwai (2015): 'Bengal Local Poll Results Don't Bode Well for the BJP, Left', *DNA*, 30 April.

40 This had little to do with intimidation by the Trinamool's student union, and was described by senior party leader Gautam Deb as 'not acceptable'. Sabyasachi Bandyopadhyay (2015): 'Bengal's Political Drama, Now Playing in Calcutta University', *The Indian Express*, 12 January.

41 Several media accounts reported this, including Akshaya Mukul (2015): 'After Night of Long Knives, Yechury Elected CPM Boss', *The Times of India*, 20 April and J.P. Yadav (2015): 'Sita Nips Night of Long Sickles', *The Telegraph*, 20 April. Both these, apparently based on party leaders' briefings, say that Yechury's backers wanted or threatened a secret ballot. But Prakash Karat has said in an email to me (14 May) in response to an article of mine reproduced in *Mainstream* ('Reimagining Strategy, Returning to Grassroots: Challenges Before Yechury', 2 May 2015) that 'there is no such thing as a secret ballot for elections in committees. The provision of secret

ballot is for election of committees by delegates in a conference. In the elected committees, we do not have provision of secret ballot. In fact we do not allow it. We hold elections by show of hands. Because the principle is that members must have confidence in one another to openly display their opinion and vote.' Karat also said that it is not 'correct to say that some state units like Kerala, Bengal and Tripura took the specific stances that you allege, nor is it true that I had backed somebody else …' I do not contest Karat's statement on the secret ballot, but my point about divisions in the politbureau stands.

42 Bose was later quoted as saying: 'I had to fight to get him [Yechury] elected.' Yadav (2015). There was media speculation, based on background briefings by party leaders, that Yechury's backers wanted to have the issue put to the vote in the new central committee; Pillai's supporters did not want a show of hands because it would probably have exposed divisions within the Kerala party, as well as between it and the West Bengal unit. This would have embarrassed Vijayan because some of the congress delegates picked by him were reportedly opposed to Pillai being made the general secretary and apparently made their opposition known to some of the new central committee members.

43 Appukuttan Vallikunnu (2015): 'Yechury and the Kerala Selfie', *Mainstream*, 2 May.

44 Both are available at www.cpim.org, accessed on 4 May 2015.

45 This is not a public document, but the author has access to it through journalistic sources.

46 Brinda Karat (2015): 'The Vizag Line', *The Indian Express*, 23 April.

47 Saubhadra Chatterji (2015): 'We Want Congress Support for India's Future', *Hindustan Times*, 21 April.

48 HT Correspondent (2015): 'Parties Greet Yechury on New Role', *Hindustan Times*, 21 April.

49 He identified these thus: 'One, in unitedly fighting against the Modi government's anti-farmer and anti-poor and pro-corporate policies such as land acquisition Bill. Two, the mounting communal activities of the Sangh Parivar since the Modi government took charge. Three, to resist the NDA regime's tendency to tweak Parliament's rules and procedures to get laws through by unleashing what I have

called the tyranny of the majority in the Lok Sabha. At the same time, we are not thinking of forming an alliance or front with the Congress'. When asked if he would be 'open to a tactical alliance or understanding with the Congress in West Bengal polls next year', Yechury responded: 'Our priority in West Bengal is to check our erosion and resist the murderous attack on our cadres and supporters. The rest of the things we will see at the time of elections.' He also revealed that many leaders of the West Bengal CPI(M) are in favour of bringing Somnath Chatterjee back into the party. C.L. Manoj and T.K. Arun (2015): 'No Alliance, But Will Work with Congress, says Sitaram Yechury', *The Economic Times*, 28 April.

50 Anita Joshua (2015): 'CPI(M), CPI Discuss United Action', *The Hindu*, 22 April; also J.P. Yadav (2015): 'Yechury Brings Party to Office', *The Telegraph*, 22 April.

51 Earlier, he was suspended from the politburo, and reprimanded in February 2015 for defying party discipline by walking out of the Kerala party's state conference.

52 Venkitesh Ramakrishnan (2015): 'Guarded Hope', *Frontline*, 29 April.

53 See 'Trade Unions in India 2010', the latest available report on aggregate union membership, at www.labourbureau.gov.in, accessed on 4 May 2015. The claimed membership figures of most unions are highly exaggerated and the Labour Bureau's system of verification has broken down. Yet going by all appearances, and business estimates, the CPI-affiliated AITUC remains bigger than the CPI(M)-affiliated CITU and the HMS, and probably slightly smaller in size than the INTUC, affiliated to the Congress, and the BJP-sponsored Bharatiya Mazdoor Sangh. See, for instance, *India Business Yearbook 2009*, New Delhi, Vikas Publishing House.

54 http://www.business-standard.com/article/economy-policy/indian-trade-unions-are-getting-bigger-coinciding-with-slowdown-113040600392_1.html, accessed on 4 May 2015.

55 There have been militant struggles at the Maruti Suzuki and Honda units in the Gurgaon–Manesar area near Delhi and Bajaj Auto in Pune. See, for instance, www.mazdoorbigul.net, and http://column.global-labour-university.org/2014/04/workers-unrest-in-automobile-plants-in.html, accessed on 18 May 2015.

Chapter 10: Towards a New Left

1 Some efforts have been under way at the national level since August 2014 to create such a platform, which emphasizes 'common actions' at the grass-roots level. But there is little clarity about precisely what is meant by 'Left unity' and what the discussion seeks to achieve by way of evolving a common understanding before attempting joint actions.

2 In 2006–07, the CPI(M) leadership flatly refused to disclose to its own Left Front partners the details of the memorandum of understanding signed with the Tata group for the Nano car project at Singur, despite countless requests. Chief Minister Buddhadeb Bhattacharjee told the cabinet that it was a state 'secret' that could not be shared even with his ministers.

3 There are scores, if not hundreds, of such movement and structures, region- and issue-specific, as well as national. They include the National Alliance of People's Movements, National Fishworkers' Forum, All-India Union of Forest Working People, Mazdoor Kisan Shakti Sangathan, Indian Social Action Forum, New Trade Union Initiative, Kisan Sangharsh Samiti, Samajwadi Samagam, New Path, All-India Agricultural Workers' Union, New Socialist Initiative, Radical Socialist, Bharatiya Khet Mazdoor Union, All India Krishak Khet Mazdoor Sangathan, Socialist Centre, Mahan Sangharsh Samiti, Chhattisgarh Mukti Morcha, Lok Sangharsh Morcha, Lokadhikar, Adharshila Learning Centre (Madhya Pradesh), Delhi Solidarity Group, Uttarakhand Mahila Manch, The Left Collective, Yuva Kranti, Sarvahara Jan Andolan, Jansangharsh Samanvaya Samiti, Adivasi Gothra Mahasabha (Kerala), Chhattisgarh Bachao Andolan, Lokayata (Pune), Medico Friends' Circle, Jan Swasthya Abhiyan, Faridabad Majdoor Samachar, and Ghar Banao Ghar Bachao Andolan, to mention only some groups.

4 Besides state hostility, RTI activists have faced threats to their life and limb from those against whom they unearth embarrassing or incriminating information; more than forty activists have been killed, according to Nikhil Dey of the National Campaign for People's Right to Information.

5 This has been documented in several reports, including Parivartan and the Right to Water Campaign (2005): *The 24×7 Myth: An Analysis of the Proposal to Restructure the Delhi Jal Board and Intervention from*

the World Bank, New Delhi, Parivartan; Amit Bhaduri and Arvind Kejriwal (2005): 'Urban Water Supply: Reforming the Reformers', *Economic and Political Weekly,* 31 December; Suchi Pande (2007): 'World Bank Arm-Twisted DJB', *Combat Law,* March–April.

6   Some of this might appear to be a wish-list. In some ways, that is inevitable when social movements and political activists look into the future and search for the horizon of the possible. At any rate, it is not my personal wish list, but the result of sustained contact and conversations with many activists.

7   There is nothing sacrosanct about the number five. Some activists have suggested eight; some believe the number of axes should evolve as more ideas and plans of action emerge in the People's Charter discussion.

8   Achin Vanaik has discussed this in (2011): 'Subcontinental Strategies', *New Left Review,* 70, July–August.

9   The case for autonomy derives from some of the arguments advanced in Chapter 8.

10   These are often not dialects at all, but full languages with literary traditions going back to the late Middle Ages.

11   These estimates are amply documented in various studies and reports—e.g., http://www.rediff.com/news/column/p-sainath-how-states-fudge-the-data-on-farmer-suicides/20140801.htm, accessed on 20 May 2015.

12   This is discussed further in Chapter 7.

13   Even Thomas Piketty, no flaming radical, calls for punitive taxation in his (2014): *Capital in the Twenty-First Century,* Cambridge (Mass.), Harvard University Press.

14   Documented in an outstanding recent report of the Transnational Institute in Amsterdam, http://www.tni.org/briefing/our-public-water-future, accessed on 7 April 2015.

15   Also see Vanaik (2011), p. 112.

16   These are among the demands taken up by the Pension Parishad led by Aruna Roy and Baba Adhav, who have run a remarkable campaign. See http://pensionparishad.org.

17   See http://www.worldbank.org/en/news/press-release/2013/07/17/india-green-growth-necessary-and-affordable-for-india-says-new-world-bank-report, accessed on 2 May 2015.

18   Of great relevance here is the Latin American experience, recounted in Daniel Chavez and Benjamin Goldfrank (eds) (2004): *The Left in the City: Participatory Local Governments in Latin America*, London, Latin America Bureau.

19   These are estimated at 20,000–40,000 passengers per hour per direction. For analysis of this, see http://tripp.iitd.ernet.in/.

20   See Chapter 3 above on the work of the Shaheed Hospital and other public institutions in Chhattisgarh, built and run by his trade union, which attracted public health activists like Binayak Sen.

21   The Soviet communist party made this claim disingenuously and undemocratically—and then imposed its vanguardism upon the citizenry by undemocratic and repressive means.

22   At the same time, the Left did little sustained popular mobilization on its own, except for staging bandhs and holding token demonstrations—often more an expression of their cadres' party loyalty than of passion or real comprehension of the issues at stake—on limited economic or political demands. It remained too preoccupied with parliamentary politics and Third Front coalition building even to offer effective resistance to the privatization of public sector companies like Bharat Aluminium Company Ltd (Balco) in 2001–02 or the indiscriminate sell-offs of chunks of the equity of several other public corporations. The Left's passive response to the Balco sell-off to Sterlite Industries (of Anil Agarwal's Vedanta Group) became a litmus test and encouraged the government to pursue privatization of other public sector companies with greater zeal.

23   There should be no expulsion except where elementary norms of public decency are violated or the equivalent of a party 'whip' is defied on a critical make-or-break issue.

24   An exception was 1992, when Cuba was reeling under food and petroleum shortages caused by the collapse of the Soviet Union. Indian parties, including the CPI(M), the CPI and the Congress, took a political initiative and sent 20,000 tonnes of rice and wheat to the Cuban people. See http://www.telegraphindia.com/1130903/jsp/frontpage/story_17305364.jsp, accessed on 6 March 2014.

25   The Aam Aadmi Party won an impressive 53 per cent of the total vote in Delhi. A Lokniti–CSDS survey estimates that it won a stunning 66 per cent of the votes of the poor and 57 per cent of those of the

'lower middle class' (compared to the BJP's share of 22 and 29 per cent respectively). http://indianexpress.com/article/india/india-others/poor-already-behind-it-aap-tapped-rich-too/, accessed on 3 March 2015.

Appendix 1: The Mode of Production Debate

1   Paul M. Sweezy and Maurice Dobb (1950): 'The Transition from Feudalism to Capitalism,' *Science & Society*, Vol. 14; No. 2, Spring, pp. 134–67; and Rodney Hilton (ed.) (1978): *The Transition from Feudalism to Capitalism*, London, Verso.

2   Ashok Rudra, A. Majid and B.D. Talib (1969): 'Big Farmers of the Punjab: Some Preliminary Findings of a Sample Survey', *Economic and Political Weekly*, 27 September; Ashok Rudra (1969): 'Big Farmers of Punjab: Second Instalment of Results', *Economic and Political Weekly*, 27 December.

3   Utsa Patnaik (1971a): 'Capitalist Development in Agriculture—a Note', *Economic and Political Weekly*, 25 September; (1971b): 'Capitalist Development in Agriculture: Further Comment', *Economic and Political Weekly*, 25 December; (1972): 'On the Mode of Production in Agriculture: a Reply', *Economic and Political Weekly*, 30 September.

4   Paresh Chattopadhyay (1972a): 'On the Question of the Mode of Production in Indian Agriculture: A Preliminary Note', *Economic and Political Weekly*, 25 March; (1972b): 'Mode of Production in Indian Agriculture: An Anti-Kritik', *Economic and Political Weekly*, 30 December.

5   Cited in John Harriss (2013): 'Does "Landlordism" Still Matter? Reflections on Agrarian Change in India', *Journal of Agrarian Change*, July, pp. 351–64.

6   Amit Bhaduri (1973): 'A Study in Agricultural Backwardness', *The Economic Journal*, March, pp. 121–22. Bhaduri defines the small cultivator whom he terms the kisan as 'any peasant 75 per cent or more of whose income comes from tilling as a sharecropper other people's land, and also who provides virtually no capital for cultivation'.

7   Ibid., pp. 135–36.

8   Pradhan H. Prasad (1973): 'Production Relations: Achilles Heel of Indian Planning', *Economic and Political Weekly*, 12 May.

9   Pradhan H. Prasad (1974): 'Reactionary Role of Usurers' Capital in Rural India', *Economic and Political Weekly*, 10 August.

10 Nirmal K. Chandra (1974): 'Farm Efficiency under Semi-Feudalism: A Critique of Marginalist Theories and Some Marxist Formulations', *Economic and Political Weekly*, 10 August.

11 Ibid.

12 Nirma K. Chandra (1975): 'Agrarian Transition in India', *Frontier*, Vol. VII, No. 29, pp. 3–9.

13 Ranjit Sau (1975): 'Farm Efficiency under Semi-Feudalism: A Comment', *Economic and Political Weekly*, 29 March.

14 Ashok Rudra (1974): 'Semi-Feudalism, Usury Capital, Etcetera', *Economic and Political Weekly*, 30 November.

15 Ibid.

16 Ashok Rudra (1978): 'Class Relations in Indian Agriculture', *Economic and Political Weekly*, 3, 10, 17 June.

17 Aparajita Chakravarty and Ashok Rudra (1973): 'Economic Effects of Tenancy: Some Negative Results', *Economic and Political Weekly*, 14 July. 'It would thus seem that the generally held idea about tenant farms' economic performance being worse than that of owner farms might be valid when the comparison is confined to small-sized farms, but not so when medium or big farms are thought of.' This is true of fifteen variables, including yield per acre, cost of production, labour intensity, etc.

18 Jairus Banaji (1977): 'Capitalist Domination and the Small Peasantry: Deccan Districts in the Late Nineteenth Century', *Economic and Political Weekly*, 20 August.

19 Ibid. Italics in the original.

20 Ibid. Noteworthy here are the similarities and (limited) differences with the Brenner thesis, discussed in Chapter 2 earlier.

21 Ibid.

22 Ibid. Italics in the original.

23 Ibid.

24 Ibid. Italics in the original.

25 Ibid. Italics in the original.

26 Ibid. Italics in the original.

27 Hamza Alavi (1981): 'Class Struggle, Production and the Middle Peasant', *Economic and Political Weekly*, 21 March.

28 Kathleen Gough (1980): 'Modes of Production in Southern India', *Economic and Political Weekly*, 16 February.

29 Gail Omvedt (1981): 'Capitalist Agriculture and Rural Classes in India', *Economic and Political Weekly*, 26 December.

30 Ashok Rudra (1981): 'Against Feudalism', *Economic and Political Weekly*, 26 December.

31 Ratna Ray and Rajat Ray (1975): 'Zamindars and Jotedars: A Study of Rural Politics in Bengal', *Modern Asian Studies*, February, pp. 244–79.

32 For a superb recapitulation of the debate, see Alice Thorner (1982): 'Semi-Feudalism or Capitalism?: Contemporary Debate on Classes and Modes of Production in India', *Economic and Political Weekly* (in three parts), 4, 11 and 18 December. The 'majority opinion' is not shared by Utsa Patnaik (1976): 'Class Differentiation within the Peasantry: An Approach to Analysis of Indian Agriculture', *Economic and Political Weekly*, 25 September; and (1986): 'The Agrarian Question and Development of Capitalism in India', *Economic and Political Weekly*, 3 May.

33 For instance, Pranab Bardhan (1979): 'On Class Relations in Indian Agricuture: a Comment', *Economic and Political Weekly*, 12 May.

34 Alice Thorner (1982): pp. 2063–65.

35 Ibid.

36 Ibid.

37 Ibid..

38 Chakravarty and Rudra (1973). See note 17 above.

39 Ibid.

Appendix 2

1 For thirteen seats, twelve in Assam and one in Meghalaya elections were not held in 1980.

2 Elections were not held in fourteen constituencies of Assam in 1989.

3 Elections were not held in six constituencies of Jammu and Kashmir in 1991.

Appendix 3: Seventh Term in Tripura

1 Harihar Bhattacharyya (1999): *Communism in Tripura*, Delhi, Ajanta Publications, pp. 1–3. Bhattacharyya also describes communism in Tripura as a 'third-generation phenomenon'.

2 In the 2009 Lok Sabha election in West Bengal, the Left's tally dropped from thirty-five seats (of the state's forty-two seats) to fifteen. By contrast, the Left in 2014 won both the Tripura seats, with a 64 per cent vote share.

3 Subir Bhaumik (2012): *Tripura: Ethnic Conflict, Militancy & Counterinsurgency*, 'Politics and Practices 52', Kolkata, Mahanirban Calcutta Research Group, pp. 5–6.

4 Probin Kalita (2013): 'Manik Sarkar: Poorest CM in the Country', *The Times of India*, 26 January. Sarkar reportedly launched his assembly election campaign in 2013 with Rs 1,080 in hand, compared to Rs 3,000 in 2003. According to his declaration to the Election Commission of India, he had only one bank account, with a balance of Rs 9,720.

5 http://indiatoday.intoday.in/education/story/tripura-aims-at-100percent-literacy-rate-in-next-six-months/1/381763.html, accessed on 2 May 2015.

6 For details, see Government of Tripura (2007): *Human Development Report*, Agartala.

7 Much of this and the following paragraphs is derived from Bhattacharyya (1999): and from his joint contribution with T.J. Nossiter, 'Communism in a Micro-State: Tripura and the Nationalities Question' in Nossiter (1988): *Marxist State Governments in India: Politics, Economics and Society*, London and New York, Pinter Publishers.

8 Bhattacharyya (1999), pp. 110–14.

9 K.S. Subramanian (2013): *Security Forces, Special Laws and Human Rights: India's North-Eastern Experience*, New Delhi, Council for Social Development, p. 162.

10 Bhattacharyya (1999), p. 3.

11 Bhaumik (2012), p. 6. Datta argued that had Deb been made the chief minister, that would have gone a long way in assuaging the tribal's apprehensions and helped the communist movement. 'Tribal

extremism would never have taken off ... and we would have been able to spread the communist movement to other tribal-dominated states of the North-East. But we missed that great chance by foisting Nripen Chakrabarty who was then described by tribal extremists as the refugee chief minister.' Ibid.

12 Nossiter (1988), p. 160.

13 Ibid., p. 167.

14 Ibid.

15 Based on table compiled by Gayatri Bhattacharyya (1998): *Refugee Rehabilitation and Its impact on Tripura's Economy*, Delhi, Om Sons Publications, pp. 38–39.

16 Subir Bhaumik (2014): 'Agartala Doctrine: A Small Indian State Plays Smart Geo-Politics', *South Asia Monitor*, 26 July.

17 Bhaumik (2012), p. 9.

18 Interview with V.K. Bahuguna, additional chief secretary (agriculture and forests), Agartala, 5 September 2014.

19 Bhaumik (2012), pp. 16–17.

20 K.S. Subramanian (2000): 'CPI(M)'s Record in Tripura', *Economic and Political Weekly*, 7 October.

21 Samir Kar Purkayastha (2014): 'CPI-M needs new leadership to recover politically', *Business Standard*, 4 August.

22 Bhaumik (2012), pp. 16–18.

23 The use of AFSPA came under sharp criticism not merely from civil liberties groups but also from former director general of police K.S. Subramanian (intervention at a seminar organized by me for the Council for Social Development at the India International Centre on 8 August 2012).

24 See for instance, 'Right Thing to Do for People's Rights', editorial in *Hindustan Times*, Delhi, 29 May 2015.

25 Government of Tripura (undated): *Approach to People's Plan in Tripura*, Agartala.

26 Interview with Sarkar, Agartala, 6 September 2014.

27 Bhaumik (2012), p. 22.

28 Ibid., pp. 24–25.

Select Bibliography

Books and Articles in Books:

Adhikari, Gangadhar (ed.) (1942), *Pakistan and National Unity*, Bombay: People's Publishing House, also available at http://sacw.net/article5487.html

Adhikari, G. (ed.) (1974), *Documents of the History of the Communist Party of India*, 1917–1922, Vol. I, New Delhi: People's Publishing House.

Adhikari, G. (ed.) (1974), *Documents of the History of the Communist Party of India*, 1923–35, Vol. II, New Delhi: People's Publishing House.

Adivasi Adhikar Rashtriya Manch (2010), *National Convention for Tribal Rights: A Report*, New Delhi: Adivasi Adhikar Rashtriya Manch.

Agarwala, Rina (2013), *Informal Labour, Formal Politics, and Dignified Discontent in India*, Delhi: Cambridge University Press.

Ahmad, Muzaffar (1959), *Communist Party of India: Years of Formation*, Calcutta: National Book Agency.

Ahmed, Talat (2009), *Literature and Politics in the Age of Nationalism*, New Delhi: Routledge.

All India Kisan Sabha (1982), *Proceedings and Resolutions*, 24th Conference, 8–11 November, 1982.

Alexander, K. C. (1989), 'Caste Mobilization and Class Consciousness: The Emergence of Agrarian Movements in Kerala and Tamil Nadu', in Francine Frankel and M.S.A. Rao (eds), *Dominance and State Power in Modern India,* Vol. 1, pp. 362–414, London: Oxford University Press.

Aliyar, Sabu and S. Irudaya Rajan (2004), 'Demographic Change in Kerala in the 1990s and Beyond', in Prakash, B.A. (ed.) *Kerala's Economic Development: Performance and Problems in the Post-Liberalisation Period*, pp. 61–81, New Delhi: Sage Publications.

Ambedkar, B.R. (2014), *Annihilation of Caste*, New Delhi: Navayana.

Anderson, Perry (1976), *Considerations on Western Marxism*, London: Verso.

Anderson, Perry (2012), *The Indian Ideology*, Gurgaon: Three Essays Collective.

Appu, P.S. (1996), *Land Reforms in India*, Delhi: Vikas Publishing House.

Austin, Granville (1966), *The Indian Constitution: Cornerstone of a Nation*, Oxford: Clarendon Press.

Balakrishnan, E. (1998), *History of the Communist Movement in Kerala*, Kochi: Kurukshetra Prakashan.

Banaji, Jairus (ed.) (2013), *Fascism: Essays on Europe and India*, Gurgaon: Three Essays Collective.

Bandyopadhyay, D. (1980), *Land Reforms in West Bengal*, Calcutta: Bureau of Applied Economics and Statistics, Government of West Bengal.

Bandyopadhyay, Sekhar (2014), 'Does Caste Matter in Bengal? Examining the Myths of Bengali Exceptionalism', in Mridula Nath Chakraborty (ed.), *Being Bengali: At Home and in the World*, New York: Routledge.

Banerjee, Mukulika (2010), 'Leadership and political work', in Pamela Price and Arild Engelsen Ruud (eds.), *Power and Influence in India: Bosses, Lords and Captains. Exploring the Political In South Asia*, New Delhi: Routledge India.

Banerjee, Sudeshna (2012), 'Overseeing the Disappearance of an Ecosystem: Governance in West Bengal and the Wetlands to East of Kolkata', in Jayanta Bandyopadhyay, Nilanjan Ghosh and Kanchan Chopra (eds), *Approaches to Environmental Governance*, New Delhi: Bloomsbury.

Banerjee, Sumanta (1980), *In the Wake of Naxalbari: A History of the Naxalite Movement in India*, Calcutta: Subarnarekha.

Banerjee, Sumanta (1999), 'Strategy, tactics, and forms of political participation among left parties', in T.V. Sathyamurthy (ed.), *Class Formation and Political Transformation in Post-Colonial India*, Delhi: Oxford University Press, 1999, pp. 202–38.

Banerjee, Sumanta (2012), *Marxism and the Indian Left: From 'Interpreting' India with 'Changing' It*, Kolkata: Purbalok Publication.

Bardhan, A.B., and M. Farooqui (1997), *Communists and India's Freedom Struggle*, New Delhi: Communist Party Publications.

Bardhan, A.B. (2003), *Crisis of Corporate Capitalism*, New Delhi: People's Publishing House.

Barrett, Patrick, Daniel Chavez and Cesar Rodriguez-Garavito (eds) (2008), *The New Latin American Left: Utopia Reborn,* London/Amsterdam: Pluto Press/Transnational Institute.

Basu, Amrita (1992), *Two Faces of Protest: Contrasting Modes of Women's Activism in India,* Delhi: Oxford University Press.

Basu, Amrita (1992), 'Democratic Centralism in the Home and the World: Bengali Women and The CPI(M)', in *Two Faces of Protest: Contrasting Modes of Women's Activism in India,* Delhi: Oxford University Press.

Basu, Jyoti (1998), 'Introductory Note', in *Documents of the Communist Party of India*, Vol. XIV (1970), Calcutta: National Book Agency Private Limited.

Baviskar, Amita (2005), 'Red in Tooth and Claw?: Searching for Class in Struggles over Nature', in Raka Ray and Mary Katzenstein (eds), *Social Movements in India: Poverty, Power, and Politics*, Lanham, MD: Rowman and Littlefield.

Bellamy Foster, John (2000), *Marx's Ecology: Materialism and Nature*, New York: Monthly Review Press.

Bhagat, K.P. (1962), *The Kerala Mid-term Election of 1960: The Communist Party's Conquest of New Positions*, Popular Book Depot.

Bhambri, C.P. (2010), *Coalition Politics in India*, Delhi: Shipra Publications.

Bhattacharya, Buddhadeva, (1982), *Origins of The RSP: From National*

Revolutionary Politics to Non-conformist Marxism, Calcutta: Lokayata Sahitya Chakra.

Bhattacharyya, Gayatri (1998), *Refugee Rehabilitation and Its impact on Tripura's Economy*, Delhi: Om Sons Publications.

Bhattacharyya, Harihar (1998), *Micro-foundations of Bengal Communism*, Delhi: Ajanta Publications.

Bhattacharyya, Harihar (1999), *Communism in Tripura*, Delhi: Ajanta Publications.

Bhaumik, Subir (2009), *The Troubled Periphery: Crisis of India's North East*, New Delhi: Sage Publications.

Bidwai, Praful and Achin Vanaik (2000), *South Asia on a Short Fuse: Nuclear Politics and the Future of Disarmament*, New Delhi: Oxord University Press.

Bidwai, Praful (2012), *The Politics of Climate Change and the Global Crisis: Mortgaging Our Future*, New Delhi: Orient BlackSwan.

Blackburn, Robin (1975), *Explosion in a Subcontinent: India, Pakistan, Bangladesh, and Ceylon*, Harmondsworth: Penguin Books in association with *New Left Review*.

Blackburn, Robin (1991), *After the Fall: the Failure of Communism and the Future of Socialism*, London: Verso.

Boyce, James K. (1987), *Agrarian Impasse in Bengal: Institutional Constraints and Technological Change*, London: Oxford University Press.

Brass, Paul R. and Marcus F. Franda (eds) (1973), *Radical Politics in South Asia (Studies in Communism, Revisionism, and Revolution)*, Cambridge, Massachusetts: The MIT Press.

Breman, Jan (1996), *Footloose Labour: Working in India's Informal Economy*, Cambridge, UK: Cambridge University Press.

Breman, Jan, Aseem Prakash and Isabelle Guérin (eds) (2009), *India's Unfree Workforce: Of Bondage Old and New*, Delhi: Oxford University Press.

Breman, Jan. (2013), *The Long Road to Social Security: Assessing the Implementation of National Social Security Initiatives for the Working Poor in India*, Delhi: Oxford University Press.

Broomfield, John H. (1968), *Elite Conflict in a Plural Society: Twentieth Century Bengal*, Berkeley: University of California Press.

Burkett, Paul (1999), *Marx and Nature: A Red and Green Perspective*, London: Palgrave Macmillan.

Centre for Equity Studies (2012), *Promises to Keep: Investigating Government's Response to Sachar Committee Recommendations*, New Delhi: Centre for Equity Studies, with Centre for Budget Governance and Accountability.

Chakrabarty, Saroj (1978), *With Bengal Chief Ministers: Memoirs, 1962 to 1977*, Calcutta: Orient Longman.

Chakravarti, Uma (2003), *Gendering Caste through a Feminist Lens*, Calcutta: Stree.

Chandra, Bipan (ed.) (1983), *The Indian Left: Critical Appraisals*, New Delhi: Vikas.

Chakraborti, Anil K. (2003), *Beneficiaries of Land Reforms: The West Bengal Scenario*, Kolkata: Spandan, for Government of West Bengal.

Chavez, Daniel and Benjamin Goldfrank (eds) (2004), *The Left in the City: Participatory Local Governments in Latin America*, London: Latin America Bureau.

Chhotray, Vasudha. (2011), *The Anti-Politics Machine in India: State, Decentralisation and Participatory Development*, London: Anthem Press.

Chattopadhyay, Gautam (2010), *Subhas Chandra Bose and the Indian Communist Movement*, New Delhi: People's Publishing House.

Chaudhuri, Tridib (1970), *Why RSP? Historic Need For a Party of Socialist Revolution in India Today*, Calcutta: Lokayata Sahitya Chakra.

Chakravartty, Gargi (2007), *P.C. Joshi: A Biography*, New Delhi: National Book Trust.

Chakravartty, Gargi (ed.) (2014), *People's Warrior: Words and Worlds of P.C. Joshi*, New Delhi: Tulika Books.

Chatterjeee, Partha (1997), *The Present History of West Bengal: Essays in Political Criticism*, Delhi: Oxford University Press.

Chaudhuri, Asim Kumar (1980), *Socialist Movement in India: The Congress Socialist Party, 1934–1947*, Calcutta: Progressive Publishers.

Chenoy, Anuradha M. and Kamal A. Mitra Chenoy (2010), *Maoist and Other Armed Conflicts*, New Delhi: Penguin Books India.

Chibber, Vivek (2011), *Locked in Place: State-Building and Late Industrialization in India*, Princeton and Oxford: Princeton University Press.

Choudhury, Saifuddin (2002), *World For Change: Our Stand on Some Ideological and Political Issues*, Kolkata: Notun Path.

Chowdhury, Prafulla Roy (1985), *Left Experiment in West Bengal*, New Delhi: Patriot Publishers.

Cristy, Carmel K.J. (2015), 'The Politics of Sexuality and Caste: Looking through Kerala's Public Space', in Satheese Chandra Bose and Shiju Sam Varughese (eds), *Kerala Modernity: Ideas, Spaces and Practices in Transition*, New Delhi: Orient BlackSwan.

Damodaran, Harish (2008), *India's New Capitalists: Caste, Business, and Industry in a Modern Nation*, Ranikhet: Permanent Black.

Das, Arvind Narain (ed.) (1982), *Agrarian Movements in India: Studies on 20th Century Bihar*, London: Frank Cass.

Davey, Brian (1975), *The Economic Development of India: A Marxist Analysis*, Nottingham: Spokesman Books.

Degras, Jane (1971), *Communist International: Documents 1919–1943* (3 vols), London: Routledge.

Desai, A. R. (ed.) (1986), *Agrarian Struggles in India*, Delhi: Oxford University Press.

Desai, Manali (2007), *State Formation and Radical Democracy in India*, Abingdon, Oxfordshire: Routledge.

Desai, Neera (1998), *A Decade of Women's Movement in India*, Bombay: Himalaya.

Devika, J. and Binitha V. Thampi (2012), *New Lamps for Old: Gender Paradoxes of Political Decentralisation in Kerala*, New Delhi: Zubaan.

Dey, Ishita, Ranabir Samaddar and Sujit K. Sen (eds) (2013), *Beyond Kolkata: Rajarhat and the Dystopia of Urban Imagination*, New Delhi: Routledge India.

Dhawale, Ashok (2000), *The Shiv Sena: Semi-Fascism in Action*, New Delhi: CPI(M) Publications.

Djurfeldt, Göran (1982), 'Classical discussions of capital and peasantry:

a critique', in John Harriss (ed.), *Rural Development*, London: Hutchinson.

Dreze, Jean and Amartya Sen (eds) (1997), *Indian Development: Selected Regional Perspectives*, Delhi: Oxford University Press.

Dreze, Jean and Amartya Sen (2013), *An Uncertain Glory: India and Its Contradictions*, New Delhi: Penguin Books.

Duttagupta, Sobhanlal (1980), *Comintern, India and the Colonial Question 1929–1937*, Calcutta: K.P. Bagchi.

Easvariah, P. (1993), *Communist Parties in Power and Agrarian Reforms*, Delhi: Academic Foundation.

Farooqui, Amar (ed.) (2000), *Remembering Dr. Gangadhar Adhikari: Selections from Writings, Part II*, New Delhi: People's Publishing House.

Fic, Victor M. (1969), *Peaceful Transition to Communism in India: Strategy of the Communist Party*, Bombay: Nachiketa Publications.

Fic, Victor M. (1970), *Kerala: Yenan of India: Rise of Communist Power, 1937–1969*, Bombay: Nachiketa Publications.

Franda, Marcus F. (1971), *Radical Politics in West Bengal*, Cambridge, MA: MIT Press.

Franke, Richard W. and Barbara H. Chasin (1994), *Kerala: Radical Reform as Development in an Indian State*, San Francisco: Institute for Food and Development Policy, also available at http://files.eric.ed.gov/fulltext/ED400149.pdf

Franke, Richard W. and Barbara H. Chasin (2000), 'Is the Kerala Model Sustainable?: Lessons from the Past: Prospects for the Future', in Govindan Parayil (ed.), *The Kerala Model of Development: Perspectives on Development and Sustainability*, London: Zed Books.

Gandhi, Nandita and Nandita Shah (1991), *The Issues at Stake: Theory and Practice in the Contemporary Women's Movement in India*, New Delhi: Kali for Women.

Gandhi, Nandita (1996), *When the Rolling Pins Hit the Streets: Women in the Anti-Price Rise Movement in Maharashtra*, New Delhi: Kali for Women.

Gaur, Raj Bahadur (1970), *Makhdoom: a Memoir*, New Delhi: Communist Party of India.

Gaur, Raj Bahadur and Shameem Faizee (1995), *Tribute to CR*, New Delhi: People's Publishing House.

Gayer, Laurent and Christophe Jaffrelot (eds) (2010), *Armed Militias of South Asia: Fundamentalists, Maoists and Separatists*, London: Oxford University Press.

George, K.K. (1993), *Limits of the Kerala Model*, Trivandrum: Centre for Development Studies.

Ghatak, Ritwik (2000), *On the Cultural Front: A Thesis Submitted by Ritwik Ghatak to the Communist Party of India in 1954*, Calcutta: Ritwik Memorial Trust.

Ghosh, A. and K. Dutt (1977), *Development of Capitalist Relations in Agriculture: A Case Study of West Bengal (1793–1971)*, New Delhi: People's Publishing House.

Gopal, Priyamvada (2005), *Literary Radicalism in India: Gender, Nation and the Transition to Independence*, New York: Routledge.

Gopalan, A.K. (1959), *Kerala—Past and Present*, London: Lawrence and Wishart.

Gopalan, A.K. (1973), *In the Cause of the People: Reminiscences*, Bombay: Orient Longman.

Gupta, Amit Kumar (ed.) (1987), *Myth and Reality: The Struggle for Freedom in India, 1945–47*, New Delhi: Nehru Memorial Museum and Library/Manohar Publishers.

Gupta, Monobina (2010), *Left Politics in Bengal: Time Travels among Bhadralok Marxists*, New Delhi: Orient BlackSwan.

Haithcox, John Patrick (1971), *Communism and Nationalism in India: M.N. Roy and Comintern Policy 1920–1939*, Princeton: Princeton University Press.

Hallas, Duncan (1985), *The Comintern*, London: Bookmarks.

Hardgrave, Robert L. (1973), 'The Origins of the Communist Party in Kerala', in Paul R. Brass and Marcus Franda (eds), *Radical Movements in South Asia*, Cambridge, Massachusetts: MIT Press.

Harnecker, Marta (2007), *Rebuilding the Left*, London: Zed Books.

Harriss-White, Barbara (2008), *Rural Commercial Capital: Agricultural Markets in West Bengal*, Delhi: Oxford University Press.

Harriss-White, Barbara and Sugata Bose (eds) (1999), *Sonar Bangla? Agricultural Growth and Agrarian Change in West Bengal and Bangladesh*, New Delhi: Sage Publications.

Hauser, Walter (ed.) (2003), *Religion, Politics and the Peasants: A Memoir of India's Freedom Movement*, Delhi: Manohar Publishers.

Hauser, Walter (ed.) (2005), *Sahajanand on Agricultural Labour and the Rural Poor*, Delhi: Manohar Publishers.

Haynes, Mike (2002), *Russia: Class and Power, 1917–2000*, London: Bookmarks.

Heller, Patrick (2007), 'Kerala: Deepening a Radical Social Democracy', in Sandbrook Richard, Marc Edelman, Patrick Heller and Judith Teichman (eds), *Social Democracy in the Global Periphery: Origins, Challenges, Prospects*, Cambridge, UK: Cambridge University Press.

Hensman, Rohini (2011), *Workers, Unions, and Global Capitalism*, New York: Columbia University Press.

Herring, Ronald (1983), *Land to the Tiller: The Political Economy of Agrarian Reform in South Asia*, New Haven: Yale University Press.

Hirway, Indira, Amita Shah and Ghanshyam Shah (eds) (2014), *Growth or Development: Which Way is Gujarat Going?*, Delhi: Oxford University Press.

Hobsbawm, Eric (1995), *Age of Extremes: The Short Twentieth Century, 1914–1991*, London: Abacus.

Irshad, S. Mohammed (2015), 'The Pipe Dreams of Development: Institutionalising Drinking Water Supply in Kerala', in Satheese Chandra Bose and Shiju Sam Varughese (eds), *Kerala Modernity: Ideas, Spaces and Practices in Transition*, Hyderabad: Orient BlackSwan.

Jalil, Rakhshanda (2014*), Liking Progress, Loving Change: A Literary History of the Progressive Writers' Movement in Urdu*, Delhi: Oxford University Press.

Jeffrey, Robin (1992), *Politics, Women, and Well-Being*, London and Delhi: Oxford University Press.

Jeffrey, Robin (1994), *The Decline of Nair Dominance: Society and Politics in Travancore 1847–1908*, New Delhi: Manohar Publishers.

Jenkins, Rob (1999), *Democratic Politics and Economic Reform in India*, Cambridge, UK: Cambridge University Press.

Josh, Bhagwan (1979), *Communist Movement in Punjab*, 1926–47, Jaipur: Anupama Publications.

Josh, Sohan Singh (1977–78*)*, *Hindustan Gadar Party,* (Vols 1 and 2), New Delhi: People's Publishing House.

Joshi, Shashi and Bhagwan Josh (1992), *Struggle for Hegemony in India, 1920–47: The Colonial State, the Left, and the National Movement*, New Delhi: Sage Publications.

Joshi, Shashi and Bhagwan Josh (1994), *Struggle for Hegemony in India (1920–47): The Colonial State, the Left and the National Movement, Vol. III: 1941–47: Culture, Community and Power*, New Delhi: Sage Publications.

Kaifi, Shaukat (2010), *Kaifi and I: A Memoir,* (tr.) Nasreen Rehman, New Delhi: Zubaan.

Kanhere, Sujata and Mira Savara (1980), *A Case Study on the Organising of Landless Tribal Women in Maharashtra, India*, Bangkok: Asian and Pacific Centre for Women and Development.

Kannan, K. P. (1988), *Of Rural Proletarian Struggles: Mobilization and Organization of Rural Workers in South-West India*, Delhi: Oxford University Press.

Kannan, K.P. (2007), 'From Human Development to Economic Growth: Kerala's Turnaround in Growth Powered by Human Development, Remittances and Reform', in A. Vaidyanathan and K.L. Krishna (eds), *Institutions and Markets in India's Development: Essays for K.N. Raj*, Delhi: Oxford University Press.

Kannan, K.P. (2012), *Interrogating Inclusive Growth*, New Delhi: Routledge.

Karat, Brinda (2005*)*, *Survival and Emancipation: Notes from Indian Women's Struggles*, Gurgaon: Three Essays Collective.

Karat, Prakash (1988), *Foreign Funding and the Philosophy of Voluntary*

Organisations: A Factor in Imperialist Strategy, New Delhi: National Book Centre.

Katzenstein, Mary Fainsod (1979), *Ethnicity and Equality: The Shiv Sena Party and Preferential Policies in Bombay*, Ithaca and London: Cornell University Press.

Kaul, Jolly Mohan (2010), *In Search of a Better World*, Kolkata: Samya.

Kautsky, John H. (1982), *Moscow and the Communist Party of India: A Study in the Post-war Evolution of International Communist Strategy*, Westport, Ct: Greenwood Press.

Kaviraj, Sudipta and Sunil Khilnani (2001), *Civil Society: History and Possibilities*, Cambridge, UK: Cambridge University Press.

Kiernan, Victor G. (2003), 'Some Reminiscences of India and the CPI', in Prakash Karat (ed.) *Across Time and Continents: A Tribute to Victor G. Liernan*, New Delhi: LeftWord Books.

Kishimoto, Satoko., Emanuele Lobina and Olivier Petitjean (eds) (2015), *Our Public Water Future: The Global Experience with Remunicipalisation*, Amsterdam, London, Paris, Cape Town and Brussels: Transnational Institute (TNI), Public Services International Research Unit (PSIRU), Multinationals Observatory, Municipal Services Project (MSP) and the European Federation of Public Service Unions (EPSU), http://www.tni.org/briefing/our-public-water-future (accessed on 7 April 2015)

Kohli, Atul (1987), *The State and Poverty in India: The Politics of Reform*, Cambridge, UK: Cambridge University Press.

Kohli, Atul (1990), 'From elite activism to democratic consolidation: the rise of reform communism in West Bengal', in Francine R. Frankel and M.S.A. Rao (eds), *Dominance and State Power in Modern India: Decline of a Social Order* (Vol. II), Delhi: Oxford University Press.

Konar, Hare Krishna (1977), *Agrarian Problems of India*, Calcutta: Gaur Sabha.

Kosambi, D.D. (1957), *Exasperating Essays*, New Delhi: People's Publishing House.

Kothari, Smitu and Zia Mian (eds) (2001), *Out of the Nuclear Shadow*, New Delhi: Lokayan and Rainbow Publishers.

Kumar, Radha (1993), *The History of Doing: An Illustrated Account of Movements for Women's Rights and Feminism in India 1800–1990*, New Delhi: Kali for Women.

Kumaramangalam, Mohan (1973), *Communists in Congress: Kumaramangalam's Thesis*, New Delhi: D. K. Publishing House.

Kutty, Raman (1999), 'Development of Kerala's Health Services', in M.A. Oommen (ed.) *Rethinking Development: Kerala's Development Experience*, Vol. 2, New Delhi: Institute of Social Sciences.

Lahiri, Ranjit Kumar (1981), 'Land Reforms in West Bengal—Some Implications', in Manjula Bose (ed.), *Land Reforms in Eastern India*, Calcutta: Planning Forum, Jadavpur University.

Lerner, Daniel (1958), *The Passing of Traditional Society*, New York: Free Press.

Lewin, Moshe (2005), *The Soviet Century*, London: Verso.

Lieten, G. K. (1992), *Continuity and Change in Rural West Bengal*, New Delhi: Sage Publications.

Lieten, G. K., (1996), *Development, Devolution and Democracy: Village Discourse in West Bengal* (Indo-Dutch Studies on Development Alternatives 18), New Delhi: Sage Publications.

Limaye, Madhu (1951), *Communist Party: Facts and Fiction*, Hyderabad: Chetana Prakashan Ltd.

Limaye, Madhu (1990), *Indian Polity in Transition*, New Delhi: Radiant Publishers.

Limaye, Madhu (1991), *Socialist-Communist Interaction*, Delhi: Ajanta Publications.

Lokayata Sahitya Chakra (2010), *A Nefarious Design to Control India's Agriculture: Indo-US Treaty, New Seed Act, Second Green Revolution*, Kolkata: Lokayata Sahitya Chakra.

Lokayata Sahitya Chakra (2011), *A Positive Programme for Indian Revolution*, Kolkata: Kranti Press.

Mallick, Ross (1994), *Indian Communism: Opposition, Collaboration and Institutionalisation*, Delhi: Oxford University Press.

Mallick, Ross. (2007), *Development Policy of a Communist Government: West Bengal since 1977*, Cambridge, UK: Cambridge University Press.

Mandel, Ernest (1992), *Power and Money: A Marxist Theory of Bureaucracy*, London: Verso.

Mathur, Hari Mohan (2008), 'Development and Displacement: Introduction and Overview', *India Social Development Report 2008*, New Delhi: Council for Social Development/Oxford University Press.

Mazdoor Mukti (2008), *A Timeline of Nandigram: One Year and More (22 August 2005 – 22 February 2008)*, Bikrampur, West Bengal: A Mazdoor Mukti Publication.

Mazdoor Mukti (2009), *A Timeline of Nandigram: One Year and More (18 May 2006 – 15 June 2008)*, Bikrampur, West Bengal: A Mazdoor Mukti Publication.

McCallum, Jamie K. (2013), 'Organizing the "Unorganized": Varieties of Labor Transnationalism in India', in *Global Unions, Local Power: The New Spirit of Transnational Labor Organizing*, New York: Cornell University Press.

McGarr, Paul Michael (2013), *The Cold War in South Asia: Britain, the United States and the Indian Subcontinent, 1945–1965*, Cambridge, UK: Cambridge University Press.

Menon, Achuta (1969), *What Happened in Kerala: Review of the 30 Months of Namboodiripad Government*, New Delhi: CPI.

Menon, Ritu (ed.) (2011), *Making a Difference: Memoirs of the Women's Movement in India*, New Delhi: Women Unlimited.

Miliband, Ralph (1994), *Socialism for a Sceptical Age*, Cambridge, UK: Polity Press.

Mitra, Ashok (1979), *The Hoodlum Years*, New Delhi: Orient Longman.

Mitra, Ashok (2006), *From The Ramparts*, New Delhi: Tulika Books.

Mitra, H.L. (ed.) (1990), *The Indian Annual Register* 1928, New Delhi: Gyan Publishing House.

Mohanty, Manoranjan (1977), *Revolutionary Violence: A Study of the Maoist Movement in India*, New Delhi: Sterling.

Mohanty, Manoranjan and Partha Nath Mukherji (eds) (1998), *People's Rights: Social Movements and the State in the Third World*, New Delhi: Sage Publications.

Moore Jr, Barrington (1966), *Social Origins of Democracy and Dictatorship*, Boston: Beacon Press.

Mukherjee, Arun (2014), *Unknown Facets of Rajiv Gandhi, Jyoti Basu, Indrajit Gupta*, New Delhi: Manas Publications.

Mukherjee Reed, Ananya (2008), *Human Development and Social Power: Perspectives from South Asia*, Oxford: Routledge.

Mullick, B.N. (1972), *My Years with Nehru, 1948–64*, New Delhi: Allied Publishers.

Nair, M.N.V. and Praful Bidwai (eds) (2005), *Labour Movement in India: Documents 1941–1947*, New Delhi: Pragati Publication/Indian Council of Historical Research.

Nair, R. Ramakrishnan (1965), *How Communists Came to Power in Kerala*, Trivandrum: Kerala Academy of Political Science.

Namboodiripad, E.M.S. (1943), *A Short History of the Peasant Movement in Kerala*, Bombay: People's Publishing House.

Namboodiripad, E.M.S. (1952), *On the Agrarian Question in India*, Bombay: People's Publishing House.

Namboodiripad, E.M.S. (1966), *Economic and Politics of India's Socialist Pattern*, New Delhi: People's Publishing House.

Namboodiripad, E.M.S. (1968), *Kerala: Yesterday, Today and Tomorrow*, Calcutta: National Book Agency.

Namboodiripad, E.M.S. (1974), *Conflicts and Crisis: Political India*, Bombay: Orient Longman.

Namboodiripad, E.M.S. (1976), *How I Became a Communist*, Trivandrum: Chinta Publishers.

Namboodiripad, E.M.S. (1984), *Kerala: Society and Politics: A Historical Survey*, New Delhi: National Book Centre.

Namboodiripad, E.M.S. (1985), *Selected Writings*, Vol. 2, Calcutta: National Book Agency.

Namboodiripad, E.M.S. (1986), *History of the Indian Freedom Struggle*, Trivandrum: Social Scientist Press.

Namboodiripad, E.M.S. (1987), *Reminiscences of an Indian Communist*, New Delhi: National Book Centre.

Namboodiripad, E.M.S. (1994), *The Communist Party in Kerala: Six Decades of Struggle and Advance*, New Delhi: National Book Centre.

Namboodiripad, E.M.S. (2010), *The Frontline Years: Selected Articles*, New Delhi: LeftWord Books.

Namboodiripad, E.M.S. (2011), *The Mahatma and the Ism*, New Delhi: LeftWord Books.

Namboodiripad, E.M.S. (2011), *History, Society and Land Relations: Selected Essays*, New Delhi: LeftWord Books.

Nanda, Meera (2011), *The God Market: How Globalisation is Making India More Hindu*, New Delhi: Random House.

Nayyar, Rohini (1991), *Rural Poverty in India*, Delhi: Oxford University Press.

Nossiter, T. J. (1982), *Communism in Kerala: A Study in Political Adaptation*, Bombay: Oxford University Press.

Nossiter, T. J. (1988), *Marxist State Governments in India: Politics, Economics And Society*, London: Pinter Publishers.

Nove, Alec (1964), *Was Stalin Really Necessary?: Some Problems of Soviet Economic Policy*, London: Routledge.

Nove, Alec (1988), *Stalinism and After: The Road to Gorbachev*, London: Taylor and Francis.

Nove, Alec (1993), *An Economic History of the USSR: 1917–1991*, Harmondsworth: Penguin Books.

Nove, Alec (2003), *The Economics of Feasible Socialism Revisited*, London: Routledge.

Omvedt, Gail (1993), *Reinventing Revolution: New Social Movements and the Socialist Tradition in India*, New York: M.E. Sharpe.

Omvedt, Gail (1995), *Dalit Visions*, New Delhi: Orient Longman.

Omvedt, Gail (2006), 'Kerala is Part of India', in Joseph Tharamangalam (ed.), *Kerala: The Paradoxes of Public Action and Development*, Hyderabad: Orient Longman

Oommen, M.A. (2007), *Kudumbashree of Kerala: An Appraisal*, New Delhi: Institute of Social Sciences.

Oommen, M.A. (ed) (2009), *Rethinking Development: Kerala's Development Experience*, (Vols. 1 and 2) New Delhi: Institute of Social Sciences/ Concept Publishing Company.

Oommen, T. K. (1985), *From Mobilization to Institutionalization: The Dynamics of Agrarian Movement in Twentieth Century Kerala*, Bombay: Popular Prakashan.

Oommen, T.K. (ed.) (2010), *Social Movements II: Concerns of Equity and Security*, Delhi: Oxford University Press.

Osella, Filippo and Caroline Osella (2000), *Social Mobility in Kerala: Modernity and Identity in Conflict*, London: Pluto Press.

Overstreet, Gene D. and Marshall Windmiller (1959), *Communism in India*, Berkeley: University of California Press.

Panikkar, K. N. (1989), *Against Lord and State: Religion and Peasant Uprisings in Malabar, 1836–1921*, Delhi: Oxford University Press.

Paranjpe, Suhas (1975), *Das Kapital: Subodh Parichaye* [Marathi], Pune: Shankar Bramhe Samajvigyan Granthalaya Prakashan.

Parayil, Govindan (ed.) (2000), *Kerala: The Development Experience*, London and New York: Zed Books.

Parthasarathy, G. (1998), 'Minimum Wages in Agriculture: A Review of Indian Experience', in R.S. Radhakrishna and A.N. Sharma (eds), *Empowering Rural Labour in India*, New Delhi: Institute for Human Development.

Parulekar, Godavari (1975), *Adivasis Revolt: The Story of Warli Peasants in Struggle*, Calcutta: National Book Agency.

Paul, Manas (2009), *The Eyewitness: Tales From Tripura's Ethnic Conflict*, New Delhi: Lancer.

Petras, James (1999), *The Left Strikes Back: Class Conflict in Latin America in the Age of Neoliberalism*, Boulder: Westview Press.

Prakash, Gyan (2010), *Mumbai Fables*, New Delhi, HarperCollins.

Prakash, B.A. (2004), *Kerala's Economic Development: Performance and Problems in the Post-Liberalisation Period*, New Delhi: Sage Publications.

Prakash, Shri (1983) 'CPI and the Pakistan Movement', in Bipan Chandra (ed.), *The Indian Left: Critical Perspectives*, New Delhi: Vikas Publishing House.

Rai Chowdhuri, Satyabrata (2011), *Leftism in India, 1917–1947*, New Delhi: Macmillan.

Rajimwale, Anil (2007), *Life and Works of P.C. Joshi*, New Delhi: People's Publishing House.

Rajimwale, Anil (2012), *A Brief History of the CPI*, New Delhi: People's Publishing House.

Ram, Mohan (1969), *Indian Communism: Split Within Split*, Delhi: Vikas Publications.

Ram, N. (1999), *Riding the Nuclear Tiger*, New Delhi: Leftword Books.

Ramachandran, V. K. (2010), 'On Kerala's Development Achievements', in Jean Dreze and Amartya Sen (eds), *Indian Development: Selected Regional Perspectives*, Delhi: Oxford University Press.

Raman, K. Ravi (2010), *Global Capital and Peripheral Labour: the History and Political Economy of Plantation Workers in India*, London: Routledge.

Ramana, M.V. and C. Rammanohar Reddy (eds) (2003), *Prisoners of the Nuclear Dream*, New Delhi: Orient Longman.

Ramana, M.V. (2012), *The Power of Promise: Examining Nuclear Energy in India*, New Delhi: Penguin Books/Viking.

Rao, M.B. (ed.) (1976), *Documents of the History of the Communist Party of India*, Vol. VII: 1948–1950, New Delhi, People's Publishing House.

Reddy, Ravi Narayan (2011), *Heroic Telangana: Reminiscences and Experiences*, New Delhi: People's Publishing House.

Retzlaff, Ralph (1965), 'Revisionism and Dogmatism in the Communist Party of India', in R.A. Scalapino, *The Communist Revolution in Asia*, Berkeley: Prentice Hall.

Rogaly, Ben, B. Harriss-White and S. Bose, (eds) (1999), *Sonar Bangla? Agricultural Growth and Agrarian Change in West Bengal and Bangladesh*, New Delhi: Sage Publications.

Rohini (1990), *To Do Something Beautiful*, Bangalore: Streelekha.

Roy, Arundhati (2014), 'Introduction' to B.R. Ambedkar's *Annihilation of Caste*, New Delhi: Navayana.

Roy, M.N. (1964), *M.N. Roy's Memoirs,* New Delhi: Allied Publishers.

Roy, M.N. (1981), *Men I Met*, New Delhi: Ajanta Publications.

Russell, Ralph (1977), 'Leadership in the All-India Progressive Writers' Movement, 1935–1947', in B.N. Pandey (ed.), *Leadership in South Asia*, New Delhi, Vikas Publishing House.

Ruud, Arild Engelsen (1999), 'From Untouchable to Communist: Wealth, Power and Status among Supporters of the Communist Party (Marxist) in Rural West Bengal', in Ben Rogaly, Barbara Harris-White and Sugata Bose (eds), *Sonar Bangla? Agricultural Growth and Agrarian Change in West Bengal and Bangladesh*, New Delhi: Sage Publications.

Ruud, Arild Engelsen. (2003), *Poetics of Village Politics: The Making of West Bengal's Rural Communism*, Delhi: Oxford University Press.

Sathyamurthy, T.V. (ed.) (1996), *Class Formation and Political Transformation in Post-Colonial India*, Delhi: Oxford University Press.

Sahni, Kalpana and P.C. Joshi (2012), *Balraj and Bhisham Sahni: Brothers in Political Theatre*, New Delhi: Sahmat.

Samaddar, Ranabir (1994), 'Caste and Power in West Bengal', in K.L. Sharma (ed.), *Caste and Class in India*, New Delhi: Rawat Publications.

Samaddar, Ranabir (2013), *Passive Revolution in West Bengal, 1977–2011*, New Delhi: Sage Publications.

Sandarbh Kendra (ND), *Khwab Martay Nahin: Kamrade Lagon Ko Lal Salaam*, Indore: Sandarbh Kendra.

Sarkar, Sumit (1983), *Modern India*, New Delhi: Macmillan.

Schaffer, Howard B. (2003), *Ellsworth Bunker: Global Troubleshooter, Vietnam Hawk*, Chapel Hill and London: University of North Carolina Press.

Sen, Abhijit (2010), 'Unfinished Tasks of Land Reform', in Michael Lipton, (ed.), *Land Reform in Developing Countries: Property Rights and Property Wrongs*, Routledge Priorities in Development Economics, Abingdon, Oxfordshire: Routledge.

Sen, Arup Kumar (2011), 'Workers' Control in India's Communist Ruled State: Labour Struggles and Trade Unions in West Bengal', in Dario Azzellini, Immanuel Ness (eds), *Ours to Master and to Own: Workers' Control from the Commune to the Present*, Chicago: Haymarket Books.

Sen, Bhowani (1962), *Evolution of Agrarian Relations in India*, New Delhi: People's Publishing House.

Sen, Gautam (2000), *Against Substitutionism: A Journey from 'What is to be Done?' to What ought not to be done*, Sonarpur: SEARCH.

Sen, Gautam (2008), *Nandigram: A Critical Evaluation*, Bikrampur, West Bengal: A Mazdoor Mukti Publication.

Sen, Ratna (2009), *The Evolution of Industrial Relations in West Bengal*, Geneva: International Labour Organization.

Sen Gupta, Bhabani (1978), *Communism in Indian Politics*, New Delhi: Young Asia Publications.

Sen Gupta, Bhabani (1979), *CPI(M): Promises, Prospects, Problems*, New Delhi: Young Asia Publications.

Sengupta, Sunil and Haris Gazdar (1997), 'Agrarian Politics and Rural Development in West Bengal', in Jean Dreze and Amrtya Sen (eds), *Indian Development: Selected Regional Perspectives*, Delhi: Oxford University Press.

Sen, Ilina (ed.) (1990), *A Space within the Struggle*, New Delhi: Kali for Women.

Sen, Mohit and M.B. Rao (eds) (1968), *Das Kapital: Centenary Volume*, New Delhi: People's Publishing House.

Sen, Mohit (1970), *The Indian Revolution; Review and Perspectives*, New Delhi: People's Publishing House.

Sen, Mohit (1970), *Communism and the New Left*, New Delhi: Communist Party Publication.

Sen, Mohit (ed.) (1977), *Documents of the History of the Communist Party of India*, Vol. VIII: 1951–1956. New Delhi: People's Publishing House.

Sen, Mohit and Bhupesh Gupta (1978), *CPM's Politics X-Rayed*, New Delhi: Communist Party of India.

Sen, Mohit (2003), *A Traveller and the Road: A Journey of an Indian Communist*, New Delhi: Rupa & Co.

Seth, Sanjay (1995), *Marxist Theory and Nationalist Politics: Colonial India*, New Delhi: Sage Publications.

Shah, Alpa (2010), *In the Shadows of the State: Indigenous Politics, Environmentalism, and Insurgency in Jharkhand, India*, Durham: Duke University Press.

Shah, Ghanshyam (1977), *Protest Movements in Two Indian States*, Delhi: Ajanta Books International.

Shah, Sonal (1994), *Indian Socialists: Search for Identity*, Bombay: Popular Prakashan.

Shani, Ornit (2007), *Communalism, Caste and Hindu Nationalism: The Violence in Gujarat*, Cambridge, UK: Cambridge University Press.

Sharma, Shalini (2010), *Radical Politics in Colonial Punjab: Governance and Sedition*, New York: Routledge.

Siraj (ND), *Conversion of Parliamentarism to Social Fascism: An Indian Experience*, Revolutionary Publications.

Sood, Atul (ed.) (2012), *Poverty Amidst Prosperity: Essays on the Trajectory of Development in Gujarat*, Delhi: Aakar Books.

Srinivas, B. (1993), *Worker Takeover in Industry: The Kamani Tubes Experiment*, New Delhi: Sage Publications.

Stree Shakti Sanghatana (1989), *We Were Making History: Women and the Telengana Uprising*, New Delhi: Kali for Women.

Subramanian, K.S. (1989), *Parliamentary Communism: Crisis in Indian Communist Movement*, Delhi: Ajanta Publications.

Subramanian, K.S. (2013), *Security Forces, Special Laws and Human Rights: India's North-Eastern Experience*, Delhi: Council for Social Development.

Sud, Nikita (2012), *Liberalisation, Hindu Nationalism and the State: A Biography of Gujarat*, Delhi: Oxford University Press.

Sundarayya, P. (1972), *Telengana People's Struggle and its Lessons*, Delhi: Foundation Books.

Tawa Lama-Rewal, Stephanie (2009), 'The resilient bhadralok: A Profile of the West Bengal MLAs', in Christophe Jaffrelot and Sanjay Kumar (eds), *Rise of the Plebeians? The Changing Face of Indian Legislative Assemblies*, New Delhi: Routledge

Teitelbaum, Emmanuel (2011), *Mobilizing Restraint: Democracy and Industrial Conflict in Post-Reform South Asia*, New York: Cornell University Press

Tharamangalam, Joseph (1981), *Agrarian Class Conflict: The Political*

Mobilisation of Agricultural Labourers in Kuttanad, South India, Vancouver: University of British Columbia Press.

The Pratichi Trust (2002), *The Pratichi Education Report*, New Delhi: The Pratichi (India) Trust.

The Pratichi Trust. (2009), *The Pratichi Education Report II: Primary Education in West Bengal – Changes and Challenges*, New Delhi: The Pratichi (India) Trust.

Thomas Issac, T.M., Richard W. Franke and Pyaralal Raghavan (1998), *Democracy at Work in an Indian Industrial Cooperative: The Story of Kerala Dinesh Beedi*, Ithaca: Cornell University Press.

Thomas Issac, T.M. and Richard W. Franke (2002), *Local Democracy and Development: The Kerala People's Campaign for Decentralized Planning*, Maryland, USA: Rowman and Littlefield Publishers Inc.

Thomas Issac, T.M. and Patrick Heller (2003), 'Democracy and Development: Decentralised Planning in Kerala', in Archon Fung and Erik Olin Wright (eds), *Deepening Democracy: Institutional Innovations in Empowered Participatory Governance*, London and New York: Verso Press.

Thorner, Daniel (1956), *The Agrarian Prospect in India*, Delhi: Delhi University Press.

Törnquist, Olle (1995), *The Next Left?: Democratisation and Attempts to Renew the Radical Political Development Project: The Case of Kerala*, Copenhagen: NIAS Books.

Törnquist, Olle (2000), *Political Violence: Indonesia and India in Comparative Perspective*, Oslo: Centre for Development and the Environment, University of Oslo.

Vanaik, Achin (1990), *The Painful Transition: Bourgeois Democracy in India*, London: Verso.

Varkey, Ouseph (1974), *At the Crossroads: Sino-Indian Border Dispute and the Communist Party of India, 1959–63*, Calcutta: Minerva Associates.

Venugopal, N. (2012), *Understanding Maoists: Notes of a Participant Observer from Andhra Pradesh*, Kolkata: Archana Das & Subrata Das.

Verghese, B.G. (1996), *India's Northeast Resurgent – Ethnicity, Insurgency, Governance, Development*, New Delhi: Konark.

Weaver, Suzanne (1979), *A Dangerous Place*, Bombay: Allied Publishers.

Webster, Neil (1992), *Panchayati Raj and the Decentralisation of Development Planning in West Bengal (A Case Study)*, Calcutta: K.P. Bagchi.

Williams, Michelle (2002), *The Politics of Socialism from Below: Democratic Communists in South Africa and Kerala, India*, S.G. Distributors.

Wolff, Richard D. (2002) *Class Theory and History: Capitalism and Communism in the USSR*, New York: Routledge.

Yagnik, Achyut and Suchitra Sheth (2005), *The Shaping of Modern Gujarat: Plurality, Hindutva and Beyond*, New Delhi: Penguin Books.

Zachariah, Matthew and R. Sooryamoorthy, (1994), *Science in Participatory Development: The Achievements and Dilemmas of a Development Movement – The Case of Kerala*, London: Zed Press.

Zelliot, Eleanor (2013), *Ambedkar's World: the Making of Babasaheb and the Dalit Movement*, New Delhi: Navayana.

Theses:

Bhattacharya, Dwaipayan (1993), 'Agrarian Reform and Politics of The Left in West Bengal', PhD Thesis, University of Cambridge.

Chakraborty, Indranil (2011), 'The Market Odyssey: Why and How Was "The Market Discourse" Incorporated in the Party Program of The Communist Party of India (Marxist) During the Days of the Communist Party of China's "Market Socialism"?', MA Thesis, Simon Fraser University.

Chakrabarty, Bidyut (1985), 'Middle Class Radicalism in Bengal: A Study of the Politics of Subhas Chandra Bose', PhD Thesis, University of London.

Cleaver, Harry (1975), 'The Origins of the Green Revolution', PhD Thesis, Stanford University.

Das, Ritanjan (2013), 'History, Ideology and Negotiation: The Politics of Policy Transition in West Bengal', DPhil Thesis, London School of Economics.

Datta, Anisha (2009), 'Syncretic Socialism in Post-Colonial West Bengal:

Mobilizing and Disciplining Women for a "Sustha" Nation-State', DPhil Thesis, University of British Columbia.

Desai, Manali (1999), 'Nationalism, Class Conflict and Socialist Hegemony: Towards an Explanation of "Development Exceptionalism" in Kerala, India 1934–1941', PhD Thesis, University of California, Los Angeles.

Hauser, Walter (1961), 'Peasant Organisation in India: A Case Study of the Bihar Kisan Sabha, 1929–1942', PhD Thesis, Chicago University.

Jayaraj, D (1977), 'Democratic Governments in Kerala, 1957–1970', PhD Thesis, University of Kerala, Trivandrum.

Jha, Gulab (1987), 'Caste and the Communist Movement in Bihar with Special Reference in Madhubani District', PhD Thesis, CSSS, Jawaharlal Nehru University.

Josh, Bhagwan (1985), 'Left and the Indian National Movement, 1934–41', PhD Thesis, Centre for Historical Studies, Jawaharlal Nehru University.

Kochuthressia, M.M. (1994), 'Women and Political Change in Kerala', PhD Thesis, Cochin University of Science and Technology.

McConnochie, Adam (2012), '"The Blessed Land": Narratives of Peasant Resistance at Nandigram, West Bengal in 2007', MA Thesis, submitted to Victoria University of Wellington.

Nair, Jaideep (1993), 'State Intervention and the Politics of Reform: Communist-Led United Front Regimes In Kerala, 1957–90', PhD Thesis, Centre for Political Studies, Jawaharlal Nehru University.

Roy Chowdhury, Arnab (2013), 'Subalternity, State-Formation and Movements against Hydropower Projects in India, 1920–2004', PhD Thesis, National University of Singapore.

Sivadasan, E.N. (2010), 'A Comparative Study of the CPI(M) and CPI-led Coalition Governments in Kerala Politics and Policy Implementation', PhD Thesis, Department of Political Science, St. Thomas College, Palai, Mahatma Gandhi University.

Thangavelu, S. P. (1991), 'Communist Parties' Understanding of the Indian State: A Study of the Congress and Janata Period (1966–1979)', Ph.D thesis, CPS, Jawaharlal Nehru University.

Thomas, Jayan Jose (2003), 'State Policy, Industrial Structure and Industrialization: The Case of Kerala', PhD Thesis, Indira Gandhi Institute of Development Research, Mumbai.

Williams, Glyn (1996), 'Socialist Development? Economic and Political Change in Rural West Bengal under the Left Front Government', PhD Thesis, University of Cambridge.

Research Papers:

Aravind, Anivar (2008), 'Subverting Peoples Power & Needs: Asian Development Bank in Kerala', South Asian Workshop on IFIs and Debt, 15–17 January 2008, http://cadtm.org/IMG/pdf/ProtestAgainstADB_in_Kerala.pdf

Bandyopadhyay, Tirthankar (2010), 'Crisis of the Left in West Bengal', MSc Dissertation Paper, Department of Development Studies, SOAS, London, UK.

Bandyopadhyay, Tirthankar and Soumyananda Dinda (2013), 'Neo-Liberalism and Protest in West Bengal: An Analysis through the Media Lens', King's India Institute, Kings College, London.

Breman, J. and J. Varinder (2012), 'The Long Road To Social Security: Implementation of NREGA in India – A National Overview', Hivos Knowledge Programme Paper 9.

Das, Arvind N. (1997), 'Swami and Friends: Sahajanand Saraswati and Those Who Refuse to Let the Past of Bihar's Peasant Movements Become History', paper for the Peasant Symposium, 23–25 May 1997, University of Virginia, Charlottesville, Virginia.

Devika, J., Binitha V. Thampi, S. Anitha et al. (2008), 'Final Report Gendering Governance or Governing Women? Politics, Patriarchy, and Democratic Decentralisation in Kerala State, India', Trivandrum, Centre for Development Studies.

Dey, Subhasish (2009), 'Evaluating India's National Rural Employment Guarantee Scheme: The Case of Birbhum District, West Bengal', Research Paper, Institute of Social Studies, The Hague.

Erwer, Monica (2003), 'Challenging the Gender Paradox: Women's Collective Agency and the Transformation of Kerala Politics',

Goteborg: Department of Peace and Development Research, Goteborg University.

George, K.K. and N. Ajith Kumar (1999), 'What Is Wrong with Kerala's Education System?', CSES Working Paper No 3, Kochi: Centre for Socio-Economic and Environmental Studies.

George, K.K. (2011), 'Kerala Economy: Growth, Structure, Strength and Weakness', Working Paper 25, Kochi: Centre for Socio-economic and Environmental Studies (CSES).

Harris, John (1979), 'The Modes of Production Controversy: Themes and Problems of the Debate', Working Paper, Madras Institute of Development Studies.

Harris, John (1980), 'Contemporary Marxist Analysis of the Agrarian Question in India', Madras: Madras Institute of Development Studies, Working Paper 14.

Jandhyala B. G. Tilak (2001), 'Higher Education and Development in Kerala', Working Paper No. 5, Kochi, CSES.

Kannan, K.P. (2014), 'The New Panchayat Raj and Its Development Initiatives: Reflections on Kerala's Record and its Successful Cases: Study prepared for the Research Unit in Local Level Development', Trivandrum: Centre for Development Studies.

Kranz, Susanne (2008), 'Feminism and Marxism in the All India Democratic Women's Association: A Leftist Approach to the Women's Question in Contemporary India', paper presented at the Annual Conference of the Economic History Society, 28–30 March 2008, University of Nottingham.

Loomba, Ania (2014), 'Indian girls in search of the party or the lost worlds of Indian communism', Typescript.

Mehra, Ajay K. (2008), 'India's Experiment with Revolution', Working Paper No. 40, South Asia Institute, Department of Political Science, University of Heidelberg.

Mukhopadhyay, Swapna. (2006), 'The Enigma of Kerala Women: Does High Literacy Necessarily Translate into high Status?', Working Paper 5, MIMAP Gender Network Project, New Delhi: Institute of Social Studies Trust.

Ramachandran, V.K., Madhura Swaminathan and Vikas Rawal (2003), 'Barriers to Expansion of Mass Literacy and Primary: Schooling in West Bengal: A Study Based on Primary Data From Selected Villages', Working Paper 345, Center for Development Studies.

Rana, Kumar and Santabhanu Sen (2008), 'The ICDS Programme in West Bengal: Scope and Challenges', paper presented in Regional Consultation on the Status of the Young Child, organized by FORCES in March 2008 in Ranchi, Jharkhand.

Rao, R.S. and S. Brahme (1973), 'Capitalism in Indian Agriculture: An Enquiry', paper presented to a seminar on the political economy of Indian agriculture, March 1973, Calcutta.

Shah, Mihir (1980), 'On the Development of Capitalism in Agriculture', Working Paper, Centre for Development Studies, Trivandrum.

Tharamangalam, Joseph (2012), 'The Kerala Model of Development in the Era of Neoliberal Reforms: New Contradictions, Old and New Questions', IDS Working Paper, 11/1, 16 September.

Thomas Isaac, T. M. (1983), 'The Emergence of Radical Working Class Movement in Alleppey, 1922–1938'. Working Paper No. 175, Trivandrum: Centre for Development Studies.

Westergaard, Kirsten (1986), 'People's Participation, Local Government and Rural Development: the Case of West Bengal, India', Centre for Development Research, Report No. 8, Copenhagen.

Zachariah, K. C. and S. Irudaya Rajan (2012), 'Inflexion In Kerala's Gulf Connection: Report on Kerala Migration Survey 2011', Working Paper No. 450, Center for Development Studies.

Official Publications:

a) Official documents:

Centre for Development Studies (2006), *Human Development Report – Kerala 2005*, Trivandrum: State Planning Board, Government of Kerala.

Government of India (1992), Ministry of Rural Development, *Annual Report 1991–92*, New Delhi.

Government of Tripura (2007), *Tripura: Human Development Report 2007*, Government of Tripura.

Government of West Bengal (1981), *Land Reforms in West Bengal: Statistical Report—V*, Calcutta: Board of Revenue.

Government of West Bengal (1981), *Land Reforms in West Bengal: Statistical Report—VI*, Calcutta: Statistical Cell.

Government of West Bengal (2004), *West Bengal Human Development Report 2004*, Development and Planning Department, Government of West Bengal.

Government of West Bengal (2004), *Economic Review 2003–04*, Calcutta.

Joint Committee of Ministry of Environment and Forests and Ministry of Tribal Affairs (2010), *Report of National Committee on Forests Rights Act*, Government of India. www.moef.nic.in/downloads/public-nformation/FRA%20COMMITTEE%20REPORT_FINAL%20 Dec%202010.pdf, accessed on 1 March 2015.

Mukarji, Nirmal and D. Bandyopahyay (1993), *New Horizons for West Bengal's Panchayats: A Report for Government of West Bengal*, Calcutta: Department of Panchayats.

NCEUS [National Commission for Enterprises in the Unorganised Sector] (2008), *A Special Programme for Marginal and Small Farmers*, New Delhi: NCEUS, Government of India.

Programme Evaluation Organisation (2006), *Evaluation Report on Decentralised Experience of Kerala – Report No. 195*, New Delhi: Planning Commission, Government of India.

Sachar Committee Report (2006), *High-Level Committee on the Social, Economic and Educational Status of the Muslim Community of India: A Report*, New Delhi, Cabinet Secretariat, Government of India.

http://www.minorityaffairs.gov.in/sites/upload_files/moma/files/pdfs/ sachar_comm.pdf, accessed on 2 September 2014.

United Progressive Alliance (2004), *National Common Minimum Programme of United Progressive Alliance Government*, http://nceuis. nic.in/NCMP.htm

Party Documents:

Basavapunnaiah, M. (N.D.), *Our Views on E.M.S. Namboodiripad's Critique of Draft Programme*, Communist Party of India (Maoist) (2004)

Party Programme. Central Committee http://www.bannedthought. net/India/CPI-Maoist-Docs/ accessed on 2 April 2013.

Communist Party of India (Maoist) (2004*)*, *Strategy and Tactics: Central Committee (P) Communist Party of India (Maoist)*, http://www. bannedthought.net/India/CPI-Maoist-Docs/ accessed on 2 April 2013.

Communist Party Publication (1948), *Who Rules Pakistan?* Bombay: People's Publishing House.

CPI (1950), *Imperialist Aggression in Kashmir*, Bombay: Mashal Publishing House Ltd, also available at www.sacw.net/article5453.html

CPI (1951), 'Statement of Policy of the Communist Party of India' (adopted by the Calcutta conference and first published in November 1951, in Mohit Sen (ed.) (1977) *Documents of the History of the Communist Party of India*, Vol. VIII, 1951–1956, New Delhi: People's Publishing House.

CPI (1978), *Documents of the Eleventh Congress of the Communist Party of India*, New Delhi: Communist Party of India.

CPI (1985), *On Certain Harmful Practices in Internal Party Life*, Resolution of the National Council of the CPI.

CPI (1993), *Communist Party of India 15th Congress Documents, Hyderabad – 10 to 16 April 1992*, New Delhi: Communist Party Publication.

CPI (2007), *Report on Political Developments, Tasks and Resolutions –* Adopted by National Council at Kolkata: National Council Meeting January 4 – 6, 2007, New Delhi: CPI Publication.

CPI (2012), *Draft of the Party Programme*, New Delhi: Communist Party of India.

CPI (2012), *Political and Economic Developments Since Patna Party Congress: Report and Resolutions adopted by National Council on September 5–7, 2012*, New Delhi: CPI Publications.

CPI (2012), *Political Resolution – Adopted by XXI Congress in its session at Patna from March 27 to 31, 2012*, New Delhi: CPI Publication.

CPI(M) Kerala State Committee (N.D.), *Communist Party In Kerala*, http://www.cpimkerala.org/eng/history-2.php?n=1

CPI(M) (1964), *Communist Party of India (Marxist) Programme*, http:// www.sacw.net/article9639.html

CPI(M) (1967), *Divergent Views Between Our Party and The CPC on Certain Fundamental Issues of Programme and Policy,* New Delhi: Communist Party of India (Marxist).

CPI(M) (1968), *Ideological Debate Summed Up by Politbureau,* Calcutta: Communist Party of India (Marxist).

CPI(M) (1969), *Central Committee Statement on Moscow Conference,* Calcutta: Communist Party of India (Marxist).

CPI(M) (1972), *National Question in India,* Calcutta: National Book Agency.

CPI(M) (1979), *Report and Resolution on Organisation,* adopted at the Salkia Plenum, New Delhi: Communist Party of India (Marxist).

CPI(M) (N.D.), *The Left in India: Facing the Challenges of Liberalisation and Communalism,* New Delhi: Communist Party of India (Marxist).

CPI(M) (N.D.), *Left Front Government of Bengal: A Saga of Struggle.* http://www.cpimwb.org.in/upload_all_docs/pdf/lf_govt/L.F._Govt._of_Bengal_-_A_Saga_of_Struggle.pdf, accessed on 20 January 2014.

CPI(M), (N.D.), *Formation of the Communist Party of India at Tashkent (1920),* http://cpim.org/history/formation-communist-party-india-tashkent-1920

CPI(M) (1992), *On Certain Ideological Issues,* Resolution adopted in the 14th Party Congress, www.cpim.org/documents/1992-14-Cong--ideological-issues.pdf, accessed on 22 January 2015.

CPI(M) (1997), *Report on Political Developments – Since The Last C.C. Meeting,* (Adopted in the Central Committee meeting 12 to 14 May 1987), New Delhi: Communist Party of India (Marxist)

CPI(M) (1998), *Documents of the 16th congress of the Communist Party (Marxist), Calcutta, 1988.* New Delhi: CPI(M).

Central Committee, CPI (M) (1988), 'On Recent Developments in the Soviet Union', *The Marxist,* Vol. 6, No. 2, April–June.

CPI(M) (2000), *Programme CPI(M),* Communist Party of India (Marxist).

CPI(M) (2001) *Report on Political Developments,* (Adopted at the 11–12 August 2001 Meeting of the Central Committee). New Delhi: Communist Party of India (Marxist).

CPI(M) (2002), *Political-Organisational Report* (Adopted At the 17th Congress Hyderabad, 2002). New Delhi: Communist Party of India

(Marxist), http://www.cpim.org/documents/2002-17Cong-pol-org-rep.pdf

CPI(M) (2005), *Political Organisational Report* (Adopted at the 18th Congress, April 6–11, 2005, New Delhi), New Delhi: A CPI(M) Publication.

CPI(M) (2005), *Party's Perspective On Women's Issues And Tasks*, New Delhi: CPI(M).

CPI(M) (2006), *Proceedings of the First All India Convention on Dalit Rights*, New Delhi: CPI(M) Publication.

CPI(M) (2008), *Documents of the 19ᵗʰ Congress*, New Delhi: Communist Party of India (Marxist).

CPI(M) (2008), *Political Resolution* (adopted at the Congress of the Communist Party of India (Marxist) March 29 to April 3, 2008, Coimbatore,) http://cpim.org/documents/19 per cent20Congress. Political.Resolution.pdf

CPI(M), CPI, RSP and All-India Forward Bloc (2008), *Left Stand on the Nuclear Deal*, New Delhi: the CPI(M) on behalf of the Left Parties.

CPI(M) (2008), 'Part II of the political-organisation report of the 19th Congress of the CPI(M)', *The Marxist*, Vol. XXIV, No. 2, April–June.

CPI(M) (2009), *Review of the Work on Kisan and Agricultural Workers Fronts and Future Tasks* (Adopted at the Central Committee meeting held during 7–9 June 2003 at Kolkata). New Delhi: Communist Party of India (Marxist).

CPI(M) (2010), *Political Resolution and Review Report* (Adopted at the Extended Meeting of the Central Committee, August 7–10, 2010, Vijayawada), New Delhi: Communist Party of India (Marxist).

CPI(M) (2010), *Programme*, New Delhi: Communist Party of India (Marxist).

CPI(M) (2011), *Constitution and The Rules Under The Constitution*, New Delhi: Communist Party of India (Marxist).

CPI(M) (2011), 'LF government and Development of Muslim Minorities in West Bengal', CPI(M) Campaign Material, West Bengal Assembly Election, April–May 2011, available at http://www.cpim. org/documents/2011-minority.development_wb.pdf accessed on 2 September 2014.

CPI(M) (2012), *Draft Political Resolution For the 20th Congress* (Adopted by the Central Committee in its meeting held from 17 to 20 January 2012 at Kolkata), New Delhi: Communist Party of India (Marxist)

CPI(M) (2012), *Draft Resolution on Some Ideological Issues* (Adopted at the Central Committee meeting held from January 17 to 20, 2012 at Kolkata), New Delhi: Communist Party of India (Marxist).

CPI(M) (2012), *Political-Organisational Report* (Adopted at the 20th Party Congress at Kozhikode).

CPI(M) (2013), *On Approach to Mass Organisations* (Adopted by the Central Committee at its 29 to 31 October 2004 Meeting), New Delhi: Communist Party of India (Marxist).

CPI(M) (2013), *Sangharsh Sandesh Jattha* [Hindi]. New Delhi: Communist Party of India (Marxist).

CPI(M) (2014), *West Bengal Verdict 'Distorted'*, 16 May, http://www.cpim.org/content/west-bengal-verdict-distorted, accessed on 25 May 2014.

CPI(M) (2014), *P.B, Communiqué*, 18 May, http://www.cpim.org/content/pb-communique-22

CPI(M) (2014), *On Lok Sabha Verdict*, http://www.cpim.org/content/lok-sabha-verdict, access on 25 May 2014.

CPI(M) (2014), *Review of Lok Sabha Election*, Press Communiqué, 9 June 2014.

CPI(M) West Bengal State Committee (2015), *The Left Front Government in West Bengal: Evaluation of an Experience*, (Adopted on the 29th Session, CPI(M) West Bengal State Committee, 23–24 February), www.cpimwb.org.in, accessed on 10 March 2015.

Fourth International (1942), *A Transitional Program for India: The May 1942 Program of the Bolshevik–Leninist Party of India*, Fourth International, Vol. III, Number 10, October 1942, http://www.marxists.org/history/etol/newspape/fi/index.htm#fi42_10

Grigorian, V. (1951), *Record of Discussions of J.V. Stalin with Representatives of C.C. of the Communist Party of India Comrades, Rao, Dange, Ghosh and Punnaiah*, [February 1951], Translated from Russian by Vijay Singh, *Revolutionary Democracy*, September 2006.

Gupta, Bhupesh (1962), *Forward to the Defence of Our Motherland under the Banner of Jawaharlal Nehru*, New Delhi: Communist Party of India.

Gupta, Bhupesh (1964), *Critical Note on the Programme Draft and Comments on Namboodiripad's Critical Note*, New Delhi: Communist Party of India.

Gupta, Bhupesh. (1970), *CPM Terror in West Bengal*, New Delhi: Communist Party of India.

Articles in Journals, Newspapers, Magazines and Websites:

Abdi, S.N.M. (2012) 'Bengal Hasn't Produced A Jagjivan Ram or Even a Mayawati', outlookindia.com, 10 August.

Acharya, Poromesh (1989), 'Education and Communal Conflict in Bengal: A Case Study', *Economic and Political Weekly*, 29 July.

Acharya, Poromesh (1993), 'Panchayats and Left Politics in West Bengal', *Economic and Political Weekly*, 29 May.

Acharya, Poromesh (2002), 'Education: Panchayat and Decentralisation – Myths and Reality', *Economic and Political Weekly*, 23 February.

Ahmad, Aijaz (1994), 'Fascism and National Culture: Reading Gramsci in the Days of Hindutva', *Social Scientist*, March–April 1994

Ahmad, Aijaz (1996), 'In the Eye of The Storm: The Left Chooses', *Economic and Political Weekly*, 1 June.

Alam, Javed (1991), 'State and the Making of Communist Politics in India, 1947–57', *Economic and Political Weekly*, 9 November.

Alam, Aniket (2008), '"National Interest" Not the Issue in Nuclear Deal', *Economic and Political Weekly*, 27 September–3 October.

Ali, Ahmed (1977–78), 'The Progressive Writers' Movement In Its Historical Perspective', *Journal of South Asian Literature*, Vol. 13, No. 1/4, Fall-Winter-Spring-Summer.

Ali, Tariq (1975), 'Memoir of an Indian Communist', Interview by K. Damodaran, *New Left Review* Vol. 93, No. 1, pp. 35–59.

Appa, Gautam (1970), 'The Naxalites', *New Left Review* I/61, May–June.

Bag, Kheya (2011), 'Red Bengal's Rise and Fall', *New Left Review* 70, July–August.

Bagchi, Jasodhara (1990), 'Representing Nationalism: Ideology of Motherhood in Colonial Bengal', *Economic and Political Weekly*, 20–27 October, pp. WS 65–71.

Bal, Hartosh Singh (2014), 'Lapse of Doctrine: Why the CPI(M) is now just another regional player', *Caravan Magazine*, April.

Banaji, Jairus (1974), 'Nationalism and Socialism', *Economic and Political Weekly*, 7 September.

Banaji, Jairus (2013), 'A short history of the employees' unions in Bombay, 1947–1991', sacw.net [http://www.sacw.net/article5805.html]

Bandyopadhyay, D. (2010), 'Census of Political Murders in West Bengal during CPI-M Rule', *Mainstream*, 14 August.

Bandyopadhyay, Krishna (2008), 'Naxalbari Politics: A Feminist Narrative', *Economic and Political Weekly*, 5–11 April.

Bandyopadhyay, Sarbani (2012), 'Caste and Politics in Bengal', *Economic and Political Weekly*, 15 December.

Bandyopadhyay, Sekhar (2008), 'The Story of an Aborted Revolution: Communist Insurgency in Post-independence West Bengal, 1948–50', *Journal of South Asian Development*, Vol. 3, No. 1, June.

Banerjee, Partha Sarathi (2011), 'Party, Power and Political Violence in West Bengal', *Economic and Political Weekly*, 5 February.

Banerjee, Sudeshna (2012), 'The March of the Mega-city: Governance in West Bengal and Wetlands to the East of Kolkata', *Sudasien Chronik – South Asia Chronicle*, Vol. 2.

Banerjee, Sumanta (2007), 'Moral Betrayal of a Leftist Dream', *Economic and Political Weekly*, 7–13 April.

Banerjee, Sumanta (2010), 'End of a Phase: Time for Reinventing the Left', *Economic and Political Weekly*, 13 November.

Bardhan, Pranab (2011), 'The Avoidable Tragedy of the Left in India – II', *Economic and Political Weekly*, 11 June.

Baruah, Sanjib (1990), 'The End of The Road in Land Reform? Limits to Redistribution in West Bengal', *Development and Change*, Vol. 21.

Basu, Amrita (1990), 'Feminism, Tribal Radicalism and Grass Roots Mobilization in India', *Dialectical Anthropology*, Vol. 15, No. 2/3.

Bhaduri, Amit (2007), 'Alternatives in Industrialisation', *Economic and Political Weekly*, 5 May.

Bhattacharyya, Debashis (2006), 'In God we trust', *The Telegraph*, 24 September.

Bhattacharya, Dwaipayan (2010), 'Left in the Lurch: The Demise of the World's Longest Elected Regime?', *Economic and Political Weekly*, 16 January.

Bhowmik, Sharit K. (1988), 'Strangling Workers Initiatives—Fate of Worker Co-operatives in Tripura', *Economic and Political Weekly*, 3 December.

Bijoy, C. R. (1999), 'Adivasis Betrayed: Adivasi Land Rights in Kerala', *Economic and Political Weekly*, 29 May–4 June.

Bidwai, Praful and Achin Vanaik (1997), 'An Open Letter to the Left', *Economic and Political Weekly*, 18 January.

Biju, B.L. and K.G. Abhilash Kumar (2013), 'Class Feminism: The Kudumbashree Agitation in Kerala', *Economic and Political Weekly*, 2 March.

Bose, Prasenjit (2014), 'Left's Debacle in 2014: Who's Responsible?', www.pragoti.in

Chandavarkar, Rajnarayan (1997), 'From Communism to "Social Democracy": The Rise and Resilience of Communist Parties in India, 1920–1995', *Science & Society*, Vol. 61, No. 1, Communism in Britain and the British Empire, Spring.

Chatterji, Joya (2007), '"Dispersal" and the Failure of Rehabilitation: Refugee Camp-dwellers and Squatters in West Bengal', *Modern Asian Studies*, Vol. 41, No. 5, September.

Chatterjee, Partha (2009), 'The Coming Crisis in West Bengal', *Economic and Political Weekly*, 28 February–6 March.

Chowdhury, Debdatta (2011), 'Space, identity, territory: Marichjhapi Massacre, 1979', *The International Journal of Human Rights*, Vol. 15, No. 5.

Da Costa, Dia (2008), '"Spoiled Sons" and "Sincere Daughters": Schooling, Security, and Empowerment in Rural West Bengal, India', *Signs*, Vol. 33, No. 2, Winter.

Dasgupta, Indraneel (2009), 'On Some Left Critiques of the Left', *Economic and Political Weekly*, 1–7 August.

Devika, J. (2010), 'Egalitarian Developmentalism, Communist Mobilization, and the Question of Caste in Kerala State, India', *The Journal of Asian Studies*, Vol. 69, No. 3, August.

George, K.K. (1998), 'Historical Roots of Kerala Model and Its Present Crisis', *Bulletin of Concerned Asian Scholars*, Vol. 30, No. 4.

Hardgrave Jr, and L. Robert (1970), 'The Marxist Dilemma in Kerala: Administration and/or Struggle', *Asian Survey*, Vol. X No. 11.

Harris, John (2013) 'Does "Landlordism" Still Matter? Reflections on Agrarian Change in India', *Journal of Agrarian Change*, Vol. 13, No. 3, July.

Herring, Ronald J. (1989), 'Dilemmas of Agrarian Communism: Peasant Differentiation, Sectoral and Village Politics', *Third World Quarterly*, Vol. 11, No. 1, January.

Jeffrey, Robin (1987), 'Governments and Culture: How Women Made Kerala Literate', *Pacific Affairs*, Vol. 60, No 3, Fall.

Kjosavik, Darley Jose and N. Shanmugaratnam (2004), 'Integration or exclusion? Locating indigenous peoples in the development process of Kerala, South India', *Forum for Development Studies*, Vol. 31, No. 2.

Kodoth, Praveena (2005), 'Fostering Insecure Livelihoods: Dowry and Female Seclusion in Left Developmental Contexts in West Bengal and Kerala', *Economic and Political Weekly*, 18–24 June.

Kumar, Amiduyti and Tarun Sanyal (2006), 'Citizens' Chargesheet On West Bengal Government's Development Policies', *Mainstream*, Vol. XLIV, No. 49, 25 November.

Kushry, Sweta (1991), 'Mandal Commission and Left Front in West Bengal', *Economic and Political Weekly*, 23 February.

McGarr, Paul Michael (2014), 'Quiet Americans in India: The CIA and the Politics of Intelligence in Cold War South Asia', *Diplomatic History*, 4 January.

Mitra, Ashok (2012), 'Lumpenland – The cause of West Bengal's gloom lies in its people's naiveté', *The Telegraph*, 4 May.

Mondal, Parthasarathi (1992), 'Privatisation of healthcare and the Left', *Indian Journal of Medical Ethics*, Vol. 9, No. 3.

Mukharji, P.B. (2009), '"Communist" Dispossession Meets "Reactionary" Resistance: The Ironies of the Parliamentary Left in West Bengal', *Focaal – European Journal of Anthropology*, Vol. 54.

Naqvi, M.B. (2007), 'Appeal To The Indian Left From A Progressive Pakistani: Evolve Alternative Paradigm of Economic Growth', *Mainstream*, 19 May.

Noorani, A.G. (2011), 'Of Stalin, Telangana & Indian revolution', *Frontline*, Vol. 28, No. 26.

Nussbaum, Martha C. (2008), 'Violence on the Left: Nandigram and the Communists of West Bengal', *Dissent*, Spring.

Öktem, Kerem Gabriel (2012), 'A Comparative Analysis of the Performance of the Parliamentary Left in the Indian States of Kerala, West Bengal and Tripura', *Journal of South Asian Studies*, Vol. 35, No. 2.

Omvedt, Gail (1978), 'Towards a Marxist Analysis of Caste: A Response to B.T. Ranadive', *Social Scientist*, Vol. 6, No. 11, June.

Pederson, J.D. (2001), 'India's Industrial Dilemmas in West Bengal', *Asian Survey*, Vol. 41, No. 4, July–August.

Phadke, Anant R. S. (1992), 'Left Response to Drought in Maharashtra', *Economic and Political Weekly*, 8 February.

Prabhash, J. (2000), 'CPI(M)'s Muslim League Dilemma', *Economic and Political Weekly*, 19–25 August.

Rogaly, Ben (1998), 'Containing conflict and reaping votes: Management of rural labour relations in West Bengal', *Economic and Political Weekly*, 17–24 October.

Roy, Biren (1993), 'Left Trade Unions and New Economic Policies', *Economic and Political Weekly*, 18 December.

Rudra, Ashok (1985), 'Jyoti Basu and Multinationals', *Economic and Political Weekly*, 27 July.

Sarkar, Abhirup (2007), 'Development and Displacement: Land Acquisition in West Bengal', *Economic and Political Weekly*, 21 April.

Sarkar, Sumit and Tanika Sarkar (2009), 'Notes on a Dying People', *Economic and Political Weekly*, 27 June–10 July.

Scrase, Timothy J. (2002), 'Globalisation and the Cultural Politics of Educational Change: The Controversy over the Teaching of English in West Bengal, India', *International Review of Education / Internationale Zeitschrift fur Erziehungswissenschaft / Revue Internationale de l'Education*, Vol. 48, No. 5, September.

Shah, Alpa (2011), 'Alcoholics Anonymous: The Maoist Movement in Jharkhand, India', *Modern Asian Studies*, Vol. 45, No. 5, September.

Simeon, Dilip (2010), 'Permanent Spring', *Seminar*, No. 607, March.

Special Correspondent (2006), 'Corporates in West Bengal Laud Govt', *The Hindu*, 1 May.

Stern, Robert W. (1965), 'The Sino-Indian Border Controversy and the Communist Party of India', *The Journal of Politics*, Vol. 27, No. 1, February.

Vanaik, Achin (1986), 'The Indian Left', *New Left Review*, I/ 159, September–October.

Varkey, Ouseph (1979), 'The CPI-Congress Alliance in India', *Asian Survey*, Vol. 19, No. 9, September.

Williams, Glyn (2001), 'Understanding Political Stability: Party Action and Political Discourse in West Bengal', *Third World Quarterly*, Vol. 22, No. 4, August.

Wood, John B. (1965), 'Observations on the Indian Communist Party Split', *Pacific Affairs*, Spring.

Zacharia, Paul (2012), 'Conduct of A Perfect Murder: The recent brutal killing of a former CPM leader exposes the grisly workings of political violence in Kerala', *Caravan* Magazine, 1 June.

Zagoria, Donald S. (1971), 'The Ecology of Peasant Communism in India', *The American Political Science Review*, Vol. 65, No. 1, March

Index

Acknowledgements

I owe a debt of gratitude to scores of people who inspired me to write this book, and helped me by providing analytical insights, new ideas, reference material and contacts, and in countless other ways. They include independent Marxist and socialist analysts, Left party leaders and cadres, trade unionists, kisan sabha activists, members of non-party political formations, and activists and researchers of Dalit, feminist, civil rights and environmental movements. I must also acknowledge the help I have received from social scientists belonging to numerous disciplines, people involved in initiatives in cultural, literary and artistic fields and the performing arts, independent scholars who have delved into issues such as health, education, energy, the urban environment, housing and people's science movements, and experts on tribal and ethnic questions.

I have greatly benefited over forty years through my comradeship and interaction with many remarkable individuals and independent Marxist organizations, of which I was an active participant and which shaped my politics and outlook on life. These include the Magowa Group, with members such as Kumar Shiralkar, Sudheer Bedekar, Vinod Mubayi, Anant Phadke, Suhas Paranjape, Ashok Manohar, Waheed Mukaddam, Achyut Godbole and Chhaya Datar. I later joined the Platform Tendency, which included Jairus Banaji, Rana Sen, Rohini Hensman, Neeladri Bhattacharya, Dilip Simeon, and several other outstanding scholar-activists. I have been deeply influenced by my interaction with D. Thankappan, Sadanand Menon, Lawrence Surendra and Achin Vanaik.

This book owes a great deal to the many conversations, interviews and formal and informal interactions I have had with Romila Thapar, Tanika and Sumit Sarkar, Ritu Menon, Achin Vanaik, Kamal Mitra Chenoy, Anuradha Chenoy, Ashok Mitra, Debabrata Bandyopadhyay, Amrita Chhachhi, Pamela Philipose, Rajeev Bhargava and Harsh Kapoor. I must record my gratitude to Harsh, a prodigious archivist and a tireless activist, who assisted me with research and documentation of exceptional quality, without which this work would not have been possible.

Among the political leaders I talked to in connection with the book, I must particularly thank A.B. Bardhan and Prakash Karat, former general secretaries respectively of the CPI and CPI(M), Deepankar Bhattacharya of the CPI(ML-Liberation), CPI(M) leaders V.S. Achuthanandan, T.M. Thomas Isaac and M.A. Baby, RSP leaders T.J. Chandrachoodan and Manoj Bhattacharya, and CPI leaders S. Sudhakar Reddy, D. Raja, and Binoy Visvom. Among the trade unionists who helped me a great deal were D. Thankappan, N. Vasudevan, Mukta Manohar, Datta Iswalkar and Vivek Monteiro. Special mention must be made of my gratitude to CPI leader Govind Pansare, whom I interviewed three times recently, and who was gunned down by fanatics in February 2015.

I have benefited a great deal from my meetings and conversations with Sumanta Banerjee, Kumar Rana, B.R.P. Bhaskar, Aruna Roy, Nikhil Dey, Anil Chaudhary, Kumar Ketkar, Zoya Hasan, Sumit Chowdhury, Anand Teltumbde, K.P. Kannan, Chandra Dutt, M.P. Parameswaran, R.V.G. Menon, B. Ekbal, K.N. Panikkar, Anitha Sharma, J. Devika, Sobhanlal Dattagupta, Ratan Khasnabis, Jean Dreze, Reetika Khera, Colin Gonsalves, Dunu Roy, Rakhshanda Jalil, Prabhat Patnaik, Michael Tharakan, Barbara Harriss-White, Manoranjan Mohanty, Amit Bhaduri, Deepak Nayyar, Harish Damodaran, Ranabir Samaddar, Romi Khosla, Kalpana Sahni, Rohan D'Souza, Prasenjit Bose, Gautam Sen, Subhanil Chowdhury, Ashim Chatterjee, Vasanthi Raman, Sonal Shah, Sujata Gothoskar, Partha Chatterjeee, Kunal Chattopadhyay, Sushil Khanna, Prakash Reddy, K.T. Ravindran, Vibhuti Patel, K. Ravi Raman, Sujata Patel, Rajat Roy, Akshaya Mukul, Venkitesh Ramakrishnan,

Vidyut Bhagwat, Mohan Deshpande, Bodhisattva Ray, Sushovan Dhar, Sharad Dudhat and Sunil Kumar Kurup.

I must record my gratitude to Shreyas Sardesai and Himanshu Bhattacharya of Lokniti for their generous help with statistical analysis of the Left parties' performance in the Lok Sabha and the West Bengal and Kerala assembly elections.

Special thanks are due to Janaki Nair of the P.C. Joshi Archives on Contemporary History at Jawaharlal Nehru University, and to Mahesh Rangarajan of the Nehru Memorial Museum and Library, both in New Delhi, for giving me access to books and other material in these institutions.

Among those whom I shall miss sorely are friends whom I recently lost, in particular Mike Marqusee, Sharmila Rege, Ninan Koshy and Bipan Chandra.

My very special thanks for reading the manuscript at various stages, and making insightful and incisive comments on its content, organizational structure and style, are due to Achin Vanaik, Tanika Sarkar, Muchkund Dubey, Amrita Basu and Mark Kesselman. Mark, professor emeritus at Columbia University, went through the manuscript with a fine-tooth comb, and with the intellectual acuity, brilliance, rigour and tenacity befitting the editor of the *International Political Science Review*. Film-maker and designer Rafeeq Ellias was a constant source of inspiration and encouragement.

I have over the years gained richly from interactions with my scholar-activist colleagues at the Transnational Institute, Amsterdam, of which I have been a fellow for more than twenty years. No less important for me has been my involvement in activism on environmental, human rights and peace issues, in particular through the Coalition for Nuclear Disarmament and Peace.

This book owes a great deal to the Council for Social Development (CSD) in New Delhi, at which I held the Durgabai Deshmukh Chair in Social Development, Equity and Human Security for three years until September 2014. This enabled me to devote time to research, meetings and interviews with Left leaders, civil society activists and independent scholars, and to organize a seminar on 'The Indian Left: Social

Development Visions and Political Challenges' in August 2012, which was attended by top leaders of the Left parties and non-party activists. I could travel to various cities, meet people and conduct interviews thanks to the travel grant I received with the Chair.

I must especially thank Muchkund Dubey and T. Haq, CSD president and director, and the Council's staff, in particular librarian Gurmeet Kaur and technical assistant Dev Dutt, for their help.

My special thanks are due to V.K. Karthika and Antony Thomas of HarperCollins.

The errors and misjudgements that remain are all my own.